THE
DESERT
WAR

Mediterranean Front

A Year of Battle

The End in Africa

ALAN MOOREHEAD

INTRODUCTION BY
RICHARD OVERY

Aurum
Press

Brimming with creative inspiration, how-to projects and useful information to enrich your everyday life, Quarto Knows is a favourite destination for those pursuing their interests and passions. Visit our site and dig deeper with our books into your area of interest: Quarto Creates, Quarto Cooks, Quarto Homes, Quarto Lives, Quarto Drives, Quarto Explores, Quarto Gifts, or Quarto Kids.

This edition first published in 2017 by Aurum Press, an imprint of The Quarto Group,
The Old Brewery, 6 Blundell Street, London N7 9BH, United Kingdom.
www.QuartoKnows.com
First published by Aurum Press 2009
First published by Hamish Hamilton 1944

A catalogue record for this book is available from the British Library.

ISBN 978 1 78131 673 3
eBook ISBN 978 1 78131 106 6

10 9 8 7 6 5 4 3 2
2021 2020

Printed by CPI Group (UK) Ltd, Croydon CR0 4YY

CONTENTS

Route of 1st Army: ENGLAND TO TUNIS

THE MEDITERRANEAN AREA

PREFACE

THE WAR in Africa and the Middle East fell naturally into three phases, each lasting twelve months. At first General Wavell had command from 1940 to 1941, and that was the year of tremendous experiments, of thrusting about in the dark; the year of bluff and quick movement when nobody knew what was going to happen. Whole armies and fleets were flung about from one place to another, and in its frantic efforts to find a new equilibrium the Middle East erupted at half a dozen places at once. At one stage Wavell had five separate campaigns on his hands—the Western Desert, Greece, Crete, Italian East Africa and Syria—and there were other side-shows like Iraq and British Somaliland as well. Most of this was essentially colonial warfare carried out with small groups of men using weapons that would be regarded as obsolete now.

Looking back, I see what a feeling of excitement and high adventure we had then when we went off on these little isolated expeditions. We did not quite realise the real grimness of war except at certain moments. The honours between the sides were fairly even. The Germans held Greece and Crete; we held Syria, Abyssinia and all Italian East Africa. The Axis and the British were balanced in the desert.

Then General Auchinleck arrived to take command, and 1941–42 became the year of set battles and eventual retreat. It was no longer colonial warfare, but the war of modern European armies fighting out a decisive issue in Africa. This fighting was focused on the desert, and in that flat and limitless arena the war developed into a straight-out issue between man and man, tank and tank, army and army.

There are a thousand considerations to be taken into account, but it will have to be admitted that the Germans had the better army. They had better weapons, more soundly trained men and better generalship than we had.

Despite this stiffening and enlargement of the desert fighting, the war in the Middle East became something of a side issue through this year because Russia, Japan and America had now entered the war. Instead of being an isolated theatre, the Middle East was becoming part of world strategy. In that black summer of 1942 it even began to look as if the Germans would reach out from Stalingrad in Russia and from Alamein, Middle East, and eventually join hands with the Japanese in India. But Stalingrad and Alamein held, and that was the turning-point of the war. Then the final year, 1942–43, the year of Eisenhower, Alexander and Montgomery, the year of success. As Montgomery struck from the desert, the Anglo-American forces landed in North Africa. The tumultuous and victorious meeting of the Eighth and the First Armies in Tunisia must go down as one of the great military strokes of history. The Middle East was secured. The Mediterranean was reopened. And far off in the East the Japanese dynamic had at last expended itself on the borders of India. Practically the whole of the British and American Empires in the Far East had fallen, but for the moment the Japanese could do no more. And at Stalingrad the Russians had begun their great westward sweep. With Africa freed, we could at last look forward to the invasion of Europe.

As each of these three separate years of battle ended in the Middle East I wrote a book describing the operations—*Mediterranean Front, A Year of Battle* and *The End in Africa*. These three are now combined in this volume.

The text is essentially the same except that here and there I have made minor corrections and deletions.

When I first began to put the three books together I planned to remove many of the personal references and shape the material into a more cohesive and historical form. But I soon found this quite impracticable. It is impossible to write a definitive history of the campaigns at this stage. Too many matters are still the subject of controversy, too much is secret, so much material remains to be gathered. The war diaries and the dispatches of the commanders have still to be published.

And so these books must remain what they are—a rambling and personal story. I think every major happening is included, and I have tried to bind the sweep of these great events into a perspective. But it is essentially an intimate picture of the Mediterranean war from one man's point of view. There are long digressions, such as the Indian chapters and the description of my journey round the world when I left Egypt in the summer, called at New York in the fall and London in the winter, and ended a little breathlessly in Tunisia in the spring.

These journeys were essentially part of my search to obtain a wider and fuller knowledge of the war, and the digressions will be justified if they establish only this—that the struggle which began in the desert as a simple military issue became in the end a vast imbroglio of politics and warfare in which the whole world was concerned. Very little here has been suppressed through censorship: I have said almost all I wanted to say. Inevitably there are many mistakes. Since one is writing so close to events, one cannot weed out all the errors, and for those that remain, unknown to me, I apologise. I was present at most of the events described here, and very often I discussed them on the spot or shortly afterwards with the soldiers and their commanders and the politicians. But I must emphasise that one man can see very little of a battle, and the opinions expressed in that highly charged atmosphere not always complete and balanced.

Throughout these three years I was writing dispatches for my newspaper the *London Daily Express*, and here and there at perhaps half a dozen places I felt I could not improve on those messages, and I have threaded them into the narrative.

I was also strongly tempted to add an account of the Sicilian and Italian campaigns. But these are not part of the pattern of this book; they belong not to Africa but to Europe, and the invasion of Europe is another story.

Among all the many people who have helped this book to publication I must place first my wife. She shared in many of the adventures. Quite apart from the tedious business of handling the proofs, the results of her correction and suggestion are on every page. A great part of the book is hers. Next I must thank Lieutenant-Colonel J. O. Ewart, of the Intelligence staff, who has patiently combed through these many thousand words and given me his account of the battle of Alamein.

I cannot easily repay my debt to Lord Wavell, for his encouragement to me through these years.

At different times General Montgomery, General Auchinleck and many of their senior officers like the late General Gott discussed their battles with me and gave me access to certain documents and war diaries, and I am particularly grateful to them. I have also profited greatly from the conferences given to correspondents by General Eisenhower, General Alexander, Air Chief Marshal Tedder, Air Marshal Coningham, Admiral Cunningham and their British and American staff officers.

The late Mr P. P. Howe, who was editor to my publisher Hamish Hamilton, did a great deal of work on these books. I must also thank the hundreds of correspondents and reviewers who have used me kindly in the past; and the companion of so many of my journeys, Alexander Clifford. Evelyn Montague of the Manchester Guardian has also checked many facts. And there is my editor, Mr Arthur Christiansen of the Daily Express, who has kindly consented to the publication of this volume.

Beyond this there were the thousands of meetings I had in the field with the soldiers and sailors and airmen who are the actors of this story, and who unaffectedly and simply described to me what they had done. So many are dead now or wounded, my own colleagues among them. And this brings me to the only possible dedication of this book, which I set down here with much pride and, I hope, without presumption: *To the men who fought.*

Alan Moorehead
London, 1944

INTRODUCTION

In 1944, the Australian journalist and travel writer, Alan McCrae Moorehead (1910–1983), published this remarkable trilogy on the war in the desert of North Africa, where he had been posted as a correspondent for the British newspaper *The Daily Express*. He stayed in North Africa and the Middle East throughout the campaigns he describes. What distinguishes his account is not only the immediacy of his own experiences as he shared many of the dangers faced by the regular forces, but also his ability to shape the whole history of the war in the desert when information was still thin on the ground, or veiled in secrecy or simply incoherent. Moorehead's account is real contemporary history—vividly conveyed, intelligently assessed, and richly detailed.

Moorehead arrived in Egypt from Paris in June 1940, avoiding the collapse of France but just in time for Mussolini's declaration of war on Britain, which suddenly made Egypt a potential war zone if Italian armies bunched in Libya decided to invade. For the next three years he followed the British and Commonwealth armies back and forth across the desert in the see-saw war against Italian and, from February 1941, German forces under General Erwin Rommel. Except for a brief interlude in Iraq, Syria and Palestine, where British Commonwealth forces secured the area from any Axis threat, and a trip to South Africa and America in autumn 1942, he was tied to the desert war with all its inconveniences of climate, its isolation and its monotonous topography. In the end the desert got too much for him. 'I felt I knew every grain of sand,' he wrote, '…quite surely, I felt I could not report the desert any more.' When he returned to Africa in November 1942 it was to report the Torch campaign when American and British forces landed in Morocco and Algeria. Though he is sometimes counted as an eye-witness of the final battle of El Alamein, he missed the denouement. Indeed the battle hardly features in his account. For Moorehead the moment of triumph came in May 1943 when he witnessed with other correspondents the final surrender in Tunisia of all Axis forces, the largest haul to date in the war. 'All Africa was ours,' are his final words.

Moorehead was an acute observer, as any fine correspondent should be. His rich descriptions of a now vanished world of European ascendancy is a reminder that the wars he chronicled were more colonial in character than the vast and savage campaigns waged across Eastern Europe and in China. The number of troops involved in Africa was modest by comparison, and the setting in Egypt, a nominally independent state by 1940, was still oddly imperial. The war Britain fought from summer 1940 to the invasion of Italy will strike modern readers as strangely distant from the reality of the European war; it was a war for the defence of empire, fought far away from the motherland. That British security seemed to depend on holding Malta, Palestine, Iraq, Egypt, Suez and Aden was taken for granted. Moorehead shared those assumptions. That he was reporting war from an exotic imperial setting would not have struck his newspaper readers as odd either. But it did strike the British Tommies as odd. Moorehead records the question many British soldiers asked him: 'Why aren't we home defending England?' Moorehead found it hard to explain to them his view that fighting on the Nile was also an important way of defending Britain, India and his native Australia.

It is remarkable how much access correspondents had to British news in the desert war. Regular press conferences and press releases were matched by an evident willingness on the part of commanders to discuss off-the-record what was going on. Nevertheless, there are things evidently missing from any account of the desert war written while the conflict was still going on. No one outside a closed circle knew about the impact of ULTRA intelligence on the war in the Middle East, and not until the 1970s was the secret finally revealed. Moorehead had little access to Italian or German records and reported the enemy as best he could. He, like many others at the time and since, assumed that the Germans were just better at fighting—better weapons, better training, better tacticians. As a result there is little sense here of how Montgomery was able to prevail at El Alamein when Egypt seemed all but lost to Rommel's advancing forces. Air power features less in Moorehead's account, partly perhaps of the difficulty of piecing air fighting together from scattered units and bases, whereas the army was solid and visible.

But air power played a critical part in the campaign. The desert was the place where the RAF finally learned how to support ground forces in the field, and used that knowledge to great effect in Normandy a year later.

Moorehead was quite frank himself about the gaps in his story, but there is still a great deal to learn here about the experience of desert war and the men who fought there, and about the travails of newspapermen as they scrambled for news behind the fighting front. This was the British Empire's longest campaign. It was fought with less bitterness and savagery than conflicts elsewhere between 1939 and 1945 but it still left thousands dead and wounded. At one point on the eve of Operation Crusader in November 1941 Moorehead confesses to a morbid revulsion against the war: 'within thirty-six hours all these placid, peaceful men, were going to rise up and start killing each other. Nothing could stop the battle taking place…It seemed a calculated cruelty.' Around Tobruk where the battle raged he saw graves of German and British soldiers intermingled, the squalid wreckage of war all around them. As a war correspondent, Moorehead was never sentimental or cynical about what he witnessed. He appreciated the efforts of the soldiers around him and brought to life their fearful environment of combat. For anyone who wants to understand what it is like to be at the sharp end of battle, Moorehead's account is as fresh and relevant today as it was when he wrote it.

Richard Overy
University of Exeter, 2017

BOOK ONE

Mediterranean Front: The
Year of Wavell 1940–41

One

Operations such as these begin with a phase
in which each commander struggles, on the one
hand, to obtain information, and on the other to
deny it to his enemy. One of the few advantages
that soldiers experience in having a desert
for their theatre of war is that the auditorium
is empty. -EXTRACT FROM A STATEMENT ISSUED BY
G.H.Q., CAIRO, JUNE 19TH, 1940.

I REACHED Egypt by way of Greece. Nothing could disturb that timeless apathy in the eastern Mediterranean. In Athens the diplomats talked leisurely around the point of whether Greece would fight or not. They were rather agreed on the whole that she would not. They talked too, of course, the Greeks. They said that every Italian would be thrown into the sea. But they had been talking in that strain for a long time. Anyway, Metaxas had a Fascist régime. Anyway, he was friendly with the Germans who seemed to be arriving in steadily increasing numbers at Athens and Salonica. Anyway, the Greeks were utterly divided against themselves, the army was robbed of all its Venezilist officers and intrigue was festering all the way through the Peloponnese to Thrace. I took a car to Phaleron Bay and swam far out into the gentle sea while they prepared a luncheon of shrimps and strawberries in the taverna on the beach. High on a crag above the lake at Marathon I came on three aged and gaitered British bishops taking tea. They exchanged sonorous reminiscences about the Royal Family, an unusual scene, occasioned, I found later, by the fact that they had been summoned to the Balkans to investigate the possibility of the fusion of the Anglican and Orthodox Churches. Differences only of ritual apparently existed. Seeking relaxation from their discussions, the bishops had motored out to Marathon and there they sat, as peaceful a group of old gentlemen as ever lingered over their tea in the vicarages of nineteenth-century England. Neither here nor anywhere in Greece was there a hint that a second Marathon was coming. This was the end of May 1940. Flying over Crete and the dreaming islands of the Aegean, it was more difficult still to understand or feel the importance of the news from France. Rethel...Amiens...Arras...all the places to which only a few months ago when I was living in Paris I used to drive with my friends for the weekend. All these were falling.

I flew on to Cairo where we bathed in the pool of the green island, Gezira, in the Nile, or watched the cricket. The Turf Club swarmed with officers newly arrived from England, and a dozen open-air cinemas were showing every night in the hot, brightly lit city. There were all the leftovers from the dollar years when all Egypt swarmed with rich American tourists. We had French wines, grapes, melons, steaks, cigarettes, beer, whisky, and abundance of all things that belonged to rich, idle peace. Officers were taking modern flats in Gezira's big buildings looking out over the golf course and the Nile. Polo continued with the same extraordinary frenzy in the roasting afternoon heat. No one worked from one till five-thirty or six, and even then work trickled through the comfortable offices borne along in a tide of gossip and Turkish coffee and pungent cigarettes. Only the radio and the ticker-machine kept monotonously insisting...Lille... Brussels...Cherbourg. Madame Badia's girls writhed in the belly-dance at her cabaret near the Pont des Anglais. Grey staff cars ran back and forth over the Kasr el Nil bridge. The boatmen on the feluccas cursed and yelled and chanted as they have always done. The first Australian division, sent to the Palestine deserts, was cursing and complaining too. They wanted action instead of route marches in the sand. They were said to be so poorly equipped at this early stage that they were using sticks tied with red flags as anti-tank guns and sticks tied with blue rags as Brens. A sergeant, so the story ran, was court-martialled for cynically demanding a new anti-tank gun of the quartermaster, on the grounds that his old one was eaten by white ants. No, the war was not serious in Egypt at this stage. It was merely a noise on the radio. There were known to be British troops in the Western Desert, of course, but no one doing the round of the parties and the polo in Cairo and Alexandria ever seemed to see them. It was known, too, that they were impatient, and that they nursed an especial hatred of Lady Astor who had recently risen in the Commons to ask why British troops were idling in luxury along the banks of the Mediterranean.

The war correspondents were grouped into a unit known as Public Relations, and they began to gather in Cairo with bright green-and-gold tabs on their uniforms, to seek information. Nothing will quite convey the astonishment and abhorrence with which the elderly colonel and the polo-playing messes received the newspapermen. The officers in charge of Public Relations battled loyally to break down the general and firmly entrenched belief that publicity and propaganda had nothing whatever to do with the army, were in fact anathema to the army. 'The only time

I want to see anything about my men in print is when the honours lists come out,' a brigade-major told me sourly. Incredible conversations occurred over the Public Relations telephones:

'Who are you?'

'Public Relations.'

'What in the name of God is that?'

'It's the unit, sir, which—'

'Never heard of you. Might be a bunch of fifth columnists or something.'

And so on. Pure *Punch*. And like every other unit, we squabbled and laughed and complained and muddled along. But for that cold news from France it didn't seem to matter very much. Censors were established by the three services in offices so far apart that a correspondent had to travel a full fifteen miles in order to visit them all and obtain their stamps on his messages. We thought of organising a censorship Derby in which each correspondent would mount a horse-drawn gharry outside Shepheard's Hotel, and set off to get a message stamped by all three censors. Since the censors were frequently at golf or in their clubs or at parties, it was reckoned that four hours would have been fast time for the course which was to have ended at the cable office.

It was while this nonsense was amusing us that the news broke: France fallen; Italy at war; June 10th, 1940. Slowly, painfully, reluctantly, the Middle East dragged itself out of its apathy. For the first time it realised fear over Dunkirk and worse fear too, closer at hand, for Italy's armies loomed menacingly all through Africa and the Mediterranean. How long could Malta hold out? What was to stop Balbo advancing to the Nile? What forces had we in the Sudan and Kenya to withstand Aosta's three hundred thousand in Eritrea and Abyssinia? And above all, how were we to maintain communications with England?

The answer came in the first week. The Italians attacked by land, sea and air. Communications with England were broken. Released from the menace of the French along the Mareth line in Tunis, Balbo hurried his Western Libyan army in thousands of lorries across to the Egyptian border. One after another the lights in the cities round the Mediterranean went out, and in the darkness the fleet in Alexandria was bombed from the Dodecanese Islands. But surely, we thought, Weygand's army in Syria would stand true. He had done the best he could in France. He couldn't, he wouldn't fail to send us all those tanks in Syria, those Glen-Martin bombers, those five or ten divisions of spahis and foreign legionaries, Moroccans and Senegalese. And Legentilhomme in Djibuti was with us. That would help hold Aosta. Through the rest of June and later still we reasoned like that. The awakening was not quite complete yet. It came in the Middle East not so much when it was realised that the French Empire had capitulated as when, doggedly, the British people turned towards the Empire forces and said: 'All right. We're strong. We'll fight alone.'

Then, at last, it was discovered that we had virtually no forces in the Middle East. All the regiments in Cairo and the Western Desert, all the ships at Alexandria, all the garrisons in Sudan and Kenya, all the raw Australians and New Zealanders training in Palestine and Egypt, all the aircraft that swept occasionally over the burnt-out land—all these amounted to not one-tenth of the forces that Mussolini alone was gathering for his great drive on the Suez Canal. In every department of modern warfare, especially in such equipment as tanks and guns, we were pitifully, hopelessly weak. If you will find greatness in General Wavell, trace it back to the summer months in 1940 when he was beaten on paper before he ever fired a shot. He shut his mouth, confiding in practically no one. He put his trust in the surrounding deserts, he sent appeal after appeal to Churchill for more forces at once, and he held on. It required no great genius, that strategy of simply digging in one's toes and waiting for the enemy to come on. What did require brilliance was the game of bluff on which the General now deliberately embarked.

It was not until some days after the opening of hostilities on the Egyptian border that I got down to the front at Sollum and saw what was happening. Driving out into the desert one early morning from Cairo, I made the first of many journeys to Alexandria, and then turned west along the coast through El Daba, Fuka and Maaten Bagush to Mersa Matruh. This road, some three hundred miles in length, had a relatively good macadam surface, especially on the Cairo–Alexandria section, and running parallel to it beyond Alexandria was the single-track railway. Nothing in the desert justifies either road or railway. El Daba, Fuka and places farther on, like Buq Buq, are merely names on the map. No houses exist there. Bedouin, perhaps, coming on intermittent water-wells, may have given names to these places, but they have nothing to attract either man or beast except this one thing—a spotless white beach that runs steeply into a sea tinted the wonderful shades of a butterfly's wing. To Mersa Matruh went Antony and Cleopatra to enjoy that glorious bathing. On that same beach I found some hundreds of sun-blistered Scots trying to get the desert dust out of their mouths by wallowing naked in the water. Behind them stood Mersa Matruh, and the village at that time was intact. Driving in from the open desert, you suddenly breast a rise and your sun-strained eyes are immediately refreshed by the white township spreading out below and the cool greenish-blue of the bay beyond.

Mersa Matruh had been for years a small watering-place to which the Egyptian pashas and a few of the foreign colony in Egypt used to send their families. Hillier's Hotel, a collection of low, white walls under a flat roof, stood by the water's edge; there was the governor's cottage, the railway station, the church and the mosque, a few shops down the central village street, and not much else.

Artesian water, as at many places along this coast, was drawn from wells, and at Matruh the water was good. Yet only a few weary date-palms and a patch or two of coarse grass and saltbush pushed up through the hot, grey ground.

Yellow rocks, saltbush, grey earth and this perfect beach was the eternal background wherever you looked in the north of the Western Desert. Except at spots along the coast and far inland it never even achieved those picturesque rolling sandhills which Europeans seem always to associate with deserts. It had fresh colours in the morning, and immense sunsets. One clear hot cloudless day followed another in endless progression. A breeze stirred sometimes in the early morning, and again at night when one lay on a camp bed in the open, gazing up into a vaster and more brilliant sky than one could ever have conceived in Europe. I found no subtle fascination there nor any mystery, unless it was the Bedouin who appeared suddenly and unexpectedly out of the empty desert as soon as one stopped one's car. There was a sense of rest and relaxation in the tremendous silence, especially at night, and now, after nearly two years have gone by, the silence is still the best thing I remember of the desert. So then the silence, the cool nights, the clear hot days and the eternal flatness of everything was what you learned to expect of the Western Desert.

But the morning I drove toward Mersa Matruh, looking for Force Headquarters, a khamseen was blowing, and that of course changed everything. The khamseen sandstorm, which blows more or less throughout the year, is in my experience the most hellish wind on earth. It picks up the surface dust as fine as baking powder and blows it thickly into the air across hundreds of square miles of desert. All the way through Daba's tent-hospital base and past Fuka it gathered force along the road until at Bagush it blocked visibility down to half a dozen yards. In front of the car little crazy lines of yellow dust snaked across the road. The dust came up through the engine, through the chinks of the car-body and round the corners of the closed windows. Soon everything in the car was powdered with grit and sand. It crept up your nose and down your throat, itching unbearably and making it difficult to breathe. It got in your eyes, matted your hair, and from behind sand-goggles your eyes kept weeping and smarting. An unreal yellow light suffused everything. Just for a moment the billows of blown sand would open, allowing you to see a little farther into the hot solid fog ahead, and then it would close in again. Bedouin, their heads muffled in dirty rags, lunged weirdly across the track. You sweated, returning again and again to your water-bottle for a swig of warm sandy water, and lay back gasping. I have known soldiers to wear their gas-masks in a khamseen, and others to give way to fits of vomiting. Sometimes a khamseen may blow for days, making you feel that you will never see light and air and feel coolness again. And this, my first, was a bad khamseen. I have been through many shorter and lesser ones since, and some even worse, but I hate them all and I hate the desert because of them.

Groping along from point to point, we found headquarters at last, an inexpressibly dreary place. Dugouts nosed up to the surface amid sandbags and rocks. A few low tents flapped pathetically in the wind. Camels plodded about moodily through trucks and armoured vehicles that were dispersed over a couple of miles of desert. Down on the beach in the yellow gloom a group of naked men were trying to wash the dirt away with salt-water soap. One or two grounded aircraft, their engines swathed in canvas, loomed up out of the sandstorm from the airfield across the other side of the camp. Clearly the war was halted by the weather. Inside the dugouts deepening sand covered everything. In the mess-tent we poured lukewarm beer from cans into gritty glasses, and waited for a luncheon of tinned sausages that was frying in a mixture of fat and sand. There was no ice. Only war could have brought men to this place at such a time, and now we were here we could see less sense in war than ever. The storm eased slightly in the evening, but I slept that night on the ground with my sleeping-bag zipped over my head. Another hot sand-swept morning broke—one of those dreary, lifeless mornings which bring no promise or freshness or feeling of having rested.

The road leading on from Mersa Matruh to Sidi Barrani was still good at this time. Camouflaged water-wagons bound for the forward units were moving along, averaging perhaps six or seven miles an hour. At intervals of twenty miles or so little groups of these supply-wagons turned off into the open desert to the south. Moving by compass across that waste, they would eventually meet brigade, battalion and company headquarters that would be resting briefly at some point that was nothing more than a number on the map. Units were seldom directed to places in the desert. They were simply ordered to proceed on a compass bearing to a certain point, and there camp down. Except in action, there was wireless silence, and communications were kept up by a few light aircraft and motorcyclists.

More and more I began to see that desert warfare resembled war at sea. Men moved by compass. No position was static. There were few if any forts to be held. Each truck or tank was as individual as a destroyer, and each squadron of tanks or guns made great sweeps across the desert as a battle- squadron at sea will vanish over the horizon. One did not occupy the desert any more than one occupied the sea. One simply took up a position for a day or a week, and patrolled about it with Bren-gun carriers and light armoured vehicles. When you made contact with the enemy you manoeuvred about him for a place to strike much as two fleets will steam into position for action. There were no trenches. There was no front line. We might patrol five hundred miles into Libya and call the country ours. The Italians might as easily have patrolled as far into the Egyptian desert without being seen. Actually these patrols in terms of territory conquered meant nothing. They were simply designed to obtain information from personal observation and the capture of prisoners. And they had a certain value in keeping the enemy nervous. But always the essential governing principle was that desert forces must be mobile: they were seeking not the conquest of territory or positions but combat with the enemy. We hunted men, not land, as a warship will hunt another warship, and care nothing for the sea on which the action is fought. And as a ship submits to the sea by the nature of its design and the way it sails, so these new mechanised soldiers were submitting to the desert. They found weaknesses in the ruthless hostility of the desert and ways to circumvent its worst moods. They used the desert. They never sought to control it. Always the desert set the pace, made the direction and planned the design. The desert offered colours in browns, yellows and greys. The army accordingly took these colours for its camouflage. There were practically no roads. The army shod its vehicles with huge balloon tyres and did without roads. Nothing except an occasional bird moved quickly in the desert. The army for ordinary purposes accepted a pace of five or six miles an hour.

The desert gave water reluctantly, and often then it was brackish. The army cut its men—generals and privates—down to a gallon of water a day when they were in forward positions. There was no food in the desert. The soldier learned to exist almost entirely on tinned foods, and contrary to popular belief remained healthy on it. Mirages came that confused the gunner, and the gunner developed precision-firing to a finer art and learned new methods of establishing observation-posts close to targets. The sandstorm blew, and the tanks, profiting by it, went into action under the cover of the storm. We made no new roads. We built no houses. We did not try to make the desert liveable, nor did we seek to subdue it. We found the life of the desert primitive and nomadic, and primitively and nomadically the army lived and went to war.

I make these points at length here because in my belief the Italians failed to accept these principles, and when the big fighting began in the winter it was their undoing. They wanted to be masters of the desert. They made their lives comfortable and static. They built roads and stone houses and the officers strode around in brilliant scented uniforms. They tried to subdue the desert. And in the end the desert beat them.

Already on this midsummer morning when I drove down the road to Sidi Barrani, Marshal Balbo was piling up his great luxurious army along the Egyptian frontier and preparing to roll on across the Western Desert to the Nile. Only a tiny, experienced and toughened little British force stood against him. We came into Sidi Barrani, glaring white in the sun, and the storm was lifting at last. The civilians had long since been evacuated—only a few hundred of them—and the empty houses had been looted by the Bedouin. The first exploratory Italian air raiders had been over the village that morning, and half a dozen dwellings and a general store had been split open. The road was dotted with small, three-foot bomb-craters. There was no sign of the army although half a squadron of British fighter aircraft rested on a remote rise, immobile.

Now we had something almost as bad as the sandstorm to face. The made road ceased in Sidi Barrani. We plunged into knee-deep fine sand that blew up through the floorboards of the car in billowing stifling waves. Every vehicle on the track set up an immense column of dust behind it, creating almost the impression of a destroyer at sea laying a smokescreen. Drivers of passing vehicles manoeuvred to get to the windward of one another so that they would not be overwhelmed in one another's dust. With each man seeking his own track, a full half-mile width of desert was broken up into drifting sand, and sometimes a car plunging through this uneasy surface would crash upon a hidden rock with a force that knocked the breath out of the passengers. Petrol tins burst. Rations flung madly about in the interior of the trucks. I sat there holding the side of the car, hating the desert.

At a saltpan beside the sea, which for some reason bears the name Buq Buq, we came on one of the advance headquarters. It was clearer and cooler here, at last, and the soothing whisper of the waves came across the sand-dunes. Guns, tanks and cars were dispersed about rather like an American middle-western caravan at a halt. In the centre of the dried-up lake stood the officers' mess—a plain trestle-table with a camp stove burning beside it. We took tea there, and as we drank, a whistle suddenly shrilled from the edge of the camp and we ran for the slit trenches. These trenches were to become as famous as the Anderson shelters in London. They were simply narrow graves dug about four feet into the earth. Whenever it stopped for the night, the first job of the crew of every fighting vehicle was to dig one of these trenches. Apart from retaliation, it was the only protection the desert could give against air raids, and it was nearly a hundred per cent effective. I myself have been in a trench when a bomb has burst three yards away, and come to no harm beyond being partly buried in sand. And so on this day we huddled into the trench and crouched there while a three-engined Savoia bomber, flying low enough for us to see its pilot, swept leisurely over the horizon. We had at that time no effective gun for hitting him. It was just a matter of crouching there and seeing if our camouflage was good or not. He came down to two thousand feet and circled slowly round. The afternoon was now sparkling clear, and it seemed so certain that he must see and dive that it was a curious unlooked-for disappointment when he turned away and nothing happened. We went back to tea.

Now at last we were close to the front and able to see Wavell's game of bluff in action. It was vitally necessary, the general saw, to convince the enemy that we were much stronger than we actually were. This was not easy in so open a place as the desert. Yet it was being done—how successfully we only learned months later. The painfully thin British forces were scattered for hundreds of miles across the desert facing the Libyan frontier. They had one all-important standing order: make one man appear to be a dozen, make one tank look like a squadron, make a raid look like an advance. And so this little Robin Hood force, being unable to withstand any sort of a determined advance by the half-dozen Italian divisions across the border, did the unpredicted, unexpected thing—it attacked. It attacked not as a combined force but in small units, swiftly, irregularly and by night. It pounced on Italian outposts, blew up the captured ammunition, and ran away. It stayed an hour, a day, or a week in a position, and then disappeared. The enemy had no clear idea of when he was going to be attacked next or where. Fort Maddalena fell, and Capuzzo. Sidi Aziz was invested. British vehicles were suddenly astride the road leading back from Bardia, shooting up convoys. Confused and anxious, the Italians rigged up searchlights and scoured the desert with them while British patrols lay grinning in the shadows. Soon, from prisoners we learned extraordinary stories were going the rounds behind the Italian lines. There were two…three…five British armoured divisions operating, they said. A large-scale British attack was imminent. Balbo drew in his horns, cut down his own patrols and called for more reinforcements from Rome. The bluff was working.

Back in Cairo, Wavell, consulting with Air Marshal Sir Arthur Longmore and Admiral Cunningham, knew that it had to work. He had to have time. Every day brought the first convoys of reinforcements nearer Egypt, and without them he knew he would not withstand a large-scale Italian attack. Somehow that attack had to be delayed through the summer. Somehow the enemy had to be kept timid, anxious and in doubt. But there were signs that Balbo would not be deluded for ever. Already after the first few weeks he was cautiously trying out his hand, cautiously testing the strength of the British.

It was at one such moment that I had arrived from Buq Buq at Sollum, geographically the most distinctive spot in the Western Desert. The coast here sweeps round in a great curve to the Libyan frontier. Locked in the arc of this shallow bay lies the lower half of the village of Sollum, a customs post, sheltering among a group of some thirty white-topped stone huts beside the sea. A small jetty has been constructed to accommodate coastal steamers bringing supplies to the unfortunate people who lived monotonously in this monotonous spot. But easily the most arresting thing, the thing that riveted your eyes from miles away, was the escarpment. This is an immense cliff rising six hundred feet sheer from the Egyptian plain. The cliff, buttressing on its heights the Libyan desert and reaching at its depths the Western Desert, cuts on to the Mediterranean roughly at right angles on a north-south line.

South of Sollum, however, it strikes south-east and runs away from the strict north-south line of the Egyptian–Libyan border. Two routes wind up the cliff-face from lower Sollum: one which climbs precariously over the very edge of the sea is a wide modern road. The other, Halfaya Pass—Hellfire Pass was the troops' word for it—is no more than a track. It starts from the coast a few miles east of Sollum, and over broken grey rocks and rubble lifts you steeply on to the Libyan desert. Once on the top there you command a broad vision of the Egyptian coastline sweeping far away to the east. Upper Sollum was then a collection of sun-baked white barracks, the home of an Egyptian frontier force, and a stony airfield. Fifteen or twenty miles away on the coast to the north-west lies Bardia, the first Libyan township, and at this time an important Fascist headquarters. Dividing Sollum and Bardia, and along the whole frontier, Mussolini had constructed a wire fence. This ran southward some hundreds of miles, and was built, it was said, to prevent the Libyan natives escaping into Egypt from the Fascist régime. It consisted of a quadruple line of five-feet metal stakes bedded in concrete and closely woven with barbed wire. It must have been some twenty feet in width. The cost of the fence must have been enormous, its conception absurd, its uses nil. It revealed how strongly a man may be driven by the acquisitive instinct, how ridiculous a lust for property can be. The escaping Libyan threw out his cloak over the barbed wire, and crawled through. The British tank setting out on patrol into Libya simply nosed the fence aside. Yet that absurd fence, like many another absurd Italian device in the desert, seemed to give the Fascist soldier a sense of security, and he patrolled it with the persistence of a goldfish edging along the confines of his glass jar.

It was black night when I joined one of our forward companies on the heights above Sollum. Since they were within range, the soldiers lived in caves among the rocks and slept by day. At night they crawled out and, mounting trucks and Bren-gun carriers, bowled confidently across the face of the desert up to the Italian lines. Reaching the point where their car engines might be heard, they disembarked and crept forward afoot until they came on an Italian outpost. Then with the bayonet they set about taking prisoners of those who submitted quickly, and killing those who did not. It was heady, exciting work. From far across the desert as I stood talking to an outgoing patrol the Italian searchlight would turn full upon us. I was tempted to duck and hide though we were much too distant to be seen.

Fort Capuzzo, some five miles down to the south-west, had just been taken though not occupied by us for the very good reason that we had not the troops or the vehicles to spare to man it. But wrecking-parties were going into the fort each night to deal with ammunition stores and vehicles the Italians left behind. Capuzzo was little else but four white stone walls with crenellated battlements enclosing a central courtyard. Around the edges of the courtyard were the men's quarters. It was a typical desert post of the type that was valuable for keeping Arab tribesmen at bay. In modern warfare its walls crumpled under even the lightest shell.

It was arranged that we should return the following night and go in with a patrol to see this Fort Capuzzo. To cross there in the daylight meant bringing down certain fire from the Italians. Of course, the company commander agreed unemotionally, it was always possible that an enemy patrol might be entering the fortress in the darkness about the same time as we would be. Additionally, the approaches to the fort were mined. These land mines, like the fence, were another illustration of the Italian passion for defence. The whole distance from Sollum to Benghazi he strewed them across the desert. Later we were to get sufficiently used to them to be able to treat them with contempt. Yet they were good mines. They were about four feet long and divided into three compartments. The two end compartments each contained four pounds of explosives, the central one the detonator. A green lid snapped down over the top of the whole mine. Originally the mines were designed to explode at the pressure of an ordinary wheeled vehicle, but the detonator wires rusted and they were often sensitive even to the footfall of a man. These mines were laid in lines across the roads and around all fortified positions. Usually they were buried just deep enough to allow a thin layer of sand to rest on top of them, but the depressions could be clearly seen as a rule. A mine going off on the driver's side of a vehicle would have sufficient force to break the legs of the driver or even destroy him and the vehicle altogether. Tank tracks could be broken by a mine. So special sapper squads were formed to deal with them, and always when an advance was on you would see the sappers going on ahead. The chief danger was that one would stumble on these mines in the darkness, and that, I remember, was the uppermost thought in my mind as we drove up to Sollum the following night to make our expedition into Capuzzo.

As we crept round the bay in the darkness the whole black silhouetted edge of the escarpment above suddenly erupted with high explosive. It came so unexpectedly that it was impossible to say what it was—mines, shells or bombs. But then a second and a third line of explosions lit the cliff-top and thundered in billowing, acrid smoke across Sollum toward the sea. We stopped the car and watched. It began to look like shelling…yes, certainly Italian shelling. As we watched, a truck came flying down the cliff road and raced past us, then another and another. A staff car loomed up from the same direction and, bumping to a standstill, deposited the brigade-major on to the sand beside us.

'Where the hell do you think you're going?'

'Capuzzo, sir. We arranged—'

The major was tired and harassed. 'All right,' he snapped. 'Just let me know how you get on. I'm getting out myself. Fifty enemy tanks have just gone into the fort, and I'd like to know what else is coming. They're laying down a barrage now along the escarpment.' He need not have told us. Another burst of shells whined overhead and broke the darkness with yellow flashes. So Capuzzo was retaken, then. Balbo was showing his hand. I had wanted badly to see Capuzzo, for it was important war news in those days, but there was nothing for it but to turn back toward our rear positions.

We cut south from the road at Buq Buq and, travelling over a broken track all the next day, we climbed the escarpment deep in the desert. On the Libyan plateau there we found units of our armoured forces. It was the first time I had seen these men who were eight months later to make their great march to the Libyan Gulf and overwhelm the last of the broken Italian armies at the battle of Beda Fomm. Already they had been months in the desert. Their faces had blistered red in the sun and after so long an isolation from civilisation they were eager to meet any stranger. We were taken to the brigadier and with delight we heard from him that he intended to try to recapture Capuzzo with his tanks that same night. We went forward to a slight rise some four miles out of Capuzzo, and waited there in the blazing afternoon sun for the attack to begin. Before us the tower and the white walls of the fort rose above the lip of the horizon. On the left flank a half-squadron of our medium tanks had broken through the frontier fence and lay silently waiting for the arrival of a heavily armed enemy squadron which, our intelligence had learned, was making its way from Sidi Aziz toward Capuzzo. On the right flank the main body of British tanks which were to carry the main assault at dusk was creeping in open formation toward the fort. At our feet stood a battery of twenty-five-pounder guns. We had been told that was the battle plan. Now in the hot tense silence of the late afternoon we waited for the drama to unroll. As the sun, growing redder and larger, dipped on Libya, it began to unfold stage by stage. First came the British aircraft to sweep the sky of enemy raiders. They plunged on an Italian flight of three Savoias that was bombing rear headquarters behind us, and put them to flight. Then, a line of black geese in the red sky, the British fighters wheeled over the expectant battlefield, found the sky clear and turned away. The battery before us opened up, not shrilly or loudly for the heavy air seemed to deaden the sound. There was just the steady rhythmical coughing of each gun firing in turn. They were sighting on an Italian battery to the left of the fort, and as each hit registered a great pillar of black sand and smoke flowered upward and spread in the form of a mushroom, making a great stain on the clear blue background of the sea beyond. The Italians did not reply. The British tanks, no more than silhouettes now in the waning light, waited motionless. A desert fox ran across the battlefield. Someone laughed. I went over to our car and got out a pot of raspberry jam and some biscuits and handed them around. The attack would come any moment now. I dredged up another spoonful of jam and felt absurdly that I was again sitting in the Haymarket Theatre in London at a Saturday matinée, and I wanted to laugh. My shirt had gone dirty black with soaking perspiration. Then the tanks attacked. They had half a mile to go, and each tank, shooting as it went, attacked one of the Italian guns spaced around Capuzzo's walls. The enemy guns waited perhaps two minutes. Then they spouted out a deafening salvo that enveloped the whole fort in smoke. Smoke rose everywhere. A full expanding cloud of blown dust split by gun-flashes rolled out across the desert toward us, and one after another the British tanks dived into it and disappeared. In a moment the battle lost all shape. There was only noise and light growing louder and brighter under the pall of smoke.

We waited, straining our eyes until it was full night, and then, while the firing began gradually to die away, we turned back to brigade headquarters to find out what had happened.

Nothing good had happened. The Italians had driven our tanks off. The British colonel in command was wounded. One or two of our tanks were wrecked, others for the moment missing. As we ate bully stew in the mess, ambulances lumbered back over the rocky track.

This, the first action I had seen in the desert, was a defeat. With one minor exception late in the Benghazi campaign, it was the only British reverse at the hands of the Italians that I was going to see for more than a year.

Two

Graziani has taken command. . .an attack must be expected. -STATEMENT ISSUED BY G.H.Q., CAIRO, AUGUST 6TH, 1940.

IN THE full midsummer of 1940, Mussolini saw his great chance. Italy had earned only contempt for her entrance into the battle of France when the battle of France was done. Now, with England preoccupied with home defence, her Mediterranean and African possessions seemed an easy prey. Conquest in Africa would elevate and enrich Mussolini at home, increase his standing with Hitler, and justify Italy to herself and the world. With the French armies in Tunis and Syria removed, there was no saying how many British mandates and possessions and spheres of influence might not fall. There were Malta, the Sudan, Palestine, Cyprus, British Somaliland, Aden, Iraq, Kenya and, richest of all, the Nile valley. Nowhere was there anything like a strong British garrison. Even at sea the Mediterranean fleet was outgunned and outnumbered. In the air the odds were ridiculously to the Fascists' advantage. There were not at this stage more than half a dozen Hurricanes in Africa. So orders went out from Rome to the Italian commanders in Libya and Abyssinia to attack. In Tobruk easygoing Balbo had met his death in an air crash that may or may not have been accidental; 'Butcher' Graziani took command. In Addis Ababa the Duke of Aosta had a score of good generals and ample stores for a colonial campaign.

Soon the Italians had retaken all the frontier points in Libya, like Capuzzo and Fort Maddalena.

Kassala, the border town between the Sudan and Eritrea, was captured easily by Italian forces advancing northward. Gallabat, on the Abyssinian border farther south, was the next, together with Kurmuk. Around to the westward the British were driven out of Gambela, a trading post, and southward on the Kenya boundary, Fort Harrington was swiftly overwhelmed. Fascist columns began marching deep into Kenya. There was worse to come. Pro-British General Legentilhomme, the French commander in Djibuti, was ousted from his command by Vichy and forced to flee into British territory, leaving behind a group of French leaders who were willing, even eager, to parley with Aosta. That meant a Red Sea port for the Italians as well as Massawa, and, better still, a guarded flank for their next move. In August Aosta threw two partly mechanised divisions into British Somaliland. They were split into three columns, one striking directly at Zeila on the coast; the other two farther east advancing through the mountains on Berbera, the capital. Two British battalions largely of native troops fought a rearguard action. But it was soon over. A British colony—a poor one, but still a British possession—was at last in Axis hands. It was the empire's first territorial loss with the exception of the Channel Islands. The propaganda effect was considerable. In England, now enduring the full weight of the first heavy daylight attacks, people began to despair of the Middle East. In Italy Mussolini rode on a sudden wave of enthusiasm and popularity. Italians everywhere after generations of inferiority complex began to tell themselves: 'We are a revived nation. We can fight.' They had felt that a little over the Ethiopian, Spanish and Albanian campaigns. But now they were opposed to British, and to beat the British was a high excitement. Mussolini, no fool, would not deny this rising wave of high morale. Even his lukewarm supporters were eager for more victories.

Even Germany was smiling politely and with just a shade more respect. In Rome, then, in that romantic grandiloquent room in the Palazzo Venezia that had seen so many Fascist chances taken and won, the Duce hatched his grand plan for the conquest of the Middle East and the enlargement of his African Empire to more than three times its size.

With France out of the way, the Italian grand strategy had clearly four main themes: a full-scale holding raid southward of Kenya; another northward through Kassala down the Atbara River to the Nile to isolate Khartoum and cut the British retreat from Egypt; an invasion of Egypt direct with motorised columns advancing along the coast to Alexandria and Cairo; and attack in the later stages on Greece through Albania in order to draw off British forces to Athens and thus weaken the resistance against Graziani in the Western Desert. The importance of the two southerly raids was also to keep the British dispersed and weak in Egypt, which was to be subjected to the full shock of the Libyan army. In conception the plan was excellent; in execution deplorable. Mussolini did not even have especially bad luck. He simply once again overstrained and overestimated the Italian people. His thoughts reached upward heroically. The people remained tied to the ground, artistic, erratic, shiftless, individualist and irresponsible.

But all went well at first. The most southerly column plunged farther and farther into Kenya, where General Cunningham's South, West and East African forces were still unprepared for battle. In Eritrea forces were gathering rapidly to sweep on to the Sudan. In Libya, Graziani gave the order to advance. Down the escarpment came the Fascist armies, a host several divisions strong, as brave and confident as a crusade on the march. Wavell's bluff had been called. The Italians had come out at last to do battle, and there was nothing for it but to beat a retreat with the tiny British forces in as dignified a way as possible.

Only two very minor but significant incidents relieved the depressing effect of this new withdrawal. At Sollum British gunners noted that enemy vehicles coming down the winding escarpment road into Egypt caught the sun on their windshields at one exposed corner. A few seconds later each vehicle exposed itself again very briefly on another bend lower down. Our gunners had merely to note each reflected flash from the windshields and then aim at the lower corner. In this way numbers of enemy transports were knocked out and the Italian advance was delayed.

At Sollum also, British engineers had mined a number of buildings and dumps before they retired to a point farther up the coast, taking their detonating wires with them. They were about to start exploding Sollum at this safe distance when an Italian artillery observation plane appeared over the village, and the enemy gunners directed by the pilot began to lay down a barrage. The situation was piquant. Both sides were allied in destroying the same object. With a nice sense of humour the British commander ordered his men to wait until they heard an Italian gun fire, then, before the shell landed he gave instructions for one of his mines to be exploded. Inevitably the mine went off in a part of the village where the Italian air-observer had not directed his fire. One knew that the enemy observer, utterly mystified, was signalling back to his guns demanding they should correct their fire and asking the reason for the double explosion. Undoubtedly, too, he was getting equally confused replies from his gunners. The farce went on until the British mines were exhausted. The Italian plane flew off and Sollum was released at last from the fury of the two armies. I say these two episodes were significant, for they revealed that the British under fire from a heavy enemy advance showed no panic and, indeed, even at this early stage held the Italian in some contempt. Then, too, our casualties in the withdrawal were scarcely a score of men and vehicles, and not the two thousand which Graziani with grandiose stupidity claimed in his first communiqué.

But no one in Cairo that September knew how far and how fast Graziani was going to go. Wavell had determined to avoid serious engagement until the Italians reached Mersa Matruh, about one-third of the way to the Delta. We had been digging traps and entrenchments in the sand for months at Mersa Matruh, but would they hold? Down the escarpment came more and more water-trucks, guns, donkey teams, tanks, armoured cars. There were thousands of vehicles against our hundreds, divisions of men against our brigades, squadrons of Savoias and Capronis against our handful of Blenheims and Gladiators. Graziani, who could hardly be called a hot-head, pulled up short at Sidi Barrani after the first sixty miles to consolidate and wait for the Greek stage of the Italian plan to mature. Slowly, methodically and with immense labour he began to fortify and build up his lines of communications.

By the late autumn he had at Sidi Barrani a sure base from which to embark on the second leg of his advance to the Suez Canal, and some hundred thousand men all well equipped were ready to set out in the cool of the winter. His new road, the Via della Vittoria, linking Sollum with Sidi Barrani, needed only light screenings and tarring for completion. He had abundant supplies of all kinds. He had control in the air—in numbers anyway. The British victory at Taranto, though serious, had not knocked out the Italian navy. The battle of Cape Matapan was still to come.

Mussolini's Greek invasion came in November with nice timing. No one could have foreseen the disaster ahead. It was in Greece that both Mussolini and General Wavell had their major setbacks. Both started in Africa, both failed to wait until they had consolidated their African victories, both went to Greece hastily, too lightly armed and taking too little account of the differences between colonial war in Africa and world war in Europe. The only major difference between the adventures of the two men was that Mussolini himself elected to go to Greece. Wavell was forced to it.

No one could have guessed how deeply Mussolini had been misled by his intelligence services on two vital points. It seems he really believed the Greeks would not fight. That was his first error. He failed to learn the lessons of the Republicans in Spain, the Finns in Finland. Nor was Mussolini alone in failing to see that war was still made with men first and machines second, and that a people once fired with a passionate hatred and an emotional patriotism are the most dangerous enemy in the world though they lack every essential piece of equipment. His second mistake was in believing Wavell was stronger than he actually was. He did not know that Wavell, apart from a few aircraft, simply did not have more than a brigade or two at the most to spare for Greece at that time. He did not know that the Greeks had said to Wavell: 'Give us a strong force of five or six equipped divisions or no men at all, otherwise, if you send a small force, it will merely provoke the Germans against us without our being able to withstand them.' So what British troops there were in Egypt stayed there to meet Graziani.

Part of Mussolini's plan had miscarried. No British expeditionary force was sent to Greece at that moment for the embarrassing reason that there was none large enough to send. We were a small but united command.

It is conceivable that Mussolini might have done better if he had reversed the later stages of his plan: i.e., to have attacked Greece first and then sent Graziani into Egypt. Then possibly Wavell might have been induced to send troops to Greece and left himself exposed in Egypt. That, anyway, was what happened later.

I personally had seen none of the reverses which led up to the triumphant Italian position at the beginning of the winter of 1940. I had left the Western Desert before Graziani advanced to Sidi Barrani and had gone down to the Sudan with the first party of war correspondents. In mid-July we had boarded the biweekly train in Cairo and in stifling heat travelled overnight to Shellal where two riverboats festered in the mud much in the same way as they did when Kitchener passed by on his way to conquer the Sudan from the Khalifa forty years before. One of the boats, I believe, was actually built by Kitchener. They were squalid double-decked affairs designed like houseboats, square shaped, with rows of cabins lining each deck. Rows of flat barges piled with grain or cotton or peanuts and swarming with natives were lashed to either side of the parent boat, and bathed it with the perpetual odour of cooking fat and human offal. A giant waterwheel thrashed out the stale Nile water from the square stern, and there was an open space forward set out like a lounge where we sat and sweated and stuck to the wicker chairs and imagined we were gathering a breeze from the snail- like motion of the boat. For two days and nights we sat there climbing the river between Shellal and Wadi Halfa where the first cataract starts on the Sudan border. A month later I did the same journey in twenty minutes in the cockpit of a Blenheim bomber.

Nothing is quite so slow as the deadly excruciating slowness of the Nile boats. It was before the annual flood, and I gazed across the mud flats at the strip of green on either bank—palms, wheat, reeds, grass huts—that always seemed the same and never revealed any motion in the boat. Farther up, nearer the White Nile sources, a planter told me, one sees the same tree sticking out of the river for three days. One day is spent steaming up to the tree, another in winding around it, a third in watching it disappear on a horizon of dun-coloured lifeless reeds and sleepy water. To do this in cool winter, to do it in peace-time on holiday in the company of women when the moon at night is brighter than an English winter sun—all this would be fine. To do it in midsummer, in war, when there are no women and the drinks are warm and the flies innumerable, and one is in a hurry and suffering from the mild dysentery everyone gets in Africa, is my idea of slow torture. Yet this journey I see now was an oasis in the rush with which we lived, and we really did enjoy parts of it. Edward Genock of Paramount News stowed his film in the overworked icebox to stop it melting. Ronald Matthews of the *Daily Herald* summoned what bottles of cool Allsop's beer he could. Richard Dimbleby of the

B.B.C. found a chaise-longue and a grass fan. I stripped to the waist and read through *The River War*, that classic book on the Omdurman campaign, written by Kitchener's young second-lieutenant in the Twenty-first Lancers, Winston Churchill. Churchill, already beginning his career as a war correspondent, records with powerful accuracy just what the Upper Nile was like when he went up it at the end of last century to take part in the Lancers' great charge at Omdurman. The description holds still, will always hold. With feeling I read: 'This great tract which may conveniently be called The Military Sudan stretched with apparent indefiniteness over the face of the continent. Level plains of smooth sand—a little rosier than buff, a little paler than salmon— are interrupted only by occasional peaks of rock—black, stark and shapeless. Rainless storms dance tirelessly over the hot crisp surface of the ground. The fine sand, driven by the wind, gathers into deep drifts and silts among the dark rocks of the hills, exactly as snow hangs about an Alpine summit; only it is fiery snow such as might fall in hell. The earth burns with the quenchless thirst of ages and in the steel-blue sky scarcely a cloud obstructs the unrelenting triumph of the sun.' Then again: 'It is scarcely within the power of words to describe the savage desolation of the regions into which the line and its constructors now plunged. A smooth ocean of bright coloured sand spread far and wide to distant horizons. The tropical sun beat with senseless perseverance upon the level surface until it could scarcely be touched with a naked hand, the filmy air glittered and shimmered as over a furnace. Here and there huge masses of crumbling rock rose from the plain, like islands of cinders in a sea of fire.'

Despite the heat, one had to agree with Churchill that the

transformation of the colours of the river and the desert at sunset had a beauty that was quite unearthly. Churchill, then still in his twenties, abandoned for a moment his Gibbonesque phrasing to describe it like this: 'There is one hour when all is changed. Just before the sun sets towards the western cliffs a delicious flush brightens and enlivens the landscape. It is as though some titanic artist in an hour of inspiration were retouching the picture, painting in dark purple shadows among the rocks, strengthening the lights on the sands, gilding and beautifying everything, and making the whole scene live. The river, whose windings made it look like a lake, turns from muddy brown to silver grey. The sky from a dull blue deepens into violet in the west. Everything under that magic touch becomes vivid and alive. And then the sun sinks altogether behind the rocks, the colours fade out of the sky, the flush off the sands, and gradually everything darkens and grows grey—like a man's cheek when he is bleeding to death. We are left sad and sorrowful in the dark, until the stars light up and remind us that there is always something beyond.'

Much of Churchill's time was spent around Wadi Halfa and that is where now one goes ashore, passes through the Sudan customs and takes the train—Kitchener's train—on through Atbara to Khartoum. There, Dimbleby was taken at once to hospital with diphtheria. The rest of us, Matthews, Genock and myself, were summoned to Lieut.-General Platt, the man who under the native title of the Kaid was responsible for guarding this territory almost the size of Europe from the Italians.

He told us bluntly at once his position was precarious. Some two thousand men—a little more than one man to a mile of frontier—was the entire army with which the imperial government had provided him. He had the use of four obsolete Vincent aircraft, and down near the Red Sea a couple of squadrons of obsolescent Wellesleys had been loaned by the R.A.F. to keep the British sea-lane free of Italian raiders. That was all. The Sudan Defence Force, though well trained, had no tanks, no artillery, and its thin native ranks were a joke compared with the legions Aosta was preparing to bring against us. Even in the last few weeks an ominous warning had come in the fall of Kassala, and with Kassala one branch of our railway to Port Sudan had been cut. The affair was all the more serious as we ourselves, using the offensive patrol tactics of the Western Desert, had been planning to attack the Italian positions behind Kassala at the time. A cypher clerk had failed to send on the final action orders to the British forces at the vital moment. In the confusion that followed, when the British were regrouping, the Italians themselves had taken the initiative, swooping on Kassala on the very day when the Gash River, since time immemorial, came down in flood. Since the river runs between the town and the railway station, and there was no bridge, this meant that the little British garrison in the town was all but cut off. General Wavell had been up to Khartoum, the Kaid said, and there was some prospect of reinforcements and better staff work. But at the moment things were in a very anxious state indeed.

Nor were we more than a few days in Khartoum when we found how sorely unprepared for war both psychologically and materially was the place. Most of the white men had been in the colony for years, building by sheer hard work in a difficult climate an administration and an economy that was a model of government anywhere. Unlike the administrations of Egypt, the Sudan officials had made their homes there and established families and identified themselves with the country. They had won the confidence of the natives. They had, moreover, a great deal of sympathy for the Italian settlers and administrators across the border who in the few years they had been in Abyssinia were making a titanic effort to produce another model colony as well. Friendships had naturally grown up between Italians and British. Military outposts exchanged gifts of whisky and chianti across the border. Italian officers visited British messes and the British went back across the border where the hospitality was returned. Sir George Symes, the British governor-general, had become intimate with the Duke of Aosta who had stayed at the palace in Khartoum, making friends everywhere with his charm, his command of English, his 'Englishness.' Everyone liked Aosta, and friendships spread among the white staffs of the two races. The Italians from the first had said frankly that war with Britain was unthinkable, and the British had agreed enthusiastically. But now suddenly, on that black day in June, Mussolini declared war, and the former friends found themselves enemies. An Italian colonel had to cancel a social visit to a British unit on the Abyssinian border.

Now all that these administrators had painfully built up through the years was to be torn down and thrown away in warfare. The bridges they had built, the roads they had forced through mountains and across deserts, the railways and fine new houses and waterworks they had forged in this barren waste, were suddenly to be destroyed. The friends with whom they had played polo and drunk were to be cut down. It was, in all truth, unthinkable. Here, remote from the play of politics in Europe, it was hard to reverse one's ideas overnight. Here, where every white man, Italian or British, was an ally in the labour of gathering the natives into civilisation, it was a flat denial of all sense to stir the tribes. So British Sudan and Italian East Africa went to war reluctantly and slowly and with immense misgiving. It was a gentleman's war. There was some undefined but quite real understanding that there would be no bombing of civilians or helpless native settlements. When Balbo, one of the same gentlemanly cut as Aosta, died, his death was announced in the *Sudan Herald* with black borders around the printed column. I found an unexpressed, undercurrent feeling that the two colonies, Italian and British, were not really concerned in the war, and since their battles could not affect the general situation there was no point in carrying the fighting to extremes. Germany was the real enemy. I was to see through the months ahead how this lax but very understandable feeling was to harden into animosity and how in deadly engagements like Keren real hatred was to emerge. But to the end our campaign in East Africa was conducted on lines that never approached the fury and bitterness of Europe, or left scars comparable with even a single week's fighting in the battle of France or Russia.

Back in the late July of 1940, when the rains were beginning to cool the torrid air a little, there was apathy in Khartoum. The lions and more dangerous beasts had been killed in Khartoum's famous zoo, lest, being wounded in an air raid, the animals might run amok through the streets. The white civilians, many of them middle-aged men, had contrived to collect a few Lewis guns and, banding themselves into a home guard, they trained with astonishing vigour on the flat stony ground across the Nile at Omdurman. But it was an exuberant half-measure, and there was nothing in Khartoum to withstand any sort of an attack either by land or air. Haile Selassie had arrived from England by air a day before us and was installed in a shoddy pink villa surrounded by a garden of lifeless shrubs along the Blue Nile. Thither we were conducted one morning, and in the first bright heat of the day the emperor emerged on to his balcony and gravely shook us by the hand. He himself had still that impassive dignity that carried him through defeat and humiliation in Geneva. His eyes were quick and watchful, and his bearing still imperious. But his surroundings were shabby, his hopes remote and his whole cause a tiny dagger in a world of heavy bombers and battleships. The ceremony that morning verged on the ridiculous. It was only Selassie's extraordinary restless spirit and his overwhelming seriousness that made the occasion seem at all real. Ethiopian chieftains who had lately crossed the Italian lines to Sudan were brought before him. They were barefoot, clad in unclean, shapeless robes, their fuzzy hair, stiff with grease and lice, was piled on their heads, their bodies were wound about with huge cartridge belts filled with bullets from the wars of another century…bullets for which they had no guns anyway. They prostrated themselves before Selassie, who sat in the bright sun under an enormous topee, evincing no interest whatever. Genock, surrounded by native boys, toiled round the emperor, filming hard. He crouched, sighted, squatted, took angle-shots and close-ups, while the rest of us stood about saying nothing; and faintly in one's head one heard the Italian jeers. Truly that morning the chances of the King of Kings did not look auspicious. Nor could one find much hope in the contemplation of the youthful Duke of Harar, the emperor's son, who had changed from the pyjamas in which we had first met him into a suit of khaki drill that hung shapelessly on his slight angular body. Presently we went inside the house with the emperor, and drank warm beer laced with lemonade. Selassie unbent toward Genock, an old friend, but they talked mostly about a camera the emperor wanted to sell, and his monosyllabic replies coming through to us by way of an Amharic interpreter advanced neither our information about the present nor our hopes for the future. Through his chief aide, a cultured and attractive little Ethiopian, Selassie issued a proclamation that day saying he had returned to free his country from the Italians. Plans were on foot for getting this proclamation into the dissident tribes in Abyssinia, plus a few guns and golden thalers. But privately the emperor had been surprised and deeply disappointed at the lack of arms in the Sudan and the failure of the British to offer him anything concrete. In London he had understood that he would be furnished with bombers, guns, trucks, tanks, ammunition, and he did not hesitate to express his disappointment to the Kaid in Khartoum. Yes, that was a grey day in the African war, and the affairs of the emperor looked stale, flat and painfully unprofitable. Matthews and I went off the next day on the long train journey to the front outside Kassala. It was a convivial train. The railway officer in charge had a suite with a bath, and there we would go in the evening to bathe and drink warm whisky until the train stopped at a convenient halt, when we would walk back along the track to our carriage. Food one either brought oneself and gave to one's native boy to cook, or accepted what the railways had to provide. It was customary for the passenger to bring his own drinks, which were kept by the boy in some remote ice-chest on the train and produced before luncheon and dinner. The train brought life to the primitive grass-hut settlements in the interior.

Natives swarmed up to the track to post and receive letters, gossip, and gather their merchandise.

Passengers as green as we were would jump down and wander through the poor village bazaars and buy daggers made from bits of steel looted from the railway track. Extraordinary things were for sale at every halt—bundles of aromatic twigs used for the cleaning of teeth, camel sticks for guiding camels, sweetmeats violent in colour and taste. But these black Fuzzy Wuzzies, Hadendoas and Nubas were magnificent in physique, and after the riverine tribes of the lower Nile they appeared as a race revived and refreshed. Their teeth were perfect and they smiled constantly. No hawker pressed his wares or molested the stranger. Their tight glossy skins shone with a luminous blackness, and the naked children played with a gaiety and vigour seldom seen south of the Egyptian border. They were as statuesque and natural as animals as they stood stork-like upon one leg, holding the other foot against the knee—a comfortable stance once you can manage it. The grass conical-shaped tukals in which the villagers lived were as natural and attractive as a field of wheat, and a relief to anyone used to the broken-down mud-hut villages of the Nile Delta. There was cleanliness and breath here.

The Mohammedan, stricter than any town dweller, religiously spread his mat on the earth, washed himself from a stone water-jar as it is prescribed in the Koran, and prayed with a sincerity that made him oblivious to all that went on around him. Many of the adults worked on the railway—worked on tirelessly, regardless of growing age but dropping the labour as soon as they tired of it with childish irrelevance. They would go off to the villages for a month or two and then return to work again. I heard from the railway officer of one old man who was told he was too old to work. He protested he was only thirty-five—a point which he could not have proven anyway, since the natives take no numerical account of the years. He was eventually given a job and worked stoutly at carrying sleepers and rails. Then one day the overseer heard him chatting to his mates about the battle of Omdurman. It appeared that he had fought Kitchener there.

Then, too, after months of dry heat in the Egyptian desert, we were seeing rain again—warm scented rain that deluged on the black cotton soil in the evenings, turning the ground into a muck and bringing a sense of relief after the long hot day. And trees appeared again as we advanced on Sennar Dam—thorn scrub, perhaps twenty feet high, the country of elephant and lion and baboons and antelope. Like schoolboys we rode across the roaring buttress of the dam in the cab of the locomotive and watched the snow-white ibises rising in lazy clouds against just such a sunset as awed Churchill here over a generation ago. This was the Blue Nile that flows from Lake Tana in the heart of Abyssinia. Here at Sennar the annual flood is locked and released with such exactitude during the following dry season that engineers can assess almost to the inch how much water is flooding through the irrigation drains of the fellaheen in Lower Egypt, over a thousand miles away. The flood was early yet, but already the water thrashed through the sluices with a roar that drowned conversation.

Later, the Blue Nile would rise to such strength that at the confluence at Khartoum the slower flooding White Nile would be forced to flow backwards. Then later again the White Nile that flows out of the rotting swamps in central Africa would gain its own impetus and restore the current at Khartoum to its normal direction. Together, then, the White and Blue Niles would sweep on to the Mediterranean, bringing life to twenty million people. Idly it had been suggested that the Italians might withhold the supply from Lake Tana or even poison the water. The hugeness of Sennar alone denied that nonsense, and later in Khartoum I met a British officer who had explored the reaches of the Blue Nile for the express purpose of proving that theory false.

Near Gedaref we approached the front. Sometimes in this final stretch Matthews and I would go ahead of the train in a rattling petrol-driven trolley. This used to proceed to the next station after every halt to report washaways on the line—a frequent happening that sometimes held up the traffic for days. From the trolley we watched the antelope bounding across the line or stopped and followed the bell-like calls of the baboons through the trees.

Gedaref is a malarial spot where one sleeps beneath netting, and it is wise to wear long trousers and poke the turn-ups under your socks. Here on a cool windy hilltop the British had established divisional headquarters in a wide verandahed villa.

Away southward, four days' march by she-camel, lay one front at Gallabat. Northward at Kasm el Girba outside Kassala was the farthest point you could reach before the enemy. The Sudanese Defence Force was astride the Atbara River there, ready to blow up the bridge if the Italians came on. Gedaref itself was a bigger cluster of grass huts than usual. It was lightly held by native troops dressed in their one-piece knee-length khaki robes, khaki turbans and stout openwork leather sandals. The British officers ate bacon and eggs and marmalade, read the *Bystander* and the *Tatler* and hoped for mail from home. They were hospitable, friendly, experienced men, feeling a little forgotten but apparently ready to carry on in this wilderness so long as it pleased some remote command thousands of miles away. It is never in London that you get a sense of Empire. It is here on the edges where they really do dress occasionally for dinner and cling pathetically to habits that were made in Eton and Piccadilly. It's absurd, of course. And quite unusually stoical and brave.

I was taken to see a group of about three hundred natives whose chief preoccupation up to the war had been horse-stealing and various forms of highway robbery. They were great marksmen, which was notable since before the war they had been forbidden to carry arms under threat of heavy punishment. They had come in readily to enlist, but when they were offered rifles they had shaken their heads emphatically, saying they had never seen such curious instruments before. Overacting heavily, each man had insisted on being shown how to load and fire. Then they were offered targets at three hundred yards. Each man plugged his entire clip of bullets clean through the bulls-eye. Now they were going off under a British officer behind the Italian lines to shoot up convoys.

For the first and only time in the Middle East I rode up to the front on a railway. Nearing Kasm el Girba we saw small bomb-craters pitting one or two of the sidings. The line had not been hit, but Fascist aircraft were up, and once we had to stop and wait while a bomber cruised over. It was feared that at any moment a land raid might come across from the Eritrean border and cut the line. Nor was there any real reason why Fascist aircraft might not have actually landed on the flat desert beside the railway in a thousand remote places. They might have torn up and dynamited miles of track. As it was, even their bombers never ventured low. Regularly at night the people in Atbara in central Sudan used to hear Italian communication planes riding high overhead. These were making the long twelve- hundred-mile flight between Eritrea and Libya. The aircraft used to come down at Kufra oasis in southern Libya to refuel and then continue on over the Sudan to Asmara. The Sudan was defenceless to do anything about it. Little too could have been done to save the vital bridge over the Atbara—the bridge that carried all traffic from Egypt and the Red Sea to Khartoum—had a determined attack been made upon it.

But now, unmolested, we bowled down the line to the Atbara at Kasm el Girba. At that friendly mess we found the war languished. If the Italians failed to come on soon, the rains would start and it would be too late. It did not seem that they would come on. Only a few nights previously a British demolition squad, sent out to tear up a section of the railway track outside Kassala, had come on a squad of Italian sappers engaged on exactly the same job a little higher up the line. The Fascists, moreover, were digging machine-gun posts and breastworks for the defence of Kassala, and seemed to be in such a state of nerves that the noise of a British patrol at night was enough to make them cover the desert with heavy machine-gun fire. As for us, we were powerless to attack. Containing Kassala at that moment were exactly three companies. The Italians had perhaps a division or more.

Life at Kasm el Girba moved calmly except for the bombing. Down in the river two officers were wading in the mud. Every few minutes they cast a circular native net into the fast-moving shallows. Then drawing the weighted ends of the net together, they hauled fat muddy fish on to the bank. The day before, a seventeen-foot crocodile had been shot, and gazelle meat was available. Far across the plain we could see Kassala clearly—a township partly European, mostly native, clustered under a great black hump of rock that rose startlingly out of the plain like a huge potted jelly that had been turned lately from the mould. That was Jebel Kassala, and a smaller jebel lay behind it—the most notable landmarks for hundreds of miles.

We dined that night in the open, fighting the insects and listening to the B.B.C. intoning from a set perched in a thorn-bush. It was a quiet war. We went back to Khartoum.

Three

A successful attack was made against Massawa. . . one of our aircraft failed to return. -R.A.F. COMMUNIQUÉ ISSUED IN CAIRO, JULY 14TH, 1940.

THREE DAYS later I was seeing all the fighting I cared for. Matthews and I had put in for a flight on a bombing raid and to our surprise it was granted. Such requests had always been turned down in France and England.

We flew down from Khartoum to R.A.F. headquarters, north of

Kassala at Erkowit—an intolerable journey of four and a half hours in a rattling Valencia. Erkowit, about three thousand feet up in the Red Sea Hills, had a resthouse to which the overheated white people of the Sudan used to go to relax and cool off a little. It recalls Mexico or the Texan desert. Cactus with long upward-reaching fingers grows out of the grey rocks. Lizards scuttle in the shadows. Donkeys cart you around the barren hilltops. There was nothing to see, nothing to do, but the governor-general of the Sudan and members of his staff had built themselves houses round about, and it was enough just to be cool. Now the rest- house was crowded with wives and children unable to make the usual summer-leave trip to England. Each night the R.A.F. officers used to come to the rest-house from their two steaming landing-fields on the plain below. There would be music and dancing and mild flirtation and drinking. From every direction on the dark cool terrace in the evening would come the voices of the guests shouting 'Walad', which was the signal for a soft-footed native waiter to come up and take orders for the bar.

Every day the British bombers would whirl up from the desert and fly off to Eritrea and Abyssinia. Old and few as the machines were, they were having it pretty much their own way against the Italian air force. And now today a squadron of Blenheims had come down from the Western Desert to lay on a few days of really intensive bombardment in order to distract the Fascists from an important convoy of ships which was due to sail up the Red Sea to Suez. Tired after the flight from Khartoum, Matthews and I went to bed in tents pitched beside the house. We had to be up at five-thirty the next morning since we were promised a flight in one of the raids which were to bomb Kassala throughout the following day.

There can, I think, be no exact analysis of fear or any complete assessment of courage. This raid as I know now was of little importance and less danger. But it was my first, and I went to bed that night with a little constriction in my throat, a faster, uncomfortable beating inside my chest. This was danger, I thought, asked for and accepted and one might be dead tomorrow. Or wounded or crashed somewhere beyond that jebel without water. One of the pilots had shown me a little card they all carried written in Amharic and English. It said something about the bearer being a British officer and asking that he be given food and water and taken to the nearest settlement. 'Since the bastards can't read,' the pilot had said lightly, 'I guess some of the tribesmen will slice you up in the usual way and start asking questions afterwards.' He hadn't seemed worried about it. And, strangely, neither did I. I was just afraid of being hit at all while in the air. I started examining this, searching round and round in my head for a way of dealing with myself, and I felt angry with myself and ashamed. This was the hard moment. In the morning it was not nearly so difficult.

An R.A.F. truck fetched us in the yellow early light, and down at the nearest landing field we bundled into the unaccustomed heaviness of flying kit and parachutes. Already the machines, some ten of them, had been 'bombed-up' and now their engines were turning over in a scurry of desert dust.

The wing commander was very precise. He had photographs of Kassala showing clearly the two jebels where the air currents were sometimes difficult; the straggling native village a mass of grass huts; the river Gash, now in yellow flood; the rectangular compound of the railway yards which was our target. Inside the compound were neat lines of concrete tukals built in the shape of the other conical huts. These had been erected by the railway company to shelter native railway workers. Now it was believed that they housed Italian troops and native levies and our object was to bomb them out. Machine and possibly A.A. guns were noted at either end of the compound. We were to dive-bomb down to about three or four hundred feet. The aircraft would go out in flights of three.

I sweated in the hot flying kit as I walked over the far side of the field smoking a last cigarette with the flying officer who was leading our flight. I will give this man a fictitious name, Watson. He was perhaps twenty-two or twenty-three. He was six foot, unusually slim and boyish with dark hair and a serious shy face, and he had been very gay last night at the rest-house. Someone had said to him, 'I hear you are going to do something pretty intrepid tomorrow.' 'Yes,' he had said, 'pretty intrepid.' They had got the word out of some newspaper report and it was a joke among them to use it. I do not think that they ever felt brave. They felt tired or exhilarated or worried or hungry and occasionally afraid. But never brave. Certainly never intrepid. Most of them were completely unanalytical. They were restless and nervous when they were grounded for a day. They volunteered for every flight and of necessity some each day had to be left behind. They lived sharp vivid lives. Their response to almost everything—women, flying, drinking, working—was immediate, positive and direct. They ate and slept well. There was little subtlety and still less artistry about what they did and said and thought. They had no time for leisure, no opportunity for introspection. They made friends easily. And never again after the speed and excitement of this war would they lead the lives they were once designed to lead. They were no material for peace.

So then Watson and Matthews, the other pilots and I climbed into three separate Blenheims and squeezed down among the instruments. We carried no observer, so there was a spare seat for both Matthews and me with a good view. Matthews was in the left-hand machine, Watson in the centre, and myself in the right being piloted by a laconic young Canadian who handed me a stick of chewing-gum—a welcome thing at that moment. I wanted now only to get into the air. But one of the other machines heaved and stopped in its take-off. A tyre was punctured, and endlessly, it seemed, we waited for the wheel to be changed. Then quite suddenly we were off—Watson first, us next, then the third machine; and soon all three were coasting evenly over the dried-up land in an immaculate V. There was a flight of an hour and a half to the target— ninety minutes of pondering what it would be like. I hated that ride. It was slightly bumpy, and the other machines, so close that one felt their wings would touch, kept rising and sinking out of sight. I watched the other rear gunners spinning their glassed-in turrets in search of enemy aircraft. I traced the path of the Gash River and the thin ribbon of railway that led us to Kassala. I tried to work out the meanings of the dials before me. But it was no good. There was nothing to do, nothing to arrest the mind and lift it up and away from its dread and senseless apprehension.

In despair I fingered my wristwatch again and again, believing it must have stopped. Then, unexpectedly, my Canadian bumped me on the arm and pointed ahead. There was Kassala breaking through the ground mist. There the jebels, there the town, there the railway yards. And in a few seconds we were going down to bomb. It wasn't necessary to wait any more. With huge overwhelming relief I leaned over for a fuller view. As I moved, the three aircraft dipped in a long easy dive and, inexplicably, I was suddenly lifted with a wave of heady excitement, more sensuous than relief from pain, faster than the sating of appetite, much fuller than intoxication. I felt keyed to this thing as a skier balancing for his jump or a surfer taking the first full rush of a breaker. There was no drawing back nor any desire for anything but to rush on, the faster the better. Now the roar of the power-dive drowned even these sensations, and with the exhilaration of one long high-pitched schoolboy's yell we held the concrete huts in the bomb sights and let them have the first salvo. I saw nothing, heard no sound of explosion, as the machine with a great sickening lurch came out of the dive and all the earth—jebels, townships, clouds and desert—spun round and sideways through the glass of the cockpit. Then, craning backward, I glimpsed for a second the bomb smoke billowing up from the centre of the compound. It all looked so marvellously easy then—not a human being in sight on the brown earth below; all those ten thousand men huddled in fear of us in the ground. A burst of tracer shells skidded past the slanting windows of the cockpit. So they were firing from the ground then, and it meant nothing. Nothing now could interrupt the attack. Already Watson was shaping for his second run and closer in this time. We followed him into the dive, skidding first left then right at over three hundred m.p.h. to throw off the aim of the gunners below. Then the straightening at last for the final swoop dead on to the target. This time I heard the machine-gun spouting from the leading edge of our machine, felt the lift as the load of bombs was released and heard again the rear gunner blasting from his turret as the aircraft nosed upward into the sky again. Watson was away ahead on a long sweep round the jebels and into Eritrea trying to pick up transport on the roads leading back to Asmara and we followed him hotly. But everything back along the yellow grey country was quiet. Over the border even the villagers were pressed to the ground in terror of the raid. We turned at length, all three of us, for the last attack, flying back over a forest to the west of the town. Coming now at this new angle we found new points to bomb, and faintly Watson's salvo sounded through our motors as we came down for the last time. Looking across as he dived, I saw where his starboard wing was ripped in two places and the fuselage was peeling back under the force of the wind. Then again the earth was turning and pitching as we came out of it and I felt sick. Sick, and nursing a roaring headache. Like that I was borne up and out of it into the pure air beyond the ground-fire, beyond harm's way. I experienced pleasure then, calmer but deeper than my earlier excitement. To have had that dread, to have lost it in excitement at the crisis, and now to have come sailing back safely into this clean open sky—that was much and more than one could ever have foreseen. In a lazy pleasurable daze I sat back through the journey home. I could have laughed at anything then. It was all very intrepid. As we came down toward the home field three more aircraft setting out for Kassala passed us in the air. Three more were warming up on the ground. We made an easy landing. My Canadian slid back the transparent roof. I stepped out along the wing, caught my foot in a piece of splintered fuselage and fell flat on my face on the ground.

While we slept and wrote and enjoyed life at the resthouse Watson went up again that day on reconnaissance far down the Red Sea. At Massawa he came on a dangerous thing: a concentration of Italian warships. His neat square photographs showed at least two destroyers and a cruiser and two or three submarines tied up around the mole. And still our convoy was not safely through the Red Sea. It was decided to organise an attack on the harbour at once, drawing the Wellesley squadron at Port Sudan into the action as well. Watson, having had the honour of discovering the enemy, pleaded to go out on the opening dawn raid the following day. By now his brimming eagerness, his modesty and his laughter had made him specially interesting to us. Among so many it was always valuable in writing dispatches to attach your descriptions to some personality. The story gained point and clarity that way. And since the correspondent was not permitted by the censorship to mention a man's name, it did not matter that there were a hundred others like him. One man stood for all. So now I fixed on Watson. He was a strange lad in that part of his character that had never yet had a chance to develop. Girls scared him. It was naturally a joke among his friends. When his squadron leader married one of two sisters at Alexandria, Watson was induced to act as best man and in an agony of embarrassment attended the bride's sister at the wedding. There you are, the others told him afterward, there is a fine girl for you. Watson retaliated to his squadron's astonishment by announcing quietly a little later that he was engaged to marry the girl. Now here he was in the Sudan waiting for leave to go back and get married and filling his days with high adventure.

Genock had joined us and saw at once he might use this attack to get a film that had never been taken before—action shots of a dive-bomber taken from the bomber itself. There was no room for him in the first raids so he attached his camera to one of the rear gunners' turrets, focused and sighted it and arranged a button which the gunner had only to push when he went into action. Off went the first flights in the morning. They came against opposition so stiff that the gunner was too busy and too preoccupied to press Genock's button. Genock himself got a seat and went out, but he too found the pace too hot, the action too fleeting and erratic to allow him to focus. Reconnaissance photographs taken after the first day's blitz showed some hits, but still the Italian warships were there. And now the three squadrons—the two in the Red Sea Hills and the other at Port Sudan—felt baulked and stirred up in their determination to have the Italian ships. Watson after two long flights in the one day, including well over an hour over the target, had bloodshot eyes and his wing commander would have laid him off had he not again pleaded so strongly to go on.

Matthews and I flew down to Port Sudan to watch the other squadron operating. The town festered in a humid shade temperature of 110 degrees and sometimes more. In the cockpits of the aircraft patrolling down the Red Sea the temperature rose sometimes to 130 degrees. Many in the town were suffering from prickly heat, the rash which blotches your face and arms and back with red scabs. The water in the pool at the front of the Red Sea Hotel was so warm that it was a slight relief in the evening to emerge from it into the less warm air. In the hotel it was wise to fill your bath in the evening so that by the morning the standing water would have dropped a degree or two below the temperature of the flat hot fluid that steamed out of the tap. One wondered how the crews of submarines in the Red Sea got along.

We watched the Wellesleys take off, great ungainly machines with a single engine and a vast wing spread, but with a record of security that was astonishing. For weeks now they had been pushing their solitary engines across some of the most dangerous flying country in the world—country where for hours you could not make a landing and where the natives were unfriendly to the point of murder— and they had been coming back. Often their great wings were slashed and torn with flying shrapnel.

Sometimes they just managed to struggle back with controls shot away and the undercarriage would collapse, bringing the machine lurching down on the sand on one wing like some great stricken bird. But always they seemed to get back somehow. Now again on this second day of the attack on Massawa the control room at Port Sudan got signals that some of our aircraft had been sorely hit. We knew how many aircraft had gone out. It was a strain counting them as they came in, knowing always from hour to hour that there were still due three or two or perhaps just one machine and the chances of the lost airmen ever getting back were diminishing from minute to minute. In the late afternoon we first heard, then saw, the last flight over the sea. They cast their recognition flares; then two of the three aircraft fell behind. The progress of the leading machine was very slow. It was obvious that since this was the one most badly hit it had been sent on ahead to make its landing as quickly and as best it could. It circled twice, then settled for the landing. Crack went one wheel; down in the sand went the engine; over on one wing went the whole machine. The ambulance, fire-brigade wagons, doctors and ground staff raced across the aerodrome. Out of the machine almost unharmed came the crew.

There were many incidents like that in the days that followed. The old Wellesleys were cracking up and we had no newer aircraft to replace them. They were too slow. Always the Italian fighters would wait over Massawa until one machine more badly hit than the others would lag behind. Then the enemy fighters would come and give it hell. That happened to a young squadron leader who after months of staff work on the ground had asked to take part in this all-important raid. He was given the job of rear gunner and his guns were blown away. The pilot was hit. The airman manning the two makeshift guns that sprouted out of the belly of the machine was mortally wounded. The squadron leader fixed a tourniquet, tightened it with his revolver, and got the dying man to hold it in place. Then he manned the two side-guns until the pilot, lacking blood, was failing. Then the squadron leader took over the controls. That machine, too, came back though they lifted out of it a dead man still holding the revolver that tightened his tourniquet.

I had to go back to Khartoum. Into the Grand Hotel there came Watson at last with a bandage round his arm and a spell of leave. He had got his submarines. The British convoy had got through to Suez.

There was a wedding in Alexandria a little later. Watson went off with his bride for a week. The week after he was on his way back to the Sudan. He was last seen going down on to that spot in Massawa habour where the warships he had attacked lay wrecked and awash.

Four

I intend to act offensively. –ADMIRAL CUNNINGHAM

ALL THROUGH this early period Admiral Sir Andrew Cunningham had been becoming more active in the Mediterranean. I had lunched with the Admiral some months before in Malta, and had come away from the meeting so inspired that I suggested to my paper that I should be allowed to join the Mediterranean Fleet as a naval correspondent. This was in January 1940 when as correspondent in Rome I had been finding things slack and had induced the naval attaché there, Sir Phil Bowyer- Smythe, to submit a proposal to the admiralty that I should make a tour of the Mediterranean on British warships to observe how the blockade was being enforced. Both the admiralty and my paper agreed, and at the end of January 1940 I had flown down from Rome to Malta by the Italian Ala Littoria Line. Ala Littoria aircraft were obliged to stick to set schedules and to cross to Malta from Sicily only a few feet above the sea. They were also required to avoid the Grand Harbour and fly between the island of Gozo and Malta before making a brief landing on the more southerly of the island's airports. Nevertheless there was no doubt that already in January the Italians were keeping a close check on Malta through their pilots, and the Italian consul in Valetta was using this convenient Fascist airline to send Rome all the information he could about our defences.

In Malta the navy had greeted me with an efficiency and understanding for which I was pathetically grateful after so many hostile months in Italy. To get properly served bacon and eggs and tea and toast again before a coal fire and hear the English language all round me was a vision of home. After going round the island's defences (an admiral's barge my transport) I was put aboard the destroyer flagship *Galatea*. For ten days we steamed off Italy and round the mouth of the Adriatic picking up freighters, searching them and directing some into Malta. It was all done with a dispatch and judgement and a taste for adventure that promised well for the great months ahead. Though Italy, of course, was not yet at war we travelled blacked out, and action stations were called with precision at sunset. But it was a gay voyage for me with a crew which had the reputation of being one of the most friendly and amusing of any in the navy. I spent hours on the quarter-deck talking with Vice-Admiral Tovey about Italian opera and politics and books. He then had no inkling that he was to be appointed to the command of the home fleet, and was feeling slightly baffled at being left in the Mediterranean while most of his destroyers had been taken away from him for service in more dangerous waters to the north. I spent long hours on the bridge, where the captain, on sighting other vessels, had constantly to take snap decisions which all affected the tortuous diplomatic game Whitehall was then playing in Italy and the Balkans. We picked up all manner of craft—Jugoslav freighters sneaking down the Dalmatian coast, Greek contraband runners lurking in the mouth of the Corinth Canal waiting for us to pass so they could make a dash for the open sea, Italian merchantmen bound for the east, Turks coming west. Once we stopped an evacuating Balkan royal. Always we hoped to grab some Nazi agent and his papers aboard a neutral ship.

Always we were busy, and twice I had to abandon a speech I was making to the ship's company on the quarter-deck when the cry came down from the masthead, 'Ship ahoy!'

For some reason I remember clearly this incident of Mulvaney, the captain's personal servant. In a vulgarly brilliant sunset we had sighted a small sailing vessel heading down the Adriatic. Her master responded neither to flags or Morse, and, since he might have been carrying even a few tons of valuable contraband, *Galatea* decided to run alongside and question the stranger, through a megaphone. The admiral's A.D.C., the officer with the most powerful voice aboard, was summoned to the bridge. The great grey cruiser and the tiny freighter, her sails dripping gold from the over-gaudy sunset, drew together. The freighter flew no flag, and her master, now genuinely disturbed, leaned over the bridge-rail not two hundred yards from us. 'Who are you? Where are you going?' yelled the A.D.C. in English. The master shook his head, unable to understand. '*Qui êtes-vous? Où allez-vous?*' Again no response, and *Galatea*, not holding the slow pace, slid past. As we turned to come up on the other vessel's port side, *Galatea's* captain said briefly, 'Try him in Italian.' The A.D.C. answered limply he had no Italian, and I was instructed to help by giving the A.D.C. the Italian for the questions he was to shout. It worked well enough. We got the answer back he was an Italian freighter bound from Leghorn to Genoa with a cargo of wheat. It seemed genuine enough, and he was too small fry to cause us further delay, so the captain decided he could proceed. 'What is the Italian for "All right"?' he asked me. 'Just say "Va bene," ' I told the A.D.C. He, not hearing correctly, shouted into wind at the top of his lungs, 'Mulvaney'. Out of the captain's sea cabin shot Mulvaney the steward, rigid at the salute. Over on the sailing ship the Italian master was shouting quite happily, 'Va bene,' and pursuing his course. We all looked steadily at Mulvaney for a moment. 'All right, Mulvaney,' said the captain dryly, 'I just want a cup of tea.'

All this was luxury to me. I had sailed these same waters only a year or two before in dirty downtrodden tramps during the Spanish War. I had been trying to discover whose were the mystery submarines which were sinking our vessels off the north coast of Africa (they were Italian all right). At Algiers I had joined the German tramp *Achaea*, and had had many a talk with her fat captain on the long trip up through the Straits of Messina to Piraeus and the Dardanelles. Even then in 1938 he would end every conversation with, 'It is impossible to continue. The English will not understand. It will be war. You might think nothing of my little ship, but she will be minelaying or patrolling or doing something in the service of the Führer.' Well, *Achaea* wasn't doing much. I had seen her only a month before I had joined *Galatea*, when I had made an overland trip up to Venice and Trieste, at the head of the Adriatic. Tied up and mouldering without a crew or a cargo in Trieste docks, I had found *Achaea* and half a dozen other German vessels. They were bottled up there by just such patrols as the *Galatea* was making.

I returned to Malta enthusiastic about the British blockade. Admiral Cunningham, then in command at Malta, had me to lunch at Admiralty House. Sitting on the terrace there with his family, I found it easy to talk, as it always is with men of unusual talent. He was engrossed in Balkan politics and the possibilities of Mussolini's devious politics. Like Tovey, he, too, seemed to me restless for action.

When I met him again seven months later at Alexandria that quick, slight, electric figure was in the thick of it. That was in August 1940. The Italian war had been going two months. I had left the Sudan to return to Egypt, and when I got to Cairo I was told to join the fleet in Alexandria. This was something new. Through the last war and the first months of this the navy had set its face against publicity. But now it was seen at the admiralty that propaganda had to be used to counter the German broadcasts, and since the navy was going to be written about anyway it had better be reported at first hand. I was posted to the flagship *Warspite* and went at once to see Admiral Cunningham. Action and responsibility had made small but very definite changes in him. He was obviously enjoying life. He sat at his desk in his sea cabin under *Warspite*'s towering bridgeworks dressed in white shirt, shorts and socks. He had colour in the flat cheeks crisscrossed with tiny red veins. His cornflower blue eyes were brisk and alight. He talked no politics. He hinted briefly that we were going to undertake an unusually important sweep through the Mediterranean, told me that I would get every assistance, and asked me to say there and then what I wanted. I wanted nothing but a handy place to watch what was going to happen, and they sent me up to the searchlight platform just astern of the admiral's bridge.

There, occasionally during the days ahead, Cunningham would come across for a few words and to drop information.

We steamed out of Alexandria in the early morning past the five sullen captive French warships at anchor there. Coming out of the overheated mess deck at daylight I saw how big this venture was. The whole Alexandrine fleet was out. It was 6 a.m., and at that moment the sky was flaming pink, the sea jet black, and the whole great steel arrowhead was pointed down the shaft of the rising sun toward Italy. Astern of *Warspite* steamed *Eagle*, the old converted aircraft-carrier, and closely following her *Malaya*, huge, castle-like and lifting rhythmically up and below the line of *Eagle*'s wide flight-deck. Starboard and port of us steamed lines of cruisers, some of the great names of this war, *Gloucester* and *Liverpool*, *Orion* and *Sydney* and *Ajax*. Beyond them in a great protective V that stretched to the horizon were the destroyers. Forward and astern of the whole fleet flew *Eagle*'s reconnaissance aircraft, looking for submarines and enemy warships and aircraft.

Warspite was like a central telephone exchange. There were never less than two lines of flags going up or coming down the signalling masthead, never less than two or three lamps flashing out Morse; never less than half a dozen other ships signalling us with lamp and flag. Orders poured out of Cunningham's office; information poured in. It was a brilliant thing to see the order go out for the whole fleet to change direction, bringing each ship into a different position. Far out on the horizon the destroyers would weave in and out between one another; cruisers would cut suddenly across our bows or drop behind; *Eagle* and *Malaya*, following doggedly astern, would start upon new directions. For a few minutes ships seemed to be steaming helter-skelter anywhere over the ocean as disorganised as a river picnic. Then it would come out straight again—the wide V, the battleships coasting along steadily in the centre. And always each ship kept swinging starboard and port in her course every so often, to throw lurking enemy submarines off their line of fire.

Three days of this and nothing much happened. The Italians were well aware something was doing. Shadowing planes—usually old Cant flying boats that hugged the surface of the sea—kept following in our wake. As often as *Eagle* sent out fighting aircraft to destroy them another shadower would turn up again. There was a story told of how the Admiral summoned one of our giant Sunderland flying boats to deal with one of these tiny shadowers. The Sunderland swept up and over the fleet on her mission. Presently she reported, 'Sighted Cant flying boat.' Then later, 'Destroyed Cant.' The admiral signalled back, 'You big bully.'

Toward the third evening one of our scouting planes returned with the news that the Italian fleet, with two battleships and seven cruisers screened by destroyers, was steaming straight toward us at fifteen knots. It seemed that a decisive action was certain, and that unless we or they changed course we should meet in the darkness about 1 a.m. Here, then, was a major decision for Cunningham to take. He was outnumbered and probably outgunned; he was within a short distance of Italian bases from which new enemy vessels, submarines and aircraft might be called up within an hour or two. More important than either consideration was the fact that night actions are risky, uncertain affairs, where luck might defeat training and the best gunnery in the world might be overreached in the obscurity of a battle fought in the darkness. One factor helped Cunningham to his decision—every man on this, his own ship, and I believe on every other vessel under his command, was eager for an encounter after training for so many years for a meeting just such as this. But an engagement would deter the fleet from its main object, and, holding that point in mind, Cunningham decided neither to seek nor avoid action. The fleet was to continue on its course, which was then obliquely approaching the Italians. If we met the enemy in the night, then we would fight him.

The decision delighted everybody. Officers in the wardroom, men in the galley, bolted their dinners and hurried on deck wrapping greatcoats over their white tropical shorts and shirts. Torpedoes were swung seawards for action. Searchlights were spun round ready to push their beams across the sea. A stream of signals flashed from *Warspite*'s bridge, bringing the rest of the fleet into position for battle before their silhouettes vanished into the darkness. The wind rose sharply, and soon cascades of black water were seething over the bows past the fifteen-inch guns which stood loaded and ready.

Stumbling in the darkness round the decks, I passed hundreds of men. They were laughing, whistling, yarning excitedly.

Ten hours later in the first light of the new day they were still there. But the Italians were not.

Somewhere in the night the enemy had changed course and disappeared. Our dawn air-patrol found them at length well on their way home to Italy. But a British submarine struck first. Roaming by chance well ahead of the British fleet on an independent course, she had reached the Italian battle squadron in the failing light the night before. Two torpedoes were launched, and before the British commander dived he ascertained through the periscope that one Italian cruiser at least had been hit. It was one of the most important successes of British submarines in the Mediterranean since Italy had declared war. Still after this, had the Italian fleet wanted action on terms greatly favouring itself, there was nothing to stop it. Overwhelmingly large numbers of aircraft could have reached us within an hour. As it was, the enemy waited until it was too late.

During these first three days we were distracting the attention of the enemy from a convoy bound for Malta. The attack when it did come on the convoy was a half-hearted one, as all the Italian attacks were. The steering-gear of one of the merchant ships was damaged, and she made port. All the high brown cliffs surrounding Malta's Grand Harbour were thronged with cheering excited Maltese as the warships steamed in at last with their convoy. After many anxious weeks of isolation these ships brought life and hope to the island. It was solid proof to the Maltese that they were not being deserted. It was the first of the big wartime convoys, the first of many that have been going there ever since.

But outside Malta's Grand Harbour something much bigger yet was happening. Only the night before I had been told that here under the very lee of Italy a rendezvous had been arranged. To buttress Cunningham's relatively weak position in the Mediterranean the admiralty had ordered to his command its newest aircraft-carrier *Illustrious* together with her forty-odd high-speed Fulmar fighting aircraft, the two anti-aircraft cruisers *Coventry* and *Calcutta*, with the battleship *Valiant*, escorting destroyers and supply ships. These new vessels almost doubled Cunningam's striking power. Better still, they meant air protection from the Italian raiders which had been harassing his ships whenever they put to sea. They had made the voyage from England with nothing worse than light raids. They had passed unharmed through the field of mines which the Italians had declared they had laid from Sicily, past the island of Pantelleria, to Libya. And now, exactly on the appointed hour, while we watched and waited tensely aboard *Warspite*, the huge square hulk of *Illustrious* heaved steadily over the horizon framed in a background of Malta's brown misty cliffs.

No ship like *Illustrious* had ever been seen in the Mediterranean before; nothing of its kind, so fast, so modern, so reassuring. Emotionally, sailors cheered as they saw her, and gazed and gazed across the flat steady water much as a schoolboy will look at a new motor car his father has brought home.

Then other smudges on the horizon resolved into *Valiant* towering above *Illustrious* and the attendant cruisers and destroyers. Cunningham signalled his welcome to all of them. Then, since we were within half an hour's flight of the enemy, there was a brisk business of getting the new vessels into line. *Illustrious* steamed into the place of honour behind the flagship, with *Valiant*, *Malaya* and *Eagle* following. The rest of the ships, a grand fleet now, took up position on the flanks. Within fifteen minutes of sighting us, *Illustrious* had flown off two of the new two-hundred-and-forty-miles-per- hour Fulmars. They set out on a slow flight round the fleet to accustom the Mediterranean gunners to their appearance, but, sighting two Italian aircraft on their way, shot them down and returned to their parent ship. In two minutes they had vanished on electric lifts into the belly of the aircraft-carrier. The whole operation had taken ten minutes. Grinning widely, a sailor walked over to the hangar on *Warspite* which housed two ancient hundred-mile-an-hour Swordfish fighters and scrawled on the doorway, 'This way to the museum.' There was a great feeling of exhilaration around the fleet that morning.

And then the Italians came. They attacked with aircraft, mines and submarines, a new kind of naval warfare. From the Sicilian airfields they kept sending up small waves of bombers, flying very high and fast. Beneath the sea, meanwhile, enemy submarines were reported from several different directions and mines were bobbing to the surface. I was standing on the searchlight platform when the first salvo of bombs came down. A curtain of grey smoke and spray, mast-high, blotted out *Illustrious* steaming only a few hundred yards astern. Then another salvo, smaller bombs this time, reared up the sea along *Warspite*. Then single fountains spurted from among the cruisers and destroyers.

Liverpool's guns were the first to hit back. One after another the other warships synchronised their pom-poms and ack-ack guns into the concert of the fleet's barrage. On *Warspite* you saw first smoke from the muzzles, then flames, then, seconds later it seemed, you felt the impact of the explosion that lifted your feet from the deck.

Far out to the horizon ships were racing to new positions making sudden turns and dashes. The destroyers, like wild cats tearing up the sea, dashed between the larger vessels to get at the enemy submarines. Each depth charge—they were exploding very deep—sent slow trembling blasts across the sea. Here and there ships were sent off to explode floating mines with their pom-poms. *Illustrious* was working at speed. Fighter after fighter wheeled off her flight deck, and I caught glimpses of distant air battles.

All this action was scattered and spread over a long period, and, since few had any clear idea of what was going on, the flagship's commander would broadcast reports over the ship's microphone. It was part of an excellent psychological understanding that men fight better if they know what and how they are fighting and with what support. The commander finished each broadcast with the words, 'This is the end.' Once he announced, 'Large numbers of Italian aircraft are expected in five minutes' time. This is the end.' A shout of laughter went from one end of the battleship to the other.

Then late in the afternoon there was an incident that brought the fight to a close. There had been another near miss beside the battleship, and shrapnel was rattling down on the deck when I got a perfect glimpse of the silver wings of five enemy machines flying in the clear sunlight thirteen or fourteen thousand feet up. At once *Warspite*'s four-inch guns went into action. One silver plane slowly detached itself from the rest, turned from silver to black, then flaring yellow as it crashed headlong into the sea. As it hit the water a dense pillar of billowing black smoke spurted a hundred feet into the sky. Shell-bursts were ringing the other four raiders very closely now. Soon another machine lost height and speed, and finally spun down, a burning moth before the flame of the late afternoon sun. After it, falling like white ashes through the black smoke, came three parachutists.

Along with thousands of British sailors I watched fascinated, as the white dots hovered delicately into the sea to drown. Two British fighters cruised over the dying Italian pilots and with wide graceful sweeps alighted on *Illustrious*. The fight was finished.

That night the fleet split up, one half going straight back to Alexandria, the rest, including *Illustrious* and her attendant ack-ack cruisers, following *Warspite* into a new adventure that was to prepare the way for the later victory at Taranto. We were bound for Rhodes.

The Dodecanese Islands were still a mystery at this time. They were known to harbour Italy's yet untried E-boats for which the Fascists had long been hinting great things. The E-boat was something that especially appealed to the flamboyant and individualistic Italian nature. Count Ciano's father, Admiral Constanzo Ciano, had already in the last war stirred every Italian's imagination by his daring strokes in the Adriatic. With the use of small motor boats he had taken torpedoes right into the Austrian anchorages and succeeded almost single-handed in sinking two major warships. When I was in Italy there was much talk of 'death's head' volunteers who were willing actually to sit astride torpedoes and guide them onto their targets. The project meant death if the rider stayed too long aboard the torpedo, or capture if he managed to slip off into the water a little before the explosion took place. But the E-boat was the practical expression of this desire for fast, stealthy night raiding which brought spectacular results if successful and cost little in life or material if it failed. So the E- boat was designed to travel at speeds of over forty knots, launch at least two torpedoes whilst travelling at this high speed, and then race quickly to safety. Its range was small, its crew a handful of highly trained men. In so small a sea as the Mediterranean the Italians hoped much from these tactics, and at least two hundred E-boats were reputed to be ready when Mussolini declared war.

The Dodecanese was furthermore an ideal pirate's nest to harbour these boats in addition to submarines and aircraft. All of them could make raids on British and neutral vessels trading up to Greece and the Dardanelles from the Suez Canal.

Rhodes, when I had last landed there from a Turkish merchantman in the spring of 1939, was still a dreaming summer island of roses and wine, of fisherfolk and holiday-makers, peaceful monasteries and pine forests. But even then Mussolini was preparing it for war. Two landing fields, one at Maritza, the other at Calato, with satellite fields in other parts of the island, had already been prepared. An energetic governor, Count Da Vecchi, had been sent across from Italy, and in an excess of the usual Fascist passion for building he was busily engaged in tearing down his predecessor's public works and putting up his own instead. There was a fine new opera and cinema house, new quays, new roads ringing the island, and the big hotel on Rhodes harbour, the Albergo delle Rose, had been remodelled in yellowish sandstone on grandiose lines. Only the lovely forts and buildings of the Knights of St John remained the same, though some of them were destined to be turned into air-raid shelters. At the Albergo delle Rose in 1939 I found the bar, the terraces and the beach swarming with Fascist officers and German tourists. I was in fact offered the room occupied only a week or two before by Dr Goebbels and I slept very soundly in it for three nights. Apart from a few Maltese fishermen, who still clung to their British nationality despite the special tax imposed upon them, the only Englishman on the island was the British consul, a tough old sea captain who was much perturbed at the continuous influx of soldiers and the aircraft which he then estimated to number about two hundred.

I attempted to take the ferry northward to Leros, the island which had been especially developed as a submarine base, but was firmly told that the boat was booked out indefinitely. It seemed, too, that Stampalia, the island farther west, was being organised as an additional air and sea base. Rhodes itself sported four submarines, but these were forced to sail out of the town's exposed harbour to the northern shores of the island when any sort of a wind was blowing out of Africa. Here, as everywhere I have been in the Fascist Empire, it was impossible not to admire the Italian genius for fine buildings, roads, ports and public works. They built with skill and artistry, and only that strained nervous atmosphere that followed Fascism everywhere indicated that this was a civilisation of the master for the master which the resident subject peoples must accept and support or else...

Up to the time of my voyage in *Warspite* Rhodes had never been raided. Its aircraft had made one or two attacks on Haifa and Alexandria, but nothing of any importance. And now we were steaming past Crete in a generous warm sea to bait the Italians in Rhodes and see what opposition they could offer to a naval and air force coming unexpectedly on them in the night.

The plan was for the *Illustrious* and *Eagle* pilots to combine in attacking the two airfields at Maritza and Calato, while the cruisers *Orion* and *Sydney* with two destroyers shelled the adjacent island of Scarpanto lying to the south-west.

An hour before sunrise the fleet was in position. One after another, over fifty miles of ocean, one could see the dark shapes of warships detach themselves from the sea mist. One after another fighters and bombers were brought up to the flight-decks of the aircraft-carriers and flown off until there were some twenty or thirty in the dark sky. This take-off in the half dark was dangerous, and one aircraft, its engine failing at the crucial moment, poised for a second on the lip of *Illustrious*'s flight-deck, then plunged sickeningly into the sea to be cut to pieces by the warship's bows. While this was happening *Sydney* was already in action. She was stealing round the island of Kaso to get at an airfield at the southern tip of Scarpanto when three or four E-boats emerged and, apparently caught by surprise, were forced into action. The E-boat commanders at once went into full speed, heading straight towards *Sydney*. *Sydney*, at several thousand yards' range, engaged and blew the first E-boat in a sheet of flame out of the water before she had time to fire or even aim her torpedoes. An attendant destroyer, *Ilex*, cut in to protect *Sydney*, demolished a second E-boat, and forced two others, apparently hit, to retire into Kaso. *Sydney* methodically went ahead with her shelling, while her sister *Orion* carried out a similar bombardment on the other side of the island at Pegadia Bay.

The importance of the action was, of course, that it showed the E-boat could be sighted and destroyed in daylight before it could even get into action. Provided he had air protection, Cunningham thereafter had a clear indication that he could approach Italian coasts with no fear of this new weapon. The point was to be proved even more completely in later actions off Malta and Gibraltar.

The second half of the admiral's plan also went forward with unexpected success—again largely the result of surprise. At Calato the sleeping Italian garrison awoke to find itself beneath a major air attack. The petrol dump and the barracks were blazing and half a dozen aircraft burning on the ground. At Maritza, the other field lying under a monastery in a cup of the hills, five-hundred-pound bombs went straight through the main hangars. Workshops and barracks took fire, and another petrol tank engulfed in the flames precipitated a whole series of explosions which trailed black smoke across the horizon clearly visible to us eighty miles away. Italian airmen, recovering from their first shock, ran from the blazing barracks and took off in time to bring down four of our Swordfish which were trying to return to their mother ship.

We expected some stiffer reprisal than this. It came at 10 a.m. when the Fascist bombers now out in force found the fleet steaming for Alexandria. The first salvo of bombs came straight out of the sun and thrust up a green wall of water to the starboard of *Warspite*. The fleet's guns opened with an aching, shuddering crash. Shells were bursting everywhere over the whole bowl of the sky from one horizon to the other. I was caught typing behind one of the four-inch guns, and the typewriter flew from my hands among a pile of books and pictures that tumbled to the floor. Bits of shrapnel spattered the deck, and I ducked and ran for the fifteen-inch gun turrets where I remained all morning watching the fight. By noon the Italians had had enough, and as they came out of the zone of British gunfire *Illustrious*'s fighters leaped in. They had two Italian bombers down in ten minutes, and three more disappeared, casting off bits of fuselage as they went.

In all we had destroyed some twenty enemy aircraft. *Warspite*'s chaplain came down to the mess cabin in the evening to post his text for the day: 'We came into Rhodes.' Next morning we were in Alexandria. Not a single warship had been hit throughout.

I trace the turning of the tide in the naval war in the Mediterranean from that one brilliant week.

Many things had been done for the first time—a convoy had been got through to Malta; reinforcements had been brought straight through the Mediterranean instead of round the Cape; the E-boat had been proven of little worth in daylight; the Italian bombers had been shown to be inaccurate, slow and unwilling to press their attacks home; and finally the pirates' nest at Rhodes had been badly shaken up.

With this experience to guide him, Cunningham was soon appearing off Taranto with his fleet air arm to cripple nearly half a dozen enemy warships at anchor there. Throughout the winter he was coming close inshore to bombard the whole length of the Libyan coast. Only the long-drawn-out agony of the crippling of *Illustrious* by German dive-bombers marred his inevitable progress to the battle of Cape Matapan when another seven of Italy's best ships were demolished.

Matapan was the Mediterranean's last great naval battle. The fate of *Illustrious* had been an earnest that the whole character of the sea war was changing. German dive-bombers off Greece and Crete put an end to Cunningham's brief but brilliant anachronism that capital ships and aircraft- carriers can operate in a land locked sea. The Italians had never really believed in that principle. The Italian navy had no aircraft-carriers. It relied on numerous convenient air bases in Sardinia, Sicily, Libya, the Dodecanese and Italy itself. For the rest it put its faith in E-boats, submarines, fast light torpedo-boats and destroyers. Its thirty-five-thousand-ton battleships like *Littorio*, though of fine design, evoked nothing from the Italian talent for short, sharp, stealthy action. The Italian navy suffered deeply from inexperience and the Italian high command knew it. It could not hope to use battleships as cruisers and cruisers as destroyers, the way Cunningham did.

So for ten extraordinary months, from June 1940 to April 1941, the British navy ruled the Mediterranean with a daring and judgement that possibly eclipsed anything of its kind at sea before. It was not that the Italian navy was no good at all. It was simply that the British fleet, taking many borderline risks, was brilliant. Cunningham deliberately spread a zest for attack. As he was sailing out of Alexandria to attack Taranto he signalled his other ships, 'I intend to act offensively in the Ionian Sea.' He was deeply admired. Nor did he take his losses during this venturesome 'sea' period of the Mediterranean war. It was when he could no longer act offensively, when he had to convoy to and from Crete and Greece and elsewhere and came at last against overwhelming air power overwhelmingly pressed home, that he lost one good ship after another. From Crete onward it became blindingly obvious that sea and air would have to go together. The fleet could not put to sea without air protection. Except for submarines and light fast surprise raids by destroyers, the purely 'sea' period was done. A bigger, more intricate, scheme of operation binding ship and plane had to be devised. Fleets alone cannot act offensively and get away with it. Neither the *Bismarck* nor any other battleship could range the seas, raiding, hunting down its foes, bombarding up the Main. Which is a pity, for every great captain, Cunningham included, is at heart a pirate.

Five

In the Western Desert elements of our forces are now in contact with the enemy on a broad front. In an engagement south of Sidi Barrani we have captured 500 prisoners. -GENERAL WAVELL'S FIRST COMMUNIQUÉ ANNOUNCING HIS OFFENSIVE INTO CYRENAICA, DECEMBER 9TH, 1940.

BY EARLY winter 1940 Mussolini was already in difficulties in Greece. Cunningham at sea and Longmore in the air were doing pretty much as they liked. Only the army of the Nile apparently was doing nothing. Week after vital week slipped by in November, and still Wavell did not move. People pointed to the Greeks and said, 'They can beat the Italians. Why can't we do something?' November drifted into December, all good campaigning weather in the desert, and I began to hear criticism everywhere in the Middle East. There was a feeling of despondency about the army. One retreat had followed another—Norway, Dunkirk, British Somaliland. People talked of 'Headquarters Muddle East,' and it became the fashion to make jokes about the staff officers in Cairo angling for promotion. And as the Greeks continued through Koritza into Albania newspapers went as far as they could in an effort to say, 'Why doesn't Wavell attack in the Western Desert now that the Italians are tied up in Greece?'

Actually the position in the desert was this. General O'Connor, the corps commander, had placed his old armoured division as a holding force at the front between Mersa Matruh and Sidi Barrani.

They had in support an Indian division including some British regiments, nearly a division of New Zealanders, and two divisions of Australians either training or simply waiting in the Delta and Palestine. There were in addition heterogeneous groups like the Poles whom it was not thought desirable to send against the Italians since Italy had never broken off diplomatic relations with Poland. Shipments had lately been arriving of twenty-five-pounder guns, new thirty-ton infantry tanks, and aircraft of various kinds including Hurricanes, Wellingtons and Long-nosed Blenheims.

On the Italian side Graziani had established one Libyan and one Metropolitan division at the front around Sidi Barrani under the command of General Gallina. Reaching inland, south, south-west and westwards in a great arc from the coast, some half-dozen fortified camps had been established: Maktila, some miles east of Sidi Barrani on the coast; Tummar East and Tummar West; Nibeiwa and Point Ninety—all more or less due south of Sidi Barrani; and finally Sofafi, deep in the desert near the Libyan border. As desert architecture goes, these camps were pretty lavish affairs. The general design was a convenient rise perhaps half a mile or a mile square surrounded with a stone wall.

Inside the Italians had established messes, hospitals and sleeping quarters by scooping holes in the sand and rock, putting a stone wall round the holes and surmounting the tops with pieces of camouflaged canvas. Outside the camps they built watching-posts by digging holes in the desert.

Minefields were embedded on the eastern, northern and southern approaches. Rough, incredibly dusty tracks linked one camp with another. Sidi Barrani had in addition to its ring of outlying camps two lines of fortifications where they had dug anti-tank traps and furnished niches for machine-guns, anti- tank guns and artillery. In command of the camps immediately adjacent to the central fortress of Sidi Barrani was General Maletti, a veteran of the Abyssinian campaign. He had been given what I suppose was an Italian Panzer division. It had a special name—the Raggruppamento Maletti, or the Raggruppamento Oasi Meridionali—and there is some evidence that when the time came for the race across to the Nile, Maletti and his shock troopers were to be in the van. But for the time being he and Gallina were resting, digging in, building up supplies and waiting for their great new road, the Via della Vittoria, linking Sollum with Sidi Barrani, to be completed.

Back on the escarpment in reserve were two more divisions under General Bergonzoli—the famed Electric Whiskers—and General Berti. These had been acting as garrison troops to Corps Headquarters at Bardia and holding the escarpment. Still another division—General Giuseppe Amico's 'Catanzaro' division—was designed to act as a relief at the front. There were then some six Italian divisions—perhaps a hundred thousand men in all—available to Graziani for use as attacking troops. Facing him between Sidi Barrani and the Nile there were some four British divisions or not more than sixty thousand men. In guns of all classes, in all kinds of transport and tanks except heavy tanks, Graziani's forces enjoyed a numerical superiority of probably not less than three to one and in some cases very much more. In the air he certainly had a three to one numerical advantage. Even if his initial assaults failed, he stood—on paper—little chance of a major setback.

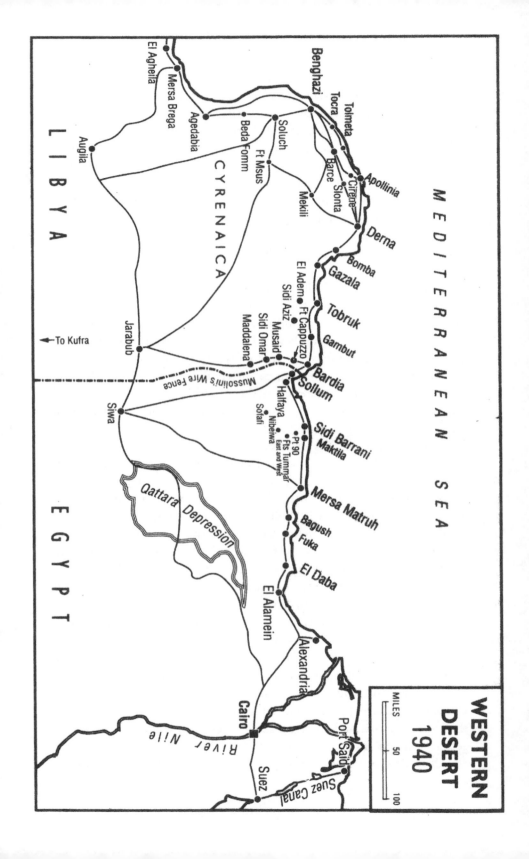

Strong garrisons of more than a division each were centred at such key points as Tobruk, Derna, Benghazi, in addition to many strong pockets of supporting infantry in desert posts like Mekili south of Derna.

It was generally assumed that in all Libya Graziani disposed of some quarter million troops against Wavell's hundred thousand based around the Nile and the Suez Canal. It was apparent then that nowhere, not even at sea, did we possess equality in numbers (though both British pilots and sailors had proved in the preceding months that this was by no means necessary for success). In fact, Graziani was sitting pretty—even though he was sitting in the imponderable Western Desert which had once swallowed up a Persian host under Cambyses and brought disaster to many conquerors since then.

The general disposition of his armies was arranged with strong Latin logic. Everything fanned out exactly from a base. From Tripoli, his chief supply port where ships were then unloaded undisturbed by air raids, his lines of communication stretched east to Benghazi and far south into the Libyan desert oasis at Kufra. From Benghazi, his most vital base, the lines fanned out again to Barce, Cirene, Derna and Tobruk in the north on the coast, and in the south below the mountains to the desert fort of Mekili. Then from Tobruk the northern line reached to Bardia and Sollum and fanned south to the border desert post at Jarabub. And now he had created his latest fan stretching into Egypt as far as Sidi Barrani; thence describing an arc down to Sofafi. Every section hinged on pivot, and the pivots were Bardia, Tobruk, Benghazi, Tripoli. Each sector fitted into the one behind it, so that the successive termini of each of the northern arms of each pivot were Sidi Barrani, Bardia, Tobruk and Benghazi. And the southern termini were the chain of desert posts, Sofafi, Jarabub, Mekili and Kufra. Doubtless other fans were planned from Sidi Barrani and Mersa Matruh until the Nile Delta was reached.

The obvious point in this grand strategy was that while you had to mass your main forces on the coast where the good roads and the ships and airfields were, yet you still had to guard your desert flank against sudden encircling inland raids. In the end it was Graziani's failure to hold this principle or realise just how far and fast an encircling raid could go that brought him to utter ruin. It was Wavell's and O'Connor's strength that from the first moment they never relaxed these encircling movements or their pressure on the desert flank. And always governing every engagement from a siege or a pitched battle down to a skirmish were the opposite theories of the two commanders: Wavell with his policy of light fast mobile forces; Graziani with his theory of defensive positions. Wavell stabbed with a lance. Graziani presented a shield.

The story of the Benghazi advance begins far back in November 1940. The Italians as was their custom, had not been patrolling except for occasional heavily armed parties which in a great cloud of dust toured the forward area. Our patrolling was done in small groups, sometimes a single vehicle, and nearly always at night. A lieutenant and a dozen men would drive far out into no-man's-land in the darkness, camouflage their vehicles with nets and salt-bush before dawn, and lie motionless on the floor of the desert throughout the day. More often than not, aircraft would fail to spot them, but at the first sign of superior land forces on the desert horizon they would try to identify the enemy and then quickly escape back to our lines. Thus a considerable amount of information was always coming into British Corps Headquarters. O'Connor was well aware that these fortified camps, like Nibeiwa and the two Tummars, were being built, but he did not know how many were completed or exactly where and what further forts were projected. He tried one frontal tank attack on Nibeiwa, and when some of our tanks came to grief on the Italian minefields and were met by considerable artillery fire it became obvious that these forts were of some strength. Each was reckoned to have about three thousand men with a very high rate of fire power.

But a British Intelligence colonel began to notice among the reports which the patrols were constantly bringing in that those scouts who penetrated the area between Nibeiwa and Sofafi invariably returned with no news at all. No contact was made with the enemy. Puzzled, he went out himself, just he and a driver, and lay in the desert south of Nibeiwa getting the same result. He returned on the succeeding night. And then again and again, each time going a little deeper into enemy territory. Still he struck nothing. Could it be possible that there was a gap—a considerable gap— between Sofafi and Nibeiwa which the Italians had not yet fortified nor were even patrolling? It was improbable that they would blunder like this. But there it was—over this whole area as large as the home counties in England no opposition was to be found. It was reasonable to assume that the Italians had not fortified on the inward western side of their chain of camps. After all, their own supply columns had to reach each camp from the west, so the supposition was that their minefields and anti- tank traps were concentrated on the outward eastern side. Moreover it followed that their artillery would be facing toward the British. Suppose then that this weak point, this gap between the forts, really existed? Suppose the British were to rush this gap and then, wheeling north, attack the camps one by one from the unfortified inward side? Might not then the whole Italian front be like an egg with a rotten inside? It was not impossible that we might penetrate as far as Sidi Barrani and even reach the coast behind the village to cut it off from its lifeline to Sollum. Given that, what then? Sidi Barrani could be besieged by land, sea and air. The British could push down the coast to Sollum, isolating the garrison of Sofafi to the south and forcing its members to retire up the escarpment on to Bardia.

Everything would depend on surprise. The navy as well as the air force would have to be called in. Even so in November these conjectures appeared visionary and super-optimistic, so strongly were the Italians entrenched, so few were the forces Wavell had to bring against them. But the scheme was one which would have appealed to every man in the desert. O'Connor came back to Cairo and put it up to Wavell—Wavell who was very ready indeed to listen. The generals had one good card— the new infantry tanks had arrived, the famous 'I' tank. Their surprise effect would be redoubled in an important engagement. Wavell sounded out the other two services. Cunningham, reinforced from home, was agreeable. He would send some of his heaviest units ahead of the army to bombard first the outlying coastal camp Maktila, then Sidi Barrani itself, then, if need be, he would get to work on Sollum too. Longmore was less strong, but he had been reinforced also. His pilots had lately been showing a very definite superiority against the large bodies of Italian aircraft which used to come over Mersa Matruh. He also was agreeable. At home Churchill gave support. There were strong political reasons for attempting an offensive. England had endured the worst of the autumn air raids, but now the long nights had set in and Nazi raiders were expanding their damage again at little cost to themselves. Sinkings in the Atlantic were growing. Apart from the repulse of the Italians in Greece there was nowhere the public could turn for some sign of hope and encouragement.

A campaign in the Western Desert was the soundest possible way to remind the people of Britain that they were not alone, that they had outside forces fighting for them and toward them through Africa and Europe. Churchill was more than approving. He was enthusiastic. It remained now solely to choose a date and somehow keep the thing secret. That was the problem. To keep it secret in a land where gossip runs wild; where enemy agents were known to lurk in every port from

Alexandria to Haifa and Aden, where so many half-allies were expecting to be 'kept informed,' where such arrangements as the unloading and movement of ships were plain for anyone to watch. How to get at least two divisions and artillery up to the front in the open desert without the enemy reconnaissance planes seeing them? How to get ships out of Alexandria and up the coast unobserved? How to get extra foodstuffs, extra transport, medical supplies and ambulances forward without Cairo buzzing with the news that 'something was going to come off soon'? How indeed to confine the information to a few key men at G.H.Q. that was strewn over Cairo and Alexandria and split into separate commands for the three services?

Wavell himself was a past master at saying nothing and appearing and acting in exactly the same way before a tea-party or a major offensive. But he was an island in a sea of garrulousness. It was as essential to keep the secret from our troops as from our enemy. There was another simple device— keep the desert and Cairo apart from one another. Communications between the desert and Cairo, as every war correspondent knew only too well, were terrible. Now while the preparations were being made in the desert no troops were allowed back on leave to the Delta where they might inadvertently spread hints and suggestions. Tickets of leave were choked off, not suddenly but gradually, so no suspicion was aroused. Another thing helped Wavell. He had delayed so long now that the public and the services—and presumably the enemy—had given up guessing when he might attack, or had even abandoned hope of it altogether. The flying fields were isolated in the desert and that again helped.

Further to confuse the troops in the field, as well as to give them some training and to perplex the enemy, many units were ordered out on manoeuvres long before the actual attack and then withdrawn again. In G.H.Q. Wavell selected half a dozen men who had to have the exact information in advance. He swore them to silence: he ordered them to turn aside awkward enquiries among their junior officers.

But by far the most valuable aid in this campaign of secrecy was the misjudgment of the enemy. All the Fascists knew of the British army at this time was that it had retreated before the Germans in Belgium, Norway and France, and before the Italians in British Somaliland and the Western Desert.

To the Italians in December 1940 it was inconceivable that the British could really seriously attack. They were on the defensive and had been all along. Moreover there was an interior rottenness in the Italian

Intelligence, something that grew naturally out of the national weakness for exaggeration.

There is, as anyone who has lived in Italy will know, nothing especially unethical in this desire to enlarge and aggrandise and embroider. Nearly every Italian I have met has a passion and a talent for bombast and display. He just can't help himself. It is a foible that has led many people into the error of believing the Italian is stupid, which he certainly is not. He proceeds with cold unsentimental logic in his inner reasoning, and makes allowances for the colourful descriptions of his friends and indeed for his own embroideries. He expects exaggerations in himself and everyone else. Nor has this in any way diminished the Italian genius for design and logic. Exaggeration never, as far as I could see, deterred the Italian from reaching decisions as well as anyone else in peace-time. But in war everything is different. Information becomes a commodity in itself. It has to be as exact as the cornerstone of a building or the barrel of a gun. And you could not overnight cure the individualistic Italian lieutenant and captain of his boastfulness. Indeed the war had spurred officers and politicians on to still greater efforts in exaggeration. The Italian communiqués were absurd. Again and again some hit-and-run Italian pilot would return to his Libyan base with stories of how he had shot down ten…fifteen…twenty aircraft, or destroyed two, three or more battleships. The Roman newspapers outdid the communiqués that faithfully repeated these fables. When Graziani destroyed a dozen vehicles he claimed two thousand. Without doubt the Italian high command, knowing that the cynical public would discount something, always added a few more imaginary and lurid details to every pronouncement. Anyway, they might have argued, we are a mercurial, imaginative people, and one solid victory will prove all our earlier claims correct. Yet the net effect was that the Italian people (I saw this before the war) lived in a state of cynical, distrustful confusion about the news. They were never quite able to say that Mussolini was wrong, since he kept serving them victories and allowed no information in from outside; but still the doubt was there. Furthermore there was the natural desire for victories; the wish that the news would be good. More than anyone the Italian wanted to believe what he was told was right.

And indeed until now the Duce had been able to give him successes. But the dangerous thing was that right through the Italian army down to the rawest ranks a stream of wrong information was flowing. If a few shots were exchanged, the Italian private called it a skirmish and quite groundlessly claimed that he had killed and routed the enemy.

If a lieutenant was sent out on a raid, he expanded it in his reports to an engagement. An engagement became a major action or even a battle. From company headquarters to battalion, to brigade, to division, a supply of inaccurate details kept arriving at Italian G.H.Q. Even if G.H.Q. discounted what they heard by half, they were still left in the dark, not knowing where to draw the line between truth and fiction.

So Wavell in that first week of December might reasonably have expected some measure of surprise. His plan was simple in arrangement, simple in detail but somewhat complex at the edges. He could not possibly know how far or how fast he would go—if he went at all. So he planned his offensive first as a major raid. If the raid went well, then his troops would be so disposed that they could pursue the enemy even as far as Sollum, if need be, or beyond—though nobody quite hoped for that. If he got into difficulties, he could again withdraw back on Mersa Matruh. The air force, first, then the navy, would start the action. For forty-eight hours Air Commodore Collishaw, the R.A.F. commander in the desert, would send over almost continuous raids on to the airfields of Libya—high- level and dive-bombing and ground strafing. The object here was to keep the Italian air force on the ground until the British troops took up position and accomplished at least the first leg of their advance. The navy meanwhile would make a dawn shelling of Maktila, the most forward Fascist post on the coastal road, and if the fort was reduced, would continue to Sidi Barrani, where the fifteen- inch naval guns were to demolish whatever they could find there. While this was going on the army would move up.

Two divisions were to be employed—the 7th Armoured Division under Major-General O'More Creagh and the 4th Indian Division under Major-General Beresford-Pierce. The more experienced and more mobile armoured division would form the spearhead of the assault. Having gone through the gap, that unexplained but undeniable gap between Nibeiwa and Sofafi, Creagh would wheel northward sharply and attack one by one with the all-important infantry tanks the Italian camps at Nibeiwa, Tummar West, Tummar East and Point Ninety. He would also endeavour to reach the coast in the neighbourhood of Buq Buq between Sollum and Sidi Barrani, and hold a position there, thus outflanking the Sofafi garrison and cutting the retreat of the Italians, if any, from Sidi Barrani. Other units would also be sent directly upon Sofafi. Creagh's position might be a very awkward one indeed if he were not supported. Accordingly the Indian division would also plunge through the gap in close support and carry out the mopping-up operations upon Nibeiwa, the two Tummars and Point Ninety.

This would bring them to the southern approaches of Sidi Barrani which they were to attack if still able to do so. On the coast units of the British garrison at Mersa Matruh were to emerge from their entrenchments and engage Maktila fortress which by then, it was hoped, would have been much reduced by the navy. On the fall of Maktila the Mersa Matruh force would proceed straight toward Sidi Barrani and attack it from the east while the other two divisions were attacking from the south. Sappers would go ahead of our forces tearing up our own mines and dealing as far as they could with the Italian traps.

The weak point in the whole scheme was that somehow the armoured and the Indian divisions had to be got into position for attack without the Italians knowing it. There was no complete answer to this problem. The only course was to go ahead and see what happened. This is what happened.

On the night of December 7th when the desert air was already icy with the coming winter, the two British divisions made a forced march of seventy miles through the darkness up to points a few miles back from the Italian lines where they could still not be observed from ground level. All through the day of December 8th the thousands of men in full kit lay dispersed and inert on the flat desert. Luck held. An Italian reconnaissance plane came over, but apparently neither saw nor suspected anything. No Italian patrol came out far enough to discover what was afoot. The air was busy with Collishaw's planes passing back and forth to the Libyan airfields and they were having a wonderful time. The score of enemy aircraft damaged on the ground or caught aloft mounted from ten to twenty to the fifties. Everywhere, at Gazala, Bomba, El Adem, Tobruk, Benina and beyond, the Italian air force was being pinned to the ground. Through the night of the 8th, while still the two divisions lay pressed to the desert waiting for the morning, the Royal Navy stole on Maktila in readiness for its bombardment at first light.

In Cairo at 9 a.m. General Wavell summoned the war correspondents into his office. We were a small group of seven or eight and as we filed into the general's room and sat in a semicircle around him he got up from his chair and stood before us, leaning back on his desk. He was in his shirtsleeves. His desk was tidy; his ten-foot wall maps non-committal. He wore no glass in his blind eye and for the first time in my knowledge of him he was smiling slightly. Quietly and easily and without emphasis he said:

'Gentlemen, I have asked you to come here this morning to let you know that we have attacked in the Western Desert. This is not an offensive and I do not think you ought to describe it as an offensive as yet. You might call it an important raid. The attack was made early this morning and I had word an hour ago that the first of the Italian camps has fallen. I cannot tell you at this moment how far we are going to go—it depends on what supplies and provisions we capture and what petrol we are able to find. I wanted to tell you this so that you can make your own arrangements.' I asked if the weather was favourable. The general answered yes. He questioned us then to discover if any of us knew that the attack had been planned. It was important, he said, since, if the correspondents had not known, then, presumably, no one else except the authorised few had known. Not one of us was able to say he had had any hint of it. The surprise was complete.

There was a scatter then to get to the front—a full day and a half s journey away. And there began for us, on that brilliant winter morning, such a chain of broken communications and misunderstandings and mistakes that no correspondent who took part in the campaign is ever likely to forget. The press arrangements for correspondents in peace-time had been sketchy. In the face of a British victory they broke down almost entirely, though later conditions were greatly improved. It was days before we reached the front. Forever the forward troops vanished ahead of us as we sat stranded in our broken vehicles. Messages went astray for days or were lost altogether. We scraped what food we could from the desert or went without. We hitchhiked when our vehicles broke down. Often we abandoned sleep in order to catch up. None of this, of course, was comparable to the difficulties the soldier in the line was putting up with. But it was a new kind of reporting: exasperating, exciting, fast-moving, vivid, immense and slightly dangerous. And what we had to say had such interest at that time that our stale descriptions were published fully when at last they did arrive in London and New York. It was a job that was for ever a little beyond one's reach. But I personally emerged from it two months later very glad to have been there and much wiser than when I went in.

Six

We have taken twenty thousand prisoners with tanks, guns and equipment of all types. ~CAIRO COMMUNIQUÉ, DECEMBER 12TH, 1940.

THE ITALIAN crust had been cracked already while Wavell was speaking to us. In the first sickly grey light of the morning a small frontal attack had been sent upon Nibeiwa, and it blinded Maletti to the far greater danger that was threatening him from behind. Rising up from their hidden positions, British forces began to pour through the gap with new infantry tanks in the van. These fell on Nibeiwa from the rear, while Maletti's men, rushing from their beds, were still engaged with the smaller frontal attack. Italian guns were swung upon the infantry tanks, but the tanks, carrying heavier armour than any seen before in the desert, swept on through the barrage. By now British shells were falling squarely on Nibeiwa itself, combing through the clustered stone huts, the parked lorries, the gun emplacements embedded in the surrounding wall. Maletti, a stoutish bearded man, was wounded even as he attempted to call his men to counterattack. He retired into his tent with a machine-gun and was firing from his bedside when at last he was killed. It was all over in half an hour. The camp's thirty tanks had not even been properly manned. Everything the Italians had built through three hard months collapsed in bewilderment and chaos in that quiet morning hour when they would normally have been going about the first routine duties of the day.

Following in the wake of the army while it was hammering in the same way and at the same speed on Tummar West and Tummar East, we came on strange pathetic scenes at Nibeiwa. A cluster of broken burnt-out lorries and Bren-gun carriers proclaimed from a distance where the first British attack had fouled a minefield. Coming nearer, we found all the approaches pitted with small square holes let into the surface of the desert, and surrounding these empty cartridge cases and overturned machine-guns—the last remaining evidence of how the Italian outposts, straining their eyes through the darkness, had fired upon the approaching enemy and fled. Here and there trucks which had been carrying supplies and reliefs up to these outposts lay smashed by artillery fire beside the tracks, or were simply abandoned by the passengers who had fled back afoot to the temporary safety of the fort. Minefields were still strewn over large areas of the desert.

Cutting south and west to avoid these, and clinging closely to the tracks the heavy infantry tanks had made, we came at last into Nibeiwa itself. Here and there before the breaches in the walls a dead man lay spread-eagled on the ground, or collapsed grotesquely at the entrance of his dugout under a gathering cloud of flies. Some sixty or seventy mules and donkeys, recovered now from their shock at the noise of battle, nosed mournfully and hopelessly among the debris in search of fodder and water.

Finding none, they would lift their heads and bray pathetically into the heavy dust-laden air. Italian light tanks were grouped at the spot on the western wall where they had huddled for a last stand and there surrendered. Others had bolted inside the fort itself and were turned this way and that, indicating how they had sought at the last moment for some formation to meet the attack. Maletti's body covered with a beribboned tunic still lay sprawled on the threshold of his tent, his beard stained with sand and sweat.

Sand was blowing now out of the immense ruts cut up by the tanks, and, walking through it, we went from one tent to another, from one dugout by subterranean passage into the next. Extraordinary things met us wherever we turned. Officers' beds laid out with clean sheets, chests of drawers filled with linen and abundance of fine clothing of every kind. Uniforms heavy with gold lace and decked with the medals and colours of the parade ground hung upon hangers in company with polished jackboots richly spurred and pale blue sashes and belts finished with great tassels and feathered and embroidered hats and caps. An Indian came running to us through the camp with one of those silver and gilt belts—a gaudy shining thing that the Fascists sling around their shoulders on parade. We came on great blue cavalry cloaks that swathed a man to the ankles, and dressing-tables in the ofificers' tents were strewn with scents and silver-mounted brushes and small arms made delicately in the romantic northern arsenals of Italy.

We sat down on the open sand and ate from stores of bottled cherries and greengages; great tins of frozen hams and anchovies; bread that had been baked somehow here in the desert; and wines from Frascati and Falerno and Chianti, red and white, and Lacrimae Christi from the slopes of Vesuvius above Naples. There were wooden casks of a sweet, heady, fruity brandy, and jars of liqueurs of other kinds wrapped carefully in envelopes of straw. For water the Italians took bottles of Recoaro minerals—the very best in Italy—and these, like everything else, had been carted out to them in hundreds of cases across a thousand miles of sea and desert by ship and car and mule team.

The spaghetti was packed in long blue paper packages and stored with great sacks of macaroni and other wheat foods as numerous as they used to be in the shops of Italy before the war. Parmesan cheeses as big as small cart-wheels and nearly a foot thick lay about in neat piles except where some hungry soldier had slashed one open with his sword. Ten-pound tins of Estratto di Pomidoro—the tomato extract vital to so many Italian dishes—formed the bulk of the tinned stuff, which also contained many excellent stews and delicate tinned tongue and tunny fish and small round tins of beef. The vegetables were of every kind. Potatoes, onions, carrots, beans, cabbages, leeks, cauliflowers, pumpkin and many other things had been steamed down into a dry compact that readily expanded to its old volume when soaked in warm water—a fine food for the desert. We sampled one package that seemed at first to contain dry grass, but brewed itself over a stove into a rich minestrone soup.

I stepped down into at least thirty dugouts, coming upon something new and surprising in every one. The webbing and leatherwork was of the finest; the uniforms well cut and of solid material such as the civilian in Italy had not seen for many months. Each soldier appeared to have been supplied with such gadgets as sewing-bags and little leather cases for his letters and personal kit. The water containers were of new improved design—both the aluminium tanks that strap on the shoulders and those that one fastened to the flanks of a mule or stowed in a lorry. And over everything, wherever I went, fell a deepening layer of sand. For two days now it had been blowing, and before one's eyes one saw stores of clothing, piles of food, rifles, boxes of ammunition, the carcasses of animals and the bodies of men fast disappearing under the surface of the desert. All this richness and its wreckage, all the scars of the battle and all the effort of ten thousand men, it seemed, would not prevail longer than a week or two, and soon Nibeiwa would be restored to the featurelessness and monotony of the surrounding waste.

Moving round in the sand, one stumbled on cartridge clips, rifles, machine-guns, swords and hand grenades that had been flung aside, especially at the entrance to dugouts, in scores of thousands.

These hand grenades came to be known as money boxes or shaving sticks or pillar boxes. They were tiny things that fitted easily into the palm of your hand. They had a black cylindrical base, a rounded top coloured vivid red, and one pulled a small leather flap to explode them.

I must have seen ten thousand that morning.

I went into the tented hospitals where the British and Italian sick were still lying tended by British and Italian doctors. These hospitals were large square khaki-coloured tents of a good height for the coolness and fitted with ample mica windows. The stores of bandages, splints, liniments, drugs, surgical instruments and folding beds would have served this or any other comparable army ten times over. Here as everywhere there was precision and immense planning with immense quantity of materials. I sat in an operating theatre and drank wine with a soldier who had fought over the places I knew in the Spanish war. He pressed more food upon me and cases of wine—indeed it was he, the vanquished, who had everything to give and we who were tired and hungry. And somehow out of relief and boredom he had achieved a sense of fatality that had given him peace of mind. He was accepting the prospect of imprisonment much as a schoolboy will accept his lessons as painful but inevitable. Yet the Italian minded the absence of his family and his friends perhaps more than we did.

Never did an army write home or receive as many letters as this one did. For five miles the landscape was strewn with their letters. In the offices of the adjutants I came on bureaux stacked with thousands of official postcards which expressed the usual greetings and to which a soldier had only to attach his name and an address. But most preferred to write their own letters in a thin spidery schoolboy scrawl full of homely Latin flourishes; full of warm superlatives like 'carissimo'...'benissimo'. The theme forever ran on children and religion. No postcard ever closed without some reference to the day when the family or the lovers would be reunited. They were not the sort of letters British troops would have written. But underneath the (to us) flamboyant emotionalism they were, I suppose, the same.

I read: 'God watch and keep our beloved Frederico and Maria and may the blessed Virgin preserve them from all harm until the short time, my dearest, passes when I shall press thee into my arms again. I cry. I weep for thee here in the desert at night and lament our cruel separation. But in the day I am filled with courage as our glorious campaign sweeps on from one more magnificent victory to another...' The shabby, dirty and not very courageous little soldier explaining away the dirt and the shabbiness to himself with great sounding adjectives, and reaching out to high thoughts and his God to comfort him. He got his comfort, too. He had to. The Italian would not and could not accept the desert and the hardship of this unwanted war. He had little heart for it and still less training. He could only think, 'This is an evil time that must pass quickly.' So he turned to his family and his church with an emotionalism which was pathetic, even absurd, but very sincere. He wrote, too, a stilted literary style, using long Latin words in the same surprising way as the Spanish peasant. Often he put down his message on the back of a highly coloured postcard of extraordinary vulgarity.

Yet it was only really the correspondence of the more sycophantic officers that turned out to be amusing. The men usually did not believe in the war or care much how it went so long as they personally did not get hurt: the officers as a rule were astonishingly Fascist. Their letters, betraying the monotony of their life, would often contain a string of perfunctory entries like: 'English bomber passed over us this morning, but did not see us'…'Tenente Recagno has received his promotion'… 'Nothing of importance today.' But suddenly they would burst out with: 'But for the cowardice of the English, who flee from even our lightest shelling and smallest patrols, we would have committed the wildest folly in coming into this appalling desert. The flies plague us in millions from the first hour of the morning. The sand seems always to be in our mouths, in our hair and our clothes, and it is impossible to get cool. Only troops of the highest morale and courage would endure privations like these, and even prepare to press the advance to still greater triumphs in the cause of Fascism and the Duce. The colonel at dinner last night made a brilliant exposition of our prospects, toasting in the name of the Duce the defeat and annihilation of the English armies. We shall soon be at Alexandria.

We shall soon now be exchanging this hellish desert for the gardens on the Nile. As I came out of the mess into the starlight last night I found my breast stirred and thrilled with a transcendent emotion, as though I could feel the lifeblood of the new Italy coursing through my heart, urging me on to still greater courage and greater achievements.'

I read one letter which contained a piece of doggerel that, roughly translated, runs like this:

Long live the Duce and the King.
The British will pay for everything.
On land and sea and in the air
They'll compensate us everywhere.

But there was much hard commonsense besides. One letter-writer insisted: 'We are trying to fight this war as though it is a colonial war in

Africa. But it is a European war in Africa fought with European weapons against a European enemy. We take too little account of this in building our stone forts and equipping ourselves with such luxury. We are not fighting the Abysinnians now.'

There was the whole thing; the explanation of this broken, savaged camp. Maletti's panzer division was as tame as an old lion in the zoo. Undoubtedly they had courage, some of them. But they were living on a preposterous scale. The British coming into the camp could scarcely believe their eyes when they saw that each man had his own little espresso coffee percolator with which he brewed his special cup after meals. The British brigadiers in this action had not for many weeks or even months lived as the Italian non-commissioned officer was living. In the British lines there were no sheets, no parade-ground uniforms, and certainly no scent. The brigadier dressed in khaki shorts and shirt. He got bacon for breakfast, bully stew and tinned fruit for lunch, and the same again at night. His luxuries were the radio, cigarettes and whisky with warm water. But wine, liqueurs, cold ham, fresh bread— no, seldom if ever that. Even the Italian trucks, of which there were several hundred scattered about Nibeiwa and the other camps, carried all kinds of equipment never seen in the British lines. The field telephones, wireless, typewriters and signalling gear were far more elaborate than anything we had used. Booty, in fact, worth several millions of pounds lay here if it could only be reclaimed in time. (It wasn't.)

Sappers were at work, getting vital parts off the Italian machines so that they could keep their own vehicles on the road. We ourselves, already short of transport, endeavoured to takeover one of the great green ten-ton Lancia trucks standing about. But though we inspected dozens, all had either been wrecked at the last moment by the Italians or were hit or had gear too complicated for us to start.

Later many hundreds of these vehicles, together with Fiats and the S.P.A. brand, were on the road carrying British troops and supplies to the front. Indeed, as Wavell had indicated, the advance could not have gone forward without them. In guns, too, we had at Nibeiwa a foretaste of the prizes ahead. Many were of old stock and small calibre like the Breda, but ammunition lay about in great abundance.

Of the thirty-odd Italian tanks some half were fit for service and some were already being dragged off to workshops when I arrived. But the light Italian tank and the lighter flame-thrower were failures, and men asked for death in riding behind their thin armour. Curiously, in all essential things—guns, tanks, lorries, ammunition—the Italian equipment was not good. And vast numbers did not make up for their deficiency. The ten-ton Lancias ran on diesel—as did most of the Italian vehicles—but they had solid tyres which shook the vehicles to pieces after a short time among the boulders on the desert. Moreover, when a ten-ton lorry which was also a good target broke down, ten tons of supplies were held up. We preferred to run on petrol, using five-tonners or lighter machines. If one broke down, then no more than five tons were delayed, and repacking onto a sound vehicle was easier. Nevertheless, from this moment on, more and more captured Italian equipment was pressed into service against the Italians.

Nibeiwa was our first storehouse. As I drove away from it northward in the early afternoon the blown sand cleared for a moment revealing two big desert birds that circled and twisted some twenty feet above the ground until, seeing what they wanted, they dived and settled amid the stench where an Italian mule team had gone down to death with its crew under British machine-gun fire.

Northward, toward the coast beyond Nibeiwa, things had gone with a precision and speed that outstripped all communications. After Nibeiwa, according to the plan, one section of the armoured division had branched off on the lonely desert route in the direction of Sofafi; another had struck for the coast between Buq Buq and Sidi Barrani; and the other had made straight toward Sidi Barrani, mopping up forts as it went. This last northerly column was the one I was following. Tummar West and Tummar East had gone that same first day almost as quickly as Nibeiwa. Nothing, it seemed, could, withstand the new infantry tanks. Travelling only twelve miles an hour, they lunged out of the dust of the battle and were on the Italians or behind them before anything could be done. The Italians in despair saw that their light anti-tank shells just rattled off the tanks' turrets, and even light artillery was not effective against them. The whole of this advance, then, was done with this surprise weapon—surprise, not because the enemy did not know about it, but because they did not know it was in Egypt and they had nothing to bring against it.

Maktila on the coast had been heavily plastered by the navy, and by the time the British garrison from Mersa Matruh came to attack they found many of the enemy already fled. These fugitives turned back to strengthen Point Ninety, the two Tummars and Sidi Barrani itself. But the infantry tanks rode upon them with artillery in support, and by the time I reached the battlefield all Italian forces who had managed to get away had retired into Sidi Barrani and were already attempting to escape farther down the coast road in the direction of Sollum. In spurting dust we drove past the Tummars, a richer arsenal yet than Nibeiwa. For miles on either side of the track the undulating surface of the desert was honeycombed with ammunition dumps, each dump about ten feet by eight by two feet high and spaced a hundred yards apart. These were the shells Graziani had stored against the day when he was to have advanced on the Nile. Every rise was dotted with stationary and abandoned Italian trucks and vehicles of all kinds. Notepaper flew forlornly across the battlefield in every direction, and here and there a gun stuck in the dust in a ring of empty shell cases.

A bitter artillery duel had been fought out with the Italian guns on a height near the coast. And now on the morning of the third day the British flung themselves on the defences of Sidi Barrani itself. Unwilling to delay their advantage until more artillery caught up with them, the tanks and infantry went in together against the first line. This was a series of zigzag trenches on a rise buttressed from other positions among the sand-dunes. As the fine sand whirled up in monstrous yellow clouds visibility shut down first from a hundred, then to fifty yards. The battle locked in choking heat over two miles of rocky desert. Constantly in the sand-dunes the Italians kept up enfilading fire upon the central British thrust. But by 11 a.m. at the bayonet point we had gained the first ridge and Sidi Barrani lay in view. The tanks then felt their way around east and west of the Italians, and suddenly in the early afternoon appeared right amongst them. Artillery posts were charged direct. Everywhere in the yellow light of the dust storm men were running, shouting, firing, diving for shelter. A regiment of Scots charged from the ridge they had gained earlier in the day, and though their best N.C.O.'s went down, the rest came on. Groups of Italians began bobbing up from their trenches, waving white handkerchiefs, towels, shirts, and shouting, 'Ci rendiamo' (We surrender).

The tanks now were upon Sidi Barrani itself and the infantry came pell-mell after them. General Gallina was there with his staff. They knew it was useless. Their surrender was received while still the ragged edges of the battle were sounding with rifle and mortar fire. This was about 3 p.m. Toward evening the Mersa Matruh troops, having pushed all opposition on the coast out of their way, entered the town from the east. Gallina drew the remnants of his army together and, addressing them quietly, an elderly general with a general's sweeping grey beard, he said, 'You have fought bravely.' They took him and his officers off to captivity by aeroplane.

The British now found themselves in a place of utter desolation.

Sidi Barrani, so the Italians had been broadcasting, had been a thriving city, its trams running, its shops open, its beaches thronged. Even its nightclubs were said by Rome to be flourishing—a picturesque way of saying that two small brothels of unexampled dreariness were open and doing business. One of the women had been killed and a grave was made for her on the battlefield. In actual fact, Sidi Barrani's twenty meagre houses had never required a tramway and certainly never had one, and the only shop I ever saw there was the village store with a bomb through the middle of it. Nevertheless there did exist one or two substantial white stone buildings on the seafront. But now all was in ruins. At the climax of many heavy aerial bombardments the navy had come and flung round after round of fifteen-inch shells upon the village.

No house maintained its roof; none had its walls intact. Everything within was a mass of whitish grey rubble. Shell-holes pitted the scrawny streets and twisted the barbed wire round the port. A shell seemed to have blasted each window in such a manner as to leave every wall with an aperture like a huge keyhole driven through it. Wrecked vehicles lay about, and a great quantity of petrol and crude oil drums—some of which, being hit, were burning yet and staining the sand a grimy stinking black.

On the outskirts there were many guns—Bredas, eighteen-pounders and anti-tank weapons. Some of these, by a new Italian device, were mounted upon turntables which in turn had been set upon lorries with the object of giving them the mobility of ordinary desert transport. Together with the booty at Nibeiwa and the other camps I counted over fifty captured tanks, over five hundred captured vehicles.

The troops who had swept through from the east had found the same eloquent story of surprise—half-eaten breakfasts (served with silver pepper and salt stands, china plates and cups); clothes half bundled into boxes and then abandoned. And there was the same business of bedside lights, book-racks, tents emblazoned with flags, officers' cloaks thick with decorations, quantities of freshly baked loaves, cases of chocolate, sweetmeats, coffee, jam, cigarettes, tobacco both Italian and English.

Down by the Sidi Barrani sea-cliffs an important base hospital had been established under canvas. The Italian staff in the hospital had vanished, leaving an appendicitis patient cut open on the operating table. Instruments were still sticking in the body when it was found.

Exhausted by hard travel and sightseeing, we camped down by the hospital for the night. Savoia bombers came over and we did not wake.

Starting fresh in the morning, we came at once onto the Via della

Vittoria, the new Italian road that ran straight and true to the Libyan border, over those sixty painful miles that once were strewn with deep dust and boulders. At the point where it met the British road at Sidi Barrani the Italians had erected a six-foot cement monument decorated with the fasces and carrying an inscription which declared 'despite wind and sand and the wiles of the enemy' Egypt and Libya were inseparably joined together under Fascist rule. And indeed the Italian engineers deserved praise. All through the late summer and autumn they had slaved with labour gangs at that road, and now the track was heavily metalled and waiting only for a covering of light metal and bitumen. It was banked and graded with the precision of an auto strada, and of a good width and flanked by deep ditches for the draining. Here and there culverts led off to sidetracks and offered an opportunity for the heavier vehicles to turn.

Steamrollers which had come from Italy to put the finishing touches lay along the highway, and as we progressed we found more monuments that proclaimed how such and such a unit had finished a section in record time. On one crest rose a stone bust of Mussolini bearing a quotation from one of his Genoa speeches, 'He who does not keep moving is lost.' British soldiers ahead of us who had no taste for irony had bowled the head over into the sand.

Now only ten miles west of Sidi Barrani we saw signs that Creagh's dash to the coast to cut the retreat of the Italians had succeeded. Italian lorries caught unawares by British tanks lay twisted in smoking ruins on the road. Guns stood about dejectedly. All the roadside camps and storage dumps were deserted and bore signs of having been passed over by an invading army. Diesel oil drums were tumbled about, spilling their contents on the sand. Every few minutes we had to make a detour to avoid more Italian vehicles left by their drivers astride the road. Food, ammunition and oil dumps followed one another among the sidetracks, all marked with Italian direction posts. Dugout villages roofed with camouflaged waterproof sheets pitted the landscape. The Italians had dug in so completely and comfortably that this was not Egypt any more—it was a part of Italy. They had found and developed a water supply with genius. They had all but completed a pipeline from Bardia. Soon, no doubt, they would have produced market gardens in the desert. At Buq Buq, which I remembered as a Bedouin waterhole dug in the sand, there stood now a line of high pumps like those used for filling locomotives and two large underground storage tanks.

It was approaching Buq Buq that we came suddenly upon a sight that seemed at first too unreal, too wildly improbable to be believed. An entire captured division was marching back into captivity. A great column of dust turned pink by the sunset light behind them rose from the prisoners' feet as they plodded four abreast in the sand on either side of the metalled track. They came on, first in hundreds, then in thousands, until the stupendous crocodile of marching figures stretched away to either horizon. No one had time to count them— six, possibly seven thousand, all in dusty green uniforms and cloth caps. Outnumbered roughly five hundred to one, a handful of British privates marched alongside the two columns, and one or two Bren-gun carriers ran along the road in between. The Italians spoke to me quite freely when I called to them, but they were tired and dispirited beyond caring. I found no triumph in the scene—just the tragedy of hunger, wounds and defeat. These were the men of General Amico's 'Catanzaro Division,' I discovered.

Soon we pieced the whole story together. Creagh had reached the coast two days before. His tanks and Bren-gun carriers had burst over the last desert rise onto the new road to find themselves confronted with the Catanzaro Division, which was then moving up on normal relief to Sidi Barrani. The Italians were smoking and singing, since none had expected action so far back behind the front.

The British joined action at once, and a smart tank and artillery battle was fought out in the saltpans between the road and the sea. When their tanks failed, the bewildered Italians simply gave themselves up, and here they were upon the Via della Vittoria, marching to Sidi Barrani and away out of the war without having fired a shot.

Thousands more were clustered round the water points at Buq Buq, a more broken collection of men than I had ever seen. Many were Libyans. They sat upon their haunches in disordered groups awaiting turn to draw water from the cisterns and receive an issue of their own cheese and tinned beef which had been gathered from one of the Italian food dumps nearby. A company of British troops was guarding them—a company that could have been overwhelmed at any moment. But there was no fight in these Italians, and their fear of the waterless desert overmastered any wild idea they may have had for gaining freedom. They were confused, too, and had no inkling of the smallness of the British forces.

In the morning three Libyans approached the unarmed war correspondents' camp which we had pitched among the white sand-dunes beside the sea. They were so utterly dejected and miserable no one thought to take their guns away from them, and they sat watching us stolidly and pathetically while we finished breakfast, wanting only to be taken prisoner. We put them in our truck and drove them back to the prisoners' depot by the water wells.

Now at last we had caught up with the front. In the far south Sofafi had fallen with rich loot. It was voluntarily abandoned by the Italians before it had been attacked, and its garrison was making up the escarpment toward Bardia under R.A.F. bombardment. Other British troops were moving across to cut them off. Others again were pressing on Sollum and Halfaya Pass. There was artillery fire along the escarpment at Sollum, and once again I saw the cliffs curtained in smoke and aircraft battling in the sky above. Two Caproni fighters lay upended grotesquely beside the road. More and more prisoners were coming in, bringing with them many guns, tanks, vehicles and truckloads of captured documents. These last were fascinating. One of Bergonzoli's orders of the day, written just before the British attacked, read: 'The emblems of the British Army that tried to bar your way are trampled underfoot. The first steps of the march to Alexandria have been covered. Now onward! Sidi Barrani is the base of departure for more distant and much more important objectives.' Then again, how truly, 'Surprise is always the mastery of war.'

Light rain fell. There followed a wind so sharp and piercing that one could not imagine it had ever been hot in the desert. Goose-flesh pockmarked our bare sunburnt arms, our faces felt blue and bloodless, and the sand came up, stinging, icy and cruel, to bite into our bare knees and arms and stun our eyelids until we could bear it no longer and reached for our towels or waterproof sheets to bind round our heads. Our food and petrol gave out, and we spent hours each day ranging round the desert in search of abandoned Italian dumps. At night six of us slept huddled in one car for warmth. Edward Kennedy of the Associated Press of America lost his voice. Alexander Clifford of the *Daily Mail* caught sandfly fever and jaundice and we left him one day huddled in blankets in the lee of a sand- dune by the sea. For an hour that night we could not find him as we hunted through the sand-dunes. When at last we made camp together we succeeded in building a fire of brushwood. On it we cooked the one good meal I can remember of this stage of the campaign—a spaghetti stew of Italian tomato, Italian bully beef, Italian Parmesan cheese, washed down with Italian mineral water.

Standing on the top of the dunes that night we watched for an hour the R.A.F. turning one of their full-scale raids on Bardia. Looking across the wide intervening bay in the darkness, we saw it all stage by stage—the first bombs, the answering fire; the hits, the misses; the flames as the aircraft came away; drama as rounded and directional as a motion picture and watched with the detachment of a spectator in the stalls. Parachute flares with their fresh blinding light hung in the sky above the town, while bombs fell at the rate of two a minute in a regular pendulum motion—right, left, right, left. The A.A. fire in reply turned right, left, in search of the unseen raiders; then, losing contact, broke into crazy patterns over the sky. 'Like a bullfight,' someone said. 'And Bardia the bull.' Two flaring lights opened high above the town and descended straightly. Two planes gone; two picadors. Then more swerving light in the sky; more interplay of light and the counterthrust of bomb noise against gun noise. Then the great flash as the ammunition dump went up and a slower flame advanced steadily up into the night. The bull. The surviving planes homewarding sounded over our heads. It was finished and we went to bed on the sand.

At last on December 16th—one week after the fighting had begun—Sollum fell; and with Sollum, Halfaya Pass, Fort Capuzzo, Sidi Omar, Musaid and a new line of forts several kilometres long which the Italians had built on the lip of the escarpment. Halfaya's old rocky track had been graded and surfaced, and as one mounted to the top the old familiar view spread out below—the sweep of Sollum bay round into Egypt; the village below and the western cliffs reaching round into Bardia.

Breasting the top of the pass into the high Libyan desert, a wind of such sharpness and force swept upon our open truck that the driver was momentarily forced to stop. No one without glasses could travel looking ahead into that sand-laden wind that hit everything raised above the floor of the desert with the force of an aeroplane slipstream. British camps loomed up among the debris of the broken Italian forts.

We returned and entered Sollum where already half a dozen British warships and merchant vessels were discharging water and stores for the army. The Italians here had erected a barbed-wire compound to house British prisoners, and now it was full of their own people. In the desert, too, we found a camp exclusively for captured Italian generals, who plodded about dispiritedly in the sand.

Upon every wall were scrawled caricatures of Englishmen, jibes at Churchill and Vivas for the Duce. Prisoners in their extremity were offering the equivalent of an English pound for a loaf of bread.

Their units were inextricably mixed and confused, since in their flight the Italians had broken up, and many small groups had struck out for themselves in that last frantic rush to gain the safety of Bardia.

It was within a day or two of Christmas, and since it did not seem possible that the advance could continue at once, we decided to return to Cairo for a few days' rest. But first we set out for one last visit to the front around Bardia. We were too cold and miserable to be much interested, but we felt we should do it. On the way down the Via della Vittoria all but one of our trucks broke down.

Standing in the tearing wind we drew matches for who should go on. Clifford and I won. We left the others to hitchhike the best they could back to our base camp, and we crept on into Sollum. The Italians were lobbing shells into the village, and we turned back into a wadi below Halfaya Pass, where we camped under a thorny clump of palms. We smashed a wooden petrol case and lit a fire under the rocks. Someone produced a tin of plum pudding and half a bottle of whisky, and as we ate and drank, the Italian 'flying circus' came over. This was a flight of about twenty Savoias protected from above by a similar number of fighters. They bombed haphazardly up and down the escarpment just above our heads, and in the night they came again, their flaming exhausts making weird flashes above us as we crouched in that frozen wadi. Clifford had not eaten for three days and clearly we could not go on. In the first grey light we turned back.

So then the first stage was ended. A rough score could be totted up. Some thirty thousand prisoners, including five generals, were in our hands. Hundreds of guns, lorries, tanks and aircraft were captured. Equipment worth millions of pounds had been won. The attempted enemy advance to the Nile had been smashed, and the last fighting Italian soldier had been flung out of Egypt. The enemy numbered their dead and wounded in thousands. Our casualties stood at the incredibly good figures of seventy-two killed and 738 wounded. The Italian egg had been cracked and it was rotten inside. It was largely a victory of the infantry tanks and scarcely one of these had been lost. Of the six Italian divisions that had been mustered for the capture of Egypt, less than half remained, and these, largely without guns and equipment, were crowded back into Bardia, which was even then being surrounded by our armoured forces. More than this, the Italian morale was broken and the prestige of the British army restored. I went back to Cairo for one of the pleasantest Christmases I can remember.

Seven

General Bergonzoli is still missing. -CAIRO
COMMUNIQUÉ, JANUARY 8TH, 1941.

ON CHRISTMAS morning I drove across the Bulaq Bridge in Cairo
to the Church of England cathedral which stands, a pile of very
modern yellow brick, beside the Nile a little distance down from the
embassy. After the service a great congregation streamed out into the
bright sunshine. Among the brigadiers, the diplomats, the army nurses,
the wives—few of these: most had been evacuated—and the soldiers,
General Wavell stood chatting with his friends. People paused as they
passed to gaze with open curiosity at this quiet thick-set man whose
name now stood higher than that of any soldier in the empire. He never
failed to impress and puzzle slightly everyone who met him, but all the
same there was nothing very much to be learned from the first meeting
with the general. His voice was high, rather nasal, and unless he was
actually engaged upon some definite business he seldom said anything
at all. His dark deeply tanned face was lined and heavy to the point
of roughness. His thinning hair was grey, and the one good eye left
him from the last war gleamed brightly from a face that was usually as
expressionless as a statue.

Wavell had just published a book about his old master, called
Allenby—A Study in Greatness, and the London *Times* was reprinting
a series of lectures he had delivered a few years before on generalship.
He was essentially a well-bred, well-groomed writer, without humour,
without sparkle, and more concerned with getting his subject written
than with making it palatable for his audience.

But the book and lectures were valuable in revealing an unsuspected
sensitivity and daring.

Whatever Wavell was before the last war, he had gained from Allenby
a talent for taking responsibility with suppleness and decision and for
drawing others after him. In this year in the Middle East he won respect
by his silence, and a good deal of admiration through his habit of
confidently deputing authority to others. Wilson, O'Connor, Creagh—
all of them were bound very strongly to Wavell. One other thing he
had, and that was modesty. Now in his fifties, after half a lifetime of
military training and planning, he had the great fortune to be able to
put his ideas to the test. There was nothing very new about them—to

use secrecy and surprise to the utmost, to hit hard and quickly and keep following up, to establish strong lines of communication, to be mobile—all sound military practices. But Wavell brought them to life by his own particular ingredient—a touch of daring.

I recall very clearly each of my meetings with him—more clearly perhaps than I recall meetings with any other public figure. First, there was Wavell standing on the forward deck of a troopship at Suez in February 1940, welcoming the first Australian contingents and saying very clearly and firmly: 'I am glad to have Australian troops under MY command, and I am sure MY orders will be fully carried out.' The capitals are the general's. Then, Wavell in blue overalls climbing out of an aircraft in the desert, where he had just made a low reconnaissance of the enemy front line. Wavell walking dourly alone under the trees at a race meeting at Gezira. Wavell sitting in his shirtsleeves in the war-room at G.H.Q., taking a conference and saying very little or nothing. Wavell in stout whipcord breeches sitting opposite me for three and a half hours on a Sunderland flying boat journey to Crete.

For an hour he fished papers from a pigskin case and made notes upon the margins, reducing those notes to paragraphs and those paragraphs to one-line headings. Then for half an hour he browsed quietly through a volume of Browning's love poems and slept a little and read his verse again.

Finally, he chatted with me a little, and when Crete came in sight he was back on his notes. It was almost the same on the way home. It was his invariable practice to invite his companion to talk while he asked the questions. Nearly always our short conversations opened with his 'Getting along all right?' He remembered all our complaints (there were many) and those that did get through to him were settled. The troops liked him. At Keren in Eritrea, at Merj Ajoun in Syria, at Capuzzo in Libya, you would often find him, just before an important engagement, sitting in a tin hat at an artillery observation post. He encouraged the front-line habit among his generals and liked them to stay in the field.

When he left the Middle East he left behind the feeling that he had not been an especially able domestic administrator, but the sweep and movement of his campaigns had raised his name high as an aggressive general. His talents were in the field. He had two important phases—the period of the Greek campaign (I can write of this later), and now during this winter of 1940–41, when all his abilities were sunning in success and approval from his prime minister, his generals, his troops and his public.

After the reconquest of the Western Desert, the character of the fighting in Libya changed radically. The surprise element was now gone. It was to recur only once more and very dramatically at the end of the campaign. The Italians were back on their fortified bases. They still outnumbered us, they were dug in, and they were expecting us to come on. Graziani's theory of roughly parallel lines of coastal and inland defence on set positions was coming into play. Both Bardia and Tobruk were surrounded by strong double perimeters which it had taken the Italians several years to construct. The desert bases—Jarabub, Mekili and Kufra—were remote. It was the British now who were on long lines of communications with all the problems of water and petrol supply before them. The winter, too, had risen to a harshness that made additional hardships for advancing troops. Through the long nights Graziani could reasonably expect the arrival of reinforcements by sea at Tripoli.

The marshal's policy was very simple—in fact it was the only one he could follow. He would hold Bardia and Tobruk, and so long as they lay across Wavell's lines of communication the British would be unable to push on. Should Bardia and Tobruk fall, then a line could be established against the invader southward from the neighbourhood of Derna to the desert post of Mekili. Here the country was riven by immense wadis and rocky heights ideal for defence. Should even this line fall, then an easy retreat over two good mountain roads could be made to Barce and Benghazi. If Benghazi was not reinforced by this time, then the whole Italian army could withdraw intact down the coast road to Tripoli. When we were far extended there in the Libyan desert, Graziani would meet us and destroy us.

Every one of these plans miscarried. They miscarried because the tactics Wavell now put into effect were of so brilliant a nature that they must remain throughout this war at least as a model for the reduction of strongholds in the desert. Briefly the plan was this: no matter how weak our forces were, every enemy stronghold had to be surrounded and cut from its supplies until we were strong enough to make a frontal attack. Conversely, no position was to be attacked until it was surrounded. The navy and the R.A.F. would leave no enemy position on the coast in peace even for a single day. Thus Bardia was to be surrounded, plastered from sea and air, then attacked directly. As soon as the attack was favourably launched, the encirclement of Tobruk would start, and the reduction of the town be essayed in the same way. And so on to Bomba and Derna. Beyond that no one yet cared to conjecture anything definite.

To accomplish this, Wavell regrouped his forces with rare

psychological insight. He was still going to use only two divisions—throughout the whole campaign he never had more than two divisions in the operational area. The experienced and fast 7th Armoured Division would undertake the inland swoops and the encircling movements. The India division, having well done its job at Sidi Barrani, would be withdrawn, together with the New Zealanders, and they would be replaced by most of the untried Australian divisions. In this Wavell aroused a very definite animosity among the New Zealanders, who had been thirsting for action. They were additionally hurt when their transport was taken away from them and given to the Australians. But with the Australians Wavell's action brought him immense popularity. They had been growing increasingly, even dangerously, restive after their year's enforced idleness. Wisely now these men, already noted as shock troops, were to have their chance while their health was at its freshest, their morale at its highest and their aggressive qualities most eager. The New Zealanders, with their reputation of being solider and more disciplined holding troops, would be a valuable rock on which to fall back if anything went wrong.

Many of the technical services—machine-gunners, signallers, railways operators and supply columns—were to be given to English or allied units. The navy and the air force would dispose of equal or even greater forces than in the December advance.

Bardia as a defensive position was much stronger than Sidi Barrani. The town itself, a picturesque Fascist settlement of white-walled houses and straight streets, stood high upon the cliffs sheer above a small, almost landlocked bay. Coastal boats of shallow draught could enter and discharge their supplies in the storehouses on the flat delta of the Wadi Gefani. This wadi effectively protected the town from the landward side and indeed left the town isolated on a spit reaching over the sea.

Attacking troops had first to penetrate a ring of forts and an anti-tank trench stretching round Bardia from one coast to the other, and then cross the Wadi Gefani. It was not easy. But the armoured division was astride the road westward to Tobruk, and the morale of the Italian troops was not high. They numbered some thirty thousand men under the command of Bergonzoli, who had lately been carrying on a high-flown wireless conversation with the Duce in Rome, the theme of which was 'Bardia will never surrender.'

All through Christmas week Australians kept pouring up the desert road from the Nile Delta—a vast procession stretching three hundred and fifty miles from Cairo to the front. The Via della Vittoria was quickly cut to pieces, and bus-loads of troops came up onto the escarpment matted in dust, the eyes of each man two dark slits peering out of a grey mask under a steel helmet. Before New Year's Day they were in position and shelling the Italian perimeter. Patrols were nightly going into the Italian barbed wire. On January 2nd shallow-draught gunboats from the China station bore down upon Bardia's harbour, and all through that night the navy and the R.A.F. raked the town and its surroundings with probably the heaviest bombardment of its kind that had ever been seen in the Middle East. The day, as I remember, had been full of warm, yellow, winter sunlight. Now in the evening, like flights of migrating birds, British bombers kept sliding across a sunset magnificently red. And far into the night the red fires in Bardia expanded and continued the sunset. Waiting at our camp in Mersa Matruh, we knew the attack was coming, and the desert had an almost tangible atmosphere of expectancy and strain.

At dawn the Australians attacked. They had chosen a spot in the perimeter to the west of the town, and here the sappers ran forward under machine-gun fire to bridge the anti-tank trench by blowing in its sides. The infantry tanks and the infantry were soon across, and, with this spearhead always pressing nearer to the heart of the enemy defences, the battle started along a ten-mile front around the Italian chain of forts. The effect of the British assault was as though one had tightly gripped an orange, at the same time piercing it with a fork. This went on all through January 3rd.

On January 4th the day began for me at 3 a.m., when the correspondents started from Mersa Matruh aboard an army truck. For miles along the road into Sollum we watched the final British artillery barrage being laid down along the five-hundred-foot cliffs that supported Bardia on their crest. In blinding icy dust we crawled up Halfaya Pass and continued on aslant the artillery fire into Libya.

Italian shells, mostly of small calibre, were crumping steadily away to the west. At force headquarters, a labyrinth of underground Roman passages, a young staff officer barked laconically: 'Whole of the southern defences encompassed and we're breaking in from the north...ten thousand prisoners taken and God knows how many more coming in... four enemy schooners stopped outside Bardia, three more captured... enemy artillery getting weaker...no, I don't know where the hell the enemy air force is; we haven't seen it all day.'

We drove on along the broken border fence to the Australian headquarters, a Roman labyrinth twenty feet below the surface of the desert. The Italian gunners were getting the range there, but unevenly and spasmodically. Right and left of the camp explosions were going up in short gusty clouds of black smoke. The staff officers, deaf to it all, were diving in and out of dugouts with messages, shouting out over the telephones new orders for new positions to the men at the front about to take Bardia.

We drove on down the Capuzzo road, and there it was again, the sight I was beginning to know well—the unending line of marching prisoners with their weary, stony faces. They were herding like a football crowd into roughly thrown-up barbed-wire compounds each holding two or three thousand men. Down the road leading to the fighting more British troops were pressing on in trucks travelling at breakneck speeds. Over Capuzzo British spotting planes ranged back and forth checking the last Italian gun positions from the white flashes that spouted up for ten miles along the coast. Capuzzo itself, as we drove past with the troops, was empty, more torn about than ever. Our lighter truck got on ahead of the troop-carriers as we approached Bardia. Shells were shrieking down along the whole length of the road, though never hitting it exactly as we went through. A sharp smell of explosive washed across the track in sudden bursts as each new mushroom of smoke billowed up—sometimes two hundred yards away to the left, then, erratically, far out to the right below the spot where an Australian battery was belching black fumes at the speed of half a dozen bursts a minute. Surrendered Italians were huddled on either side of the road, sheltering from their own shellfire. Others made desperate by their hunger rushed across the open to us. They swarmed round our truck in hundreds, crying: 'Food… water…cigarettes.' We flung out biscuits and they scrambled for them in a heap on the ground, forgetting the shells in their frantic hunger.

We were reaching the most forward troops now, down a road that drove through empty Italian trenches. Rifles and machine-guns were lying unmanned along parapets; dead and wounded were mingled together in ditches. Clearly the majority of Italians had surrendered as soon as their positions were invested. Over toward the coast another long line of prisoners moved across the desert without a guard, blindly seeking shelter, blindly looking for anyone to surrender to. In a branch of Wadi Gefani, half a mile from Bardia, the front-line Australians in full kit were awaiting the order to go over the top for the last time. They lay about in groups in the dry riverbed, smoking comfortably. You could almost trace the trajectory of the Italian shells as they screamed a hundred yards above and hit empty sand on the back edge of the wadi above us. The commanding officer limped up and took a drink from me gratefully. 'It's my birthday today,' he said. 'Just remembered it.' He was wounded.

It was 3 p.m. now and very near the end. I crawled up the Bardia side of the wadi and looked over.

There it was, the white township with its church spire and the road leading in across two bridges. Just in front of the church, six hundred yards away, the last Italian gun was mouthing white flashes toward us. The final assault started just after 3 o'clock—British heavy tanks moving through a belt of machine-gun and even anti-tank gunfire right up to the gates of Bardia. I watched them go on spurting out shells from every gun. Crouching as they ran and calling out their war-cries, Australian infantry followed up and joined the Bren-gun patrols which had already advanced under the lee of the town in the early afternoon. I could see only a hundred or two of infantry now, and even these disappeared from view as the Italian gun turned upon them. Then that last gun hiccoughed and stopped altogether. The attack swept past it and eastward from the town.

It was easy then. We grabbed a place in a line of Australian Bren-gun carriers moving in on the town, outdistanced them at the gates, and drove down the burning main street to the town hall, where the leader of the Australian company which had just occupied Bardia stood wiping black sweat from his face. They had been in possession just over an hour. They had gone in in extended order through the neat right-angled streets, firing bursts into the houses. But only one machine-gun near the church hit back. All round us now Italians were coming out of caves and houses to surrender. Prisoners swarmed in every direction, and even in the light of the fires which were licking up the white walls of the houses it was impossible to distinguish enemy from friend. All they wanted was food, shelter from fighting, and a guarantee of life.

One Australian officer with eight men walked up to the mouth of the biggest cave in the cliffs. As he stood at the entrance with cocked revolver, over a thousand Italians came out into the daylight, holding up their hands. Half a dozen guards were told off to get them away. Except for a few who escaped by schooner or stole across overland by night, no Italians slipped through the British net. The great majority were captured unhurt, since the Italian machine-gunners had continued firing only so long as the Australians were out of range. As soon as the Australians began to set up their own guns to retaliate, the Italians came out with white towels and handkerchiefs.

I walked down through the burning town, stopping here and there to peer into the houses.

Everything had been cleared out down to the last drawer. A table was laid for ten in the officers' mess, but there was no food anywhere. We went to the harbour. Down in Bardia's lovely blue bay (where a group of naval ratings had been captured) several ships lay half-submerged and deserted. Through the clear water you could see slime already clinging to the sunken cabins and fish darting among the stanchions and sodden timbers. Thousands of tins of bully beef littered the sea floor like scattered silver coins. Birds were already nesting in the slanting masts showing above water.

The shooting and shelling stopped at last as we came back to the centre of the town. The fires in the back streets fed quietly. A little handful of us stood about in the gathering darkness, waiting for the other units of the Australian army to come up and occupy finally the cliffs and outlying forts. It was deathly quiet now after the battle. It was hard to realise we had won and it was over.

Straightaway we set off on the frigid all-night drive back to Mersa Matruh, where we could send off our messages. Often in the darkness (no car lights were allowed) we swerved to avoid lost and bewildered Italians roaming over the desert trying to find their units. Many knew nothing of the rout of the Italian army. Many slept beside their guns or turned over and shouted to us in Italian for food or water or news. We picked up a wounded Italian officer and drove him along to one of the dumps where they were collecting prisoners. 'We should never have been fighting you,' he kept insisting. 'All this should never have happened.' Four of his men hoisted him shoulder-high in the darkness and carried him off to some dressing station they knew about.

Australians, cigarettes in the corner of their mouths and steel helmets down over their lined eyes, squatted here and there among the prisoners, or occasionally got to their feet with a bayoneted rifle and shouted, 'Get back there, you,' when some Italian started to stroll away. These men from the dockside of Sydney and the sheep stations of the Riverina presented such a picture of downright toughness with their gaunt dirty faces, huge boots, revolvers stuffed in their pockets, gripping their rifles with huge shapeless hands, shouting and grinning—always grinning— that the mere sight of them must have disheartened the enemy troops. For some days the Rome radio had been broadcasting that the 'Australian barbarians' had been turned loose by the British in the desert. It was a convenient way in which to explain away failures to the people at home. But the broadcast had a very bad effect on the Italians waiting in Bardia for the arrival of the Australians. I saw prisoners go up to their guards to touch the leather jerkins our men were wearing against the cold. A rumour had gone round that the jerkins were bulletproof. More than anything for the defenders of Bardia the last few days had been a war of nerves. And now the Italian nerve was gone.

We drove on slowly, endlessly, chilled to the bone, past streams of ambulances and supply-wagons going up to the front where they were badly needed. By midnight we were down the escarpment. Just before dawn we were approaching Mersa Matruh, Richard Dimbleby driving to relieve our chauffeur. Six of us and our kits were jumbled somehow in the back of the tiny 8-cwt. truck, too frozen to move, but beyond sleeping. Only Dimbleby slept. The truck struck two concrete drums placed across a newly completed bridge and plunged into space over the ditch beside the road. Painfully but unhurt we picked ourselves out of the wrecked vehicle and stood beside the road.

Out of the gloom emerged an engineer who stared glumly at the wreckage for a moment. Then in a tired hurt voice he said: 'I've been working for a solid month in this bloody hole. I built that bridge. I finished it today. I was just putting up a nice little memorial to say, "Bridge begun by the 21st Company of Engineers, December 1940, Completed January 1941." I don't suppose it matters now.' Then, more bitterly: 'Or would you like to add something to the inscription? Would you like to say, "Destroyed by War Correspondents, January 1941"?' But kindly he gave us tea and we were packed up and taken into Mersa Matruh. And there we wrote and slept. We had been travelling two days and nights.

Eight

Early this morning our attack was launched on Tobruk. ~CAIRO COMMUNIQUÉ, JANUARY 21ST, 1941.

ALREADY WHILE Bardia was falling Tobruk was being surrounded. Those elements of the 7th Armoured Division which had guarded Bardia's outlet to the west cut back deep into the desert once the Bardia battle had been joined. They arrived presently at El Adem, one of the

Italians' three main air-striking bases, just south of Tobruk. Here eighty-seven aircraft lay burnt out or broken on the ground. Many of the machines had been just sufficiently damaged by the R.A.F. to keep them on the ground while the offensive was going on, and now, unwilling to abandon valuable engines and air- frames, the Italian air force had set fire to them. Several blocks of fine concrete workshops, hangars and living-quarters stood beneath El Adem's high wireless tower. Climbing it, we had a view on to the white roofs of Tobruk itself.

The machinery captured here was the first real booty that had fallen to the R.A.F., and the field itself was destined to become a valuable air junction for the British forces. But at the moment it was under shellfire, and when I arrived there, only a handful of British troops were keeping guard over the workshops. A sheikh with seven magnificent solid gold teeth came riding out of Tobruk to meet us.

The town was running short of water and food, he said, and he had had enough. He had escaped the Italians and was returning to the desert with his wives, his camels and his sons.

Keeping just beyond the point where the Italians were laying down a barrage, I drove on up to the coast to the west of Tobruk. We hit a fine road some twenty miles outside the town, and now at last the colours and contours of the desert were subtly changing. A low yellowish scrub sprouted here and there, and the overnight dew lying heavily upon the desert had brought forth thin tender shoots of grass. The colours were greyer than the Western Desert, more liquid and softer. The sun lost the edge of its harshness, and one's eyes, strained from the glare of the yellow sand in Egypt, were rested. As we pushed on westward toward Derna and Bomba, Bedouin tribesmen ran from their scrawny sack-and-kerosene-tin settlements beside the way, crying, 'Sayeeda,' which means, 'May you be lucky,' or perhaps 'Go with God.' The war was bringing them loot. We found they had already rifled a hospital and two roadhouses which the Italians had erected in the empty desert. This road was a wonderful thing, solidly tarred, well banked and straight, and running a thousand miles to Tunis. Mussolini had all but driven it through to the Nile. And it was a strange sensation to ride here on this sound motor road through enemy territory, one Italian army behind us at Tobruk, another in front at Derna. Yet beyond Bedouin we saw no one, not even our own troops. It seemed impossible that the Italians should not try to rush this gap and break the siege on Tobruk.

At Gazala we judged it wiser to go back. True, the Derna garrison, immobile and undecided, was too fretful to patrol even the intervening cliffs, but the night was approaching and we had not one gun between us. To encircle Tobruk again we made the great loop southward through a desert as empty as the sea. We came only upon occasional British units that had pushed forward into the waste. These men, charged with the job of forever slamming the back door on the Italians, had all but lost touch with civilisation. They had little contact with the rest of the army. They lived on bully and rationed water. They were never out of the danger zone. Nor was it possible here to tell enemy from friend in the distance, and convoys sighting one another on the horizon would manoeuvre and reconnoitre like ships at sea. Once, seeing a long line of tanks descending a chain of sand-dunes to the south, we put on speed and fled. It was not worth the risk of enquiring whether they were British.

Back at Bardia we found the Australians had already moved into position for the siege of Tobruk. A great quantity of new twenty-five-pounder guns was moving up the road, and the supply convoys stretched back to Sollum where half a dozen British merchant ships were dumping ammunition and foodstuffs and taking off prisoners. The problem of Tobruk differed only in detail from that of Bardia. The perimeter of the town was larger here—some thirty miles round the outer line of forts, nineteen round the inner. Tobruk itself, more than double the size of Bardia, housed a garrison of some twenty thousand, and for the first time civilians were enclosed. The town's long straight harbour was the most valuable port between Alexandria and Benghazi. Given it, we knew we could supply our forward troops from here and push on perhaps as far as Benghazi.

The town of Tobruk itself, like Bardia, was perched on a spit of white cliffs that formed the seaward flank of the harbour. Italian naval forces were established there, and from the half-sunken cruiser *San Giorgio* and other vessels the Italians had brought ashore several naval guns. 'Bardia Bill' had been the troops' name for the big gun with which the Fascists had pounded Sollum. And now Tobruk gunners were carrying on the tradition of Italian artillery, which was the one department of Italian arms that survived this campaign with honour. At Sidi Barrani and Sollum, at Bardia and Tobruk and again later at Derna, it was the enemy artillery that stuck to the end often long after the infantry had fled. The Italians used old guns, some dating from the last war. Many of their shells were duds and their precision instruments far from precise. But especially when firing upon fixed targets they showed a skill and endurance beyond the level of the rest of the Italian army.

Heavy responsibility fell upon the gunners, for from this time forward the Italian air force dwindled and finally disappeared altogether from the sky. Day after day went by and fewer and fewer Fascist airmen came against us. There was still some strafing of the troops, but now Hurricanes flying only thirty or forty feet above the ground were ranging back and forth over the whole of eastern Cyrenaica, blowing up staff cars and transports, machine-gunning troops and gathering information of the movements of the enemy. By the time Tobruk fell, the Italian air force was utterly defeated, and it was never afterwards restored to superiority. When the enemy came again in the air it was largely with German machines piloted by Germans.

Longmore's policy had succeeded brilliantly. From the first he had concentrated on damaging enemy aircraft on the ground by low-level machine-gun attacks. This put the enemy machines out of action long enough to enable our troops to come up and seize the airfields. Around Tobruk I had already seen nearly a hundred aircraft caught in this way. From the town appeal after appeal was going out to Italy for help. From Mussolini came back only promises and encouragements. Il Duce had no warships able to risk encounter with Cunningham in the Mediterranean—the tonnage he had a- plenty, but not the men. His Libyan air force had already seriously drained the air armada at home both in men and machines. Graziani, back at Tripoli, still had more than double the numbers of the one and a half divisions we were sending against him. But much of their transport and equipment was lost in Libya, and his generals, discouraged and bewildered at their failures, were eagerly electing to hold a line farther back rather than sally out rashly to the relief of Tobruk.

There were good grounds for believing that Tobruk might hold. Its troops were seasoned and well dug in. They had learned lessons from Bardia. The British were extended and it was reasonable to assume that their infantry tanks would soon be forced back for overhaul. Graziani was still clinging to his theory of defensive positions. Even so, it seems impossible that he would not have come out to meet us in pitched battle if he had known how few we were. Fantastic statements came pouring out of Rome. Four hundred thousand men, they said, had been sent into Cyrenaica by the British. Cut that figure by five times and it was still a gross exaggeration. Yet it is possible that the Italians really believed they were outnumbered. One longed to meet and talk of these things with such a man as General Bergonzoli. He had eluded us on the escarpment. When the troops entered Bardia they found he had flown again, though when and by what route no one could say. Some believed him to be in Tobruk, where an Italian admiral was in command.

The weather now was holding a steady sharp coldness, the days tempered with sunshine, the nights starry and bitter. But toward the twentieth of January a sandstorm of such violence blew up that telegraph poles were uprooted, trucks overturned, and troops huddled to the ground, wrapping their blankets over their heads. Nothing in living memory approached it, the veterans said. I tried to drive out of Bardia, but it was impossible to see even either side of the road, and we came back to the flimsy shelter of a bombed house where soon everything was deep under layers of sand. In this tempest where an enemy might come up to within ten yards unseen, the Italians at the more remote outposts in the perimeter kept firing off rounds every few minutes. Obviously they were seeing imaginary shapes in the eerie half-light. All this was excellent.

Then on January 20th the R.A.F. and the navy were upon the town with an even greater weight of explosive than fell on Bardia. It was the same all over again. At dawn the Australians attacked. They broke the perimeter and applied the general squeeze, English and Free French units coming in from the west. By that evening the attackers had reached every objective, and the troops in the vanguard were eight miles inside the perimeter. The attack continued under brilliant artillery fire all through the night. By noon of the following day the first troops were in the town and mopping up along the dockside.

This was our biggest capture yet. In the harbour some dozen ships lay sunken or awash, among them the *Marco Polo*, fine passenger vessel, and the cruiser *San Giorgio*, now so battered that she looked like that last photograph of the *Graf Spee* going down. On the waterfront valuable stores of water, petrol, foodstuffs and ammunition were discovered in buildings sheltering under the portside rocks. The docks and some of the heavy cranes were intact. Black trails of smoke floated from burning buildings across the harbour and the town. A lorry park was found outside, covered with more than two hundred vehicles ranging from ten-tonners to tiny 'Toppolino' Fiat touring cars. The channel of the harbour was open, and soon British destroyers were feeling their way in with stores and water to speed the army on their way. With the capture of this port we had achieved here much more than Bardia, and there was begun on that morning a tradition of the British occupation of Tobruk that is likely to emerge as one of the vital phases of the war.

The surrender was accepted in the town by an Australian brigadier. The Italian admiral commanding and his staff, all shaven and immaculate in white, and a group of four haggard generals, received him. It had been a bitter engagement. The dead were still lying out, and the wounded were everywhere. It was no time for mincing words. 'You have landmines laid in and around the town,' the Australian said. 'I will take reprisals for the life of every one of my men lost on those mines.' Quickly the Italians led Australian sappers to the mines and they were torn up. Booby traps were revealed, storage dumps opened, some two hundred guns handed over. More than fifteen thousand prisoners were gathered in for the long journey, some by sea, some by land, back to Alexandria. We had now in all some hundred thousand prisoners, but Bergonzoli had got away again. Twenty per cent of the prisoners were found to be suffering from some form of chronic dysentery.

Sickness, death and wounding enveloped Tobruk. Inside the town fires blazed. Shops, homes, offices, were torn up and their furniture and household goods strewn across the roads. Walking through it, I felt suddenly sickened at the destruction and the uselessness and the waste. At this moment of success I found only an unreasoning sense of futility. The courage of the night before had been turned so quickly to decay. And now the noise and the rushing and the light had gone, one walked through the street kicking aside broken deckchairs and suits of clothes and pot-plants and children's toys. A soldier was frying eggs on the mahogany counter of the national bank. A new fire leapt up in a furniture storehouse in the night, and the wine from the vats next door spilled across the road. Stray cats swarmed over the rubbish. In the bay a ship kept burning steadily. By its light the wounded were being carried down to the docks.

Nine

The capture of Derna was completed this morning.
–CAIRO COMMUNIQUÉ, JANUARY 30TH, 1941.

AFTER TOBRUK the character of the campaign changed again. It had been fluid at its start, then static at the Bardia and Tobruk stage; now it was fluid again. This was desirable for the British cause, since it was manifestly to our advantage now to keep the enemy on the run. At all costs he should not be given time to form a line.

Nobody expected that Derna, a hundred miles by road to the west, would be able to make a substantial stand. Nor after Derna was there any strongly fortified place before Benghazi. But the country here humped itself up three thousand feet into the range of the Green Mountains— the Jebel Achdar—and was difficult. After Derna the road through the mountains split into two branches, one taking the more northerly route past ancient Cirene, the other in the south passing through Slonta and Maraua. The two roads enclosed the rich moorland area where Mussolini had settled thousands of his model colonists. At Barce, the western junction of the two ways, the settlement scheme flowered out into a rich valley. Thence a coastal road and an inland railway ran down to Benghazi. The rains were at hand, the distance great and the dangers of ambush considerable, but already there were strong hopes that we would arrive at Benghazi.

It was resolved then to send two Australian brigades directly along the coast toward Derna. Before the town the two brigades were to split, one to take Derna and proceed beyond it to Giovanni Berta, the other to take the cross-desert route south of Derna to the same destination. At Giovanni Berta the brigades would split again, one taking the higher road to Barce, the other the lower. Then both would advance on Benghazi together. .And, in fact, it all fell out better than anyone hoped: Derna fell on January 30th, Cirene February 3rd, Barce February 7th, Benghazi February 9th.

More than anything else it was a war of engineers and artillery. Sometimes the Italian gunners would stand for a day or two firing upon fixed targets along the roadway. Often their engineers would explode great slabs of the mountainsides to block our path, or demolish bridges and hairpin bends along the roads. Everywhere they could they laid landmines—I met one company of sappers which had degaussed fifteen thousand, uprooting many of the metal boxes and stacking them beside the roadway. Time and again Italian labour gangs flung themselves upon some job of trench digging or building gun emplacements, only to find it was too late. The Australians advancing quickly upon them would discover nothing but freshly turned earth and equipment thrown away by the enemy in their flight.

The kilometre stones told the story of the accelerated pursuit very clearly. An Italian gang had been set the rather futile job of destroying these stones so that we should never know how far we were from the towns ahead. Outside Derna the numbers were chipped off and the stones themselves uprooted bodily and dumped across the roads as tank-traps. A few miles farther on the Italians contented themselves with merely chipping away the numbers. Then, with time getting shorter and the Australians hard upon them, they merely painted out the numbers. Finally, the kilometre stones outside Benghazi stood in their places untouched. The engineers' chisels were flung aside in a ditch.

Time was everything, and in that hectic three weeks between the fall of Tobruk and the taking of Benghazi the Italians were never given a moment's rest. Through every daylight hour Hurricanes were swooping on them at three hundred miles an hour, or the Blenheims were bombing. Fighting patrols with anti-tank guns were forever running far ahead of the advancing army and taking garrisons by surprise. The Italian system of communications, always their weakness, broke down altogether, so that sometimes whole brigade staffs fell into our hands before they guessed we were within fifty miles of them.

Soon transport was the only thing that held the British back. The roads were good, but there were many detours to avoid mined bridges, and the trucks were overloaded. As each vehicle fell out, ordinance units set to work to replace it with a captured lorry. Since the majority of these captured lorries were in poor condition, the advance of the whole army was constantly checked and delayed by breakdowns. We never went a whole mile in some places without seeing some broken vehicle tossed aside in a ditch. In the end the brigade convoys, something over thirty miles in length, struggled through the mud with a collection of every type of vehicle in northern Africa; some with broken springs and bodies lashed with fencing wire; others being towed in groups of twos and threes and even more; others which were a conglomeration of the good parts of several vehicles thrown together. Motorcycles, touring cars, road-menders' trucks and vehicles for drawing tractors and tanks—all were forced into service. In the end every able-bodied man got through.

The country the men were asked to penetrate after Tobruk was vastly different from the desert. Derna was an oasis of banana plantations and pomegranate groves, of lush vegetable gardens and leafy trees. Beyond, in the Green Mountains, you might have thought you were on the Yorkshire moors. A fresh mountain wind blew and with it came heavy rain and hailstones. The reddish-brown earth undulated into green valleys and hilltops dotted with shepherds' flocks and neat white colonial homesteads, all built to the same standardised pattern, all modern, all surrounded with neat hedges and home gardens. The villages were trim, hygienic and attractive—if your taste runs to ordered rows of white cottages and streamlined town halls and sewerage works. All this was a great change from the desert. It relieved us of the problem of water and presented us with another difficulty—mud…red, clinging, loamy mud that frothed up round the axles of the cars and sent them skidding round in the opposite direction to the one in which they were going; mud that bogged tanks and stained the men up to their waists; mud that got into your food and your eyes and your hair; mud that was cold and very very dirty.

But the first hundred miles were the best. In fair weather we rode on past Bomba toward Derna on a perfect road. Little by little the scattered bushes grew to shrubs and even at last to clumps of trees and a few palm groves. Bomba fell easily. But on Derna aerodrome, a great red plain lying above the thousand-foot sea cliffs with the town below, the Italians stood and fought. Wadi Derna, a ragged valley that struck into the hills, was for a few days death to enter. A few companies of Australians charged the aerodrome above with the bayonet and made themselves masters of its storehouses and buildings. The two sides were so mingled at first that the leading Australian platoon lodging in a hangar heard Italian voices through the night. In the first light of morning they saw, not three hundred yards away, four Italian tanks. The tank crews were cooking breakfast. Scarcely daring to breathe, the Australians whispered urgently down their field telephone for anti-tank guns, and the Italians were blown up before they finished breakfast.

The aerodrome with its twenty wrecked machines was now ours, but unexpectedly about forty Italian guns firing from the other side of Wadi Derna turned upon it an uninterrupted cannonade of shellfire. The shells kept bursting and bursting as though they would never stop. I crouched beneath the flimsy protection of a hangar door, with a Libyan prisoner who kept saying to me: 'I don't want to stay here. I've surrendered. Why don't they take me back behind the lines?'

'What does he say?' asked the Australian sergeant. 'He says he doesn't like it,' I translated.

'Tell him we don't like it either,' said the sergeant.

I told him.

'Then,' the Libyan protested, 'why don't we all go back?' It did seem at that time a first-class idea.

This was a bad shelling while it lasted. And it lasted three or four days. The Italians had every building on the aerodrome registered, and the buildings were the only cover. One evening they shelled a platoon of Australians back from the open into the administrative block; then they hit the block and shelled the Australians out the back door and up the hillock behind. Once again the Italians got onto them, and the Australians were pursued with a chain of bursting shellfire across the aerodrome into another building and out of that.

Watching from only four hundred yards away, where it was quite safe, that incident seemed funny to the rest of us. I do not think it is funny now, but it was then, at a moment when one was keyed to meet the tension at the front and the small manners of living were diminished or forgotten entirely.

One lived there exactly and economically and straightly, depending greatly on one's companions in a world that was all black or white, or perhaps death instead of living. Most of the things it takes you a long time to do in peace-time—to shave and get up in the morning, for example—are done with marvellous skill and economy of effort at the front. Little things like an unexpected drink become great pleasures, and other things which one might have thought important become suddenly irrelevant or foolish. In a hunter's or a killer's world there are sleep and food and warmth and the chase and the memory of women and not much else. Emotions are reduced to anger and fear and perhaps a few other things, but mostly anger and fear, tempered sometimes with a little gratitude. If a man offers you a drink in a city bar, the offering is little and the drink still less. You appreciate the offering and often give it more importance than the drink. At the front the drink is everything and the offering merely a mechanical thing. It is never a gesture, but a straight practical move as part of a scheme of giving and receiving. The soldier gives if he can and receives if he can't. There is no other way to live. A pity this is apparent and imperative only in the neighbourhood of death.

We would spend the day at the observation post of our sixty-pounder guns that were demolishing the enemy batteries one by one, and return to our lodgings in a deserted garage on the aerodrome at night. It was exposed and under fire, but the walls were fairly solid and the Italians did not seem to be interested in it. One night while the blitz was on we achieved, in honour of the artillery major and his captain, a dinner of wine, vegetable stew, sauce, fruit, tea and brandy—a rare meal at that time.

The fall of Derna depended greatly upon the fall of a certain Fort Rudero, which the Italians were using as an observation and sniping post. In the first advance one Australian company was all but wiped out trying to take it from the seaward side, and another company attacking it from the wadi inland had to be withdrawn. The final attempt came one forenoon, when the red earth was washed and new after a heavy shower at night. The barrage had begun afresh, and a staid slow fight of Savoias— the last we were to see—had been over bombing until it ran into a lone Hurricane coming back from patrol into Libya. The Australians forgot the shelling, forgot momentarily the wounded nearby and their hunger, and raised a cheer as the Hurricane dived straight through the Italian machines and sent one dropping with that breathtaking fateful slowness to the red desert. Its bursting flames rose from behind the wreckage of the other broken aircraft on the field.

The Italian shells were falling twenty and thirty yards away from us, tearing off bits of the hangar, blasting our eardrums and raising billows of red dust from the quickly drying earth. Through the noise and blast another Australian company advanced toward us—dark little figures marching slowly with heads down in little lines across the open airfield. 'Good troops,' the brigadier had been saying back at brigade headquarters, just before this engagement, 'will never be stopped by shelling.' Yet this was hard. The Italian artillery observers could actually see them. The little lines drew level with the hangar and passed on up to the ridge beyond which no one had yet advanced. For a moment I watched them pause in the full face of the enemy shelling on the open crest of the ridge and then they disappeared over the top of it. By the time I had crawled up to the ridge in a lull in the firing they had crossed the valley to the next rise, the one that ran straight down into Derna only three miles away.

I joined a Vickers-gun unit that was shooting the Italian positions just ahead of the advancing Australians. The British sighted first on an enemy observation post, silenced it, and then turned their fire on some trucks. My ridge and the ridge on which the Australians were advancing lay parallel. The intervening valley was filled with Italian shellfire. We gave it an hour or two and then followed. It seemed certain that Rudero, the objective, had fallen. We went on foot, taking a wide sweep round to the right away from the Italian positions, and came up under the fort with a party of Australian water-carriers.

Rudero had not fallen, but there was something strange and quiet about the place. After the heavy fighting along the beach yesterday its guns had not spoken. We were clinging now to the side of a cliff so precipitous that it was not easy to stand upright, and the soldiers in this sector had been here twenty-four hours without food or water. As soon as they had eaten, the company was ordered forward to take the fort. We clambered first onto a pinnacle of the cliff where all Derna broke suddenly into view, a thousand feet below...the most startlingly pleasant sight one could conceive after so long a time in the desert. We were looking right into the town as from an aeroplane. Row after row of stout, snow-white houses reached down to the graceful sky-blue harbour. A steamer, bombed by the R.A.F. and fired by the Italians, lay sinking at the jetty. Close by rose a high modernistic hotel and beyond that was the main street leading to the lighthouse. One or two cars were going along this street. A few people were moving in front of the shops. A great grove of spreading palms made a cool green pool of colour in the centre of the town.

While we gazed down, the Australian riflemen had gone ahead through the barbed wire and surrounded Rudero, a rough stone pile perhaps five hundred yards square. No sign of the enemy appeared and the soldiers relaxed a little. Some of them made in a bunch toward the side door. Once more then the enemy had vanished in the night. Concerned that he would miss a good picture, an officer with me, who was taking photographs for the War Office, called the men back and asked them to re-enact their passage through the barbed wire. Readily the men agreed. Twice the photographer rehearsed them through it, and then, the pictures taken, we all went up to the fort together to see what the enemy had left behind.

It was full of Italians. While we had posed for photographs fifty yards away outside, they had stood there with their rifles waiting dumbly to surrender. They lurked in the cellars and the stone passages; they stood in the central courtyard surrounded by the wreckage of our shell-bursts. They smoked, they stood packing their kits, or kneeling to get a last drink of water from a broken wooden barrel.

The Australians, recovering from their surprise, presented their bayonets and ran through every room and dugout until the prisoners were herded together in the main courtyard. They even unearthed a couple of white puppies born just before the bombardment began. Revolvers were grabbed from the Italian officers and rifles from their men. It was all done very quickly, and soon a platoon was on its way down the other side of the ridge to silence an Italian machine-gun post that was still pinging spasmodically up the hill. Farther back, six hundred yards away, I could still see odd groups of Italians on the run, but suddenly our artillery got onto them and they disappeared in clouds of blown dust and rock.

Three of us—the photographer and two war correspondents—were asked to escort the three senior Italian officers back to our own lines. The Italian major was obviously overstrained and tired. He leaned heavily on his dignity. The junior lieutenant, scarcely more than a boy, had wept under the machine-gun fire and again when he had asked me whether he would be shot out of hand or later. (It was a lie deliberately fostered by the Fascist command that Australians took no prisoners.) So then the six of us—the three Italian officers and we three—set off together afoot. The major was so confused he led us straight onto a field of Italian landmines and we circled back to the main road just in time.

I was beginning to chat freely with Tenente Alberto Pugliese, a lawyer from Rome, when a round of machine-gun bullets tore through the space between us. I was the first to hit the ditch beside the road, with the tenente on top of me, and there we lay while the bullets ripped up the road a foot away. Clearly the Italian snipers had that spot marked. Every time we raised our heads bullets started spurting past again.

'It's your machine-gun,' Pugliese said.

'It's not,' I said.

'All right,' he said. 'I'll stand up, and if they don't fire when they see my uniform, we'll know it's Italian and I'll ask them to stop. If they do fire, we'll know it's British. Then you stand up and ask them to stop.'

I looked at him hard, but he was apparently serious. 'You stay right where you are,' I told him coldly. Not for anyone on earth was I going to stand up. My further embarrassment was saved by the arrival of an Australian officer who called us to come on. We ran for it then until we had cover and were behind our own lines. Pugliese and the others went off toward the rear by truck with their two fox-terriers, Tobruk and Derna (Bardia, their third dog, had been killed).

These officers were typical Italians, voluble and assertive once they were certain no reprisals were going to be taken upon them. Pugliese had argued with me in the ditch: 'We would have gone on shooting, but where was the point when your guns are twice as good as ours? Anyway, we could not have gone back to Italy after this failure. As for Italy—well then, if what you say is true and the Germans are taking over the country, then good, the farce is over. But don't think there will be revolution yet. There are many like me who have got nothing out of Fascism, but we don't dislike it enough to rebel against it. Even if we hated it, what could we do about it?'

Yes, what could they do? The machine had started turning and only exhaustion now would stop it. They could surrender to us. But never to themselves.

We drove back to force headquarters that night to send our messages. It was a strange sensation, writing dispatches away here in the blue, never knowing whether they would get back to Cairo, let alone London and New York. We had been away now so long without word from the outside world that I, for one, had lost my 'news sense'—that sense of proportion you have that tells you whether a thing is worth writing or not. Everything here to us at this minute was vital and crammed with interest. But was it interesting to the Home Guard in England, to the sheep farmer in Australia and the commuter in New York? You just couldn't know. So in the end I used to find myself putting down what I had seen and felt without trying to make a rounded 'story' of it, and without the slightest idea of whether it was worth publishing or not.

The circumstances in which we wrote were strange. We typed on the backs of trucks, on beaches, in deserted houses, in gun emplacements and tents. We hoisted our typewriters on kerosene cases, on bathtubs and rolls of kit, on humps of sand and the steps of cars, or just perched them on our knees. We wrote by candlelight or lamplight, or with an electric torch shining onto the paper. And in the end we could write anywhere at any hour of the day or night—anywhere, that is, except during a bombardment, for I tried it and failed miserably.

And now, driving through a thickening sandstorm, we groped about in the collection of galvanised huts for a place to sit down and write. We found the Intelligence hut at last, and a corner of the table there, and wrote. That night we slept in another iron shed, dignified with the name of Force Headquarters Mess. Other strays like ourselves had wandered in, and we bedded down around the concrete floor as soon as dinner was done. The wind ripped part of the roof off during the night, sheet by sheet, and rain splashed in. The banging of iron against iron was like an air raid, only more irritating. Bomba was a desolate place. We were glad to get back to the front.

Two nights after this, shortly before midnight, the Italians stopped firing. They had held on gallantly. Now their ammunition was running out. They packed what they could of their equipment and escaped quietly down the coastal road in the darkness. The first Australian patrols entered the town the following morning. The road that plunged off the cliff into Derna had been cruelly blasted, but the sappers had it clear enough before the day was out, and the troops rode down.

We did not ride with them. We missed all this. It was one of those wrong decisions, inevitable sooner or later. We had thought that Derna would hold a day or two longer, and while the town, unknown to us, was actually being evacuated by the enemy, we were driving far southward across the desert to visit the armoured division at Mekili. It was an all-day run over a fresh rolling stretch of semi-desert in brilliant sunshine. We should have been warned that we were making a false move, for along the bad open stretch at the beginning which was under enemy observation we were not fired on. Following likely tracks, by compass and by guessing and by questioning a Roman Catholic priest who suddenly appeared across the desert, we found Mekili at last and the armoured division. They had had none of the spoils that fell to the men on the coast and were very short of supplies. We exchanged a couple of cases of Italian mineral water for a tin of army biscuits, and spent the night pleasantly beside the broken fort.

The armoured division had fought a quick engagement here, and now that the Italians had fled, the officers did not know what was to be their next objective. But they suspected. Already the plan for the great desert march that was to come had been discussed, and a brigadier hinted something was in the wind. But next morning a signaller came casually to our truck and said: 'Derna's gone.' I poked my head out of my sleeping-bag. 'What?'

'Just heard it on the B.B.C.,' said the signaller.

We could not believe it. It seemed impossible that the B.B.C. thousands of miles away had beaten us to the news of something only fifty miles from us—something which we had waited for days to happen. We packed, jumped into the truck, took a compass bearing straight across the desert, and set off for the coast. As we drew into another British camp on the way, a wireless was blaring out across the desert: 'Derna fell last night.' It was true, then. The official communiqué, as always, had beaten us. And we had made a first-class blunder in leaving the coast front.

Miserably we drove on through the midday heat, arguing about our compass direction. I was convinced we were driving straight into the enemy lines; the others thought we were heading for the Nile. This is just something the desert does to you. In the end we hit our objective dead centre—a dry water well—and ran on at a speed that bumped our reserve petrol tins into shapeless empty lumps of metal. The silence of the coast when we got there made it all too painfully clear—Derna had fallen.

We were met in the town by the other correspondents who had been there for hours. Competition among us was strong. It was, in a way, the most galling moment of the whole campaign.

Ten

Benghazi is in our hands. –CAIRO COMMUNIQUÉ, FEBRUARY 7TH, 1941.

DERNA WAS all that its distant view had promised. The main road wound between palms into streets of high cool buildings and spreading bougainvillea and flowering shrubs. Big gardens lay round the hospital, and the governor's palace stood among shaded lawns and fountains at the edge of the sea. The local Arabs had gone through the town and the bazaars, looting, the night before, after the Italians had left, and there had been a paying off of old scores in the few hours before the arrival of the Australian army. Front doors had been broken open and furniture looted and destroyed.

Everything in the European quarter was modern—modern and standardised to the nth tiresome degree. It was strange to come down from the desert into this super-suburbia where the curtains and the chair coverings came in three natty shades; where the dining-room suites in real old mahogany and three-ply were in strict neo-Fascist tradition, and china Cupids stood upon the standardised mantelpieces. Some three or four designs had been selected for the houses, and the colonist apparently just picked the one he liked best, ordered a set of furniture, and moved in. Much of the stuff was good and comfortable, but the tinsel and the regimentation broke through. Yet nothing could have destroyed everyone's pleasure in these gardens, or the luxury of a roof from the rain, and a hot bath.

We selected a white single-storey villa close to the sea, richly hung with flowering bougainvillea, and moved in. Except for minor looting, everything had been left as it was, and soon we had good wines on the table and a fire going. I wallowed in the bath, washing away a week's dirt, and, walking naked into the next room, was somewhat taken aback to find a telephone with its owner's name let into the base of the instrument—'His Excellency Marshal Graziani.' Several soldiers tramping in long columns through the town that night slipped aside to splash a bit in the marshal's bath, while we drank his wine and ate from his dinner service.

Old Electric Whiskers had bobbed up again. He was in command here, they said. But once more he had vanished.

For three nights we slept in Derna on made beds. We lived luxuriously, and friends would drop in to taste our cooking and selection of wines. Two officers driving up from the rear left cards on us, and we sent them a couple of bottles of the marshal's better brandy. Each day we would drive out to the front that kept eating steadily into Cyrenaica. Since we had come down off the cliffs we had to ascend them again outside Derna, and here the Italians had chosen to blow three large holes out of their fine road that wound up the mountainside. Once over those we were well on our way to our rendezvous with the other brigade at Giovanni Berta. The advance was going so quickly now that it was not always possible to tell whether the forts and villages off the main line of advance had been taken or not. In this way, Clifford of the *Daily Mail*, Captain Geoffrey Keating, our conducting officer, and myself came to the fort of Ain Mara, just before Giovanni Berta.

We had been cruising along in our truck for an hour or two behind the advancing Australian troops, enjoying the freshness and greenness of the hills and the sight of occasional farmhouses. As there had been no contact with the enemy since the previous night, we decided to cut across from the front line to the left of the main road. The rough track, through high scrub and rocky red hills, took us to an ancient Turkish fortress. From that high point an Arab shepherd showed us the landmarks in the no- man's-land that lay ahead. Ain Mara, we had heard back at advance headquarters, was to have been taken that morning, and we swept its two stone forts carefully through glasses. No soldier showed on the ramparts and no flag flew from the watchtower. A few Arabs in brilliant red cloaks made tiny spots of colour on the cultivated hillside. The colonists' white houses just over the crest of Ain Mara ridge seemed deserted. Shellfire sounded well around to the left—doubtless where the other brigade was coming up. The first brigade was somewhere out of sight on our right as we began to bump forward over the rocks to the fort. Twice we jumped from the truck and scrambled for shelter among the underbrush when low-flying bombers went by. Then, watching for landmines, we drove up the broad gravel path to the nearest of the two stone forts.

Clearly, the Australians had not arrived. I kicked the gate open.

The cobblestoned courtyard was empty. A key stood invitingly in the door of the guardhouse. Over the place was the unnatural hush you got sometimes at the front. It seemed even to drive the birds and the animals away. Then a turbaned head shot up over the stone wall opposite, followed closely by two more. I called out to them, and three Libyan soldiers scrambled quickly over the wall and came forward, grinning and repeating, 'Buon arrivata.' Then things began to happen more quickly. From holes and caves in the rocks, men, women and children began pouring out over the hillside. Every group waved a white flag—bits of sheeting torn from the Italian officers' beds. The biggest flag of all was tacked to a sapling and borne down the road by an Arab sheikh—a fine, grey-headed old man wearing an Italian army tunic, and supported on either side by two native non-commissioned officers. The men from the village fell into step in a ragged crowd behind them.

Ten paces from us the sheikh halted, hitched his banner up a little higher and flung out his right hand in salute. He made us a formal speech in Italian that went something like this:

'On behalf of the village and the fort I welcome you to Ain Mara. Your enemies the Italians have fled. After lunch yesterday they retreated over the hills beyond Giovanni Berta, and now we formally surrender the fort to you. We are most thankful you are here. We have been waiting three months for this happy day. Long live liberty. Long live England.'

I really think he meant it. He led us onto the main fort, ceremoniously produced the keys, and flung back the door. In we all went, though there was nothing much to see. The Italians had taken everything of value. From the battlements one looked down on the ploughlands of Ain Mara's green valley where the purest and freshest spring in all Cyrenaica flowed from the rocks. The Fascists had been at work on a powerful new pumping plant here. Here, too, was the spot where they used first to sight raiding British aircraft and raise the alarm in Derna.

As we came down from the fort to join the main road by another route, the women of the village gathered on the rocks ululating shrilly, a simple greeting, but embarrassing. We rejoined the road ahead of the main column of Australians at a point where the Italians had blown Ain Mara bridge. A patrol of sappers had just arrived. Afoot we scrambled up the culvert to meet them, and then stood rooted where we were as a hearty Australian voice roared across the stream: 'You are standing in the middle of a minefield.' It was only just possible to see the long sinister outline of the boxes at our feet as we tiptoed past them up to the wrecked bridge. A few minutes later the sappers walked boldly onto the field. One after another they prodded at the mines, knelt and flipped back the lids, dug the detonators out with their fingers and flung them away. In seven minutes they had thirty useless mines stacked beside the way. Overnight they had the bridge restored.

And so it went on after this, the Italians forever seeking somehow to delay and harass the steady oncoming lines of tanks, lorries and guns. Giovanni Berta fell, and the two brigades rode on again. Tert on one road offered nothing against us; nor did Abragh on the other. Luigi di Savoia collapsed, and we came into Cirene, once a place of a million Romans and the birthplace of the man who went to the help of Christ on the Cross. Nobly still its ruins rose out of the hillside, the marble tinted pink when I saw it in the late afternoon. Below law Roman Apollonia on the sea: all this valley was rich in antiquity.

Graziani had lately made his headquarters here in the cumbersome hotel that stood massively on the hill beside the delicate Roman columns. Here, as everywhere, there had been much looting. The Arabs had turned at last on the Italian settlers left defenceless by the retreating Italian army. In the gap before the arrival of the British they had cut loose to pillage and burn and loot and destroy. With tears the Italian settlers implored us everywhere to stay and guard them. Even their women were not safe, they said. They brought us gifts of fresh eggs and loaves and fruit and cheese and wine.

The whole problem was presented neatly to us here in Cirene. In the barracks on the hill above the modern village we came on two Italian gendarmes still armed. They had rounded up some twenty Arab looters and locked them in barracks without, so far as one could discover, food or water. For days the Arabs had been confined there with these guards watching them. And now what to do? We had no guard to leave. Manifestly men could not be imprisoned without food or water. Nor could enemy soldiers be left at large with their rifles. The choice of action was not mine to take, but I did not agree when the British officer in charge took the rifles from the gendarmes and liberated the Arabs, who immediately ran delightedly across the compound, shouting: 'Viva Inghilterra!' This treatment could have been interpreted by them as no other than licence to continue their looting, and I suspect they were already at it before we left the village.

For my part, war or no war, I would have left the gendarmes with their rifles, for the old hates among the Arabs were running high. Many in this fertile region had been dispossessed of their lands or thrown off the communal holdings to make way for the Italian settlers. The fact that the Italian was developing Cyrenaica beyond the Arab's furthest capabilities was no compensation to the Arab. He was being forced to work and even to pay taxes. The coming of the British was taken by some to mean that all the Italians had built up would be immediately handed over to the Arabs. Obviously that could not be, since the farms, the butter factories, the waterworks and sewerage and the power plants would have collapsed into chaos in three months.

But the Senussi tribesmen had waged bitter war with the Italians and they were not forgiving. Was it not Graziani himself, Graziani the butcher, who had taken the chieftains of the Senussi in chains and had them flung down upon Kufra from an aeroplane? True or not, the story was believed, and fed by the natural wild spirits of the youths, the Arabs were now carrying the knife into the Italian settlers' homes.

It was no easy problem for General Sir Henry Maitland Wilson, who had just been appointed military governor of Cyrenaica. But at this moment the problem was secondary, and we were concerned only to push on. Slonta fell, and Maraua, and now every man knew that it was Benghazi itself that was our object.

Clifford, Keating and I, with our driver, a lad from south Wales, ran on again in our Morris truck to the head of the column travelling down the southern road. For a time we kept with the Bren-gun carriers, scouting on ahead, and as prisoners were being roped in, we acted as interpreters. The danger of mines ahead was the chief concern, and when one prisoner protested to us that there were neither mines nor opposition of any kind between us and Barce, the Australian colonel commanding said: 'All right. Tell him to get into that truck and drive two hundred yards ahead of us. Tell him if he tries to make a bolt for it we will machine-gun him.' We told him. The man was haggard and very afraid, but he had no choice but to obey. And if we had taken a hint from the wisdom of the colonel, then Clifford and Keating and I and our driver might have been more comfortable that night. But at that moment a major of the armoured division suddenly appeared with a fighting patrol of armoured cars. He had cut across from the open desert to the south. And now this major offered to patrol ahead of the Australian army, and we were invited to go along.

Steadily the tracks of the retreating enemy got warmer along the road. An Italian colonel and staff officer who were trying to round up their utterly disorganised forces were captured. Then we came on whole bunches of Italians. They said the road ahead was clear for some miles at least. Hurricanes had just passed that way, making a frightful wreckage on the road where they had caught and overturned several lorries full of men. The vehicles were uprooted bodily from the track, and the unwounded passengers frantically waved white handkerchiefs at us as we passed by. The road now in the early evening turned into wooded undulating hills.

And then at last we were on the enemy. A group of Italians in green uniforms were laying mines in a bend in the road. They dropped the mines and fled into the bushes at the sound of the leading armoured car and our truck following next in line. There were two more armoured cars following immediately behind us. We could still see and hear the Italians in the bushes, but, having seen so many surrender already, it did not seem worthwhile giving them a burst of machine-gun fire. British officers and men jumped out of the vehicles and began tearing up the mines to make the road safe for the Australian troops now advancing up the road some miles farther back. As they worked, the Italians, about half a dozen in all, emerged onto the road a little higher up and stood watching us. It was strange they did not surrender. 'Give them a burst,' someone began to say, and then from the hill ahead a long whining scream of bullets came at us down the roadway. We were ambushed. The enemy were in force. Breda guns, two-pounders and mortars crashed their shell dead among us. Clifford and I made for the wooded bank on the left, but it was hopeless—the enemy were firing almost at point-blank range, two or three hundred yards away. The rest of the British patrol also tried to make for cover, some of them shooting as they ran. One Breda-gun burst set the armoured car next to ours ablaze, killing the men inside. I heard the muffled scream of another man, hit half a dozen times in the legs, being gallantly dragged back along the gutter by his comrades. The enemy's tracer-bullets made long crisscross sheaths of light down the road.

Then I saw Keating, full in the face of the fire, running down the line of empty armoured cars trying to get a first-aid kit. Our driver had been cruelly hit on the arm by an explosive bullet as he had leapt from the truck. I ran over to him, tearing off a bandage from a sore on my knee, but he was huddled crookedly in the shallow drainage gutter, quickly drenching in his blood. Clifford joined me, and together we tore off his greatcoat and cut away his sweater and shirt. But then the Italians creeping closer saw us—the last of the British left around the cars. They blew our truck to bits while we lay four yards away trying to stem the wounded man's flow of blood. Then Keating, who had somehow got up the roadway, joined us with a first-aid pad which we fixed in the wounded man's arm. The fire was very close and very heavy and our cover not more than eighteen inches, so we had to stop and be still from time to time. Then a piece of shrapnel struck Keating in the forearm, while a bullet tore a ragged hole in his leg. He fell forward softly upon the driver in the shallow trench. Clifford was nicked neatly in the behind. Another bullet passed through the folds of the sleeve of my greatcoat, and, certain I was hit, I remember waiting frigidly for the pain to come.

By now the line of cars was blazing, and although the enemy could see Clifford and me alone, trying to bind up the wounded men, they concentrated all their fire upon us. It was madness then to stay. We dragged the driver into a bush—I pulling him by the heels, Clifford pushing his shoulders. Keating, who continued directing us, urged us to go ahead while he looked after himself. He, too, succeeded in following slowly. Forcing the driver to his feet—he was in great pain, but trying very hard to help us—we crouched and dodged from bush to bush. All this was at dusk, and as we crossed each open space the Italians unloosed their fire again. Three hundred yards back in a ditch we were forced to stop and dress the wounded men again. Then with my arm round Keating, and Clifford's supporting the driver, we began a long bad walk back to our own lines. The shelling eased slightly after a few minutes, and soon our only concerns were whether we would make the distance and whether or not we would be fired upon by our own troops. But with a rush of gratitude I heard English voices in the darkness, and, raising our voices, we got an answer.

Even as we hoisted the wounded onto a Bren-gun carrier, Australian patrols were coming up to encircle the hill and take it. In a chill bare cottage by the roadside a doctor operated upon the two men under the light of hurricane lamps. Someone gave Clifford and me a swig of water and some cold tunny-fish. In the night an ambulance came and took our wounded off. Clifford and I lay on stretchers and slept.

We went back next day when the hill was won, to salvage what we could from the wrecked truck, but it was next to nothing. Smashed cameras and typewriters, bedding rolls riven with bullets, suitcases battered into shapelessness, lay strewn about. Even our fine Parmesan cheese was pitted like a Gruyère, and a tin of army biscuits had all but reverted to its original flour. Razors, glasses, compasses, revolvers, water bottles—everything was smashed.

We had no food now and practically no clothes. Apart from my greatcoat, all I was able to salvage was the uniform of an Italian sailor—

stuff I had got at Tobruk—and in that uniform I stayed until the end of the campaign.

We were sitting forlornly there among our wreckage when the other war correspondents arrived, and we clambered aboard their vehicles. There was no time to lose. The advance was going very quickly now.

Barce, when we first sighted it, was erupting with a series of heavy explosions. The Italian rearguard, working with time-bombs, were smashing the waterworks, the electric-power plant and anything else they could lay hands on. Smoke, black, white and red, billowed up in great mushrooms over the neat white town. It did not seem to matter to the Fascists that the thousands of Italians they left behind would have no water, light or heat. Across Barce's wonderfully fertile valley that might have been anywhere in Dorset or Devon, the colonists' trim white houses were stretched in rows to the horizon, all of them sheltering little groups of frightened, anxious people. The steep road before us winding into Barce had been blown at many places and sown with mines. Half finished anti-tank trenches made scars across the mountainside.

An Australian officer and six men went down afoot and restored order to that lovely valley. Settlers escorted them to the town's best hotel for a hot dinner, and soon the hastily reformed town council was getting the life of the town back to normal. The rest of the Australian army, who would not wait for the repair of the coastal road, cut inland over earth tracks beside the railway running directly into Benghazi.

We came to the railway in the darkness and pouring rain, and groped along it until we got to a deserted railway station. An Arab boy with a lamp lit us through the empty ticket office and upstairs to the bare stone-floored rooms, where presumably the last stationmaster had lived. His reports showed that the last train had gone through at 3.10 p.m. two days before. The telephone to Benghazi was still working, but when we tried to ring through there was no answer—just a confused buzzing on the line. We built fires in the house to make tea and a stew.

As we ate, more troops came in—about half a dozen of them. They were in high spirits. They had been generously served with wine by the peasants, and now they were determined to go on to Benghazi by themselves without waiting for orders. They had picked up an ambulance somewhere in Barce and now they wanted petrol from us. One of the men was festooned with captured Italian revolvers. He was full of good noisy humour, and he twirled the revolvers round and round on his forefingers. We gave them a little petrol, and the ambulance set off crazily in the darkness. Amazingly, we saw it still going the next day.

Deep in the night I woke and heard a loud tearing noise on the railway outside. Some of the others heard it too and sat up. It was a heavy rumbling in the rain, and whether it was a runaway truck or some ghost train in the night I do not know—we were too sleepy to care.

A kind of frenzy possessed the Australians now in their utter determination to have Benghazi at once. I cannot conceive that anything would have stopped them from that Wednesday night on. But now hail and rain came that turned the countryside into red mud and slush. Every few kilometres the tracks were blown away by the Italian rearguard, which was fighting only for time and still more time in which to organise and make a stand. Australian engineers slaved at the head of the column until men in their ranks were forced to drop out through sheer exhaustion, while others came forward to take their places. Soon it developed into a contest between the engineers and the squads of Italian minelayers and dynamiters. All that first day after Barce, while the storm still gathered force, the Australians kept flinging boulders into craters along the roads or breaking open new roads along the goat tracks. Kilometre by kilometre—yard by yard sometimes—the troops moved forward. It was a forty-mile-long column of vehicles that crashed over tank-traps and plunged headlong into valleys and across ruined gaps in the railway line. Nowhere could the Italians destroy the way sufficiently to hold them more than an hour or two.

At El Abiar, where the Delmonte division used to be quartered in barracks nearly half a mile square, we came on the brigadier in command bolting cold poached egg and toast, while he kept on issuing the same order to every officer who came in: 'Push on. Push on.' I lunched in the officers' mess on hot rum and cold bully beef. The room showed every sign of panic-stricken flight—swords flung away, meals left on the table, shaving things strewn about. An Italian orderly was protesting: 'I don't know what happened. They have all gone off and left me.'

We went on again. All the way down the track vehicles were fighting with the mud. Prisoners began to pass by, cold and weary men, utterly confounded by the debacle, who stared in astonishment at the convoys of British vehicles that appeared suddenly out of the driving rain. At Regima we were held up again for an hour on an icy hill. Everyone's nerves were strained now as the end of this interminable thousand-mile journey from Cairo was in sight. We bumped on again past two blown-up railway yards, and round by a goat track, and suddenly a burst of cheering went up from a gun-crew travelling ahead of us. Benghazi lay in view.

It stood there clearly, a long line of white rooftops by the sea, a cloud of smoke shot with flame rising from the centre of the town. Nearer on the coastal plain were the red and grey roofs of Benina— Benina, through which Mussolini for a year past had provided most of his bombers and fighters with their ammunition for the destruction of Egypt and the army of the Nile. All of us had been bombed by aircraft from Benina. Now that whole airport was deserted and in ruins. Through glasses I counted twenty-two wrecked aircraft on one end of the airfield alone. A water-tower had been blown bodily out of the ground by the R.A.F. Half a dozen hangars, each large enough to accommodate a goods train, were shattered and savaged into a state of uselessness.

In the airport's living-quarters, where we slept for a few hours, Italian pilots had lived well with their private baths and neat dressing-tables equipped with double mirrors and scent-sprays. But all was in wild disorder by the time we got in. Electric light, heating and water had been sabotaged only thirty hours before. While we rested here Italian couriers came posting out from Benghazi to beg for a parley. The emissaries followed—the lord mayor, a Roman Catholic bishop and a few police officers—and the Australian brigadier, known from his vivid red hair as 'Red Robby,' received them in a draughty airport building. The Italians came to offer the complete submission of the capital, of the naval base and of all military establishments, of the Italian, Arab and Greek populations of all the surrounding country, and anything the British chose to regard as theirs. The Italian army, navy and air force, they said, had fled. The brigadier sent them back with promises of protection. The carabiniere, he said, could retain their rifles to keep the peace and prevent looting.

It hailed and rained, and even the red mud itself seemed to be flying in the wind that night. A bleak windy morning followed and we drove into the town, Benghazi. It was, in the end, the unsung soldiers of the line who had the honours that morning. While it was still very cold and grey they got down from their trucks in the streets—just one company—and marched into the square before the town hall. They were unkempt, dirty, stained head to foot with mud. They had their steel helmets down over their eyes to break the force of the wind. Some had their hands botched with desert sores, all of them had rents in their greatcoats and webbing. They had fought three battles and a dozen skirmishes. They had lost some of their comrades, dead and wounded, on the way. They had often been cold, hungry and wet through in these two months of campaigning in bitter weather. The townspeople crowding round the square had half sullenly expected brass brands and a streamlined military parade. Instead they got this little ragged group of muddy men. They hesitated. Then a wave of clapping broke down from the housetops along the pavements and across the square. One felt like clapping oneself in that highly charged moment. The applause was thinnish and no doubt would have greeted any other conqueror who had come in. But at least it was spontaneous and unasked for, and an earnest that the people would peacefully accept British rule.

The troops stepped out into the centre of the square and swung round with a full parade-ground salute as the brigadier drove up and alighted on the town hall steps. The mayor of Benghazi, wearing a tricolour sash across his chest, was waiting for him, surrounded by civil guards, officers and the bishops. They listened tensely while the brigadier issued orders through an interpreter. 'I reappoint you and all civil officers in their present positions. You will continue with your normal work. Get the people to reopen their shops and businesses. Your civil guard will act in conjunction with my own garrison troops.'

In five minutes it was done. As I came away from the square a tobacconist was pulling down the shutters from his shop. Everywhere people saluted my khaki cloth cap. I walked down to the Albergo d'Italia and ordered coffee with a roll of bread. Someone put half a lire in the café music-box. And then it came again, that same feeling of unreality and futility. Suddenly I felt very tired.

I went upstairs to a room with a bed and clean sheets. There was a hot meal waiting—a meal I had not prepared myself in a ditch by the roadside. And it all seemed very uninteresting. More than anything I wanted to get away quickly and to see and hear no more of the campaign and the fighting and the booty.

The quietness and peace of Benghazi were extraordinary. Fifteen days ago the newspapers had stopped publishing; the banks had closed and most of the businesses had shut down a week since. Three days previously the buses had stopped running. A Fascist gunboat had cleared out, and some thousands of civilians, their cars stacked high with household goods, had fled toward Tripoli.

Benghazi's garrison had followed hard on their heels. The small force left behind had started blowing up oil stocks, burning papers and wrecking instruments too cumbersome to take away. Refugees had begun pouring down the road from Cirene, Barce, Tolmeta and Tocra, and wild rumours had spread through the town about the British advance—rumours that were all too true. Some had panicked then and rushed their women and children into the country. One passenger plane that was not airworthy had tried to make a getaway and crashed, killing forty people.

Looting began among the townspeople themselves. The R.A.F. came over on the last of many raids, and by the Wednesday the frightened people had sworn they could hear the Australian guns getting nearer. Yet there was little damage in the town at that time. Many of the portside houses bore marks of shrapnel bursts, but the civilian quarter, including the Arab markets spreading a square mile, was intact.

I went down to the Hotel Berenice where I had stayed just before the war. Graziani had used it as a headquarters. Like most of the other principal buildings in the town, its corridors had been faced with an additional stone wall as a protection against bombing. Little remained there to show how the marshal had worked for his abortive campaign against Egypt. The cathedral just behind the hotel was safe, but in the harbour, noisy then with its thunderous surf, I came on two sunken Italian destroyers that were hit on the day of the R.A.F.'s first long-range raid on the town the September before. Half a dozen other vessels, small supply ships mostly, lay about at their moorings, either beached or awash. In the town, water and light supply was working—an unbelievable luxury to men who had had weeks on a gallon of water a day and had grown used to seeing the stub end of a candle at night. Here and there posters of Mussolini had been defaced. A group of Arabs had hastily stitched together a crude Union Jack, and were parading in through the town while they gave vent to a weird and horrible victory chant. The churches and monasteries continued placidly.

I lingered on for a day or two aimlessly waiting for transport back to Cairo. I was determined not to face that journey of a week overland. When I did leave, I left by air in strange circumstances and with a feeling of intense relief. But there was first another job to do. When we were in Benghazi we got word for the first time of the battle of Beda Fomm, which had been fought by the armoured division while we were coming along the coast. Now we drove south to see what had happened.

Eleven

UNKNOWN TO us, while we had been following the Australian army, a manoeuvre that was destined to alter the whole character of desert fighting and put an effective end to the campaign had been carried out by the British armoured forces inland. It had been foreseen by Wavell and O'Connor that the mere occupation of Benghazi would not mean the destruction of the still very strong forces which Graziani had under his command. These would simply escape down the coastal road toward Tripoli to fight another day. So it was resolved that an attempt should be made to cut them off. This would involve a forced march of some two hundred miles at speed straight across an open desert that was largely unmapped, in circumstances so unfavourable as to be almost prohibitive. No army had ever crossed this wasteland south of the Green Mountains before. Even the Bedouin seldom attempted it. The camel tracks led nowhere. The surface of the desert was rough in the extreme. The vehicles were already badly strained, and it would be necessary to steer by compass, carry all supplies without hope of replenishment, and leave the rest to luck. And all had to be done against time

But the generals were encouraged in their resolve to go forward when units of their armoured forces made contact with the enemy at the Beau Geste fort of Mekili, fifty miles south of Derna (where I had met them during the fall of Derna). A squadron of British tanks there came unexpectedly upon a large force of Italian tanks and mechanised infantry, and, unwilling to wait until reinforcements came, gave battle at once. Some twenty Italian tanks were destroyed in the running engagement that followed, but the main body of the Italian army slipped away before it could be encircled. This was galling. It had seemed at headquarters for a moment that the battle of Cyrenaica might have been settled there and then. Now there was nothing for it but to risk this adventure across the open desert.

It seemed obvious that this, the main effective striking force left to the enemy, would return to Benghazi through the mountains, perhaps interfering with the advance of the Australians on its way. If all went well for us on the coast, however, it was reasonable to assume that the Italian commanders would not stay to fight but would make back towards Tripoli, where they would have time to form an effective line. The only real question at issue was, 'Could we get to the coast in time to stop them?'

On February 4th two columns were ordered to move out on the big march from Mekili—one to strike toward Soluch, thirty-five miles south of Benghazi, and the other toward Beda Fomm, close by near the coast. The trucks were stacked to capacity, the men's drinking water cut down to the equivalent of about a glass a day, and the regulation halts for food and sleep reduced by half or more. There was only one order of the day: 'Get to the coast.'

The wind blew shrilly and bitterly at first. Then a storm of full gale force sprang up against the last convoys. While the forward units were often battling against fine sand that reduced visibility sometimes to nothing, those that followed on were faced with frozen rain that streamed down in front of the wind. Standing in their trucks like helmsmen, the commanders of vehicles had their fingers frozen claw-like around their compasses. Through day and night the long lines of tanks, armoured cars, Bren-gun carriers, trucks, ambulances and guns bumped onward. If a vehicle fell out, that was just too bad: its drivers had to mend it or jump aboard another vehicle and press on. The going was the worst the men had known after a year in the desert—bump over a two-foot boulder, down into a ditch, up over an anthill into another boulder— and so on hour after hour.

They travelled bonnet to tailboard in the darkness and spaced out again for protection against air raids in the daylight. O'Connor's own car broke down when he came out to urge them on. At places it was impossible to do more than six or seven miles an hour. The drivers, muffled up to the ears and strapped in leather jackets and goggles, became unrecognisable under a caking of sand or mud. Several times they had to deploy and fight against Italian outposts. Yet they did it in thirty hours. Two hours later would have been too late. The Italians would have slipped through.

On February 6th the report that the two columns had reached their objectives was followed by the dramatic news: 'We have contacted the enemy on the coast. Three large columns are moving south from Benghazi.'

The road from Benghazi, in fact, was packed with enemy vehicles. It was the last of Graziani's forces, escaping with all his eight senior generals, and with some 130 tanks, 300 guns of all calibres, more than 20,000 men and many hundreds of lorries and trucks. The British were outnumbered five to one in tanks, five to one in men and three to one in guns. They were up against a fresh and desperate enemy.

At midday the British opened the battle along a broken desolate stretch of the coastal plain, some ten miles in length. The tanks swept forward and all three columns were engaged. The artillery deployed and opened fire. For the last time the Italians turned and fought, fought out of desperation more fiercely than they had ever done since the war began. This in fact was the only time they honestly gave battle, battle to the death or surrender.

The British commanders, meeting under shellfire, hastily made their plans, and, since there were some hours of daylight left, those plans were simply to go straight ahead, cut the enemy's retreat in the south, and smash him in the centre. In the southern sector thirteen British cruisers gave chase to the main body of Italian tanks and destroyed forty-six of them. Mines were laid in the southward path of the remaining enemy formations, and as they ran upon them they were attacked again.

In the centre the Italians were themselves attacking fiercely. But British artillery had got the range on the coastal road from which the enemy were operating. By nightfall burnt-out tanks, trucks and guns were lying everywhere, just great smoking steel carcasses on the sand.

Twice the British tanks exhausted their ammunition and had to go back for more. All night the shelling continued, while one after another Italian field-guns were registered by their flashes, straddled with shot, and finally hit. General Tellera was in command of the enemy. He turned, as every Italian general had done before him, and looked for some loophole through which to escape. 'I cannot believe,' he told his staff before he died, 'that the full strength of the British has got here so soon, or that they can have blocked us to the south.'

But he was wrong. In the darkness the British regrouped for the final crushing blow. One section spun fanwise round his north flank and reached the sea. Another, rushing south, straddled the road to Tripoli. When the morning came with the threat of heavy rain these jaws began to close. The Italians counterattacked then. Their infantry still remained confused, undirected, inactive, and much of it still embussed. But their artillery spoke out violently, and a charge of such resolve was made upon the British that one tank succeeded in reaching a brigade headquarters before it was shot up.

Then the jaws shut. Bofors and twenty-five pounders raked the sea plain from one end to the other. Everywhere the Italian attack was fought to a standstill and broken up. There was carnage in the centre of the battlefield. British machine-gunners and light units went in to support the tanks. They picked off one target after another, until for ten miles the road was littered with upturned smashed vehicles that had crashed into one another or upended themselves grotesquely in the air.

All through the second night the mopping up went on along the beaches and the marshy plain. White handkerchiefs began appearing as the Italians in thousands came out of hiding in the rocks. General Tellera was hit by a bullet and died on the field (his body was given full military honours later in Benghazi). General Cona took over. He had a more forlorn hope than ever Weygand had in France.

The fighting had been carried with grenade and rifle and bayonet into the sand-dunes. It was there that the British found Bergonzoli at last, and many other generals and staff officers. The rejoicing message went back to headquarters: 'Bergonzoli in the bag.'

By Friday morning it was all over, and the British were sweeping on to occupy Agedabia and Agheila, nearly two hundred miles south of Benghazi. Only a few Italian tanks and a few score vehicles had escaped the battle of Beda Fomm. And now we had in our hands seven generals and their staffs, about twenty thousand more prisoners, 216 guns, 101 tanks and vehicles in hundreds. And Cyrenaica was ours. In all this fighting, here and on the coast from Sidi Barrani to Beda Fomm, the entire British casualties had not exceeded three thousand in dead, wounded and missing. It was complete victory—even though the world never had time to realise it before the reverses set in.

Graziani's army of Cyrenaica was destroyed forever. Of the quarter million Italian troops in all Libya something more than half were either killed or in our hands. At least two-thirds of his equipment in ships, aircraft and land weapons were destroyed or captured. Nineteen Fascist generals were prisoners. An area of land as large as England and France had been lost by Italy. The Suez Canal had to a great extent been removed from the war zone. The morale of the Italian soldier was broken. Wavell and his men had been lifted to immense prestige at home and in America. All this had been done in precisely two months.

And the fall from power to weakness, from bravado to humility and despair, was displayed with brutal clarity in a mean little farmhouse in the mean little village of Soluch where I found my way after the battle. Pushing through the thousands of prisoners who stood about aimlessly in the mud, I went past the guards about the farmhouse door, and there, squatting in the unfurnished corridors or standing in the shoddy yard outside, were the captured generals, the brigadiers and the full colonels. I went from one to another—General Cona, the commander-in-chief; General Bignani, leader of the Bersaglieri; General Villanis of the artillery; General Negroni, chief of the technical services; General Bardini, head of the motorised division; and General Giuliano, chief of staff to Cona. In the yard outside, sitting in the backseat of a car with a rug wrapped round him, was Bergonzoli. He was ill; I stood outside and saluted him, and he opened the door and leaned forward to speak to me.

'Yes, I had supposed you would want to know how I kept on eluding you since last December,' he said. 'The others asked me that. Well, I walked out of Bardia on the third day of the battle. I saw it was hopeless, and with several of my officers we set off, walking by night, hiding in caves by day. It took us five days to reach Tobruk. We passed right through the British lines. We were so close we heard your troops talking. We saw their watch-fires and smelt their cooking. My staff major, a heavy man, was forced to drop out through exhaustion and I suppose he was captured.

'After Tobruk fell, I flew out aboard the last remaining plane to Derna. Derna was in some ways our best stand of all, but when at last many of our guns were out of action and we had no more ammunition I got my troops away at night and with them drove off in a Toppolino car down the coastal road to Benghazi.

'We had no time to prepare defences outside Benghazi. In any case, it was an open town. We had no wish to expose the women and children there to any more misery. We decided to leave with our army for Tripoli. You were here too soon, that is all. Your forward units found us on the coast on Wednesday morning when we were in an exposed and dangerous position. But we gave battle at once. Our tanks and artillery and men were tired and at a considerable disadvantage on the coast, but they came quickly into position and gave battle magnificently. We launched two counterattacks that were very nearly successful. Our tanks against superior numbers broke right through the English lines. Our second attack was made when our forces were largely decimated and our ammunition almost exhausted. And always, here as everywhere else, we were grossly outnumbered. So when our second attack was unable to prevail we had no choice but to make an honourable surrender.'

All this was spoken in Italian through an interpreter, but when the interpreter translated, 'I ran away,' Bergonzoli snapped in English, 'Not ran away, drove away.' I have compressed here all the pertinent things he said in answer to the correspondents' questions, and this was the theme of it—'We were outnumbered.'

Poor little Bergonzoli. I had expected a blustering, piratical sort of general. But here he was, a soft-spoken little man with a pinched swarthy face that had aged unbelievably since his great days in Spain. His famous 'barba elettrica' was a neat, bristly beard parted in the centre. A large diamond flashed on his left hand as he waved it for emphasis. He wore a plain, undecorated green uniform.

Among the Fascist generals, he was certainly the bravest of the lot. One could not help perversely wishing that after so many risks and chances he had got away in the end.

He was taken the next day to hospital in Benghazi, as it was thought he was suffering from appendicitis. But the day after that they brought him to the aerodrome at Berka on a stretcher, and lifted him into a Bombay transport plane. Then, with the six other captured generals and myself squatting on our luggage on the floor of the aircraft, we took off for Cairo.

It was a fearful trip: cold, bumpy and long. Under his fierce crop of whiskers Bergonzoli lay there looking ashen grey, not moving or speaking. He was exhausted into numbness. We flew on for four hours non-stop over the territory we had conquered—past Barce and Cirene, Derna and Mekili, Tobruk, Bardia and Sidi Barrani. The other generals too were far from well, and when they were airsick it was too much for me.

We were a wan and unhappy crew when we put down for a few minutes outside Alexandria. Then we took off again up the Nile Delta for Cairo. As the Pyramids showed through the mist, one or two of the generals turned listlessly in their seats to look at this green valley where they had dreamed they would arrive as conquerors. But they seemed to care little about it any longer.

We came down at last and they were taken away. A British ambulance, squat, trim and efficient, was the last thing I remember of the Benghazi campaign. It shunted up to the aircraft. Bergonzoli was lifted down carefully. And still he never moved.

Twelve

In all other sectors our penetration into
Abyssinia is enlarging. -CAIRO COMMUNIQUÉ,
APRIL 1ST, 1941.

I FLEW back to East Africa for the fall of Addis Ababa. Once or twice only in my life have I been seasick. Yet any sort of air journey makes me feel uneasy. If it is at all rough, then it is hopeless—I just give up and lie back, pea-green in the face, while my stomach rages and my ears buzz with a terrible low humming. Five years of travelling by air round Europe haven't made any difference. A year in the Middle East hitchhiking with the R.A.F. has made things worse if anything.

But there is one trip I can almost enjoy, and that is on a flying boat up the Nile Valley on a still day. You can make straightaway for the smoking room and order a drink. The Nile water squirts pleasantly past the windows as you take off from Cairo. You look down on the Gezira Sporting Club on its smug green island in the Nile, and the numberless reeking streets of Cairo, and you are cool and remote. Even the meaningless and utterly boring shapes of the Pyramids achieve a faint distinction from the air. All the rest of the journey is just the green ribbon of the Nile and the desert roasting itself under the 'unrelenting triumph of the sun'. You are not obliged to look at anything, since there is nothing to see. So you sit back and smoke and imagine yourself in some noisy but not too dreary club, and presently you are at Khartoum.

For this journey the British Overseas Airways Corporation exacts a fee of nearly £40, and to my mind it is not dear. The same trip takes you four days by boat and rail.

From the flying-boat anchorage upstream they drive you past a landmark called 'Gordon's tree' into the town of Khartoum which Kitchener laid out in the form of the Union Jack. Every writer on Khartoum recalls this harmless piece of Victorian jingoism—probably because it suggests the whole of the Sudan so strongly. The place is not jingoistic. It is just a well-run empire country club. They tend to pick Blues rather than dons for the Civil Service. But Big White Carstairs flourishes here in his most amiable form, a friendly hospitable man and not a bore. It is a country where every white man is something. He is Jones of the railways or Gibson of cotton or a white hunter or a district commissioner or a soldier. Almost the lowest rank any white officer can hold in the Sudan Defence Force is Bimbashi—major.

The only notable political disturbance that has occurred since the British took over was when the Sudanese objected to Egyptian officers in their army. But the motion picture, *The Four Feathers*, which was filmed in the Sudan with a good deal of painstaking attention to accuracy, is banned in the country. It is felt that it might upset the white man's station since, you may remember, a good deal of the picture is devoted to showing what the Fuzzy Wuzzies did to white prisoners when they caught them during the Omdurman campaign.

But British rule is on the whole benevolent and progressive, and certainly the best advertisement for empire I have seen. Which is strange, for the lush rich colonies seem not as a rule to have attracted diligent enthusiastic men, while the pitiless Sudanese deserts abound in the type that is just born to administer and control. This you see when you are driven on your arrival to the Grand Hotel, the place where the administrators come to take their refreshment and listen to the B.B.C. Here on the terrace, which is perhaps two degrees cooler than the smiting sunshine outside, you meet ivory hunters and coffee planters from Juba and Wau up the river. On that terrace I was introduced to the pleasant custom of taking a bottle of iced beer for breakfast. From there I saw my first wild hippopotamus floating down the White Nile.

It was always pleasant to get back to the Grand Hotel, though now when I drove up in the early summer it was much altered. There was great movement in the lounge and the terrace was crowded. Soldiers and airmen moved about everywhere—General Legentilhomme of the Free French and one of Haile Selassie's aides-de-camp, a naval officer from Port Sudan and a South African brigadier— all these in addition to the habitués. And Wavell and de Gaulle coming from opposite directions were expected on the morrow. Two Tomahawks flew by, and staff cars kept driving up to the hotel. Down the road headquarters had filled a whole great red-brick block and the place buzzed like a hive. You no longer knew each officer by name—the staff had multiplied out of all knowledge and lurked behind strings of initials placarded upon its office doors.

Khartoum was at war in all seriousness now. Keren was about to fall, and Keren to the people of the Sudan was the hub of the war. Many had been killed and wounded there. For six weeks the Italians had thrust the imperial forces off those immense slopes. And now at last we had cleared the roadblocks and won the governing peaks. The vital attack was about to be launched and there was not even time for me to make the two or three days' car journey there across the desert through Kassala. It was a little difficult to assimilate all this at a moment's notice, and people bandied about the placenames too quickly for one to follow. Sanchil and Agordat meant nothing to me. I decided then to cut my losses and abandon any attempt to report Keren at first hand. Addis Ababa, after all, was the prize, and it did not seem to me that even if Lieutenant-General Platt took Keren he could carry on down the Dessie road to the capital before the Africans under Lieutenant-General Cunningham got there from the south.

So I booked at once on the next flying boat to Kenya. In order to reach Abyssinia I was going right round Italian East Africa, a distance of 3000 miles. It was taking a chance, since I knew nothing of the transport on from Kenya; and Addis Ababa might fall while I was on the way. Covering the war in these huge countries we always tried to be at one of two places—at the front, or back at headquarters. Either way you got the news. But if you were caught halfway you got nothing, and even if you did have any information you usually had no means of sending it.

And now I had to kick my heels three days in Khartoum waiting for the next flying boat south. Keren fell all right. A holiday was proclaimed in Khartoum, and the Anglican bishop ordered the church bells to be rung. Under the eye of Wavell the attack had gone down the pass and the six- thousand-foot heights had fallen to the British. It was indeed a notable victory.

The air force, it was said, were so short of machines that the hoary Vincents were being used as dive-bombers. They were used on a mail run first thing in the morning, an R.A.F. pilot told me, and then they went delivering stores and ammunition by parachute to the imperial troops who were perched in almost inaccessible positions on the heights. After that the same machines with the same pilots went bombing throughout the day until it was time to go back on the mail run again.

The fighting on land, too, had been very heavy. Many of our troops had received slight flesh wounds from a three-inch mortar the Italians were using, and these festered and became flyblown before the men could be got down to the dressing stations. Temporary casualties then were high.

Viscount Corvedale, son of Earl Baldwin, had been down there speeding up desertions from the Italian lines. He had rigged up a big loud-speaker at the front to broadcast across the valley to the enemy. The British commanders demurred at first at this new-fangled idea, on the ground that it would draw fire. Apparently it had the reverse effect. It used to stop the war. Corvedale would play selections from Italian opera and then put across a short talk full of bad news about the Italian army.

The Italians, fascinated, stopped shooting to listen. Corvedale got deserters, as he richly deserved to. Everything here to do with propaganda and the fifth column was in fact being handled with a dispatch and vision that had not yet reached Cairo.

Selassie and his patriots were away up near the sources of the Blue Nile, holding parades among the disaffected tribes and issuing golden thalers and rifles in regal abundance. The emperor still had no tanks, but his cause was going ahead by leaps and bounds. An aeroplane was flying provisions to him, and the disappointed, pessimistic little man I remembered from the previous year was become a guerrilla leader and the throne of the King of Kings was waiting for him only a hundred miles away in Addis Ababa. Keren had opened the way at last.

Gloomily in Khartoum I read the reports saying that our men were pressing on to Asmara and Massawa. Those were two good stories I was throwing away for the sake of this doubtful and difficult journey across Africa. I tried to cool my impatience by doing one of the most soothing things I could think of—walking down to Khartoum zoo again in the evening. Once again I sat there with a book in the stuffy twilight while the birds and the animals came softly round me and the deer nuzzled up to my hand. The place was pure Walt Disney. I sat before a round pond overgrown with vivid purple weed, and it was twenty minutes before I realised that two big-billed pelicans squatting in the water were not concrete statues. They arose and peered at me narrowly as I sat reading. Then they went away, believing perhaps that I was of concrete too, for I sat very still, unwilling to disturb the twenty or thirty creatures that had come around me in the dusk for company—or a lump of sugar.

At five the next morning I was off. I felt terrible despite the cooling fan above my head, and went downstairs where a group of guests in evening clothes had fallen into a discussion the night before and were still continuing it. Two sleepy brigadiers emerged. A large man whom I had turned off the flying boat by claiming a priority seat was moving around the lounge alternately threatening to take legal action against Overseas Airways and to deal directly and more forcibly with the man who had been responsible for his misfortune. He had been doing this all night, the porter told me, and I would be advised to slip out circumspectly. It seemed the man would be forced to wait in Khartoum another week, and that would cost him several thousands of pounds over a business deal. I offered to leave my kit behind so that he could be accommodated. But when that was refused by Overseas Airways I was unwilling to do more, for this was my last chance of reporting the fall of Addis Ababa.

Already I was very late. It was a relief at last to step into the flying boat with the two brigadiers, and soon we were bowling up the White Nile. I dozed, feeling awful. Then, just short of Kosti, the aircraft turned round and went back to Khartoum. An engine had failed. We trooped miserably back to the hotel to wait another day. The man who had been left behind laughed bitterly when he heard the news. I fancy it would have been all the same to him if we had made a proper job of it and crashed.

The next morning at daybreak we were off again, breathing cool air above the endless desert, coming down occasionally into the steaming heat along the Nile. I was looking forward to seeing the natives along the way. Especially I had read of the Dinkas and the riverine tribes of the Sud country where the people were slim and tall and hipless. The naked girls were reputed to be of unusual beauty, and every bookstall in Khartoum sold photographs of the extraordinarily sexual native dances. The girls with their high firm breasts and long legs danced with a passion and a gaiety that had something more than the rhythms of America. Neither at Malakal nor at Juba did I see much rhythm, nor was there any noticeable passion either. At Malakal I made the flying boat ten minutes late by walking off into a native village in search of rhythm and passion. My only reward for the angry glances of the crew and the other passengers was that I had seen family life in the raw among the grass huts. Two girls had giggled as they passed me, their hair matted with grease and piled in a two- feet pyramid above their heads, fantastically Parisian. A naked man scowling sourly had offered to sell me a chicken.

At Juba, where the heat was past all bearing, a dozen piccaninnies were really having fun in the warm river. They yelled and cheered and dived about madly as the flying boat roared up to its mooring in the racing yellow current. As soon as we trailed half-heartedly ashore they bundled themselves into filthy shorts and shirts—just dirty little boys again. Nothing, it seemed, could prevent the native from wearing clothes now. Clothes were a distinction, and it didn't matter much if they did bring disease and ugliness. In parts of the Sudan the officials were trying to confine the men to a loincloth and the women to a scarf about their necks. But it was an uphill fight trying to persuade the native to be native.

In Kenya the authorities had accepted the inevitable and had managed to get a sort of uniform accepted. This for the men was shorts and a shirt, and for the women a simple one-piece cotton frock. Only in the outer villages did the native walk about in his naked savage grace, and even he did not regard this condition very highly, for he was off to an Indian clothing store as soon as he had the money. Glamour was being pushed out of Africa by a mass of cheap printed cotton. Even the grass huts were getting galvanised-iron roofs.

But in that section between Malakal and Juba, the Sud country, where the White Nile breaks into endless sluggish tributaries and swamps, you feel lost in a strange world, as different as the moon. Green reeds flourish, and the water channels meander over the brown earth with the intricacy of the veins in an old man's hand. The rotting vegetation from the swamps, called Sud, mats itself into floating islands that are borne off downstream, sometimes carrying elephants and even native villages upon them. And for weeks the captive men and animals might live afloat, while the banks slide slowly by, until at last in the quickening stream, the Sud breaks up and is carried off in small pieces.

'There was a general and his wife who were once lost down there,' the steward told me as I leaned over the rail and looked down. 'They had an aeroplane in which they used to fly home to England on leave. On this occasion the general's wife said they hadn't enough petrol. The general said they had. And he took off and landed fair in the middle of that green mush you see down there. It took weeks to get them out. They were alive all right. The plane had upended and tipped them out.'

We looked down on it again, a place reeking with fetid heat and disease and bad biting insects.

'Funny how arguments get you,' said the steward. 'After their accident that couple took this flying boat home on their vacation. And, can you beat it, when they were smack over this spot they started arguing again over whether they had had enough petrol. The general still thought he had.'

Nor is Uganda, so fresh and green and varied from the air, like anything you may see in Europe. A thousand grass fires spouted smoke into the air, like a place that has just been heavily bombed, or the factory area in the Ruhr or the north of England. We came down at Port Bell on Lake Victoria, which is so large that even flying over it you sometimes cannot see either shore. Coasting on over innumerable green islands and rocky bays, I acutely remembered Scotland.

The two brigadiers were also bound for Addis Ababa, so we joined company and decided to get off at Kisumu rather than take the longer, more official, route round by Mombasa. Kisumu is remarkable for me principally because it was my first acquaintance with a place where by law you cannot pay for another man's drink. The law ran through Kenya, and was designed to stop the soldiers from spending too much on drinks they didn't want.

With the ease available only to men with red tabs on their shoulders, my two brigadiers got a car from the local authorities, and we set off along the equator for Nairobi in the morning, an eight hours' drive. Here, at this height and at this season, the country flourished like a garden. Here again there were tall trees and greenness and a high mountain wind. We drove through endless plantations of tea and coffee, of grain and pyrethrum, of mimosa and bananas. Gazelles grazed in the open, and the white ibises flocked in every swamp.

We got into Nairobi in the evening, a garden town that looks like Surrey and has a golf course at Brackenridge that is somewhere on the South Downs. Almost anything you hear of Nairobi, I imagine, is true. At this time it was filled with soldiers—both men and women. The women in khaki, an unknown thing then in Egypt, had apparently arrived in numbers from England and South Africa and were acting as chauffeurs and secretaries. The lounge of the New Stanley Hotel was one solid rendezvous. Every soldier had his girl. A good thing, too, after Alexandria and Cairo, where nightly thousands of sailors and soldiers roamed around the blue-black streets in search of company, in a land where white women were outnumbered a hundred to one, and even that remaining one was on the point of being evacuated. Nairobi was far from being evacuated. It had developed a spirited night life, as we found when we hunted for transport onto the front.

A plane was going up the following day. There were two seats. That meant that I was left behind. It seemed I was destined always to be late. Harar had fallen two days ago. The road to Mogadishu in Italian Somaliland had packed up under the weight of transport, and it was simply not possible to get into Abyssinia overland. I had to wait for the next army plane with a vacant seat. Too add to my unhappiness, Asmara fell, and it began to seem more and more likely that I should miss the fall of Addis Ababa as well. For a full week I pleaded, argued and organised, and in the end I got away.

But the time was not all lost. You cannot entirely lose time in Nairobi. It is so improbable a place, such a survival from some lost world along the pre-war Riviera, that you pause at first unwilling to believe. Somehow a small group of people in the town had achieved a life that is something between a romance in the *Girls' Own Paper* and a good healthy boys' adventure yarn. The lovers *are* frequently tall, good-looking counts and earls; the ladies more often than not move glamorously about in Paris evening gowns and furs. They *do* drink champagne, they *do* dance through the night occasionally on soft-lit terraces, or go riding under the moon. The men *do* go out on safari with beaters and servants, and emerge later from the forest bearing the skins of savage animals. And there is a carnival of intrigue which produces many a dramatic scene involving elopements and fights and runaway marriages between nobles and chorus girls; and, just occasionally, a little genuine tragedy.

All this is known, of course, to any student of the pre-war Sunday papers, but to see it here in full cry is an unusual experience. The case over which the people of Nairobi were engrossed when I arrived was the murder of the Earl of Errol. His body had been found in a gravel pit after a lively dinner party, and one of the guests, Sir Delves Broughton, had been charged with the murder. He was later acquitted, but at that time the case was exciting almost as much attention as the war in Nairobi.

Big-game hunting was flourishing; and, dining at Muthaiga Club, I was offered trout freshly caught in the mountains, together with some last bottles of a particularly fragrant Rhine wine. Not since that last bright summer in Paris in 1939, when the wealthy of the world came flocking to spend their money lest they should not visit Paris again, had I seen women so well groomed, wearing so many lush furs. Baboon pelts and leopard skins were particularly popular. Great log fires burned in the grates of the club chimney places, though the nights were scarcely sharp. The men wore dinner- jackets or dress uniform. The conversation tended to hunting. In the day one had golf at Brackenridge, or swimming or riding or fooling round the game reserves where giraffe still roam haphazardly. Normally one looked in at a roadhouse for an apéritif around eight in the evening, and after dinner perhaps went down to Torr's to dance. They say the altitude at Nairobi makes people slightly crazy, but after the desert I found it all delightful, as though the world were enjoying one long holiday.

As for the army, that was different. The South Africans were very keen. Most of them hated lingering on in Nairobi, and wanted to follow their fellows to the distant front. I was a good deal astonished to find trained subeditors at the censorship, and a cable service to London that took only two or three hours. My messages were censored quickly, critically and accurately, and to enable me to visit the various area offices, which all seemed to be half a dozen miles apart, I was given a Ford truck and a driver. The advance had gone so quickly and so far that communications with the front had all but broken down; but here in Nairobi they were superb. The place was small enough to be efficient. And so a happy-go-lucky week went by until at last I saw the R.A.F. commodore in command, and he put me aboard one of the old Junkers planes that used to run on the South African passenger line, and was now ferrying men and supplies to the front.

Thirteen

The Emperor entered Addis Ababa yesterday, the anniversary of the entry five years ago of the Italian troops. –CAIRO COMMUNIQUÉ, MAY 6TH, 1941.

AS I reached Nairobi airport in the morning a friend dropped me the information that Addis Ababa was falling. I scrawled a hasty message to my paper and gave it to a runner who carefully stuffed it in his turban. That was the nearest I ever got to using a cleft stick. We flew a thousand miles over Africa that day. We came down for petrol among the northern wastes of Kenya and flew on over the Juba River (where a battle had been fought) into Italian Somaliland to Iscia Baidoa, where an ostrich darted suddenly under the wheels of the machine and we rose unsteadily over the grass huts again. Then onward interminably northward. I woke once to see a mob of giraffe racing in panic below us and many wild camel strewn through the wadis. Then we were over the Ogaden, that much be one of the most desolate and savage regions of the world, a place where the dead earth has been twisted and warped into long ugly ridges of stark yellow rock, and the heat reached up to us thousands of feet above. We came down onto the burning sand at Gorrahei, but there was no one there and no petrol, and the pilot decided to take a risk and try to make Harar that night.

We rose then majestically into Abyssinia, and the deserts changed suddenly into green mountains and lakes, and wild cold rain thrashed against the wings of the machine. It was nearing sunset now, and this was the difficult bit when the Italian raiders came over and we were an easy mark. Great ragged bits of rain cloud filled the sky, and we twisted this way and that to find a passage through the storm. Mountains loomed up suddenly around us, and we came low down into the valley that leads into Harar. At last, in a tremendous sunset that was full of yellow light behind purple thunderclouds, we flew over Harar itself, a walled town upon a wet green rise, and landed in the mud of a landing field some miles beyond. It was cold there and wet, and no one came to meet us. Half an hour later soldiers found us in the darkness. They had been hunting us with the radio all afternoon to warn us not to land at Harar since the field was wet and dangerous.

Well, here we were, and since no truck could risk being bogged on the field, there was nothing for it but to struggle across a mile of mud with our baggage in the darkness. A truck bumped us into Harar, where Corps Headquarters had been set up in the European quarter. It was much like the newer settlements of Libya. White stone buildings rose out of the native town. Broad fine roads ran east and west. And flies innumerable and persistent clustered like blackcurrants upon every living thing.

From far up the road at the front near Addis Ababa the news was good. Aosta had sent an envoy into Diredawa that day. It was not the armistice, but the capital had been declared an open undefended town, and we were entering it in the morning.

There then began for me a ten days' struggle for transport. No plane was going onto Addis Ababa. No convoys were going. A private car I could not have, since hostile banda tribesmen were swarming along the roads and attacking single vehicles. Intelligence were willing to help to the extent of allowing me to send two hundred words a day over army signals, but everyone was too busy and too harassed with their own job to bother about a stray journalist.

I slept at last in a friendly R.A.F. mess outside the town, too tired to care much what happened, and too disappointed at having missed after all this weary travel the thing I had come for—the entrance into Addis Ababa. There it was happening under my nose, only three hundred miles away, and it availed me nothing that I had come three thousand miles already. Actually communications to the outside world were so bad that it did not matter whether one was in Addis Ababa or not, but I did not know this then, and I went to bed that night with a feeling of crushing disappointment.

Another day of hanging round Harar waiting for a plane got me nowhere, so I decided to join a small convoy that was leaving that night under the command of a security major. With luck it seemed we might get through in twenty-four hours. We started in the darkness from the Italian hotel—three trucks and a staff car. Before midnight we were in wild mountains where the forest came down upon the road on either side, and heavy rain splashed across the track. The going got worse and worse, and at 2 a.m. the drivers were exhausted and we were forced to stop. In the morning we woke to find ourselves far out in unconquered territory on completely the wrong road. I was not yet grown used to disappointments, and my feeling of bitterness at our mistake half blinded me to the rest of the events on that absurd morning.

. For some reason that was clear to nobody but himself, the security major persisted in continuing on the wrong road. We drove for an hour over country of wild precipices and valleys and came out at last under a high stone fort that was thronged with enemy native soldiers. A white flag had been flying there, but now, as we approached, it was hauled down. That was the moment when I personally would have chosen to turn the cars and retreat at speed. After all, this territory had not been conquered, and we had not ten rifles between us. But the major, one of the bulldog type, rode on up to the gates where some hundred natives armed with knives and rifles were awaiting us in heavy silence.

We got out boldly, and as we walked toward them one of the natives who sported trousers instead of a white robe came slowly forward. Clearly he and his people were puzzled. Their white Italian officers had left them and they knew the enemy was expected. But here was the enemy come in a mere handful, and there must be rich booty in those trucks. Was this all the enemy? Or were there more? You could almost hear this native in the trousers thinking.

But the major gave him no time to think deeply. While our trucks were being turned on the muddy road, the major shot out a stream of quick questions in English. The native answered slowly, partly in Italian, partly in English, partly in Amharic, and the rest in sign language. This was Graua, he said. And who were we?

'A South African patrol will be here to occupy the fort in half an hour,' the major said firmly. 'In the meantime see there is no trouble.' It was a nice piece of bluff.

Rather overacting, I was pushing through the natives to see inside the fort when the major called me back shortly. 'Get in quickly,' he said to me quietly. 'They will start something in a minute.'

Inside two minutes we were in the cars and away. Twice shots sounded distantly as we came round out of the valley. I do not know if they were for us or not. But it was nice to be on the road again, and as we passed through the smaller villages on the way back the elders were assembled gravely along the roadside among the flies. They arose as one man in their flowing robes and bowed deeply to us. Here, as everywhere in Abyssinia, they carried umbrellas.

By two in the afternoon we were back whence we had started the night before and on the right road.

From Harar to Diredawa the highway drops more than two thousand feet. It is an immense gorge, and when you run out among the modern Italian huts and buildings on the flats below at Diredawa you are oppressed with the stale heavy air. The Italians moreover had blown this corkscrew highway at all the most dangerous places, and the passage through at that time was not easy.

Diredawa, the place where the road meets the Addis Ababa–Jibuti railway, had been converted by the Italians into their biggest airport. The R.A.F. had been blasting the place for the past six months or more. From there the road executes an interminable series of small switchbacks through the thick scrub until, always descending, you are upon the Awash Gorge—the place where the Italians were expected to make a stand—and didn't. Then you rise steadily again and the landscape opens out flatly until you are at Addis Ababa, more than seven thousand feet above the sea. All this we passed over in the next twenty-four hours, and in the early afternoon we drove into the capital itself.

If Nairobi was slightly crazy, this was a complete madhouse. Outwardly all was quiet enough among the wooden huts and the white Italian buildings and the endless eucalyptus groves. Only an occasional shot sounded from the outskirts. But most of the Empire forces had gone off chasing the Italian army down the Gimma road, and there was only a small garrison force left to control the capital. These were outnumbered ten to one by Italian soldiers, many of whom had their rifles and were still restless. Some seven or eight thousand of these men, of whom a number had prudently changed into civilian clothes, were huddled into the centre of the town in fear of their own native troops. In all the surrounding villages the Ethiopian warriors who had lately been bound to the Italian cause—some of them terrible old men with long knives—were now out for vengeance. And driving briskly through these villages, you saw all too clearly that the one ruling thought among the tribes was to get into Addis Ababa quickly and have at those Italians. War was war in the minds of the warriors, and at the hour of victory it meant a certain amount of knife-play and booty and beating up. They seemed to be to me very discontented as they stood about leaning on their barbed spears and testing the edges of their knives.

In the outlying Italian settlements there was already hell to pay. The banda had seized this golden chance to storm the Italian settlers in their farms, and appeal after appeal was going up from our former enemies for British help. In one village the besieged Italians had spread a notice on the ground to attract the attention of airmen. It read: 'Come and save us from the Abyssinians.' British armoured cars were hurried to another settlement where they had to fight their way through the tribesmen, pack the cars with white women and farmers, and fight their way out again. At other points empire troops and Italians were fighting side by side against the angry natives.

It was all very confusing, this overnight transference of allegiances, and my Cockney driver asked darkly, 'Oo the hell are we fighting anyway—the Wops or them niggers?' I simply did not know.

The Italians inside Addis Ababa had been badly scared, and three zones had been marked out for them—one definitely safe from the Ethiopians, another probably safe, and a third definitely not safe. Into the first area they crowded thickly. This region of the town included the Albergo Imperiale, a large rambling hotel in which I booked a room. Some hundreds of Italians had taken possession of the lounge when I arrived. With that unquenchable truculence and brazenness of the Italian, they had tuned the wireless into the news bulletin from Radio Roma and were listening to a recital of British defeats and a vilification of Churchill. That went on for three days while I was in the hotel. There were even some cheers and much laughter, despite the British officers in the lounge, when Rome radio related the enemy's recapture of Benghazi.

I can conceive of no other people in the world emerging so quickly from fear to impudence. I know of no people except the British who would accept such a slight with such indifference. But to someone like myself who had lived in Italy the incident jarred. Admittedly most of the officers in the lounge could not speak Italian and did not know that they were being laughed at. But the security of the town was involved, since these people were taking heart from the Rome propaganda, and in many ways it might have made them more difficult to deal with. Not that these settlers were bad types, nor was it necessary to reduce them again to that pathetic despair of so many thousands of other Italians I had seen in Libya. But we were protecting them from the natives who ought to have been their friends, and it did seem that the Empire's forces were entitled to some gratitude. So in the first flush of my indignation

I went off to report the matter. I regretted it later. It was, after all, no affair of mine.

It was raining fairly heavily now, and the town was bedraggled and dark with its early curfew, its closed shops and half-foodless restaurants. There was no bread in the hotel, and the food was very meagre and unpleasant. But big army storehouses were found in the town. They were packed with materials of all kinds—some full of uniforms, webbing and boots, others stacked to the roof with tinned meats, vegetables, fruits and biscuits. Others again piled with spare parts, tools and electrical instruments. There were dumps of paper, leather, timber, steel. There were petrol dumps both for road vehicles and aircraft, and arsenals containing every type of small arms, larger pieces and ammunition. All had been stored for the army, and there was enough here to have kept the army going for perhaps another year.

The Duke of Aosta had rebuilt the emperor's new temple into a sort of mammoth pagoda that looked like a national art gallery. He had cleaned out most of his things from the marble halls inside, though I found a fine bronze head of Dante in the entrance hall. The emperor's old palace seemed to have been neglected, for its ramshackle wooden rooms were empty except for scattered papers of some routine department. Some attempt had been made to do up the main council chamber, where the throne of the King of Kings once stood. The Fascists had had the idea of converting this room into a sort of demonstration of their power. They had erected a number of emblematic shields made of three-ply wood. Upon each of these was painted the name of one of Mussolini's victories in the conquest of Ethiopia—'Diredawa', 'Harar' and so on. Someone had taken these down by the time I got there, and had stacked them neatly with their faces to the walls.

The walls of the council chamber had been given over to some colourist with a taste for the new Fascist art: bounding amazons and young athletes hurling spears and banners into the air, a vigorous pantomime. And now over it all floated the Ethiopian flag; the chieftains had come into the capital to kiss it, and weep emotionally as it had been hoisted up aloft.

The emperor was still a hundred miles away at this time, engaged upon the conquest of Debra Markos near the source of the Blue Nile. He had been sent the news of the fall of Addis Ababa, but it was not thought politic to bring him in just yet. There were too many Italians still in the town, and too many factional disputes among the Ethiopians themselves to make it really safe.

Down at the other end of the town from the palace, Mussolini's railway terminal stood forlornly on the edge of a cow paddock, and the South African engineers were amusing themselves by getting steam up in the twenty or so locomotives the Fascists had left behind. I watched them get two underway, and these were hitched to half a dozen wagons and sent chugging off down to the Awash Gorge, where the Italians had blown the bridge—a spectacular structure that once rose several hundred feet above the river and now lay in a mass of twisted tumbled wreckage.

I took a car up the mountains that rose still higher above Addis Ababa and looked down over its eucalyptus groves that all but embedded the buildings, and gave the place the air of being a large and well-wooded cemetery.

It was late, and by the time I got back there was no food left in the hotel. I walked around until I came upon a small restaurant, well boarded up, but with lights showing through the chinks. They took me in reluctantly at the back door, and the place was full of Italians— soldiers, I judged, who had changed into civilian clothes. The waiter explained in English (he had lived in America) that there was no food. I asked for coffee. It came hurriedly, and the entire company sat and watched me drink. I ordered more, and still they stared. They did not want me, but I was hungry. I knew there was food, for my driver had gathered himself a dozen eggs that day and quantities of green bananas and vegetables. I had not asked how he got them, but he had said, 'Plenty more where these come from.' And now I said to the waiter that I wanted some wine.

'There is no wine, signor.'

'Then some bread and butter.'

'But there has been none for three days, signor. We have nothing.' He called his wife in from the kitchen to support him and she wafted a rich smell of onions and frying meat into the room. The others in the restaurant, about twenty, kept watching me. I did not want to take their food, but I was as hungry as they were, and I did not see why they could not share it with me.

'All right,' I said, 'have a cigarette.' Every Italian had been asking for cigarettes. I brought out a packet of fifty Player's. The waiter came forward at once. 'Go on,' I said, 'take two.'

I handed them right round the room. Everyone reached forward for them. Some took two or three. It was the same as years ago in Spain. It was the lack of cigarettes that people minded almost more than anything. Some of the Italians smoked at once; others put the cigarettes carefully away in their pockets.

The waiter leaned over my table and said he was in America for five years and that he had smoked Camels. Here is Addis Ababa there were no cigarettes for the civilians, he said.

One of the Fascist officers in plain clothes came over to the table and asked the waiter to translate. 'I told him I was in America,' the waiter said. 'Sit down,' I said to the officer in Italian. 'Perhaps you know how to get some wine.'

'You speak Italian?' the officer said.

'No. I just know a few words—just enough to say I am very hungry.'

The waiter went into the kitchen and came back with a plate of stew and half a bottle of red Chianti. 'There is really no bread, signor,' he said. 'We cannot get any even for ourselves.'

Soon the whole restaurant was eating and talking and smoking, and I was battling with my Italian to keep the Fascist officer in conversation. It did not take long for him to open up.

'We knew the end was coming,' he said, pulling out a copy of the *Corriere del Impero*—the last issue that had been printed before the British came in—'when they stopped saying we were invincible and started printing things like this.'

I read: 'Consider as light the burdens you are enduring today and the bigger burdens you must expect to endure tomorrow.' The paper spoke of more towns in England being 'coventryed'.

'Most of us were for the armistice,' the officer went on. 'Now the rains are starting we might hold you for a few months in Gimma and Gondar, but what is the good of that? It will not give us back Ethiopia. It will not bring us help from outside. They kept saying the Germans were coming. It's too late now anyway, unless the whole war finishes. The duke, too, he thought it was useless going on after Keren. I know, for I was on his staff here in Addis. The papers for the armistice were drawn up. Then just a week ago there were new orders from Rome. We had to hold on. We were to give up Addis if necessary, but we were to hold on everywhere else we could. They said that the Germans were preparing immediate offensives in the north, and we should soon be relieved.

'And it seemed true when they retook Benghazi. The armistice papers were torn up. All Aosta's generals were told to hold on. Even in Massawa the admiral was told to continue the negotiations for the port as long as possible, though he was no longer in a position to fight. All this was urgent, they said in messages from Rome. It was necessary to hold up as many British Empire forces as possible to prevent them going north to strengthen Egypt. They did not exactly tell us this last bit, but we guessed it. And, anyhow, we had to obey.'

So there it was at last. I went back to my hotel working it out. The Abyssinian war was not done yet. It was going to drag on with siege after siege and skirmish after skirmish. None of it would be as important and decisive as the fall of Keren and Addis Ababa, and the British conquest could not be weakened now. And suddenly I saw there was nothing here for me among this guerrilla fighting. At another time it would have been an exciting adventure to travel with the army through this wild country, winning all the time. But the battle for Egypt was being fought out right now in the desert, and the battle for Greece would begin soon. I had to get back as quickly as I could.

Fourteen

The Duc d'Aosta has sent in emissaries to seek
terms of surrender for the whole of the Italian
forces in the area. -CAIRO COMMUNIQUÉ, MAY
18TH, 1941.

IN THE morning I met General Cunningham, and his A.D.C. took me down in his new white Alfa- Romeo to try and get me aboard the general's plane. That fell through, and I set out in a Ford staff car with two drivers, a white and a native to try and catch the same aircraft at Diredawa. Having dropped the general, it was flying on empty to Nairobi, where I could arrange to join the flying boat back to Cairo.

We left Addis Ababa at noon. The afternoon went by pleasantly as we cruised along at a steady fifty miles an hour, taking pot shots with our revolvers out of the car window at jackals and hyenas that kept crossing the track. Brilliant birds swept through the forest at every waterhole, and there was some wild creature at every turn in the road—a hyena or a gazelle or more jackals. Once a school of several score of baboons vanished into the bush with a flash of blue, red and gold.

The general's plane swept over and past us. Once of twice banda tribesmen, lean, half-naked and looking ferocious, ran out toward us from the bushes, but we were gone before they could start anything.

Once we were forced to wait with some men of a Gold Coast regiment who had been fired on and had disappeared through the bush mopping up. They came back presently with about a hundred armed prisoners, but we went on again.

By evening we were over the Awash Gorge, and taking turns at the wheel we came on past Miessa and Afdem. We were in the switchback section now, and our pace slowed to twenty miles an hour. As the car breasted each rise, the headlights showed straight into the sky and the driver for a second could see nothing. Then as the bonnet fell suddenly down the opposite side of the rise he had to move quickly, for the track in falling turned to the left or right. There was only a split second to bring the wheel round. Often we splashed through streams and passed trucks bogged in the mud, and it was necessary to feel a way cautiously around them.

At 2 a.m. we reached Diredawa at last, and drove up to the lighted signal-wagon in the airport. They knew nothing of the general's plane or its projected journey to Nairobi on the morrow. It was perhaps at a satellite landing field in the forest about twelve miles out.

We set off over a deeply sanded track and in an hour got nowhere. We returned to Diredawa, got new directions and set off again. At 4 a.m. we were stuck in the sand and hopelessly lost in the scrub. We could do no more then, and, too weary to undress, we flung ourselves down on the ground to sleep until daylight. Two hours later I half turned over on my blanket, wakened by some noise that was not the usual chorus of the forest. It was grey light and I lay for a moment waiting. Then it came clearly— a full deep-throated lion's roar, perhaps two hundred yards away. The two drivers heard it too and sat bolt upright. I was not out for adventure. I was just a reporter wanting very much to get his story back to a cable station. Inside five minutes we had the car out of the sand and were bowling off in the opposite direction to the lion. We heard him faintly twice in the distance—clearly he was very hungry—and then judged it safe to try and get our bearings for Diredawa.

I had given up all hope of catching the general's plane. All I wanted was a cup of coffee. We chose a likely-looking track and in five minutes had run straight upon the satellite landing field and there stood the general's plane. I rushed over to the tents in the middle of the thorn scrub and found the pilot in bed. 'Oh no,' he said, 'you're out of luck. The orders have been changed. The aircraft isn't going.'

We drove on up to Diredawa and Harar and fell asleep in the hotel there. Next morning I was promised a seat on a Junkers leaving from

Diredawa. We drove down to the airport in good time in the morning. The Junkers was late in arriving. It was decided to postpone its departure for Nairobi until the following day. This I did not mind, for I had talked to a young South African pilot who was also going to Nairobi. He was flying a Glen Martin straight through from Nairobi to Cairo, he said, and invited me to go with him. I would be in Cairo in three days.

That night I slept under the mosquito nets at the Diredawa hotel. Next morning, as the plane was warming up for its take-off, I was told that there had been a hitch. I could not go. The plane was overloaded. I went back to air headquarters at Harar thinking hard, hard things about the South African air force. I would try no more here. I would drive onto the Jijiga field and try to contact an R.A.F. mail plane that called there from Aden. Air headquarters wired Aden asking them to pick me up at Jijiga, and I felt better.

We drove on now over a lush green countryside, where wild duck were so thick upon the lakes they could be shot with a rifle. Slim, graceful Ethiopian girls, with bundles and baskets on their heads, were walking along the highway, their brilliant robes caught in a knot over their breasts, leaving their copper-black shining shoulders bare. Naked children swarmed in every grass-hut village. The sun shone out at last through the rain clouds, and the men were out with their oxen turning back the rich black cotton soil with wooden ploughs for the summer sowing.

We came up through Marda Pass, where again the Italians had tried to make a stand and failed. Beyond that the bridges were down, and I counted nearly five hundred South African Ford trucks waiting to get through. The convoy had been on the road for nearly a month, and the men's cursing in Afrikaans and English filled the valley from end to end. They did not know yet that Addis Ababa had fallen, and they were beyond caring much anyway at that moment. The rain began drizzling down again, and just over the next line of hills we could see Jijiga. My plane was due to leave for Aden in the morning. The roadblock, they estimated, would take anything up to twenty-four hours to get through. In desperation I made straight across the half-broken bridge and got through.

It was pouring hard when we got into the airfield, a small township of white tents, with a squadron of Junkers bombers—they were actually being used as dive-bombers—lying in the rain beyond. The commanding officer, a colonel (these South African air force officers had army rank and wore army uniform) received me kindly. 'But a mail plane from

Aden?' he said. 'There used to be a mail plane. But it doesn't come any more. I don't know how you are going to get out. You just might get a ship from Berbera in British Somaliland if you can get yourself down there. All the other roads out are blocked.'

It was too much. I gave up then. I saw myself trapped forever in this wet, impossible, benighted country. My messages were stale already to the point of uselessness. My wife and baby had been left in Cairo, and the last news I had had of Egypt was that Bardia had fallen and the Germans were advancing into the Western Desert. There was nothing I could do about it. I was utterly cut off and utterly without ideas. And I was utterly sick and tired of travelling around in the mud and getting nowhere.

I squelched through the rain down to the mess, where about forty South African pilots were raising a terrific din. The war in East Africa for them was over. Some were going down to South Africa to take over the new Glen Martins and see their families and girlfriends again. And just that morning, after a two weeks' drought, a large consignment of whisky had arrived. Nothing could have suited me better. I was swept into the party. And while the rain drove steadily onto the canvas roof through the afternoon, the evening and half the night, we sang choruses and told stories and played stupid very funny games and finished a case of whisky. I slept blissfully that night on the camp bed of a pilot who had crashed the day before.

These young South African pilots were wonderful types—big men, steady, intelligent and enthusiastic. Only a few days before, one of their Hurricane pilots had been forced onto a landing field in enemy territory. Another Hurricane pilot landed beside his comrade, and the two men tried to take off in one machine. The first pilot clung to the edge of the cockpit and was blown off at the first attempt. Then he clambered upon his companion's shoulder, and, riding like that, they came safely home together.

There was another story of a young South African Irishman who had been put on a dull communications flight with one of those big Valencias that do ninety miles an hour if they are lucky. Each day the aircraft had to pass over an Italian fort, but the pilot was forbidden to bomb while he was on communication work. It was tantalising, this Italian fort. One night the Irishman and his crew got a dustbin. They broke up an old sewing-machine and threw the bits in. They collected old bolts and nails and scrap-iron. And they rammed it all down into the dustbin with a charge of cordite on top. They constructed a homemade fuse, and carted the whole contraption over to the Valencia.

That night when no one was about they took off. Over the Italian fort the pilot yelled: 'All right. Let her go!' The crew lit the fuse, swung open the side door and shoved at the dustbin. It did not budge. It was too heavy for them. The fuse kept burning. Desperately they shoved and tugged again as the aircraft turned and made another run over the target. This time it fell out and the lightened plane lifted with a sickening lurch. The dustbin fell squarely in the courtyard of the fort where still no one stirred. The South Africans could see the fuse burning. Then came an immense deafening roar. The Valencia was flung hundreds of feet upward, and sneaked off quietly home to its landing field. When, later, troops reached the Italian fort, its entire garrison—over fifty men—was found dead.

In the bright sun of the next morning at Jijiga a Blenheim bomber sailed down upon the airport, and as the pilot climbed out he said to me: 'Is your name Moorehead? I am supposed to pick you up and take you back to Aden. And if you want to go onto Cairo, you will probably be able to arrange a lift for tomorrow.'

Inside an hour we were in the air and flying out of Abyssinia and into British Somaliland, and high over the mountains past Hargeisa. I sat in the rear gunner's transparent turret, with only the clouds round my head, and it was the finest ride in an aeroplane I had ever had.

We ate lunch in flyblown Berbera, where a native boy pulled a punkah over our heads and bits of plaster fell off the walls from the shell-holes made by the British navy before the town was reconquered. It was hot, smelly and surrounded by desert, and I still cannot see why any man should wish to conquer Berbera, let alone Mussolini, who has—or rather had—enough deserts already.

We crossed in an hour to Aden. One more disappointment there. The squadron flying up to the defence of Egypt was so overloaded already that it could not take another passenger. But a troopship was waiting in the harbour to leave for Suez first thing in the morning, and the news from the Western Desert was better. The Germans, it seemed, had run themselves to a standstill.

I sat down in the R.A.F. mess and wrote these notes on the Abyssinian campaign:

'Most of the preconceived ideas of colonial warfare went west in Abyssinia. The strategy of defensive positions was proven false. Speed and the fifth column broke the Italians. We concentrated superior firepower at a few unexpected places. Then we hit and went right on hitting so long as there was anything to hit—tactics which Hitler used in France and is using now in the Balkans. Before East Africa drops out of the war altogether, let us not forget why we won here.

'It is the story of three battles. It begins among the reeds and swamps of the Juba River that cuts British Kenya from Italian Somaliland. When Napoleon or Caesar wanted to hold a river (I am quoting one of the staff officers who designed this battle) he put a light screen along his own bank and kept his main forces in the rear. He let the enemy establish a bridgehead and send his troops across.

Then he swept forward with his cavalry and cut the invaders off.

'The modern Caesar did not believe in that.

'He spread the mass of his army along both sides of the Juba River. General Cunningham forced a passage over the stream at two points, cut through the Italian lines, and his two columns converged on one another till they met behind the enemy and formed a triangle with the river. Then a third column smashed straight across the Juba and joined the triangle at its apex. The Italian Somalis, who fought more bravely here than anywhere else, were never allowed to reform.

'In one increasing wave the British swept up the coast through Kismayu, Brava and Mogadishu. Then they wheeled left across one of the world's most hellish deserts. The lines of communication lengthened from 500 to 1000, then to 1500 miles. Great slabs of unconquered territory lay on either side, and still Cunningham pushed on.

'At one time the advance went at more than sixty miles an hour. Lorries, guns and staff cars roared up the road to Jijiga as though it was a cross-country race. As the anti-tank guns breasted each rise at one place they blew the enemy out of the valley below, and charged after them to blow them out of the next valley. It was untechnical, unprecedented, and it knocked the Italians into bewildered surrender. They stood at last at Marda Pass between Jijiga and Harar. Who wouldn't? An uncovered grassy plain leads up to a line of steep hills. Guns in the hills covered our approach for ten miles, and the hills themselves were honeycombed with machine-gun nests and traps. But the British wheeled upon the flanks and won the position. And central Abyssinia was ours.

'Now propaganda began to work. Stories of defeat at Juba and Marda Pass began to filter through to the Italians who were making a strong stand on the 6000-feet cliffs at Keren, in Eritrea. We spread those stories day and night—by pamphlets and broadcasts from Nairobi in many languages, by front- line broadcasts at Keren, by

Selassie's fifth column and by British missions in the interior. The effect was tremendous.

'In hundreds, then in thousands, the enemy conscripts began to desert. The Fascists, bewildered at the rot spreading everywhere, gave up their untakeable fortress at Keren. And that actually was the finish. After Keren, where we had fairly heavy casualties, until Addis Ababa fell, there was not any more large-scale fighting. Harar and Diredawa were confused, halfhearted affairs. The last engagement at Awash was hardly a fight at all. The Italians blew up the 500-foot railway bridge there, and banged off a few mortars across the gorge.

'But the Duke of Aosta saw there was no hope. He flew an envoy— strangely, it was an Italian naval attaché—into Diredawa to gain time while he drew up papers for complete surrender.

'Then came Benghazi, Yugoslavia and Greece—and a new set of orders for Aosta. "Hold on," these said in effect. "Tie up the British in Abyssinia as long as you can."

'The Duke hit upon the ruse of handing over to us the capital, with all the embarrassment of looking after its thousands of white women and children and his disarmed soldiers. He guessed we would not abandon them to the natives. We did not. Addis Ababa was a hindrance to us. We were diverted from the job of immediately pursuing the main Italian forces down the Gimma road and northward up to Dessie. And now the guerrilla fighting will go on. But it is peace for a time in most of Abyssinia. I make these points about the campaign that might be worth remembering in Europe yet:

'First: subject peoples will rise against the Axis if given enough support. Second: the Air Force and the Army worked here as one instrument, under a single high command. Third: we used only a few well-equipped men to risk a lot. It was actually just two brigades that made that final advance on Addis Ababa, and half of those were native troops.'

It went on for months after I wrote this. Dessie fell on April 20th, and the Emperor folded up his red tent at last and entered the capital. Amba Alagi, 'the second Keren,' fell on May 26th, and at the end of a column of seven thousand prisoners who marched out to surrender came Aosta himself.

Resistance round the southern lakes collapsed. Gimma hung on until midsummer, and then Gondar alone was left holding out in the rain to the north. There will probably always be someone holding out somewhere against somebody in Abyssinia. But for all effective purposes the conquest of Italian East Africa took us about six months. It was a more permanent success than Cyrenaica and in many ways as brilliant.

Going aboard my troopship in Aden, I was bombarded with questions about the Middle East by hundreds of officers and troops who had been months at sea with little or no news on their voyage out from England. In the short voyage to Suez I was forced to become a lecturer. My platform was the hatch, my audience men who had never seen the desert or Africa before. I spoke several times a day. They were so eager for information; so quick to learn and tie me in knots with questions. I wonder where they are scattered now.

Fifteen

Benghazi is indefensible from a military point
of view. ~CAIRO COMMUNIQUÉ, APRIL 3RD, 1941.

IN THE spring, at the moment of his triumph, Wavell was forced to decisions more difficult, more dangerous and more important that any he had faced before. After the first rosy glow of optimism had passed, it was seen that the capture of Benghazi had not reduced British difficulties in the Middle East, but multiplied them.

The first decision that had to be taken, and taken quickly, was whether we should advance to Tripoli. Tripoli was another good seven or eight hundred miles by land, and nearly all of it desert. The men who had reached Benghazi were tired, and many of the vehicles and weapons altogether worn out. Benghazi was already being mined and bombed so heavily by the newly arrived German aircraft that it was untenable by the navy and unsuitable for the time being as a supply port.

True, units of another armoured division were now arriving in the Middle East, but the men were untrained in the desert, and in any case the campaign against Italian East Africa had already been launched and materials as well as men were needed there. Then again, of what use these extra eight hundred miles of desert coastline? Valuable, of course, if Weygand in Algeria and Tunis threw in his lot with ours, but the French were a long way from doing that. Benghazi as an invasion or air striking-point was almost as near Italy as Tripoli, and both were farther off than Malta, which we already held. It would require a large garrison—a larger one than we could spare—if we did seize the rest of Libya.

Those were the main points against going on—points that were thrashed out by O'Connor and his generals as they studied their maps in the damp and gloomy bedrooms of the Hotel d'Italia in Benghazi, and by Wavell in his office by the Nile, and by Churchill and the War Cabinet in London.

But there were two big advantages in continuing the advance at once—first, the Italian army was in poor condition to resist even at the gates of Tripoli, and would probably collapse against any sort of opposition; and, secondly, we should prevent the Axis from landing reinforcements and coming on again.

There remained the political factor, and that probably tipped the balance against continuing. Greece, though still attacking, was wearying, and the Germans were preparing to march against her. Greece, in fact, sent an urgent request for help the moment Benghazi fell. If the Nazis attacked through Bulgaria, then Greece would fall and with it our last chance of getting an easy foothold in Europe.

That was the vital thing. A foothold in Europe. There alone could we land with the approval and help of the local people. Once in Greece, an expeditionary force might prop the whole tumbling structure of the Balkans. Bulgaria might stiffen her attitude toward Germany, Yugoslavia would be encouraged to turn down Hitler's demands, and, last and most, Turkey might finally drop her neutrality and come in with us. The mountains of Greece were high. We had held a line there in the last war. Could it not be done again?

Neither Wavell in Cairo nor the War Cabinet in London alone were competent to decide. So Mr Eden and Sir John Dill got in an aeroplane and flew to Cairo to thrash it out. They talked to Wavell, Cunningham, Longmore. They flew to Ankara and sounded out Sarajoglou and the Turks, they went on down to Athens. Then they came back to Cairo, well pleased with what they had seen and heard. General Smuts flew up from South Africa to give his advice. Little by little the opinion grew that we could risk this adventure, that we could organise another and better Gallipoli in the Balkans. It was not one man's opinion. It was certainly not Wavell's, but Wavell naturally was the man who would have to carry out the job.

And so, while the Middle East was still mellow with its victories and optimism still glowed in the arguments of the generals and the faces of their soldiers, it was decided that we should march out upon Germany in the battlefield of Europe.

Through March Egypt hummed with activity. The Greeks had asked for at least six divisions. Very well, then, we would give them five, anyway, and the help of the Fleet and twenty squadrons of aircraft and food and oil. Sixty thousand men were ordered to the ships—Australian and New Zealand infantry, British gunners and technicians and mechanised units. What if Germany was steadily eating into Bulgaria and putting it out that she had three hundred thousand of her best men ready to fight us in Greece? What if Hitler was announcing that he would take the offensive if the British landed? Turkey would stand at our right hand. Eden had flown to Cyprus and had had another most satisfactory meeting with Sarajoglou, and the two statesmen had been loudly cheered in a patriotic Turkish–British demonstration at Nicosia. The Yugoslavs would hold and aid us. Moreover, the snow still lay upon the Rhodope Mountains, blocking the German way south, and the Greeks were stoutly attacking still in Albania.

There was something else. The invasion of England was in the air. Hitler was declaring he felt youthful and eager in the spring. The German radio was more than hinting. Should invasion come, then the blow would be lessened if the Germans were also engaged at their back door in the Balkans. Both the Australian and New Zealand governments fully saw these points, and promised all the help they could in the coming campaign.

And finally America and the world could not fail to be impressed if we honoured our pledge of help to the Greeks.

That was March in Egypt, then—optimism, great mental activity and all the surge of ambition and hope that precedes adventure. In contrast to the opening of the Benghazi campaign, there was no secret about the expeditionary force to Greece. The Egyptians were gossiping about it in the bazaars. New war correspondents were being lined up in London for the 'new front.' In Istanbul it was the major question of the moment and every politician discussed it. In Athens the German minister was kept fully informed, and his military attaché was duly there on the quays at Piraeus when the first troopships arrived. Another member of the German legation went through the New Zealand camp on the slopes of Hymettus, chatting with the troops in perfect English. (Greece, remember, had never broken off diplomatic relations, and the German legation remained in Athens through the war there.)

The troops themselves knew all about it. They had been mustered at

Alexandria and Port Said and were looking forward to a change from the eternal desert. New soldiers had arrived from England and were eager for the fight on the romantic soil of Greece. They had good weapons. There was talk of advancing through Europe to the relief of England. Courage and hope ran high.

Wavell alone was non-committal.

Three weeks later Belgrade was in ruins, and most of Cyrenaica was lost. Six weeks later the swastika was on the Acropolis, and what was left of the British expeditionary force was evacuating on a bombed sea. Nine weeks later the Germans held Crete.

Against that Addis Ababa was ours. Tobruk held. Sections of the German forces had been decimated. And the German plans, whatever they were, had been held up and disrupted. These were some consolation. But, it might have been added, had you never gone to Greece, you might still have had Benghazi and Crete too. You might have seized the Dodecanese and taken Syria with ease. You might never have had a revolt in Iraq. You might have extended the mauling of the Italian army by the Greeks in Albania, for without your intervention the Germans would not have entered Greece so soon.

There were a dozen, a hundred 'mights'. Rising out of the welter of mights was only the courage of the men who had fought for Greece and Crete and the desert. It was that courage that in the end lifted the Middle East out of the despondency caused by the Greek campaign. That and the holding of the Russians in Russia.

Now, after the event, it is clear that there were one or two major misapprehensions ruling in the spring of 1941. First we did not even then know that the Italians were so weak or the Germans so strong. We underestimated the ability of the Germans to reinforce Libya and advance across Cyrenaica. We, perhaps deliberately, overemphasised the danger of the invasion threat to England. Politically we misjudged Turkey. Militarily we underestimated the German dive-bomber and the power of his airborne divisions.

The German offensive in the Middle East followed the most careful political planning and the most exact military preparation and timing. The German design was force and overwhelming firepower applied in restricted areas. The chief interest of the enemy lay in dispersing Wavell's already widely divided armies to the utmost. Accordingly, in strict logical sequence Raschid Ali was encouraged to his *coup d'état* in Baghdad in early April; the Italian fleet was sent out to Matapan to draw the British navy off while Benghazi was retaken; the Turks were threatened; the Italians in Abyssinia told to hold on to the last, and in the Far East the Japanese were persuaded to create new diversions; more pressure, too, was put on England's nerves. It was thereby hoped that England, threatened in the west by the Germans, and the Dominions, threatened in the east by the Japanese, would withhold supplies and men from Wavell; that within the Middle East itself Wavell would be forced to buttress Benghazi in the west, strengthen his forces attacking Italian East Africa in the south, and rescue the R.A.F. garrisons in Iraq in the east, while his unsupported expedition in Greece was destroyed by the main German army.

And in some measure this scheme succeeded. Undoubtedly extra reinforcements that would have gone to Greece were retained for the protection of the Nile after Cyrenaica had fallen. The British forces in Cyrenaica had been stripped to the bone. Then, too, the South Africans and Indians attacking Abyssinia and Eritrea were prevented by the continued Italian resistance from coming north to support the garrison of Egypt, Australia was compelled to divert troops to Singapore, and we had to land Indians at Basra to deal with the Iraqis. As later in Syria, the Germans had no intention of really supporting Raschid Ali, and he, poor little mutineer, was left in the lurch after he had served his purpose.

The presence of the Germans in Libya was not altogether a surprise. It was well known that Badoglio and the other Italian generals were removed to make way for the new commanders sent down with troops from Germany. It was known that the Luftwaffe had occupied the air-striking bases in Sicily, and their bombers and fighters were appearing in increasing numbers over Malta and Benghazi with much more resourceful tactics than the Italians had ever shown. Our own R.A.F. kept reporting the continued and increasing arrival of troopships at Tripoli.

There were several brushes between the Germans and our patrols in the desert between Benghazi and Tripoli. The first of these involved six armoured cars—three Germans, three British. The story runs that the two groups of cars were bowling down the coastal road beyond Agheila in opposite directions, and actually shot past one another. 'My God,' said the British commander, 'did you see who they were? Germans.'

The three British cars turned about and made toward the enemy, one car coming straight down the road, the other two deploying in the desert on opposite sides of the road. The Germans followed exactly the same procedure. The result was distinctly unusual. While the two cars on the road were blazing away at one another, the other four got stuck in the sand on either side. Eventually all extricated themselves, and, still firing vigorously, the three British cars crossed through the Germans again and both sides regrouped themselves, still three cars a side, much in the manner of the game of oranges and lemons. There had been no hits, no casualties. It did not seem that anyone was going to get a clear result, so both formations retired with dignity to their own lines.

But Agheila fell, and Agedabia. And then German Erwin Rommel, the Nazi commander, with his one German armoured division, supported by the residue of the Italian forces, put Wavell's tactics into reverse. One section of his army fell unexpectedly upon Benghazi; the other crossed the desert south of the Green Mountains from west to east and engaged the British at Mekili. It was the sort of military coup a commander can expect once in a lifetime.

The British in Benghazi had reduced their garrison to a skeleton. Most of the fighting vehicles were back in the Delta being repaired. For a hundred miles they had little or no support. And the suddenness of the attack spread confusion. Light British tank forces that went out to engage returned to their base near Benghazi only to find that while they were out the petrol dump had been exploded—in error. The tanks without fuel had to be abandoned.

Round Benghazi there were no defensive lines at all. There was nothing for it but to blow up equipment and munitions that could not be got away, and retire in as good order as possible until we had time to make a stand and discover the strength of the enemy. But the supply convoys that were toiling up that wearisome road from Tobruk and Egypt could not be turned about in a moment, nor could the troops suddenly be regrouped for defence. The British forces were still stressed for advance, not defence. Communications broke down. Units became isolated.

General O'Connor and General Neame sent their immediate staffs and their baggage back by the main road and themselves followed a shortcut. They found themselves blocked by a large convoy. A squadron of Nazi motorcyclists, far in advance of the main German army, drove up. The British driver who first saw them was shot dead at point-blank range, and the German motorcyclist who had shot him was in turn killed outright. But the other motorcyclists closed in, and travelling up the line of vehicles they came on the generals' car. It was the worst possible luck. With tommy-guns pointing at them through the car windows O'Connor and Neame were compelled to surrender, and were promptly taken back to the German lines. Only a few days previously O'Connor had been knighted. No army could easily afford the loss of so shrewd a tactician, and this little Irishman, with his energy, his quick forceful manners and his charm, was loved in the desert. It was a bad blow.

While the British on the coast and in the mountains were still giving ground and seeking to get some cohesion into their command, the Nazis' desert column arrived suddenly at Mekili, where the British garrison under General Gambier-Parry was in no condition to receive them. Gambier-Parry was taken in his tent, and Mekili collapsed.

It was now seen that no line could conveniently be held short of Tobruk, and on Tobruk now the Empire forces converged. From Egypt itself what reinforcements there were available were hurried up to meet the enemy on the escarpment. The Germans and the Italians, in the full tide of their success, flung themselves headlong on Tobruk. They were flung back. The Australians and British with their backs to the sea had recovered from their surprise. They manned the long outer perimeter and fought with that desperate and deadly accuracy that was soon to become memorable in Greece and Crete.

Shaken but not yet rebuffed, the enemy left a containing force round Tobruk and swept on easily to Bardia and the escarpment. But the advance had now spent itself. Indeed, some units had outrun their course, and prisoners in groups of some hundreds began to fall to the British. Rommel, hardly expecting so quick an advance, had not equipped or provisioned his men for a long drive into enemy territory. No food or water convoys could keep up, and soon his advance units were in desperate need. Provision-carrying aircraft were not enough. Germans were captured in a state of near insanity for lack of water.

Upon Tobruk, then, Rommel turned the full power of his considerable force of Stukas, Heinkels and Messerschmitts, and there began a series of violent raids which in the next three months reached the amazing total of one thousand. Heavy guns were drawn up to pound the outer perimeter. Heavy tanks and eight-wheeled armoured cars were turned upon the perimeter itself. Cut off, short of water and food, lacking sleep and many of the crudest amenities of life in the field, the Tobruk garrison fought back. Attack after attack was launched against it, and though one penetrated a little distance into the outer perimeter, making a blister in the British line, every onslaught was halted.

At the end of a month the enemy abated their direct attacks.

At the end of two months they were abandoning their heavy dive-bombing raids and were resorting to shelling. They began digging in themselves. Unable to make a surgical operation upon this angry ulcer in the side of their lines, the Germans decided to seal it up.

At the end of three months the 'rats of Tobruk'—Lord Haw-Haw's description—were taking the offensive with nightly fighting patrols. Nor was Haw-Haw's other description of them as 'the self- supporting prisoners' quite accurate. Tobruk pegged the German advance. Always it lay athwart the enemy's lines, restless, threatening and defiant.

Inside the garrison the men lived a strange restricted life without liquor or women or picture shows or amusements of any kind. They had no fresh vegetables. They were pestered by heat, sand and flies. They had no ice. They were bombed every day and every night. The ships that brought them supplies of bullets and bully beef were sometimes sunk in the harbour. But they learned to make a life out of this confinement. They played cricket on the sand. They swam. The cooks and orderlies and batmen amused themselves by collecting old pieces of Italian pre-war cannon and ammunition. These they rigged up as best they could on bits of rock and concrete. Having no precision instruments, they poked their heads up the barrels of the guns and sighted them that way before the charge was put in. They achieved elevation and direction by removing or adding another rock to the base of the cannon. And in their spare time they banged away at the enemy, alongside the modern twenty-five-pounders— banged away so effectively that the Australian general in command was forced to give them official recognition and an honoured place in the firing line. Anti-aircraft guns were lacking, so the garrison turned small arms upon the raiders, and one officer alone brought down six with a Lewis gun. Never was a more timely stand made; never one more vigorously continued.

Of many good stories of Tobruk here is the one I like best. A tiny Greek freighter was loaded with German prisoners in Tobruk harbour and told to proceed to Alexandria. Three knots was the speed of the freighter and three knots was her absolute utmost. Dive-bombers attacked the vessel, and though an escorting British minesweeper did what she could, and the German prisoners rushed on deck waving white towels and tablecloths, the little freighter disappeared beneath tons of exploded water. When the raid was over, the minesweeper drew near again. Smoke was belching from the funnel of the Greek—from the funnel and the ventilators and the bridgehead. And she was doing nine knots.

It is ridiculous of course to assert that the Germans in the course of a few days regained all that Mussolini had lost in two months in

Cyrenaica. Even a juicy morsel of the desert like Cyrenaica is of little value unless one destroys armies there. That Wavell had done with a vengeance. Our retreat cost us under three thousand men and fewer vehicles. Nevertheless, the loss of Benghazi was a bitter surprise and it affected our enterprise in Greece.

Sixteen

The enemy, by the employment of greatly superior
numbers, had obtained complete command of the
air, and by repeated attacks had made unusable
the one available good port, the Piraeus at
Athens. . .Consequently re-embarkation had to
take place from open beaches against continuous
enemy pressure on land and heavy and repeated
attacks from the air. . .Rearguards which
cover this withdrawal may have to sacrifice
themselves to secure the re-embarkation of
others. - CAIRO COMMUNIQUÉ, MAY 1ST, 1941.

TWO UNLOOKED-FOR events of the greatest help to the expeditionary forces to Greece had occurred at the end of March. On the 27th, General Simovitch made his *coup d'état* in Belgrade, bringing Yugoslavia over to the Allies; the following day Admiral Cunningham joined the battle of Matapan and sank seven Italian warships.

At that moment it appeared that fortune was really with us and that the Greek adventure would go forward with success. But then there followed, one after another in the first week of April, the fall of Benghazi, the *coup d'état* of Raschid Ali in Baghdad and the opening of the German attacks on Yugoslavia and Greece. The future clouded over.

Our expedition was landed principally at Piraeus and Volos. The force consisted of 24,100 British, 17,125 Australians and 16,532 New Zealanders. About 60,000 in all. They were fully equipped with sixty- and twenty-five-pounder guns and there was also an armoured brigade; the infantry were transported in trucks. General Wilson was in command.

I myself was going across with other war correspondents. On the morning of departure Clifford and Edward Ward of the B.B.C., my wife and myself gathered gloomily for a drink in the Hotel Cecil at Alexandria. None of us were optimistic about the campaign ahead. We ordered champagne and drank a toast to 'the new Dunkirk at Salonika'. I don't know how far that feeling went through the army, but we had it pretty strongly at the time. Morbidly, I remembered Lawrence writing in his *Seven Pillars of Wisdom* of a moment in the last war that seemed unpleasantly like this: 'Meanwhile I heard of Allenby's excellence, and of the last tragedy of Murray, that second attack on Gaza which London forced on one too weak or too politic to resist; and how we went into it, everybody, generals and staff officers, even soldiers, convinced that we should lose.'

No. We definitely did not feel cheerful that morning. With a mixture of disappointment and relief I got a last-minute cable from London ordering me to Addis Ababa instead.

The wind freshened in the bay, and we stayed on in our bedroom playing bridge while the others had to leave. When they had gone it was in my mind that anything might happen and we might not meet again.

When the correspondents reached Athens a colonel came to warn them against optimism, and Clifford, with more justice than he knew, remarked: 'All we need now is a rubber boat, a false set of whiskers, and a Bolivian passport.'

Yet still events favoured the expedition. Practically all the troops were landed without mishap. It had been decided from the first that the Greek armies should continue to hold the line against the Italians in the west—a thing they were eminently capable of doing. The Greeks also should man the forts guarding Salonika from the north and north-east, along the Bulgarian border. The British would hold the central sector—the line reaching parallel with the Yugoslav border, from the Gulf of Salonika to Florina. And when Simovitch revolted it began to appear more likely that the Turks would come in to support our right flank and perhaps even launch a side attack upon Bulgaria, which by this time was nothing more than a German camping ground. Hurricanes flew low over Athens and there was rejoicing among the Greeks at the arrival of their strong ally.

But the events of that first week in April went by almost too suddenly to be believed. The Greeks on the Salonika front, valiant as ever, turned back the first German wave, and the main enemy attack swept westwards into Yugoslavia. Belgrade was beaten down, and it was soon apparent

that the Slavs had nothing but valour to offer against the Germans. Pressing on through Skoplje the Adolf Hider division joined hands with the Italian Bersaglieri from Albania, disrupting all Yugoslavia and cutting Simovitch's army from the Greeks in the south. Meanwhile the British were hurried up from Volos and Athens, and a line was quickly formed stretching from Mount Olympus to Edessa and Florina. But now the Germans, wheeling south from Yugoslavia, advanced down the Vardar valley and fell upon Salonika. Nine days' fighting gave them the town. Still Turkey did not move.

The Greeks then found themselves in danger of isolation in the west, and began to withdraw from their positions in Albania, with the Italians hard on their heels. We had to close the gap on the Yugoslav border. On the mountains of Florina the Adolf Hitler division and the imperial forces clashed; the standardised shock-trooper against the individualistic colonel. Tank was opposed to tank; the German three-inch mortar against the British twenty-five-pounder.

And while the battle was still locked with horrible carnage in the field, it became apparent that the Germans had overwhelming mastery of the air, and there was nothing, absolutely nothing, we could do about it. The Germans had come to Greece determined to conquer the country mainly with the use of the Stuka, the bomber and the fighter—the dive-bomber was actually taking the place of artillery—

and we had come to Greece unprepared to meet them. Our advanced striking bases were pitifully few in number, and those there were came immediately under a blitz that knocked them out of action almost overnight. Hedge-hopping over the mountains, the German Messerschmitts fell upon one airfield after another, and wiped out whole squadrons of British aircraft. They never ceased coming. British crews at some places never even had a chance to get to their bombers and load them; the bombers got no chance to take off. Messerschmitts would hang about drawing the ack-ack fire, and then cut down beneath it to machine-gun the helpless British Hurricanes on the ground.

Things were little better back in our rear bases. Larissa was overwhelmed. Down in Piraeus harbour, where the German blitz touched a climax on the first night of the war, a bombed ship, instead of being towed out of the harbour, was left blazing. The flames ignited another vessel full of T.N.T., and in a second the harbour was savaged and battered with a volcanic explosion. Ships, wharves and buildings burned. Later, a whole cargo of Hurricanes went to the bottom.

And now up at the front the empire troops came under an unrestricted bombing attack that never relaxed until they escaped to Crete and Egypt. Every road was blitzed with every type of bombing— high and low level, dive-bombing and ground-strafing. Broken vehicles littered the roadsides. Communications were disorganised. The Stuka was the new artillery—the mechanical device that carried the missile over the mountains to the target and dropped it there. The Stuka pilot saw what he wanted to hit, and went at it in a perpendicular dive at so sickening a rush that he sometimes fainted. To guard against this, the Germans had fitted the Stukas with a device which automatically released the bombs and pulled the plane out of its dive, keeping it airborne until the pilot had recovered.

Dive-bombers are a sitting target for fighters, but we had none now to bring against them. For the Luftwaffe it was just a matter of hopping over from Bulgaria, getting rid of the bombs, and then going back for more. In hundreds the bombers were plying to and fro on their unmolested way. Where the R.A.F. was able to get fighters into the air they made havoc, but some soldiers went through this campaign without seeing a British aircraft in the sky.

Shaken by this airborne attack, Wilson flew back from Florina and Edessa toward the coast. On Olympus the New Zealanders stood and fought. This was their battle and they made it great. They stood to let the other British forces get through to form a line farther back. But in the west the Greeks could do no more. Six Greek generals at the front met and informed the British they would seek a separate armistice. After six months of continuous war that had even drawn women into the front line, the Greeks had been broken at last, and an armistice now was all that was left to them—all, in fact, they could expect. The Fascists alone they had disgraced for ever. Germany was too much. The Greeks had their glory. Wilson had a first-class problem in deciding how to get his men out of Greece and home again.

He retired now to a line running from Thermopylae to Delphi, where again a battalion or two of Dominion troops stood while their comrades pushed on south. By the end of April they were pouring through Athens to the embarkation ports. German parachutists disrupted the retreat; a whole body of them landed round the Corinth Canal. Some fell in the Canal. Many others, dropped from too low an altitude (three hundred feet) smashed their thighs on landing and were tended by British doctors. But others got to earth safely, and the German technique of parachuting was revealed very clearly.

A zone perhaps half a mile square was selected, and around this the bombers laid down a barrage almost too heavy for any unprotected living being to survive. While this was in progress troop- carrying planes flew through the bombers and dropped their parachutists in the protected area in the middle of the bombed zone. The parachutes carrying equipment were of different colours, so that the descending men could quickly sort out their weapons on the ground. The parachutes were opened instantly by a special device which left a puff of French chalk in the air. These tactics were a rehearsal and a warning of what was going to happen in Crete.

Upon the beaches the British set about destroying the last of their equipment, putting bullets into car tyres, ramming shells the wrong way down gun barrels and firing the charges, smashing engines with crowbars, draining oil sumps and leaving the motors running, plunging vehicles over cliffs, shooting horses, firing dumps of munitions, oil and food. The order to the men marching to the ships was: 'Don't take shelter, or if you do you will be left behind. Carry your wounded and leave your dead.'

Some were stranded and cut off in the vicinity of Volos; others got away from four embarkation ports to the east of Athens; many were taken off from Nauplion in Peloponnesos or from farther south. There were many remarkable escapes. Destroyers ran dangerously close inshore and men swam out to them. Many put to sea in small Greek fishing boats. Sunderland flying boats crossed from Crete and each packed ninety men aboard, including three standing in the lavatory.

Weeks later in Cyprus I came upon a group of two hundred Australians who in Greek caiques had sailed across to Turkey and thence passed right through the Dodecanese. And in the end some 45,000 of the original 60,000 who had landed in Greece got away. They had lost all their equipment, but the total of 15,000 men killed or taken prisoner was not in the circumstances very large. Great credit redounded to the navy.

By the end of April, then, the Germans were in Athens, and had crossed to Samothrace, Lemnos and other Greek islands where little resistance was offered. Our second Gallipoli had been lost. Our foothold in Europe was gone. It remained to be seen whether we could hold Crete and Tobruk; Mr Churchill announced on May 17th that these would be defended to the last man.

On the fall of Greece many of the evacuating ships made for Crete. In Suda Bay there was great congestion, and more than one warship was damaged or sunk by the successive waves of German raiders which continued to harass the British across the sea. We had now been in occupation of Crete for many months. One brigade, camped among the olives and vines between Canea and Suda Bay, had discharged the garrison duties. The air force had also maintained a base there, and although it was not thought necessary to dig underground hangars, two runways were cleared at Maleme, near Canea, and some attention had been given to the construction of landing fields at Retimo, midway to Heraklion (Candia) and at Heraklion itself. A few shore batteries and anti-aircraft guns had been established, and machine-gun nests commanded the approaches to the northern ports. A few Bren-gun carriers were on the island, but all of the scanty artillery was captured Italian stuff. There were six infantry tanks, but little general transport. Equipment, such as field telephones, wireless and so on, was lacking.

The island, one hundred and sixty miles of broken, barren mountains, offered little attraction to an invader. Water was short, flat stretches on which to land aircraft practically non-existent, and the serviceable ports were virtually confined to Heraklion and the deep, almost landlocked reaches of Suda Bay, six miles long. The villagers were sturdy, primitive people, who had worked a poor living in wine and cheese and olives from the rocky red soil. The local defence force amounted to nothing more than a few guerrilla fighters. But to these were added now some two Greek divisions from Greece. King George of the Hellenes and his Cabinet had also arrived on the island, and the national patriotic movement flourished strongly.

After the fall of Greece the British arrivals brought the imperial garrison in Crete up to 27,550 men, made up of 14,000 British, 6450 Australians, 7100 New Zealanders. Major-General Freyberg, the commander-in-chief of the New Zealanders, was placed in command.

At the beginning of May, Wavell and Wilson flew to Crete for a secret conference with Freyberg. They discussed then how the island should be held. Freyberg had barely three weeks in which to straighten out the tangle of evacuated troops: to send some away, to retain others; to share out the little equipment they had; to set up new strong-posts round the island—endeavouring all the time to keep the Nazi air raiders at bay. The navy especially were suffering under the incessant air attacks, and six warships were sunk around Crete. Others, capital ships among them, were damaged. Freyberg's headquarters were established upon the Akrotiri peninsula of Suda Bay, and upon that small area, reaching through from Suda Bay to Canea and Maleme, the German air attacks were insistent.

Our R.A.F. meanwhile were reporting that large numbers of enemy aircraft were massing on half a dozen landing fields in the south of Greece. On the island of Melos, which the R.A.F. had found unsuitable as a base, the Luftwaffe had established an aerodrome in the space of eight days. There was activity, too, in the Dodecanese, and the Germans were observed to be collecting numbers of caiques and small coastal vessels. The R.A.F. in its present depleted state could not hope to break up these formations; the navy and the fleet air arm were busy with raids upon Tripoli, where the Germans were still reinforcing Libya.

In Cairo it was well known that a German airborne division was gathering in Greece, but its destination was an open question. Crete was the obvious answer. But it might, too, have been Cyprus or Syria or the Western Desert, even the Delta itself. Airborne divisions were still something new in the Middle East, and since we held too vast a territory to be closely garrisoned, the presence of this one was a menace everywhere. Its strength was placed at about nine thousand men, and, as it was believed to carry its own armaments up to a 75-millimetre gun, it was a formidable opponent.

Vichy and the rebel government in Iraq were playing Germany's game to the utmost now. Raschid Ali was in open revolt, and the Germans were sending aircraft through Syria to aid him. Once again the enemy was making a very extensive and ingenious attempt to hide his real intentions. The next move was up to him, and we had to expect attack in the Western Desert, in Crete, Syria, Cyprus, Iraq—or in all five places simultaneously.

I myself took ship to Cyprus to see what I could glean there, and arrived in time for the island's first air raid on the capital, Nicosia. It was a half-hearted affair, carried out by Italians, but it showed that the Axis was casting its net far and wide in the effort to split up the Middle East command. For the moment it really did seem that the German way lay through Cyprus: as if, by establishing a chain linking Greece, the Dodecanese, Cyprus, Syria and Iraq, she was going to isolate Turkey and absorb her into the Axis.

I travelled across to Cyprus overnight in a merchantman that was carrying new guns to aid the island's slender garrison. We landed at Famagusta, where the sandstone ruins of the crusading days rise from the edge of the sea, and the Moors worship in a Norman cathedral. For twelve shillings one could take a special train from there and travel across the flattish plains of the eastern end of the island to the old walled capital, Nicosia. For two or three days we idled there, buying silk in the markets, meeting the garrison officers, lunching with Sir Wilfred Battershill, the governor, whose residence is a more than modern affair, where the interior walls slide up and down into the second storey, and Roman arches rise over a tiled swimming bath. We drove on across the lovely island to Kyrenia in the north and the ruined castle of St Hilarion, where you can clearly see the Turkish coasts and flowers bloom richly among the vines. Beyond that, at Morphon, the gold–pyrite–copper mines, run by an American syndicate, lay idle for the want of shipping.

We went down along the southern coast, where we fell in with an R.A.F. pilot who a day or two before had taken the first American Tomahawk into action in the Middle East. He had raided Palmyra, in Syria, he said, and the Tomahawk had gone beautifully. He had surprised three or four German aircraft on the ground, and his big cannon had blown bits off their fuselage as he dived at 350 miles an hour. He had lingered so long over his target that his petrol had run out in the mountains on the way home, and only after a forced landing had he managed to get back. Now he was in Cyprus with his Tomahawk to intercept any more Germans going across from Greece.

The rest of the island was slowly and reluctantly shaking itself out of its ease in this dreaming corner of the Mediterranean. Now at last they were being drawn into the war, and clearly they might be in very great danger indeed. There were a number of Polish refugees here, and these, together with British wives and children, were being sent away. Yet one could hardly believe in wars here in this holiday place of pine forests and donkeys and wine and flowers. Something in the sun and the solid earth bound the island to the more definite realities of farms and fields and crops and fishermen's homes by the sea. There was an essential 'villageness' about everything, that would not and could not absorb the possibility of war.

Crete had been like that, too. And Greece. Yet it was refreshing to meet the sense of peace again for a little, and I came back to Egypt determined to go on at once to Crete and continue on down the Mediterranean to Malta, so that I might write the story of the island front line, and trace the differences between the outright war in Malta, the preparation for war in Crete, and the peace in Cyprus. I had a theory that the waiting for war was a worse strain than actually being in war, so that Malta in the midst of its gunfire might be fundamentally a happier place than Cyprus, where the people merely dreaded and waited.

Seventeen

Early this morning German parachutists and airborne troops made an attempt to secure a footing on the island. -CAIRO COMMUNIQUÉ, MAY 20TH, 1941.

After twelve days of what has undoubtedly been the fiercest fighting in this war it was decided to withdraw our forces from Crete. - CAIRO COMMUNIQUÉ, JUNE 1ST, 1941.

WHILE I was waiting to embark for Crete, air raids of exceptional ferocity and extent began to fall upon the northern coasts of the island, and continued with rising intensity for three days. The British warships especially came under the barrage. The cruiser *York* had been sunk in Suda Bay by enemy sailors who, courageously, came riding in astride torpedoes. But the ship rested on the bottom, and although her decks were awash she kept firing on raiders with A.A. guns. *York* was repaired by divers, and a salvage party was about to raise her to the surface when enemy aircraft scored a dead hit with another torpedo—and sank her for the last time.

But now from Suda Bay other warships and the shore batteries fired back, and all the garrison—the New Zealanders round Suda, the Australians at Retimo and Heraklion, and the British and Greeks interspersed among them—lay under cover from the shock and blast of thousand-pound bombs. By May 19th it was apparent that this was no normal raid. It was the preparation for something big. Perhaps invasion.

The night of May 19th–20th was still and clear and bright. But with the first light the sky was filled with the noise of machines: machines everywhere flying very low. The biggest diye-bombing attack yet had begun.

Then the sentries along the coast saw them—little white lazy dots that looked like flung bits of paper in the sky. Parachutists. Some down by the beach, some over the hill, then parachutists dropping everywhere in scores and hundreds, falling straight down onto the villages and the vines, straight into the arms of the waiting men, onto the tents, the slit trenches, and the guns. The half-lighted morning sky was filled with twisting, turning aircraft, hundreds of them bearing down in long lines from the sea.

And now machine-guns and small-arms fire cracked through the din of bombs and exploding shells. At Heraklion and Suda and Canea and Maleme the Imperial troops were firing straight out of their trenches and rock shelters into the sky. The aircraft were spilling out the parachutists from only a few hundred feet, and as they came down, squirming and running with their legs to break the fall, the British picked them off with Bren guns and Lewis guns, with rifles and pistols, with hand grenades and bayonets. Sometimes a whole sector of the sky, crowded with parachutists, would fill the sights of a machine-gun, so that all were killed in the air and the parachutes would deposit only inert, clumsy bodies on the ground.

As the enemy soldiers came down they could be heard calling to one another to rally their spirits or warn one another of the dangers below, and those that landed safely and found a little shelter from the bullets that were flying everywhere started shouting for others to join them. It was essential for them to keep together, for alone they were helpless, and since one man might be carrying the barrel of a machine-gun, another the base, and a third the ammunition, they were not an effective unit unless they got together.

All the falling men were heavily booted and heavily harnessed with equipment. They wore camouflaged overalls with the parachutists' special badge, and a rimless helmet. They wore wrist and ankle bandages. In their packs were blankets, little stoves and utensils for boiling water, water bottles, clips of ammunition, sacks of hand grenades, knives, gloves, greatcoats, torches, underclothing and many other things the soldier carries. Most had tommy-guns and pistols. Many had as well the parts of heavier guns, bicycles, signalling and radio sets, and all manner of weapons that might be used in guerrilla warfare.

Some had a trick of turning a somersault as they were about to land in order to break their fall.

They were only a few seconds in the air, and instinctively they clutched at a device to release them from their parachutes as soon as they were down. Then they would crouch behind bushes and wriggle forward among the rocks, calling to their fellows until enough were banded together to make a knot of resistance.

But their tommy-guns had a range only of two hundred yards, and the British standing back from a safe distance would pick them off at four or five hundred yards with rifles and machine-guns. Again and again in the thick of this day's fighting the British charged into close quarters with bayonet and hand grenade, for there was a moment when the parachutist had first landed when he was dazed and could be taken prisoner, or knifed.

Every enemy soldier was working upon rigid instructions set out for him on his maps. The coast had been carefully charted, and the men were dropped according to a set design. But in the descent and on the ground all became confusion, because so many were killed and wounded, and the heavy firing not only of guns and rifles but of bombs made an already unfamiliar territory doubly strange. At scattered points all down the coast from Heraklion to Maleme it went on, while flames lifted over the burning village houses and the olive groves, and along every road and upon every village the incessant heavy dive-bombing went on and on.

Upon Suda came something that had never been seen in action in the world before—glider troops. Over the great knoll that forms the seaward side of the bay came big, troop-carrying aeroplanes, drawing gliders behind them. The gliders were attached to the mother craft by a cable, and each glider had the wingspread of a large passenger machine.

They carried ten men. As they swept up to the bay the glider pilots slipped their cables and floated out over the rocky hills looking for a landing place, and the men who saw them come said they were more sinister than the parachutists, stranger and more menacing. Some flew straight upon Corps Headquarters, as though they would land there, and each soldier below felt the landing would be made upon his own head. But the wings tilted just over the treetops, and in a swift rush the gliders were carried over the hilltop. Clearly the pilots had expected a flat space there where they could land or pancake down, but their maps were at fault. The machines crashed heavily in a sharp rocky valley and the crews and passengers were killed outright. Others wrecked themselves among the scrub and rock around Maleme, where the parachutists were falling thickly, and the British gunners were upon them before the unwounded men could rise and make a stand.

Strewn along the northern coast then for a hundred miles men were fighting in isolated groups among the rocks and the olives and the vines; and over everything rose the insistent heavy bombing and the answering gunfire.

Gradually toward evening it became apparent that the Germans had made landings in three main sectors—Heraklion, Retimo and the Suda Bay–Canea–Maleme sector. These three areas were the sites of Crete's three landing fields, so it was obvious that the Germans were intent upon getting control of these before anything else. Some three thousand parachute troops had been dropped, and of these about eighteen hundred had been killed or made prisoner by the end of the day. Others, wounded among them, were still hiding among the foothills and along the beaches. Still the bombing continued into the night, still parachutists were landing, and still the wounded and dead were being brought in.

I was with Mr Peter Fraser, the New Zealand Premier, in Cairo, when General Freyberg's message came in: 'It has been a hard day.' It seemed like a message coming out of another world, for there was little the remainder of the forces in the Middle East could do but wait and watch.

Again, as in Greece, the Germans had control of the sky. The few fighter planes on Crete had not been able to deter the invasion, and now they were finished. Bombers might reach the island on the morrow, but the distance was too far for fighters to accompany them, and what could they bomb when they got there? And the morrow promised to be as bad or worse than the first day.

The news from Crete was painfully and pitifully scarce through the night. The Germans, unwilling to publicise an adventure before it was a success, were saying nothing either in their communiqués or on their radio. Freyberg had the use of a military wireless, but his own communications on the island were poor. Sometimes for many hours no news at all came from Crete. But it was becoming clear from our air reconnaissance reports that the Germans were operating from at least half a dozen landing fields in the Peloponnesos and southern Greece, as well as the island of Melos and the Dodecanese. All these points were barely an hour's flight from Crete across the sea, and the German aircraft were kept ferrying back and forth, each plane making several journeys through the day. The enemy aircraft were packed wingtip to wingtip on their Greek bases. They were of all types— Messerschmitts, Heinkels, Stukas, Junkers, Focke-Wulfs—troop-carriers capable of lifting thirty fully equipped men into the air. It was the airborne division in action. Now we knew its destination. Undoubtedly it would be supported by seaborne troops sailing in those scores of Greek fishing boats which the Germans had been so busily collecting through the past few weeks. Crete was going to be subjected to the most violent and desperate storming that had ever yet fallen upon the island.

Our hope lay in Freyberg's men, and the Greeks already on the island, and their thin equipment. But there were some things that could be done to help. From the neighbourhood of Mersa Matruh the R.A.F. prepared to bomb the invasion ports from which the Germans were setting out—a flight of six hundred miles each way. Other bombers were got ready to make the 700-mile journey to Crete and back. Hurricanes were stripped of ammunition and equipped with extra fuel tanks in the hope that they would be able to get to the island and have half an hour's fighting there before they were forced to run for home. But already at this early moment it was seen that the R.A.F.'s chances were limited. The Crete sky swarmed with German fighters which flipped easily back and forth to Melos and the Dodecanese. In the daylight our bombers would have little chance against them. Maleme and the two other landing fields were already untenable under the German bombing barrage. No British aircraft could be stationed on Crete. None could even land there to refuel.

Again the high command turned to the navy and asked Cunningham to do what he could. Ships to take more men, guns, ammunition and food to Crete were wanted. Somehow they would have to be landed under the German barrage—and landed quickly, before it was too late. Any attempt at a sea invasion had to be frustrated.

Once again the admiral ordered his ships out. This was to be the old fleet's last battle in the unequal fight of ships against bombers, and possibly it was the greatest battle of all. It was to take a greater toll of lives than Matapan. It will be remembered that the sailors went out well knowing that the odds against them would be much greater than in the Greek evacuation, and their chances of survival much less.

That first nightfall found a compact group of parachutists still holding out on Maleme airport. It was essential for the British to expel them, reoccupy the central aerodrome, and wreck the two runways that ran down to the seashore in a 'V' formation, the arms of the 'V' uniting on the beach. Only then could we prevent the enemy from getting his troop-carriers down on the morrow. The gliders had been a failure, and it had been proven that parachutists by themselves could be dealt with. The whole battle now hinged on whether the Germans could get the main body of their airborne troops down by landing them from aircraft on Maleme. Freyberg attacked. His New Zealand infantry made headway, and in the morning they were in possession of a part of the airfield.

The second day—the day that was to decide the battle of Crete— broke clear and warm. Over most of the island the colours still glanced up from the pale blue peaceful sea along the high cliffs, and gulls wheeled unmolested through a quiet sky beyond Ida and the White Mountains. But on that strip of northern coast the battle was continuing in a fury that was not to reach its peak until the end of the day. From dawn the dive-bombers were over in hundreds; and the parachutists; and now something in addition—troop-carriers and supply planes. Three-inch mortars that had done deadly work in Greece were floated down in big cylinders. Light field artillery supported by three separate parachutes were released. Then came motorcycles, boxes of medical supplies, ammunition, signalling sets, tinned food, barrels of water—all suspended on parachutes, all dropped at a steady rhythm and on a set plan. Little by little the group of parachutists fighting at Maleme added to their numbers. They began to get machine-guns into action. Soon they had a mortar assembled, and were winning back the ground they had lost in the night. And still more and more German aircraft filled the sky with the noise of rushing express trains as they dropped more men, more supplies.

By evening Freyberg was ready with a new attack—tanks first, then the New Zealand infantry coming in, and at the end, as they wearied, an Australian brigade was to break through.

It came as near to success as any failure could. The tanks went in, but in the confusion after Greece some had been furnished with the wrong ammunition and were smashed up without their crews being able to fire an answering shot. The New Zealanders advanced, but when they looked for the support of the Australian brigade, it had not yet arrived. Poor communications had made it late in starting, and the heavy air blitz along the roads had delayed its progress. The New Zealanders had almost but not quite gained their objectives, but now they were not able to go on alone.

And now the Germans sent down their big troop-carriers onto the Maleme runways. The first dozen aircraft pilots, with the deliberation of men committing suicide, landed their machines straight into the line of British artillery fire, and were smashed to pieces with their passengers. And still others followed them into the arena of flaming wrecks and wounded and dying men. At last one troop-carrier got down. Then another. Then others were destroyed. Then another got down. In five minutes the Germans were out of each machine and taking cover, and the pilot was off again. Some of the aircraft were blown up as they steadied for a landing, others as they taxied to a standstill, others again as they rose from the take-off. At immense cost the Germans were getting a few men aground—just enough to hold back the British from the aerodrome.

It was useless now to regret that we had not laid obstacles across the runways before, or dug pits, or exploded the surface with dynamite. The field had to be won back first. And Freyberg at this stage could not draw off more men from the other sectors. At Retimo several hundred fresh parachutists had succeeded in holding a building by the sea and were engaging an Australian brigade. Farther east, at Heraklion, it was the same. The Germans had taken a hospital near the ruins of Cnossos, and the fighting was bitter. Many of the parachutists had been wiped out, and others had been ambushed and killed with knives by the Cretan irregulars who lay in wait round the waterholes. But more kept arriving.

Had Freyberg been able to summon the R.A.F. at this moment to bomb the Germans on Maleme, he might still have won the field back, but the means of communicating with the R.A.F. command in Cairo were archaic. An officer from Freyberg's headquarters had to find the R.A.F. group captain and bring him back to Freyberg. The R.A.F. officer had then to return to his office to put a message to Cairo into code. Cairo had to decode it and send instructions to the Western Desert bases—by which time it was too late.

So on this second evening while the sun shone warmly across a still sea, the battle of Crete swept up to its crisis. Freyberg knew that a sea landing was likely to be made at any moment. Indeed, the shore light signals which were to guide the convoy of enemy caiques into Suda had been captured from parachutists. The navy was warned that the British forces ashore would make an attempt that night to decoy the enemy convoy toward Suda at a convenient moment. But a British destroyer came upon that convoy first in the darkness. An Italian escorting destroyer failed to release its torpedoes in time to damage the British vessel, and soon the navy was on the spot in strength. This was about 11 p.m.

There began then one of the most fantastic actions ever fought in the Mediterranean. The British ships found themselves in the midst of a fleet of caiques, each carrying about a hundred Germans so closely packed they were standing shoulder to shoulder. The Italian destroyer was sunk outright, and the navy turned its pom-poms and four-inch guns upon the caiques—often at point-blank range. In a few minutes the sea was in chaos. In the gun-flashes the sailors could see thousands of Germans swimming about in the sea, calling hysterically for help. Caiques were rammed head on and smashed to pieces or raked by the pom-poms or sunk by the four-inch guns. For hours the British warships cruised back and forth, ramming, sinking, killing. In some vessels the Germans attempted to hide below and hoisted the Greek flag. In others they jumped overboard in terror as the big warships bore down upon them. A few who got near the shore were met with machine-gun fire or ran foul of booms and, overturning, drowned their crews among the rocks. Not a living man landed that night. Some nine thousand Germans were either drowned or killed. They were the staff of the Eleventh Fliegerkorps and part of the Fifth Mountain Division with their artillery.

Their destruction gave Freyberg sufficient respite to hold on for another ten days. But already that night he had seen the vital danger at Maleme. 'All depends on the next few hours,' he wirelessed to Cairo. But in the next few hours he could not retake Maleme. His hope was that sooner or later the Germans would have to stop coming. Sooner or later they would have no more aircraft. But the Germans still kept coming. They never ceased till they had won, and had landed some thirty-five thousand men on Crete.

We had successes within the structure of the whole invasion. The Germans were turned out of Retimo. They were reduced to impotency at Heraklion. These two sectors were of minor importance to Maleme, but they helped greatly in the process on which broadly we were now embarked—that of destroying as many Germans and German machines as possible. At Heraklion those parachutists who had escaped death in landing took shelter in a valley where they could be heard calling to one another all night long. It was expected that in the morning they would emerge and attempt to win a better position. Accordingly, British guns were trained on the outlet of the valley. The enemy came out. They were entirely destroyed.

It was in this sector, where the casualties among the falling Germans had been very heavy, that the British found the bodies of the parachutists turned a vivid green a few hours after death. The colour suffused the dead men's cheeks and arms and chests. Clearly they had been drugged. Already something of the sort had been suspected in Greece, and now an Australian soldier reported he had come upon a packet of the drug and had taken some. His story was that through the next few hours he felt uplifted on a glorious wave of enthusiasm and energy and recklessness. His comrades said that he had shouted and cheered, and they had had to hold him down when he wanted to rush from cover alone upon a position strongly held by the enemy.

Upon the bodies of the parachutists also was found the parachutist's code. It made a strong appeal to the ideals of late adolescence—and most of these parachutists were boys of twenty or thereabouts. All were volunteers. Here are the most interesting points in the code:

You are the *élite* of the German Army.
Know everything yourself; don't leave it to your officers.
Your guns are more important than you; look after them first.
Support your comrades always.
Treat an honest enemy honestly; be merciless with snipers or spies and saboteurs.
You will win.

Drugged or undrugged, they came with a high purpose, these boys. And the letters upon their dead bodies revealed much romanticism and idealism. There was more family feeling than national patriotism; more concern for their families in Germany than enthusiasm for the cause of Greater Germany. And the theme of many of the letters was 'when the war is over...'

They did in fact reveal themselves at times as honest fighters. At Heraklion they protested to the British that a wireless set was being used in Cnossos Hospital. When the wireless set was broken up, the German commander agreed that the place should be used as a joint hospital for the wounded of both sides, although the building was now inside the German lines. German doctors who had parachuted down joined the British staff of the hospital. British ambulances were driven through the German lines with British wounded. A British orderly, before he was taken off the island, was permitted to go first to the hospital and say goodbye to his colonel, lying wounded there. These things were exceptional in a battle of such bitterness and speed as Crete, but they did happen. The report that the Germans landed in New Zealand battledress was not true. It arose from an unfortunate but honest error. The hospital near Canea was taken in the first downrush of parachutists, and the New Zealand walking wounded there were forced to advance down the road ahead of the Germans as a cover. From a distance it appeared to the defending troops that these men were disguised parachutists, and the mistake was not discovered till later.

There was nothing much to destroy in Crete; no power plants, no railways or tall buildings. The majority of the villagers drew their water from wells and used oil lamps. But after the third day had brought them no definite result, and still their aircraft were being destroyed in scores, the Germans embarked on a ruthless campaign to obliterate Canea, the capital of the island.

Canea was a town of 27,000 people, many of whom had by this time evacuated to the hills. Before the Nazis came I had wandered one whole day through its quiet back streets and along the ancient stone wharves where fishermen had been fishing since before recorded history. The town's two best restaurants were the London Bar (with a Chinese chef) and the Caprice. They swarmed with flies, and you could not always be sure of getting a tablecloth or a table napkin or a clean knife and fork. But you could get the tart, resinous wine of Crete, and the goats-milk cheese, and omelettes made with vegetables gathered that morning from the mountainside. The market was rich with oranges and grapes and vegetables and cheese packed inside a goat's skin (with the hair of the goat turned inwards). Last war the Royal Navy was here, and it left a legacy of naval photographs on the walls of the London Bar, and a smattering of English words among the townspeople. Venizelos and Byron were the heroes of the people here. But history had left this place untouched in the sunshine for the last twenty years, and even tourists passed it by.

Now that it was suddenly become the battlefield of the most modern war the world had seen, it was hopeless for Canea to try and bridge the gap between its timeless stolid peasantry and this fighting in the sky. A few slit trenches were the town's only answer. For the rest, it lay half empty, its life paralysed, its importance in the war nothing at all. But between dawn one morning and the evening, the Germans came and laid most of Canea in ruins. The plan for its destruction had been worked out to the meanest detail at the Nazi air headquarters in Greece, and it was translated perfectly and methodically into action. The bombers, heavily protected by fighters, came at intervals of one every three minutes. They worked back and forth, bombing one side of the town, then the other. The sticks of bombs came down in neat exact pattern, reducing street after street. Then when the outskirts were demolished, the last of the raiders set fire to the centre of the town, and left it there smoking, battered and ruined forever under its own red glow in the evening.

When Geoffrey Cox, with whom I had worked in Paris, came from Crete and wrote his story of the invasion in my flat in Cairo, he described how he had gone down in the morning to see how his 'Crete News' was progressing. It was a single broadsheet he and a few soldiers and local people were continuing to produce for the troops, invasion or no invasion. And this, the day of the destruction of Canea, was publication day. From the morning throughout the day the staff of the paper worked in a printing shop in the centre of the town, setting type, writing copy, reading proofs, running the machines. When the bombs came too close they would lay off for a bit and lie with their faces to the ground against a wall. An Australian, filled with the goodwill of the heady Greek wine, and completely oblivious of the bombs, kept roaming in and out of the printing shop through the day, bringing them food and drinks and cigarettes from the broken shops and the burning houses outside.

And in the evening the printers presented themselves in the darkness at Corps Headquarters with the printed bundles of 'Crete News' under their arms.

The destruction of Canea did nothing much to advance the German foothold upon Maleme, but it added to the horror and the unreality of the war which now, through this last week in May, resolved itself into a series of heavy, slogging engagements, with the British giving way foot by foot. Plane after plane crashed and blew up until the beach was piled with wreckage, and some three hundred machines were strewn about the airport and the foothills reaching up to the White Mountains beyond. The Nazis, it seemed, were prepared to accept an insanity of wastage, and the assault took no account of lives or wounding. Once on the ground, the Germans alone could not have hoped to stand against the defenders but for the endless bombing and machine-gunning from the air, which never relaxed. Not even a single man or a cyclist exposed on the roads was too small a target for the Nazi fighters. They shot at everything and anything. And as the wrecked machines mounted in number from three hundred to four hundred and higher yet, they still kept coming.

Through this last week aircraft had been dropping supplies everywhere for the Nazis who were now gradually increasing their positions round Maleme. The parachutists brought down with them canvas signs and numerals which told the Nazi pilots above what to drop. At places along the beaches the British captured some of these signs and laid them out. Down upon them floated guns, rifles, medical supplies, tobacco, bicycles, barrels of water. One gun-crew received a piece of light artillery mounted upon rubber wheels. Forgetting to remove the wheels and steady the gun upon the ground, they promptly unloosed it at the enemy. The gun recoiled at speed upon the gunners, then came charging back on them and finally bowled over a cliff to destruction.

The New Zealand Maoris in the first battle rose out of their rock shelters and, shouting their native war-cries, charged upon the German machine-gunners—a wonderful charge, against the rules of tactics, but brilliant in its success.

King George of Greece and his staff, and the British legation from Athens, were taken by New Zealanders through the parachutists, over winding tracks and through the mountains, and were brought to a place on the south coast where they were embarked and got to Egypt.

The R.A.F. came in the night and bombed the Germans on Maleme, but the bombing was too slight, and they could not come in the day without fighters. The Hurricanes, which had been fitted with extra tanks, could do nothing against the clouds of Messerschmitts. As one fighter after another failed to get back to Mersa Matruh, the British air offensive was at last abandoned. Bombers still crossed to the Greek bases which the Germans were using, but there, too, the British met overwhelming fighter defence. The royal navy, coasting round Crete, was under ceaseless dive-bombing—sometimes thirty and forty bombers upon a single ship. Inevitably casualties at sea began to mount. Reinforcements sent out from Egypt were unable to make a landing in the face of the blitz, and had to turn back.

So when this bitter last week in May was ending, Freyberg gave the order to the Suda Bay troops to retreat through the White Mountains to the southern port of Sphakia. The others at Heraklion were taken off directly by destroyers. Two whole battalions in the Retimo area had to be abandoned. Through the last day of May and the first two days of June the retreat through the White Mountains went on. Once for two hours the general and his staff lay sheltering in a narrow valley, while the Messerschmitts raked it from end to end. In the groves the branches of the olive trees caught fire. Units became divided, and men lost in the hills had to fend for themselves. There was no hot food and water ran out. Villagers in the mountains led the weary, unshaven, dirty men to wells where they lowered their water bottles on ropes to the springs below. The walking wounded walked at first, were carried in the end. Outside Sphakia they funnelled down through a narrow village in a long, tightly packed queue, none knowing whether there would be room or not for him in the warships lying out in the bay.

Nor was there room for everyone. The navy was losing ships. The Luftwaffe was pressing hard on the evacuation. When the last warship and the last caique drew off, there were still hundreds of men—New Zealanders, Australians, British—strewn over the mountains and along the beaches and in the villages. Many were still fighting because there was nothing else to do. Even when the warships were at sea they were harassed from the air through all the daylight hours on their journey to Egypt. Once when a destroyer was hit it was lashed to a sister ship and the crew and passengers transferred. As the sound ship stood off again she put a torpedo into the other destroyer.

But at last the ships came home, and the men from Crete came down the gangplanks at Alexandria. They had fought for twelve days. They had destroyed nearly one thousand German aircraft, and so mauled the German airborne division and two other divisions that it was many months before they could fight again. They had killed or wounded between fifteen and twenty thousand Germans. They had blocked the march of the Germans through Syria to Iraq and the oil wells. For this, we had paid with the loss of half a dozen of our best warships at sea and many of their crews. Of the 27,550 men sent to Crete, 14,850 had come back. Much equipment had fallen to the Germans. And we had lost Crete.

It seemed at first through that depressing early summer that we had paid too highly for too little. There was anger at our failure in the air, and bitterness at the mistakes that were all too clear after the event. But little by little it was seen that some good was emerging from the conflict. First, we had met the parachutist and the airborne fighter—the men they were threatening to send to England—and we had proved him weak, vulnerable, an easy mark in the air and not much good on the ground. He would never get anywhere if he did not have overwhelming support in the sky. Then it gradually became more and more apparent that the Germans were too weak now to press their advantage. Cyprus at that time might have fallen like a ripe plum. Dentz in Syria would have welcomed the Nazis. But they did not come on. The forces the German high command had allotted to this theatre of the war had been exhausted.

As later intelligence came in we learned that the Germans had expected to find no more than five thousand men in Crete, but once embarked on the adventure they had to press on and take appalling losses. By midsummer it began to seem that we had not paid too dearly. Crete was the low point for the fortunes of the British in the Middle East. After that, the British position painfully and gradually but steadily improved.

Eighteen

Early this morning Allied forces under the command of General Wilson crossed the frontier into Syria, with the object of eliminating German personnel. –CAIRO COMMUNIQUÉ, JUNE 8TH, 1941.

FOR ONE year—June 1940 to June 1941—Syria lived on its nerves. In all the world it was the one neutral place whereof you could say with absolute certainty: 'Here will be war.' The only surprising thing was that it remained at peace for so long. Whenever news was slack (it seldom was) you could always turn with confidence to Syria for a story, since the place hummed with rumour and intrigue.

Before France fell, Weygand built a great army there, and it stood upon the right flank of the Middle East as solid as a rock. Even after the Franco–German armistice it was expected that Weygand would come back and lead this autonomous command to the side of the allies. And when that failed to happen, Syria was bombarded with propaganda from every direction and riven with factions. The Arabs wanted independence, the Turks wanted Aleppo, Vichy wanted to maintain its mandate, the British wanted an ally, the Germans wanted a springboard in the Middle East, and the polyglot, restless, mercurial people of Syria itself wanted fifty different things and set about intriguing for them with a vigour remarkable even for a country that has bred intrigue since Alexander the Great. Vichy tried a succession of administrators and generals in command—Mittelhauser, Puaux, Fougère, Chiappe (who was shot down and drowned on the way out) and lastly General Dentz. Inevitably every one of them made a mess of it. And the worst mess of all was made by the Italian and German armistice delegations in Beyrout, who were the real masters of the place. The Italians had command at first, but failed to make much headway against the solid mass of contempt from nearly everybody. One Fascist general after another went trailing home to Rome, and the Germans took control with the eager assistance of General Dentz. When the battle of Crete was fought and German aircraft were passing through Syria to assist Raschid Ali against the British in Iraq, it became obvious to everyone that the country was going to be occupied by one side or the other. The only question was who would get there first.

After Crete I had gone up by train to Jerusalem, hoping to get a week's holiday in the cool air there.

As I stepped down from the train on Sunday morning an American correspondent met me with the news that the empire forces and the Free French had crossed the border a few hours before. There was nothing for it but to get a car and chase after them.

We drove fast down to Haifa, and, having no military transport of our own, clambered aboard an ambulance called 'Bloody Mary' at the border. The French were fighting back, and there were casualties. We rode on into the Phoenician port of Tyre which had been captured that day, but the coastal road farther on was blocked with heavy machine-gun and tank fire. It was going to be no walkover.

Back in the mountains in the central sector, the Australians, expecting a friendly reception, had walked up to the French frontier post with their slouch hats on. They were mown down by machine-gun fire and a battle was now raging round Merj Ayoun below the slopes of Hermon, still capped with snow. Farther east General Legentilhomme's Free French had gone through Deraa easily enough and were well up the road to Damascus. But they, too, were getting a hot reception. Away round to the far east two other British columns were making their way in from Iraq along the general direction of the Euphrates valley, but they had miles of desert to cross before they got anywhere.

We settled down to a protracted campaign. When the German and Italian agents in Syria fled the country and Berlin announced that the affair was no concern of the Axis, the result was a foregone conclusion. But General Wilson, again in command, had to find the solution of the extremely bristly problem of how to subdue thirty or forty thousand angry French subjects with the least possible number of people on either side getting hurt. He tried sending in officers to parley under a white flag, but they were shot down. There was nothing for it but to fight a way through to Damascus and Beyrout.

I chose at first the coastal sector and never was a war so convenient for the war correspondent. We lived in a Jewish hotel high up Mount Carmel at Haifa—a lovely place overgrown with pines and flower gardens. Looking down from here—the very place where Elijah saw the cloud no bigger than a man's hand and beheld below him on the site of Haifa the priests of the temple of Baal—one had a panorama of the whole sweep of coastline around to Syria. Across the plains of Armageddon came the French and Axis bombers to raid the fleet in the port of Haifa at our feet.

In the night we stood on our balconies and saw the heavens open with tracer shells, flaming onions and the flowering bursts of the navy's ack-ack fire. Sometimes in the moonlight you caught the silver outline of a bomb going down, and, knowing it was not headed in your direction, you watched fascinated for the explosion in the sea or along the shore directly beneath. Sometimes a raider, misjudging the sharpness of Carmel's slopes, would all but brush the pine trees above our heads and we would hear the pilot open his throttle for the next dive on the port. It was the nearest thing to being in one of the attacking machines oneself, and Mount Carmel must assuredly have been the world's best air-raid grandstand.

Over this chain of hills where the Carmelite Order had been founded and David and Jonathan had their last quarrel, the Jews had built big modern hotels and restaurants among the trees. Here every afternoon and evening the people came from the hot town below to listen nostalgically to lieder from Germany and hot rhythm from America, and to dance under the trees. It was possible, if you wanted, to attend a tea dance on the mountain and afterwards drive down to the front in Syria for an hour or two in the evening. Returning at dusk, you would be in time for dinner in a German beer hall in the town and a nightclub on the mountain. Each morning from my bedroom window I could see the fleet steaming out along the Syrian coast, and soon the noise of shelling would come sweeping across Armageddon into my window as the breakfast coffee came in.

The road through Acre into Syria was almost perfect, and the coast itself dissolved into rolling hills and plantations of wheat and olives and bananas reaching down to a yellow beach and a soft and warm green-blue sea. Usually before going up to the forward positions we would strip on the beach and swim for half an hour and drink the bottles of Carmel Hock we had brought from Haifa. It was still not too hot, and always the snow sat pleasantly on the mountains inland.

It was not quite so idyllic as all that for the soldiers at the front. They were being opposed by tough Algerians and Foreign legionnaires, and more and more Dewoitine fighters and Glen Martin bombers were arriving from French North Africa by way of Italy and Rhodes to bomb and strafe the British positions. Talking to captured Frenchmen, we got to know how bitter was this fight which had started as a skirmish and was developing into a war. The better-informed Frenchman would argue like this: 'Why shouldn't we fight? We're professional soldiers obeying orders, and you came here on a deliberate aggression. You think it would have been easy for us just quietly to submit; but what about our friends and our relatives imprisoned by Germany? The Boches keep threatening us. They say they will take reprisals and they mean it. We've got to fight.'

And there was another subtler impulse. It was expressed perfectly by a French sergeant near Sidon. 'You thought we were yellow, didn't you? You thought we couldn't fight in France. You thought we were like the Italians. Well, we've shown you.' They were fighting for something that was almost as fundamental as self-preservation—for human dignity, for the right of walking among others as an equal. And since we brought against them forces much inferior in numbers to their own, the French could not out of sense of pride surrender at once.

I am speaking now of the early stages in June when it was touch and go as to whether they would go on or not. When we tackled them with too few men and guns and they beat us back, they naturally gained confidence and wanted to continue the fight. And that old deadly frontline bitterness sprang up—Jean's comrade Gaston is killed and he wants to avenge him. And so the war gathered impetus, snowball fashion, feeding on itself. Everyone on the British side hated it. No one enjoyed killing Frenchmen. And it was naturally painful to be destroying the men and the arms which once had been drilled and built to help us. Even the very propaganda posters the French had printed to bring in volunteers to help the Allies in 1939 were being used now to recruit men against the British.

The greatest animosity of the Vichy French officers (not the men) was reserved for the Free French. In the first day or two a captured Vichy captain turned his back upon Legentilhomme, and that genial, courageous little man's blue eyes hardened suddenly when he realised what he was up against. Frenchmen fighting Frenchmen. It was unthinkable. But, by God, now the Free Frenchmen decided, we're going through with it. And they went battering on at Damascus.

On the coast the Australians struck their first real snag beyond Tyre at the Litani River. The Litani came down freshly from the snows of the Lebanon, a green fast stream bearing rich banana groves on its banks. As the troops came up to the river, a British force, lads from Scotland mostly, was landed behind the French positions on the enemy bank. There was some confusion in the darkness. The men were put into boats a mile or two out, and when they got near the shore they waded up to their necks in water straight onto a beach that was covered by a French seventy-five-millimetre battery. The French had been forewarned. 'You were twenty minutes late,' one of the Vichy officers said later to a captured British soldier. There was a murderous sweep of fire down the seashore. By the time I got up to the Litani River in the evening the force had been badly broken up and those that could were getting out. Their colonel, some of the survivors told me, had got ashore among the first, carrying his walking-stick and a revolver, and had made straight up to the French battery with a sergeant and some others. Both the colonel and the sergeant were mortally wounded, but they led a charge up to the Frenchmen and actually succeeded in grabbing a gun and turning it on the other enemy guns in the battery.

Another soldier at the colonel's order had gone off down the coast where he had swarmed up the mast of a French barracks and pulled the tricolour down. There were many skirmishes of fantastic daring through that bad day, while the bullets kept ripping through the broad green leaves of the bananas and scorching the olive trees. In the end the force did what they were sent to do. They distracted the enemy while the Australians won the river and threw a pontoon bridge across.

I rode back in a convoy of two trucks with what was left of the British force. The men were utterly exhausted—almost beyond smoking—but when we stopped to pick up stragglers on the road they leaned out shouting excitedly: 'There's Jock. He's out of it'; or 'Andy, where's the rest of your section?' They rode back to Haifa counting their dead on the way, and those who had gone ahead in ambulances and those who were simply missing. Barely half had come back. The war was taking a serious turn.

There was to be an attack again the next day, and I stayed on the hills all night watching the barrage. In the morning the war correspondents rode back into the village of Tyre which lay a little off the main road. We wanted breakfast. We saw something was wrong as we approached. The Union Jack was down from the Gendarmerie. There was no guard, no Australians in the town. The people who had thrown scent and rose petals at us as we came in a day or two before stood about sullenly in the village square. Some gave us the Nazi salute. The chief of the Gendarmerie bobbed up suddenly beside our cars and hissed at us doubtfully: '*Vous étes Anglais?*' He drew us into a café for an urgent consultation. 'You have been beaten,' he announced. 'The flag is down, the soldiers have gone. You are in retreat. The Boches are coming.' He was very agitated.

Little by little the story came out. It seemed that the Australian security company which had been posted in the town had been wanted elsewhere, and, all being quiet on the surface at Tyre, they had been withdrawn. Having only one Union Jack, and that one only an old yachting flag, they had pulled it down and marched off. The next thing the wondering people heard was heavy gunfire along the Litani River. Villagers sent to the main road came back with reports that British ambulances and staff cars were travelling fast down the road toward Haifa. At once the people jumped to the conclusion that the Empire forces were retiring. Out of their nooks and crannies in the village came the pro- Nazis, and there had been a wild night of arguments and Fascist demonstrations in the village square. When we arrived, the people had not been sure if we were Vichy French or Germans or Italians. They had routed two Vichy destroyers that had come out of Beyrout. But now the chief of Gendarmerie stepped briskly forward into the square. Throwing up his hand for silence, he announced with superb simplicity: 'The British are not beaten.' There was a cheer from the ranks of the anti-Axis clique, and dark troubled looks among the pro-Nazis. From somewhere another Union Jack was produced, and as it went up we sent off for another platoon of Australians to occupy the town.

Of no importance all this, except it was probably symbolic of all Syria. These Lebanese had been so twisted and confused by rival propagandas that nothing seemed definite and true, and they were ready to swing any way so long as it would give them peace to go on with their farms and their fishing.

When Sidon fell and we drove in on the heels of the first Australian patrols, the town was half sullen and doubting. Two Senegalese soldiers lay jumbled in horrible death at the gateway to the town, where a naval shell had hit them, and the people had been badly scared. All the French had decamped. Dentz had been here only two days before to tell the troops straight out that unless they fought reprisals would be taken upon their kinsmen imprisoned by the Germans. They were to shoot all British who attempted to parley. More and more as we progressed with this campaign Dentz was emerging as a very sinister figure indeed. And as yet we had not begun to know how far he would go.

The town was painfully short of things like bread, sugar and petrol, and goods had apparently been cornered by a few merchants to put up prices.

The English fleet had been steaming steadily ahead of the advancing troops, shelling French positions on the coast from four or five thousand yards out. They had routed two Vichy destroyers that had come out of Beyrout. But now in the evening an unusually heavy force of German Junkers appeared suddenly over Sidon. The British ships were at once obliterated in fountains of bombed water, and as the bombers turned for their second run a great widening shaft of black smoke arose from one of the destroyers. It was badly damaged. This misfortune, coming after several other encounters in which British warships had been hit, made it imperative that the fleet should have air protection if it was to go on.

On land we were flourishing. We had taken Merj Ayoun, in the centre, and Jezzine. Kinetra on the road to Damascus had fallen, and we drove into it the following night and slept there in the Stade Pétain.

Two days later Merj Ayoun had been retaken, Jezzine was menaced, and a Vichy column fell suddenly upon Kinetra and captured or killed most of the British regiment holding it. The stone wall against which I had slept at Kinetra two nights previously was all but blown away. There was nothing for it but to bring up more aircraft, more guns and men, and recover the position. After a day in the central sector where the French were methodically shelling Palestine territory at Metulla with seventy-fives, I was glad enough to get back to Haifa for a quiet night.

These drives across northern Palestine and southern Syria went by like tourist outings. From Rosh Pinna you turned down upon the lower road past the Sea of Galilee and Tiberias and Nazareth. Or upon the higher road you came past Mount Canaan and a succession of villages almost too Biblical to be real. Military traffic was on the road everywhere, and the general awakening to the war was very like what I had seen in the Sudan.

When I had come to Palestine a year ago the place was drifting along on the edge of the war with a happy-go-lucky round of dinner dances at the King David Hotel in Jerusalem, and swimming on the coast at Tel Aviv. Prices in the hotels and restaurants and for such things as taxis had been allowed to rise to unreasonable heights—a legacy from the tourist days—and now they had gone higher yet. A day and a half at the King David Hotel cost my wife and myself seven pounds. It was the old business of cashing in on the war, and from one end of the Middle East to the other now the British army was paying through the nose. For the hotel-keepers and the merchants it was a time of abundance. Only the mass of the people, the fellah in Egypt, the farmer in Palestine—who had had no direct means of tapping the flow of gold from England and the Dominions—had a hard time, for they got no increased income to meet the artificial prices. And immediately any part of Syria was occupied, the old bad profiteering business was begun, for we were determined to placate the people and the best way of doing that seemed to be to let them have a free hand at their business.

Two weeks of fighting had not got us anywhere much, but now, late in June, the reinforcements had come, British–American Tomahawks were fighting French–American Glen Martins. Damascus was overlooked by Indians and Australians who had got around to the left flank. We regained Kinetra and I set off fast for the Damascus front. We were almost there when the car broke a spring and we had to return all the way to Haifa. Damascus was falling. Once again I was going to be too late. Once again it wasn't going to matter.

We drove hard all the next day up out of Palestine and across that arid black lava country where the Arabs were threshing a brilliant yellow harvest on the ground, and on up the road where Legentilhomme had been wounded, and so into Damascus, which had been entered a few hours before. Nothing comparable to the excitement of Lawrence's entry twenty-four years before had taken place, though the last fighting had been bitter enough.

Here, then, was the garden town on the edge of the desert, which was so beautiful that Mahommed had refused to enter it lest he anticipate heaven. This was the burial-place of Saladin and John the Baptist who is also a saint of the Arabs; the largest city in Syria, the oldest inhabited city in the world, and probably the most ancient hotbed of intrigue in the Middle East. I see Damascus must be a delight to a man coming into its green gardens from the desert—rather as Derna was to me in Cyrenaica; but, with my head filled with the lively colours of the coast, I found the streets dusty and noisy and the buildings shabby. We drove to the Orient Hotel and booked rooms, much as you could in Marseilles or Bayonne in the years before the war. It was very French. But the crowd milling round in the square outside was largely Semitic. Again the French had left in a body down the Beyrout road.

There had been a three-way thrust into the city at the end. Colonel Collet with his troop of wild Circassian cavalry had come in from the east without opposition. Legentilhomme had come straight at the town up the main road from the south; and round in the west the Indian and Australians had had a stiff fight in an outlying suburb called Mezze. At Mezze, while the Australians won the heights, an English gunnery officer had used the most original tactics of charging with twenty-five-pounder guns. Starting near a British military cemetery of the last war, he had unloosed a salvo, and then, harnessing his guns, he had rushed forward to a new post where he swung his artillery round into action again.

And then once more they charged. Unorthodox, risky and highly successful.

There was still a proper mix-up in the hills above Mezze. An Australian brigade headquarters had been surprised and captured by the French, and the French and their prisoners had had to face the Allied counterattack together. But now the prisoners were retaken and General Catroux was coming into the town to take over in the morning. There was a curfew but no blackout that first night. I looked out of my window and saw for the first time in a year a city glowing with light. Like some Venetian carnival, electric lamps gleamed right through the oasis and threw their warm colour up on the bare heights beyond the city where the battle was still going on.

In the morning we drove through the city, looking, for some reason, for 'The Street Called Straight,' and found only endless bazaars and byways filled with hideous prostitutes of whom Lawrence used the disgusting and brilliant phrase, 'raddled meat'. We put on slippers and walked through the Ommayyad Mosque to the tomb of St John the Baptist, and later climbed a hill above the town.

Coming back we went into a Roman Catholic church where Collet's Circassians had come to hear Requiem Mass for one of their number killed. A plain deal coffin stood at the altar. In the pews were these wild, stable-smelling, leathery men with their knives and rich robes. They bore the coffin out into the sunlight and placed it in an army truck. As it went down to the cemetery, the Circassians walking behind, I ran ahead in my car with Christopher Lumby of the *Times*, and a little farther down the road an Australian soldier shouted at us: 'Get back, there. Get out of it.' We had run straight into the front.

Here, three minutes from the centre of the town, two minutes from that solemn pathetic little funeral, machine-gun bullets were coming down the road, and dead and wounded men were lying out on the hillside. Even round at Mezze, French guns were still lobbing shells onto British transport going along the road. And it was then I heard the news that Germany had gone to war against Russia.

My story of the fall of Damascus could not mean much against such news as that. So I left quickly and returned to Cairo, for my paper was endeavouring to get me to Moscow. When no visa arrived, I returned to Syria for the fall of Beyrout. There had been a hard fight at the village of Damour just outside the capital. And now at last, after a month's hostilities, Dentz had asked for terms to end 'the bloody and unequal battle.'

Acre, the place where Napoleon was beaten back from the Middle East by the British Commander Sidney Smith, was chosen as the place for the negotiations. It was well back from the front in Palestine, and the conference room in the barracks stood pleasantly beside the sea. Firing stopped around midnight Friday, July 7th, and in the morning General de Verdillac, whom the Germans had recently released from prison to fight in Syria, crossed the British lines with his staff. General Wilson and General Catroux were waiting to conduct the negotiations for the Allies. All day long the conference went on. Journalists, radio broadcasters and photographers waited outside to report the signing of the armistice. Occasionally, during breaks in the conference, the delegates strolled out on the lawn by the sea, and more than once I saw Catroux and de Verdillac chatting amicably enough. There had been one minor incident when a certain M. Conti, one of the Frenchmen, had refused to be served luncheon by a Jew. But, on the whole, the negotiations went peacefully enough. Yet it was annoying to discover at the end that de Verdillac had come without full powers and could do no more than initial the drafts. The actual signing, they asked, should take place forty-eight hours later on the Monday. It looked then as if the French wished to gain time for some motive of their own.

However, at 11 p.m. all was ready for the initialling, and the journalists were ushered in. Edward Genock, the Paramount cameraman, had been concerned that the lights in the conference room would not be sufficient for his newsreel. He had obtained several reading-lamps in the barracks, and these he had joined together ready to plug into a power point in the conference room. As soon as the correspondents were admitted, Genock's assistant strode forward and took up a position with his makeshift candelabra at General Wilson's elbow. The general, a large and benign-looking man, allowed himself one astonished glance at this sudden visitation and dipped his pen for the initialling. The candelabra was plugged in, and all the lights in the room went out. Someone produced a fountain- pen torch and flashed it aimlessly among the blacked-out delegates. Others brought a staff car to the door, and turned its lights in a blinding stream upon the Frenchmen at the conference table.

It was proposed then that a motorcycle should be brought right into the room in order to shed its light upon General Wilson's papers. A dispatch rider accordingly bowled his machine up the steps and into the position lately occupied by the unfortunate holder of the candelabra. Then before the fascinated gaze of the company the soldier began to set his motorcycle in motion: a performance which would have utterly deafened everyone in that confined space. 'But I can't light the light unless I start the motor,' the soldier protested glumly. He was ordered to take his machine away and hurricane lamps were called for. During the period of waiting it was seen that a number of unauthorised persons, hangers-on around the barracks, had crowded into the conference room to enjoy this entirely unusual spectacle. The order was given for their removal. The order, however, was not quite understood by a sergeant of police who had possibly had a training in raiding nightclubs before the war. He now flung his arms solidly across the door and announced: 'My orders are that no one who was in this room when the lights went out can leave.' At length the hurricane lamps were brought, and in an atmosphere that was beyond either laughter or tears the papers were initialled. The further meeting was called for the Monday.

All next day the two armies lay in the positions they had occupied when the ceasefire order was given. Wilson's five columns, that looked on the map like the five fingers of a man's hand, stood clutched about the heart of the country waiting for the order to go forward and occupy. On Monday de Verdillac came back, and another long day of negotiation brought the final signing of the armistice. There was nothing unexpected in the terms. The French were given all the honours of war. There would be an exchange of prisoners, and those French soldiers who wished to return to France could do so. The Allies were to have their choice of the French war material, and there was to be no sabotage of the essential services of the country by the vacating French command.

The terms were generous, and Syria itself had suffered very little by the campaign. The men who had suffered were the front-line troops. There had been no fraternising between the two sides during the negotiations. The two armies had kept a rigid no-man's-land between them.

On Tuesday, July 15th, when the Australians were ordered forward and it was clear to everyone that the war was over, the people came out in thousands to see the entry into Beyrout. We drove slowly forward along the coast into Damour's rich gardens which had been ravished by the fighting. I counted some fifty houses in the village, and every one had a shell-hole through it. The big bridge over the Damour River was down, and broken tanks and armoured cars lay about. An undertaker's shop in which the French had secreted a tank to fire down the road was blown up. As we drove on toward Beyrout, through the world's largest olive plantation, Lebanese villagers ran from their houses to wave and cheer. Since it was finally the Allies and not the Germans who had the honours of war, the population were content to welcome them. In the suburbs of the city itself girls ran along the streets waving hastily made Free French flags with the cross of Lorraine upon them. We came out at last into the big Place des Canons, where between ten and twelve thousand people had lined the pavements and the windows and the rooftops in a compact mass.

A brass band was hurried forward, and now in the bright sunshine they came marching into the square playing 'Mademoiselle from Armentières.' A long column of infantry followed behind with their tanks and Bren-gun carriers.

I had arrived now at the scene of the third British victory in six months. Benghazi, Addis Ababa, Beyrout. In this tangled, fluid war it was impossible yet to assess them clearly or know how to set them against our reverses. We were simply profoundly grateful that this Syrian campaign, with all its unpleasant implication of civil war, was done. We were very ready to forgive and forget and make friends with the Vichy people that morning.

I went down to the St George's Hotel, a luxury place that rises like a Chinese pagoda out of the sea on the edge of the town. The bar was filled and luxurious Lebanese girls were swimming idly in the sea below the hotel. Over across the bay the Lebanon rose up mistily cool and remote. It was a little like Toulon. It was as though the war had never been. General Dentz and the Vichy army had gone off up the coast to Tripoli where they were to sort themselves out—some to stay, others to go off to France. The rest of Syria was ours to go wherever we liked; the forests, the vineyards and the mountains, the ancient ruins, the cities and the beaches. In the streets you could drink syrups cooled by the snow brought down from the mountains, or buy rich silks and silverware in the bazaars, or knives with long chased handles. The motor roads led off to places with romantic-sounding names—Baalbek and Palmyra, Homs, Rayak and Aleppo. In the winter there would be skiing in the Lebanon, and high above Beyrout at Aley one could stay in great tourist hotels and see the lighted city spilled out below. All this new country was rescued from the war and could expand now in peace.

In a relaxed and grateful frame of mind we arranged for a large and very French dinner at one of the town's best restaurants, and, coming home late that night, we plunged naked into the warm sea that broke away in shafts of phosphorescent light from our bodies as we swam. Russia was in the war now, and for the first time in a long busy year the Middle East correspondents were not expected to fill the news pages and keep up a daily stream of messages. It was good to win like this.

I woke abruptly from my idyllic daydream next morning. Syria was not passing out of the war quite so easily as all this. You could not take a country to war and avoid leaving running sores behind. As I moved round the town, meeting people, I began to see Syria was pretty well raddled with running sores at that moment. Bit by bit I pieced together the story of the last month—the story from the French side. And the thing that emerged from it was that Syria was only the beginning of an eruption in the French Empire and an estrangement between England and Vichy that was to eclipse anything that had gone before. It became clear that cooperation between Vichy and Germany was much stronger than had been guessed. And the essential link in this theatre of war was General Dentz.

Dentz and his henchman Conti were no longer Frenchmen any more. They had sold out completely to Germany. Here briefly is what I discovered. After his reverses in the first days Dentz had approached the United States Consul-General in Beyrout, Mr Engert, and asked him to sound out the British for terms. But by the time a reply had come through Washington, the position had altered and Dentz decided not to parley. He had had some successes in the interim, plus a strong injunction from Berlin to hold on. Two divisions of French prisoners held by the Germans were being released and sent overland to Salonika. The Vichy undersecretary of state was on his way to Turkey to ask permission for these troops to be transferred through Turkey to Syria. New aircraft were being sent across from France and French North Africa, and several French naval vessels were *en route* to Beyrout. It began to seem that Vichy (i.e., the Axis) would hold out in Syria.

But things did not go according to plan. Turkey refused to give the French troops right of way, and the British navy was intercepting the vessels that endeavoured to bring them across by sea. Damascus fell, and then the strong position at Damour. Dentz, who had been in daily communication with Darlan (not Pétain) and Berlin, as well as surrounding himself with the Italian and German delegations, decided to ask Mr Engert to approach the Allies again.

You can judge the feeling that was running at Beyrout at this time by an incident that occurred over two American correspondents with the British forces—Robert Low of *Liberty* magazine and Kenneth Downs of the International News Service. They were captured in an ambush outside Damascus, and when they were brought to Beyrout they were confronted by M. Conti. Conti said: 'You are spies and I intend to have you shot.' The charge was absurd, and in the ensuing argument Conti revealed himself as entirely in German pay.

But now the armistice intervened, and Dentz set himself to protract the negotiations as long as possible. While the armistice was pending and his delegates were at the conference table, he flew off the British officers in his hands to Europe, where some of them were delivered to the Germans. He flew off all his remaining aircraft to other French possessions. He took the British tanker *Pegasus*, then a prize in French hands, to the mouth of Beyrout harbour, and, with two other British vessels, sank her there. He removed the last of his own serviceable warships to Turkish waters for internment. He tried to coerce the French conscripts into returning to France instead of giving them a free vote. And he set in motion a most intricate organisation for the supply of information to the Axis and the political disruption of the country.

Every one of these actions was a violation of the understanding of the armistice. Yet some weeks intervened before Dentz and thirty-five of his immediate and most dangerous followers were interned by the

British in surety for the British officers so treacherously handed over to the Germans.

Driving after the fall of Beyrout to the far north of the country, I saw many French airmen in Aleppo and soldiers along the route. They had a very understandable coolness, but would stop and give one directions upon the road with good grace. Everything was being done by the occupying troops to leave them at peace until they made up their minds whether to go back to France or join the Free French. But at Tripoli, where the main French army had retired, a most active campaign was begun by the Vichy officers to dissuade foreign legionaries and others from coming over to the British side. I drove on to the Turkish border and saw the first meeting of British and Turkish soldiers there. But as I drove back and out of Syria I could see no permanent settlement in the country—not at least until it was purged of Vichy French and the mounting Axis influences. That lovely troubled little country was still far from working out its destiny in peace.

Nineteen

We have had some setbacks, some successes.
-GENERAL WAVELL.

AND NOW, in July 1941, the first phase of the war in the Middle East was done. It had actually ended on June 22nd when the Germans marched upon Russia. Just as the R.A.F. had saved England until the help of the United States arrived, so Wavell had stood in the Middle East until the imponderable Russian army rose to fight with us. It had been a big and tiring year. I alone had travelled, I suppose, some thirty thousand miles and seen something of three of the five campaigns. From next to nothing the army of the Nile had risen to half a million men, despite its reverses— English, Australians, New Zealanders, South Africans, Indians, Poles, Czechs, French, Palestinians, Cypriots, Sudanese, Belgians, Ethiopians, East and West Africans. And at least they were being armed from the United States as well as from England and the Dominions.

As the Russian war rolled on into the late summer, and one peaceful week succeeded another in the Middle East, it began to become clear that something had been done here to earn this rest and prepare the way for bigger offensives. Something like a quarter of a million Italian soldiers were safe in concentration camps in Egypt, India and South Africa. Ethiopia had been won back, and two other Italian colonies were conquered. Berbera was recovered. The Western Desert and Tobruk held strongly. The Canal was open and secure. But by far the major achievement had been in the sphere of our reverses—the sphere that inevitably will be the centre of argument. Whatever were the demerits of our tactics and planning in Greece and Crete (which were the cause of the Benghazi reverse), it could not be denied as the winter of 1941 set in that our campaigns there had delayed Hitler's plan for the Middle East and perhaps baulked them altogether. If, as it seems likely, Hitler had proposed to sweep quickly through Crete and Cyprus and Syria to the Iraqian and Persian oil wells, then we had impeded him by going out to meet him in Greece and Crete. Presumably he already had the Russian campaign in view, and could allow only a certain amount of time to his Middle Eastern adventures. By delaying him, it well might have been that we forced him to cut short his drive at Crete. That, anyhow, is the British case, and it appears fair and reasonable to those of us who have followed the war out there.

There are many criticisms, for there were many errors in these twelve tumultuous months. The Benghazi reverse was a bad blow, and would have been averted had we gone on to Tripoli in the first place. Greece and Crete showed that we underestimated the Germans, and had failed to accommodate ourselves to meet the new fast blitz of war of the air. Iraq and Syria showed we needed a deeper understanding of the peoples of the Middle East, and a firmer hand. Both those countries might with clever diplomatic handling have been won to us without revolt or war.

But it would have needed a brain of genius and more forces than we possessed to have averted all these mistakes.

There is much here I have not touched on, either because I had no personal knowledge or because I did not think the event contributed greatly to the theme of this book. Malta, for instance, is a book of itself. There were many Maltese who had no cause to love British administration before the war, and the story of their loyal fight for England is a thing of grandeur and deep pride.

The revolt in Iraq truly was nothing. When the British dead were counted they numbered scarcely a dozen. It was a political rising that had just this significance—it showed that the Germans will stoop to use any tool however small. And it indicated that skilful propaganda among the Arabs will achieve results as great or greater than actual wars. It was a warning, too, for us to keep watch and stem the intrusion of German agents into the Middle East or Asia.

Against this, there were many other more vital things not noted here. There were the garrisons in Palestine and along the Suez Canal; the merchantmen who bring the weapons and men from England; the men in the outposts like Aden; the A.R.P. in a hundred cities through the Middle East; the people who slogged at their desks in G.H.Q. in Cairo; the civil airways pilots, and many a civilian who was stuck in some Godforsaken place on the route between Cairo and England.

In all these people's minds there was one overriding thought—how are my family and my friends?

Nearly everyone in the Middle East was cut off from his family. The mail means much to every soldier. And it was not easy for men to fight in the Middle East knowing that their families were being bombed in England or menaced in any of a dozen other places I can think of. I heard this a thousand times: 'Why aren't we home defending England?' It was difficult to make it clear to the soldier on the Nile that he was doing as much to defend England or Australasia or India as he would have been in his own village.

Wavell saw this clearly. He understood his troops. And I for one was deeply sorry when at the close of this hard year's fighting the papers came out with the announcement that he was going.

The war correspondents went down to G.H.Q. to say goodbye. The general was in his shirtsleeves again. And for once he was full of words.

'We have had some setbacks, some successes,' he said, and he went on to sum it all up. It wasn't a particularly good summing-up. The theme was 'More equipment.' But I saw suddenly how sincere he was, how hard he had tried—tried, fought, organised, argued and held on. There went out of Cairo and the Middle East that afternoon one of the great men of the war.

BOOK TWO

A Year of Battle: The Year
of Auchinleck 1941–42

One

August 1941 in Cairo

I THINK we first began to realise it was all over for the time being at the end of July. There seems to come this moment of anticlimax at the end of every campaign. The excitement and enthusiasm abruptly die away. Overnight the roads become half deserted, and you find the troops making camp in the fields. Tents begin to spring up, and at their doorways you see men shaving and taking baths in the open. The steel helmets have vanished.

Some of the local people come out of hiding and begin to sell fruit and eggs along the roadside and then you see the most definite sign of all—red-capped security police. They begin to appear in every village. They mean that law and order have returned. They mean that the fighting is done, that the banks can reopen their doors and the shopkeepers pull down their shutters. Peace, plenty and profit and loss have come back into the world again.

It was like this in Syria. I was far up in the north on the Turkish border where the road runs across to Antioch, and we were resting briefly by a ruin with the improbable name of Chateau des Dames. Without my being aware of it at first a thought suddenly jumped into my mind: 'What are we doing here? How many hundreds of weary miles is it back to Cairo?' Everyone appeared to have the same idea at once and we all began talking about going home. The Syrian campaign was done.

Yet we had never had this feeling of anticlimax so strongly before. As we drove back through Aleppo and Homs and across the Lebanon Mountains to Beyrout we began to see that this was more than a single campaign that was finishing—it was a whole cycle of the war. First there had been the collapse of France, then the air battle of Britain, and now the long untidy series of Middle Eastern campaigns was ending on this hot midsummer day in the deserts of Syria.

Russia had taken over the struggle: cycle number four. As we drew near Cairo we were arguing hotly, not about the Middle East, but Russia. Some thought she would hold out only a couple of months.

As I crossed the Nile in Cairo to my flat on Gezira Island, I decided to use the inevitable lull ahead by writing a book. I remember I was full of the idea at the time and could scarcely wait to unpack my typewriter and make a start. It was not quite so easy as I expected. I got out of bed at six o'clock and set the typewriter up in the front room without waiting to dress. At 7.30 the telephone rang in the hall and I answered it. Then it rang again. Then a third time. Hassan the suffragi came in and swept the floor until I drove him out.

Outside the street vendors came by, and the cries of the Cairo street vendors are just what you would expect them to be—entertaining and romantic in the evening and merely damnable in the early morning when you are trying to work. There was one man who brought such nameless pain and misery into voice that I was forced to the open window to listen. He was selling bath mats.

In the nursery at the far end of the flat I could hear my son John rising like a bombshell from his twelve hours' sleep. The nurse was battling with him against that inevitable moment when he would elude her and go thundering through the flat in search of amusement. The telephone rang again.

Lucy at that time had a job in General Staff Intelligence at G.H.Q. and she had to be at work at 8.15. I could hear the shower going in the bathroom. Alexander Clifford rose heavily from his bed in the front room and put his head in my door.

'Are you writing a story at this time of the morning?'

'No,' I said. 'A book.'

'Good God!'

I could hear him telling Lucy the news through the bathroom door and I shouted at them, 'Will somebody answer this damn telephone?'

By eight o'clock the noise of my typewriter was getting on everybody's nerves and we had a sultry and irritable breakfast. The heat glared fiercely outside. Most of this August went by like that.

Yet it was a nice flat and a pleasant place to live when one was in Cairo. Looking across the green lawns of Gezira Club we had often admired these two tall modern blocks in the Sharia El Gezira. They were known as the Elephant and Castle. Most officers in G.H.Q. had tried to get a flat there at some time or other. It was just by chance one day that we saw the notice go up 'appartement à loyer' and the following week we moved into number three on the rear and shady side of the Elephant's first floor.

General Catroux of the Free French, a lean, quiet, leathery man with a deft sense of humour, lived on the top floor. Directly above us was the Japanese legation full of bland little men in striped trousers who kept tumbling out of the lift into Packard motor cars. The Hares and Williamson Napier of the British Embassy were our neighbours on the same floor. Just across in the Castle lived John Shearer, known as the Cairo military spokesman. Colonel Philip Astley, who controlled the war correspondents in the Middle East, lived there too, and many red-capped brigadiers and generals came and went. The club lawns were convenient for my baby and nurse. We were, in fact, in the right spot.

So then it was an additional irritation this August when we received word that our lease was finished and that we must find another flat at a time when Cairo was doubling its population and flats were wellnigh impossible to find.

I wrote quickly because I did not know how long the lull in the news would last. Each day we half expected some new front to develop, and then Clifford and I would have to pack our bedding rolls and make off. It had happened so often in the past year. There had been Wavell's campaign in the desert; Ethiopia and East Africa, Greece, Crete, Iraq and Syria. Even when Damascus fell and the Russians entered the war, we could not grow used to the idea that the long series of campaigns was done and that for the moment there was nothing of any real importance to report in the Middle East.

The lull in the Middle East was, of course, no lull. The two opponents had simply drawn off from one another in order to re-equip and fling themselves forward again more violently than ever before. There was tremendous activity behind the lines. Wavell had gone to India and his place had been taken by Auchinleck. Stemming from this, immense changes were taking place right through the Army of the Nile. The Army became three armies—one the Eighth in the Western Desert, another the Ninth in Syria and Palestine, and the third the Tenth based on Baghdad and territories to the east.

A spate of new people came in from England and India, bringing with them new machines, new tanks and guns, and one or two fresh ideas. Air Marshal Longmore had gone, and his place at the head of the Middle Eastern air force was taken by Arthur Tedder who had been second in command. Under Tedder the R.A.F. was doubling and tripling itself with Beaufighters and Bostons, Wellingtons, Hurricanes, Marylands, Tomahawks.

At sea Andrew Cunningham still had command, and new warships were sailed to him from England to replace those he had lost in his great actions off Crete and in the Ionian Sea. The time of the big naval sweeps through the Mediterranean was finished now. Against increasing and unremitting opposition from the Luftwaffe, the navy was getting supplies into Tobruk and Malta and sinking the Axis convoys that slipped out of Naples on dark nights and made for Tripoli by way of the Tunisian coast.

From England to Australia, fourteen thousand miles away, our chain of naval bases was still holding—Gibraltar, Malta, Alexandria, the Suez Canal, Bombay, Colombo, Singapore. The route around the Cape of Good Hope was being developed by both belligerent and neutral vessels. Possibly because of the Russian campaign, U-boats and German raiders were less active through this summer, and most of our convoys were getting through.

Only the isolated garrison of Tobruk was seeing real fighting and this was for the most part a matter of shelling, offensive patrols and bombing. This book is partly concerned with the story of Tobruk and it is good to remember the garrison as it was this August during the great days of the Tobruk tradition. The town and its thirty-five-mile perimeter were manned by British tanks, artillery and infantry, and by the Ninth Australian Division, all under the command of Major-General Morshead. German and Italian forces were encamped right under the perimeter and several divisions of enemy troops lay on the Egyptian frontier. Although the main part of our desert army was little more than a hundred miles away from Tobruk, it was impossible to send fighter support to the garrison or maintain British aircraft there. An experiment was made in landing Hurricanes on Tobruk airfield, but they were sighted at once and shot up within a few minutes of landing. No flares could be lit to bring in aircraft at night. Morshead had to rely solely upon anti-aircraft fire to hold off the German bombers that were coming over every day on their five minutes' run from El Adem field just across the perimeter. Our men holding the perimeter could actually hear the German aircraft warming up to take off from El Adem.

Tobruk itself was a maze of broken, tottering buildings though still they gleamed white and clear in the sun. Shells fell constantly among the wrecks in the harbour. All that dusty and ravished plain reaching up to the minefields, trenches and barbed wire of the perimeter was under enemy fire, so that reliefs on the front had to be carried out at night. Even the food of the front-line men had to be cooked near the town and taken up to the trenches in the starlight. The men who had lain all day in the sun facing the enemy would crawl through the trenches to the dugouts where the bully stew and brackish tea was served out. And they would relax there for an hour or two at night to smoke, talk and read.

Before the morning came they would walk back to their posts. By any standard they were very fine troops. They were the Rats of Tobruk,

All these men—some twenty-five thousand—were maintained solely by the navy and the merchant fleet. Destroyers crammed with men and stores would steam out of Alexandria and Matruh and make the quick dash through the night into the treacherous darkness of Tobruk harbour. Only a narrow channel was kept open through the sunken ships and the entrances to the harbour were mined.

Landing crews—and these included a little band of picked Indian troops—would be waiting on the improvised docks and lighters. They worked feverishly through the midnight hours getting ashore the shells, tanks, spare parts and boxes of food. The reinforcements came off silently and under the spasmodic glare of bombs and gun-flashes they marched off somewhere into the darkness. Then the wounded were carried down to the ships and borne off into the open sea before the morning broke. At sea the ships were often followed and bombed by the enemy until they reached port in Egypt.

In all this there was none of the stir and excitement of battle action. There was no thrill of closing with the enemy, of seeing the torpedoes go out and the big guns straddle their targets on the horizon. Seldom, if ever, were the men on the Tobruk run able to see that most terrible and exhilarating sight on the ocean—an enemy warship that billows suddenly into flame and casts up its stern for the long dive to the seabed.

All this was stealth, speed and essentially defence. Yet still I carry a photographic picture in my mind of the dark harbour of Tobruk. Over on the right somewhere lies the wreck of the Italian liner *Marco Polo* and another vessel that by some freak of the weather or high explosive had edged a good twenty feet of its bows onto the yellow cliffs on the southern side of the harbour. On the left lie the broken buildings of the town rising tier on tier up to the crest of the promontory which binds the harbour on its northern side. In between is the heavy darkness of the harbour itself. All around is the noise and sharp light of gunfire.

The dockside labourers straining their eyes can just make out the low hulk of a moving ship. It is probably no more than a triangular shadow weaving in and out of the wrecks, until it comes alongside. The decks are crowded with men in full kit. No one smokes. There is an exchange of shouted orders from the destroyer's bridgehead and answers from the quay and then the men begin filing off. The winches are moving before the gangways are down.

Thousands of men have stood on Tobruk quays watching this scene while they, too, waited in full marching kit for the order to go aboard...

to go aboard and leave Tobruk and get a spell of rest and quietness and good food back in Egypt or Palestine. While they pondered on cool beer and how it would be to see women again and trees and gardens, many have thought, 'Will there be room for me?' There always was room.

It is a notable thing in seafaring that through this period I have called a lull, nearly the whole of the Ninth Australian Division was taken off Tobruk and replaced by two English brigades and a brigade of fighting Poles. The casualties in the changeover were almost nil. The Australians left their trucks and guns behind and the new troops simply moved into the perimeter and took up the struggle. It was done so secretly and quickly the enemy never knew of the changeover until it was completed. Even if this manoeuvre lacked the excitement of a battle, it had the importance of a victory.

Meanwhile on the frontier Rommel was doing little more than digging in. He was mounting entire turrets he had taken off captured British infantry tanks. They were embedded in concrete on the high points of Halfaya Pass, overlooking the British forces that were sprawled across the Egyptian desert below, and down across the road to the sea. There was shelling, minelaying, patrolling. But not much else. Rommel had his plans for the winter and so had we.

We suspected but did not know definitely that Rommel was consolidating this frontier so that he could assault Tobruk unmolested by the rest of the Eighth Army. On one side we were filling the Western Desert with such numbers of guns, tanks and vehicles as had never been seen there before. We planned to go around his frontier positions and relieve Tobruk before the enemy could launch his attack on the perimeter.

There was no great concern at this point about the rest of our Mediterranean bases. The heavy raids on Malta had not yet begun and the island was holding strongly. The middle arm of the Nazi Drang Nach Osten had stopped at Crete so that the island of Cyprus and newly occupied Syria were secure and fairly heavily garrisoned. From Persia there was an ominous rumble of Axis activity at our back door, but it was no more than political intrigue and underground sabotage.

In the south the East African war was finished. Haile Selassie sat on his old throne in Addis Ababa. The disposal of thousands of Italian settlers there was proving a first-class problem, but they were showing no desire to make trouble. British Somaliland was again ours. Italian Somaliland and Eritrea, with its valuable Red Sea base at Massawa, had been added to our war-time empire. Vichy French still clung to the flyblown waste about Jibuti and were supplied to some extent by submarine from Madagascar. But this was a minor problem. Three-quarters of Africa was now behind the British. Vichy and the Axis still held the north-west corner reaching from Dakar to Sollum. Two valuable and large South African Divisions, with their attendant aircraft, were released for service in Egypt.

Until now the British dispositions in the Middle East had resembled a huge wheel with Cairo at the hub. One spoke of the wheel had reached south to Addis Ababa, another west to Tobruk and Malta, a third north to Greece and Crete and a fourth eastward toward Baghdad. But now all this was changing. The northern spoke of the wheel had been removed by our expulsion from Greece and Crete and our conquest of Italian East Africa had made the southern spoke unnecessary. The wheel was a wheel no longer. It had been shaped into a huge shallow V, one arm of which stretched toward Baghdad and the countries of the east; the other arm reached toward Tobruk and the central Mediterranean. Cairo stood at the angle of the V.

It required no great foresight or knowledge to see what were the British plans for the winter or to understand that, despite our losses, our grand strategy had passed from the defensive to the offensive stage. We had to guarantee the Mediterranean and somehow re-establish a footing in Europe. The way to do that was by the conquest of Libya. Holding Benghazi and Tripoli we could give land-based fighter protection to our ships; we could supply Malta and send air raids deep into Sicily and Italy; we could mount an expedition to land on Italy itself. This was the long-range hope for the western arm.

In the east there was still a little plugging and filling to do. In neutral Persia, with its all-important oilwells in the south, German technicians and agents were steadily white-anting British interests. The Turkish government, temperamentally democratic but anxious to offend no one, poised itself on an awkward triangular foreign policy. The Turks took arms from Britain and America, barter agreements from the Axis and fair words from Russia. To Turkey it seemed that she would be swamped overnight if one of the great powers decided to invade. She feared that her great wastes might suddenly be turned again into a battlefield. She believed that the only logical object of her foreign policy was this—to keep out of the war until she was invaded and then invoke the aid of the other belligerents. In the meantime, Turkey was a weakness in the chain of our eastern positions, for she would accept no allied troops on her soil lest she offend the Nazis.

The position of India—so closely linked with the Middle East—I deal with later. At this moment, before Japan and the United States had entered the war, India was chiefly a great workshop and emporium for the Middle East. She was an immense reservoir of men, ships, guns, clothing and food, and she was committed to the rôle of supplying Auchinleck's armies wherever they went—into Europe if need be.

The situation generally was not bad so long as Russia held. But there was an immense job of coordination and supply to be done in the Middle East, and the War Cabinet sent out Mr Oliver Lyttleton as its minister of state and highest authority.

I saw Lyttleton only half a dozen times while he was in the Middle East, and then at semi-public meetings. He worked hard, travelled a good deal, held many private conferences, and those things he did achieve were kept secret. Very possibly we had an unfortunate view of him. His press conferences were so appallingly dull, his words so banal and evasive that it was impossible to put him before the public as a leader; when he came to leave Cairo he was scarcely known. I remember once when we had spent months following a campaign in the desert and were temporarily back in Cairo, Lyttleton summoned us to a conference. He then revealed to us that he himself had made a short visit to the desert, and he proceeded to describe in some detail the geography of the places we had been visiting all winter. However, he appeared to hold a good balance between the generals and the diplomats, and those who dealt directly with the minister spoke highly of him.

There was through this quiet time something definitely and deeply wrong with the mental attitude of the British forces in the Middle East. Not since Mr Eden's visit just before the disasters in Greece and Crete had we heard words of such optimism and confidence. The complacency was contagious. Everywhere you went the men were 'in good heart'—or so their officers told you. Probably this was true enough, but it was largely the good heart of ignorance. Apart from Greece and Crete we had not seriously met the Germans anywhere, and Crete and Greece were sliding comfortably into the background. Everyone looked forward to the coming winter campaign in the desert with enthusiasm and dangerously brimming hope.

Shipload after shipload of fresh troops and machines came round the Cape from England and soon we had thirty thousand vehicles in the desert. New American light tanks and medium bombers and fighters kept pouring in. Everyone was impressed. Unlike Wavell's first campaign, there was no secret about this offensive whatsoever. The only question was—When?

There began, too, at this time a widening political and emotional gulf between the soldiers of the Middle East and the people of England. The real grimness of warfare had scarcely touched Cairo. We had never been bombed in our homes. The men here never knew the long weariness of working day in, day out, in a factory. They never fully realised that human beings at war crave some of the excitement and movement of war to offset the discomforts they are enduring. In the Middle East it was impossible to understand how the rationing of food, the lack of heating and the crowding of railway trains and buses can reduce the spirit. We got plenty of everything to eat, we seldom wanted any heating, there was petrol to burn and motor transport for nearly everyone.

In the Middle East the war was a thing of fast movement and new places. For many it was a matter of tactics and strategy and the high excitement of playing the most dangerous game on earth. No civilian populations were being destroyed. It was straight, clean warfare, a battle of courage and wits. If Benghazi fell, then it was just a manoeuvre of war, very important to the game, of course, but it did not mean that one's wife and family were imprisoned or that one's house and car were destroyed.

I do not mean to suggest that the men did not fight bravely—possibly they fought more intelligently and clearly since their minds were not fogged with immediate worries about families and places that were dear to them. I simply say that for the most part that essential grimness of total war could not be experienced here because this was not total war. The women and children were not involved. Their immediate fate did not depend on the battle.

Certainly the men worried about their families, but that cut both ways since the families in England were presumably worrying just as much about their menfolk out here. Certainly many who died would far rather have done their fighting at home—but then relatively very few died in the Middle East. This open mechanical warfare tended to destroy machines, not men. The huge numbers of prisoners taken were nearly all unwounded because there was practically no trench warfare in the desert, and once the protective armour was gone there was little the infantry could do in many cases except surrender.

I conceive that to the workers and soldiers of England the war did not appear in this light. I conceive that in a certain sense Benghazi was almost as real to them as London. It was the symbol of the success of the weapons they had made and the calibre of the men they had sent out as their champions. They saw the fate and worth of England in the desert.

Living here on the threshold of the war, a strange blank spot appeared in our minds, and we did not see Benghazi as clearly as the people of London did. Perhaps we were too close. Nor again did we see Russia as clearly as it must have been seen from England. The troops in the Middle East were too much involved in their own war.

The Middle East was almost an all-British sphere, full of all-British ways of thinking and some of them a little behind the times. The ritual of the salute and the hierarchy of the commissioned officer survived very strongly. That increasing left-wing movement among the soldiers and workers of England scarcely touched the Middle East. It is understandable that the political moves at the heart of an empire do not penetrate its edges at once. Isolated in the desert and scattered outposts, the men craved reading matter more than anything else—and did not get it. This cut them off from the political and social trends at home.

In this self-contained and intensely unpolitical world the entrance of Russia on our side caught the serving officer off balance. The prime minister's prompt and lucid speech on the Nazi attack upon Russia did a good deal toward making our position clear. But after that there was an immense gap in our internal propaganda on the subject. It was not easy for men reared in the public-school-university- city-regular-army atmosphere to adjust themselves suddenly to the idea that they were fighting side by side with the Communists. It was embarrassing and painful to see them struggling against their old loyalties. Some made no attempt. Others avoided the whole issue. The majority in the end achieved the necessary mental transition, and as the Russian resistance went on from day to day they began to take pride in the Red soldier.

For the average soldier in the British ranks no such mental upheaval was necessary. The conditions of labour in England in the late 1930s and the conduct of our foreign policy up to Munich had not exactly made him a passionate admirer of the Conservative Party. He had already travelled some little distance toward the left. He was at this point a long way ahead of his officers in his appreciation of the Russian question.

But the soldier's approach to the new political line-up was slow and cautious. He was starved of information. Where his officers lagged so far behind him politically he could not make much progress. All this may not have been important, but for the fact that still there came no pronouncement from London about the aims of this war. Through the previous winter in the Middle East it had been enough for the private soldier to know that his home in England was in danger and that he was fighting for his life. But now that the crisis was past he could reasonably hope for the defeat of the enemy. To what end? Were we going to annihilate Germany? Were we going to rebuild the English cities and improve working conditions? Were we going to make a union with the United States? In the desert and the Delta, at sea in the merchant ships and in the remote garrisons of Malta and Cyprus, Aden and Basra, the men debated these points endlessly. Inevitably every argument turned toward Russia, Red Russia the Mysterious, the place of Moscow Trials, Bolsheviks, whiskers and Volga boatmen dressed in smocks. The ignorance was pitiful.

Yet as each day went by, the seeds of admiration for the Reds began to take root through the camps and barracks of the Middle East and there was a growing feeling, 'We must do something too.' This was healthy and the high command at once encouraged that feeling. It was most desirable before an offensive. And so out of the complacency of the diehards, out of the high-spirited ignorance of the younger men and out of this new political half-awakening, the morale of Auchinleck's men rose strongly through these burning weeks of the early autumn, and their hopes ran dangerously high.

If I have set down these things clearly, then the events which followed will be understood at least in part. The optimism of the Cairo spokesmen was no accident, nor were the reverses in the field. They flowed logically and arithmetically from the sort of system we were busy erecting in Egypt through this August. No one man was to blame. The false and easy optimism was spread because we misjudged the temper of the people in England; the reverses occurred because we misjudged the enemy.

We had not then, nor, as far as I can see, have we yet learned the simple equations—understate your early successes so that your later successes will appear the greater and later failures will seem the less. And—never underrate your enemy whether you win or lose.

It was natural that later on a good deal of the criticism should attach itself to G.H.Q. in Cairo. G.H.Q. has always been a favourite Aunt Sally. I suppose every journalist who visited Cairo this war wrote at least one dispatch about the glamours of its nightclubs and the luxury of its restaurants.

The truth was, of course, that the lures and excitements of Cairo were just as tawdry and provincial as they always were. But the place gained by contrast and monopoly. Apart from Alexandria (incidentally a much gayer and more cosmopolitan city), Cairo was the only place in Egypt where the troops could go on leave to spend their money. A soldier coming in from the desert luxuriated in hot baths and cold beer. A soldier coming from England was overwhelmed by the richness and variety of the food. Between the two, Cairo achieved its Babylonic reputation, and the men who were destined to work there on the general staff came to be regarded by some as modern sybarites.

It goes without saying that this was silly and unfair. Few people who have tried both G.H.Q. and desert would have chosen a permanent job in Cairo. There is an enervating quality about the heat which lies upon the city from March until November every year. In this month of August the Blue and the White Niles gather their overload of tropical rain from the highlands of Ethiopia and the swamps of Uganda. The flood joins at the confluence of the two rivers at Khartoum and sweeps on across the Sudan deserts, past Luxor, Assuan and Upper Egypt. At Cairo all this muddy water is carefully distributed in a thousand canals across the rich soils of the Delta. The land becomes sodden and out of the soaking fields rises a steamy foetid heat which seems to intensify itself in the pall of dust and filth that hangs forever over the dirty streets of Cairo. Innumerable minor complaints beset the unacclimatised men when they first come to work in Cairo. Few set foot in Egypt without contracting 'Gyppy Tummy', which is a mild stomach disorder lasting usually a couple of days. It recurs at irregular intervals and it makes you feel terrible.

The river itself is not unclean, but no white man bathes in it because of the fear of being infected by the bilharzia. The most dire warnings are given to everyone about this bilharzia disease. You are told that it is practically death to fall into the Nile. Let me pause just a minute to go into this matter since it is so typical of a thousand other errors in the Middle East. I quote Colonel Ralph Bagnold of the Long Range Desert Group who knows Egypt as well as anyone. It seems that the bilharzia is one of the few germs that will penetrate straight into human skin and does not need to enter the bloodstream through a sore or an abrasion. It lives in stagnant water and seems to enjoy fastening itself upon wood or reeds. In Kitchener's day the British troops quartered in the Kasr el Nil barracks in Cairo were accustomed to taking a daily swim in the fast waters of the river. None came to any harm. But one day a sergeant was borne off downstream by the rising current and before stronger swimmers could reach him he drowned.

Swimming was at once forbidden to the troops, and workmen set about building an enclosed bath at the edge of the river. A line of stout wooden stakes was driven into the mud and when the thing was completed the troops returned to their daily bathe. At once they began to contract bilharzia and it was often fatal in those days. One after another the men died and the death-roll in the barracks became serious. Debarred from entering the clean, fast-moving waters in the centre of the Nile, the troops were contracting disease from the worms that clung to the wooden stakes of the bathing-pool. But this was not clearly investigated at the time and the whole river was condemned as infectious.

The baths long since have disappeared. The superstition of the worm survives.

Swimming such as you will find nowhere else on earth can be found along the white beaches of the desert where the nights are cool and the air clean most days of the year. In Cairo the dirt is persistent. Yet the fact is that if towns have gender, Cairo is a lady. It was meant by the high command to be a basic fortress in the Middle East, as Spartan as Gibraltar, as grim as Malta. But something in the climate thwarted that design. Twenty centuries of easygoing soporific life have made it impossible for Cairo to be like Liverpool or Malta.

Swollen to nearly two million by the influx of troops, artificial and dirty, filled with rickety noisy streets and tumbledown buildings, the city sprawled over the lush mudflats at the apex of the Nile Delta. Its mood was gay, rather flashily romantic in the evening, shrill and ugly in the morning. By instinct, I am afraid, the lady was a prostitute.

Egypt generally, too, seems to have been as much misunderstood as the bilharzia worm. Our relations with the country were very clearly laid down by the Anglo-Egyptian treaty signed in London in 1937 and its broad lines were followed. The Egyptians broke off relations with the enemy—they were not obliged by the treaty to go to war. The canal and the strategic bases like Alexandria were handed over to us together with the desert. We had the use of the docks and the railways, the roads and the rivers.

The essential thing about the treaty was that the British government was determined to regard the Egyptians as a free people with sovereign rights in their own territory. This meant that there could be no all-out war effort in Egypt. Private enterprise must have its profits. No special demands could be laid on the people. Martial law was not declared.

Everything we wanted of the Egyptians had to be asked for and voted in Parliament. It had to have young King Farouk's approval. Sir Miles Lampson, the British ambassador, had a very difficult and delicate mission. The instructions laid on him by the Foreign Office seldom allowed him to go beyond the bounds of ordinary peace-time negotiation. When the railways ran late, when the unloading of ships at Suez was held up through strikes, when the opposition parties in Parliament strained away from their allegiance, when there were irregularities in the internal administration, when, in fact, anything occurred that impeded our war effort, Lampson could do little more than protest as a diplomat and ask for correction. There could be no compulsion.

The powerful and subtle weapon of propaganda could have greatly assisted Lampson in his job. There were one or two people who worked hard and intelligently, but at this stage our propaganda was still childish and inept and the censorship, both ingoing and outgoing, remained capricious, slow, misinformed and utterly uninspired. The British Empire was hawked through the mud villages of the Delta like a dud second-hand motor car. In the face of the witty and virile Axis broadcasts, our propaganda was a poor limp thing, essentially prim and correct, essentially unenthusiastic.

On his side King Farouk had his difficulties. He was the absolute monarch of a hybrid population of sixteen or seventeen million people. They were much divided by class, money, language, race and temperament. Practically all the wealth was gathered into the hands of less than 5 per cent of the people. There were Greeks, Levantines, Jews, Syrians, French, British and Italians of fabulous wealth. They took rich profits from the war and gambled heavily at the races, on the stock exchange and the property market. They lived in lavish homes. They bought the best cars and clothes and wines from abroad. Prices trebled and all the display of monopoly and wealth came crudely and flagrantly to the surface.

Under this upper crust laboured the vast mass of the fellaheen, more than 80 per cent of them diseased, illiterate and abjectly poor, and they supported a birth mortality rate that vied with India. Egypt indeed was no advertisement for British rule during the early decades of this century. Can you wonder then that there were many here who were not ardent supporters of the British cause? That there were occasional street demonstrations when they shouted 'Up Rommel'? That the Axis was able to find agents among the politicians? That corruption spread?

I emphasise all this confusion here because one of those strange unobserved social phenomena of the highest historical importance was taking place in Egypt. Despite the inefficiency and delay, despite the self-interest and misunderstanding, Egypt rose to the crisis when it came, and behaved very well indeed. Just as the Jews and Arabs in Palestine temporarily sank their differences when we went to war, so Egypt when the vital moment came stood solidly behind her agreement.

All these things and many more besides made up the atmosphere of the Middle East during this hot August. Many of them I failed to observe at the time, for I worked ten and sometimes twelve hours a day on my book. In the end it was finished and I emerged from my flat to find that already events were on the march again. The new cycle in the Middle East was beginning. It was going to be a much more serious affair than anything we had ever seen here before.

Two

September in Persia

LATE IN August Arthur Christiansen, the editor of the *Daily Express*, cabled me: 'Can you fly to Persia at once?'

I drove across the Nile to the Persian Embassy in the suburb of Giza below the pyramids, and presently they took me into the ambassador's study. Ali Akbar Behman was a pert and shrewd little man, his clothes European, his language French. He sat amid his splendid Tabriz carpets and gave me a little eggshell cup of sweet Turkish coffee. He said, 'I am going to give you a visa. I have refused many others, but I want you to go and see for yourself whether all these stories about German agents are true. Persia (he called it Iran) is pro-British, pro-German, pro-Russian and pro-everybody. We are utterly neutral. It's nonsense to talk about Nazis running the country.'

He marked my passport as valid for crossing the border at Khanakin and nowhere else, and on a certain date. The visa was valid for thirty days and I had to proceed straight to Teheran. I was to report to the Persian police on the way. 'You will see everything,' he said. 'You will be able to expose these lies.'

The conversation had not gone much further when I realised that the ambassador was puzzled. He was probing me. What he was really saying was, 'I think the British are going to invade my country. Why, then, are you coming to me asking for visas? Is this a deception scheme?' I could not have answered him at that moment. Clearly Christiansen had some information about it in London as I had, too, in Cairo, but I knew nothing for certain.

I went down to Colonel Astley at G.H.Q. and he was mysterious. 'Go and see Randolph,' he said. Major Randolph Churchill, the prime minister's only son, had lately taken over the army's propaganda branch and he said flatly, 'No, I strongly advise you not to go off to Persia on your own. I have something better arranged for you.'

I cabled Christiansen evasively and waited. Randolph kept stalling. He would not say what he was planning. I even wondered whether it could be Dakar or Jibuti.

Randolph had come into G.H.Q. like a hot gusty wind. He was an unabashed reflection of his father, whom he always referred to as Winston. He was aggressive, headstrong, opinionated, full of rushing energy and he went around G.H.Q. mortally offending one brass hat after another. He was a notable figure with his heavy leonine head, his thick greying hair, his husky voice and big shoulders.

His politics, to me, were deplorable, and he had a habit of riding roughshod over everyone he could. He disliked advice. Inevitably he made many enemies and many mistakes. But that limp, lifeless and pathetic thing we called British propaganda in the Middle East suddenly revived under his impulsion. He got things done. He broadened the censorship and let in criticism. He revived the local press which at that time consisted of Reuters Foreign News Service and not much else. Sound and comprehensive as Reuters can be, I defy anyone to digest at breakfast seven or eight solid columns of that particular sort of circumlocutory English. Randolph brought in a new service of foreign cables, articles, pictures and cartoons.

He brightened the press conferences and he dared to publish for the army a weekly digest of the best magazine and newspaper articles appearing in America and England. Some of these articles were frankly critical of army methods. They were packed with well-written information and some contained left and liberal opinions (not that Randolph was left-wing—far from it). To the news- starved men of the desert, this sheet was the most stimulating reading they had seen in months, even years. An hysterical die-hard British brigadier had one copy of the paper publicly burnt at his desert camp. Other reactionary minds of the type that was blocking all originality in the British army wrote bitter and abusive letters to the editor. One officer I remember protested that the troops in the desert did not need this kind of subversive literature. What they really wanted, he said, were magazines like *Country Life*. Certainly Randolph was shaking things up.

When he left, his *World's Press Review* declined steadily. It was no longer distributed free and it became in the end just another flat, orthodox news magazine.

At this moment, however, Randolph was in his heyday and thoroughly enjoying himself. He had succeeded in persuading the authorities that if we were going to enter Persia then the war correspondents should be on the spot beforehand. They had given him something we had been begging for for years—an aircraft of our own. It was Randolph's idea that we should set off from Cairo the day before the occupation began, but things went wrong, and a senior Intelligence officer managed to get us delayed an extra day. His reason was that we would have given the show away if we had arrived the day before. It was not quite clear to me how half a dozen correspondents were going to give the show away if the arrival of some twenty thousand troops at the border of Persia had not done so already.

However, there it was, and one hot morning at the end of August while the British and Russian troops were entering Persia, a thousand miles away we assembled beside our Bombay aircraft on Heliopolis airfield outside Cairo. There was Kim Mundy, our conducting officer who was known as the Flying Tank because he had joined the R.A.F. in the last war and the Tanks Corps in this; Geoffrey Keating, the War Office photographer, who had been wounded when he was with us in the Cyrenaican hills earlier in the year; Edward Kennedy, a veteran of the Associated Press of America and one of the best correspondents in the Middle East; Desmond Tighe of Reuters, who had been trapped in Oslo when the Nazis arrived the previous year and had got away; Russell Hill of the *New York Herald Tribune*, who had arrived in Egypt by sailing down the coast of Yugoslavia in an open boat just one jump ahead of the Nazis; and myself.

We flew east from Cairo in the fresh morning light and, crossing the canal and the Eastern Desert, we came down among the orange groves of Lydda near Jerusalem. Then all through the hot midday hours when the heat struck up at us thousands of feet above, we cruised across the Iraki desert. We played bridge on a suitcase and over Habbaniyeh, the R.A.F. base on the Euphrates, the air pockets were so severe the cards jumped up and hung briefly in the hot atmosphere.

Habbaniyeh is the place which the Iraki rebels besieged in the spring of 1941. When we went into the mess-rooms, the bullet holes made by

Nazi fighters were still letting in shafts of sunlight.

As we ate a late lunch under the fans, a sandstorm blew up and we were grounded for the rest of that day and night. It was agonising to sit there and do nothing. Just a few hours away we knew the British and Russian troops had gone into action. All we could do was to play billiards and wait.

I got a seat in the glassed-in nose of the Bombay as we flew on next morning along the brown course of the Euphrates and over the confluence with the Tigris and so on to the green swamps of Basra on the Persian Gulf.

Basra is one of the keypoints of this war and it is a hateful place. It festers along the banks of the Shatt-el-Arab River and the prevailing colour of this flat unlovely landscape is lifeless grey. On the left bank of the river are the date-palm groves which once they say were part of the Garden of Eden. On the right bank lies the scattered township, a collection of wharves, one or two office blocks and the rest just grey mud huts and a bazaar. Withered trees struggle out of the grey earth.

The hotel has an air-conditioned bar and here you might meet Russian and American pilots, British and Dominions officers, Indian traders and all the rest of the odd collection that usually gathers at an overnight stop at any of the crossways of the world.

The river is more or less the boundary between Iraq and Persia. Across it the British Indian troops had thrown a rough strong bridge. It consisted of about thirty Arab dhows lashed side by side, their midships covered with planking. Across this the rear remnants of the Indian army were hastening into battle. We began a weird drive in their wake.

We motored through palm groves and came out on the dry mudflats of the Delta, where hundreds of army vehicles were bouncing pell-mell toward the east. In this southern sector the great oil refineries at Abadan, the largest in the world, were the objective. We could hear no firing as we coasted along. No aircraft flew overhead. No ambulances passed. In the brutish mud-hut villages the people merely stared and they were unafraid. So we came at last into the riverside port of Khormanshah and met the British general.

The battle was all over. Khormanshah and the other ports like Bandar Shapur were in our hands and Abadan was likely to capitulate in a few hours. The Persian navy—a few sloops—had been sunk or silenced. A dozen merchant ships were either burning, beached or captured. Some were good German ships of the Fels Line, capable of eighteen knots. Our men had gone down the winding waterways of the Delta and overwhelmed one Persian settlement after another. What was left of the southern Persian army had withdrawn northward onto its base at Ahwaz.

There was a pathetic story of the Persian admiral, Bayendor, who had an English wife. At the first alarm at Khormanshah, the admiral had rushed to mobilise his sailors and for a while a couple of sloops kept up a running fight along the river. Seeing it was hopeless, the admiral came ashore to the radio station and manned a machine-gun. British Intelligence officers, meantime, had come up with the troops. The admiral, they knew, was a close friend of the Shah. It was hoped that, once captured, he could be persuaded to get in touch with the Shah and induce him to negotiate. Documents had already been made out for this purpose. But when the British penetrated into Khormanshah they found the old admiral dead at his machine-gun. He was buried with full naval honours in the river.

All this we heard in the comfortable security of a house by the river which was temporarily British headquarters. It was like no war I had ever seen before. We sat around in easychairs drinking whisky and soda and it was all explained to us on maps like some new parlour game. It suddenly occurred to me that it must often have been like this with the Germans. In Austria and Czechoslovakia, in the Lowlands and Norway—how often had it all been over in a few days, the régime finished, strange soldiers in the streets and at the railway station, and the people standing about not knowing what to do because everything had gone too quickly to be grasped. Months of planning had preceded this invasion. Months more were going to elapse while Persia was conditioned into her new rôle in the war. But the actual fighting, the actual event which changed the country's history, was really a very small thing. There was nothing here to be greatly excited about, nothing, apart from the technical smoothness of the operation, to be very proud of.

There was a soft velvet quietness along the riverbank now that the sun had gone down. We drove along the earth track in the darkness until we reached a garden—one of those many lovely Persian gardens which are still as good as all one reads about them. Groping through the flowers we came on a swimming bath and plunged in naked.

I for one felt no desire to write a message. All my enthusiasm had gone. The whole scene was an anticlimax after our long impatient flight. But we went back to the English Club, wrote our dispatches, and slept on the floor among the billiard tables.

Before it is too late and all the English clubs of the tropics are gone, let me just record my memory of this one. It was almost a perfect specimen… a ramshackle single-storeyed wooden building by the river, with a library, a billiard room and a bar. A wide verandah and a big reception room for the dances and social evenings on Saturday night. Barefoot servants in white robes and turbans, a broad table on which lie six months' old copies of the *Tatler*, the *Bystander*, the *Sketch*, the *Sphere*, the *Illustrated London News*, *The Times* and the *Daily Telegraph*, the *New Statesman*, the *Forum*, *Truth*, *Punch*—a lot of *Punches*, bound copies too—the *Windsor* and *Strand Magazines* and a pile of engineering and trade papers and one or two local journals. The wicker chairs are just as they should be and always have been. So is the boy who presents a chit for you to sign for your drinks. So are the silver cups and the shield in the corner. Only the wireless set is out of place. When the day's work is done, launches slide down the river and drop off the white-trousered English residents and they call for drinks as they slump down in the wicker chairs among their friends.

'Have the other half?'

'No. I'm in the chair. What'll you have?'

They drink whisky. They talk about themselves until the eight o'clock B.B.C. news comes on, and after that they talk for a little about the news. This they do every night.

The English Club is the place where you 'get away from the local people for a bit'…the place where you can talk English and be English, the place where you can rest and be cool after the long day. Here you sit quietly in the darkness and calculate how many weeks, months or years it is to your next leave—in England. It is the social centre of your life, the only real compensation for the heat and boredom and the endless work of the day. If you are English, you are no longer an alien here. This, at second best, is your home.

All down the southern coasts of China and out along the Malay Peninsula to the East Indies the English clubs were scattered. There were more of them in Burma, and the subcontinent of India was almost becoming one great big English club. Wherever you went in all this heat and ugliness, there was always a club where you could shut yourself away from the world, away from the politics and the shiftless squalid lives of the natives. The Japanese could not enter the English Club, nor could the Hindu or the Tamil, the Eurasian or the Malay. What the natives did was their own affair, so long as they obeyed the English law. One began to lose touch a little with the native. It was rumoured that he was plotting something, but then he was always plotting.

What a crude and tragic Hollywood thriller it has since turned out to be—the natives creeping through the jungle, the sudden arrow embedded in the bar-room door, the settlers spilling their drinks as they run for their guns, the war whoops in the jungle, the ammunition gone and the final overwhelming rush of the enemy, and then the house going up in flames.

All this was about to happen in the Far East. One after another the English clubs were going to go up in flames—at Hong Kong and Penang, at Singapore, Rangoon and Mandalay.

If you had hinted at this to these Indian army officers in Persia, they would have stared at you coldly and put you down as an alarmist. To them the situation was 'well in hand.' That was true enough as far as Persia was concerned. For once we had arrived in time. We had arrived, in fact, at the second half of the programme. The White Man's revenge was on its way. Here in Khormanshah the sheriff had actually ridden into the town in time to save the English Club. One could not help feeling perversely that it might have been a better thing if the Club *had* been burnt down, and some of its old ideas destroyed with it. Then perhaps when we came to rebuild after the war, the native would be invited inside.

Feeling too tired to sleep and turning over these ideas turgidly in my head, I spent the night on the billiard room floor, and woke with a jump at the sound of an explosion in the early morning. Momentarily I half expected to see an arrow quivering in the woodwork above my head. We got up and looked down the steamy reaches of the river. Something was still going on across on Abadan Island. We got a boat and went over.

Like the skyscrapers of New York, the towers of the Abadan refinery rise out of the flat Delta. All around lie the cottages and gardens of the officials and the workers. They have an air-conditioned restaurant and a section of the desert is roped off to form a golf course. It is not an attractive place. The Sikhs were just completing their encirclement of it as we came in. What a crazy war it was. The British employees of the Anglo-Iranian Oil Company, several hundreds of them, including some wives and hospital nurses, had stayed in the town throughout the fighting. They were simply told to 'stay indoors until it is all over.' Only three of them who ventured out into the streets had been hit and killed. A handful of Persian soldiers in their mustard-coloured uniforms had fired a few desultory rounds through the streets. One or two had been sniping from the rooftops, but most of the Persian army had decamped in a body across the river. Who could blame them? The odds were hopelessly against them. At the administration block where the bullets had gone crashing through the adding machines and office desks, there had been a skirmish. The Indians had settled it by bowling a heavy railway truck through the iron fence. Then they charged over the wreckage. Only a score or two had been killed or wounded on either side.

We went into the hospital where the English nurses had lain for an hour or two on the floor while the bullets ripped holes out of their bedroom cupboards and windows. They were a little breathless, but no one had come to any harm. Among the palms nearby a dead Persian boy was lying, and close beside him I turned through the ruins of a little arms dump. There were boxes of new Bren guns marked Skoda Works, Czechoslovakia—stuff evidently brought in at the last minute by the Germans.

Down by the river ferry a British officer was camped with a company of Indians. 'About six hundred of the enemy got across in the ferry,' he said. 'We have just sent messengers to them to say that unless they surrender in two hours' time, we will round them up.' We all sat down in the sun and waited for the surrender. Presently a perspiring messenger turned up. 'The enemy are having a conference,' he reported. 'They can't make up their minds what to do.'

After another half-hour we got tired of waiting and went back to the air-conditioned restaurant for lunch. Its temperature was a good thirty degrees less than the sweltering heat outside. I shivered over the beer and bacon and eggs, and emerged into the sun an hour later with the most violent cold I have had in my life. You can judge of the unreality of all this action in the south by the fact that throughout the fighting the Persians never cut the oil supplies. The oil flowed out of the territory held by the Persian army to the British oil refineries at Abadan and the British continued to pay their royalties.

Next morning at 5 a.m. the majority of the British army went coursing up both banks of the river in pursuit of the Persian army at Ahwaz. It was an incredible drive. Thousands of vehicles were moving northward at high speed across the dusty plain. It was a sort of mass hue and cry, and everyone wanted to get there first. When the horn of one of our vehicles jammed, the Indian driver crawled out along the running-board as we rushed along at forty miles an hour and fixed it.

Every few miles yellow-furred gazelles would leap across the horizon. Arab villagers, astounded and delighted at this apparition rushing like a tidal wave across the desert, came out to cheer us on. All morning we continued, and then in the full midday heat we came at last to the head of our columns. Once more it was all over.

The Shah himself had telephoned his army commanders to abandon the fight. The defenders of Ahwaz had not had much time to lose. Already they could see the columns of dust from the British vehicles bearing down on them. They sent out an emissary in a civilian car, but he, poor man, was soon hopelessly lost in the long lines of British vehicles. No one at first took any notice of him and he went from one Indian truck to another vainly trying to surrender. At length he reached the brigadier in command and the guns were silenced just as they were about to open up their barrage.

We drove on ahead of the army into Ahwaz and at once lost our way in a huge barracks. Persian soldiers came running out excitedly and jumped on the running-board. A sentry lifted his gun and we stopped. In the barracks the Persians had been told nothing definite—they had simply been confined there—and now they wanted to imprison us. 'It's all over,' we shouted at them in English. 'There is a truce.' And at length they understood and doubtfully let us through.

We drove onto the big modern block by the river where the surrender was taking place. British and Persian generals stood chatting amiably on the verandah. It was indeed all over. Then for us began a fantastic drive through the night to Basra to get our stories away. Half a dozen times we were bogged in the sand. For hours we wandered among the tributaries of the Delta, bumping into slit trenches and barbed wire, doubling around the swamps and coming back onto our own tracks. At length we got across and, more tired than I can ever remember, we flung ourselves down in the lounge of the hotel.

This was the southern sector of the occupation. Next morning we went by train to Baghdad to find out what had happened in the north. It was much the same. After two days the Shah had capitulated. For the first time in this war the Russian and British armies had joined hands.

We hired three Baghdad taxis to make the three-day journey over bad roads to Teheran, the Shah's capital. Now a Baghdad taxi is no ordinary vehicle. Its broken springs are bound together with rope, the rope is soaked in water which has the effect of tautening it, and this contraption is the only liaison between the body and the wheels. The first taxi had proceeded some two hundred yards down the main streets of Baghdad when both doors and the back fell off and the engine exploded. We hired another which boiled but did not explode. There were two or three punctures and once we fell into a ditch, but all three vehicles reached the border at Khankain that night. Immediately the three drivers mutinied. They wanted more money and they wanted to go home. We bargained and finally went to sleep on the stretchers of a hospital train which had been shunted into a siding.

At six the next morning we were on the road again. We bumped along the earth tracks past incredible stone forts and palaces on the frontier and up the formidable Paitak Pass. Then on, endlessly, across the flat-baked land. Gaunt hills flowed past. Villagers came out offering sweet melons and sticky drinks. Occasionally we ran down from the desert into tiny valleys, so green, so shady and refreshing that it was a great hardship not to stop and wash one's burning feet in the streams. But stop we dare not. Each time we did come to a standstill the three drivers at once refused to go on and demanded more money.

My driver was the first to realise that our plan was to keep the three vehicles going, day and night, until they collapsed or reached Teheran—whichever was the sooner. He decided to wreck his vehicle and that was child's play. He ran it over a monstrous rut and smashed what was left of all four springs.

It took a village blacksmith two hours to repair the damage and, meanwhile, the drivers plotted a *tour de force*. It started with non-violence and non-cooperation. They lay down in the shade and slept. We wakened them. They said they had no petrol. We got some. They said their carburettors were not working. We fixed them. They said they had no food. We gave them food. Then Mohammed, the big one, fingered his knife, folded his arms and said, 'Finish. We stop.' Mundy pulled out his revolver.

'You're in the army now,' he said dramatically. 'Come on. Get started.' It was more the way he said it than anything. Scattering broken springs and spare parts, we bumped into Kermanshah at last and lunched off Persian beer and bad eggs. Mundy was practically unconscious with his cold and lay down for a little.

Through the hot afternoon, when the bumping of the taxis became an agony, we passed many demobilised Persian soldiers on the road. They tramped along stolidly, sometimes raising enough energy to throw a curse or a stone, but mostly they were just bored and anxious to get home. In one village the people brought us sweet Persian tea and would not accept money. In the evening we came to Hamadan and slept for a few hours among the bugs in that mockery of an hotel.

All this time we had been passing groups of Indian soldiers encamped beside the road, and now on the third morning we came on their farthest outpost, a company of Gurkhas.

Their officers told us the great meeting between the British and Red forces had taken place the previous day, and now the Russians had withdrawn to Kasvin, some seventy kilometres farther on. Well, that was another story we had missed. We were too weary to care much about it anyway. I was beginning to loathe the whole adventure. We went on doggedly and presently someone said, 'Good God, what's that?'

It was a truckload of troops who seemed at first sight to be Nazis. They sat four abreast in gabardine tunics and jackboots. They had German helmets on their heads, and each man, sitting bold upright, clasped a rifle with a fixed bayonet. Where had I seen this before? A newsreel showing the Nazi entrance into Vienna? We ran alongside. Looking up into their faces, we saw young men with fair hair and blue eyes and round brown cheeks. Hand grenades were strapped to their waists and on their superb shoulders were strapped cartridge belts. Every rifle was an automatic.

They never turned to look at us. They looked straight ahead, sitting there stiffly on the hard wooden seats of their truck, and the truck was running on caterpillars. I looked keenly at the nearest boy and his pleasant, peasant's eyes were blank and rigid, and his great countryman's hand was corded tightly round the barrel of his rifle. He was as erect as a birch tree. He wore a red hammer and sickle badge. In that moment the great Red bluff was exploded for me forever. What about the poor anaemic Russian infantryman who had no boots in Finland? And the dumb herds slaughtered by the Germans in the last war? And the amateur factories that turned out amateur guns and rusty ammunition? And the peasant crushed by the OGPU?

It had been a fine bluff and it had been working steadily for more than two decades. Now at last the Soviets had been forced to show their cards.

And their cards were these young men, athletes all of them, with their iron discipline, their brand new modern weapons, their wonderful shining health. They had that strange thing you see occasionally in young men's faces. It is a mixture of adolescent strength and spiritual resolve, and something else—pride, maybe. I had never seen troops like this before.

As we drove on into Kasvin, we came on one remarkable thing after another. There were multiple pom-poms mounted on tractors that were designed to meet low-flying aircraft. These travelled with the convoys of lorried infantry and filled the rôle a destroyer takes at sea. They had field guns too far off for me to see clearly, but obviously of a recent design. They had armoured cars with a two- pounder gun and two-inch armour on the turret. These cars had eight wheels, two of which in the front could be jacked up clear of the road and used as spares or lowered to help the car across bad ground. They had steel field kitchens and wireless vans. They had streamlined aircraft, faster than our latest Spitfire (though these we did not see until later). They had many tracked vehicles and small scout tanks. All these weapons were in a spotless condition.

The men were in grey-green uniforms and light half-length black knee boots. Woven badges on their arms showed who was an electrician, who a wireless expert, who a tank mechanic and so on. The officers' ranks were marked by little red enamelled badges attached to their tunic lapels—four badges to a general. They all had heavy steel helmets.

Sentries twice sprang from ditches with hand grenades and stopped us. They carried Russian tommy-guns.

We came in the early afternoon to the hotel at Kasvin, the Russian army headquarters. There were Red sentries and armoured cars at the door, and the Persian servants, obviously frightened, were setting out a late luncheon on the dining-room table. One after another the Russian staff officers and commissars came in.

There must have been about twenty of them. They were rough, leathery, sweaty and cheerful. The senior political commissar, a round, porcine little man, looked at me narrowly and said, 'We met in Valencia in the Spanish war.' I could not remember, but it seemed to reassure him greatly. I suppose he was doing one of those underground political jobs in Spain. The general, the last to arrive, was a soft-spoken little man with deceptively gentle manners. A civilian interpreter had bobbed up from somewhere and explained that we were a party of British and American war correspondents on our way to Teheran.

'Ask them to lunch,' said the general; 'we will discuss it later.' The lunch continued until six in the evening. There was the stage where we ate cold chicken and chatted politely through the interpreter. The stage where we toasted Stalin, Roosevelt and Churchill. The stage where we denounced the Germans and filmed one another with my miniature movie camera. The stage where we exchanged badges and sang folk-songs together. And, last scene of all, the stage where I drew off to my bedroom with a splitting head to type my dispatch.

Through all this toasting in fierce Persian vodka, the general was charming but adamant. Teheran, he said, was not yet occupied by the

Allied troops. He, for his part, would be delighted to let us go through, but he had just made an agreement with the British general that no one should pass along the road. Let us produce a pass from the British general and he would countersign it at once and off we should go.

There was nothing for it but to drive back to British headquarters. Mundy and Patrick Crosse of Reuters, who had joined our party, volunteered to make the journey while the rest of us slept. They drove all night, were twice arrested by Red sentries, and in the early morning got back with the pass. By ten o'clock we were on the road again.

Just outside Teheran we stopped to remove our badges and then drove on into the broad streets of the city ostensibly as ordinary civilians.

Teheran just then was playing out the last act of a long and not always comic opera. All the pent-up and bitter feelings of many years of despotic misrule were rising to the surface and ready to break loose. In his palace the Shah, Reza Pahlevi, was beginning to see at last that the game was up. He had gone through all the scenes of which a ruthless and self-willed old man is capable. He had summoned his beaten generals and raged at them and beaten them with the flat of his sword. He had thrown politicians and commanders into prison and shot some of them. He had locked himself up in his room and sulked. He had threatened suicide and revenge. It was too much for this limited and arrogant mind to see its dream of empire broken in a day.

Almost alone he had created this new city with its absurd and empty opera house, its stock exchange and pretentious railway station. They were toys from the western world and he loved them. Year after year he had flung out new highways and built new palaces for his private use, and no one had dared challenge him. He had broken all opposition ruthlessly. Persia was his private domain and its fifteen million people were his slaves. Every one of his childish whims was a high part of the internal politics.

Coming suddenly into this city, one looked down into a dark gulf of medievalism as barbaric as the days of Genghis Khan, as primitive as a fifteenth-century ghetto. Much as he loved the flying machines and the motor cars of the modern world, the Shah disliked the intrusion of modern foreigners in his country. Now that they had come to overturn him, he hated them. There was only one greater hate in Persia and that was borne by the Persian people against their Shah.

A state of corruption and misery unexampled even in war-time Europe had been uncovered by our invasion. Much of the Persian army was unpaid and in a state of semi-mutiny. The Kurds were, in fact, mutinying at that moment. Many thousands of peasants had been impressed into road gangs and set to work in the gorges of the Elburz Mountains where daily more than one was accidentally killed. The only payment was food. Disobedience meant the whip. As a population, the people were in rags and the swollen bellies of the children I had seen in the villages showed how far famine and disease were spreading. The gaols were full and filthy. The scale of taxation was only matched by the prevailing system of bribery.

The great wealth of the country—much of it from royalties paid by the Anglo-Iranian Oil Company—was being slowly and steadily drawn into the Shah's own hands by a network of monopolies and taxation. His wealth was immense and he was spending it with the egocentric vulgarity of a pork-and- beans millionaire on his first trip to Paris.

When he came to go, the old man still had his soldierly bearing and his pride, but this was not enough to diminish the outraged feelings of his people. At the end there was scarcely one man left in Persia to weep for him.

All this had been a pretty easy market for the German minister Count von Ettel. Herr von Ettel played heavily upon the Shah's vanity and cupidity. For example, when he had heard that the British were wrangling with the Shah over the price of a wireless transmitter for the capital, he had hurried to the palace and offered the finest set Germany could produce as a free gift from the German people. It cost, I suppose, some thirty thousand pounds, which was cheap, considering the advantages it brought in its wake. Soon Germany began to flood Persia with cheap manufactured goods, house fittings, garden tools, electrical equipment, plumbing odds and ends, and anything that could be made with bakelite and ersatz.

Never in my life have I seen so many shops filled with electrical goods as I saw in Teheran. The majority of the people in Persia have no electrical current.

Germans had begun to arrive in increasing numbers. They edged their way into the broadcasting and newspaper business so that the majority of the news items were from the Axis. They began to get the contracts for such state monopolies as the airways. The Shah owned all the hotels in the country, and they did business with him there. Little by little they were beginning to undermine the oil concessions granted to the Anglo-Iranian Oil Company. It was a grand game while it lasted.

But now von Ettel himself was in trouble. He was locked up in his summer legation in the hills above the town, and some six hundred

German subjects were encamped in the legation gardens, hoping that Hitler would find some way of getting them out. The Italian legation was in much the same position. So were the Bulgarians, Rumanians and Hungarians. Just for once, the Allies had got in first and put the Axis on the spot.

Governing everything was one dominating fear—fear, not of the British, but the Russians. In the last war the Russians had come into this country, they had seized Kasvin, the very town they now held again, and they had been ruthlessly severe. Every Persian I spoke to seemed mortally afraid of the Russians. The people of Teheran were spreading the most hair-raising stories of Red rape, pillage and violence.

The German and Italian nationals also were petitioning that they should be handed over, not to the Russians, but to us. It was interesting to see that even after the bombing of England these remote little hangers-on of the Axis believed that there was still goodwill to be found for them among the British. And they had a proportionate fear of the Russians. I had seen the same thing at the fall of Addis Ababa. Even at the moment of their capture Italians and Germans will adopt a confident, almost insolent, manner because they have a conviction that they will be treated well by the British.

Von Ettel exploited this now to the utmost. While the two allied armies waited outside the capital, he haggled over the lists of names of those who had diplomatic privileges and those who had to be handed over. He argued, delayed and bargained. He pretended to be ill. He made agreements and broke them on a technical point to gain just a little more time. Even when the trains were sent, he at first failed to deliver the wanted men, and when they finally appeared they went off in a hail of salutes and Sieg Heils which I suppose was a snub to us. The presence of just one platoon of Red soldiers in the town would have made such a difference.

There were comic moments, of course. One day we drove up to the nearby hills where the Shah had built a sort of pleasure garden and tourist hotel which was a nice blending of Bournemouth and Montreux. Sitting high upon the terrace there was Raschid Ali's rebel cabinet. They had fled here after the failure of their revolt in Baghdad a few months previously, and now they sat moodily gazing into a fountain. Poor little men in their striped trousers and black coats. I wonder what has become of them.

Then we dined one night in a restaurant where a couple of German youths, half drunk, were sitting at one of the tables. When they saw us they began to shout their Sieg Heils. One of them banged his fist on the table and glared at me. I suppose I should have offered to fight. As it was, they got up after a bit and staggered out. They, or someone, staged a small demonstration for us when we emerged later. We were often hissed and booed in the streets on our way to and from the Firdausi Hotel. Despite the absence of our badges we were still in uniform, since we had no civilian clothes, and the town was full of demobilised Persian officers who were feeling bitter.

At the censorship—all through this charade we had to send out messages through the Persian censor—we sometimes used to run into Japanese, German and Italian correspondents who still kept filing dispatches to the Domei, D.N.B. and Stefani agencies. Since Nazis still controlled the radio station they managed to get some of our messages delayed or stopped until we protested and got the Nazi controller sacked.

There were pleasant moments when we went through the shops and bazaars buying German cameras and Persian sheepskin coats, when we lazed in the Luards' swimming bath or spread ourselves on Persian vodka and kebab. The wines were bad, the beer passable. The caviare brought freshly from the Caspian was no pleasure to me since I dislike it, but the others gorged themselves.

While we were waiting in Teheran for the departure of the Axis nationals and the dethronement of the Shah in favour of his son, we decided to visit the Caspian Sea where the Red fleet was in occupation. I set out in the same deplorable taxis with Clifford, Sam Brewer of the *Chicago Tribune* and one or two others. All of us had travelled widely in Europe, but none had seen such fantastic country as this. The road across the Elburz Mountains climbed ten thousand feet into a tumbled mass of fiery peaks. These peaks, utterly barren, were fashioned by some convulsion of the earth into monstrous shapes, so that sometimes a vast scarlet and yellow razorback rose up in front of the road, and all the heights beyond fell into crenellated ridges. Great synclines and anticlines of vivid rock arched like bridges across the valleys and the mountains or tumbled into screes of broken stone.

Except along the torrents below, not a single tree grew, and the effect of this awful country was to fill the mind with images of huge sprawling dragons and fabulous monsters. I looked and looked until I became dizzy with the tremendous spectacle. It was a relief at the summit to plunge into a long tunnel where the damp rocks were sweating runnels of mountain water and the hot sunlight at the other end shone like a candle through the intervening darkness.

We came out on the northern side into a new world where trees grew and bright ferns lay heaped on each other on the walls of the gorges. This was the road where the labourers clinging to the sheer rocks had lost their foothold through fatigue and giddiness, and gone screaming down into the pits and crevasses of the range. Few gorges were less than two thousand feet deep. At the foot of the range we came upon the most irresistibly lovely sight I had seen since I left England eighteen months before.

We drove into a beech forest dripping with fine rain, and along the muddy country lanes willows, oaks and elms were growing. It was almost too much to accept after so long in the harsh colours of the Middle Eastern deserts. It was as though someone had suddenly lifted a curtain and the whole world had turned itself into a stage. They told us that bears, wolves, leopards, wild boar and occasionally tigers roamed through the woods. We heard the sound of an axe on a wet tree trunk, and ran past meadows of a Devon greenness where cattle were grazing. We saw farms and hunting lodges, and I suppose the wet fresh smell of the forest had the same nostalgia for all of us for we said nothing.

We dropped at last below sea-level to the shores of the Caspian and drove into the flowering gardens of Chalus. Six Red sentries blocked the road.

Sam remembered a few Russian phrases and Clifford seems to be able to speak any language he likes after about ten minutes. Between them they made the introductions. Cluttered up with his tommy- gun and his hand grenades, the Russian corporal bowed from the hips, an astonishing gesture, and told us to report to his officer a few kilometres east along the coast.

Now we were really enjoying ourselves. The Caspian was grey and limitless, a wonderful vision after the desert. From the green forests little mountain streams raced across the road into the black sand beaches. Two Russian destroyers lay at anchor, and again one felt that sudden uplift of excitement about the Red forces. From a distance these ships looked exactly like our latest destroyers, only a little more rakish and modern in outline. If fresh grey paint goes for anything, they were beautifully maintained. Two more sentries, tommy-guns braced evenly in their hands ready for action, blocked the way to the wharves. Strange uniforms only meant enemy to them, and we went forward keeping our hands elaborately away from our sides. Then the lieutenant came along in blue gabardine with a blue cap and an anchor badge on the band. He was absurdly handsome and his teeth were like an American toothpaste advertisement.

As soon as we approached, the two sentries saluted and jumped to attention; and at attention they stayed throughout the whole interview. When the officer called a marine along the beach the marine RAN toward him, saluted, stood to attention while he got his orders, saluted again, and then RAN back to his post.

These men were keyed to a discipline I have yet to see in our army, or any other army. It may be that they are all comrades together, but the Red officer on the job gets the sort of skilled and immediate obedience we don't often see off the parade ground. At Kasvin a sentry had been posted outside my bedroom door. It had been almost unnerving the way he had swept up to attention and a full salute when I merely appeared in the distance. Here on the Caspian this was no rehearsed parade for the benefit of foreigners. We had arrived unexpectedly, their first visitors, and probably, apart from Persians, the first foreigners these men had ever seen.

The lieutenant wrote us out a safe conduct at once. He grinned and seemed to take the whole thing in his stride and I would much like to have talked at length to him. All the rest of that afternoon we drove along the southern littoral of the Caspian to Ramsar.

At Ramsar the Shah had built himself a monument to his vanity. It was an hotel. He resolved that this hotel should outdo the hotels of Europe, and now here, reaching up the sea plain before us, was the result. I suppose there were some two square miles of gardens in the French style with a Casino stuck at the edge on the black beach. Terraced stone steps flowed everywhere like rivers. Marble statues bobbed up out of every nook and alcove. The façade of the hotel was a vast and heroic bas- relief done in some sort of grey composite. The Armenian architect had fairly let himself go inside. It was a mad dream of scarlet and gold, of chandeliers and plush. Rich and riotous Persian carpets were flung about with the confusion of confetti.

It was like entering a Victorian museum or a funfair or Madame Tussaud's. A neat little Swiss presided over the empty rooms, and he told us sadly of the great days when the Shah and von Ettel and all the diplomats came down here to stay.

The head policeman of Ramsar, bulbous, sweating and surmounted by a Prussian helmet, had met us on the steps. It seemed that the Russians had not called here yet, and in a long lyrical speech he offered us the surrender of the town. We took him inside and sat with him far into the night eating caviare and drinking vodka and lemonade. We were asked to go pig-sticking in the forest on the morrow, but declined.

Each time the policeman spoke, he clipped his heels, bowed and raised his glass in a toast. He was very hot and very thirsty.

It soon turned out that all the stories of Red atrocities were untrue. True, the Cossacks had frightened the people badly by riding through the town at a gallop. True, they had seized certain stocks of sugar and other provisions they needed. True, their aircraft had bombed Pahlevi, the town along the coast.

But their fleet had not opened fire. What had happened at Pahlevi was that at the last moment the Persians had attempted to camouflage their warships by decorating them with branches of trees and shrubs, which they had brought down from the hills. But then a Russian cruiser appeared and the crews took to their heels. The Belgian consul had saved the day by rowing out to one of the Persian ships and hoisting the white flag before the Russians attacked.

A word here about the Russian commissars. They wore the same uniforms as the soldiers and held similar ranks. They were responsible directly to Moscow and not to the army command. In all matters apart from operations, they appeared to have control. They handled the administration of conquered territories, the financial and economic affairs of the army and propaganda. They were the liaison between the soldier and the state. They were the governors of the army. They watched morale and were the authorities on all normal civilian affairs. They exerted considerable power. Thus when one Red officer, an engineer, wanted to show me a medal he had in his pocket and a photograph of his wife and children, I noticed that he first glanced quickly over his shoulder at the nearest commissar— in this case my fat friend from Valencia. The commissar nodded and the engineer displayed his souvenirs.

Clearly the suspicions of the Russians were boundless. They trusted no foreigner unless they had to. Yet before I left Persia the British and Russian commanders had worked out an agreement and it seemed to be operating smoothly enough. Little by little, relations became closer in Persia. A great highroad for supplies to Russia was developed through the country. With the occupation of Persia a continuous front from Murmansk to the Western Desert of Egypt was secured. The Russians had gone into Persia with six divisions, we with two. Not ten per cent of those forces were needed in action.

The casualties were trifling—perhaps a few hundred in all. For the Persians themselves only good could flow from the occupation, for their new Shah, who was crowned in Persia in September, broke the royal monopolies, opened the political prisons, paid the army, reduced the taxes and took advice. Food was quickly brought in to feed his famished subjects. It began to appear that there was some reasonable future ahead of the country despite the war.

I made that romantic journey back to Cairo by road, passing through Baghdad, Damascus, Nazareth and Jerusalem. It was time enough. Things were beginning to move again in the desert.

Three

October in the Desert

BACK IN Cairo friends had loaned us another flat on the island and we were in the turmoil of moving—a crazy business of donkey carts in Egypt. Lucy had left her old job and it was decided that she should go to the commander-in-chief as his private secretary. I was opposed to this partly because it meant very long hours of work in the heat and partly because I felt it would lead to a difficult and somewhat absurd situation between us. As General Auchinleck's secretary, she would be handling his correspondence with the War Cabinet and the most secret messages in the Middle East. I felt that if I obtained any exclusive information in the normal course of my job and wrote it, I would be accused of having got it from my wife. I also wanted to be free to criticise the high command up to the limits allowed by the censorship. However, we agreed to see how things worked out, and Lucy went to work in a converted scullery adjoining the general's office in the block of flats which was G.H.Q.

Auchinleck up to this time had been something of a mystery. He had slipped quietly into this job from India, and for some reason through a long career he had escaped or avoided the publicity which clung so relentlessly to the other generals like Gort, Ironside and Wavell.

His record did not promise genius. His had been the most regular of all regular army lives. He was even born at Aldershot, the Vatican of British soldiering, and his father was a gunner. They said— inevitably— that as a boy he used to dig trenches round the family orchard and that he drilled his younger brothers and sisters. He went, of course, to Sandhurst, and one might almost guess the rest— the commission in the 62nd Punjabs in India at the age of twenty, the fighting against the Turks in the Middle East through the last war, the lonely soldier home on leave during the early 1920s when everyone wanted to forget soldiering, the marriage with the pretty girl he met in France, the return to the India of polo and rhythmical promotion.

Up and up he went, with never a move out of character. There was the fighting on the north-west frontier, the term at the Imperial Defence College in England, that nursery of generals, then back to rising commands in India. Colonel, brigadier, major-general, lieutenant-general. This war had brought him a brief command in Norway, a brisk administrative job preparing the south of England after Dunkirk, and then finally that ultimate goal of every regular officer in the empire army—commander- in-chief, India.

No, none of it was very exciting. It was believed in the Middle East, with reason, that something more than an efficient but average general was wanted to restore our losses and take the offensive. Wavell's personal magnetism, which seemed to survive every setback in the war, had made it very difficult for a successor to step into the Middle East command. The sudden removal of Wavell to the India command was not liked in Cairo, or the desert.

The man who stepped out of his aircraft one hot morning in June 1941 to take command in Cairo was, of course, utterly different from his reputation…or, rather, different from what everyone expected him to be. But when people had got over their first surprise at finding him so different, and Auchinleck had taken his two defeats in the desert, it was again fashionable to point to his prosaic career and say, 'He lacked new ideas, drive, initiative.'

Both views—the early reaction in his favour and the subsequent tendency to regard him as just another regular officer—were hopelessly mistimed and misinformed. This book is no defence of General Auchinleck. But it is an attempt to describe his two campaigns in the desert and explain how they went wrong under the direction of this vigorous and intelligent mind.

There is a strange contradiction in nearly everything about Auchinleck, and this in the end is probably the reason why success was always snatched away from him just at the moment when it seemed secure. He had extraordinary charm and gentleness in conversation, and he could be utterly ruthless. Half a dozen times he sacked some of his closest associates who failed—sacked them overnight so that one day they were in charge of a sector of the battle in the desert and the next on their way to England and retirement. In each case he maintained a bigoted loyalty to these men until they made their major mistake, and you might argue from this that he was no chooser of men.

For a man who had been ridden by British army drill and discipline for forty years, Auchinleck had a mind of quite exceptional freshness and originality. He would seize on every new idea and explore it at once. He was ready to meet everyone and anyone. He brimmed with ideas himself. He was very easy to talk to. With all this he was still scarcely known to his men or the public. That curious psychology by which everyone in the Middle East felt that they knew Wavell personally never operated in the case of Auchinleck. With all the instincts of a social and gregarious human being, he had never learned how to make contact with the world at large. He loathed public speeches as much as he enjoyed private conversation. He almost never broadcast. He avoided social engagements.

Almost the first thing Auchinleck did on his arrival in Cairo was to turn his house on Gezira into a combined barracks and officers' mess. Wavell with his large and youthful family used to hold open house there every Sunday, and often the place was full of the noise and laughter of young men and girls. The last time I had gone there in Wavell's tenure, a wedding reception was being held, and as the general stood receiving the guests, orderlies kept coming up with urgent messages. Undisturbed by the wedding scene, Wavell would open and read his telegrams and then turn back to his guests again.

A few months later I went there with Tony Phillpotts, Auchinleck's personal assistant. I went through one empty, flowerless room after another. The place had become what the general intended it should be—a barracks.

Auchinleck was an ascetic. He had no private life. Despite his charming manner and his sense of humour, he was deeply and irrevocably serious. The army was the ruling passion of his life. He had no interests outside the war. He did not smoke. He could never really relax for two minutes.

There were no children in Auchinleck's family, and because the rest of the men in the army were forbidden to bring their wives to Cairo, he left his own wife in India. When I crossed to India I met Lady Auchinleck in New Delhi, and it seemed to me—as indeed it seemed to her—that she should have been with her husband in Cairo. I can only imagine the difference she would have made to that barracks. It was not only that she was an American, that she was many years younger than her husband, nor even that these two were deeply attached to one another. Lady Auchinleck had a vivacity which would have acted benignly on that serious house in Cairo, and I think she would have brought a good deal of comfort and encouragement there when things were going wrong.

As things were, Auchinleck was set upon his own course—alone. He enjoyed command. He had enough moral courage to accept any situation, and some of his biggest decisions, like the dismissal of General Cunningham at the moment when Rommel was breaking through, were taken on his own responsibility. Yet Auchinleck was forever deputing his authority, and kept believing that his commanders in the field possessed the same foresight and rapidity of decision that he did.

He believed that he could control the battle from Cairo, and that it was possible to galvanise his men with a stream of advice and encouragement sent out from headquarters. In the light of the last two campaigns, it is apparent that the desert is not geared to remote control. No admiral has succeeded in fighting a naval battle from a shore base. Things move too quickly on an open front like the desert. It was not until after the fall of Tobruk in the midsummer of 1942 that Auchinleck at last accepted this fact and went down to the front to take personal command. Rommel had been at the front the whole time. Often he was in a tank and directing his men 'in clear' over the radio telephone. He was stopped only when Auchinleck took up a similar position on the opposite side of the line.

It is only fair to say here that Auchinleck had an amazing run of bad luck with his generals. There had been in the desert since the outbreak of the war a number of young commanders of exceptional ability and toughness. One after another they were killed, usually in accidents, or captured through some trifling unforeseeable reason. Air Marshal Boyd and Lieutenant-General Carton de Wiart were shot down near Italy on the way out and captured. Lieutenant-General O'Connor, a dynamic little Irishman, led that first fantastic march south of the Jebel Akdar and annihilated the Italian army at Beda Fomm. He was very nearly the ideal desert commander, but he took a wrong turning on the way back from Benghazi and was picked up by the Nazis with two other experienced British generals.

There were two brigadiers, Russell and Gott, who were outstanding leaders in Wavell's first campaign, and Gott through his brilliance and tenacity and personal courage was becoming a legend in the desert. Both were killed in aircraft. Tilly, another general, contracted pneumonia and died as soon as he reached the desert. Pope, an expert in armoured fighting, crashed in the same aircraft as Russell. Jock Campbell, a sort of Francis Drake of the desert, the man with the greatest daring and enterprise on either side, died on the Sollum escarpment when his car overturned. Young veterans like Coombes, O'Carroll and Garmoyle were killed or captured at critical moments in the fighting. Other irreplaceable men like Freyberg, Gatehouse, Briggs and Lumsden were wounded by Stuka bombs or stray bullets when they were most needed.

This total of nearly twenty commanders goes beyond mere coincidence or the normal fortunes of battle. The loss of O'Connor, Gott and Campbell alone was a far more serious disaster than the loss of Benghazi or even possibly of Tobruk. When they and the others went, it meant that Auchinleck simply did not have the men to lead his troops in the desert. Even those who had failed—half a dozen or more—had been sent home or to other jobs, and could not be recalled.

However, during September 1941 most of these misfortunes lay ahead, and all we knew of Auchinleck was that he was working with great urgency and speed in G.H.Q.

His personal appearance and address had made a great impression, for he was a strikingly handsome man, looking at least ten years younger than his fifty-eight. Many senior officers went to his room with some misgiving, for it was rumoured that a purge was about to start among the staff. They went in like lambs and came out like tigers. Auchinleck, they found, was a pleasant, amiable fellow. He had friendly blue eyes, thick reddish hair, a strong vigorous face with the usual faint military moustache. Physically he was a fine sight, a tall distinguished officer who had no affectations. He wore the shorts and shirt which had now been adopted right through the ranks. There was no stuffiness about him. The new general was feeling his way carefully. The purge did not come until later.

I went down to the desert to see this new Eighth Army which Auchinleck was creating. It was nearly seven months since I had been in the desert and I cannot say I was very enthusiastic about going back. The road down from Cairo to Alexandria was just the same except that there was more traffic on it. We turned left outside Alexandria and drove along the coast road as I had done so often—past the fig plantations and the wonderful turquoise sea at Alamein, where the sunlight strikes the white seabed and is reflected back to the surface so that the water is full of dancing light and colour. Then over the bad bumpy part of the road that takes you into the supply base at Daba, where there always was and always will be a sandstorm. Daba had a restaurant now with paper flowers on the tables and bacon and fresh eggs on the menu. That was something quite new. After Daba we got into a traffic jam which was a wonderfully encouraging thing to see. It went on and on for many miles— tanks, heavy lorries and twenty-five-pounder guns, staff cars, transporters and signal wagons, anti- tank guns and anti-aircraft guns, travelling workshops, water wagons, ammunition trucks and still more tanks. This procession reached all the way to Cairo, two hundred miles away, but it had thickened here. Everything was moving forward to the front.

Beside the road, at places like Fuka, I saw many squadrons of new aircraft, new tent cities, new dumps for petrol, spare parts, food and general stores. There were a couple of new prisoners' camps. Many aircraft kept sweeping by overhead. That little piratical force Wavell had sent to Benghazi had become a great army. The war correspondents' old camp at Bagush I simply could not recognise. It was like coming into a hotel. An officer met us, took our names, allotted us to tents—*tents*, we never had tents before—and our bed-rolls were carried off for us. They said dinner would be ready in an hour, and if we did not want a swim we could go into the bar. This was the first time anyone had cooked a meal for us, and as for bars, those were the sort of things one talked about nostalgically and never saw. There were enough new vehicles for everyone; enough petrol, enough rations, enough maps. The only thing lacking was war. It was dead quiet at the front, a day's run farther on.

Russell Hill, Alaric Jacob of Reuters and myself made up a party to run down to the desert oasis at Siwa. It was a journey of a day and a half, and in this late October weather the air was clean and sharp in the morning and the evening, and we slept under two blankets a night. I still had the Italian mattress and waterproof sheet I had captured in the last campaign, and in addition to these a blue Italian canvas jacket which I had lined with a sheepskin bought in Teheran.

It was mostly a joy ride. For miles the surface of the desert was as unspoiled as a mountainside after a fresh fall of snow. Travelling at nearly forty miles an hour in our two Ford trucks, we just broke the crusty surface of the sand, and it was like travelling on a speedway. The shells of white desert snails crunched under the tyres. Along the track, which we avoided because of the dust, long lines of ten-ton lorries were coasting down to the oasis, and in the evening they sometimes had the appearance of a convoy of ships moving in line across the horizon.

At Siwa the floor of the desert broke suddenly into steep-sided valleys and weird little plateaux studded with gravel and pink rock. We ran down below sea-level, past the new barbed-wire entanglements and the notice saying, 'You are in a malarious area. Do not forget your precautions.'

Siwa is the sort of place you see described in the *National Geographic* magazine. It is a long lozenge-shaped depression, sprinkled with clumps of date-palms which bear, they say, the finest dates in the world. Fresh crystal springs flow from the hot soil, and these, in ancient times, were locked in stone-sided pools full of strange fish and malarial mosquitoes.

There are a series of small mud villages, and since all are in ruins it is not easy to distinguish which are inhabited and which are not. When your home collapses in Siwa, which is fairly often, you simply erect a new one on the ruins. This practice has been going on for some hundreds of years and the result is a series of ramshackle skyscrapers and labyrinthine passages. The general effect is of a huge and dilapidated beehive.

The Siwans themselves enjoy a lurid reputation for wickedness. Many of the women who passed us wearing scarlet robes and their hair matted with grease practised Lesbianism, we were told. This apparently had developed of late years as a retort to the men who had long since fallen into the vice of homosexuality. The war had accelerated this moral decline, and young girls were being offered for as little as two Egyptian pounds a head.

Siwa was once an Egyptian army base and a number of concrete bungalows had been built to house the troops. In one of these we settled down among the mosquitoes for the night. We got a ration of one quinine pill each. In the morning an Italian three-motored reconnaissance machine came over low enough for us to wave at the pilot. The enemy were very suspicious of Siwa at this time, and machines were coming over almost daily to photograph those long lines of British transports travelling southward into the oasis. It was conceivable that when the British attack began, a large- scale flanking movement might strike northward from this point or from the more westward oasis of Jarabub.

We swam in the rock pools and clambered over the temple of Ammon Ra which was supposed to have been visited by Alexander the Great. Then we struck out along the uneven floor of the valley toward Jarabub.

Jarabub is the spiritual home of the Senussi tribe, and its claim to a place on the map is based on a waterhole and a mosque. You reach it by crossing the tail end of Mussolini's famous fence which divides Egypt from Libya. The fence is some four hundred miles long on a north-south line, and its ten-foot thickness is made up of tangled barbed wire and steel stakes bedded in concrete, a notable and useless engineering achievement. At Jarabub the shifting sand had silted up the fence and you drive straight over the top of it. To the south the sand sea sprawls majestically. Its immense dunes flow for hundreds of miles like the endless swell of a tropical ocean, and in the evening the sand turns to vivid pinks and purples. It is possible in a light car to travel across that awful waste, but in Arab legend it is a place of mystery and disaster. Certainly no heavy armoured vehicles could get through, and so the war stopped at the edge of the sand sea.

Even here on the northern shore near Jarabub we stuck for hours in the heavy sand. In Jarabub itself we found nothing happening—just the steady preparation for battle, the troops digging into rock caves in the wild and ragged cliffs, the armoured cars going out each day on patrol into Libya.

At Melfa, close by, we found a wide lake of sparkling water too salt to drink but fresh and cool for swimming. The flies swarmed in billions. We turned slowly back to the coast. In the early evening we stopped and camped in the open, beside the trucks. In the morning we took our compass bearing again and drove on through empty and featureless desert, sometimes passing the derelicts of earlier skirmishes, sometimes sighting convoys in the distance. Over many hundreds of miles the desert was quiet and undisturbed. Sometimes we saw gazelle, which do not drink but simply suck the dew and moisture from chance shrubs. Sometimes birds passed overhead, part of those great migratory flocks that swing back and forth across Africa with the seasons. Once I caught sight of a desert rat, the jerboa, one of the tribe which preys upon the occasional birds that weaken in their long flight and fall in helpless exhaustion to the sand. A round and lovely moon began to come in, and our little party would sit talking by its light. All around was perfect, unbroken silence. We felt so secure in that endless space that we posted no sentries at night to guard against the approach of German patrols. The enemy seemed very distant, and the fact that their patrols did occasionally come exploring only added a sense of mild excitement to the other sensations of remoteness, of quiet and of deep peace.

It was the last time I was to see the desert at peace for nearly a year. The old days of small piratical raids were gone. The desert was filling up with thousands upon thousands of armed men. Two great armies, as mobile and heavily armed as any in Russia, lay camped within half a day's distance of one another. As more and more guns and tanks were pressed into the desert, the days of peace were running out rapidly. The new battle when it came would no longer be a border skirmish but a full-scale test of strength between the Germans and the British.

Little by little, as I moved around the desert, I began to piece together the dispositions of both armies and weigh the chances of success. On our side General Sir Alan Cunningham, who had done so well in Ethiopia against the Italians, had two army corps of roughly three divisions each. In the extreme north opposite Sollum and Sidi Omar lay the Indians and the New Zealanders, and they had a division of South Africans in reserve. In the centre were three newly equipped British armoured brigades with supporting artillery. In the south, the line was held by another division of South Africans and more Indians—these last based in Jarabub. In addition there were about twenty thousand British and Polish troops in Tobruk with something up to one hundred infantry tanks.

In all, Cunningham could call upon about one hundred thousand men, eight hundred tanks and nearly one thousand aircraft of all kinds.

Rommel had somewhat more men. Spaced mostly around Tobruk were the following Italian divisions—Brescia, Trento, Trieste, Pavia and Bologna. These were infantry, some of them motorised. The 90th Light German Infantry with more Italians held the frontier bases, Bardia, Sollum, Halfaya Pass, as well as positions around Tobruk. The Axis armour consisted of the German 21st Panzer Division under the command of Major-General Ravenstein, the 15th Panzer Division under Major-General Neumann-Silkow, and the Italian Ariete Division. In all Rommel could count about one hundred and twenty thousand men, four hundred tanks and somewhat fewer aircraft than we had.

Both commanders were planning to attack about the same time. Rommel proposed to bring the main weight of his armour and guns upon the south-eastern sector of Tobruk perimeter and take the garrison by assault. On the border he proposed to do nothing more than hold for the time being.

Cunningham planned to contain the enemy garrison on the border by running a horseshoe formation round it—the Indians to hold the eastern arm, the New Zealanders to hold the western arm. The British armour, supported by the South Africans, was to go through the wire fence at Fort Maddalena in the centre and hunt for the enemy armour. They were to force the Axis tanks to fight by running a cordon round them—a cordon reaching from Maddalena to the outskirts of Tobruk.

While the tanks were engaged, the Tobruk garrison was to sally out in the south-east as far as El Duda and there link hands with the New Zealanders coming along the coast road through Gambut. In the far south the Indians were to make a diversion by sending out an expedition to the desert post of Jalo south-east of Benghazi. Once the German armour was destroyed—and this was paramount—the whole army was to sweep on to Benghazi and beyond to Tripoli if possible.

The British were to attack on the morning of November 18th. The Germans proposed to start their assault of Tobruk about November 23rd. Neither side was quite sure of the other's plans, though each had a pretty shrewd idea. We would not have attacked on the 18th if we had known definitely that Rommel proposed his Tobruk adventure for a few days later. It would have been pleasant to have allowed Rommel to get his main forces stuck into Tobruk and then to have taken him in the rear. On Rommel's side, it is evident that had he known of our zero hour he would have shelved his Tobruk attack and disposed his forces differently.

Four

November in Attack

GENERAL SIR Alan Cunningham, the brother of the admiral, and at that time in command of the British forces in the desert, called the war correspondents into his concrete dugout at Bagush on the night of November 16th. He was a blue-eyed, ruddy-complexioned man with a soft voice, and he smiled a good deal. He looked more like a successful businessman than a general even when he said to us, 'I am going to attack the day after tomorrow…everything depends on how the battle goes.'

We trooped up and out into cloudy night. There were no stars and Matt Halton and I stood still for a moment to accustom our eyes to the darkness. Then we began to move slowly across the sand-dunes to our camp. We were too preoccupied to talk much or watch where we were going. Out in front of us a hundred thousand men lay camped in the sand, British, Germans and Italians, and others like the Poles who had drifted into this arena by the haphazard course of war. No shot was fired.

All around us men were asleep. The sea moved easily and quietly along the beach. The one irresistible thought that filled my mind was that within thirty-six hours all these placid, sleeping men were going to rise up and start killing one another. Nothing could stop the battle taking place. All the orders were given, the guns placed, the tanks grouped and ready, and the empty beds standing row on row in the field hospitals. It seemed a calculated cruelty. The inevitability of the battle was the hardest thing to accept. I kept perversely remembering one night nearly two years before when I had stood hour after hour on the cobblestones outside the prison in Versailles waiting for the murderer Weidmann to be beheaded. They had erected the guillotine, tested it, roped off the crowd, backed the hearse into the square and then with the utmost punctuality they had brought Weidmann out at dawn and cut off his head. Now it was not one man but a hundred thousand.

I began to say something about these morbid ideas to Matt and we fell into argument. He saw the colour and the movement of the battle. In the end we agreed that the inevitability of a catastrophe—the actual knowing of the zero hour—was the hardest thing to take. It was easier to be left: in doubt.

By this time we were hopelessly lost and we roamed about for an hour by the sea before we reached our camp where the others were finishing off the last of the beer. There was an air of nervous excitement as we marked our maps and made our plans to move up to the front at dawn.

It took us all next day. We ran down the good coast road beyond Mersa Matruh and then turned deep into the open desert down the Siwa track. Clifford, Richard Busvine of the *Chicago Tribune*, a little Scots conducting officer and myself rode ahead in a Humber staff car. Our two trucks filled with bedding, water, petrol and provisions followed on behind.

It rained in squalls of bitter sleet that night. Like artillery, the lightning came rushing from the Mediterranean and, as we lay awake and watching in the open, the water seeped through bedding, blankets, groundsheets—everything. Men crouched against the sides of tanks and guns in the futile struggle to stay dry. The infantry sat numbly in their trucks with their greatcoat collars turned up over their ears. No aircraft could take off from the sodden sticky sand. It was a cold, miserable and disheartening start for the battle. Bedraggled and wet, we trailed on in the wake of the soldiers. Every track we took was the wrong one. Somehow the great lumbering Eighth Army had got itself into motion, and there were hundreds upon hundreds of vehicles all bumping across

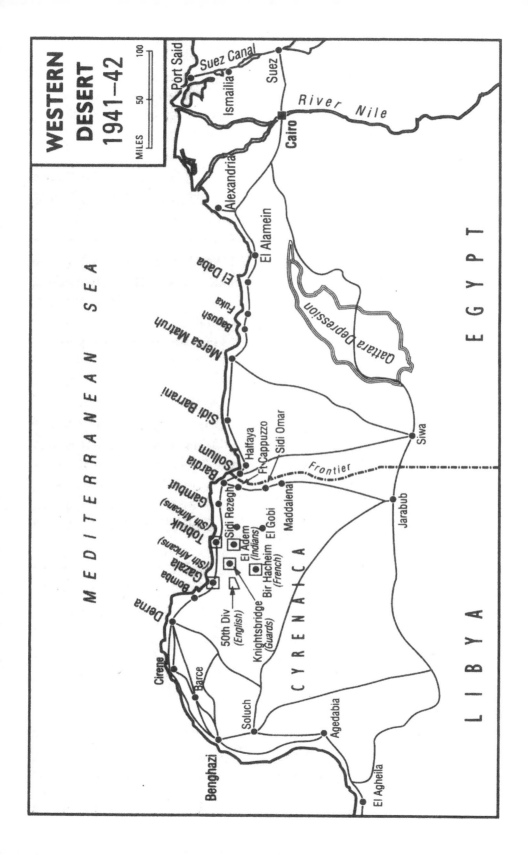

the sand in different directions. The general trend was west into Libya, but no one seemed to have a clear idea of what was happening or where we were going. Sometimes for hours we coasted along with South African supply convoys, and then, giving that up, we turned aside to chase a few stray guns on the move or paused miserably to brew a cup of tea and make some new plan for getting where we wanted to go— the front where the tanks were in battle.

Still that night we had seen no action and we camped a few miles east of the frontier wire near Fort Maddalena. A cold fierce wind had succeeded the storm. In the morning it was better. We passed the ruins of Fort Maddalena in the early sunshine, and the sky now was full of British fighters and bombers passing on to the front. A great part of the southern part of the army had swept through this break in the wire at Maddalena, and now we began to catch up with it. There were remarkable mirages in the desert that day. At times you could see on the horizon a towered city that floated on a lake and undulated as you watched like a stage backcloth blown in the wind. Small bushes looked in the distance like great trees, and each truck was a two-storeyed house passing through the dust. Often we saw groups of castles on the horizon. As we approached, these turned to battleships and then at last from a mile away they resolved into the solid shapes of tanks. We were getting up among the fighting troops at last. But still no one could direct us to Corps Headquarters, and when we did find the location it was too late—Corps had moved on. Again in the evening when we were tired and angry and had seen nothing, we were still embroiled in the endless and meaningless cavalcade of lorries. Once a stranded tank crew had prevented us from driving straight into the Italian lines. We had heard firing then, and there was talk of forty Italian tanks having been knocked out, but we could get nothing definite.

Unknown to us, much of the army was in the same condition as ourselves. The tanks, guns and lorries had poured helter-skelter into Libya and at first no enemy was to be found anywhere. There was a very good reason for this. Rommel, incredible as it may sound, had been taken by surprise. He was far behind the front when scouts came rushing to his headquarters with the news that the British army was on the move and that it was no 'reconnaissance in force' but a full-scale offensive.

Hurriedly Rommel had called off the Tobruk affair and, with that sure instinct of his for organisation, had begun bunching his tanks together. A large body of these German tanks now came scouring down the border fence to test the strength of the invaders.

By this time Cunningham had succeeded in laying his various layers round the Axis forces. The Indians were entrenched with their minefields east of Sollum and had approached Sidi Omar farther to the south on the frontier. The New Zealanders had rounded the German frontier positions and were making up toward Sollum, inside the German lines. The three British armoured brigades, a band of steel in these soft layers of infantry, had strung themselves in a shallow arc from Maddalena to the outskirts of Tobruk, and south of them the sprawling mass of the South African division lay in support.

The other two British moves were also in operation—the garrison at Tobruk had begun to sally out toward El Duda, there to await the arrival of the New Zealanders coming along the coast; and the diversionary column from Jarabub had set out on its long forced march to Jalo, south of Benghazi.

The whole British plan seemed to be based on the assumption that the Germans once surrounded would be forced to fight from inside while their dumps and lines of communication lay outside. But you cannot isolate a force in the desert. We were committed to the policy of getting behind the enemy and forcing him to battle. It was like penning a savage bull in a hencoop.

Although we outnumbered the enemy in tanks and guns, the forces were far too small to surround him. In the attempt to carry out the manoeuvre that ancient and fatal error of desert warfare was committed on a mammoth scale—the three British tank brigades were divided. The first of these, the 4th Brigade, under Gatehouse, consisting of the fast light American tanks, stayed in the east. The newly arrived 22nd Brigade, with its Valentines, was placed in the centre in the direction of Bir Gobi, and the 7th, with the support group under Brigadier Jock Campbell, was sent up to Sidi Rezegh on the outskirts of Tobruk. There we were—like a pack of wolves round a lion waiting for the kill.

These forty-eight hours must have been a time of puzzlement for Rommel. Overnight he suddenly found the desert—his bit of desert— overrun for hundreds of miles. Now cautiously he had moved his tanks southward near the border to see what it was all about. Late in the afternoon of the second day they bumped into Gatehouse and his American Honey tanks, and by the merest luck I saw the action from a distance.

My party had blundered into the British armoured division headquarters and the first officer I saw there was the welcome figure of

Colonel Bonner Fellers, the United States military attaché.

Bonner Fellers was often in the desert. He liked to gather his facts at first hand. In the Wavell campaign we used to see him buzzing round from place to place in an ordinary civilian saloon car. And now here he was again looking quizzically across to the east where quick heavy gunfire had suddenly broken the quietness of the afternoon.

I called across to him, 'What's happening?' He just had time to answer, 'Damned if I know,' when we had to duck for shelter as two Messerschmitts came over ground-strafing. Then, clambering on top of our trucks, we saw the opening of the strange confused battle that began on the evening light of November 19th and finished in almost the same spot some eight or nine days later.

Dark rain clouds were pressed solidly onto the eastern horizon. Against this backcloth a line of grey shell-bursts flared up, and soon there were so many of them that a series of twenty or more were hanging together on the skyline. As the battle joined more closely these bursts grew together and made a continuous curtain of dust and smoke and blown sand. This was the battle of the guns reaching its climax—German guns on our tanks, our guns on the Germans; the range perhaps five thousand yards. Then came the tanks.

What a moment it was. These light Honeys with their two-pounder 37-millimetre gun, their ugly box-shaped turrets, their little waving pennants, had never seen the battle before. They had come straight from the steel mills of America to the desert, and now for the first time we were going to see if they were good or bad or just more tanks.

Gatehouse, with his heavy head, his big hooked nose, and his deep-set eyes, sat on his tank watching the battle, estimating the strength of the enemy, the position of the sun, the slope of the ground. Then he lifted up his radio mouthpiece and gave his order. At his command the Honeys did something that tanks don't do in the desert any more. They charged. It was novel, reckless, unexpected, impetuous and terrific. They charged straight into the curtain of dust and fire that hid the German tanks and guns. They charged at speeds of nearly forty miles an hour and some of them came right out the other side of the German lines. Then they turned and charged straight back again. They passed the German Mark IVs and Mark IIIs at a few hundred yards, near enough to see the white German crosses, near enough to fire at point-blank range and see their shell hit and explode.

I saw nothing of all this infighting. I doubt if anyone saw it at all clearly. Dust, smoke, burning oil, exploding shell and debris filled the

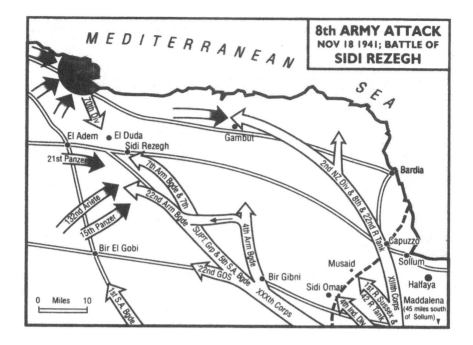

air. From a distance it was merely noise and confusion.

Fires on the battlefield delayed the early winter night a little. But by six o'clock it was too dark to see any more and one after another the guns hiccoughed into silence. Both sides drew off.

Through the sharp cold of the night the Nazi recovery units crept forward onto the battlefield and they were not unkind to our wounded lying there. They handed hot drinks to the men who lay helpless beside the smoking wrecks of their tanks and threw blankets over some of those who would otherwise have died of exposure before morning. Working at speed, they hitched up the partly damaged vehicles, both British and German, and dragged them off to repair shops. They seized on all the food and clothing left about in the mêlée of battle and bore it off.

A few miles away my little party had gone into a protective leaguer for the night. In the last light we had cooked and eaten our bully-beef stew. The 'soft' vehicles—those that had no armour—had lain dispersed about the desert all day to minimise the danger of air attack. Now we drove these together into a compact group for the night, and a ring of tanks and armoured cars lay about us on guard against surprise attacks in the darkness. But neither side reopened the fighting through the night, and I was woken half an hour before dawn by a burst of Bren-gun fire. This was the signal for the leaguer to disperse again and drive on to a new stretch of desert lest our position had been plotted by reconnaissance aircraft the day before.

As we came to rest in our new base the darkness began to weaken under the red glow of the coming sun. Visibility extended first a few yards, then a hundred, then two hundred, and the formless silhouettes of a few hours before resolved into tanks and trucks and guns. A few miles off the battle began again at the point where it was broken off the night before. Gunners and tank crews, straining their eyes through the mist, now suddenly caught sight of the enemy again and put their gloved hands to the frozen metal of their guns. At some places Germans and British had lain right alongside one another through the night and the men opened up with machine-gun fire as they scrambled for cover. Then for a brief hour the firing ran in bursts along the eastern horizon, and once again the men on the tank radio link could hear the tank commanders shouting at one another in the thick of the battle—'There they come, Bill…half right, two thousand yards, six of 'em…right, let them have it, the bastards…Christ, that was a beauty!' Scarcely before the sun was over the horizon the Nazis drew off, and turning west avoided further engagement.

All this time—through the engagement the previous night, during the night itself, and now again this morning—the battle arena had been cut off from the rest of the world. No one at headquarters had any clear knowledge yet of how our experiment had gone forward or of how the Honeys had behaved in their first encounter.

But now some of the crews, young English boys, began coming back, and they had remarkable information. It seemed that the German tanks with their heavy 50- and 75-millimetre guns had opened up an effective barrage at ranges of up to fifteen hundred yards. At this distance the Honeys' two- pounder was quite unable to reply, and Gatehouse had accordingly ordered his men to charge forward until they were within shooting distance—about eight hundred yards. To cover that terrible seven or eight hundred yards under continuous enemy fire, the Honeys had zigzagged back and forth across the sand and to some extent had thrown the German gunners off. The great speed of the American tank had helped, and once they got well up to the Germans they had done great execution. But some thirty of our tanks had been lost in the process of getting into battle—some of them had not even had a chance of firing a shot. The German losses were unknown because so many of their tanks had been salvaged in the night.

The first day of battle then had revealed the two grave disadvantages which were to handicap the British for the whole of this campaign and for many months to come. It was known on this first morning that all our tanks were out-gunned, and that however many vehicles the Germans lost they were going to get a far greater number back into action than we could because of their efficient recovery system. Their huge tracked and wheeled tank-transporters were actually going into battle with the tanks themselves. Even while the fighting was still on, the men in the transporters were prepared to dash into the battle, hook onto damaged vehicles and drag them out to a point where they could start repairs right away.

Rommel, on his side, was finding out that he was up against a very much more numerous enemy than he had reckoned with. He had broken off his engagement with the American tanks in order to regroup nearer to his main forces about Tobruk. But as he went west and north he continued to bump into British armour. In the south-west at Bir Gobi, the Italian Ariete Tank Division had had a brush with the British 22nd Armoured Brigade and also been forced to withdraw. These Italian tanks now began to slide along the southern side of the British armoured line trying to find a weak spot while the Germans were doing exactly the same thing in the inside of the British ring. And so both German and Italian tanks fetched up together at the north-western extremity of the line at Sidi Rezegh just below Tobruk. Rezegh airfield had been surprised and won by Campbell's support group and the 7th Armoured Brigade the day before.

Rommel now decided to fling the bulk of his armour onto the British at Rezegh and so force a gap out to the west. Rezegh became the decisive battlefield of the campaign. All day the 7th withstood the full weight of the Panzer divisions while they waited for the other two British armoured brigades to come to their assistance.

General Gott himself was at Rezegh and I saw one of his messages come into divisional headquarters in the late afternoon. It said: 'We are all right, but we would like to know when the other brigades are arriving.' Gott had begun the action on Rezegh with over one hundred tanks. By the end of the day, when help at last arrived, he had barely a dozen serviceable vehicles left.

Both the 4th and 22nd brigades were late in arriving—the 4th because it had delayed to attack a large soft convoy of German lorries, the 22nd because it was a new brigade sent far too hastily into the desert and some of its elements got temporarily lost. There were already large numbers of inexperienced British troops wandering about the desert uncertain of their direction.

So now the battle of annihilation on Sidi Rezegh began. I drove with Edward Ward of the B.B.C. and one or two others into that spit of flat land we were holding just above the Tobruk escarpment. It was ringed with fire. In the east the Germans were counterattacking the airfield and Jock Campbell was like a man berserk. He led his tanks into action riding in an open unarmoured staff car, and as he stood there, hanging onto its windscreen, a huge well-built man with the English officer's stiff good looks, he shouted, 'There they come. Let them have it.' When the car began to fall behind, he leaped onto the side of a tank as it went forward and directed the battle from there. He turned aside through the enemy barrage to his own twenty-five-pounder guns and urged the men on to faster loading and quicker firing. He shouted to his gunners, 'How are you doing?' and was answered, 'Doing our best, sir.' He shouted back, grinning, 'Not good enough.'

They say Campbell won the V.C. half a dozen times that day. The men loved this Elizabethan figure.

He was the reality of all the pirate yarns and the tales of high adventure, and in the extremes of fear and courage of the battle he had only courage. He went laughing into the fighting.

From El Adem in the north and the rocks of the Tobruk escarpment the enemy was attacking too. I saw his guns ranging on our forward tanks in the north and they stood like knockovers in the shooting gallery of a country fair. Like an endless chain of artificial ducks, British vehicles passed across the horizon, and every now and then a shell burst, belching black smoke, would fall among them.

Then in the third sector, around to the west, more enemy were pushing forward. As the darkness came in Very lights spurted up from every direction. These were the signals of the Germans showing where their forward troops were closing in. We had at this time just this narrow promontory of territory reaching up from the southern desert toward Tobruk—the British armour in the end of the promontory at Rezegh and the mass of South African infantry forming the stalk and base.

The airfield fell, and as my party struggled back in the mud and darkness I saw the enemy's Very lights creeping rapidly around us. They rose, a series of reds, greens and yellows, to the east, north and west and then they began to close in on the south. That meant we were surrounded…at least temporarily. On this night the firing did not cease, and the broken burning tanks glowed fitfully and grotesquely across the damp sand of the desert.

In the morning we left Ward behind and made a bolt southward to reach rear headquarters. Even as we bumped along the uneven track German armoured cars came in again from the west and east driving in front of them, like stampeding cattle, hundreds of British lorries, ambulances and supply wagons.

At divisional headquarters we had to pack and run quickly, and we went back to Corps to write our messages and spend one quiet night out of the battle.

I was strolling in the sun at Corps and the others of my party were lazily washing in the open when the enemy breakthrough came. We were in a slight hollow lightly studded with camel thorn and saltbush— just fifty or sixty vehicles dispersed about with a few armoured cars to protect us. Into this hollow about a hundred British trucks suddenly burst in a whirl of dust. We looked up wondering.

Some convoy perhaps with urgent supplies? Then from another direction several hundred more vehicles, tanks among them, came flying pell-mell across the desert, racing past our stationary vehicles without stopping and covering us in great billows of fine sand.

This was no organised convoy. The others got the idea at the same time as I did. As I raced back toward our trucks Clifford and Busvine were already flinging the bedding, the cooking pots and our clothes into the back of the trucks. Everyone was packing at speed. The big three armoured vehicles which housed the Intelligence, Operational and Signalling staffs were being warmed up. One of our officers, shaving soap on his face, came over when he saw us packing and enquired with all the confidence of ignorance, 'What's the flap? Ops will tell us if we have to get out.'

'Take a look at Ops,' said Clifford briefly. The Ops crew was flinging aboard beds, maps, cases of food and everything they possessed.

Another great swarm of vehicles rushed through the camp and now shells began to fall among them. It had been a bright early morning, but now the churned-up dust had blotted out the sun and visibility became reduced to two hundred yards or less. In this semi-darkness and confusion thousands of vehicles got hopelessly mixed so that men and vehicles of entirely different units travelled along together, and since many of the drivers had no orders they simply rushed ahead following anyone who would lead them.

My party stuck to the Signals vehicle, but unknown to us the young officer inside had jammed his hand in the door and was semi-unconscious. His driver simply went on as hard as he could in the direction away from the firing which was south-east and we followed blindly. Twice we stopped and while men ran from one vehicle to another asking for orders and trying to find out what was amiss, more shells came over the horizon. We were being followed—and fast. So the hue and cry went on again. Occasionally vehicles around us ran onto mines or were hit by shells or were simply fired by their bewildered drivers who believed the enemy to be upon them. Once when we paused on a rise— an odd collection of tanks, cars, lorries, light guns and command vehicles—a squadron of British aircraft came toward us flying low. Everyone ran to their places and the stampede began again.

All day for nine hours we ran. It was the contagion of bewilderment and fear and ignorance.

Rumour spread at every halt, no man had orders. Everyone had some theory and no one any plan beyond the frantic desire to reach his unit. We were just a few hangers-on of the battle, the ones who were most likely to panic because we had become separated from our officers and had no definite job to do. I came to understand something of the meaning of panic in this long nervous drive. It was the unknown we were running away from, the unknown in ourselves and in the enemy. We did not know who was pursuing us or how many or how long they would be able to keep up the pursuit and whether or not they would outstrip us in the end. In ourselves we did not know what to do. Had there been someone in authority to say 'Stand here. Do this and that'— then half our fear would have vanished.

So I began to realise, sitting there in the swaying car, how important the thousand dreary routine things in the army are. The drill, the saluting, the uniform, the very badges on your arm all tend to identify you with a solid machine and build up a feeling of security and order. In the moment of danger the soldier turns to his mechanical habits and draws strength from them.

On the battlefield the individual vanishes. Men turn with absolute trust to one another; they need one another as they seldom do in the even time of peace. The leader should be the product and best expression of the system; not an individual experimentalist. The system should be flexible and inspired enough to throw up the best men into leadership so that when the leader comes to take a daring decision it will be just the decision all his men would have taken. And this must be still more true of guerrilla fighting and the partisans of Russia, even though the trappings of the military machine are missing there.

These matters, I suppose, should have been obvious enough, but I personally only began to see them clearly during this ignominious retreat back into Egypt. I wanted badly to receive orders. And so, I think, did the others.

It was a crestfallen and humiliated little group of men that finally felt its way towards the frontier wire fence as dusk fell. We found a gap in the wire and as we plunged through it with a feeling of relief— even a fence between us and the unknown pursuer was something—a British major came up in a truck and began to organise us and knock some sense into us. We stopped and grouped the vehicles in three close-packed lines for the night. Lights and gunfire were still showing a few miles to the north and men came forward to act as sentries. Food, water and petrol were portioned out.

Cigarettes were forbidden. Once or twice through the night we heard tanks—ours or the enemy's— rumble past, but when the morning came, grey and damp, the desert was clear. So we rode on into our own rear lines.

The war correspondents' base camp was at Cunningham's headquarters and we were the last party to get in. Our colonel, Philip Astley, was waiting for us anxiously. We could give him no news of Eddie Ward or Harold Denny of the *New York Times* or Godfrey Anderson of the Associated Press, or half a dozen South African correspondents. Later we heard they had been overrun the night before and were last seen standing in the prisoners' lines being searched by Nazis.

Two others had run their truck onto a mine, a third had been lost at sea, one or two more were simply missing. The correspondents had taken a bad beating and the loss of Eddie, with whom we had so often gone campaigning, was more than an ordinary distress to Clifford, Busvine and myself.

We shaved, washed, ate breakfast and slept, and presently began to sort things out a little more coherently. It had been a bad reverse for the Eighth Army but not nearly so bad as we had imagined. While the tanks were still locked in this bloodiest of all battles in the desert Rommel had decided upon a gamble that had the elements of genius and the wildest possible folly. He had detached a part of his tanks and armoured cars and flung them straight across the desert through the British lines of communication. A tank among unarmed lorries is like a shark among mackerel. In a spectacular night attack, the German Panzers had almost entirely overwhelmed the 5th South African Brigade and then they had plunged straight into Egypt and attempted to rejoin their infantry forces left on the frontier.

British soft transports had scattered before them and confusion more deadly than shellfire spread everywhere. And now lost groups of men roamed about, passing and repassing through enemy lines. Convoys of vehicles were scattered over a hundred miles of desert, not knowing where to go.

Batteries of guns and groups of tanks were left stranded in the empty desert. Men who believed they were holding the end of a continuous salient suddenly found the enemy behind them. And north of them and south of them and all round them. Then the enemy in turn would seek to carry off his booty and prisoners only to find that his own base had vanished and that he was in the midst of a strong British formation. Prisoners became gaolers. Men were captured and escaped three or four times.

Half a dozen isolated engagements were going on. Field dressing stations and hospitals were taking in British and German and Italian wounded impartially, and as the battle flowed back and forth the hospitals would sometimes be under British command, sometimes under German. Both sides were using each others' captured guns, tanks and vehicles and absurd incidents were taking place. A British truck driven by a German and full of British prisoners ran up to an Italian lorry. Out jumped a platoon of New Zealanders and rescued our men. Vehicles full of Germans were joining British convoys by mistake—and escaping before they were noticed. Generals themselves were taking prisoners and corporals and brigadiers were manning machine-guns together. On the map the dispositions of the enemy and ourselves looked like an eight decker rainbow cake, and as more and more confused information came in, Intelligence officers threw down their pencils in disgust, unable to plot the battle any further.

It seemed indeed that Rommel had achieved a masterstroke. Cunningham had little hesitation in pointing out that the wisest course was to retire his army out of Libya to regroup. Most of his tanks appeared to be lost. He was out of touch with a great part of his army. The New Zealanders had succeeded in making contact with the Tobruk garrison at El Duda but only for a few hours. The Germans had surged forward, broken the bridgehead, and now Tobruk was again a besieged fortress with barely forty-eight hours of twenty-five-pounder ammunition left.

Of the two British Corps headquarters, one, the 13th, had bolted into Tobruk and was besieged there and the other, the 30th, was split up and out of touch. Among the South Africans alone we appeared to have lost an entire brigade—more than two thousand men.

At this grim moment Auchinleck exhibited a touch of brilliance and moral courage that was the high-water mark of his career. He flew to the desert and opposed a final and absolute 'no' to the proposal for retreat. He refused to acknowledge that Rommel's spectacular breakthrough had disorganised the Eighth Army. He argued vehemently that it was only a matter of sticking to what positions we still held and that the enemy must break and give way. He said finally that in order to maintain our stand the last man, the last gun and the last tank in the Eighth Army would be sacrificed. The Eighth Army would go through or never come back.

In this hour of great crisis Auchinleck cast about for any expedient that would delay the enemy until we could return to organised attack. He found it in the Jock Column. Brigadier Jock Campbell had previously spent some time in the desert organising small fighting patrols. Each was just a handful of vehicles—perhaps a troop of armoured cars, two or three troops of guns and a company of lorried infantry. They were provisioned for a few days or a week or more and the command handed over to a young lieutenant who knew the desert. Each commander's orders were simply these—'Get out and behind the enemy. Attack anything you see.' It was an order that had a peculiar attraction to a certain type of young Englishman. The elements of the Drake and Raleigh tradition were in it. Piracy on the high sands. Where the British army still bungled hopelessly in massed fighting, there were still the individuals who fought brilliantly in small guerrilla groups, who had the inspiration of feeling free and the taste for quick and daring movement.

So the partisans of the desert were born. As fast as they could be put together Auchinleck rushed them out into the desert. Within a few days he had twenty or more groups behind the enemy lines, burning, looting, shooting, cutting in and running away, laying ambushes in the wadis, diverting enemy tanks, breaking signal wires, laying false trails, breaking up convoys, raiding airfields, getting information. It was a make-shift while the Eighth Army worked desperately to reorganise itself, but it began taking immediate and heavy effect.

Returning to Cairo Auchinleck drove to his house on Gezira and late at night wrote the letter to Cunningham which removed him from his command. There was no time to consult Churchill or the War

Cabinet. Auchinleck himself had to take the decision to depose the man he had sent for so hopefully only a few months before. The letter was handed to Major-General Neil Ritchie, Auchinleck's deputy chief-of-staff and Ritchie flew down to the desert the following morning to take command. Already now in the last days of November the situation was righting itself slowly—righting itself for the last great onslaught of Sidi Rezegh. It had turned out that the fighting troops at the front had not been shaken nearly so much as the soft transport behind by Rommel's breakthrough. The breakthrough itself had petered out to nothing after the first wild dash—the enemy tanks had come within five miles of our main dump and missed it altogether. They had not touched our railhead. General Gott and all the troops north of the breakthrough had simply driven northward and carried on the battle from the coastal area. The Indians were successfully attacking Sidi Omar in the centre. The Germans and Italians bottled up in Halfaya, Bardia and Sollum were trying to send out some of their men but ineffectively. The New Zealanders under Freyberg, the finest infantry division in the Middle East, were still defending the coastal ridge about Gambut. Tobruk still held. More tanks were coming up and the broken loose ends of the army in the central desert were being brought together. In the far south the Indians had reached Jalo and overwhelmed it.

My little party flew back to Cairo for a day or two to refit. What an exquisite pleasure it was going back to Cairo! The first hot bath, the first cold drink, the good meals and the clean clothes: these were the things that made the war suddenly fall away and become unreal. Lucy had been told I was missing and was astonished and relieved when I walked in covered from head to foot in fine sand and dirty with three weeks of dirtiness. We had a pleasant meal with Quentin Reynolds of *Collier's Magazine*. Reynolds had also been pretty freely bombed and shelled at the front but nothing could shake that breezy good humour. When Lucy invited him to lunch on our baby's first birthday, he sent her a telegram: 'I hear there was a man in your room a year ago tonight.'

But it was no time to stay eating and drinking in Cairo.

Refitted, refreshed and reprovisioned Clifford, Busvine and myself set out with Randolph Churchill for Sidi Rezegh to see the tank battle that was going to decide everything for good and all.

We reached Gatehouse just as he was going into action. His headquarters had been overrun and he had lost all his possessions. He had a Scottish plaid rug wound round his waist and fastened by a leather strap. He had an armchair strapped to the top of his tank and he sat there directing his men. The tank was blasted and pitted with shell-holes, but Gatehouse was uninjured. All but five or six of his original Honeys had been destroyed but he had reinforcements. He had been in almost continuous action for nearly a fortnight and he was feeling good.

'You better keep close behind me,' he said, and off we went into Sidi Rezegh. The battlefield now was a scene of extraordinary desolation. Several aircraft had nose-dived into the ground and stood up-ended grotesquely. I recognised the one that had attacked us the previous week. About thirty Stukas and Messerschmitts had come along the British column making their slow graceful dips to the earth and shooting upward as the bombs sprang downward and burst. Then one Messerschmitt had peeled off and come after us about twenty feet above the ground machine-gunning. The air hummed and screamed with bullets. I was wearing my blue Italian sailor's jacket and I remember thinking as I pressed into a wheel rut, 'He can't help seeing me.' And as I had glanced up I had seen the white taut face of the German pilot. A young South African sergeant close to me had stood up to him with a Lewis gun and in a daze I saw the machine falter in its course, lurch to the sand and erupt into a streaming plume of black smoke. I had seen the pilot's face in the second of his death and it had showed no fear or hate or excitement—just intense concentration. Death had leapt on him too quickly to be felt. Now we passed by the blackened aircraft and the grave.

Every few hundred yards there were graves—the dead man's belt or perhaps his helmet flung down on top of the fresh earth and over it a cross made of bits of packing case: 'Cpl. John Brown. Died in Action.' Then the date. This scrawled in pencil.

Sometimes there were mingled German and British graves as though the men had gone down together, still locked in fighting. Sometimes the dead were laid alongside the blackened hulks of their burnt-out tanks. The tanks themselves still smouldered and smelt evilly. Their interior fittings had been dragged out like the entrails of some wounded animal, for you would see the mess boxes, the toothbrushes and blankets of the crews scattered around together with their little packets of biscuits, their water bottles, photographs of their families, hand grenades, webbing, tommy-guns, mirrors, brushes and all the mundane ordinary things that fill a soldier's kitbag and are a part of his life.

Empty petrol tins, the flimsy and khaki-coloured British and the stout black German ones, were scattered everywhere. Like great lizards, the broken tracks of tanks were sprawled across the sand with their teeth gaping upward. One tank newly hit was fuming and spluttering with interior explosions and every few seconds ignited Very lights would burst through the overhanging coils of black smoke. Its petrol tank crashed open in a sheet of flame. Nobody seemed to take much notice. The ground itself was crisscrossed a thousand times with the deep crenellated ruts of tanks and these, with indifference, had smashed rifles, bullets, machine-guns, tins, boxes, papers and even human beings, into the mud. Muddy water was seeping steadily into shell and bomb holes. Over everything hung the same bleak winter's sky. Across this wilderness, made doubly a desert by the past week's fighting, the British tanks went forward once more.

We had barely reached the lip of the airfield when Gatehouse, still sitting in his armchair, suddenly swung his tank about, and began looking with his glasses toward the spot where the sun was setting among a knot of dark clouds. It was usual for the enemy to attack in the evening with the light behind them and now some eighteen or more of their tanks were coming on to our rear.

Speaking into his mouthpiece, Gatehouse turned his forces about, sending some of his Honeys out to the west, some to the north. He had with him a battery of twenty-five-pounders of the Royal Horse Artillery that day and these he posted in the centre close to his own tank. The twenty-five-pounder was never intended to be used as an anti-tank weapon. For one thing it is a gun-howitzer. For another it has to be towed, then uncoupled and swung about before it can be brought into action. It cannot be retired or shifted as quickly as an anti-tank gun should be. But the short range of our two-pounder gun had forced Gatehouse to bring twenty-five-pounder artillery right into the front line to cover the Honeys until they got into range.

I could just see the dark dots of the enemy tanks against the sunset light as the R.A.F. came in and laid a stick of bombs across their path. One bomb fell far short and killed one of our gunners, but his comrades worked on in the face of the enemy fire. It all happened within the space of twenty minutes. I saw two tanks ablaze on either flank and a doctor's car racing out towards them. The crews were leaping from the burning hulks like sailors leaving a sinking ship. Then the twenty-five-pounder troop posted in front got the range—three thousand yards—and the plain lit with their shell bursts. Still the Germans came on through the barrage and I heard the artillery major shorten his range down to fifteen hundred yards, then one thousand. By this time the enemy was very close, firing straight out of the battle clouds toward us. The forward artillery ceased fire, hitched up their guns and came careering back. As they came, the rear troop took up the barrage and they in their turn fought the enemy down to a thousand yards before they were forced to retire. Then again the original troop was ready to take up the fight from a position farther back. By this time our ranks were near enough to open fire from either flank and all Sidi Rezegh was raked back and forth with their shells. It was beautiful timing and wonderful coolness considering that if the enemy tanks had got through the guns and their crews could not have escaped.

In the last light of the day the Axis tanks drew off and this time the battlefield was ours. Such skirmishes were going on at several other spots around that same flat stretch of ground which both sides had decided should be the final testing place. As I came away, I began to sense something new in the fighting. No longer the Very lights closed around us in the darkness. The enemy opposition was getting weaker.

Freyberg meantime was reopening the way into Tobruk with the bayonet. His men had withstood two tremendous charges of tanks and anti-tank gunfire and now they were coming forward again. Far back on the frontier Sidi Omar had fallen to us. The guns of Tobruk were still spouting their barrage from the sea. It was very near the point where one side or the other must collapse through sheer exhaustion. Some five or six hundred tanks had fought one another to destruction or impotency. Just a few were left on either side. The fact was that the hard armoured coating of both armies was destroyed. The softer, slower infantry was exposed at last and left to decide the battle. The Eighth Army had come out of its mortal crisis, and had gathered its second wind. Most of its original tanks were gone. Many of its dead lay in that torn stretch of ground reaching along the coast from Tobruk to Bardia, then south along the frontier to Sidi Omar, then east to Bir Gobi and so back to Tobruk.

The first stage of the battle was over. No one could say clearly yet who had won. British, Germans and Italians lay around Tobruk too exhausted to go on, almost too tired to pick up the spoils of war.

As December came in, the coldest month of the year, the semi-quiet of utter weariness had settled over the front.

Five

December in Benghazi

CAIRO WAS going through all the spasms of despair, hope, exhilaration and back to despair again. A myopic and confused propaganda was trying to sublimate all these moods and at the same time keep track of this most incoherent of all battles. Little or nothing had been allowed out about our losses or the German gains. A new British victory had been served out to the world's press and radio each day. The breakthrough had been ignored. Newspapers were encouraged to come out with such headlines as 'Rommel Surrounded,' 'Rommel in Rout,' 'Germans Desperately Trying to Escape British Net.'

Now, in early December, the amateurs controlling propaganda began to see what a bogey of over- optimism they had raised. Before the battle had fairly begun they had told the world that we outnumbered the enemy in guns and tanks and so any future victory of ours had been discounted in advance and any setback made to appear doubly severe. They had even suggested that the battle might be over in a few hours. Hardly one colourful and dramatic guess had been overlooked. And now all the guesses and easy prophecies were coming home to roost. People all over the world were beginning to suspect that Rommel had been overlong in a state of rout; that just possibly something had gone wrong. Each day a new estimate of the number of enemy tanks destroyed had been made and now people with mischievous minds began to add up the total and find out that each German tank appeared to have been destroyed at least twice. Somehow now the facts had to be given, and given in such a way as to maintain morale and not disturb the public's faith in the news they had already received.

To those of us who came back from the front at this time, it seemed that we saw the last fortnight's battle as though reflected in distorting mirrors in Cairo. There seemed to be no sense in it.

I do not suggest that the British high command deliberately put out false information—I am even sure that they did not. I simply suggest that unskilled men who were confused and bewildered by the events had been put in charge of propaganda and that they were painting their rosy pictures not from bad faith but bad judgment. The old bad dictum that you must always give the public good news had been the theory they had fallen back upon in their distress. They were urged to this course in support of all those lightly made prophecies of success with which the troops had gone into battle. Already this strained and artificial policy was finding out its authors. They had not graduated to the realisation that the public of both America and the British Empire was quite able to accept the news of defeats and delays; what the public disliked intensely was having its hopes raised high only to be plunged into the disappointment of reality later on. There was no need either before this campaign or any other to raise the hopes of the people. A tremendous disservice was being done to the fighting soldier. His problems and difficulties were being misunderstood. He was being applauded for victories which he had not won and his real successes were being overlooked in the backwash of disappointment and disillusion.

So now, when the Eighth Army, by a moral triumph of its general and by the fighting stamina of its men, was about to move forward to a victory, there were few to applaud, still fewer to understand how it was done. The earlier glowing heroics had soured into cynicism and boredom.

Feeling a little as though we had been cheated, Clifford and I went down to the desert again. We had to take that appalling Mersa Matruh train and it was on our first night out that we got the news of Pearl Harbour, of the *Repulse* and the *Prince of Wales* and the entry of America into the war. We spent a freezing night in a siding when our train was disrailed and we went on in a hospital plane to army headquarters. Busvine flew down and joined us an hour or two later. He had covered our three- day journey from Cairo in three hours. Kim Mundy, too, was ready to come forward with us, and we set out, a caravan of three vehicles, for Gambut and the coast.

From the outset it was clear that the shape of the battle had altered. At Gambut we came on the wreckage of many Nazi planes—Stukas, Messerschmitts, Dorniers and Junkers. Then as we rode along the coast road the news came through that Tobruk was released at last. Such of the enemy who were not locked up in the Sollum area were heading westward. It was the break at last. Worn out, short of supplies and badly short of armour, Rommel was clearing out. We stopped beyond Gambut and turning off the track ran down to the sea where a German workshop had been established. The place was lying exactly as the Germans had left it, when they had hurriedly turned to escape, and there in these tents and bivouacs lay the private life of an army. It was like some Doré etching of a forgotten and spellbound village, a place that reminded one of the mystery of the sailing ship, *Marie Celeste*, which was found intact upon the ocean without a man on board.

The tents were equipped with concrete floors and electric lights. They had tables and chairs, canvas baths and alarm clocks. There were tables covered with a confusion of little comforts which had apparently been issued to each man in the Afrika Korps—highly coloured boxes of bakelite filled with buttons and cotton and thread, endless bottles of mouthwash, eye lotion, body powder, toothpaste, liquid soap, water purifiers, headache powders, ointments, hair oils and shampoos, even a special chocolate that was supposed to 'pep you up' according to the label. (I tried some; nothing happened.) A year before during Wavell's advance I had seen how lavish the Italian camps and equipment were. But whereas a good deal of the Italian equipment had been showy ornament, all this stuff was ingeniously designed and must have greatly lightened the burden of living in the desert.

The Nazis had neat little cooking stoves with telescoping pots and pans and little blocks of white concentrated methylated spirit with which to boil a pot quickly and easily. They had those electric torches you pump with your hand and varieties of camp lights and other gadgets. There were many cigarettes, many tins of British bully beef they had captured earlier in the year. The field kitchen was stocked with sacks of fresh potatoes, onions and lemons, and there was evidence they had been getting fresh meat up from Benghazi and Tripoli. In a clothing dump I came on thousands of pairs of woollen gloves and underclothing, stockings, sweaters, shirts, tunics and caps. There was no shortage of anything. It was a profusion the people of Germany have not seen for years and although much of the stuff was ersatz it was warm and well-made.

The tank workshops eclipsed anything we had in the forward areas. Bedded in concrete and under canvas were big lathes and a heavy smithy. Cases of tank precision instruments worth many thousands of pounds lay about. One was full of periscopes. Several huge boxes contained new 50-millimetre guns which apparently could be fitted to damaged tanks in this place. There were sheets of armour, new tracks and tyres, a mass of woodwork and steel parts. It almost seemed that they could have built a tank here in the desert by the sea.

The richest prize was about thirty tanks of all kinds which the Germans had left lying about. These tanks had been brought in for repair and when the retreat was ordered, they had been set on fire. Some still smouldered. At the same time German officers had run down to the sea and cast many of their maps and papers into the waves. But these had been thrown up again by the high tide so that we were able to gather some of them. One was a large coloured sheet showing the uniforms of all the British forces for identification purposes. The artists had drawn his models with strong virile faces—a slight but interesting point. Unlike us, the Germans in their domestic propaganda never underrated their opponents.

In one tent we found little bags of real coffee which a soldier had been parcelling up as Christmas presents for his family at home. Clifford, of course, dived for the letters and correspondence lying about. He translated revealing extracts from the letters the men had received by a fast bi-weekly airmail from Germany. One German wife wrote: 'You must insist on leave. It has been ten months now since you were sent to the desert and others who arrived in Africa after you have had leave.' Then there were passages like this: 'We have no news of Hans, but we think he went to the Russian front. Rudolf has gone there too, and there were some others from the village whom you knew. But we have no news from any of them.' The soldiers had apparently been complaining of the conditions in the desert for there were many letters from mothers commiserating with their sons over the dust and the heat and the flies. All the letters referred to Russia and spoke hopefully of success there. For some reason the writers insisted that the fall of Leningrad had taken place. (Rommel at the height of the campaign had officially circulated the news that Moscow had fallen.)

The troops were well supplied with the latest German illustrated weeklies and they had their own desert paper, the *Oasis*. It contained a lurid serial story entitled 'The Heroes of Hellfire Pass' and Clifford went hunting through the camp to get the back numbers. In most of the official papers we saw that the general motive seemed to be the suggestion that the Germans on the other fronts were doing exceedingly well and that it would be a humiliating thing if they were let down by the Afrika Korps. Good propaganda that. Even units in the Afrika Korps were set against one another in friendly rivalry.

At various places in the camp stone and concrete monuments and emblems had been set up. They bore such inscriptions as 'We Germans die but never surrender.'

We loaded our truck with some of the excellent dried vegetables and fruits the Germans used and packets of rusks and black bread covered with silver paper. I picked up a couple of their tidy little green bivouac tents, and we drove on to Tobruk. As we left Bedouin were roaming through the camp, looting. A German major who had fallen asleep just before the British arrived sat miserably in the back of a truck with a guard over him. A gleam of hope had come into this officer's eyes when Clifford went up to him and spoke in German. 'You're a German, aren't you?' said the major. He hoped that he had met a fifth columnist.

It was a memorable moment driving down into Tobruk. Coming from the east, you do not see the town until you are right upon it. Then, as you wind down from the El Adem crossroads, the scarred white village breaks suddenly into view. On this day it had the appearance of utter dreariness and monotony as though the very earth itself was tired. Every foot of dust was touched in some way by high explosive. The sand was full of shrapnel and broken bits of metal. Countless thousands of shells, bombs and bullets had fallen here among the rusting barbed wire, the dugouts and the dust-coloured trucks. You could distinguish the men of Tobruk from the other soldiers. Their clothing, their skin, and especially their faces, were stained the same colour as the earth. They moved slowly and precisely with an absolute economy of effort. They were lean and hard and their lips were drawn tightly together against the dust. They seemed to fit perfectly into the landscape and it was impossible to say whether their morale was good or bad, whether they were tired after so many months of bombing and shelling and isolation—or merely indifferent. They had become identified with their underground and dusty existence. Certainly they were not exuberant at their release—it had been too hard and grim a business for that, and the realisation of it would only come after weeks or even months. The base troops were still going about their normal duties as though nothing had happened. They stood patiently in queues at the water points and the food dumps. They talked laconically about the things they had talked of for months— the weather, last night's raids, the quality of the rations. Of the high excitement and heroism that had held this place for nine months there was no sign whatever. There were no flags, no bands, no marching men. The war seemed to have reduced nearly everything to a neutral dust.

Except for the lines of crosses in the cemetery and an occasional passing ambulance there was not even any suggestion of pain. Tiredness and boredom governed this place where no green thing grew, where everything had been designed for death for long over a year of warfare.

The Germans and Italians were forming a new line about forty miles farther on—the Gazala Line. We joined General Kopansky and the Polish brigade just a few minutes before they went in to break the northern sector of this line. The Poles had burst out of their confinement in Tobruk with the exuberance of Red Indians and now, as their infantry deployed under shellfire, their chief of staff said to us with no intention of being funny, 'It makes a nice change for the boys. A very nice change indeed.'

It did too. They went into battle as though they were buccaneers boarding a fifteenth-century galleon. Zero hour was at 3 p.m. At ten to three the barrage went over our heads on to the enemy and the anti-tank guns slid forward on either flank. At three precisely the horizon about a mile to the north- west of us suddenly sprouted a line of men and this line began to tramp forward straight into the enemy fire. Without glasses I saw the shells bursting among them and as the smoke hung on the desert for a minute you would be sure that that sector had been wiped out. But when the cloudburst cleared there they would be again—the fighting Poles, still going forward and shooting as they went. The quick staccato noise of machine-gun and tommy-gun fire came ringing along on the bleak wind as the Poles closed right in and covered the last few yards to the enemy positions with the bayonet.

On our left flank the New Zealanders and Indians were going forward as well. It was mainly an infantry fight now. That night the German Gazala Line was broken and Rommel gave up Cyrenaica. He gathered what was left of his Panzer divisions and, abandoning Derna, Barce and Benghazi, he cleared right out for three hundred miles along the desert route south of the Green Hills. It was only fair after so many British reverses to remember that this was the second time that the Axis had bolted from the desert…their own desert.

Many Italians were left behind to be captured. I sat on Gazala cliffs that night looking down on the coast road some hundreds of feet below. Through the glasses I could see a group of British Tommies going forward on foot up the road towards a bluff that blocked their view to the west. From my perch I could see a platoon of Italians marching toward the bluff from the other side and it was obvious that they wanted to surrender.

It was like watching an early Mack Sennett comedy. The Italians and Tommies reached the bend in the road at the same moment. The Italians at once threw up their hands. The Tommies, intent on gathering some loot beside the road farther on, marched straight ahead. The Italians ran after them and threw up their hands again. The Tommies waved them away. The Italians began to argue—I longed to be closer so that this silent movie would turn itself into a talkie—and some of them threw down their guns to make their intention absolutely clear. At last one of the Tommies jerked his thumb back in the direction of the British lines. Dejectedly the Italians picked up their arms, formed into a double file and trailed off down the road again, seven soldiers in search of a captor.

The drive into Derna was like a recapitulation of a day in the Wavell advance in 1940...except that the enemy did not defend the place this time. Eight or nine German troop-carrying Junkers full of soldiers who had not yet heard the bad news came down onto Derna aerodrome just at the moment when our forward Indian platoons were occupying the place. The Indians laid low while the big planes swooped slowly round and settled into their landing. Then the Indians blew them to bits. Only two of the Junker pilots managed to get into the air again.

Then the British troops scrambled down the steep thousand-foot cliffs into Derna. Derna was still a lovely village. But in that interval between the departure of the Italians and the arrival of the British, the Arabs had cut loose. They had gone through the township looting and destroying, paying off old scores by firing the shops and warehouses. The streets were covered in broken glass. A number of British wounded lay in the hospital and the Arabs had gone shouting and looting through the wards.

They set fire to the west wing of the hospital in order to obtain more light by which to loot. The sick British patients struggled out of bed and fought the fire through the night and drove the Arabs out.

When we entered the town in the morning the wounded men were lying exhausted among their dirty sheets. Some, too tired to get up, were on the floor among the puddles of water they had used to fight the fire the night before. The stench of sickness was awful.

All night these broken men had watched the hills above the town hoping and praying the British army would come and rescue them. In the early morning they had given up hope. In utter weakness and despair, they had abandoned the vigil and slumped down into sick sleep or a coma that served as sleep. The major who led the first British troops into the town thumped heavily on the door of the hospital and shouted: 'Any British here?' There was no answer. The wounded prisoners lay there like cattle, uncomprehending. Some raised their heads and stared at the smart figure in the doorway and it meant nothing to them. Again the major shouted, 'Any British here?' Suddenly a young R.A.F. pilot, less badly wounded than the others, jumped up and yelled hysterically, 'It's all right. It's all right. It's all right. It's the British.'

Fresh bandages, food and doctors were rushed to the hospital.

When we captured Derna the previous year we had found wine in the town and fruit, butter, eggs and chickens. This time there was little except the good clean spring water. We stayed again in the governor's house by the sea but it was only a shell and its polished woodwork was scarred by the boots of young Nazi soldiers. Even the banana groves and the pomegranates seemed to have gone sterile. Yet still the place was a green pool of colour in the desert and it was pleasant to walk through the shaded courts and know that the Axis soldiers had been here only a few hours before.

Beyond Derna lay Giovanni Berta, the first of the Italian settlers' villages in the Green Hills. We approached it by the back road above the cliffs. Everywhere the British army was in hot pursuit.

Columns of vehicles thirty and forty miles long were coasting along the red mud tracks and we wound on steadily up into the green slopes where flocks were grazing on the first natural grass we had seen for many months. An occasional three-engined Savoia kept darting out of the low rain clouds to spring a bomb on the long procession of British vehicles. By this time my party was reduced to Mundy and myself travelling in the forward car with a driver and Clifford following on behind with the truck and another driver. One of the Savoias made a dead set at Clifford on a lonely stretch of the road. We stopped our car and looked back just in time to see the big unwieldy machine leave the clouds and two black bombs leap out of the undercarriage. Clifford and his driver were like two animated Walt Disney figures. They sprang straight out of the truck into the air and landed neatly on top of one another in the ditch beside the road. The bombs burst harmlessly a few yards away.

Up in the air sprang Clifford and his driver again in search of safer cover; and down they went again as another bomb landed beside them. Until these things turn to tragedy they seem really very funny at the front. When the bomber had gone Clifford came up and found Mundy and me still laughing. He stared at us coldly.

At a brigade headquarters they told us Giovanni Berta was already occupied, so we passed on to the front of the column and went ahead until we were in clear view of the sparkling white township only a mile away. A stray shell went overhead and through the glasses I could see Indian troops moving forward to a group of old Roman pillars that dominated the township on the south. There was something strange about the Indians, but I could not think for a moment what it was. They crouched as they walked. They moved up the slope with hunched-up shoulders. Where had I seen that walk before? I was still idly trying to puzzle it out as we drove up to the pillars and there was a quick urgent shout from someone—'Get those vehicles in here. Get them in here quick.' We drove under the cover of a shed and got out in front of a bearded Indian doctor. He was saying excitedly, 'Where the hell have you come from? Down that road? There has been no vehicle along it yet—it's under fire.' So Berta had not fallen. We asked where the enemy was shooting from. 'Come on,' said the doctor.

We went on foot up to the three Roman pillars. Now I remembered what it was. It was, for want of a better description, 'the frontier crouch'. Unconsciously as a man goes up toward enemy machine-gun positions he stoops and falls into a sort of animal lope. Stooping in this way we got to the crest of the rise and looked over—straight into the enemy four hundred yards away. They were on the rise of the opposite side of the valley. As we watched, British artillery raked the slope from one end to the other, and like hunted rabbits the Italians ran blindly hither and thither. Alongside me some Indians were firing mortars and shells. They made a fussy whistling and screaming, arched over the valley, and fell at the mouth of a cave where I could see a number of Italians were hiding. There seemed to be an argument going on in the mouth of the cave. One Italian was holding a white flag on a stick and the others about him kept preventing him from hoisting it aloft.

Then the Indians got the order to creep forward and take the position by assault before the darkness closed in. The British shells were landing in a regular rhythm now. It was all very confused.

Machine-gun fire was snapping right along the floor of the valley. Grey ranks of Italians began to break from cover all over the place and advance toward us. They carried no white flags. They were getting nearer and nearer—only three hundred yards away now. A counterattack then? An Indian soldier went racing past us and Kim shouted to him in Hindustani, 'Are they counterattacking?' The soldier shouted something over his shoulder that Kim interpreted to mean 'Yes,' and at that we bolted down the slope. It was not until we got to the bottom that we saw the Italians coming in without their arms to surrender. It had been a nice hundred yards sprint we had done all the same.

So Berta fell, and we motored on past the villages of Savoia and Tert and on to the ruins of Cirene, the place where they say a million people lived in Roman times. Geoffrey Keating and Russell Hill and Fred Bayliss of *Paramount News* were routing about there. Keating and Hill had been in Tobruk at the breaking of the siege and it was an interesting reunion. Not far from this spot ten months before, we had dragged Keating trailing his broken arm and ankle out of an Italian ambush. Now we drove down the road together to the same place to get to the head of the British column. It was absorbing to see the approaches to the place again—the ditches where Clifford and I had stopped to rest our wounded, the spots where we had dressed their injuries and the curves in the wooded hills where we had dashed across the road.

I was saying rather fatuously, 'It's like doing a Cook's tour of the battlefields after the war,' when Preston Grover of the Associated Press came up and said, 'You can't go any farther. There has been an ambush.' It had happened all over again in exactly the same spot except that we were not in it this time. The poor devils in the leading armoured car had been caught by crossfire from the undergrowth.

We slept that night in an Italian hospital at the front. Its priceless equipment—surgical instruments, bandages, drugs, beds and bedding—had been strewn through the mud by looting Arabs and the rain soaked down steadily. The ambush was cleared on Christmas Eve and we drove down into Barce.

This lush valley was once a thriving dairy settlement and its white homesteads and creameries were among the finest in Africa. The barren moorlands had been made to give out fruit and flowers and all the rich things of modern farming. Four armies—Graziani's, Wavell's, Rommel's and Auchinleck's— had crossed the valley in advance and retreat. They left a curse upon the place. The fences were broken and the doors of the homesteads flapped open admitting the wind and the rain. The crops grew rank and the fields were falling back into the morass of their original mud. A few settlers lingered on and they stood in their doorways staring vacantly and without comprehension. When the soldiers called to them only one or two of the younger girls answered and then automatically and without smiling. Over everything was that same air of neglect and decay and utter weariness. This final catastrophe in the valley was too much. Nothing here now was able to struggle against the war any more. Rain poured through the dilapidated roofs and it was no longer worth the effort to make repairs. Ploughs rusted in the fields and cattle mooed in anguish for someone to milk them. The fight to maintain civilisation here was too unequal, too disappointing, too hard.

The valley was simply given up. Under our eyes the land was returning to its old sterility.

At Tocra the retreating Germans had blown away part of the cliff onto the road, so we had to spend the night at Barce. Bayliss had captured a couple of turkeys in the cellar of the hotel and we badly wanted to eat our Christmas dinner in Benghazi. We debated whether we would stay at the Hotel d'Italia there or one of the other places. We promised ourselves hot baths and clean sheets and some urgent shopping through the town.

Early on Christmas Day we set out. The Arabs were friendly as we ran into the suburbs and we hastened on, hoping that the best rooms in the hotels had not yet been taken by the leading British patrols. Then gradually as we drove through street after empty street, the realisation came on us— Benghazi, too, had collapsed. It was no longer a city any more. The plague of high explosive had burst on the place and left it empty, apathetic and cold. The shops were shuttered, the markets closed and ruin succeeded ruin as we drove along. The façade of the Albergo d'Italia where we hoped to stay, bulged outward sickeningly. The Berenice by the sea, where the Luftwaffe headquarters had been, was burnt out, and all that was left inside were the cords from which the valuable silk parachutes had been cut away. Blasts had pockmarked every building, direct hits had ploughed the waterfront and dashed the anchored vessels onto the seabed. For nearly a year the R.A.F. had gone on and on, night after night, and here we were looking at the scoresheet—a ravaged, ruined city.

We found a block of flats fairly intact where two scared Christian Brothers alone remained. While I cleaned out a couple of rooms in the flat of the chief of police, Mundy, Bayliss and Clifford, all famed cooks, went down to the Berenice which had the only decent sized stove in the town. Somehow they cleared the cinders from the kitchen, killed, plucked and cleaned the turkeys and basted them with hot fat as they sizzled on top of the stove.

We all felt so forlorn that day that we had decided to abandon any real idea of celebrating Christmas. Then in the midst of our depression everything went well. The turkeys were a miracle of tenderness and flavour—even though they had to be rushed half a mile in a truck to our flat. Out of Bayliss's kit came Christmas puddings, brandy, wine, chocolates, raisins, and a tinned ham. Others brought more wine, whisky and liqueurs. Cigars and nuts appeared. I found a dump of Italian mineral water and Chianti and someone gave me a bag of fresh oranges.

Outside in the harbour the Germans were dropping delayed action mines. The wind leapt against the windows, and flung beams and broken bits of plaster onto streets. We were horribly dirty after the long thousand-mile journey from Cairo. But here we sat on this Christmas night eating, drinking and singing, and beyond any other Christmases it will be a time for me to remember.

Boxing Day we scoured round the desolate flats to the south of Benghazi as far as Magrun, Soluch and Beda Fomm, the scene of last winter's great battle. But the action flagged. The Axis troops had retreated fast to beyond Adjedabia and at this point we were not strong enough to harry them strongly or cut them off.

We turned to the long drive back through the rain and mud. At Bardia I paused briefly to watch de Villiers launch his assault on the Germans still holding the border positions. By the time Bardia had fallen I had reached Cairo and the second stage of the campaign was done. It was New Year's Day.

Six

January 1942 in Retreat

RAIN FELL. The people in western Cyrenaica declared they had never seen such rain before. You might have expected them to say that since the weather is always believed to be worse in war-time— probably because the people are more exposed to it. Even so this was exceptional. Day after day heavy grey storm clouds hung over the Green Hills and drenched the countryside. Great hailstones came down, an almost unprecedented thing, and away to the south near Adjedabia the front-line troops reported they had seen flakes of snow on the desert.

The rain began in the neighbourhood of Derna and beyond Derna it engulfed one village after another—Giovanni Berta and Slonta, Cirene and Barce, Tocra and Benghazi. Everywhere the troops stood about huddled in their greatcoats and every spare bit of clothing they could lay hands upon.

Some protected their faces with woollen balaclava helmets; others draped captured bivouac tents about their shoulders and went foraging through the deserted houses in search of firewood.

Convoys of motor vehicles crawled along the roads to the front, with painful, agonising slowness—the slowness that Lord Milne meant when he spoke of war as consisting of short periods of intense fear and long periods of intense boredom. They started out from the dry desert of Egypt and made an immense and dusty tour around the Halfaya positions where the enemy garrison was still holding out. When they regained the road again in Libya they ran into the rain and the cold.

The roads were jammed. For hours the vehicles stood still, thousands of vehicles, and there was nothing to do but sit and wait in the pouring rain for the blockage to be cleared. Wherever the enemy had blown the road engineers and road gangs worked in the knee-deep red mud easing the vehicles through one by one over temporary bridges and half-finished bypasses. No one on the road had any news. No one seemed to know what was going on at the front. The journey from Cairo lengthened from four days to a week to two weeks and still the front line lay somewhere out in the remote and elusive horizon of the wet desert.

Near Tocra, where the plateau suddenly spills into broken hills and cliffs, the vehicles were being pushed along by hand over a dangerous blowout. It was no use going round. We tried it. We drove for hours along a sodden track and every so often our big station wagon would pitch and slither into the green underbrush, and we had to tug and heave until we got it out again. The country here behind Barce still held enemy refugees and wandering Bedouin but the war had driven them into the cover of the hills. Even above Barce itself where the enemy had hastily thrown up a series of tank ditches and side roads, the war had forced the people away. Farmhouses, orchards, cattle, sheep, crops—everything—were abandoned to the rain and the mud and the invader.

In the desert south of Benghazi it was far worse. Red mud stretched interminably across the dreary landscape. I went out to the airfields of Berka and Benina—those two key fields that were going to be the springboards of our next great air sweep through to Tripoli. Inch by inch the grounded enemy aircraft were sinking into the mud. There were scores of aircraft, all useless. Those which had not been wrecked or broken up at the last minute by the Luftwaffe were falling to pieces in the wind. The rain did the rest. All morning I splashed through the muck and wet, and it seemed to me then that no aircraft would use these fields for weeks to come. As though to prove it, a light British reconnaissance plane came down. It bucked and bounced away as it touched down. The wheels skidded madly, flinging the wet earth over the fuselage, and the machine finally came to rest in a pond. There it stayed immovable; after that no aircraft attempted to take-off or land.

It was the same at Barce and Maraua, at Magrun and Soluch. Only Msus was left as the one available field in the forward area that could be used. There was no question of supplying the troops by air, even if we had the transport planes, which we hadn't.

But it was vital to get supplies to the troops. So long as this problem was unsolved, everything else had no importance. The British tried the sea. They loaded ships in Port Said, in Alexandria, Mersa Matruh and Tobruk and set sail for Benghazi. Given Benghazi as a port the rest became fairly easy.

But Benghazi could not be used as a port. Within an hour of my first going into the town on the heels of the leading patrols, it was being bombed and mined. When I came away it was still being bombed and mined. The Germans came over in waves from Sicily. Their mines lay on the seabed in the narrow confines of the harbour and there was no equipment to deal with them, no means of spotting where the danger lay. U-boats lay in wait outside. The docks and the rail-ways leading to the docks were a chaos of exploded stone and steel and concrete. There were no lighters to take off the cargoes, no cranes to lift the boxes of ammunition, no pumps to draw off the petrol from the tankers. A tangle of wrecked steamers blocked the channel through the bay. Benghazi was no use. Only the land route was left. And the land route was choked.

The Eighth Army was like a healthy plant that had suddenly been denied water. The young leaves at the top suffered first. Around Adjedabia the troops first went short of tinned fruit and vegetables, then jam and cheese. Finally they had bully beef, biscuits and tea, and nothing else. Little by little all the supplies fell away. Petrol was the most serious. The men could keep going on bully and biscuits, but until the petrol came they were unable to move. All over the desert I saw parties out scouring for enemy fuel dumps. Squadrons of new tanks which had toiled all the way by train and road to the front found they could do nothing. Even spare parts failed to arrive. There was not enough ammunition and what they had was rapidly running out. There were not enough radio sets and soon the last commodity of all began to fail them—information.[1]

For hundreds of miles isolated groups of men were strung across the wet desert with no orders and no notion of what to do. The sap was being drained out of the Eighth Army, not by the enemy, for Rommel had withdrawn around the Gulf of Sirte, but by the desert and the weather and the distance.

The ancient law of the desert was, in fact, coming into play. Once more the British had proved that you can conquer Cyrenaica. Now unwillingly they began to prove that you cannot go on. It had been the same for both sides. Tripoli and Cairo were equidistant from Cyrenaica. The enemy had shown that he was capable of sallying out of Tripoli, of crossing Cyrenaica and digging his nose into the Egyptian desert. But there he stopped. And now coming in the reverse direction, here were we stopped at Adjedabia. The trouble was that the farther you got away from your base, the nearer the retreating enemy got to his. Consequently as you got weaker, the enemy got stronger.

Four trusted and able generals had tried to disprove that rule. In the summer of 1940 the Italian, Graziani, had advanced as far as Sidi Barrani in Egypt, and there he stuck. In the following winter Wavell had driven through to Adjedabia and he could do no more. In a few days Rommel had reconquered all that lost Axis territory, but he, too, collapsed in exhaustion at the Egyptian border. Now, finally, Auchinleck had swung the seesaw back the other way and his army was already floundering in the mud.

Auchinleck would not give up. Despite everything he was determined to go on to Tripoli. While still the rain swept across the Cyrenaican waste through the early days of January he kept pushing his generals to make haste. They must get Benghazi open. They must clear the roads. They must speed the unloading at Suez. There was no fighting to speak of—just the long dreary struggle against inefficiency and delay in the great problem of supply.

The most urgent thing, of course, was to wipe out the enemy garrison at Halfaya. It was blocking the coast road and putting an extra one or two days on the journey from the Nile Delta to the front. Bardia had fallen on New Year's Day after a brief struggle, but still the enemy gunners were able to lob shells on the coast road from Halfaya. At last, in the middle of January, Halfaya fell and the route was clear right through to Benghazi.

The news was received in Cairo with a good deal of excitement and pleasure. Now all Cyrenaica was in our hands and the fall of Bardia and Halfaya had yielded us 13,500 prisoners, as well as a large quantity of war material. A rough check showed that in all the enemy had suffered somewhat less than fifty thousand casualties. Clearly it was a victory. The conquered territory and the long lines of prisoners were there for anyone to see. But still there remained the fact that the bulk of Rommel's army had escaped clean out of Cyrenaica and even in retreat it had made many sudden and damaging forays against our vanguard. And still the rain came down in the desert.

Rain never really falls on Cairo. The place is bathed in perpetual sunshine and at this time of year it is just strong enough to take the chill out of the air and make the climate ideal. Men back on leave flooded the bars and clubs of the city. The movies were crammed. At Gezira there were football matches every day. Shepheard's Hotel and the Continental–Savoy did a roaring business. New nightclubs sprang up—one of them on a houseboat on the Nile. There was no shortage of anything.

Prices were leaping up but then the men in the desert had nothing to spend their money on except their leave. Cairo was gay and secure. Each day at the Turf Club or Gezira I used to see the ticker machines typing out the non-committal news from the front. It seemed to be a stalemate, nothing more. There was no need to worry. The breaking open of the bottleneck at Halfaya had released many damaged tanks and vehicles and these were being hurried back to the delta workshops as fast as possible. There were hundreds of tanks in the workshops. Soon all these would be ready for the great new drive on to Tripoli. True, there was a good deal of stuff now being diverted from the Middle East to Singapore and Java and India, but still new American aircraft were arriving for duty in the desert. It was machines we wanted, not men. Just a few more machines and we would be set to go again.

Only very few in the high command saw the dangers ahead. I lunched one day with Auchinleck and afterwards, as we walked back and forth through his rose garden, he traced the history of the campaign for me step by step. He made me see how much he had been compelled by events to do what he did do, how impatiently and emphatically he had urged his men on to certain courses of action only to find that they were baulked or diverted by the weather or by some move of the enemy or some mechanical thing that happened unexpectedly. He revealed how often a general has to shift his ground and change his orders because the situation is never static. He saw the mistakes all too clearly. I found him modest and direct and extraordinarily clear-sighted that day. He had no rosy pictures of the future. There was his determination to go forward at all costs and he clung to that through all the fog of mishaps and delays and setbacks that were constantly going on. We stopped in our talk to see some of his pictures and once or twice he paused to admire his flowerbeds. But his mind kept darting back to the war. This was his one hour of leisure through the day and he kept pacing back and forth hunting for new ideas, rearranging the old ones, analysing and comparing the things that had happened. Nor did Gott or Willoughby Norrie, the two most active generals in the field, seem to me to be particularly confident. Lucy and I lunched with them both one day at Gezira and I did not like to press them for information. They were taking just one or two days off from the fighting. Norrie, in fact, was hurrying down to the front the next day, for already there were signs that things were going wrong.

Gott turned over to me his maps and papers on the campaign at his Cairo headquarters. He said that he wanted me to use them in the writing of this book and I found them fascinating. His lecture to the officers' training school was especially brilliant. He emphasised in it the necessity for good supply, the necessity for always keeping your supply line in the desert at a right angle to your front so that it would present the smallest possible target and ensure the quickest delivery.

All Gott's theories on supply were being ignored at that very moment. This was not so because the men in command were ignorant or pigheaded. It was happening because the Eighth Army was simply incapable of overcoming the physical difficulties of distance and time. It was too far away from its base. Nor was there cynicism in the ranks about the generals. Gott in particular was loved. I had seen him in Benghazi just a few days previously. He had come in from the front, dirty, unwashed and tired. He drove through the shattered streets to the hospital which was still intact and full of British wounded who had been left there by the retreating enemy. As I stood in the doorway I heard the whisper go round the ward, a filthy evil-smelling place, that Gott was coming in. And with him was Jock Campbell. Gott and Campbell together were a remarkable sight, both of them very tall and heavily built, both soldiers who fought at the front alongside their men, both, as far as one could guess, indifferent to any form of high explosive. The sick men heaved themselves up on their elbows and grinned as the two leaders went down the ward. It was, in some ways, a pathetic little thing, that current of enthusiasm that swept through the hospital and I do not know why I remember it so clearly. Still, there it was—the men still had their leaders and they were willing to fight their way on to Tripoli if they could get there.

The trouble was that they could not even get to the front. As one vital day succeeded another the most the British could get into the Adjedabia region was two brigades. A full brigade of new Valentine tanks had arrived in Suez and these, after a painful journey, did reach the firing-line in addition to the other two brigades. The 4th Indian Division was posted as a garrison for Benghazi, and scattered back along the recent battlefields were South Africans, British, New Zealanders, Poles and Fighting French—about five small divisions in all. They could hardly be called a coordinated force. They sprawled across three or four hundred miles of desert and only that small group around Adjedabia was in actual contact with the enemy.

There was another and entirely separate British force—the Long Range Desert Group. Their numbers were so tiny that they could never seriously affect any battle one way or another. Yet their exploits about this time had become so famous and they were so successful that they were a factor in the fighting. The Long Range Desert Group was a collection of young men of the commando type. They were volunteers and trained men. They had their headquarters in the caves of Siwa Oasis and from there they used to set out on incredible journeys many hundreds of miles inside enemy territory. Their safety was the vastness of the desert. They struck unexpectedly by night and got away.

If you had a taste for piracy and high adventure, then the L.R.D.G. was the unit to join.

Their leader at this time was a young New Zealand major, whom I had met at Siwa one day when one of the most daring raids was being carried out. Just a handful of men had set out in ordinary army trucks. They had measured out their water and petrol to the last spoonful. Every spare pound of weight had been given to machine-guns and bullets, grenades and flares and dynamite. On a clear hot morning they set out into that part of the southern desert where no one, not even the Bedouin, ever penetrates. For many thousands of square miles the country has been scorched into a useless waste, entirely waterless. For the first few hundred miles they knew they were safe enough. No enemy patrol would venture down there, no aircraft was likely to reconnoitre so far south.

As usual they rationed themselves to a cup of tea in the morning and another at night. Another cupful of water was enough for washing. They did not shave but instead grew beards that matted with fine dust as they went along. They travelled slowly—on the good stretches about ten or twelve miles an hour. Often they would have to get down and dig their vehicles out of the sand. One or two of the trucks broke down and, since to abandon the trucks would mean abandoning their crews to death through thirst, the whole caravan waited until repairs were made. Inch by inch and remote from all the world they edged their way across the map. There were no tracks in this desolation and they were guided by compass.

Five days out they came on their objective—a secret Axis airfield, so far behind the front that the usual guards were not stationed around it. Leaving their trucks a few hours' drive away, the men went forward afoot to reconnoitre. Creeping across the sand in the half-light of the evening, they saw a squadron of German bombers lying dispersed near a group of tents. Many camouflaged vehicles were standing around and there were dumps of petrol and bombs spread about near the aircraft.

Everything depended on their taking the place by complete surprise.

That night they attacked. Some ran to the German mess tents and sprayed the enemy officers with tommy-gun fire. Others attacked the aircraft with crowbars and hand grenades. They smashed the instruments in the cockpits and set fire to the fuselage. One after another the petrol dumps went up. It was very quickly done. The Germans ran wildly about among their tents not knowing from what quarter they were being attacked or by how many. Machine-gun bullets were spitting across the airfield from a dozen different directions at once.

As soon as the enemy aircraftsmen ran across to one fire, another started somewhere else. Flares went up over the weird scene and in the yellow light men fought one another with pistols and bayonets. When most of the aircraft were smashed and confusion in the camp was complete, the British commander drew off his men. Driving several prisoners before them, they tramped off to their trucks and drove at full speed into the empty desert. It had been a heady and exciting night, brilliantly successful, but there still remained the long journey back to the British lines.

Enemy aircraft picked up the British car tracks the next morning. They were bombed that day and again the next and again after that. But somehow all came back. Incredibly dirty, tired and dishevelled, they drove into their base bringing their prisoners with them.

There were many raids like this. Sometimes several occurred at the same time. Through the winter they had paved the way for a strong British column that crossed the desert to the tiny oasis of Jalo not far from Adjedabia, and in the middle of January Jalo was still in our hands.

All this time Rommel had been planning his counterattack. It was not done quickly. Among the marshes of the Gulf of Sirte coastline, near El Agheila, he decided to make his stand and prepare. Tanks, guns and men were sent across to him from Italy. Some were landed on the beaches close to the front. Others were dropped off at Tripoli and brought around the coast road. Rommel was only two days' hard drive over a good road from his supply centre at Tripoli and every kind of material began flowing up to him at a time when the supplies in the British front line were running short.

In the middle of January, he began with a series of flanking raids on the British vanguard. These were not serious affairs but they gave Rommel the information he wanted and they forced the British to keep using their ammunition and fuel.

About the time I was lunching with Gott and Norrie in Cairo Rommel felt strong enough to attack. His air reconnaissance had shown him the disposition and size of the British front line. He knew that if he could once get through the front he could fan out inside the British line and create havoc among the soft transport on the supply lines inside. Beyond that lay Benghazi, and Benghazi never was defensible. Neither side had ever attempted to use it as a battleground. The sea-cliffs receded at this point of the coast leaving the town on an open exposed plain. The roads leading northward up the cliffs are bottlenecks and so make retreat difficult. Rommel had abandoned Benghazi on his retreat, and given a first success he could reasonably expect to retake it now.

There is not much to tell. In open pitched battle the heavier German tanks fell on the Valentines near Adjedabia. Some of the Valentines ran out of petrol before they were ever engaged or had to be abandoned on the battlefield. Others lost contact with the supporting anti-tank guns and so faced the German barrage alone. Others again were lost because the Germans overran the British petrol and ammunition dumps.

Communications seem to have failed badly almost from the first moment. Hard-pressed infantry could not get support and reinforcements either lay idle or when they attempted to reach the threatened quarter found their path blocked by the enemy. In three strong columns then the Axis forces streamed straight into the British lines. They fanned out and it was the same old story—isolated British groups being mopped up one after another. In two days the British cutting edge was gone. In three days the British advance had definitely turned into a retreat.

One after another the bases south of Benghazi fell—Adjedabia, Saunu, Antelat, Soluch, Ghemines. There remained only the important operational point at Msus where the British had built up their main supplies. After a confused series of skirmishes Msus fell and then there was no hope for Benghazi.

The British garrison had to act quickly. Demolition squads set to work on all those priceless supplies which had been dragged with such pain and difficulty to the town. Once more Benghazi was ringed with fires at night and big explosions towered up from the cliffs. Two of the Indian brigades were safely got back up the coast road in the Green Hills. A third brigade was cut off in the Benghazi area. It was a bad moment.

When Rommel had driven Wavell out of western Cyrenaica a year before he had ignored the coastal route and cut straight across the desert to Mekili south of Derna. This time he ignored the desert route and instead cut the road leading out of Benghazi. The commander of the trapped Indian brigade rose to the crisis and provided the only really satisfactory British action in the whole engagement. He fought his way out of the German ring. He not only fought his way out but he gathered a number of prisoners and brought them with him.

After that some order was got into the British retreat. A defensive line was thrown up at Gazala, reinforcements were hurried with the hurry of desperation from Egypt and the retreat was ended. For many days after, well into February, British troops kept drifting back to the Gazala Line from Benghazi and all that area we had held so flimsily and vainly for a few weeks.

This, then, was the bitter end to the winter campaign that was to have carried us to Tripoli. On balance we still had the advantage— we had relieved Tobruk, we had destroyed one Axis tank force and taken a respectable number of prisoners. And we had conquered half Cyrenaica. But still it seemed an inconclusive and unsatisfactory end to the adventure.

I put down six reasons for our setback:

The failure to get supplies forward.
The failure to get Benghazi working as a port and air-base.[2]
Poor communications.
The slow recovery of vehicles.
The exceptional weather.
The superiority of the German guns and tanks.

One might make such lists indefinitely. But in the end all lists will bring one to the same inescapable conclusion—that there had been a straight fight and the Axis army was better than the British army. There were no tricks, no great inequality in numbers, no exceptional runs of luck, and no surpassing genius anywhere. The cold fact was that somehow the British had to build a better army. And build it quickly. In the meantime it was a stalemate. The Axis forces were as exhausted as were the British. Too weak to strike, they stood watching one another warily across the Gazala Line while they gathered their strengths again. They were to stay like that until high summer.

Seven

February in Syria

IN FEBRUARY we wanted badly to have a spell away from Egypt and the desert. Lucy had been working hard at G.H.Q. The hours had lengthened and soon her two days off each week dwindled to one, then half, then sometimes none at all. She loved the work, but she was very tired at the end of each day when she came home to organise the flat, the two servants, Hassan and Mohammed, and the baby.

For my part, the campaign had been followed by an outburst of writing. Besides the many thousand words of reporting from the desert I had written several long series on the campaign as a whole and on the German army, and I had completed a scenario for the Army Film unit in addition to my normal work. The stabilisation of the fighting on the Gazala Line had also brought a sense of anticlimax and we all needed some sort of change. So Lucy and I got short leave from our jobs. There was no question of our leaving the Middle East, and the most dramatic opposite to the desert near at hand was the snow. We decided to leave the baby behind with his Armenian nurse and go up to the snowfields in the Lebanon. They said the skiing was best at this time of year.

Lucy's last skiing had been in the Alps at Grindelwald long before the war. Mine had been in the mush at St Cloud during that cold winter in 1938 when all Paris was sheeted with snow. We had had a Christmas tree in my flat and, seen through my frosted windows, the Bois de Boulogne was a lovely tangle of white crystals cupped in the bend of the river. At night the lights of Paris bobbed and twinkled across the snowfields like a million points of phosphorus on the sea. Warmed with warm brandy we had stood there on Christmas Eve looking down on this vision and it had been an overflowing pleasure.

In the morning Geoffrey Cox had come round with his skis and we had gone off to the woods of St Cloud where the snow was lying almost a foot thick. Later we had Christmas dinner at the Coxes' with Walter Kerr and Ed Hartrich, and some of us had gone down to the Boeuf sur le Toit off the Champs Élysées where a dark girl was singing 'You Go to My Head.' It had been almost the last time we were going to find Paris quite like that. It was just a little sad to recall it as Lucy and I drove down to Cairo Central Station to catch the Haifa train. Now the Haifa was no ordinary train. It was a sort of appendix to the old peace-time

Orient Express. It ran from the vicinity of the Pyramids and the Sphinx to the Plain of Armageddon in northern Palestine. Thereafter, with a few connecting bus trips, it resolved itself into the Taurus Express which eventually landed you up in Istanbul and the Golden Horn. Thence the Orient Express took you through Sofia, Belgrade, Turin, Paris and the English Channel to Victoria Station, London. I doubt if anyone made the whole through trip during the war. But still the wagon-lits of the Haifa Express gallantly carried advertisements for 'Hotel Splendide, Ostende,' for many succulent and quite unobtainable French liqueurs. 'Express' was a euphemism in the Middle East meaning 'train which may or may not stop for half an hour at every station.'

Usually it left on time—around 3.30 in the afternoon. But first you had to battle with Cairo Central Station. The entrance seethed with soldiers, Egyptians, Arabs, horse cabs, fly-whisk vendors and mountainous piles of army kit. As your taxi pulled up, three or four Egyptian porters flung themselves inside, tore your luggage out and disappeared with it into the crowd. The best tactics then were to split your forces, sending one party for the tickets and another to find the porters and the luggage. On your way to the ticket office you were offered in turn by the vendors a fly-whisk, an officer's stick, a pornographic magazine, a glass of yellow syrup, a lottery ticket, a bar of partly unused chocolate and a booklet on how to avoid paying income tax.

The booking clerk sends you back to the railway transport officer for a voucher. The transport officer tells you that you don't need one, so you return to the end of the queue at the booking office. It is not the custom latterly to bribe the railway clerks, so you argue in a mixture of French, Arabic and pidgin English and emerge just in time to go sprinting up the platform after the baggage which has been placed in a third-class carriage going to Alexandria. With luck you can get it all transferred to the pullman going in the Haifa direction before the train leaves. The three porters with whom you started out have now swollen to six, and the man selling the pornographic magazines dumps his parcel on a nearby seat and lifts his palm up with the others. You pay the official rate of a piastre a bag with a little extra and a cry of fierce anger goes up from the entire crowd.

The more sophisticated porters laugh with harsh contempt and fling the money onto the platform, taking care to keep their sandals over it. The juniors shrill in chorus, 'No good, no good. Gib ten piastre.' In their wrath and excitement they turn upon the pornographic magazine man and someone deals him a great blow on the back of the head. He hits back viciously and the fight is developing warmly as the train begins to pull out. Immediately all the combatants turn and scream Arabic curses at you as long as you are within earshot. Your last view of them is a line of figures walking contentedly hand in hand down the platform.

The first part of the journey lies through the Delta and the desert to the Suez Canal at El Kantara, not far from the spot where Moses led the Israelites across the Red Sea to the Promised Land.

Not all Egypt looks like one of those lurid lithographs of purple sunset and palm trees with a line of camels walking across the sand-dunes. The Delta gleams with bright subtropical fields of wheat and maize, cotton and tobacco, bananas and sugarcane. It has a warm, moist greenness, all intensely artificial since the water flows in a thousand man-made canals from the Nile and the overworked soil is forced into fertility with nitrates. Every few yards oxen clump stolidly round and round their waterwheels or thresh the grain in an endless circle with their hooves. Every village in Egypt looks as though it has been bombed the night before. There are thousands of these crazy unfinished mud-hut compounds all of pitiless squalor and unbelievable dirt. Sipping weak tea in the pullman, you watch it all go by through the windows. The fan over your head stirs the flies and dust from one end of the carriage to the other. Your compartment might contain a couple of English officers going on local leave, a sheikh in his native robes, a Polish ensign and a couple of Australian privates who have got into the pullman because it looked comfortable. The Australians are waiting with pleasurable anticipation for someone to come along and tell them to remove to a third-class carriage. They will then enquire if anyone wants a fight.

Kantara is the spot on the canal which the Germans liked to bomb. They swooped across from Crete sometimes carrying thousand pounders, sometimes carrying mines. For some reason the Germans never really succeeded in blocking the canal by sinking ships in it. They have caused delays while the canal was swept after a raid, but the traffic was never seriously disrupted. After the first year they found daylight raids too costly and came only on moonlight nights. The Haifa train with Olympian indifference to all this continued to reach Kantara in the evening and proceeded to send its passengers across the canal to connect with the Palestine train on the other side just at the moment when the enemy was most likely to bomb.

There was, of course, a blackout in Kantara and the business of the porters there achieved an added virulence and mystery. There was one remarkable night when all the military passengers were carrying the same sort of leather suitcase, bought from the same army depot in Cairo. It was child's play for the porters to get a couple of hundred cases mixed up on the ferry and then began the long exciting hours in the darkness when we roamed up and down the platform opening each other's baggage in search of our own.

At Kantara station you saw a little cross-section of the Middle East. A squad of German prisoners surrounded by fixed bayonets comes marching down the platform on its way to some camp in Palestine, or some ship at Suez. Quietly the young Nazis whistle 'We March Against England.' They are quiet, well disciplined and their taut young faces are full of defiance. It is interesting to see the reactions of the polyglot crowd waiting on the platform. The English colonel elaborately turns his back. The young sous-lieutenant, who escaped from Bordeaux, makes some bitter sneer in French.

The Tommies exchange barnyard jokes with the escort. The Australians mutter unprintably. The Indian soldiers merely stare in a curious childlike way, uncomprehending and indifferent. The Arabs grin vacantly.

It was not like this at all when the Italian prisoners went by. Once out of the battlefields, I seldom saw Italian prisoners when they were not fatalistically laughing, singing or swapping comments with British troops. Their attitude seemed to be—'In the African army we never got home leave and we had to fight. Now we still don't get leave, but we don't have to fight. So what the hell.'

But the Nazis created an aura of dislike and bitterness wherever they went. That tense, uncompromising and almost fanatical look on their faces seemed to isolate them from other people. They invited hatred, even when they were prisoners, and hatred made a wall around them. The young ones I spoke to coming freshly from battle did not appear to be like ordinary young people any more. Something human and kindly had gone out of them. None of those I saw were blue-eyed, fair-haired Aryan giants, but just ordinary little mechanics from the Rhine and clerks from Berlin, many of them thinnish, with rather a pinched look on their faces and under normal height. But they were unquestionably fine soldiers, these of the Afrika Korps, with their transcendent *esprit de corps* and faith in their mission. They had a military habit of mind which made them automatic and correct.

Clearly they thought it was a degrading, humiliating thing to be captured—rather as we would have felt, perhaps, to be captured by the Japanese. They took refuge in their isolation and their discipline.

So there they go, these young men of the 19th Light Infantry, while we sit around on our baggage waiting for the Palestine section of the Haifa train to come in. If you have a sleeper from Kantara, the Haifa express is tolerable and easy—and Lucy and I were lucky. But it's in the rest of the train that you get the real flavour of the journey. Men lie sleeping or trying to sleep wherever they can—on the floors of the corridors, under the seats, between the seats, and on the seats and in the lavatory. Another time I made this trip there was simply no room at all and about twenty of us laid siege to the locked restaurant car. We had no sooner broken in and settled down on the floor when a South African was sick and so we stormed the kitchen and spent the night perched among the cooking pots.

The morning brings you to the oases of El Arish and Gaza with Beersheba nearby, the place where Allenby launched his big offensive against the Turks in the last war. Then at last, toward midday, you creep into the promised land around Lydda where orange groves cover the earth and you get the first real breath of cool air. You are not doing badly. True, the train was due in Haifa at 9 a.m., but there is still a reasonable chance of your reaching there before dark.

All this coast is a lovely place, rich with farmlands and lines of eucalyptus trees and a cool breeze comes off the sea. The German-Jewish refugees have worked hard to recapture their memories of Vienna. Little biergartens lie along the way, and they have gay sunshades, string music and very drinkable beer. Haifa itself is a sparkling town, and Lucy and I came into it in the late afternoon—just early enough to hire a car and make the three hours' drive above the cliffs into Beyrout across the border in Syria. Beyrout had settled down uneasily to the rule of the British and the Fighting French. Everything had doubled or trebled in price, and the winter was bringing in serious poverty and hunger…a fruitful background for the intrigue that festers endlessly in Syria. Yet it was still a place to remind you of Toulon in the summer. The Lebanon shone frostily with snow from above the town.

The sea below rippled like shot silk. Nowhere else in the Middle East is there colour and light like this.

We went shopping through the bazaars where they sell soft gazelle skins. We crossed the mountains to Baalbec and roamed among the great ruins there. We drank brandy in a bistro by the waterfront. We priced the French scent which had now gone up to £30 a bottle. We took a rowing boat out into the harbour with Philip Astley and pretended to fish. We went to a military cocktail party.

These surely are the sort of things one does on a holiday. But it was no good. We were still too much involved in the war. Even here any day they were expecting the Axis parachutists might come. The streets were full of Australians.

We went off then on that hair-raising drive to the topmost peaks of the Lebanon where they had two hotels, one for the military, called The Cedars, the other for tourists called—God knows why—Mon Repos.

It was not easy, of course, far up there in the snow, to achieve comfort and warmth. But one felt one might expect such things as, say, a wall to your bedroom and a chair to sit on; and these things were not necessarily part of the 'service extraordinaire' at Mon Repos. The place was a 'paradis des sports d'hiver'—just that pure and simple, and you could ask for clean sheets to be thrown in as well.

We were not over-optimistic as we drove up to the ramshackle door, between ten-foot walls of snow. Two departing guests, both strong physical types, hurried up to our car enquiring, 'Is this the car to take us back to Beyrout? It is? Thank God.' We asked them what they meant, but they merely looked at us darkly, bundled their luggage aboard and departed down the mountainside. The manager, a dark little Egyptian, then approached and announced that our bookings were invalid. We would have to go away at once, he said. The 'service extraordinaire' presumably. We were rude to one another for ten minutes, more especially as I had paid £25 in advance. Heaven knows the manager had reason. About a hundred human beings were crammed into this shed in conditions that made the soldier's life look like the ultimate in riotous luxury.

In the end we were squeezed into a cubicle with one single bed on the angle of the staircase. Since the bedstead had no bedding and only three and a half legs, it seemed a little superfluous, but we found later it was doing good work in propping up the piece of three-ply that served as the wall.

There was no other furniture. Fine granules of snow, only slightly interrupted by the cracked window, were eddying across the tiled floor. In the next cubicle a husband and wife were arguing wearily about the hellishness of all life in war-time.

Lunch came in with a rush and a bang. I have no clear memory of what we ate on this or any other day. A kind of desperate hunger seized us, and we ate quickly and in silence, ignorance and loathing. I only remember one day saying to the waiter timidly, '*Pourriez-vous me donner un peu plus de vermicelli soupe?*' and he, replying coldly, '*Il n'y-a pas de vermicelli soupe aujourdui. Vous mangez pudding de tapioc. C'est une assiette anglaise. Voulez-vous encore de ça?*

'Sure,' I said. 'Give me a little more tapioca pudding, then.'

Outside all was different. Mon Repos was perched on the lip of a precipice and behind, a huge basin of snow swept up to the heights of the Lebanon. On the edge of this basin grew the hundred or so trees that were all that was left of the Biblical cedars of Lebanon, and they were still magnificent. It was pure joy to coast on skis between the old trunks, in and out of the sun and the shade, and so down to the hotel again.

Close to the trees lay the other hotel, The Cedars, which was now a school for training Australians in ski-warfare. The soldiers had been provided with white overalls in which to ski, and when they came to render these overalls waterproof the only stuff available was copper sulphate. The overalls came out of the proofing process a stimulating pale green colour. The effect of some fifty or sixty men ploughing about the white mountainside in pale green suits was a thing well worth seeing. 'Like caterpillars,' someone said. As with the seven dwarfs they all had green peaked hoods.

The Australians really enjoyed themselves. Great ringing oaths echoed from peak to peak as they came thundering down the slopes in a welter of broken skis and flying snow. With most of them it was a thing of muscle more than skill, but one or two were really good. They used to come into Mon Repos at night to buy the fluid which the barman laughingly called alcoholic drinks. Their faces were burnt brick-red by the sun-glare and all of them were bursting with health. Having nothing else to do with their money they put it into the Mon Repos fruit machine which had long been the hotel's financial triumph. That fruit machine was a remarkable piece of engineering. Every hour or so the manager would enter and extract a tinful of money from the works. There was one regrettable night when three plums turned up and the thing disgorged eighteen piastre pieces. It was the damp air, I suppose, that got at the works. At all events the whole contraption was unchained from the wall and taken into a back room. It emerged again in its old place a couple of days later and there was no nonsense about three plums turning up after that.

I talked one night with a young sergeant who was the ace of the junior instructors. He had begun his skiing on the wilds of Mount Hotham in south-eastern Australia where the bushmen use skis more as a means of conveyance than as a sport. His whole world was bounded by skiing. 'You know,' he said seriously, 'there's a time of the year, especially during a bad winter, when there's snow all the way from here to Berlin.' I found it good to hear him say it. What visions he must have had of bowling down off the Lebanon into Turkey and then on across Bulgaria, Rumania, Hungary and Czechoslovakia and through Dresden to the Unter den Linden. I fancy he pictured just a little band on skis, a tommy-gun wrapped in bedding on the shoulders of each man, and then the great adventure of hiding in villages, raiding Nazi barracks at night, mining railway trains and setting fire to barges on the Danube; a wild fanciful dream, one of the kind that wins wars.

On the lower slopes the snow was mushy and you had to climb for an hour or more to the spots where it was icy on the surface. Lying exhausted up there with all the Syrian coast fanned out below we ate oranges and chocolate until we got our breath back. Then for the next hour we traversed and practised christianias and snow ploughs or just got fed up with the drill and plunged headlong down the valleys with the sunny wind streaming through our hair. We were terribly out of practice, terribly unused to climbing, but it was gay. We stayed out as long as we could, putting off the grim moment when we would have to go back into Mon Repos for lunch.

There was a German Jewish ski club staying at the hotel and skiing to them was no light thing. They rose relentlessly before dawn, men, women and boys. The grey morning light was just beginning when they rushed with whoops and shouts out into the snow. Then they set off for the highest, most distant and most frozen peak. The rules of the club forbade them to sing until they had reached a certain height and the leader kept remorselessly hounding the stragglers on. What trials and endurance tests went on in the upper reaches I do not know, but several hours later you would hear 'Achtungs' ringing across the mountainside and down they would hurtle across the ice at forty miles an hour.

There was one little man we called the 'Brown Bomber' and he either could not or would not learn the rules. His courage was immense. He would poise himself at the edge of some awful gulf, set his jaw, plant his feet wildly apart and then launch into space. At first he flew superbly over frozen ruts and hidden rocks. At the end of the first two or three hundred yards he achieved a most terrifying speed, and as he rushed past one could see the fixed misery on his face, for he knew the end was near. Being wholly out of control, he would bear down on some other hapless tourist coming up the slope. While the tourist stood transfixed with horror and the Brown Bomber croaked a warning from his dry lips, the collision would take place. Still as rigid as stone the Brown Bomber would somersault into the air and finish the rest of the course in a series of arcs and parabolas like some great boulder that had avalanched from the heights above. At the bottom he would pick himself up and trudge wearily up the mountain again. The stunned and frightened tourist would be taken back to Mon Repos and given a little parsnip wine from a gin bottle.

The Brown Bomber was one of those Germans whom you can never really defeat. Someone had told him that skiing was an enjoyable and even an easy sport and he was just damn well going to go on until it did turn out to be easy and enjoyable. He was still plunging madly into the rocks when I left.

As for the rest of the ski club, they would tramp into luncheon each day to bolt a quick meal. Then such of those who had not been injured in the morning's exercises would go out again for another three or four hours' drill.

It was pleasant to sit in the sun on the uneven roof of Mon Repos and drink beer and watch them at work. I suppose Lucy and I might have had more fun there than we did despite the food and the damp sheets. But somehow I could not shake off the feeling of the war. It was a continual disturbance in one's head, an uneasy ghost that came and sat beside one at every quiet minute. I knew I could not stay out of it for more than a few days while so many things were happening. Then when Singapore fell, it was too much. We drove down to Beyrout just in time to catch the afternoon plane to Cairo, and I sent off a cable to Christiansen asking for permission to leave for Australia. Australia appeared at that time to be the next place on the Japanese list, and my argument for going there was that the Middle East was quiet and that I was born and grew up in Australia and knew the country well.

Noel Monks of the *Daily Mail* flew in from London on his way out. Ronald Matthews, Ted Genock, and many others I knew had already gone ahead. Christiansen was at first in favour of the idea. It was nearly six years since I had been home and I booked my passage in some excitement. But then Rangoon fell, and Charles Foley, my foreign editor, pointed out that while India was in more immediate danger than Australia, we were understaffed there. Correspondents evacuating Singapore had given us all the staff we wanted in Australia. So there was nothing for it but to get aboard the flying boat at Cairo and go off into the full summer heat of New Delhi. Sir Stafford Cripps on his mission to conciliate the country was already a day ahead of me. For some reason, I had never wanted to go to India. A brief visit to Ceylon years before had not excited any further interest for me. Gloomily I left Lucy and the baby in Cairo and set off.

Eight
March in India

FROM THE air, India in summer is just another desert. A common brownness covers everything. The flying boat dumped me down in the centre of the country at Gwalior and that, too, is brown—brown lake, brown rocks, brown fields and brown villages. From this moment to the time I left India and Ceylon two months later, I was never really comfortable unless I was sitting directly under an electric fan with a cool drink in my hand. Matt Halton and I accompanied a brigadier and a young subaltern up to the Gwalior Hotel to await the arrival of the train from New Delhi. We had been warned in advance that it was impossible to find rooms anywhere in Delhi, since the people who had come to see Cripps had crowded it out. We felt too hot to care.

We lunched off curry and that permits me one more general statement—not once in India did I succeed in getting any decent curry. Obviously I went to the wrong places or did not try hard enough, but the fact remains that it was not until I got right outside the curry belt—to Ceylon in fact—that I came on a really first-class brew. I got it at the Galleface Hotel in Colombo, and it was a curry of such virulence and natural heat that it left the mouth blistered for the next twenty-four hours. Here at Gwalior the cook had not even tried, and when I came to pay the bill the Indian waiter rejected my rupees on the ground that they bore the head of King Edward VII. King Edward VII, the waiter argued, was dead. Therefore his currency was not valid.

It was my first introduction to the witch-doctory and ignorance in which a great part of India has lain sleeping these past thousand years. I played a Gilbertian game of billiards against the brigadier with elliptical ivory balls and twisted cues, and then at last we trailed across to the station to catch the train.

It was just an ordinary Indian train and therefore fascinating. Matt and I piled into a first-class compartment, took lukewarm showers, and as the three fans gently blew the hot floor-dust in our faces, men came to sell us ivory carved models of the Taj Mahal and fans made of peacock feathers. There were no connecting corridors and at every halt bearers and servants who had been locked in their own compartment came bounding along the platform to sweep the gathering dust from the floor and ply us with tea—good tea. At places like Agra we got out and walked through the restless polyglot crowds. There was a rich creamy smell of flowers and fruit. We observed some of the rites of the Experienced British Woman Abroad. She plugs all the cracks of the carriage doors and windows with newspapers to keep out the dust. Then she hoists a bucketful of ice and suspends it a foot or two below the central fan. The air sweeps cleanly and fairly coolly off the ice and there the lady sits with her tea and her copy of the *Illustrated Times of India*. Enviously Matt and I went back to our steamy cabin and tried to read the lurid magazines we had bought in Gwalior. These magazine were 'pulps' of the True Confessions type, but a local product. They were written in good circumlocutory English and the theme of most of the stories was this: The young Indian student, already married with several children, is studying at one of the universities. He is poor. His great aim in life is to obtain admission into the Indian Civil Service, which means wealth, dignity and a slice of the power of the great British Raj. He meets a girl as lovely as his wife is drab, as intelligent as his wife is illiterate. The next ten pages are devoted to describing the student's reactions, physical and mental, to his new 'soul-mate'—you have just got to get used to that phrase 'soul-mate'. The wife wants her husband back, the student wants to go onward and upward with his soul-mate and the I.C.S., and the soul-mate wants to make a sacrifice of some sort. Somehow, usually through a tragedy, the thing is disentangled and you are left with an impression of frustration and disillusionment. The stuff reeks with cheap sentimentality and snobbery of the most blatant kind. The worst of it is the sycophancy with which the I.C.S., and anything European is regarded. A thick treacle of sex, the luscious and serpentine kind, is spread over the whole dish. I remember putting the magazines down and having a good sneer. After all, I knew still less about India then than I know now.

Nobody at that time had shown me the intense repression of poverty in India. It entirely escaped me that these cheap magazines were an expression of just one of the limited horizons which the Indian has been allowed to see. Nor could I yet see in them the intense desire to 'do something better,' to 'get out of the rut,' to 'find some meaning in life.'

It was not that I was prejudiced against India—I was merely accepting the evidence as it came along. I had no conception then of the enormous uphill climb that lies in front of nearly every child born in India.

We went on steadily toward Delhi, past some of those three thousand villages where life is so degraded and short that it is only a slight departure from death—villages of cow-dung and mud, places of no sewerage, no artificial light, no meat and very little grain, of endless childbirth and disease. And so into the city of New Delhi.

It was already dark, and on the platform they laughed at the idea of our finding rooms in the Imperial Hotel. Nevertheless I insisted on driving there first. At the reception desk the clerk answered with the boredom of a man who has said the same thing many times before—'Sorry, we have no rooms. No, I don't think you will find a room anywhere in New Delhi. You might try Old Delhi, but there is almost certainly nothing there either.'

We were very tired after our three days' flight and the long train journey. I was asking for permission to sleep in the lounge, when along the corridor came Richard Busvine. Richard, of course, had everything arranged—room, bathroom, drinks, everything. So we settled down to the discovery of New Delhi and the strange case of Stafford Cripps *versus* the Indian people.

It was a moment beyond all others in which to arrive. Just for a few days the intensely complicated political life of more than 350 million people, one-fifth of the population of the world, had become crystallised. Nearly every major party and a good few of the minor ones had sent spokesmen to New Delhi. There were the Viceroy, Lord Linlithgow, and General Wavell, who composed the political and military sides of the two-headed monster, the British Raj. There was Gandhi, still the greatest personal force in India, and his followers or near followers, Jawaharlal Nehru, Maulana Azad, Rajagopalacharia Patel and the others of the All India Congress. Then Jinnah of the Muslims, their bitter enemy. Then the princes and the Untouchables, the Hindu Mahasabha, the Sikhs and the Gurkhas, the Parsees and the British businessmen, Colonel Louis Johnson, the United States minister and Major-General Brereton, head of the American military forces. There were Communists and Pacifists, pro-Axis groups like the Forward Bloc and many, many others.

Each had his case to put to Cripps and Cripps had his case to put to them—the case for the independence of India and the defence of India. To give the whole tremendous scene an atmosphere of sharpness and urgency, Rangoon fell and the Japanese forces began rapidly marching northward through Burma toward Bengal. We appeared to be on the threshold of the invasion of India and the possible collapse of the greatest and richest part of the British Empire.

Apart from reading one or two superficial books, my knowledge of India was absolutely nil.

Cripps had begun his negotiations and somehow, within the space of a few hours, I had to absorb enough to be able to write intelligible reports for my newspaper in London. I decided to begin with the people I knew best—the military. Richard took me up to G.H.Q. and the secretariat.

Sir Edwin Lutyens, the famous British architect, was the man who got the job of designing New Delhi. The British wanted an Imperial City, a place of spreading avenues and fountains, of massive administrative blocks and ponderous monuments. They got it. Lutyens spared nothing. The central post office went *here*, the commander-in-chiefs house went *there*, the imperial arch at this end of the park and the viceroy's house at the other, the shops and the banks in a neat circle down one end of the town, the clubs and the residences with their lovely gardens spaced round the curving roads at the other.

New Delhi, as a result, looks exactly like what it was in the beginning—a set of architect's drawings. With the possible exception of Canberra, the capital of Australia, which was built in almost the same way, it is the best ordered and most attractive city I have ever seen. It is a mistake, however, to imagine that New Delhi has anything to do with India. It still is an enormous English club, the finest in the world.

Its very gardens and flowerbeds isolate it from the parched brown earth of India, and the hungry people of India have no place here. They seldom penetrate into these well-kept shaded streets. As we drove along, Richard related to me an incident of the day before. It seemed that a man of deep political feeling had hired a thing called a 'tonga,' which is a sort of donkey cart. Upon this he had mounted a microphone and he drove through New Delhi shouting, 'Go home, Cripps. Go home, Cripps.' The tonga driver had sat his seat fairly and composedly, and at the end of the drive had collected his fare in the usual way. While the incident fascinated me, Richard said that it had not drawn so much as a crowd of fifty people. Rashly I took that as a sign that the public were well disposed toward Cripps.

We rounded the Imperial Arch and came within full view of those two solid redstone bastions that house G.H.Q. and the secretariat, an extraordinary sight. A fierce wall of heat, at least a hundred yards thick, was reflected outward from the buildings. Shaded wooded walls would no doubt have been much cooler, but cheap wood is unthinkable in New Delhi. We went inside and met Major Peter Coates. He was still Wavell's personal assistant and the general, lurking in the inside office, sent out a message inviting me to luncheon. I handed over some letters I had brought from General Auchinleck and went off to meet some of the I.C.S. bosses. They were friendly, confident and precise. They laid out the Indian problem neatly and clearly. They gave one the impression that here at least was calm strength and foresight in the midst of this awful muddle—and as for the muddle, well, they felt that was just hopeless anyhow. Nobody called Gandhi a blackguard or said that Nehru ought to be clapped into jail again. They were very polite about Gandhi and Nehru and referred to them always as 'Mister'. One of these men kept repeating: 'There is, of course, no question of arming the masses.' I was too new to India to realise the significance of that. What pulled my thoughts up with a jolt was the way in which most of them were confidently looking forward to the failure of Cripps' mission.

It was not expressly that they resented this 'amateur' coming in to do what the British had failed to do for so many decades—pacify India. It was more of a settled conviction that there was really no solution to the mess. India, they suggested, would just have to muddle along in her old way. In the meantime, they were perfectly open-minded about any proposal for a quick solution. They merely reserved the right to be sceptical.

Nor was the luncheon with Wavell any more informative. The general sat in the midst of his family and the talk went round the table in an easy, pleasant way without touching on the political crisis that was raging through India. Peter Fleming volunteered the information that the way to tell the difference between Japanese and Chinese soldiers was to take their boots off. The Japanese, he said, were accustomed to wearing a thong on their sandals which divided the big toe from the little toes; the Chinese were not. So if you found a man with his big toe jutting out then he was a Jap. Lady Wavell, sitting next to me, said that she had found far too many servants in the house and was economising. A Dutch officer and General Hartley, who was the commander-in-chief, India, before Wavell, were also at the table and said little. I passed on the gossip from the Middle East and said that Wavell had been reported wounded at Singapore just before the fall of the garrison. 'No,' Wavell said, 'I walked down to the end of the quay in the blackout and fell off. I am all right now.' It was an agreeable luncheon, but nothing was said that would give me any sort of a clue to the situation.

I have talked often to Wavell and seldom come away with any really vital information. Yet for some reason it is a most stimulating thing to meet him. He seems to have the same enlivening effect upon everyone he meets. Later, the American general, Brereton, said to me, 'You can say this: General Wavell is the finest soldier I have ever met.' This was said after the fall of Singapore and Java; after Wavell's reverses in the Western Desert, Greece and Crete. Alone among the British generals, his reputation survived one failure after another.

My own theory is that this is so because Wavell is so irresistibly like Tolstoy's Kutuzov. His fine heavy head, his lined and leathery face, even his blind eye, give you the feeling of strength and sagacity and patience, though there is little in what he says normally to suggest any of those qualities. He listens intently. One feels one can tell him everything.

About this time I was reading Tolstoy's *War and Peace* and had come on this passage: 'How, and why it was, Prince Andrey could not explain, but after his interview with Kutuzov, he went back to his regiment feeling reassured as to the future course of the war and as to the man to whom its guidance was entrusted… "He will put in nothing of himself. He will contrive nothing, will undertake nothing," thought Prince Andrey, "but he will hear everything, will think of everything, will put everything in its place, will not hinder anything that could be of use, and will not allow anything that could be of harm. He knows that there is something stronger and more important than his will—that is the inevitable march of events, and he can see them, can grasp their significance, and, seeing their significance, can abstain from meddling, from following his own will, and aiming at something else." '

It all fits Wavell perfectly, or at least the Wavell I had known for the past three years. How many hundreds of officers have gone back to their regiments reassured after meeting him. How many of them have said, 'It's all right. He knows what is going on. He won't forget.' Yet Wavell in nine out of ten of these interviews has done little more than listen. 'He will not hinder anything that could be of use.' That semi-negative quality, in the last resort, seems to be the thing men want in a general. It seems to give men more confidence than anything else. To know that the correct, efficient thing will be done because the commander knows what the correct efficient things is—this to my mind has more potency than all the rousing orders of the day, all the band playing and the high heroics.

After luncheon, I spoke to the general of the possibility of rebellion in India. I asked if there might not be a rising to coincide with a

Japanese attack on Bengal. 'I hope not,' he said. 'It may be, of course, but I hope not.' And he went on briefly to discuss the situation without giving any definite view. Why I found this reassuring I do not know; I simply came away with the feeling that what was coming was bound to come anyway, that there was nothing to do about it except just what Wavell was doing—impeding nothing that could be of use, promoting everything that would help the army in its defence.

Eve Curie, who was staying with the Wavells, came in after luncheon and I talked for a little with her and Peter Fleming. Neither was very hopeful about the situation.

I had letters for Lady Auchinleck from her husband. She was staying in the viceroy's house, and I went up there in the evening. The place resembles the other official buildings—redstone, heat and all—and through some quirk of the architect, you approach it through two hideous underground ramps rather like the entrance to a London tube station. They led me through winding corridors to a simple and beautifully furnished little room. Lady Auchinleck could never, even in France, have been referred to as 'La Generale'. She was too young, too unaffected, too forthright and too attractive. She had been delivering army trucks all day and was still in her sergeant's uniform, and she opened our conversation with two hopelessly indiscreet remarks about her husband. I liked her tremendously at once, and so I gather did most of the other people in New Delhi.

We went out into the garden at the back of the house and even now that the summer heat was withering every green thing, it was a breathlessly lovely place. It was huge, one of the last of the great gardens of the world. It had a golf course, grass tennis courts and big stretches of country out beyond the stables, where you could ride. Nearer to the house brilliant creepers hung over the garden walls and a pathway dotted with fountains led you down to a circular pond. Like the tiers of a Roman theatre the flowerbeds reached up from the pond row on row, and the outer circular wall was ablaze with pinks and blues and yellows. Lawns sloped away under the trees. All this was being neutralised and dried up by the summer sun; it would not bloom again until after the monsoon.

Back at the Imperial Hotel a strange group of journalists were gathering to report the Cripps mission. Philip Jordan of the *News Chronicle* had come in from Russia, and Leland Stowe of the *Chicago Daily News*, from Burma and America. Clare Boothe, whom I had seen in Cairo, was looking and talking very much like the woman who wrote *The Women*. New Delhi had not been quite able to absorb both Clare Boothe and Eve Curie at the same time. Apart from the fact that they were both highly successful, they were absurdly in contrast. Clare Boothe was blonde, lively, witty, gregarious, full of highly coloured opinions and completely American. Eve Curie was dark, quiet, aloof, full of shrewd abstract deductions and completely cosmopolitan. Both were very attractive and had invitations to stay with the Wavells and the viceroy. I never saw them together. Each went after the news in her own way. Dining with Clare Boothe you would discover that she had fallen heavily for Nehru's brilliant and cultured mind and that the root of the trouble was the repression and hopelessly inefficient imperialism of the British. Dining with Eve Curie, you would find that she had seen everyone including Gandhi and fallen for no one and that the sickness of India lay far deeper than any malady the British had caused. One could not help talking to Clare Boothe but agreeing with Eve Curie.

There were also in Delhi Sam Brewer of the *Chicago Tribune*, who had flown across from the Middle East; Inglis of the London *Times*, who knew more than anyone else; and half a dozen Americans, who arrived from all over the world. On Saturday night the hotel was a resplendent regency piece. Aged but definitely Parisian gowns and a surge of dress uniforms floated down the lounge to the dinner dance on the floor above. The Indian princes and their retainers came in with their women in jewels and saris. The leader of the band was Viennese, the cabaret Eurasian and sadly European, the wine South African, and the food a glamorous memory of the Brighton hotels before the war. Little potted trees bloomed with oranges on the terrace outside and people sat on the lawn sipping Drambuie and French coffee. There was also the grill room where you sat on leather chairs before an open furnace and watched a suckling pig and half a dozen chickens turn slowly round on a sizzling spit. Scores of overhead fans kept up the unequal struggle against the heat.

In the bar I used to meet a British brigadier, one of whose jobs was training the Gurkhas as parachute troops. Like most other people I had an affection and admiration for the little Chinese- looking men and I liked this story about them. The Gurkhas, it seems, insisted on jumping with their kukris—curved knives with which they can lop off a man's head with one blow. The British officers pointed out that each Gurkha already carried a tommy-gun, revolver, medicine chest and other oddments strapped to his legs and body, and that a knife would be dangerous in landing. But the Gurkhas were adamant—'No knife, no jump.' So the knives were fitted with a rubber tip and the Gurkhas came down like a band of Barbary pirates on the wing.

I picked up all sorts of information round the hotel. There were the lads from the American Volunteer Group, who had been doing a tremendous job flying Kittyhawks against the Japanese in Burma. I talked to everyone I could about Indian politics. I found pro-Indian British colonels and pro- British Indians. I found Muslims who agreed with Hindus and Fascists who wanted to fight the Japanese. There were Tories who wanted to get the Communists into the government and fire-eating officers who 'saw something in what Gandhi was getting at.' There were absolute princes who were moving for legislative assemblies. There must have been thousands in New Delhi of liberal or freakish turn of mind. But for every one who genuinely looked toward a compromise there were millions who were entrenched irrevocably in their own opinions. And all around this artificial and unread citadel there was this solid wall of bitterness and hatred, ignorance and misunderstanding. I found this city frighteningly soft and dilatory after the military atmosphere of the Middle East—and the Middle East, as anyone could tell you, was no model of discipline. I began to see what the I.C.S. bosses meant when they talked resignedly about the Indian problem and I felt depressed when I went back to the vice-regal lodge to see the viceroy on the day after my arrival.

It was no light thing to lunch with Victor Alexander John Hope, the Marquess of Linlithgow, and his wife. Linlithgow himself, a man who rarely if ever smiled, and whose outlook, superficially at least, was a settled melancholy, did not design the ceremony and ritualistic decoration of the viceroy's office. Nor, I imagine, did he enjoy it particularly. But there it was—the gilt-edged Victorian system, the orders of precedence, the flunkeys and the parade—and the Linlithgows took it over. You might argue that the viceroy could have made gaps in this wall that hedged him off from the Indian people, but the choice was not entirely his. The British conservative party believed—and probably still believes—that people want glamour and display in their kings, an expression of all they might have and do if they were kings themselves.

So you first took a cocktail with two or three aides-de-camp and a private secretary when you went to lunch at the viceroy's house. They talked easily and informally, but one of the aides you noticed was glancing at his watch. At one o'clock, I think it was, or perhaps 1.06 p.m. we moved in file to an antechamber of the dining room. We stood round in a semicircle, myself the only guest, at the left hand and near the central table. I was required to turn half right and so poise myself that I was facing the double doors leading off a shaded verandah. I was warned beforehand what to do and what would happen and it happened just like that. At 1.10 p.m. the viceroy and his wife, who must have been two of the tallest people in India, came through the double doors, shook hands silently, and flowed on through and out of the room without a word spoken. The young aide with the watch whipped out of his pocket a scrap of paper with a plan of the luncheon table, and the places of everybody marked on it, and we all went off in pursuit of the viceroy to the dining room.

Lunch (curry) with a brightly caparisoned servant behind each chair, the viceroy silent and intent on his port, and only Lady Linlithgow and myself chatting on matters that interested neither of us, was not a spontaneous meal. Toward the end Linlithgow lifted his head and began to speak sporadically and slowly about India. I asked him if there was any good book covering the last ten years in India which he could recommend. He thought deeply for a couple of minutes, then answered precisely, 'No. I know of no such book. But the fact that I do not know of the existence of a book, does not imply that such a book does not exist.'

As we got up from the table, the time-keeper aide whispered to me, 'Will you go over there and talk to the viceroy?' I went off in pursuit again and Linlithgow offered me a cigarette and a seat beside him. There followed for the next twenty minutes as clear and concise an exposé of the Indian scene as I was going to get during all my stay in the country. I disagreed with Linlithgow's approach to nearly everything he discussed, but his facts were there, incontrovertible, logical and persuasive. He was well aware that he was the butt not only of a great deal of anti-British feeling in India, but of liberal opinion overseas. If it had affected his judgment it had merely made him gloomy—he was none the less subtle. He worked, I knew, some fourteen hours a day, especially at this time. He had a habit of passing his hand wearily across his face, and this combined with the effect of what he was saying left me with an even stronger feeling of pessimism than the one with which I had arrived. All the paths of this argument seemed to have been trodden so often and so fruitlessly before. There was nothing one could suggest that had not already been put up and knocked down for one reason or another. It was useless to postulate a resurgent India on the lines of new Russia, new China—the seeds of new life just were not there. Civil war, invasion, intenser racial hatred, wider poverty— these made the future of all these helpless millions, unless we were very wise and strong. Even granted good luck and time, the best we could hope to do was to keep India intact as she was—to prevent the

Japanese entering and the evils multiplying. Cripps could scarcely hope to affect the future one way or the other.

I am not reporting here what the viceroy said as our conversation was a private one. I am summarising the effect left in my mind through all the discussions I had had and the things I had seen up to this time. Before I left, the viceroy traced for me the probable course of the coming three months in India, and I am bound to admit that what he said was incorrect only in this—that things have turned out a good deal better than he then hoped. On their general course he was right. Some of the blacker alternatives he suggested have yet to arise.

I drove back to the Imperial Hotel and ordered a chota-peg and on second thought changed it to a burra-peg which is a double chota-peg and still a very small whisky.

The burra-peg for a long time had been the palliative for most of the worries of official India. Clasping mine firmly I went up to my room to type a message to my paper. At the end I found it contained roughly 1 per cent of the information I had gathered that day. The rest of the stuff was unusable. Too complex, too gloomy.

Nine

March in India (continued)

STAFFORD CRIPPS had settled into an informal-looking bungalow in Queen Victoria Road. One after another, the Indian leaders went to meet him and hear what his proposals were. We were told that Cripps would broadcast his proposals to the world in a day or two. After that the Indian leaders were going to be given until the end of the week to return a 'Yes' or 'No'.

You can imagine the scene at the villa; scores of Indian journalists and cameramen prowling about the grounds and swooping upon anyone who came or went through the front door. The local newspapers, like the *Hindustani Times*, were a riot of speculation and cartooning; a favourite cartoon showed Cripps with an Indian pipe to his lips trying to do the Rope Trick while Gandhi looked on sceptically. Another showed Cripps as the young man on the flying trapeze. He wore an agonised expression on his face because his fellow-performer, Nehru, had failed to reach out his hands to catch him. Nehru's hands were bound with a heavy weight. Few politically conscious people in India had failed to recognise the weight as Gandhi.

Gandhi himself had telegraphed Cripps that he had no intention of altering his well-known views on non-violence and that he did not think he could help the mission. Cripps, however, sent a charming telegram and the Mahatma had arrived staff in hand like some strange white bird. Gandhi's headquarters were around the corner at Birla House—one of the lovely homes owned by the Indian millionaire, Birla. This, too, was the seat of the Working Committee of the Congress Party, the most powerful political sect in India. Nehru, Patel, Azad, Rajagopalacharia and other leading members of the Congress, all dressed in white cotton homespun, were in attendance upon Gandhi who, though not a member of the Working Committee, dominated it.

The incredibly thin and wiry Mr Jinnah, leader of the Muslim League, an implacable hater of Congress, was in still another pleasant residence in the town. The princes, the big businessmen and the visiting diplomats and politicians distributed themselves around the capital in large European houses. In addition there were some two hundred journalists from the Indian press.

For the first few days Cripps saw a steady flow of the party leaders at his bungalow. They came and went in dozens. Boys staggered in and out with loads of telegrams and letters from every political and religious party in India. Each night Cripps went off to discuss the day's debating with the viceroy. There was an air of good temper about the proceedings and everyone agreed that Cripps was putting his case with great persuasion and clarity. The papers praised his sincerity and agreed pretty generally that if anyone had to negotiate Cripps was the man. There was a quick-silver geniality about him and he appeared to be full of confidence. The day Gandhi came to see him I was sitting in the bedroom of Graham Spry, Cripps' assistant, and their talk went on so long I fell asleep. When they emerged, smiling, and stood exchanging wisecracks at the front door, you might have thought the whole thing was settled. Here were the empire's two ablest lawyers, and just possibly two of the best actors. When journalists started to aim questions, Cripps answered them slyly with a phrase of Gandhi's, 'I am keeping my silence.'

The press conferences at the secretariat were even better. About a couple of hundred of us gathered in a large, bare room and we came from all over the earth. There were Chinese, Hindus, Tamils, Muslims, British, Americans, Dutch, Swiss, Sikhs and French, and we wore every variety of clothing from morning coats to white cotton robes. The air buzzed with a dozen different languages, It reminded one vaguely of a meeting of the International Drug Committee at the League of Nations building in Geneva before the war.

Then Cripps, in a light grey suit, came bustling in and opened the proceedings with the air of an auctioneer selling a particularly good lot to an eager market. Questions were fired at him at a rate of half a dozen a minute—sometimes three or four of the Indians would be on their feet at once—and Cripps parried them all very slickly and quickly. You would hear this kind of thing:

Large, very black man in a white turban: If you have the luck to put this thing through... Cripps: Don't talk of luck. It is a matter of commonsense.

The Turban: Well, if you have the luck to find the commonsense to put this thing through, will you consider staying for another three months to assist with the arrangements?

Cripps: I will certainly consider it, but I am going to get an answer one way or the other by the end of next week.

The Turban: It's going to be Hobson's choice, then. Cripps: Yes. And Mr Hobson has got to make the choice.

The Turban (shouting to drown two others who are struggling to get into the conversation): Have you any political party backing you?

Cripps: I have a party of one which has the advantage of always voting the same way.

Not sparkling or very serious dialogue, perhaps, but it was quick and it pleased most people. The Indians were very shrewd and persistent in their heckling, but Cripps kept his temper. The journalists liked him. He already had a good personal press.

I called one morning at the Legislative Assembly hoping to hear something as there was a motion down on the adjournment for a discussion of the Cripps mission. The building itself, a maze of rich mahogany and leather underneath the spinning fans, was as lavish as the rest of Delhi. The assembly was moribund. As I gazed down from the press gallery the motion for the adjournment was quickly squashed and the house returned contentedly to the railway bill.

I wandered then with Richard down to Birla House, hoping to see Gandhi. It was the hour of the evening prayer. On the wide lawn outside the house many white-robed men and women were coming soft-footed into the garden. The women took their places on the grass on the left, the men on the right and Richard and I sat among the Untouchables behind. Presently Gandhi came out through the latticed french windows and squatted on the verandah before the crowd. His disciples deployed in a semicircle on either side of him. Outlined by the soft light from the french windows and with a bright moon rising beyond the house, he looked very impressive. At the Mahatma's blessing, the Untouchables rose and left, content that they had seen him. All the rest lingered on in the rich, heavily scented garden while Gandhi chanted his prayers in a thin, high-pitched wail. Occasionally the disciples joined in. The crowd simply sat and listened quietly in the hot moonlight. It was very soothing. After a little Gandhi rose and the people quietly drifted away.

It is just one of India's enigmas that no one call tell precisely to what God Gandhi prays. He is a Hindu, of coarse, but his faith of non-violence is his own and exists for all men who will hear him. I felt strongly drawn toward this little goblin-like man, who was God to many millions in India and increasingly the most powerful emotional and spiritual force in the country. All his apparent contradictions make no difference. He is adored. Even an intellect like Nehru's will shelve its logic and follow him devoutly. And since Gandhi, in addition to being God, is a politician, I resolved to press for an interview on the following day.

In the meantime Cripps announced what his proposals were. We met him briefly at a tea-party on the lawns outside the secretariat and then we all filed inside to a large domed conference room to hear the fate of India. In his clear, full barrister's voice Cripps read out:

'I am giving you this document for publication today as a PROPOSAL which has been submitted to the leaders of Indian opinion by the War Cabinet and its publication is NOT the publication of a declaration by His Majesty's government, but only of a declaration they would be prepared to make if it met with a sufficiently general and favourable acceptance from the various sections of Indian opinion.

'I rely upon you all to make that position abundantly clear.

'Secondly, I am sure I can rely upon every paper in India and throughout the world to deal with the document with the deep seriousness and responsibility it deserves. It is difficult to imagine a more weighty issue than this one, upon which the future, the happiness and the freedom of 350 million people may well depend.

'Whatever you say as to it, I know I can trust you to say it with a full sense of its importance and with a full realisation that you, too, may play a part in the solution of this difficult problem, by the way you treat the document and by the manner of your publicity.

'I have waited to make this document public until I had the opportunity of submitting it personally to the leaders of the main interests in India, and until they had been able to submit it to their colleagues. Now it is to be given a wider publicity and I commit it to your hands in the confidence that whatever your views may be you will seek to help to bring all Indian opinion together and not to divide or exacerbate differences.

'I will read the document to you slowly—and thereafter I will answer your questions.'

For once there was silence among the Indian journalists and the agents who had been sent along by the rival political parties. Just for a minute there was a sense of history in the air, a faint pale hope that after all these years of struggling and bitterness something was about to be done which would settle it all and bring some chance of unity and peace.

Slowly and carefully and with additional emphasis here and there, Cripps read out the declaration:

> His Majesty's Government having considered the anxieties expressed in this country and in India as to the fulfilment of promises made in regard to the future of India have decided to lay down in precise and clear terms the steps which they propose shall be taken for the earliest possible realisation of self-government in India. The object is the creation of a new Indian Union which shall constitute a Dominion associated with the United Kingdom and other Dominions by a common allegiance to the Crown equal to them in every respect, in no way subordinate in any respect of its domestic or external affairs. His Majesty's Government, therefore, make the following declaration:
>
> A. Immediately upon cessation of hostilities, steps shall be taken to set up in India in manner described hereafter an elected body charged with the task of framing a new constitution for India.
> B. Provision shall be made, as set out below, for participation of Indian States in the Constitution-making body.
> C. His Majesty's Government undertake to accept and implement forthwith the Constitution so framed subject only to:
>
> 1. The right of any Province of British India that is not prepared to

accept the new Constitution to retain its present constitutional position, provision being made for its subsequent accession if it so decides. With such non-acceding provinces, should they so desire, His Majesty's Government will be prepared to agree upon a new Constitution giving them the same full status as the Indian Union and arrived at by a procedure analogous to that here laid down.

2. The signing of a Treaty which shall be negotiated between His Majesty's Government and the Constitution-making body. This Treaty will cover all necessary matters arising out of the complete transfer of responsibility from British to Indian hands; it will make provision, in accordance with undertakings given by His Majesty's Government, for the protection of racial and religious minorities; but it will not impose any restriction on the power of the Indian Union to decide in future its relationship to other member states of the British Commonwealth. Whether or not an Indian State elects to adhere to the Constitution it will be necessary to negotiate a revision of its Treaty arrangements so far as this may be required in the new situation.

D. The Constitution-making body shall be composed as follows, unless the leaders of Indian opinion in the principal committees agree upon some other form before the end of hostilities: Immediately upon the result being known of Provincial Elections which will be necessary at the end of hostilities, the entire membership of the Lower Houses of Provincial Legislatures shall as a single electoral college proceed to the election of the Constitution-making body by the system of proportional representation. This new body shall be in number about one-tenth of the number of the electoral college. Indian States shall be invited to appoint representatives in the same proportion to their total population as in the case of representatives of British India as a whole and with the same powers as British Indian members.

E. During the critical period that now faces India and until the new Constitution can be framed His Majesty's Government must inevitably bear the responsibility for and retain the control and direction of the defence of India as part of their world war effort, but the task of organising to the full the military, moral and material resources of India must be the responsibility of the Government of India. His Majesty's Government desire and invite the immediate and effective participation of the leaders of the principal sections of the Indian people in the councils of their country, of the Commonwealth and of the united nations. Thus they will be enabled to give their active and constructive help in the discharge of a task which is vital and essential for the future freedom of India.

So then it was out at last. Freedom for India. The exit of the British after three hundred years. Dominion status first, then the right to get out of the Empire completely. The Muslims to have their separate state if they could get enough people to vote for it. The Congress to rule all India if they could get enough people to support them. The princes to retain their absolute sovereignty over their own states if they could get their subjects to agree. All the minorities given a chance to have their voices heard according to their numbers. Everybody, in fact, to have a chance of getting exactly what he wanted and the Indians to decide the whole thing themselves without British interference. The British were getting out lock, stock and barrel if the Indians wanted them to go. There was just this proviso—just this one all-important thing—India must fight the war first and fight it under British direction.

It looked a fair enough offer at first sight. It was a big enough offer certainly. There was a pause for a few moments in the conference hall. Many there were old and hard campaigners for India's freedom, good haters of the British. Now suddenly when they saw or thought they saw all the power and responsibility thrust into their own hands they baulked a little. They hesitated as a man might do when he has run a long difficult course up a mountain and at the top suddenly finds there is a precipice before him. It was impossible to grasp at once the immense repercussions of the thing, its vast effect upon the world. But this hesitation lasted only a few seconds. Then the questions poured in upon Cripps.

Peeling off his coat and lighting cigarette after cigarette, he gave a masterly display for the next two hours. This was the greatest case of his career and he pleaded it magnificently. Hundreds of questions were aimed at him—some friendly, some clever, some bitter and some downright stupid. Excited by the fateful and highly charged atmosphere of the meeting, one or two hecklers became abusive. A man near me rose and in a hoarse voice made some sneer at Cripps' honesty. With wonderful timing Cripps suddenly halted the headlong course of the debate. Then he turned sharply on the interjector: 'I will close this meeting if you go on,' he said. 'I am entitled to courtesy as well as the Press.' There was a moment's embarrassed silence. Then the tide of questions flowed in again.

'No,' Cripps said, 'you won't get President Roosevelt's guarantee for the scheme. If you don't trust me, you can't trust this document or anything.'

'Yes,' he said, 'the states that don't want to join the union can form a separate union of their own.'

'No,' he said, 'there is no objection to different states having different armies.'

'It would take about one year after the end of the war to frame the new constitution...if India won't agree to a new constitution, then we can't do anything more for her...new states will be able to make any arrangement they like with foreign powers...there will be no imperial troops in India unless the Indians themselves ask for them.. .India can decide to look after her own frontiers...the British government will not undertake to finance the new dominion.'

And so on. Once Cripps launched into a concise and brilliant exposition of the relationship between the Dominions and the mother country. When a really vital question came along he was ready for it. A man in cotton homespun challenged him: 'You are offering us civil war. You are throwing us into a perpetual melting-pot of disintegration.'

'No,' he answered, 'I am simply giving India the chance to govern herself like any other dominion.'

I never saw him hesitate and he knew that every word he said would be reported all over the world and that the British government would be held to it.

'Yes,' he said, 'the new states can break off relations with England. Once made, the British government will stick to its promises, but if the other parties to the agreement do not, the British government will take such steps as are necessary to induce them. Every province has got to take part in forming the constitution—to ensure this will be the last act of the British in India. We are satisfied that this is the best solution. The scheme goes as a whole or is rejected as a whole. If rejected, we do not see any possibility for another scheme before the end of the war. The end of hostilities means when Germany is beaten, not necessarily when the Japanese are beaten. It is impossible to remove British control from the defence of India at this juncture.' Then finally—'It is for me alone to judge if there is an adequate measure of acceptance of the proposals.'

It was a *tour de force*, a masterpiece of historic debate. Yet, coming out of the foetid room in the dusk, it seemed to me that there was going to be no easy passage for this scheme. The questions had revealed a mistrust and rancour which showed that the Indians were far from grateful for the offer of independence. It was something more they wanted and I could not at this stage quite see what. It appeared obvious to me that we were saying to the Indians, 'Fight the Japanese now and we will give you all you want.' The vernacular press had been repeating endlessly and uselessly that Britain was only making offers now because she was in a tough spot. But were the Indians only bargaining for a better offer? If so, what better offer? There was something in it all I could not understand.

The meeting had cleared one point in my mind. It had revealed that if the two main parties—the Congress and the Muslim League—were won over to the scheme then Cripps would go ahead and recommend that it should be put into operation, whether all the dozens of other minorities liked it or not. So the thing was for me to see Jinnah, the head Muslim, and Nehru, the leading man of Congress. But before I saw either of them it was essential to get to Gandhi, because Gandhi in the end was the man who was going to have most say in the decision. Once get the points of view of these three men and it seemed to me I would have the keys to the whole situation.

Gandhi sent for us in the full heat of the mid-afternoon. Richard and I got into our car and drove down to Birla House. Mahadev Desai, the great man's secretary, met us at the latticed doorway and led us through a number of rich corridors to a back room and there we squatted cross-legged on the blue carpet. One corner of the unfurnished room was filled with a huge and spotlessly white mattress. On this was lying a heavy bolster—one of the type called in the Far East a 'Dutch wife'. Letters and telegrams were spread about on the mattress. We talked with Desai while we waited and he told us that a telegram had just been received from Gandhi's wife saying she was not well. It was necessary for Gandhi to leave at once for his home in the village of Wardha and we would have only half an hour with him before he caught his train. This in itself was news. It meant that Gandhi had already given his decision on the Cripps proposal.

Once back in Wardha, Desai said, Gandhi would revert entirely to the simple life. He would rise at four or five in the morning and stalk through the fields, staff in hand. Then he would return to his mud hut and as the heat advanced through the day a bowl of water would be placed beside him. From time to time he would dip a towel into the water and then bind it around his head—one of the best ways of keeping cool. He would take only a little goat's milk through the day, perhaps a few dates as well. He would spin a little, go through his correspondence, dictate articles for his paper the *Harijan*, and receive visitors. At dusk he would hold his prayers for the villagers outside his hut. Gandhi was seventy-three and still wonderfully healthy and strong.

At this Gandhi himself came into the room, a twist of white cotton around his loins, his black barrel of a chest quite bare, nothing on his thin sinewy legs or feet, steel spectacles on his nose. He shook hands smiling and teed himself up comfortably against his white bolster. From that moment until we left I could never quite catch up with the argument or bring it under control. It was not so much Gandhi's quickness or his wits. Not his really overwhelming charm and the amiable warmth and patience of his pinched little face. It was more that from first to last he had the tremendous advantage in argument of being absolutely convinced that he was right. He would allow you to say anything but he would draw all your remarks gently into his own line of logic, not brusquely or apologetically, but with reason. Time and again I was forced into the intolerable position of hearing him make excuses for me. And then he would season the conversation with some slight joke. I found myself unequal to this sort of spell-binding. It is impossible to interview Gandhi. You have to argue him and avoid being trapped.

'You were so persistent,' he said, 'that I had to see you. Now what do you want to talk about?'

'Your views on the Cripps proposals.'

'I'm sorry, I cannot do that,' he spoke in soft very precise English. 'I am only a private person. I hold no office now and since I have left all these decisions to the Working Committee of the Congress Party, it would not be right for me to discuss them.'

This was undeniable, of course, but still an evasion.

'No,' he went on, 'the only thing I can talk about is my own subject of non-violence and that, I think, would not interest your principals in London at this moment. As war correspondents (Richard and I were in khaki) you will not want to discuss peace.'

Non-violence was interesting to me just so long as the violent Japanese kept making up the Burmese jungles toward India but I merely said, 'I think anything you can say at this moment will be interesting'; and there we were, he had won the toss without an effort and we were entering into his own field where he had all the answers ready.

'Then let us begin with China,' he said. 'The Chinese made the mistake of fighting the Japanese and the fighting still goes on. Had they not opposed the Japanese, neither raising their arms nor destroying the crops, had they simply refrained from cooperating with the Japanese, then in the end the Japanese would have been defeated.

'Carried to its logical end non-violence in China might have meant the killing of the last Chinese, but I do not think it would have come to that. The Japanese could not have gone on killing people. It is not human to go on killing when there is no resistance.

'In Australia and America, the natives have all but been wiped out by white men. They, too, made the mistake of resisting violently. Had they not fought and simply refused to cooperate, the white man would have stopped killing them.'

I protested here. 'But surely the evils of submitting and of living in slavery will be greater than the suffering caused in keeping the invader out.'

'No. If you fight you are destroyed anyway. If you resist non-violently you have a chance of survival. There are 350 million people in India. The Japanese cannot destroy them all.'

As the argument developed like this, half a dozen women followers of Gandhi crept into the room and quietly squatted with their spinning on the carpet behind me. They sat listening intently as they worked.

One or two men also came in and Desai, like an ancient scribe, sat perched at one end of the mattress, taking shorthand notes on a tablet. Desai was the man who recorded the best of the master's words and printed them subsequently in the *Harijan*.

'Remember,' Gandhi went on, 'non-violence requires an even higher kind of courage than violence.

You must be just as prepared to lay down your life—even more so.'

Yes, you had to concede that. Often Gandhi's followers had simply stood their ground during the police charges and had not even raised their hands to protect their faces from the blows of the lathis. But the point I kept tyring to make was that you do not necessarily die if you resist. The majority of soldiers don't die in battle. They live on—with a sense of liberty and achievement.

'But what is the point of discussing this in relation to India?' Gandhi said. 'The people aren't armed. What is the use of resisting the Japanese when they have better arms? They will annihilate us.'

'Suppose we produce as many arms as the Japanese?'

'Then we will simply destroy one another.'

'Then suppose,' I said, 'we have superior arms, as I think we have?'

'Then I still will not fight. I do not want to destroy the Japanese. If a little child attacks me I don't use my superior strength to crush it. That would not be human. It is not human to destroy.'

'Then are there any circumstances in which you would fight?' I asked.

'No.'

This for the next ten minutes was the pith of his argument—it takes two to make a quarrel. If one side won't fight, then the other side gives in or at least goes away. Gandhi would not admit that the humiliation and pain from giving in and submitting to the evils of Japanese rule were worse than the suffering from driving them out by war. He returned again to the theme that there were too many Indians for the Japanese to destroy, and at last I said: 'As far as you are concerned then, there is no hope of Cripps reaching a compromise, no hope of a settlement?'

He grinned disarmingly. 'You are very quick. You are trying to trap me into talking about the present negotiations. Never mind. This is very delicate ground but I don't mind being trapped. There is hope of a compromise between non-violence and British interests in India. I do not see why we cannot reach some settlement. But there must be two compromises—one in India along Indian lines. Another in England along English lines, if you will. You cannot tell people in England that you have abandoned active war in India but some arrangement might be made. Here in India you can allow the Indians to meet the situation in their own way and that is the way of non-violence.' He went on: 'I agree, after all, that our interests are the same; we both want an India for the Indians and we want to keep the Japanese out.

'Give me control of India and I will resist the Japanese, though not by fighting.

'I would let them land. Then by non-cooperation, even though they killed my people, I would stop them possessing India.'

There was nothing more to be said. I got up stiffly from my squatting position and thanked him. My mind was still full of his ideas as we drove back to the hotel. The conversation had gone far too quickly for me to take notes and it is probable that here and there I have misquoted Gandhi's words. But the gist is there—the passionate conviction and the determination not to fight. I hope I have not suggested Gandhi is a conscientious objector. I am convinced that he is utterly sincere in his brand of resistance. It is an entirely non-European philosophy and unquestionably it suits the temperament of millions of Asiatics. They do not think along European lines.

For me the interview threw a great flood of light on the Cripps mission—even on the future of India. It revealed that Cripps was bound to fail—had, in fact, failed already and even before he started. So long as the British were determined to defend India by force of arms then Gandhi would oppose them. He regards the ordinary human desire to fight for the protection of one's home as primitive. He believes that human beings can be lifted by self discipline and reasoning to the higher plane where they will not murder one another or seek each others' possessions. His method of reaching that higher plane is to embarrass the aggressor with pacifism, to sate him with one's own blood, to impede him by refusing to draw water for him or offer him food.

The British and all the belligerents were irreconcilably committed to the other philosophy—that if you destroy the aggressor then there will be peace on earth. There could be no compromise. We wanted peace through war. Gandhi wanted peace through non-violence.

There were two comments on this interview. Desai published his version in the *Harijan* the following week and, although I have no doubt that his text is more correct than mine, he wrote so much into it afterwards that it is more of a restatement of Gandhi's views than a report of the interview.

In England Kingsley Martin wrote a mildly patronising comment in the *New Statesman*, in which he regretted on the one hand that non-violence was not put into operation and on the other hand that it was unworkable anyhow. He pointed out that Gandhi's follower, Nehru, did not support Gandhi's non-violent creed and that he was prepared to rouse India to fight fascism—violently.

It was to Nehru's house I went now to seek further light. Nehru had come to the actual, if not the nominal, leadership of Congress by the strange route of Harrow, Cambridge and the Indian gaols. He is a Socialist of formidable intellect, an aristocrat of great charm, a lawyer with immense persuasion. Except for the Indian gaol part of it, very like Cripps in fact. The two men were friends. They had already had a number of long talks without getting anywhere particularly. But Nehru had said he would fight. There seemed to be some hope in that.

In fluent, beautiful English, he went through it all with me, as we sat in his European house surrounded by his European books. What he said boiled down to this, 'Give us—the Congress— control now and we will fight the Japanese for you.' Again and again he emphasised that India would never be aroused to fight unless Indian leaders had command and were allowed to fight in their own way. In other words that meant 'arming the masses'. I began to see for the first time the importance of that phrase. Arm the masses was the one thing the British feared to do, and for this reason—they could not be sure of what the masses would do with their arms once they got them. Some of them might even turn on the British and Britain's allies. It was all very well, the British argued, for Nehru to say 'arm the masses'. But did Nehru and the other anti-Japanese leaders have sufficient control over the masses to organise them against the Japanese? Nehru's own leader, Gandhi, was against fighting. At most, the Congress could only claim the direct allegiance of thirty million Indians out of 350 million.

Nehru's answer to this was, 'You have got to trust me and take a chance.'

He said, 'For you British, India is a foreign battlefield. We Indians have got to stay here whatever happens. We can't evacuate. So then we have the right to defend ourselves under our own leaders. In no other way are you going to galvanise the people into action against the Japanese. We must have our sense of freedom. I am ready to cooperate with Mr Jinnah and the Muslim League over defence and we can settle our political differences later. Gandhi is our seer, our prophet. He expands our long range ideal. But there are many of us who do not think that this system of non-violence is adequate to meet the present crisis.'

On the question of a separate state for the Muslims, Nehru was adamant. Again and again he said, 'No.' Jinnah was to him a 'Fascist'. The Congress which included both Muslims and Hindus—and for that matter anyone who liked to join it at the cost of fourpence a year—was the sole responsible party in India. The only hope for India was unity under the Congress.

I gathered that Nehru might be willing to accept a scheme along these lines—first: Indians to be members of the War Cabinet in London and of the Pacific Council in Washington, and an Indian to be minister of defence in New Delhi. Second: Wavell to continue as commander-in-chief and with his trained Europeans and Americans to direct tactics, but to be under the control of the Indian defence minister, whose job also included recruiting and general stimulation of the war effort. Third: a federal governing body to be set up at once in New Delhi. All states and provinces could send representatives to it and would be bound to accept the authority of the new federal council for a certain period—say ten years. Fourth: after this period had elapsed the Indians themselves to settle the future of India without outside interference.

Nehru himself was intensely sceptical about getting any such scheme accepted. He saw that the British would never turn over control of defence right away, that they would not agree to the establishment of a brand new all-Indian government at this moment of crisis. And I think he saw, too, that the British would not allow Congress to dominate all the minorities, including the Muslims, as they would be certain to do, since they would have a majority in the new government.

That Hamlet-like quality in Nehru came out strongly as he talked. He could see nothing ahead but bloodshed, endless dispute and probably civil war. He spoke like a man who sees no hope and expects soon to be blotted out himself. He kept saying, 'So many things are going to happen.' His melancholy and depression were ingrained and chronic. He was no less sincere than Gandhi but his fine mind had gone darting back and forth from Indian philosophy to the present actual horror of the war and found no comfort or solution anywhere. He had thought too long, too painfully and deeply if that is possible. He had only come out of gaol recently and clearly he was expecting to go back to gaol very soon. You have only to read his autobiography to see how the shadow of gaol hangs over him. Sitting there with him in this pleasant room watching his thin, sensitive face, his beautiful hands, hearing his soft voice, it seemed a hateful thing that this gracious and gifted man should ever be in gaol. It also seemed inevitable.

No wonder that Nehru is loved in India almost as Gandhi is venerated. Like Gandhi his private life was selflessly monastic, almost saintly. Yet his 'Europeanism' had left him isolated and despite the immense crowds who came to hear him he was intensely lonely. He was a man who had no hope of ever attaining the quiet mind. He was destined to go on searching forever.

His autobiography, *Towards Freedom*, is a remarkable document. When as a wealthy young Cambridge graduate he first went out to discover India, this is what he saw:

Presently whole villages would empty out, and all over the fields there would be men, women and children on the march to the meeting-place. Or, more swiftly still, the cry of Sita-Ram, Sita-Ra-a-a- a-m, would fill the air, and then people would come streaming out or even running as fast as they could. They were in miserable rags, men and women, but their faces were full of excitement and their eyes glistened and seemed to expect strange happenings which would, as if by a miracle, put an end to their long misery.

They showered their affection on us and looked on us with loving and hopeful eyes, as if we were the bearers of good tidings, the guides who were to lead them to the promised land. Looking at them and their misery and overflowing gratitude, I was filled with shame and sorrow—shame at my own easy-going and comfortable life and our petty politics of the city which ignored this vast multitude of semi-naked sons and daughters of India, sorrow at the degradation and overwhelming poverty of India. A new picture of India seemed to rise before me, naked, starving, crushed and utterly miserable. And their faith in us, casual visitors from the distant city, embarrassed me and filled me with a new responsibility that frightened me.

Then as a political leader after he had become a pledged follower of Gandhi and non-violence:

We looked back to find a bunch of mounted police, probably two or three dozen in number, bearing down upon us at a rapid pace. They were soon right upon us, and the impact of the horses broke up our little column of sixteen. The mounted policemen then started belabouring our volunteers with huge batons or truncheons, and, instinctively, the volunteers sought refuge on the sidewalks, and some even entered the petty shops. They were pursued and beaten down... Suddenly I found myself alone in the middle of the road; a few yards away from me, in various directions, were the policemen beating down our volunteers. Automatically I began moving to the side of the road to be less conspicuous, but again I stopped and had a little argument with myself and decided it would be unbecoming for me to move away. All this was a matter of a few seconds only, but I have the clearest recollections of that conflict within me and the decision, prompted by my pride, I suppose, which could not tolerate the idea of my behaving like a coward. Yet the line between cowardice and courage was a thin one, and I might well have been on the other side. Hardly had I so decided when I looked round to find that a mounted policeman was trotting up to me, brandishing his long new baton. I told him to go ahead and turned my head away—again an instinctive effort to save the head and face. He gave me two resounding blows on the back. I felt stunned and my body quivered all over, but, to my surprise and satisfaction, I found that I was still standing.

Unbecoming,' in the above is good.
Then the following day, still at Lucknow:

Suddenly we saw in the far distance a moving mass. It was two or three long lines of cavalry or mounted police covering the entire area, galloping down toward us, and striking and riding down the numerous stragglers that dotted the maidan. That charge of galloping horsemen was a fine sight, but for the tragedies that were being enacted on the way, as harmless and very surprised sightseers went under horses' hoofs. Behind the charging lines these people lay on the ground, some still unable to move, others writhing in pain, and the whole appearance of that maidan was that of a battlefield… the horsemen were soon upon us and their front line clashed almost at a gallop with the massed ranks of our processionists. We held our ground and, as we appeared to be unyielding, the horses had to pull up at the last moment and reared up on their hind legs with their front hoofs quivering in the air over our heads. And then began a beating of us, and battering with lathis and long batons both by the mounted and foot police. It was a tremendous hammering, and the clearness of vision I had had the evening before left me. All I knew was that I had to stay where I was and must not yield or go back. I felt half blinded by the blows, and sometimes a dull anger seized me and a desire to hit out. I thought how easy it would be to pull down the police officer in front of me from his horse and to mount up myself, but long training and discipline held and I did not raise my hand except to protect my face from a blow…

And those faces, full of hate and blood-lust, almost mad, with no trace of sympathy or touch of humanity! Probably the faces on our side just then were equally hateful to look at, and the fact that we were mostly passive did not fill our minds and hearts with love for our opponents or add to the beauty of our countenances. And yet we had no grievances against each other; no quarrel that was personal, no ill-will. We happened to represent, for the time being, strange and powerful forces which held us in thrall and cast us hither and thither, and subtly gripping our minds and hearts, roused our desires and passions and made us their blind tools. Blindly we struggled, not knowing what we struggled for and whither we went. The excitement of action held us; but, as it passed, immediately the question arose: To what end all this? To what end?

That was non-violence in action. The first visit to the villages had turned Nehru into a missionary. The experience of the cavalry charges had made him an active soldier of non-violence. Now finally leadership at the head of the great Congress Party turned him into a statesman. As a statesman he wrote of Gandhi:

Whether Gandhi is a democrat or not, he does represent the peasant masses of India; he is the quintessence of the conscious and subconscious will of those millions...Of course he is not the average peasant. A man of the keenest intellect, of fine feeling and good taste, wide vision; very human, and yet essentially the ascetic who has suppressed his passions and emotions, sublimated them and directed them in spiritual channels; a tremendous personality drawing people to himself like a magnet, and calling out fierce loyalties and attachments—all this so utterly unlike and beyond a peasant. And yet withal he is the greatest peasant, with a peasant's outlook on affairs, and with a peasant's blindness to some aspects of life. But India is peasant India and so he knows his India well, reacts to her slightest tremors, gauges a situation accurately and almost instinctively and has a knack of acting at the psychological moment...India still seems to understand or at least appreciate the prophetic-religious type of man, talking of sin and salvation and non-violence...He is obviously not of the world's ordinary coinage; he was minted of a different and rare variety, and often the unknown stared at us through his eyes.

This is the kind of beautiful and powerful English with which Nehru talked to me. Considering that his book is mainly a diatribe against British imperialism in India, Nehru writes with extraordinary restraint and courtesy. Considering how much he has suffered, how many years he has spent in gaol, he has almost a divine tolerance. That he has acted foolishly at times, he would be the first to admit. He asks only that you will believe in him and his cause. This book—his whole life—is crushed with disillusion, doubt, mental depression and extraordinary courage. If someone could find the cure for Nehru's sadness they might discover the next leader of India. As it was, during this early summer in New Delhi, Nehru could not find even enough hope to force some ray of light into the darkness of his own mind.

There remained Mr Jinnah. Now Mr Jinnah has no doubts at all. He is a violently practical man and a highly successful lawyer, who says he knows exactly what he wants and intends to get it. The Hindus call him a Fascist, and Mr Jinnah has much bitterer things to say about the Hindus than that. In appearance he looks rather like a Victorian tragedian and I believe he once toured England with a company that was producing Shakespeare. He has a mane of grey hair, an eloquent and pungent voice and at the climax of an argument his eyes burn fiercely.

His convictions are so downright that he had the strength to turn his daughter out of his house in Bombay when she married a non-Muslim and he has since refused to speak to her.

Richard and I found him reading the newspapers in his study and, surprisingly, his long spindly legs were encased in jodhpurs. Richard's methods of conducting an interview are not mine and on this morning he was feeling especially belligerent for some reason. He opened the proceedings by bluntly contradicting Jinnah three times and describing one of his allusions as ridiculous. Jinnah, a formidable opponent at any time, snapped back vigorously. Richard's last crack had been really too provocative. He had said that there was no essential difference between Hindus and Muslims, which was rather worse than telling a Nazi that there is no difference between an Aryan and a Jew.

'What!' roared Jinnah. 'They worship cow. I eat cow.' It was a strong point and he had more. 'I defile a Hindu if my shadow falls across him. A Hindu would not take water from my hand. We are utterly different.'

When the two of them were not arguing I managed to extract the following statement of the Muslim aims. On the surface it bears a certain resemblance to the Congress view:

He said: 'British and Indians are in the same boat now—whatever has gone before doesn't matter. But I want to make it clear that you are only going to galvanise a hundred million Indian Muslims into action on one condition. It isn't enough for me to tell them they are in danger of invasion. I have got to be able to tell them that their own leaders are having a say in the defence. Only on these terms will they give their money and spill their blood. I have never asked for anything more. I have never asked for a separate Muslim state immediately. I have said all through these negotiations that this matter can be settled in the future provided the Muslims get a reasonable share of the control now. Given that control I will raise the Muslims to fight; denied it we can only maintain benevolent neutrality—which is more than the Hindus have done. Hindus and ourselves must be separate, but there is no reason why we cannot get along peaceably together. I simply ask that after the war a separate state for Muslims shall be established. I guarantee to protect the rights of Hindu minorities in the new state. They can have their own religion, their own law courts. A fundamental of the new state would be a close alliance with Britain. I only fear that the Hindus are using this conference to undermine my plans.

They hope to get the power now to crush us later on.'

He spoke vehemently and with great conviction. There had been a time when he was himself a leader of the Congress Party and a believer in a united India. But now, at the age of sixty-six, he was rooted in his determination to get his Muslim kingdom, and all over India his agents were stirring up differences between Hindus and Muslims. Jinnah was as determined to divide India as Nehru was upon uniting it. He feared—with some reason—he would be swamped in an elected federal body and so he was playing fairly closely with the British and was careful not to give a yes or no to Cripps until he first heard what Congress had to say. Actually Cripps' plan as it stood promised to give Jinnah almost all he wanted.

These then, were the three main views: Gandhi's—'I will not fight the Japanese at any price.' Nehru's—'Give me control now and we will settle our internal differences ourselves later on.' Jinnah's—'Give me control now and guarantee me a separate Muslim state.'

I tried then to find out what some of the other great minorities were thinking and was plunged at once into a maze that was just as conflicting and twice as obscure. There were the British civil servants and businessmen who surprisingly seemed ready enough for the British to get out of India. They seemed genuinely eager to get on with the war beyond all else. Anyway, compensation for their lost jobs and property was guaranteed them under the Cripps scheme. There were the princes who were playing a heavy game of wait and see. The removal of the British meant the probable collapse of their states, their money, their huge powers. Yet many of the younger, more enlightened ones, foresaw that the rising of popular governments was inevitable and were already moving toward a more democratic control. There were the Sikhs, the black-bearded fighting men who had filled the ranks of the Indian army for generations and they hotly opposed the plan, fearing that their independence would be taken away from them by other Indian sects. There were the Mahasabha, who were the rigid Hindu conservatives, and the political counterbalance to the Muslim League. They wanted no compromises, no interference. There were the hill people like the Gurkhas, wonderful fighters, but not politically alive—yet. There were the Stalinist communists who temporarily supported Britain, the pro-Axis group led by the missing Chandra Bose,[3] the professional agitators in the big cities, and those were steeped so deeply in their hatred of British rule that they had no plan beyond the removal of the British. There was the great mass of mercenary soldiers and Indians who had public jobs of one kind or another, and most of these, through habit or hope of security and gain, or perhaps even through affection, wanted the British to remain. There were those who simply feared for what might happen if the British left. There were the politically minded Untouchables who wanted to break the caste system. And beyond all these, beyond them and above them and all around them, was the ragged, hungry, helpless, apathetic and confused mass of Indian peasants. Millions upon millions of them, outcasts of the world, docile followers of anyone who could lead them into some sort of life higher than that of the beasts.

They did not seem to count very much in these negotiations in New Delhi. It was accepted that they could be led or pushed or simply ignored. They were simply the rough material that was being fashioned and apparently of no more importance to the potter than his clay. I do not say that people like Nehru were not working for them heart and soul. I simply say that their mass will was not evident at New Delhi because they had no mass will.

There was one other figure at this strange charade—Colonel Blimp. I must say in all truth I never met him. It was one of the most unexpected things I discovered in India. Blimp flourishes, of course, and by the thousand. But I do not think he is quite like his public reputation. Those Indian army colonels I saw were not peppery, red-faced and bewhiskered martinets. There were narrow men, convention-ridden men and idle, stupid men, but no more, I thought, than in any government offices. One or two in private conversation with me flared up against the Indians and some of the women were furious at the insolence of their servants. Many of the Indians were venting their spleen against the British with many little insults and obstructions, and there were shootings from time to time. But the majority of the British I met were eager to discuss the possible solutions to the mess. The Indian press was allowed at that time what seemed to me to be amazing latitude. Papers like the *Hindustani Times* openly jeered at the British generals in Malaya, at the viceroy and Cripps, at everything British. Gandhi was leading an active press campaign to urge the peasants not to scorch the earth if the Japanese came. Much more drastic things than this were being done under the surface. Twice, for instance, anti-British and pro-Axis pamphlets were left in my room, and a number of fifth column movements were active in places like Calcutta and Bombay.

With so many prejudices and ambitions and all pulling in different directions it was no great boon then for the Indians suddenly to be told: 'Behold! You are free. Just fight the Japanese first and then you will be left entirely alone.' It was as though a group of schoolboys were fighting when their master came to them and said, 'Stop fighting. Weed the garden for me and then I will let you go back to your squabbling and I won't care what you do to one another. You can all murder yourselves and I won't interfere.'

It was useless for liberal and left-wing leaders in Britain and America to thunder, 'Let India be free.' Who were you going to give the freedom to? To Nehru? The Muslims, the Gurkhas, the Sikhs and dozens of other groups would not hear of it. To Jinnah? Congress would never agree. To Gandhi? He was openly declaring he would not fight the Japanese and that was the one thing the Allied nations were determined India should do. Anyway, there were millions inside India who would never follow Gandhi. Then let all the different groups have their own freedom and act in their own way? Chaos and civil war at once—the Indians themselves saw that.

The same question and seemingly impossible difficulties arose over the now vital problem of control of defence. To what Indian could the control be given? How could you get a group of these bitterly antagonistic leaders to act together? How could you be sure they would fight not themselves but the enemy? This was the crux of the matter that was agitating Cripps' mind.

No, despite all the clamour for the ejection of the British and the freedom of India, the thing Indians really wanted was a settlement of their internal disputes and the more intelligent of them saw this.

They wanted India to be free for peace, not free for internal war. And in the minds of many the Cripps plan was merely a plan for war against the Japanese now and war among themselves later.

So they hedged and stalled. Each political group tried to score off the other. Again and again the delegates went back to Cripps' bungalow with new proposals, new ideas, new compromises. Cripps on his side agreed to shift his ground slightly and he wired suggestions to London for an alteration of the original draft. The Congress were insisting on a larger share of defence control immediately and Cripps tried to get it for them.

A number of other people now began to come forward to see if they could help in reaching a compromise. Colonel Louis Johnson, President Roosevelt's personal representative, arrived from Washington, a large and vigorous man. He knew very little about the Indian problem, but he was politically tactful and naturally well disposed toward both Indians and British. Marshal Chiang Kai Shek, who had recently visited New Delhi with his wife and whose battle against the Japanese was much nearer to Indian hearts than any other foreign war, sent a letter to his friend Nehru. General Wavell was drawn into the consultations to define just what defence powers might be handed over to the Indians.

All these interventions were helpful. But then Lord Halifax, the British ambassador in Washington, who as Irwin had been viceroy of India, decided to make a speech. There was nothing very provoking in his homily, but he used such archaic expressions as 'the ancient treaties between Princes and the King-Emperor' and for some reason this maddened the Indians. Halifax to them was the embodiment of British imperialism and they kept saying petulantly, 'Why is he interfering?' 'What has it got to do with him?' Halifax presumably was doing no more than try to clarify the issues for American public opinion which had long been sympathetic to India's demands for freedom.

The speech would have done no harm but that that well-known tame white elephant British Propaganda came blundering in on the scene. With the same heavy-footed lack of subtlety the comments of the American newspapers were given wide distribution in India through Reuters. The Americans, hearing that the British had offered India her freedom, came down with a bang on the British side and lectured the Indians severely for failing to grasp the handsome offer. So, of course, did Fleet Street.

No one can blame the Indians for being irritated. To ask a man to lay down his life for you and then lecture him on his want of a sense of duty—no, it wasn't very good propaganda. To hell with you, said the Indians.

A number of people suggested to me that a section of the Conservative Party in England was deliberately trying to sabotage Cripps, whose popularity at this time was enormous at home. They said the Tories feared a New Socialist government under Cripps. Others answered this by saying that the war and the Indian problem were too vital to be baulked by party politics. I do not know.

In Delhi now we could only wait while the tide of conferences went on and on and the stew began to thicken and grow cold. Wavell had asked me to fly down with him to the Burma front with Peter Fleming, a wonderful opportunity, but I dared not leave New Delhi at that moment and as a result I never got to the Burma front. Instead Matt Halton, Philip Jordan, Richard and Sam Brewer and myself relaxed with a little local sightseeing.

We drove down to Shah Jehan's lovely palace beside the Jumna River at Old Delhi and walked through the corridors where the marble was so finely shaved that it admitted the light and where cool streams once flowed over corridors of gold and silver studded with jewels. We went, of course, into the room of the Peacock Throne and read the once magnificent arrogant and now merely ironic inscription: 'If there is a paradise on the face of the earth, it is this, oh, it is this, oh, it is this.'

Close by the British troops had once turned one of the jewelled antechambers into a cookhouse and the delicate marble lattice work and the arched ceiling were blackened irrecoverably with cooking smoke and burnt fat. The silver plates had been prised from the walls with bayonets.

We drove all one day to Agra and the Taj Mahal and though its great dome was under scaffolding and machine-gun fire sounded across the water buffaloes in the river it was the same breathlessly beautiful thing I have always wanted it to be. It did not matter much that Lord Curzon's presentation lamp had ruined the interior—the interior to me is a bit like an ornate municipal baths anyway. The building seen from a distance floated serenely in the midday heat and one felt grateful and rested. All the way back chipmunks lolloped across the road and monkeys scattered through the trees. The peasants were threshing the crop and the blown husks made an amber light among the trees. It was a restful day.

We got back to find it was all over. Congress had come out with a flat demand for a Congress dominated Indian government and control of defence right away. Cripps said that all this was something new, something impossible which they had foisted on him at the last minute. The Congress leaders said that Cripps had gone back on his word and became part of the intransigent British imperial machine. There was much bitterness.

Cripps was leaving on the following day for England—his mission a failure. First he held a dismal little press conference and he showed us his final reply to Congress: 'Nothing further could have been done by way of giving responsibility for defence services to representative Indian members without jeopardising the immediate defence of India under the commander-in-chief...The real substance of your refusal to take part in a national government is that the form of government suggested is not such as would enable you to rally the Indian people as you desire.

'You make two suggestions. First, that the constitution might now be changed. In this respect I would point out that you made this suggestion for the first time last night, nearly three weeks after you had received the proposals, and I would further remark that every other representative with whom I have discussed this view has accepted the practical impossibility of any such legislative change in the middle of a war and at such a moment as the present.

'Second, you suggest, "a truly national government," be formed which must be a "Cabinet government with full power."

'Without constitutional changes of the most complicated character and on a very large scale this would not be possible as you realise.

'Were such a system to be introduced by convention under the existing circumstances, the nominated cabinet (nominated presumably by the major political organisations) would be responsible to no one but itself, could not be removed and would, in fact, constitute an absolute dictatorship of the majority.

'This suggestion would be rejected by all the minorities in India since it would subject all of them to a permanent and autocratic majority in the cabinet. Nor would it be consistent with the pledges already given by His Majesty's government to protect the rights of these minorities.

'In a country such as India where communal divisions are still so deep an irresponsible majority government of this kind is not possible.'

Cripps added, 'I received the reply of Congress...at seven o'clock last night. It made it clear that the working committee were not prepared to accept the scheme or to enter a national government.

'As a result of this and other answers, I have had most regretfully to advise His Majesty's government that there is not such a measure of acceptance of their proposals as to justify their making a declaration in the form of the draft.

'The draft is therefore withdrawn and we revert to the position as it was before I came out here. 'Though perhaps not quite to that position...Although we must for the moment agree to differ there is no bitterness or rancour in our disagreement. There has been a large and very important area of agreement.

'The present and the future press upon us and must be faced.

'India is threatened; all who love India—as I love India and you love India—must bend our energies, each in his own way to her immediate help...We have tried our best to agree—we have failed. Never mind whose fault it is, let me take all the blame if that will help in uniting India for her own defence.'

It was a gloomy meeting.

Someone asked, 'What happens now?'

Cripps answered, 'Nothing. The offer is simply withdrawn and I do not think we will be able to make another one. The position is just as it was before I arrived.'

His smile was gone. He looked tired. It had been a tremendous blow to his prestige in England, at a time when he was being spoken of as the next prime minister. One felt a little bitter for him. He had tried so hard.

Nehru had his final say. We all went down to a shady garden on the outskirts of New Delhi. A coloured marquee had been erected on the lawn and there we gathered around Nehru who had mounted a plush armchair in the centre. Cool lemon drinks and little savouries bound up in vine leaves came round as the conference went on. It went on for two and a half hours and was in its way a masterpiece of dialectic. Nehru was sometimes acid, even spiteful, but his soft, friendly voice went on and on piling up point after point with nice logic. He had the almost impossible job of explaining that on the one hand he was determined to repel the Japanese and on the other was equally determined not to help the allies do anything about it.

He said it would have been quite possible for the British government to pass in twenty-four hours a short bill of half a dozen clauses giving India independence immediately. He said the British proposals were nebulous and that the powers offered to the Indian defence minister were ridiculous.

He said, 'I swallowed many bitter pills in order to come to an agreement. I wanted to mobilise hundreds of millions of Indians. We were not going to surrender. We were going to mobilise a citizen army. I could have doubled and trebled Indian production. There would have been hell to pay for anyone who didn't work and that would have gone for both Indians and British from the viceroy downwards. There would have been no question of this business of four-o'clock tea and dress for dinner at eight—that is not the way to fight a war. We would have been in a much better position than China to raise a citizen army. They couldn't see that in the stifling atmosphere of New Delhi. The British have an attitude of complacency peculiar to no other people. They say, "You are not only wrong, you are damnably wrong." All Cripps would say about the citizen army was that it was a matter for the commander-in-chief to decide. But he did give us the impression that the viceroy would not interfere with the national Indian government. He admitted that the India Office was an anachronism. But we were suddenly astonished to find that all these assumptions on which we had been arguing for the past ten days were wrong. Cripps suddenly became much more rigid. He had probably been pulled up by his senior partners in London. He now made it clear there would be no change in the viceroy's position. To talk of the tyranny of the majority rule is amazing fantastic nonsense.

'I cannot tolerate that I should sit idle while the battle for India is fought between foreign armies. I am not going to give in to the British but much less will I give in to the Japanese. It would be a tragedy if Germany and Japan won the war. We could have broken the British war effort here had we chosen to do so, but it is no use jumping from the frying-pan into the fire.'

And so on. I have bound together here only a few of the things that were said in a long, rather rambling but brilliant discourse. The central thing was the hopeless disagreement on every major point and even on the interpretation of the negotiations.

These differences from that day forward began to increase and deepen. Three months later Rajagopalacharia who favoured cooperation had left his colleagues, but the remainder of the Congress committee did the thing which Nehru had said he would not do—a campaign of civil disobedience was begun. Four months later Gandhi, Nehru and the rest, some hundreds of them, were arrested. The great hopes that Cripps had raised were finally broken and buried underground.

Could Cripps have succeeded? I am convinced not. His mission was based on the belief that the Indians could be brought together by persuasion, which was impossible; that they wanted to fight the Japanese, which was doubtful; that they were strong enough to decide their own fate, which was not true.

At the risk of being boring, let me repeat: Give the biggest party, Congress, its citizen army and the control. What then? Would the Muslims, the Sikhs, the Gurkhas—the bulk of the anti-Congress men in fact—obey Congress? No. Would the citizen army fight? Some like Nehru said Yes. Some like Gandhi said No. Others again like Chandra Bose would prefer to use the army on the side of the Japanese against the Allies. The British had committed terrible faults and created terrible grievances in India. But they had ruled there and kept the people together for centuries. Remove them suddenly. What then? The answer was pretty clear—civil war. It had happened so often before. The history of India is the history of barbarian tribes and dictators crossing the frontiers and annihilating the soft people of the plains.

Take it from the Indian point of view. Would the Japanese be better masters than the British? No, on the whole not. Gandhi said that the lot of the peasant couldn't be more debased under any other government, but most of the others were agreed that the Japanese were a worse menace to freedom than the British.

Take it from the British point of view. Could they entrust to doubtful allies the security of the allied land, sea and air-bases in India? Could they risk exposing China's flank? Already the incoming

U.S.A. forces were complaining that the indecision of the politicians was hampering their operations.

If the Cripps mission had revealed anything it was probably that the Indians or at least a part of them would only combine under some strong armed direction, probably from outside. Despite Nehru's view, inside India most of the forces appeared to be moving toward disintegration. It seemed clear that India would fight only under the control of the allies and would peacefully settle her own differences later only under the compulsion of the victors. Perhaps that was the solution of it all—a combined British, American, Russian and Chinese commission to meet and settle India's problem.

Such a commission at least would remove the charge that Britain was legislating in her own interest.

In the meantime Cripps was beaten by passive resistance—by that mass of weak, helpless, hesitating humanity, that lies, layer on layer, like a London fog, so that the deeper he went down into it the more it gave way in front of him and closed in behind and got darker. He could find no foothold in this slippery space. No Indian came forward with a strong enough will. Quarrelling, uncertain and ambitious, the Indian leaders failed both us and themselves.

No one can criticise them too harshly. Many of the faults lay with the British administration in the past. The system we had built up was not strong enough to meet a crisis and retain the goodwill of all the people at the same time. Somehow the Indian war effort had to be pushed on in spite of the politics. It rolls on now, immense, slow, imperfect, but still a major factor in the war. It has increased tremendously since the Cripps affair and is still increasing. The huge Indian mercenary army—the men who know no politics and have accepted British rule—is fighting and expanding as it fights. I for one am convinced that India can go on under British rule in the same way until the war is ended. It is a bad way but it seems the only way. After the war, the British will go. That is inevitable. And unless an Allied control steps in, unless the world develops a conscience for India, the exit of the British will create such a mass misery, such a chaos of want and unhappiness and death as even this war has not created yet.

Ten

April
in Ceylon

WHAT, MEANWHILE, about the Japanese invasion of India? It was going forward surely enough. General Alexander had been rushed out from England to take over the Burma command and he had arrived just in time to abandon Rangoon. No one man at that stage could have made any difference. Another melancholy British retreat was beginning up the Irrawaddy River and it was the same story of local quislings rising to join the invader, of too little equipment and of the wrong sort, of poor communications, of not enough air support, of a slow-moving European army encumbered by its baggage. Burning docksides and broken bridges marked the ending of British rule in Burma and the opening of the gateway into India for the Japanese.

General Stillwell of the United States army had taken an allied command on the left flank of the retreating British, and a few small Chinese divisions were sent in from the direction of the north Thailand borders. But this could only delay the Japanese. Step by step they pushed on through the heat, living on pills and the country. In the confusion of the retreat the enemy was able to smuggle small groups of riflemen into the allied lines to cause diversions, and snipers were constantly taking the British in the rear. It was the sad story of Malaya over again—endless infiltration by the Japanese. We had anti-tank guns and even some armoured vehicles, but the Japanese used no tanks.

Mandalay at last went up in flames, and then finally Lashio, the terminus of the Burma Road. The road was cut and China, after five years of indomitable defence, was isolated from the land-borne supplies of the outside world. There had not been a blacker moment in the war of the Far East.

Calcutta, Tatanaga and the bulk of India's heavy industry lay within bombing range and exposed to immediate attack. Something like half a million refugees had already poured northward from Calcutta into the teeming valley of the Ganges and these were joined now by streams of homeless, bewildered people and tired soldiers coming out of Burma. The feeble Allied air link with China from Calcutta to Chungking was almost breaking and everywhere to the east of Bengal the Japanese air force had control.

Even this was not all. The Andaman Islands and then the Nicobars, both Indian-administrated territory, fell without resistance and the Japanese fleet burst into the Bay of Bengal like a cyclone. Allied freighters plying up the eastern reaches of India to Calcutta were like so many fish caught in a pondful of sharks. A dozen ships went to the bottom within the space of a few days.

A considerable British fleet, probably the largest that had ever been seen in these waters, put to sea but was unable to bring the Japanese to battle. Instead, the aircraft carrier *Hermes* and two cruisers, *Dorsetshire* and *Cornwall*, and the Australian destroyer *Vampire*, were caught by enemy naval aircraft in the Indian Ocean and destroyed without our being able to make any notable reply.

There were at least three aircraft carriers operating with the Japanese and these now sent out the first raids onto Indian soil. Cocanada and one or two other places on the east coast were bombed, not seriously, but badly enough to panic the frightened people. From Madras there was a wholesale evacuation, and while refugees packed the roads inland and the railways were strained to the point of disorganisation, the ordinary life of Madras itself was almost at a standstill. For a few days food was difficult to get and even transport was disrupted in the city. Shops closed their doors and the wildest rumours of parachutists and bombing raids spread up and down the peninsula. From top to bottom the Japanese dominated the Bay of Bengal. The stage was set for invasion, fast, deadly and violent.

Then, abruptly, from out of the blue sky, a great and good thing happened for the Allied cause. The Japanese raided Ceylon. They fell upon the fuelling depot of Colombo in the west of the island and the naval base of Trincomalee in the east. Nearly one hundred Japanese aircraft were blown out of the sky. They were blown up so thoroughly that not a single Japanese airman was recovered in Ceylon.

Very few of the raiders got back to their ships and that meant that at least two enemy carriers had quite insufficient aircraft with which to carry on. For the first time in months here was victory, clear, sharp and conclusive. It was the first sign that the Japanese had begun to reach the limits of their dynamic series of conquests, that here at last was force to arrest them, that the rot in the British lines was stopped. In its very minor way, this was as important to the Far East as the Battle of Britain had been to Europe.

The Japanese never returned. Their fleet cleared out of the Bay of Bengal, probably to refuel, possibly also because the United States raid on Tokyo had raised such a scare in Japan that it was felt that the warships were needed nearer home.

The real significance of the raid on Ceylon was nowhere realised at once. It was believed to be the prelude of the invasion of the island, and my paper naturally ordered me to Colombo at once.

Invasion or no invasion it seemed to me that here was a wonderful chance for British propaganda. The attack had come at the end of a long list of British reverses and right in the middle of the Cripps negotiations. Half of India was in a state of nervous tension. Many believed that India would become a battleground within the next few weeks. Surely here, if ever, was a chance to restore confidence.

Pictures of the wrecked enemy planes should be rushed to the mainland and distributed to every newspaper. Some of the wrecks themselves should be crated and sent over at once to be displayed to the jittery crowds in Bombay, Madras and Calcutta. Newsreels should carry the story to the millions who attended India's vast number of cinemas. The successful British pilots should be interviewed and put on the air. Any captured Japanese should likewise be photographed and displayed. The people should hear of this victory and hear of it fully.

In New Delhi I prodded the old white propaganda elephant gently and he stirred just slightly. Any new-fangled nonsense about displaying aeroplane wrecks or broadcasting pilots' stories was, of course, out of the question. Similarly, it was quite absurd to suggest a special plane to fly to Ceylon. Man alive, weren't we short enough of aircraft for operational purposes as it was? However, if I liked to get myself down to Bombay an air priority (B) would be arranged on the civil airline from there onwards.

Richard and I went to the station at Old Delhi and set off. We waited precisely ten days in Bombay before we got on an aircraft for Colombo. The story was a little tired when we collected it a fortnight after it had happened. Cripps had gone home long since, anyway.

Yet it was an amusing journey. From Delhi to Bombay we travelled in a wonderful blue upholstered compartment in the air-conditioned carriage. The air-conditioning came from huge blocks of ice that were shovelled into a sort of bin under the floor. As the train moved forward the warm air coursed over the ice and blew a strong and refreshing draught into the compartment above. Except that there were still no corridors and one got trapped between stations in the steamy restaurant car, it was the most comfortable train in which I have ever travelled.

There was one quite unforgettable pleasure at a wayside station. Heavy thunderclouds were gathering in the late afternoon as we came to a standstill. Dozens of monkeys were careering about the platform, both the old and flea-bitten sort, and the young and comic that clutched at their mothers' backs. Peacocks perched majestically on the lower branches of the trees and many tiny birds were in the air. A fierce Tibetan dog leaped from the train and pursued the monkeys here and there among the flowerbeds on the platform. On the mud roads beyond, the swarming life of India went along, men, women and children and bullocks.

Suddenly the storm broke. Rain fell on the tired overheated earth like machine-gun bullets. In one wild screaming burst the monkeys scattered to the treetops; the peacocks hunched their plumes against the storm; the dog, tail between its legs, came back; and everywhere the natives ran helter-skelter for the sparse protection of the trees. It was all over in a few minutes. All the west went into a crazy vision of sunset colour, reds, greens, ambers and pinks with a rainbow amongst it, and from the earth a rich, clean smell came out. The air was washed clean. Standing in the door of the carriage I took one deep breath after another, and felt suddenly a tremendous physical affection for the country. Long afterwards, in the thick of a vile sandstorm in Egypt, I remembered that moment, and it recurs in my mind at any time now when I am hot and bored and tired.

Then Bombay. For some reason I dislike the big ports—Bordeaux, Marseilles, Naples, Alexandria—they are all the same to me, and I did not expect to enjoy Bombay. But for Bob Stimson of the *Times* of India and his wife and their books and their pleasant flat beside the sea, I would have hated it. We stayed, inevitably, at the Taj Mahal Hotel, which, like most hotels in India, was crowded. No one had heard of our air priority to Ceylon. The air priority had to be fixed in New Delhi. It was impossible for a civilian to telephone New Delhi. The only way to telephone was to put in an official call through one's own unit. There was no officer of my unit in Bombay. Anyway, the two or three three-seater machines that were the only regular air-link with Ceylon were booked with 'A' and 'Super' priorities for days ahead.

Unknown to us, General Wavell had very kindly sent a message to Admiral Somerville, the commander of the fleet, requesting facilities for us. We only discovered this by accident when we met the governor, and by then the fleet had sailed.

Twice we drove out to Juhu airfield in the early morning, and tried to get aboard the R.A.F. bombers which were being rushed to Ceylon, but they were all overcrowded. We did not like to risk getting aboard the south-bound trains which were still running hours, even days, late. It might have taken a week by train.

We killed the time by going to the movies, by playing endless billiards in the Bombay Yacht Club, by swimming and by arguing with the authorities. The seething masses in the Bombay mills had not yet felt the backwash of the Cripps breakdown, and things were pretty normal.

I used to watch the vultures in the distance. Circling round and round in the humid air, they followed the Parsee funerals down to the Towers of Silence. On the heights of the tower, so I was told, the bodies were stripped and laid out upon a grill. Then, like squadrons of dive-bombers, the vultures would hurtle downward. 'It takes them just twelve minutes to strip a body,' Stimson told me with relish. 'The bones fall through the grill onto a great heap below. It's very clean really.'

A minor strike broke out. During the luncheon hour at one of the mills a policeman ordered the men away from the place where they were eating and kicked over one of the men's luncheons. At once the workers flared up. There was some shooting and a baton charge. It was the first rumbling of the storm ahead. One morning I saw the strikers march through the town. They were more sullen than belligerent. In the back streets the usual religious processions went by and this was the time of the year when the weather was it its worst and people's tempers were frayed. Someone would throw a stone at the Muslims as they went past and then it would start.

At night it was more of a blue-out than a blackout and there were occasional beatings-up. Several times we came on drunken sailors lying on the pavement, their pockets stripped. The harbour itself was crammed with ships and some of them had been lying there for weeks waiting to be unloaded.

Hold-ups among the dockside labourers and the general muddle of war was making this a crucial bottleneck. Through this one port, the bulk of the overseas supplies for China, as well as India, was flowing or supposed to flow. The protection of the port at that time was paltry. For the first time during my stay a few ack-ack guns were mounted on the waterfront. Hundreds of thousands of Bombay people had evacuated.

In the clubs the endless debate went on. What was going to happen? The clubmen lay back on those rush-bottomed easychairs which bear the remarkable name of 'Bombay fornicators' and studied the matter carefully through the bottom of an upturned glass. There appeared to be three theories. The first was that the Japanese would make a series of landings at Calcutta and Madras. The second was that they would invade Ceylon. The third was that they would bypass the peninsula altogether and land at Karachi and Basra in order to link up with a German offensive coming through Syria and the Caucasus. Few at that time discussed the fourth theory—that the Japanese would abandon their outward expansion for the time being, and, wheeling east from Burma, concentrate upon China. They were held already in Australia.

One of the worst things about these agonising days of waiting was that we had to reject invitations to do other pleasanter things. We might have gone to Hyderabad and toured the domains of that richest man in the world. Or Mysore, probably the best run princely state. The war had made little difference to the lavish hospitality of the princes. One of them had told us that, maintaining the usual number of guests, he still had enough Heidsieck 1928 to last him five years. He promised Richard that he would send an air-conditioned Packard to meet him at the station, that he should have his own house and his own servants, and that he need see his host only at dinner each evening. He could play golf, squash, polo or cricket. He could swim in a private bath or play tennis on floodlit courts at night. He could shoot tiger or pheasant. He could fish and he could have curry.

We had invitations also to the hill stations at Khasmir and Simla and another trip was planned to some of the Hindu temples in the north. I had been promised a privileged view of the native dancing and ceremonial. Just for a little, it would have been agreeable to have ceased being a reporter and to have forgotten the war. As it was, I stayed in Bombay and talked Indian politics with Stimson, who had a sensitive understanding that was rare among Englishmen in India—or at any rate, the Englishmen I met.

At length, after an acid telephone conversation with New Delhi, we took off. We flew straight over the wild hills behind Bombay and over Poona. For days Richard had been trying to lure me up to Poona so that he could write a message saying: 'Poona, Thursday—The situation in Poona is excellent. The troops are in wonderful heart. Dammit'—or some such idiocy.

Hyderabad sizzled with heat and I felt ill with it as we bolted a heavy unnourishing breakfast on the airfield. One of the Blenheims had crashed there a few days before. Hours later we came down in deserted Madras, but they told us that the people were regaining confidence. The workers were beginning to drift back into town. The night stop was in Trichinopoly and we spent it in the railway hotel.

Our pilot was a smart young Singalese boy and he told us great tales of Ceylon. As we ran over the extreme southern tip of India, he asked us if we would like to go elephant hunting from the air. We had a wild chase then over the jungle. It glowed with a moist lush greenness, the quintessence of greenness. Here and there the undergrowth parted into a little clearing round a waterhole and then we would go zooming down a hundred feet above the treetops. Wild birds and deer leapt up screaming.

Then at last we sighted an elephant, an enormous brute with two of its young. They were drinking as we swept down and in a daze of fear the mother elephant lifted her trunk and went thundering into the trees, the two little ones in hot pursuit behind her.

We kept on a strict route over the palm trees, for another Japanese attack was expected at any time, and came down outside Colombo. Six years before I had been there and it was still a shock to see the almost crazy fertility of the place—the natives carrying huge branches of bananas and sacks of pineapples. Coconuts, mangoes and pawpaws— they grew haphazardly anywhere, and the jungle reached down to the city streets as though it would suddenly engulf everything in a wave of green fleshy leaves.

We went to the Galleface and for the first time since the war began I had the joy of sinking back into a really first-class hotel. Hotels perhaps occur too often in this story. But for us who have to spend a great deal of our lives in them, it is important to get good food and a hot bath after a long journey, and it makes all the difference if your window looks out on a great sweep of rolling breakers.

Here at last for me was an ocean I really knew. The Indian Ocean is like no other ocean except perhaps the Pacific, and I had grown up close to it in Australia, and as a boy had come to know its storms, and its colour and its peculiar warm saltiness. Looking out of my window and seeing a line of vessels making southward to Australia, I experienced homesickness for the first time in many years.

It was made the more disturbing since I had never really thought of returning since the Spanish war. In ten days I could be in Fremantle. All the forgotten memories came in with a quick sentimental rush. I had my fine curry that night. There is no sentiment in curry.

One quick skirmish round Colombo for information convinced me that I need never have come.

This was no second Singapore. The island was defended far more strongly than I could have believed. There were many old friends here, units from the Western Desert. There were Australians, Africans and Indians. There were the increasing Hurricanes of the R.A.F., as well as the fleet air arm. The sense of confusion and delay I had in India fell away. Here in Ceylon they had really prepared, and given a little more time they would be secure.

D'Albiac, the R.A.F. commander, I had met when he went to take command in Greece the year before. Admiral Layton, the commander-in-chief, had come across from Singapore. He was a squat, slow, bushy-eyebrowed man, a sailor who had been born, launched and sent into action like a battleship. He lacked subtlety perhaps, but he was a solid and sound man to talk to. One good thing was that the three services were getting together. D'Albiac had an army lieutenant as A.D.C., Layton had an airman, and so on. As Richard and I went round G.H.Q., Hurricane after Hurricane went by until there were thirty or more overhead, and from the sea, two cruisers were entering the harbour. It all looked healthy.

If they had not yet got around to dealing with propaganda as a military instrument, at least they had made a start on the political and economic security of the island. Someone with more brains than were evident in Singapore, was tackling the problem of native labour. On the docks a labour pool was being established and priority of unloading given to the most important cargoes. Labourers who did not get work were promised a free meal and one rupee daily so that there would always be a supply to draw from. Natives running the vital services like railways were being organised into a sort of civilian army and rewards were given to men who were especially good on the job. A recruiting campaign was being organised throughout the island. With a population of only six and a half million the chances of rebellion were not so good as in India, and as far as I could gather the opposition to the British was disorganised and clumsily led by certain priests. The menace of a native uprising was always there, of course, but here at least we were strong enough to keep it in check and even induce a little enthusiasm for the British cause.

The main thing was that this air victory had occurred, and in many ways the native was being shown that we had no intention of evacuating Ceylon. Many of the white women and children were remaining in the hill stations like Euralia. Others were working in the army and navy offices. The moral seems to be that if you garrison a place with fresh troops and fresh arms and show you are in earnest over the defence, then the native population will begin to throw in its weight behind you.

Force counts in the Far East. It's useless appealing to old loyalties when the Japanese are abroad.

There were also some sensible decrees for conserving the food—especially rice. The coarse, split rice of the island is not normally eaten, but now it was needed and the governor handsomely came forward as an experimenter. He fed himself a number of large meals based on the split rice and sent a long and fascinating letter about it to the local newspapers. It was rather like a piece in *Country Life*. The governor faithfully described all his reactions and pronounced the rice most eatable. It was another blow for the island's defence.

Rubber was the big thing. With the fall of the Far East, Ceylon remains almost the last source of natural rubber to the Allies. The day I arrived the island announced a scheme for stepping up production by 200 per cent. New rubber tappers were to be recruited in the villages. Trees previously tapped on a single-cut system were to be double-cut. Those already double-cut were to be submitted to afternoon cuttings as well. Even the young trees were to be cut, despite the injury to future plantations. And more ground was to be cleared for rubber.

Old airfields were being enlarged and new ones hewn out of the jungle. We drove out to one of these where the elephants had been put to work knocking down the palms, some of them thirty feet in height, and dragging them off. The need for this expansion was clear enough for an American Flying Fortress lay partly wrecked on the edge of the Colombo field. It had landed and run the full distance and the pilot had only saved himself from crashing into the palm trees by jamming his brakes. The big machine had upended on its nose.

Just about this time Tokyo radio broadcast a flamboyant account of the Colombo raid. It was given by one of their pilots and he described how he had seen his flight commander, badly hit, deliberately raise his hand in salute to the emperor and then dive headlong to his death into a ship in Colombo harbour. Did the Japanese pilots commit suicide? Were they fanatical enough to glory in a death like this? The R.A.F. pilots who had fought off the raid and many others in Malaya and Singapore were not decided.

They took me first to see the wreck of a Japanese Navy Nought fighter. It was twisted beyond all recognition. Its paper-thin metal—perhaps a magnesium alloy—had ripped bodily away from its rivets and the metal itself had taken fire. The construction throughout was extraordinarily flimsy. Even the instruments were cut down to the barest possible minimum. There was no armour protection whatever for the pilot and most of those on the Ceylon raids appeared to carry no parachutes. The identification marks were red circles on the fuselage and under the wings, and red and yellow horizontal stripes on the rudder. Some of the machines carried an additional fuel tank which could be thrown off.

These, then, were the machines that lay scattered through the Ceylon jungles. Some of the wrecks would never be found. Villagers were still coming in from time to time with reports of great flaming mechanical birds that had rocketed across the trees and then plunged into undergrowth so thick that no man could penetrate it. One native had seen a machine bounce off the underbrush into one of the jungle pools and only a tiny triangle of metal above the surface showed where the wreck had come to rest. Of the pilot there was no sign. Three Japanese only had been seen to come down by parachute and these also had vanished in the jungle. The rest presumably were under the sea. In all, about three hundred Japanese had disappeared.

The absence of armour plating and parachutes suggested that the Japanese were willing to succeed or die. But a British pilot told me: 'I chased two of them out to sea and they seemed to be concentrating on one thing only—escape.' Then another pilot: 'At Trincomalee I saw a Navy Nought so badly hit that she was grounding. The pilot had just enough control to turn his aircraft, and he directed it straight into an oil tanker. The ship and the plane went up together.' Then another: 'I thought I would be smart that morning. When we got the word to scramble (take off in a hurry) I nipped inland keeping only about ten feet above the coconuts. My idea was that no one else would think of taking that direction and that is where I was dead wrong. A Jap had exactly the same idea, except he was sneaking along at about three hundred miles an hour in the opposite direction. We saw one another just about half a second before there was a head-on collision. He flipped upwards, I flipped downwards and brushed the coconuts. He could have had a first-rate suicide then if he had wanted one.' And a fourth: 'In Singapore we captured two Japs and they asked at once for revolvers with which to shoot themselves. At the end of a week they had given up all idea of suicide. They confessed that at first they were certain we were going to shoot them if they didn't do the job themselves.'

In the end the R.A.F. men agreed that some Japanese were ready to commit suicide to get a target, others not, but all of them were strictly disciplined. The bombers would hardly ever break formation. As soon as the leader was shot down someone else would slide in to take his place.

And all the while the Navy Noughts would weave round and round the bombers, occasionally peeling off the circle to dart into combat above or below.

To mother these planes the Japanese were using some of their N.Y.K. passenger liners, which were capable of twenty-five knots under pressure. Some of the ships merely transported planes; others had flight decks fitted. The Japanese liked to approach to within two hundred and fifty miles of their targets during the night and fly their machines off just before dawn. By the time the machines returned from the raid, the mother ships were already steaming fast away from the target.

After two years of fighting, some of it in the Battle of Britain, these young R.A.F. fliers were an interesting study. One was a psychologist in private life, and it was he who arranged football competitions between the squadrons and obtained invitations for the men to spend weekends at the country estates on the island. He believed in diversion rather than relaxation on the ground. Another was the author of the American best-seller, *A Yank with the R.A.F.* A third was a school-teacher. A fourth, a banker. A fifth had come straight from school to the air force.

They had a racy, half-excited manner, all of them. They drank a good deal, but mostly beer, and less of that than they had done in the early days. A good deal of their conversation was about girls and the walls were decorated with nudes or near nudes cut from the illustrated magazines. They were fresh- faced, loose-limbed and casual in their movements, rather like undergraduates. They joked a lot, but would suddenly fall into a deep discussion about aerodynamics or some such subject. Most of them were quite unpolitical and their reading was light—detective stories, Wodehouse. They had a special language of their own and this argot was expanding every day with local additions. It amused them to invent new words and they could be unintelligible at times.

Beyond this there was something else, something that was more and more dividing them from the soldier and the sailor and the civilian. I had noticed this often before. They were just as boyishly friendly as ever, but more and more they seemed to be only really at ease when they had withdrawn into their own circle. They tended to become more critical of the army and the navy—especially the army. Something in the quick danger and independence of their lives was turning them into special men and you could see it occasionally in their eyes. The R.A.F. was becoming a club.

Buried there in the green jungle these men did not seem to me to be unhappy. They were working out the adventurous parts of their lives, and they felt they were living fully and completely. It was not quite so easy for the soldiers up-country. Apart from routine work and the forced marches they were making through the jungle as part of their new training, they had nothing to do but wait. They were badly plagued with insects and the heat. They had not the quick thrill of air fighting nor the airmen's chance of getting up and out of the island, and many of them were discontented and bored. The mail, as usual, never seemed to arrive. An invasion might have come as something of a relief. Those soldiers who had already had experience in fighting in Burma and Malaya believed or affected to believe that the Japanese were not good soldiers. They would tell you such stories as these: 'We had a wire fence in front of us and we covered it on fixed lines of fire. One of the Japs came running up to throw a mat over the wire so that the rest of his platoon could scramble across. We picked him off easily; and the second one and the third. But then they came running with mats from all over the place and one or two of them got across. It might have gone pretty badly but then we got our artillery onto them. That broke them up. They never came on in that place again until we left it.

We only left it because we didn't have any air support. We could have held it all right if we had the bombers to help us. You have only got to bring the right weapons in and you will break up the Japs every time. They don't like a bayonet charge either.'

It was agreed among the soldiers that the Japanese were good guerrilla fighters and especially quick in movement, but not very good troops in a regular action. The trouble seemed to be that there never was a regular action.

I was shown this list which was said to have been issued to the Japanese troops:

Spend as much time out of doors as possible. Bask in the sun and take plenty of exercise. Take care that your breathing is always deep and regular.

Eat meat only once a day and as far as possible let your diet be eggs, cereals, vegetables, fruit and cow's fresh milk. Chew your food carefully.

Take a hot bath daily and a steam bath once or twice a week.

Wear coarse cotton underwear, a comfortable collar, well-fitting boots. Early to bed, early to rise.

Sleep in a very dark and very quiet room with the windows open. Let the minimum of sleeping hours be six and a half, the maximum seven and a half.

Take one day of absolute rest each week as far as can be arranged even in the field. On this day refrain from even reading or writing.

Try to avoid all passions and strong mental stimulants. Do not overtax your brain at the occurrence of inevitable incidents or of coming events. Do not say unpleasant things nor listen, if possible, to disagreeable things.

Be married. Widows and widowers should be married with the least possible delay.

Be moderate in the consumption of even tea and coffee and, of course, tobacco and alcoholic beverages.

Avoid places that are too warm, especially steam-heated and badly ventilated rooms.

Not very practical for men campaigning through the jungle perhaps; but a good regimen for camp. I heard no one suggest that the Japanese soldier looked unfit.

For a few days we pottered around Colombo picking up what information we could and waiting for the arrival of a car to take us round the island. It was at this time that the monsoon began to break. The monsoon was not a crucial factor for Ceylon, since, curiously, it did not affect the northern half of the island. But it was vital for the operations in Burma, India and the Indian Ocean. It meant that roads and fields would go under mud, that flying conditions would be bad, that aircraft taking off carriers might have difficulty in finding their ships once they had left them. Already in flying to Ceylon we had come through sharp rainbursts and seen the faded tired colours of the land turn overnight to fresh greens. And still the Andaman Islands were eight hundred miles from Ceylon and the Japanese had no nearer base. They had now begun to bomb Chittagong, which is Indian soil on the Burmese border, but most of the British army appeared to be coming out intact. The defences of Calcutta, especially in the air, were being rushed ahead.

I was convinced now that immediate Japanese invasion either of Ceylon or India was not likely, and I sent a cable to my office suggesting that I should return at once to the Middle East where a new German offensive threatened at any time. I need not have bothered. A message arrived for me from Charles Foley, my foreign editor in London: 'Any dog's chance getting to Madagascar quickly?' A British force had landed at Diego Suarez in the north of the island that morning. It was too far by air. At Colombo docks they could not help me—a ship had left for Mombasa on the Kenya coast a few hours before and there was nothing else. I got aboard the next plane for Bombay, hoping to pick up a destroyer or some warship from there. I might eventually have succeeded in that, but by then the first flush of the Madagascar action was done, and London cabled me: 'Don't bother now.'

Event then I might have stayed in India. I had become engrossed in the politics of the country and would have liked to have remained and seen the results of the Allahabad meeting of Congress. But it was now obvious that the Middle East was the place in which to be. For the time being the Japanese dynamic had exploded itself. India had been saved by a very narrow margin, and not by its own defence but by the fact that the Japanese had to pause and consolidate the vast territories they had already gained. India would never again be so utterly exposed. On my way out of the country, I saw scores of American bombers arriving and met the vanguard of the new American army that was beginning to trickle into this central sector of the war. These were air force technicians mostly, but already they were assembling and repairing aircraft at several new depots scattered through the peninsula. That incredibly long ferry route across Africa and the Atlantic to Washington was beginning to run regularly, and I travelled with a man who said, 'I've got to go over to the States for a few days.' He planned to get there and back within three weeks.

Out in the Indian Ocean Japanese submarines were beginning to explore the British routes through the Mozambique Channel and the Allied trade routes leading up to the Persian Gulf and the Red Sea. But now a combined British and American fleet was getting onto them. Four enemy submarines were sunk within a few days. The remaining raiders thinned out and tended to husband their ammunition.

Ships in the Indian Ocean reported that just one torpedo was launched at them—then nothing more. So the Indian waters, too, were being lifted from the peril of this distressing early summer.

The danger had done something to bridge the gap between the India of the Great Moghuls and the present war—not much, but something. Hundreds of ships were building in the dockyards. The great steel mills, the largest in the empire, were working full time. Every day that went by was something gained in the battle to lift the country out of its muddle and apathy and disaffection.

Almost the last close-up view I had of India was at Karachi. A black and naked little girl walked through the dust near the airport. She had a delicate little face and it was heavily plastered with mud. Naked and dirty as she was, there was much dignity in the tiny creature and she had those soft and luminous eyes that follow you everywhere in India. In nearly everyone I had met in India had been this same spirituality in the faces of the people; a remarkable change from the depraved and greedy faces of the Middle East. I found it hard to dislike even our worst enemies among the Indians. God knows this war was not of their making. They had troubles enough of their own.

I kept meeting friends on the flight back to Cairo. Alaric Jacob, who had recently joined my newspaper, got aboard the flying boat at Basra. He had been up with the Russian army in the Caucasus. Donald Mallett, who was once in my Paris office, joined us at Habbaniyeh in Iraq. He was on his way to take up an appointment as head of propaganda in the British Embassy in Cairo. Both of them were convinced that Rommel was going to start something in the desert immediately. By the skin of our teeth we had held the Axis in the east on the Burmese border. Now the Axis was coming after us in the west. There seemed to be no rest anywhere. But then looking back over the past two years when had there been any real lull in this central sector of the world war? The old business of plugging and patching up the empire here and there seemed to go on and on. As soon as the balloon held in one place the pressure had to be rushed to some other spot where the balloon was sagging.

And it was leaking all over the place. When were we going to get a real striking force and strike someone?

I arrived in Cairo, glad to be back but not very cheerful.

Eleven

May in Gazala

THE DESERT baked in the midsummer sun. For fourteen hours every day the sun sat there in an unclouded sky, and long after nightfall the rocks were still warm to touch. The nights were too short to bring much relief from the glaring heat and it seemed that one day followed another almost without interruption. When the soldier woke in the early morning the sun was in his face and long before the day was over he was longing for the moment when it would go and the night close over. The sandstorms always stopped in the evenings. Sometimes a light dew fell and a man waking in the night would feel a cool dampness soaking his sleeping-bag on the sand. By the sea a light breeze sprang up occasionally and it was like taking a long, cool drink. The troops sat in the open turrets of their tanks and let the breeze go over their dark, leathery-skinned faces. Inevitably one man fried an egg on the blistering steel roof of his tank to prove something that everyone knew well enough—that the metal was too hot to touch.

It had been argued that these were no conditions in which to fight a campaign; that white troops could not endure the strain of fighting in such weather and that the atmosphere inside the tanks would be unendurable. There was the question of water, too—men and machines would require much more water in summer, more water than could be supplied.

It needed only one short trip into the desert to prove that all this was nonsense. Both sides were preparing for offensive on a scale that had never been seen in the desert before. They were amassing such numbers of tanks as had never been used up to now on any sector of the Russian front. Both Germans and British were standing up to the heat without any great difficulty. As the summer advanced the men became leaner and harder and browner, but they ate and slept just as well and moved and thought just as quickly.

In the long desperate race to pile up arms and men on the front line, it was hard to say which side was winning. Certainly the Germans and the Italians had all the advantages. Whereas they could bring a tank into the desert within one month of leaving its workshop in Europe, it took the British three months or more to get the same vehicle across from England or America. In two days Rommel could summon aircraft from Germany and Italy.

Ever since February this race to reinforce had been going on, and the history of what was to come was being written along the supply lines from Naples to Tripoli and from Liverpool to Suez. And the greatest of all battles for supply fell upon the island of Malta.

Malta when I was there, just before the war, was a place of green corn and grazing fields locked behind low stone walls; of ancient stone villages and ox carts; of quiet beaches and fishermen netting among the rocks. Coming in under the steep walls of the Grand Harbour at Valetta you took an elevator up to the little town above. The governor's palace was once a bastion of the Knights of St John, and going to see the governor one day I walked through a great dark corridor lined with the ancient armour of the Knights, a peaceful place. There were coal fires burning in the bedrooms of the Osborne Hotel, which was more like an English country pub than any pub should be. Goats prowled among the white-suited naval officers in the uneven streets outside, and you could drive unmolested round the island through the farmlands and the fishing villages. In the centre of the island there was a great domed church of which they were very proud. In the Grand Harbour there were always four or five warships standing by in addition to the freighters unloading at the docks. Dozens of little rowboats and motor-launches plied from one ship to another, or from one arm of the harbour down to the main gate of the docks. In the evening hundreds of sailors and young officers came ashore to drink in the pavement cafés and the clubs. They seemed to play football and cricket regardless of what the season was. Malta was a good spot on which to be stationed, a place for the tourists to see on their cruises across the Mediterranean. Gozo, the island no one seems to know about, lies across a narrow strait from Malta. It was smaller, quieter, more provincial.

All this was turned now into a hell. Malta was a base for British submarines and aircraft preying on the Axis lines of supply to Libya. In the spring of 1942 the Axis decided to obliterate that base. Right through the spring they turned such a blitz upon Malta as no other island or city had seen in the war. It was a siege of annihilation. One after another all the other great sieges were eclipsed— England and Odessa, Sebastopol and Tobruk. Malta became the most bombed place on earth.

I have twice made the flight between Malta and Sicily. Each time it took less than half an hour.

Within a few minutes of riding over the tops of the last of the Sicilian mountains, you are in sight of the island. The Luftwaffe took charge of Sicily. They made it their main striking base against the British fleet and Malta. They found half a dozen good fields already in existence— notably Catania which, as I remember it, is a large grassed field by the sea surrounded by many new hangars and workshops built of corrugated iron; and Palermo, the capital of the island, where one used to alight between two hills on sloping rocky ground dotted with palm trees. These fields were expanded, equipped with new barracks and workshops, new fuel dumps and hundreds of German airmen began to appear in the old and dirty cities of the island. Several hundreds of Messerschmitt 109F fighters and Junkers bombers were landed, and they set to work upon

Malta with the precision and regularity that had been used on England the autumn before.

The people of Malta had been a long time waiting for disaster. When it came in the long full days of the early summer they were still unprepared for it. They had no fighters to speak of. They still had no underground shelters for aircraft and not enough for themselves. They had just received large reinforcements in men, anti-aircraft guns and ammunition—but not enough to withstand a sustained attack. Food, too, was already rationed severely. In the last resort they had really just themselves and that ancient determination not to give in. Even when their towns were blown to bits and the emergency hospitals were full, they still would not give in.

Valetta and the Grand Harbour were, of course, the first to suffer. In the beginning the raiders came in groups of half a dozen or a dozen through the night and while the searchlights and the tracer bullets groped toward them, two and three hundred pound bombs fell on the moored ships and the piled merchandise along the waterfront. Some of the bombs missed their targets and fell among shops in the main streets like the Strada Reale. Soon the raiders were coming in groups of twenty or more and with heavier bombs and instead of being called to the shelters for an hour or two, the Maltese found themselves staying underground all night. They burrowed deep into the soft workable rock that was so good for absorbing shock and built themselves hospitals and dormitories, kitchens, lavatories. Even cinemas were run in caves thrust into the steep cliffs about the Grand Harbour.

All night firefighters were running through the streets and Valetta and its nearby suburb at Sliema glowed in the flame of bomb bursts and burning buildings. Children grew used to sleeping in caverns with the rock shuddering their cots under the force of high explosive. Mothers wrapped the babies' faces in wet cloths to protect them from the flying rock-dust. Men and women grew used to seeing each morning the growing piles of rubble and the spreading damage of the night.

Then the daylight raids started in force and these were added to the night attacks. Instead of once or twice a day the sirens screamed twenty times, and soon at the height of the blitz it became one long alarm. The guns were never silent. One after another the British fighters were lost in the air battles that swayed far out of sight across the island toward Sicily and back again. The enemy fields were so close that it was possible for the British in Malta to detect the noise of Nazi machines warming up at Catania and so our fighters, always outnumbered, were repeatedly in the air to accept battle. They tried for the German bombers. The German fighters concentrated on the British fighters.

Far to the east and west of the island, the German blitz spread out. They wanted not only to destroy Malta but to starve it as well. I saw one convoy go out from Alexandria. It was an urgent convoy. In Malta they wanted flour as much as anything—merely flour with which to make bread—and one ship was laden with it. Another carried ammunition. Another fuel. Another general stores. Every available British warship in the Mediterranean was sent out to guard the convoy. Aircraft flew from Egypt to bomb the enemy bases in Sicily and Italy, Libya, Greece, Crete and the Dodecanese Islands.

The enemy kept a reconnaissance plane constantly hanging about just outside Alexandria. Within two hours of leaving that port any ship could be reasonably sure of being bombed. This convoy was bombed. In regular waves the Germans came over with dive bombers and fighters. The Italian fleet set out and was driven back, but still the bombers came on. It is a thousand miles from Egypt to Malta—three days steaming for a convoy. Two of the supply ships were sunk.

Sometimes the convoys were more successful than this one, but always they came under deadly fire, always some ship was hit. One could have despaired about keeping Malta going. She was so defenceless out there. It seemed impossible to bring her aid quickly enough. Bit by bit the island's homes were being broken up. Civilians and soldiers alike were dying every day or going to the hospitals and no one dared say how long a people with a gallant heart could hold out against increasing odds—odds that were flung at them day in and day out.

When Lord Gort came to take over the control of the island he was warned he might have to arrange its surrender. But Gort was determined not to surrender. He greatly tightened up the defences and the work of unloading convoys. The half-starved garrison had previously unloaded no ships on Sundays.

Then one day a few Spitfires put down in the island. More followed. They had been flown in from aircraft-carriers, notably the American *Wasp*. A few hours later the German raiders began coming over on their usual run. Suddenly they found the air filled with the deadliest fighters in the Allied air armament. There was a ferocious burst of fighting in the sky. The Maltese and the British garrison, grateful beyond measure, saw some thirty Axis machines crash into the sea in the ensuing twenty-four hours. The *Wasp* sailed up the Mediterranean again and flew off more Spitfires piloted by men who had met the Germans over England, and

Churchill wirelessed the American commander jubilantly, 'Who says a wasp can't sting twice?'

For the time being it was the turning-point in the air war over Malta. From that day until these Spitfires were themselves demolished, the enemy attack on the island weakened.

But sieges are negative. The object of Rommel's Malta blitz was to prevent the British operating out of there to raid the supply fleets going to Tripoli. It is certainly probable that he intended to invade the island as well, had he been able further to reduce it from the air, but the main thing was to get his guns and men across to North Africa. The blitz enabled him to do that.

On their side the Allies were making an even greater effort in the race for supply. They had a twelve-thousand-mile journey with their reinforcements around the Cape of Good Hope from England and America. They had to cope with a bottleneck at Suez where the bulk of the labour was native and the docking and railroad facilities inadequate. Then there was the long route out to the desert.

A procession of camouflaged trucks three hundred miles long was again strung out down the coast road from the delta to the front line. It was a remarkable thing to see. Penetrating a little inland one day I came on the advance guard of the water pipeline and railroad builders. Indians and South Africans were doing their jobs. They were pushing the railroad ahead at the rate of over a mile a day. Trucks dragged the rails over the sand to the head of the track. There was little or no bridge or embankment building. The ground was simply levelled off by the Indians and the rails fitted together. Every so often a whistle would blow and the men ran and flung themselves on the sand as enemy bombers came over. The railhead especially was under fire. Soon the line had breasted the escarpment, had cut through the frontier fence into Libya near Capuzzo, and had reached the outskirts of Tobruk itself. Every day long lines of tanks on flat cars went chugging up to the front. Soon, too, we had fresh Nile water in Tobruk. Steamers and destroyers were still making that hellish run from Alexandria to the desert front line with explosives, food and men. By the middle of May we were actually in a better condition to get local supplies than the enemy, since Cairo was only half the distance to the front that Tripoli was, and Tobruk, our forward base, was much nearer the front than Benghazi. Such convenience had its danger too.

There was no doubt whatever in Cairo now that a battle was coming. Officers who usually drifted around the Turf Club and the sporting club on Gezira Island began to disappear. There were fewer and fewer troops in the crowded streets of the city. In the desert the rawest private was convinced that the lull would not last—heat or no heat. A curious air of expectancy and excitement hung over the front line. Discipline of its own accord became much better as it usually does when men are near danger.

On a featureless stretch of tussocky plain called Gambut, Lieutenant-General Neil Ritchie, the British commander, pitched his camp. So many cars laden with generals and liaison officers kept driving into the camp that soon its tracks were in knee-deep fine dust. The main British fighter base lay just across the main road and all day aircraft were overhead bringing in new supplies. At night an occasional Luftwaffe squadron went hedge-hopping over the camp and everyone jumped for their slit trenches.

Ritchie had under him two lieutenant-generals, each commanding an army corps. They were the two men I had met in Cairo—Gott and Willoughby Norrie. With Auchinleck in Cairo, these three, all physically big men, all in their early middle age, all regular soldiers, hatched a new scheme of defence between them. Gott and Norrie, covered with dust, would drive up in their jeeps and disappear inside a yellow wooden caravan with Ritchie, and there they would confer for hours on end.

Except for their scarlet tabs and capbands, the generals wore the same uniform as everyone else in the army—boots, knee-length socks, khaki shorts and 'bush jackets', which are open-necked, belted shirts worn outside the shorts like a tunic. They carried large boards on which maps were spread and covered with sheets of talc. Most staff officers went about armed with these maps and bundles of coloured pencils with which to mark the disposition of the armies. Most officers for some psychological reason preferred to mark in the German forces with black and the British with red.

Looking back now I see how much those little red and black marks entered into our consciousness.

How vital they were. How many hundreds of times did we drive up to a headquarters in the desert and cluster round the Intelligence officer and his map. One glance told you roughly how things were going. You got to know the important spots in the line. If you saw the black marks on the map had moved eastward, you knew things were going badly. Sometimes with a leap of interest in the mind, we saw a new red mark far out in the desert behind the enemy lines—and knew that we had made a sudden unexpected push. Sometimes we stood around while the radio reports came in from the different sectors of the line and we watched tensely while the Intelligence officer marked up his map accordingly. We took compass bearings on those little map marks. We altered our journeys according to how those marks went back and forth. And, as with everyone else, our lives often depended on those marks being accurate.

As we entered the third week in May, the conferences of the generals became more frequent and the red marks on their maps more and more definite. They assumed a form that was something quite new in the desert—the Gazala Line.

Somehow, without being dreary, I must describe the idea and the structure of the Gazala Line, because its design had an influence on a good deal of the open fighting in the war. Allied officers from other fronts were sent to study it on the spot.

Up to this date neither side had ever established a line in the desert which was defensible. The trouble was that while you could always base a line securely on the sea at its northern end, inevitably the southern end finished in the empty desert. Always the enemy could drive around the southern end of the line and attack the defenders from the rear as well as the front. General Wavell had taught the Axis that. And it was Wavell who had said to me in New Delhi only a few weeks before this, 'Yes, I think that Gazala is just about the natural balance in the desert.' It was roughly in the centre of Cyrenaica, and whatever army crossed this point was looking for trouble.

Ritchie and his two lieutenant-generals decided to drop the idea of having a continuous chain of defences at Gazala. They decided to define their position with a solid minefield stretching about thirty-five miles from the sea southward into the desert but they did not man the minefield. Instead they sealed up their troops in or behind the minefield in a series of isolated forts or 'boxes'. These boxes faced four-square, ready to meet attack from any direction. It was the old idea of the British square at Waterloo, adapted to modern fast armoured fighting. Each box was completely surrounded with a ring of landmines and barbed wire. Guns faced outwards in all directions. The boxes were only a mile or two square at the most, and were provided with water, food and ammunition to withstand a siege. Narrow lanes led in through the mines and wire so that the garrison could be supplied.

The underlying idea was this—the Nazi tanks were at liberty to bypass or surround these sealed-up boxes and seize all the rest of the Gazala area if they so desired…it was just empty desert anyway.

But they could not proceed far lest the British should sally out of their boxes and take them in the exposed rear or flank. Moreover, the British tanks were kept fluid outside these boxes and were in a position not only to attack the enemy in the open whenever they wanted, but also to go to the assistance of any box that was hard-pressed.

There were half a dozen or more of these boxes manned by as wide a collection of Allied troops as ever entered the desert. The main boxes were at Gazala on the sea (South Africans); at a point a few miles just south of them (northern Englishmen from the Tees and the Tyne rivers); at Knightsbridge, in the centre (English guardsmen); at Bir Hacheim, in the extreme south (French); at El Adem, in the rear centre (Indians); and there was the big box of Tobruk itself (South Africans and English base troops).

Roaming about between these positions were three large new British tank brigades and attendant guns, all under the command of Major-General Messervy, who had taken over when Major-General Jock Campbell was killed. Messervy had done well as an infantry divisional commander in the winter campaign, but he had yet to prove himself with armour. There were two great secrets about the British armour. One was the American Grant tank. The other was the British six-pounder anti-tank gun. The Germans suspected that we had something new, but they did not know exactly what or how much. The important thing about the Grant was that it was the first Allied tank to appear in the desert with as big a gun as the German tanks had—a 75- millimetre. The important thing about the six-pounder anti-tank weapon was that it could shoot faster and better than any anti-tank guns we had had previously. Elaborate camouflage and deception were used to get these weapons off the ships at Suez and into the desert without detection. The only trouble was that we did not have enough of them. The majority of our tanks were still British Valentines, Crusaders and American Honeys, mounting a two-pounder gun, and most of the anti-tank guns were the ordinary two-pounder.

As for the men on the British side, they were an odd mixture. The South Africans up in the north were led by Major-General Dan Pienaar, a lean grey wolf of a man who had come through many battles in the last war. He used to sit in his iron-roofed dugout high on Gazala cliffs above the sea and look sourly across the strip of desert where the Germans and Italians were hiding. From his headquarters one day I saw clearly a line of Axis trucks going along toward the coast. No one fired. It was one of those days when a strange lull came to the front, when no shot was fired, when the tens of thousands of men simply lay on the desert and waited—idly and unquestioningly and with patience since they knew they would have action soon enough.

Now and then the most forward boxes exchanged a shot or two with the enemy. For half an hour perhaps the shells would come over with that rhythmic and rising whine and erupt violently in the sand. Once or twice in the course of a morning Stuka dive-bombers stood high in the clear sky, then dipped their noses for the long singing slant toward earth that always ends with the graceful lift upward at the last moment and the shattering crash of the bomb below. Always somewhere out in the minefields at night there would be the distant shots of a patrol in search of prisoners and information—shots that sounded faintly and were soon over and meant nothing to the thousands of waiting men who were not directly concerned.

But the tension was there. It could be sensed right along the line. The men always knew when something was about to happen. You could tell of the tension perhaps from the way some boy from the veldt fingered his sticky bomb in a slit trench; from the marks on the map; from the rich and fruity voice of some English north countryman saying, 'Reckon it won't be long now'; from the tanks that were steaming everywhere like battle fleets on the move across the horizon and the hurrying trucks raising lines of dust like the smokescreen of a destroyer at sea; from some chance remark—or some silence—of an Intelligence officer; from the calculated casualness of the guards officers' conversation as they sat round their vehicles taking a nip of whisky before getting to bed. Everywhere in many thousands the men lay in their boxes waiting for the battle.

Most of the activity was along the lines of supply and on the airfields. The British had decided to tighten up the cooperation between the army and the air force—a thing at which the Germans had excelled since the invasion of France when tanks were directed from aircraft and had their way paved by dive-bombing. Air Marshal Coningham, who lived at Gambut with General Ritchie, had given orders to his pilots that they were to avoid independent aerial combat if possible and concentrate upon giving support to the ground forces. Thus if a flight of British Hurricanes on a sweep saw a group of Stukas dive-bombing our men they were to concentrate on the Stukas and try to avoid the Axis fighter screen overhead. Whole squadrons and fighters were to be held ready to go to the assistance of any hard-pressed sector of the line.

As yet Coningham had no Spitfires to speak of, but he was soundly reinforced in light bombers, especially the American Bostons, and he still had his Kittyhawks, Beaufighters, Blenheims, Marylands, Wellingtons and the rest. A few Hurricanes had been equipped as dive-bombers. We were probably outnumbered in the air, but not by much.

Looking at it generally then, we had a few cards to play and a sound position to start from. Coming out of one of his conferences Gott said, 'There are two places where I would like to meet the German tanks— either on the minefields or here'—and he indicated a spot on the map near Knightsbridge. He was confident. Right through the army the morale was good.

Over on the Axis side there was tremendous activity. Every day our patrols brought in reports of some new troop movements, of some great convoy of hundreds of vehicles driving down to the front- line bases from the coast. There was also news that the Germans were training parachute and commando troops at Bomba. A general order went out through the British army instructing all men to be on the lookout for parachute troops and special guards were to patrol all camps throughout the night. No one liked the idea of suddenly being taken in the rear. A sad little incident occurred over the parachute scare just before zero hour. A young British officer was worried about his wife in England— worried to the point where he was sleeping fitfully and uneasy dreams went through his head. Like everyone else he had the parachute warning in the back of his mind. One night as he was dozing in his tent he heard a slight noise and, looking up half awake, saw a dark figure at the door. In a sudden excited reflex he thought the intruder was a German. He grabbed his loaded pistol and shot the man dead. The man was a British dispatch rider coming in with a message. The officer was exonerated.

But Rommel had much bigger fish to fry than parachutists. He had brought a great host with him into the desert. There were elements of eight Italian divisions—the Sabrata, Brescia, Pavia, Trieste, Bologna, Trento, Littorio and Ariete. The last two were armoured. These were the three German divisions of the Afrika Korps—the 90th Light Infantry and the 15th and 21st Armoured Panzer divisions.

Most of these units had been brought up to strength since the winter campaign. Unlike the British, there was nothing especially new about the Axis equipment. Again they had their Mark III tank with the 50-millimetre gun (the Mark IV had a 75-millimetre); and there were Italian tanks like the L6 and MB. The most important thing was that large numbers of the mobile 88-millimetre all-purpose gun, both those made in Italy and Germany, had been brought in. This was the gun that was to dominate the battle.

In the air the enemy had the Messerschmitt 109F, still the fastest fighter in the desert, and the usual Stukas and Junkers bombers and troop-carriers. The Italians had the three-motored Savoia bomber and a considerable increase in the numbers of their fast Macchi fighters. Rommel, now a marshal, was again in command and his immediate juniors were Generals Nehring and Cruewell. Marshal Kesselring was in charge of the Luftwaffe. Colonel Marx was also coming into prominence as a leader of the 90th Light.

In all then, you might estimate that each side had about ten divisions comprising roughly 130,000 men and 500 effective tanks, and their guns and air forces were fairly evenly matched in quantity. The surprising thing was that two great powers should have so nicely balanced themselves at this remote end of the long front line that now stretched from Murmansk in Russia to Gazala in Egypt.

As with us Rommel was keeping his tanks fluid somewhere about the north centre of his line until March 26th when he swung them south, leaving behind their camouflage to trick us (as it did). The Italians mostly were used as positional troops; the Germans as a striking force. The area over which the two armies were about to fight was about as large as the home counties of England, but it was nothing more than a wide, almost featureless, strip of land and rock. There was an occasional low ridge pitted with camel thorn, an occasional cairn of stones casually thrown up by passing Bedouin pilgrims, and for the rest it was arid, limitless desert as empty as the sea—and as dangerous. Gazala had just one dilapidated Italian roadhouse—and no other building.

Travelling westwards along the coast road you recognised Gazala at once, because there was a deserted airfield on your left, with broken aircraft lying about, and beyond that the sea swept into a narrow bay. At the end of the bay the road led across a flat scrub-covered plain, and after that you were in the cliffs of Gazala itself. They came so close to the seashore the road had barely room to squeeze past. A crazy and dangerous sidetrack led up to the top of the cliffs, where there was a superb view along the sweep of coast back to Tobruk.

As a fighting arena the desert is superb. You get there as close to a straight out trial of strength as you will on any battle-front on earth. Gazala and all the thousands of miles of desert around it were not of the slightest value to the British or the Germans. They simply chanced to meet on that spot as haphazardly as a hunter will meet his quarry in a forest. Neither side came into the desert for conquest or loot, but simply for battle. It would have mattered nothing to the British if the

Germans had suddenly decided to seize a thousand square miles of desert to the south; or even if they had occupied the whole of North Africa. Provided that the British Eighth Army was still in existence at Gazala, the Germans could not hope to hold this territory. But once the Eighth Army was defeated, or even just the tanks of the Eighth Army were demolished, then not only Tobruk but the Nile Delta as well was laid open to the Germans.

It was a battle staged and announced with all the technique of an opera season and the approaching zero hour had all the studied drama of an opening night. On this tiny spot on the African map the future of the whole continent was being decided. As the month moved into its final week it was clear to everyone that the time was running out. An overture was already sounding in a sudden burst of heavy bombing. A bright full moon came up and through its clear fresh light the German raiders went rushing over the tents of the British camps. They pelted the roadways with machine-gun fire. They dived onto the airfields where the British aircraft lay dispersed about the sand. No one could sleep very well.

Early on the morning of May 26th a British tank commander saw through his glasses an unusual pillar of dust going up from the south of Bir Hacheim. Straining his eyes through the early morning haze he saw the dust cloud deepen and expand. Little black dots were spaced along the bottom of the cloud. 'Looks like a brigade of Jerry tanks coming,' he reported over his telephone to his headquarters. He looked again and added sharply, 'It's more than a brigade. It's the whole bloody Afrika Korps.' The battle had begun.

Just a handful of British tanks under this commander took the first German rush. The British tanks outside Bir Hacheim were too weak to fight a delaying action. They were too late to get clear away. So they went forward over the uneven rock and sand to accept their destruction and all the desert from one end of the Gazala Line to the other erupted into an earthquake of shelling, bombing, flame and dust. One after another the British boxes reported they were engaged. From a hundred concealed crannies in the rocks the Italians unloosed their artillery on the South Africans and the British in the north. Stukas rode over the barrage, bombing and fighting. On the ground Italian infantrymen picked their way through the minefields and rushed the British outposts on the western rim of the box. The South African machine-gunners began the killing they had awaited for months. All through the morning while the artillery came in to swell the uproar, they went on killing men. It was the same at Bir Hacheim. The French slammed the doors of their box and opened up with every gun into the pall of dust that kept swirling around them.

For an hour or two there was much confusion. Many little pockets of British troops and unarmed convoys travelling through the open desert were swept up by the German host. No one knew exactly where the enemy was attacking or with what force. One after another the British boxes sealed themselves up and simply gave battle at anything they could see. The British tanks meanwhile went rushing southwards toward Knightsbridge and the Capuzzo track where the main German thrust seemed to be developing. But there was no point of the battle zone that did not rock with gunfire or lie at times under the wrenching explosion of bombs.

By midday it was obvious that the Axis was sending its main force round the open desert south of Bir Hacheim and directing it north-eastwards into the midst of the region of British boxes. At least four hundred tanks and guns had come charging round behind our positions. All that afternoon and far into the moonlit night one small British tank force accepted the full tide of the enemy armour. Yard by yard it was forced to give ground, leaving behind the burning wrecks of its tanks and many of its men in death and imprisonment.

All that night and again next morning the main bulk of the British armour raced to get into position while still the enemy drove on. By the second evening the battle began to take shape. Rommel had done a bold thing. He had flung his men broadcast into the heart of the British positions in an attempt to take Tobruk itself by storm—and at once. It was learned from prisoners and documents that he planned to have Tobruk not later than May 30th—five days from the opening of the campaign. His four or five columns had spread out like the fingers of a man's hand. The hand reached upwards clutching at Tobruk from the south. One small Nazi tank force on the extreme left had travelled right up inside the Gazala Line and reached the coast where a group of light coastal vessels coming from Derna had arrived to supply them on the beaches. Another column on the extreme right had gone off, more as a stunt than anything, to El Gobi, the scene of the previous winter's battle. A third column under Marx was more enterprising still. Striking north-east straight past El Adem it had arrived on the high ground to the east of the Tobruk perimeter and occupied the vitally important ground at El Duda and Sidi Rezegh. The main part of the Axis forces—the armoured Panzer divisions and their two

Italian tank satellites—had stayed in the centre near Knightsbridge in order to meet and destroy the British armour there before advancing on Tobruk. The enemy seemed to be swarming everywhere. They drove through the night shooting out Very lights, banging their guns off to make as much uproar as possible and give the impression of great strength. Even at Gambut Ritchie's headquarters were threatened. Tobruk and El Adem were forced to lock themselves in. The firing sounded from every direction in the desert and by night Axis aircraft were all over the clear sky. The fingers of the hand were beginning to tighten their grip. It was a brilliant opening. It was as though a gang of thugs had invaded a house and were prowling through the passageways, while the inmates had locked themselves in their rooms. And as the intruders pummelled at the doors and the windows, it was a moment of high nervous strain for the householder and his family.

Then the British armour gave battle. The American Grants flung off their camouflage and went into action for the first time. The anti-tank guns came out of hiding. About Knightsbridge and the Capuzzo track the Nazi Panzer divisions waited to receive them. The Germans knew the British tank tactics well enough—the headlong charge to get into range, the flanking movements. They waited confidently behind their big guns, ready to break up the first onset by picking off the British vehicles one by one. But the charge never came. Instead the British tanks deployed—one group to either flank, one to the centre. Then they settled into positions, hull down on the horizon. There was a moment of puzzling silence. Then a volcanic burst of armour-piercing shell ripped through the leading Nazi tanks. Then another burst and another—big 75-millimetre shells with instantaneous fuses that kept falling from a distance that was almost beyond the Germans' own range. The British anti-tank guns, the new guns, opened up with an aching, sickening barrage. All this was something quite new. It staggered the Germans for a while. The fluid fast-moving tank movement of the winter had been turned into an artillery duel. The polka had become a minuet.

Frantic appeals went back over the Nazi radio for reinforcements in 88-millimetre guns. Because they had no choice, the Nazis rushed their tanks into hull down positions and settled into a steady answering fire. It was anti-tank guns and tanks firing together now from fixed positions. The 88- millimetre and the Mark IV against the American Grant and the six-pounder. It was almost static battle. The opponents at two thousand yards' distance or more could just see one another as dark dots on the horizon, and all the intervening space was filled with the crash of shells and dust and the rising flames and smoke of the vehicles that had been hit. Both sides sent in their bombers to augment the wreckage and confusion. Soon there were broken tanks and guns on every side. Some tanks were merely put out of action by a broken track or a jammed gun. Some blew up. Some were grotesquely upended by the force of the shell that struck them. Ambulance men rushed blindly into the chaos and the burning, and were themselves hit as they tried to get the wounded away. Recovery vehicles came forward to rescue the stranded guns and vehicles and were smashed, even before they could get their cranes working.

The battle broke into parts and spread north and south of Capuzzo track. It rolled uncontrollably across the sand and wherever they could the lighter British tanks nipped in among the fire of the leviathans and cast out their two-pounder shell at close range.

Since the Germans were attacking and their most forward infantry troops were every hour in more urgent need of support, they had to go forward. They could not afford at this stage to fight it out shot for shot with the British in a slow-moving artillery duel. Again and again Rommel sent his men forward onto the British steel. It was the Germans who were charging now and the cost to both sides was appalling. One by one the Grants were knocked out but more and more Valentines and Honeys came in with artillery support to take up the fight against an enemy who was tiring.

Nor was the news any better for the Germans from the other sectors. The tanks that had crept up behind Gazala on the coast had been driven out. The supply barges had either been sunk off the shore or forced to turn back. The Knightsbridge box, the hub of the whole battle, was withstanding every infantry attack. Up on El Duda, Colonel Marx was exposed and alone and British forces were hurrying to deal with him. It was essential for the German armour to push forward if he was going to survive.

While the tank duel still dragged on, Rommel ordered an all-out offensive against Knightsbridge. If Knightsbridge fell he could reasonably hope to hold his positions and make good the awful damage his tanks were receiving. The 90th Light combined with Italian infantrymen, tanks, artillery and dive- bombers fell upon the box in a series of massed attacks from all sides. An immense battle-cloud rolled across the Capuzzo track and the whole area was enveloped in continuous sandstorms. In this unreal gloom the men fought. The Stukas came back again and again. The enemy artillery got onto the box from several sides at once and there was hardly a yard in the target area that was not ripped and ravaged with high explosive. In regular waves the German and Italian infantry came on, right up to the minefields and there they broke, divided and fell back. It was Waterloo over again.

The English Guards with their strange and slightly automaton code of behaviour were peculiarly suited to this sort of action. It was something they understood. A position was given you to fortify and then you got the order to hold it to the last round and the last man. It was simply a matter of progressing to that final point, unless of course, the enemy got tired first. One simply had to remain there firing through the dust and something or other would come out of the muddle. Whether or not the ground was wisely chosen, whether or not victory or disaster emerged from the struggle was not the essential point. The essential thing was that the Guards had been given this piece of ground to hold and the reputation of the regiment required that it should not be given up until the regiment was wiped out or got the order to retire.

So these odd gawky officers with their prickly moustachios, their little military affectations, their high-pitched voices and their little jokes from the world of Mayfair and Ascot kept bringing their men up to the enemy, and the men, because they were the picked soldiers of the regular army and native Englishmen and Scots, did exactly as they were told. Knightsbridge did not break because it could not break. It stood through this maelstrom as a rock will stand against the sea.

Rommel gave up. It was no good: he could not go on. His tanks were getting nowhere. There were horrible losses on each side, somewhat more on the British than the German. Left in an impossible position without support or supplies, Colonel Marx evacuated El Duda in the night. From either side of Tobruk the enemy fell back toward the centre. Their blitz had exhausted itself like a spent rocket. Even at this stage things could have been retrieved if Knightsbridge had fallen, but Knightsbridge did not fall. And all night and all day the R.A.F. kept bombing, bombing, bombing.

Rommel now ordered a general retirement. It was impossible for him to get his whole army round the long route past Bir Hacheim—the British were marauding down there anyway. Some shorter route had to be found. He ordered the retreat onto the centre part of the Gazala Line. He ordered his engineers to cut a passage through the British mines so that the Axis army could escape westwards.

Mile by mile the Germans fell back. They left Sidi Rezegh. They bypassed El Adem. They came back from the coast near Tobruk. The battle-weary defenders of the British boxes and the tired tank crews suddenly found themselves disengaged. They still waited doggedly at their positions for they had not yet guessed the extent of the enemy withdrawal and they expected renewed attacks. Nor did the British leaders realise how thoroughly they had cut down Rommel in his stride. In that confusion and high tension it was difficult for anyone to see ahead and understand that a victory had been won.

Disheartened, bewildered and partly disordered the Germans and Italians struggled back over the sand toward the rallying point in the centre and the 88-millimetre guns kept up a ferocious rearguard action. They ringed the retreating men with steel and managed to get most of them under cover.

Wrecked German vehicles and guns were left in dozens on the battlefield. First one gap, then two were made in the minefields and the survivors began to straggle out to the west.

This was the position after the first five days when I arrived at the front. The British, though, still badly shaken, were just beginning to realise that they had, in fact, a victory on their hands. The German claws had been laid round them and now the fingers were relaxing their grip and drawing away. A signal came from Auchinleck: 'Well done, Eighth Army.' There was an air of exhilaration and excitement in Gambut Camp.

My first concern was to get to Knightsbridge where the fighting was still swirling about uncertainly. No one seemed to know clearly what was going to happen, so we drove first to Gott's headquarters near El Adem. Indian soldiers were dug closely into the wadis about the cliff as we turned in through the one narrow entrance between the minefields.

A light screen of armoured cars and anti-tank guns were placed round the box and the men were standing ready for action, since there were still numbers of enemy about and Messerschmitts were constantly coming over. Three huge steel-plated vehicles were dispersed under camouflage nets in the wadis. They looked like those big trucks that ply the roads between London and the north of England through the night. In one was the operational staff—the men who actually plan and direct the tactics.

In the second vehicle, the signallers were at work. In the third was the intelligence staff and they were the people we wanted to see. The truck was fitted as an office. It was a maze of telephone lines and switchboards, of radios, maps, codes, typewriters, telephones and papers. A 'blower' in one corner kept broadcasting the voices of men tuning in with information from the forward units—information not secret enough or too urgent to be put into code and sent by dispatch rider. Jeeps were buzzing about outside carrying liaison officers to different parts of the front. They were easily the most successful staff cars either side used in the desert.

Colonel Desmond Young, commanding officer of the Indian army Public Relations Unit, was standing outside the Intelligence vehicle and from him I got my first indication that something was going wrong. He had come straight from the battle an hour before and like everyone else he was cheerful about what had been done. There was no doubt about it, the Nazis were on the run.

'But,' Desmond kept saying, 'I don't understand why we aren't following up. Why aren't the Indians going in after them? We could have occupied the battlefield yesterday and grabbed all those Jerry tanks lying about. The Germans themselves are milling about all over the place. Why don't we push in and mop them up? It's a job for the infantry now. We will have to move quick or you can bet your life they will reform a line. I can't understand it. I am only afraid that it is already too late.'

He had raised the point that was going to make many a bitter argument in the days to come. Our armour was temporarily weakened but all the other positions held. Could not the South Africans and the English have come out of their positions in Gazala and burst along the coast? They would have outflanked the partly disorganised enemy in the centre, and cut him off from his supplies. They were eager to do it. The Fiftieth Division were, in fact, to show later how well it could be done. But today they rested in their positions. The Indian division got no orders to close upon the Knightsbridge area in force. Only light skirmishes occurred on the battlefield. The Axis, meantime, regrouped.

A digression here about Colonel Young before he goes out of this story. The last time I had seen him was on March 29th in the easy surroundings of the Imperial Hotel in New Delhi where we were having a talkative dinner with Matt Halton. I suggested that we should take bets against one another about the future course of the war. Here are the bets as they were scrawled and signed on the back of a military movement order and an invitation to meet Stafford Cripps. The bets are in rupees:

'Moorehead lays ten to four against India being invaded within three months.

'Moorehead lays ten to five against Turkey being invaded within three months.

'Moorehead lays ten to seven against Australia being invaded within three months.'

(This turned out to be three up to me.)

'Halton lays ten to six that Dakar will be occupied by American troops within three months.' (One up to Young and me.)

'Young lays ten to five against Halfaya Pass being occupied by the enemy within three months.' (One up to Halton and me but only just.)

Then finally this in Young's hand:

'Young lays ten to ten that of the three signatories of these bets, one of them will be killed, wounded or captured before September 30th, 1942.'

What a bet to take so lightly against fate in that crowded and comfortable room! Desmond Young left me at El Adem to go back to the front on this fifth morning of the battle. We never saw him again. We heard first that he had been killed, then wounded, and then finally that he was a prisoner of war in Germany.

We slept that night among the rocks of El Adem. We were a big party with three vehicles—the conducting officer and his three drivers; Clifford, Chester Morrison of the *Chicago Sun*, and George Lait of the International News Service, who were making their first trip to the front, and myself. Each of us found a deep grave and spread out his bed on the bottom of it. There was no great danger of our being hit by bombs in the night, but we found we slept better when we knew we were secure. The drivers brewed one of our famous stews and with a mug of whisky and water apiece we sat round it for hours in the darkness talking. Such nights were an enduring pleasure. The endless space of the desert made men turn to one another for company, and the sense of danger brought warmth and raciness to their talk. Every so often our conversation would pause and we listened to the sound of bombers low overhead or saw in the distance sudden yellow flares go up on the horizon. Atmospherically these moments had the flavour of a boy's adventure yarn.

It was midnight when we crawled into our sleeping-bags among the yellow rocks. I woke at 2 a.m. to find our little valley bright with yellow light and the sky above full of the noise of Junker bombers. One of their flares drifted like a chandelier across the dark rim of the escarpment and hung gently above us. I saw the others leaning on their elbows and watching and waiting for the inevitable sequel. But the bombs, when they fell, landed far off on the airport and we drifted into sleep again.

In the morning we drove on down the Capuzzo track toward

Knightsbridge. All through the first hour we passed through the recent battlefield and it looked good at first. Many Mark III and Mark IV tanks lay about, interspersed with the damaged hulks of our own Grants and Valentines, and upturned guns and trucks of both sides.

The thing that made Clifford and me enthusiastic was the recovery that was going on. Huge tank transporters, the largest vehicles in the desert, were bounding over the tracks. Gangs were hoisting the tanks, both German and British, onto the trailers. We stopped and talked to one of the tank crews that had just come out of battle with a jammed gun. They said that a number of defects were showing up in the Grant. The tracks were somewhat vulnerable. The precision instruments were not so good as the British, the big gun did not always eject the shell promptly and the vehicle's engine was still a little weak for the weight of the tank on heavy sand. Those were some of the teething troubles. 'But, Lord love you, what a job she is,' said the driver, 'and that gun there is a wizard. There's nothing wrong with the armour either. Take a look at that (a couple of jagged scratches on the turret) and that (a dent like a hoof print on the front) and that (a line of shrapnel holes through the rubber treads of the port track). Every one of them is a direct hit from a Jerry Mark IV.'

They were going back now to collect another tank and get into the battle again. The place where they got their new tank was a square half-mile of desert covered with vehicles that had been wrecked in the battle. I crawled over many of the damaged tanks and talked to the crews. They were all delighted with the Grants, delighted with the sweetness with which the big brutes crawled over the sand. For the first time they felt they had an instrument in their hands which was the equal of anything the Germans could bring against them. The pity was that there were not more of them.

Much that the Germans had taught us about recovery in the winter campaign had been learned and improved upon. Each British armoured brigade had its own recovery unit and mobile workshops. The transporters were going right into the battle to lug out the disabled vehicles. At this forward workshop those tanks which could be repaired within three days were handled and sent straight back into the fight again with their old crews. The others more badly damaged were sent back to a desert tank hospital or to the railhead near Tobruk and thence the trains carried them to the Nile Delta where practically any job could be undertaken. New tanks were coming up all the time from Cairo and being manned near the front. In this way a constant stream of damaged tanks was coming out of the battle and new and repaired ones going in again. It was the bloodstream of the armour, the thing that could turn defeat into victory.

Firing was now sounding intermittently from the direction of Knightsbridge and we hurried on…on into the most painfully memorable sandstorm of my experience. I do not think I can improve on the description of this day as I find it in my notes written on the spot when the dust was still in my eyes and my mind full of hate for the desert and all its parts:

'It had to come. Everyone knew that. Millions of tank and tyre treads have ground the thin crust on top of the sand into loose powder. When a hot strong wind blew from the south yesterday morning, everyone got ready. At midday the visibility was fifty yards with occasional clear patches. At 14.00 hours it was twenty yards; at 16.00 for a good part of the time it was nil.

'Except for a little shelling and one or two skirmishes the two armies lost contact with one another.

Germans and Englishmen may have lain a hundred yards apart and never have known it. Tanks that could have blown one another to bits passed by within easy range since the crews were blinded and their hearing numbed. Occasionally, when the sand lifted for a minute or two, the machine-gunners blazed away at one another, but then the pall fell again and the bullets spent themselves uselessly in space.

'I drove out toward the central front from General Gott's headquarters hoping to see something of the battle west of Knightsbridge. For the first hour it was not bad…just a matter of coasting along through the foot-deep dust of Capuzzo track. Weird shapes came out of the dust that was now rising half a mile in the air. It was like moving at sea through a heavy fog, except that the shapes which lunged up at you suddenly were five-ton lorry convoys, twenty-five pounder guns, and tank recovery vehicles.

'We threaded through last week's battlefield where mingled derelict British and German tanks lay in the positions where they had been blasted to a standstill. We fouled a slit trench. Then, reversing, we swerved madly at the last second to avoid an armoured car that towered out of the gloom.

'My conducting officer had his head poked through the roof of our truck all this time. He was on the lookout for the Stukas which had been blitzing this track for the past five days. They dive on you from behind and you have to keep watching. But no Stuka could live in this storm and the officer drew his head in. His face was like sandpaper, his eyes bloodshot, and his fine military moustache, soaked with sand, looked like a piece of wet flannel.

'Each one of us—every man in the desert in fact—looked like a clown with red-rimmed eyes peering through faces daubed with sand and with lines of sweat running down our cheeks.

'Toward Knightsbridge a line of smashed German tanks showed where British mines had been strewn. And here the storm touched its height. Vivid, lovely colours filled the air according to how the sand thickened or thinned under successive gusts of wind. Sometimes it was pink, sometimes bright orange, then greys and whitish greys strengthening again into orange.

'A towel wound round his face up to his goggled eyes, a military policeman guided us through the mines into Knightsbridge. At walking pace we felt our way toward the brigadier's dugout. This dugout was straight "Journey's End". Six officers crouched there just below ground level, and their equipment was a couple of field telephones and not much else. It was impossible to eat; at times even difficult to talk as the sand drove clean through the dugout. It coated the maps so thickly in dust that you had to brush your hand across the paper to read it. "We're shelling when we can, but God knows what we're hitting," they told us, and like noises off-stage in a stage play, the guns sounded to the left.

'From somewhere out in no-man's-land one of the company commanders was shouting through the telephone, "There's something ahead of us, but we don't know what it is."

'"How do you know it's there?" shouted the brigadier.

'"Because," answered the voice, "every time I shove my head out of this hole I get a burst of machine-gun fire." 'On the other telephone the brigade major was saying to another advanced platoon leader: "No. Tell them to stay out there and push on if they possibly can. It's no use their trying to come back here for lunch and tea and all the rest of it—we haven't got any anyway."

'These men were Guardsmen, members of the oldest families in England. The brigadier is one of the wealthiest men in the army out here. All of us sat there with just one overriding idea apart from the battle—what would it be like to have a glass of cool, sand-free water?

'These were the soldiers who took the first shock of the German offensive. They held Knightsbridge for days while it was isolated, and in the end Knightsbridge—it bears this name, but really it's only just another bit of empty desert—has become the linchpin of the whole battle. The fighting keeps swirling around it and always the Germans know that at any moment the Guardsmen may sally out through their minefields and take them in the rear. The best thing I know to say about these men is that they are no longer amateurs, no longer a group of civilians turned soldier. They are professionals. So this story they told us in the dugout seemed funny.

'A young London playboy had joined the regiment recently. He had never fired a gun in anger.

When the Germans came in with their main assault everyone—cooks, orderlies, mechanics and staff officers—was ordered to mount the spare guns and do what they could. This young officer was given one of the new two-pounder anti-tank guns. "What do I do?" he asked. They told him to pull the string. He pulled it. Out in the desert a few hundred yards away a Nazi Mark IV stopped dead in its tracks.

He had holed in one. The tank was written off for the rest of the battle.

'The story was capped with a terrific explosion outside the dugout. It shook the sand out of the bags around us and we tried to identify the noise. It was not a bomb, not a shell, not someone stepping on a mine. And it was one hundred yards away. An officer came in with the explanation—that strange electric current that plays through a sandstorm interfering with the telephone and radio had ignited a dump full of explosives.

'Out in the sandstorm again a Guardsman told us the way through the minefields to one of the British armoured brigades we had been trying to catch for the past two days. The brigade was temporarily held down by the storm only a mile or two away and we set off. I walked in front of the vehicles as it was impossible now to see anything through the windscreens. The sand stung one's bare knees as though they were plunged suddenly in very hot water. We followed a pipeline and skirted a minefield, keeping just two yards off from the tripwire. Other travellers called to us through the storm asking directions—Indians, South Africans, Tommies—but we could not help. Sometimes, unable to see anything or even think very clearly, I was forced to stop and stand for ten minutes. After a mile or two we gave it up. I am no desert expert, but I defy anyone to find anything in such a storm when even an oil compass plays tricks. I crawled back into the leading car gasping for breath—as all the others were.

'Even though our second vehicle kept three yards behind us and we made only three miles an hour, we lost it on the long return journey. It's no joke losing anyone in this area which can be overrun by the enemy at an hour's notice.

'It was not until nearly 21.00 hours when the sun, coloured pale ice-blue by the sand, was setting that the storm began to die down. One by one the things around us took shape and as visibility extended from a hundred to five hundred yards the desert began to take on its normal contours again. The whole landscape looked worn out and utterly desolate after this hateful day. In a few hours the wrecks of many vehicles have been half buried in the sand and new dunes and ridges have appeared. On the battlefield all the broken relics of the fighting have been covered over.

'Both sides suppose that the storm has been of advantage to themselves. Certainly it has helped in giving cover to troops going to new positions. But I doubt if either side really benefits. The war simply has been made tougher and more of a trial of endurance than it was. If victory comes it will have been earned as much against the weather and the desert as against the Germans.'

It was Chester Morrison and his driver who were in the lost vehicle, and we were additionally worried about them because a scare had been raised at El Adem. We were told that the entrance had to be mined and closed immediately. The enemy were reported three miles away. Any vehicles that were going in had to do so immediately. What to do? Go inside and get locked up there for days possibly, while the enemy milled around? Stay where we were? It was out of the question to go looking for the other vehicle at night.

Chester solved it all by turning up at dusk and we ran down to the sea to eat and sleep and wash the dirt out of our ears. At headquarters next day there was still an astonishing absence of news. The situation was tense. It *felt* as though we were on the edge of a considerable victory. Yet there was no real news. We drove back then into the battle area and this time there was a real scare. In the late afternoon the firing sounded clearly about ten miles away—it was another of these indeterminate skirmishes that seemed to go on and on without getting anywhere. We decided to bed down for the night. The trucks were unpacked, the beds set up beside slit trenches and a stew put on to boil.

Meanwhile the sound of firing was increasing. A few bursts of shellfire leaped up on the western horizon. This was between El Adem and Knightsbridge and we had judged ourselves reasonably secure for the night. But here were all the old ominous signs again...trucks racing through our camp, the increasing sound of shellfire. The vehicles broke over the horizon first in pairs, then in dozens, then in scores. We had been long enough in the desert to understand.

We packed up swiftly, bolted down the stew and set off for the coast. Halfway there it grew dark and there were extraordinary sights in the desert. The coloured Very lights of the enemy kept bursting up from the east and, nearer at hand, the retreating British lorries were running onto minefields. Soon half a dozen lorries were blazing around us and we ourselves were not at all too sure of our direction.

Suddenly in the darkness I heard wood splintering under the wheels of my truck and caught a glimpse of a wire fence. I expect we all had the same sickening feeling at once—'mines'. We stopped and peered out. We were in the middle of a front-line cemetery. Broken white crosses lay under the wheels and farther back we could hear the other truck blundering into other graves. Feeling guilty and confused, we got out somehow and reached the road leading down to Tobruk.

Tobruk was in an uproar. Axis bombers were coming over dropping flares and from all the perimeter the tracer bullets were arching upwards in cascades of red light. In thousands the little red balls crawled lazily upwards or got lost in a confusion of explosive bursts. On the ground the gun flashes and the gun noise mingled with the light and the explosion of the falling bombs. It was a heavy raid and it went on for hours. To the west the artillery kept up a barrage through the night.

There was no peace anywhere around Tobruk. We camped one night six miles away by the sea; the enemy planes kept passing only a few hundred feet over our heads. A wall of ack-ack was going up from the port. One enemy pilot lost either his direction or his nerve or both, and dropped his flares directly over our tiny camp. It was as though one had suddenly been stripped naked. Every morsel of sand seemed to stand out in the blinding light. Then a stray bomber came and while we flung ourselves from our beds to the ground, we heard the whistle of the bombs leaving the bomb racks.

They erupted mountainously five hundred yards away, and the earth wrenched and shuddered all around us.

Frank Gervasi, of *Collier's Magazine*, had now joined our party with another vehicle and with him we toured back and forth along the line trying to clarify the battle in our heads. Little by little, we began to realise what had happened. The chance of annihilating the Axis army on the minefields—if the chance ever existed—had gone. Whether through the lack of foresight, the poorness of communications or the insufficiency, or the combination of these things, our troops had failed to press on the heels of the enemy. He had halted his movement westwards. He had destroyed the minefields in the centre of the Gazala

Line and the gaps, which he had made for his retreat, were now being used to bring in supplies. The Axis troops lay wedged in a solid block in the centre of the minefields and it seemed we were powerless to shift them. Attacks were sent in from the north, south and east separately, in stages, and at once. It made no difference. In these few vital days Rommel had had time to build a line and behind a ring of steel he was regrouping.

Someone, without much originality, had called this central area 'The Devil's Cauldron' and the name stuck. The R.A.F. Bostons pounded the Cauldron right through the daylight hours. The British artillery got onto it. The infantry charged its flanks at night. There was some bloody and desperate fighting. One of our best tank commanders was lost and many of his tanks with him. Now it was the British who were trying to attack, and again and again they ran upon those deadly 88-millimetre guns which Rommel had posted right round his precarious position.

It was about this stage that General Cruewell, hastening to the front in a Storch communication plane, was forced down into the minefields and brought in. His dead pilot's blood was still splashed on his boots when I saw him at Gambut. But the capture of a senior general was not going to make much difference either way at this moment. The two armies had got themselves inextricably mixed up and every day that went by was to the advantage of the Germans. Soon they had transformed a very precarious position into a fortress. Our mobile patrols acting on the lines of communication to the west could not do much. It was a deadlock. Tobruk for the time being was saved. It was useless to lament that we had not pushed our victory home when we had the chance. The thing now was to devise a new offensive before the Germans were strong enough to launch one.

From now on it was almost entirely a matter of reorganisation and speed in everything. It was not a question of some general devising a brilliant scheme. On neither side had any real originality been shown. The tactics Rommel used were simply those employed by Wavell eighteen months earlier when we went round one enemy position after another. All that Rommel planned to do had been anticipated by the British and they had defeated him—or at least thwarted him. And now the British were quite powerless to initiate any new plan to shake the enemy from his positions. It was a matter of discipline, of the sticking power of the ordinary soldier, of the quality and number of weapons; or, in other words, of the whole system and construction of the armies. The army that was best trained and equipped was the one which was going to break this deadlock to its advantage. The situation required not so much a brilliant general as a large number of soundly trained young officers and N.C.O.'s Provided that he did nothing glaringly stupid, a very average general could have led the best trained army successfully out of this mess. Conversely, a very brilliant general could not have got a victory out of the army which was the more poorly equipped and officered. So now that the surprise elements were gone, the possible tactics exhausted, the morale about evenly matched and both sides clutched at one another like tired wrestlers in a close embrace, it remained to be seen which was the better army.

Twelve

June in Tobruk

GENERAL KOENIG, a dark sallow-faced man wearing his blue and red kepi and the cross of Lorraine, got word in the first days of June that the name of his Frenchmen was to be changed. There were no longer the Free French. They were to be called the Fighting French...La France Combattante.

His French, indeed, had need of all their fighting now. They had come down here to this box at Bir Hacheim in the early spring and they were a very mixed collection. Some, like Koenig himself, had been named by the Vichy government and declared traitors. All of them had been outlawed by France and dispossessed of their property, their titles and their citizen rights. They were rebels and could be shot if captured.

They had come together from the strangest places. Some had drifted in from French Indochina in the wake of General Catroux. Some had escaped in boats from France, sailing northwards to England and southwards to Algiers and Morocco. Some had come up from the Congo jungles in the south, or enlisted in Syria and Egypt, some had got away from the Balkans or crossed from America. There were regular soldiers and diplomats, Spahis and sapiers-pompiers, businessmen and Foreign legionnaires, sailors and farmers, black and white. For the past two years there had always been a couple of companies of Free French somewhere near the fighting in the Middle East, but they were never in enough numbers to be of much consequence and somehow they fitted oddly into the picture— strangers in an empire war.

But now in Bir Hacheim there was a full brigade of Fighting Frenchmen equipped like any other British brigade with anti-tank guns and twenty-five-pounders, Bren guns and Bofors and good supplies of water, food and ammunition. They were in the most exposed and isolated sector of the front. And, looking out from the bare hot ridge where his troops were lying, Koenig saw that his position was no longer only dangerous—it was critical. Rommel once more was going to attack.

The plans of the enemy were all too obvious. They were wedged solidly now in the centre of the Gazala Line, cutting Bir Hacheim off from the British positions to the north. They had repaired a great number of their tanks and guns and brought up new ones. Their infantry was rested. Since the British had failed to dislodge them and they had turned a difficult defensive position into a striking base, there was no reason why they should not return to their original plans for the quick conquest of Tobruk. And the first step in that direction was the obliteration of the Fighting French at Bir Hacheim. Once Bir Hacheim fell, Rommel could claim all the desert south of Tobruk, he could speed his communications and remove the threat to his right flank. He could make the whole Gazala Line untenable.

In the first week of June Rommel flung the full weight of his striking force onto Bir Hacheim. It was apple pie for the Stukas. They came over in batches of thirty and forty from the first daylight hour and shattered the ridge from one end to the other. Koenig called for the R.A.F. He added that the enemy was creeping round him to the east and that he would soon be cut off unless something was done. The Hurricanes and Kittyhawks went out in force, for there is nothing in the sky so helpless as a Stuka once the fighters are around. The R.A.F. caught one batch just as they were about to bomb. There was havoc over Bir Hacheim. Frenchmen, lifting their grinning faces up from the slit trenches, counted ten, fifteen, twenty, twenty-two machines with the black German cross go spinning into the sand and burst. Right round the garrison black plumes of smoke stood up. Koenig radioed delightedly, *'Merci pour la R.A.F.,'* and the R.A.F., equally pleased, signalled him in reply, *'Merci à vous pour le sport.'* From that moment the R.A.F. took the Frenchmen under their wing. There was always a bomber or a fighter squadron somewhere over Bir Hacheim. But it was not enough. The German infantry crept closer and closer up to the French outposts—little groups of machine-gunners dug into the sand in the outer minefields. The Nazi 88-millimetre guns got the range and the ridge came under a bombardment that continued through the night, and grew heavier every day as more and more guns came up to strengthen the enemy infantry. Repeatedly Ritchie enquired from his Gambut headquarters, 'Are you all right?

How are you getting on now?' From the battle Koenig answered, 'All right. All right for the time being. But we shall need more supplies.' All his guns were in operation. The gunners were reporting they had only a few days' supplies left.

Ritchie sent down a convoy with twenty thousand rounds of Bofors ammunition. It got through. The next day the Germans attacked again. They were putting in staggered attacks that came at first from the south, then the north, then the west. Again Ritchie sent out a convoy and gave it a tank screen. There was bitter skirmishing on the route, but some of the heavily laden lorries got in. After that it was hopeless. Rommel shifted his armour right round Bir Hacheim. The garrison was cut off. The enemy now was intent on two things—to starve the defenders and keep them continually awake with a non-stop bombardment. Lack of food and sleep were the things that broke men's morale.

There were two women in the garrison. They had gone down to drive staff cars and act as secretaries. Now they became nurses and stretcher-bearers, and they were all day and night among the mounting wounded. They cooked and served meals to release extra men for the front. Soon both food and medical supplies began to run out. There were no more such delicacies as coffee and that soup they used to prepare from the desert snails. It was biscuits, bully-beef and sometimes tea. The men in the outposts went for whole days without anything at all.

The R.A.F. made one more effort. Back near the Egyptian border the ground crews worked all night stowing supplies into Bombay troop-carriers. Again and again the Bombays ran across Bir Hacheim in the darkness and parachuted down drugs and bandages, spare parts and petrol, bullets and grenades. But you cannot supply a brigade with a handful of Bombays. A good deal of the stuff was smashed or lost in landing. At the end of ten days the garrison was in a desperate position. Burning vehicles studded the ridge. There was no part of that ground that had not been pitted with shell and bomb holes. All night the bombardment went on and the enemy ring closed tighter and tighter. The rest of Ritchie's men hacking and thrusting at other sectors of the line to relieve the pressure on the garrison could still make no headway.

In this crisis there was revived spontaneously in the desert all the spirit of the French soldier in the last war. In its small way there was a touch of Verdun about Bir Hacheim. As the Guards had fought with stubborn discipline at Knightsbridge, so now the French fought with art and desperate comradeship and were gallant in their own way. All the bitter accusations against the French soldier after the fall of France were being denied and proved false under this little tricolour that kept hanging in dusty folds on the ridge of Bir Hacheim. Wherever you went in the desert, you found the rest of the men of the Eighth Army full of glowing pride for the French.

Twice the Germans swarmed over the outer garrison defences in the north-west. Twice the French swept them out with the hand grenade and the machine-gun. But there were ten Germans to every Frenchman and the same defenders could not go on forever meeting fresh men and fresh guns. They wanted sleep, some pause. They never got a pause.

All this time the South Africans were held practically idle in Gazala. At no time apparently did Ritchie feel strong enough to risk getting them out of their fortified positions and sending them into attack on the enemy flank. In the end this may have been the deciding point and by June 11th it was all over. Koenig, without stores, without reinforcements, without much hope, reported he could not do more and he was ordered to come out.

At least three times through the battle the Germans had sent in officers with white flags to demand Koenig's surrender and had been contemptuously refused. They had even resorted to such tricks as sending out false instructions on the radio ordering him to capitulate. Even now Koenig would not surrender. On the night of June 11th, he began firing his remaining dumps and stores, and gathering his men into a closer ring. They hung on somehow through the 12th, and that night they boarded their trucks and set course north-eastwards to fight their way out. A rearguard was left behind on the ridge with the most badly wounded. They wrecked the remaining arms and covered the retreat.

Through the night there was bitter skirmishing. But the French now put forth their final effort. It was each man for himself and, with all the hate and desperation of soldiers in battle against odds, they ran upon the Germans in the darkness. It was a matter of the bayonet and the rifle now. And since the French were prepared to accept immediate death to get through and commit any risk, the enemy gave way in confusion before them. Koenig came out at the head of his Fighting Frenchmen and next day was safe inside the British lines. It was a tired and shaken group of Axis soldiers who went in to occupy the barren waste on the ridge.

Bir Hacheim had been an epic struggle and the results of this defeat were great. The Gazala Line was cut in half. The British defensive position in front of Tobruk now resembled a big quadrilateral with Tobruk, Gazala, Knightsbridge and El Adem at the corners—and not a very good position at that. Still there remained the British armour. So long as that was in being, Rommel could not get through.

Against this armour Rommel now sent every tank he could summon into battle.

The Germans drove forward in a great wedge eastwards along the Capuzzo track. They were taking no chances this time. Their tanks were kept bunched together and along either flank of the advancing wedge great quantities of 88-millimetre guns were spaced. These guns, in fact, formed a protective layer right round the Axis forces and there were more of them than had ever been seen in the desert before. It was not known that Rommel had so many guns or that he had rushed them forward so rapidly with his tanks. All the British scouts could see on June 12th was the approaching dust cloud under its screen of aircraft.

Again the British tanks raced to concentrate. We had to give battle now whether we liked it or not, for if the Axis forces kept going they would reach Tobruk.

The British tanks had been reduced from three to little more than one brigade, which was somewhat less than the German total. This discrepancy might not have mattered so much had we had the same proportion of Grants as before. But the Grants had taken heavy losses in the May battle and only a squadron or two were left. This meant that we were flung back on the Valentines and Honeys which were going to be outgunned from the start by the Mark IIIs and IVs. It was going to be a matter of destroyers and light cruisers against battleships.

This was one of the two vital things that governed this battle which has since been treated as such a mystery. The other thing needs a little longer explanation.

Rommel (as I know from a private source) had said to a British brigadier whom he had captured in the winter campaign: 'I don't care how many tanks you British have so long as you keep splitting them up the way you do. I shall just continue to destroy them piecemeal.'

The British commanders were well aware of the dangers of splitting their forces. But to keep tanks together in battle is not so simple as it sounds. On the evening of June 12th Ritchie had half a dozen isolated infantry groups calling for armoured assistance. The situation was extremely fluid, the direction of the Germans not yet defined and there was the possibility that Rommel might attack any one of several places—he might turn on Knightsbridge, or Gazala, or El Adem, or remain in the centre. What to do? If all the British tanks were sent in one direction the enemy might mop up a number of isolated infantry positions in their absence. If Ritchie withheld his tanks altogether he faced the possibility of the same result, plus the danger of the enemy getting right onto the Tobruk perimeter. Actually, on June 12th, the British tanks were scattered round the Capuzzo track and from that time forward it was the enemy which compelled their movements—not the general. As soon as the British outposts reported contact, events went forward so swiftly and fatally that there was no time for any effective single control.

It was usually like this in tank battles. No one on either side saw this action clearly and fully...neither the man in the tank, nor the brigade commander, nor the airman, nor the Intelligence officer, nor the general. It was too complicated, too quick, too obscured by flying sand. Each man saw or heard of only a few restricted and dramatic incidents and the whole picture was not worked out on a map until after the battle was over. And just as one man saw only a limited sector, so the battle itself was divided into a series of fast-moving incidents which were a law unto themselves.

Through this action, as through so many others, there was very little the general could do once the action was joined. The information he got was extremely meagre and quite likely to be wrong. Ritchie knew that even if he issued orders based on this information they were not likely to reach all the men for whom they were intended, and in any case the situation would almost certainly have changed before the orders could be put into effect. Even the brigadiers in charge of the British forces, who had their headquarters in fighting tanks, quickly lost sight of the whole picture. So the real responsibility fell upon the individual commanders of the tanks. Isolated in their own vehicles they had to fight with their own wits and with not much direction from outside. It was the equipment and training that counted.

Through the night of June 12th, Rommel continued his drive eastwards and before dawn of the following day he realised that he had had the great good luck to get between the two British brigades. Saturday, June 13th—the nineteenth continuous day of battle—broke warm and clear. With the first light the two armies were engaged. Almost at once the battlefield was covered over with rolling sand and the smoke of burning oil. Confused orders and messages were flying over the radio on both sides. The front line British tanks called for assistance, and launched an attack from the north to cut through the base of Rommel's wedge. They ran at once on the 88-millimetre guns that had been concealed in the night. Simultaneously, the tip of the enemy wedge threatened the British armoured headquarters which were forced to decamp hurriedly eastwards. During this move the headquarters lost contact with a great part of the tanks joined in battle. And the battle was ferocious.

In an attempt to get within range the British charged headlong upon the German positions. In a few minutes it was a massacre for both sides. From dozens of concealed positions the 88s opened up a tremendous belt of fire. Those British tanks, which had somehow escaped the opening salvoes and got right up to the enemy, found themselves exposed and deserted by their comrades who had fallen by the way. Those who were only slightly hit at first and turned to get away were caught by the second and third barrages of gunfire. Those who came in as reinforcements found themselves in a confusion of blown sand, burning vehicles and deadly shellfire that raked the plain again and again. When at last the British sighted the German tanks and went forward at them they were led onto other guns and demolished. Then and not until then, the German tanks came out and ran upon the British forces that had been largely cut up by anti-tank guns.

To a great extent it was the repetition of the oldest tactic on earth. Little brother goes down the road and the footpad springs out at him. Little brother runs back to the spot where big brother is waiting with a cudgel behind the corner. Big brother springs out and knocks the footpad down.

Both sides had many times lured or tried to lure enemy tanks onto concealed anti-tank guns. The Germans succeeded here not because it was a new tactic, but because the British were bound to attack to stop the march on Tobruk, and to attack they had to run into the 88 barrage in order to get their own guns within range.

One after another the British squadrons reported that they were taking heavy losses and needed immediate support. It was the Germans who were charging now, charging past the burning hulks and they forced the depleted defenders to give battle. In this tremendous follow-up the British became isolated from one another and were forced to fight in small groups. These groups in turn got separated from their own anti-tank guns and their supply vehicles. Many tanks ran out of petrol and had to be abandoned. All the confusion which had overtaken the Germans in their earlier retreat was redoubled here in the British lines and at a time when we had no reserves, when only a few counters were left on the board, and so each counter was vital. This was the position that Rommel had reached in his big retreat from Sidi Rezegh in the winter except that it was we this time who had no more reserves. The great battle for the annihilation of the tanks—the only sort of battle that counted most in the desert— was nearing its end.

The bad news began to come in to British headquarters toward evening. Little haggard groups of men began filtering back out of the chaos and each with a story of overwhelming German forces that had crushed them first with the gun and then the tank. The story that we lost some two hundred tanks on this day was, of course, nonsense. Actually the total was nearer to a hundred. But we had no adequate reserves.

That night, while red fires shone through the dust and still the artillery sounded from the Capuzzo track, it was seen that the British armour was gone. There was not sufficient force left to meet Rommel any longer in the open desert. Only the experts realised the full grim horror of that position. The hard armoured coating round the British infantry was gone and the experts knew all too well that once that happens the victor claims the desert. The infantry becomes a liability instead of an asset. It is largely at the mercy of the enemy tanks even in a defended position.

Ritchie had only one order to give and he gave that quickly. 'Abandon the Gazala Line. Get out, and get out before it is too late.' The most now he could hope to do was to hold Tobruk. He resolved that, if possible, he would try to keep a landward route open into the garrison from the east since it was not worthwhile for the navy to supply it by sea this time. That was Plan Number One. If the landward route was cut and Tobruk surrounded then Plan Number Two would go into action. Tobruk would seal itself up and try to hold out for perhaps a month until the British could re-form on the Egyptian frontier and counterattack for the relief of the garrison. But everything had to be done quickly even if only Plan Number Two was to go into effect. In the midst of the confusion, the sickening sense of defeat and doubt, the breaking of communications and the spectacle of the incoming wounded, the British commanders got to work. It was the blackest night they had faced in more than two years of fighting.

On Gazala Pienaar and his South Africans and the British 50th Division to the south of them heard the news with black dismay. Immediate retreat. This was the dismal end to their high hopes, to all the weeks and months of planning and working and preparing. They had stood ready to advance, not retreat, to blast through westwards along the coast and take Derna. The men felt thwarted, restless and angry. They cursed as they dug out their guns and gathered their equipment. They cursed still more when they were ordered to blow up some of those priceless guns and demolish the dumps of fuel and food and ammunition which they had dragged with such effort to high crannies in the rocks. It seemed to them there was no sense in this waste. Why couldn't they fight?

But even angry moods were a luxury in this crisis. Hurrying from trench to trench in the darkness and shouting their orders the South African officers got their men into the trucks. Bumping and heaving, the vehicles lurched down through the rocks to the coast road, a long procession of disappointed angry men. Officers went up and down the line urging them to more and more speed. The whole South African division, ten thousand men, had to get into Tobruk before it was too late. Pienaar was being warned hourly that he had not much time left. The Germans were already swarming up inside the line toward the coast. Once they got onto the cliffs above the sea and dominated the road with their tanks and artillery, then Pienaar's position would be critical. A rough line of minefields had been hastily flung along the clifftops from Gazala to Acroma, just outside Tobruk, in order to keep the coast road open. Ritchie was rushing his men there, but he advised the South Africans he could not hope to hold longer than forty-eight hours. Already, as the first South African brigade was hurrying down the coast toward the safety of Tobruk, Acroma was engaged.

British gunners turned back the first wave of German tanks but one or two of the neighbouring ridges were changing hands almost hourly.

The retreat went on all through the 14th and the 15th. As the South African rearguard came to leave its positions on Gazala, the enemy finally burst through and there was a running engagement down the rocks. The coast road came under heavy fire and every vehicle was forced to take its chance of missing the shells that pelted down from over the lip of the escarpment and fell in uproar beside the sea. Drivers simply hung tight to their steering wheels and drove flat out. Some were caught in traffic jams and hit. Others were cut off. Like wolves in some Russian snow-sled melodrama the Germans kept closing in in increasing numbers from behind. In the end most of the South Africans got through.

Far down in the centre something of the same sort was happening to the Guards, at Knightsbridge.

With the same discipline they smashed the guns which had done them great honour through the previous few weeks and began filing out of that grim and horrible stretch of sand for which they had been willing to give their lives the night before. Everywhere across the desert vehicles were streaming back to the east. Ambulances laden with wounded plunged through the dust and jostled for position on the tracks with armoured cars and tanks, jeeps and travelling workshops. All the men from Knightsbridge's satellite boxes, all the Indians on the Capuzzo track were now on the move.

They tried to keep a decent dispersal for their own safety through the daylight hours, but at night the trucks closed in, bonnet to tailboard, and without lights of any kind, felt their way eastward through the gloom. It was a moment of such wide confusion, such complex movement, that no one, neither the German commanders nor our own, could say exactly what was happening. British and Germans passed one another within a few hundred yards in the night. And one by one each box was emptied, its heavier equipment destroyed, and the men got away.

There remained only the English 50th Division south of Gazala. It was too late now for them to follow the South Africans eastwards down the coast road…the Germans were already swarming there. They had three alternatives—they could surrender, they could try to find their way through the desert to the east, or they could go west. They chose the last. It was the one stroke of leadership and imagination that lightened the whole of this stage of the campaign—a forced march straight into the heart of the enemy. By going west they were turning their backs on Tobruk and the British lines: they were taking a chance of one in a hundred that they would be able to burst clean through the Axis line and then wheel south and east through the open desert right round Bir Hacheim and so on back to the Egyptian border.

This plan had something in it that stirred the men. With the feeling of high adventure they got to work. The whole division was split into small groups of a few vehicles each. Each group was composed as a commando and told to fight like one—silently, swiftly, and to kill and get away. Rations were carefully measured out—water was the main thing. All lights, all smoking, was forbidden. Even talking was stopped. Then they sallied out into the darkness against the Italians, each man for himself.

An indescribable confusion broke out in the enemy lines as the British threaded or blundered their way through the minefields. An attack westward was the last thing that the enemy had expected at this moment. The attackers seemed to be coming at them from half a dozen directions at once. Italian commanders who sent reinforcements to a threatened area suddenly found themselves under fire and with what strength and with what objective they did not know. Italian prisoners were taken as they lay sleeping on the ground. Convoys of enemy supply vehicles were ambushed and overwhelmed. Guns were put out of action before they could open fire. Dumps of food and petrol were pilfered before the guards could understand what was happening.

The 50th burst clean through the enemy defences leaving a trail of burning vehicles, panic-stricken men, bemused commanders and confusion everywhere. Had they been on an organised and supported offensive they might have scattered the enemy in this sector in a single night and cleared the road to Bomba and Derna. As it was, they were alone and with many extraordinary adventures they came around Bir Hacheim and reached the British lines almost intact.

It was now June 16th and nearly all the British positions west of Tobruk had either fallen or were about to fall. The line was broken. Rommel was triumphant along its whole length. Acroma held out fitfully for a day or two longer, then that collapsed. Only El Adem, south of Tobruk, remained and without wasting an hour Rommel flung upon it a succession of armoured attacks. The Indians fought from their high ground for several days and they were under almost continuous bombardment and bombing. Then they, too, could do no more and they came out first into Sidi Rezegh and then down into the Tobruk perimeter. Tobruk slammed its gates. The siege was on.

All through this chaotic period the R.A.F. was rising to a climax of endeavour. It was the one arm that was on the offensive throughout. While the enemy crept closer and closer Air Marshal Coningham still refused to abandon his forward airfields about Gambut. The ground crews and the fighters kept going until the Nazi tanks were actually within ten miles of their fields, an unprecedented thing. They worked in a frenzy of energy, day and night. As the Germans closed in the British bombers made shorter and shorter runs until they were only fifteen or twenty minutes in the air at a time. The pilots would land, 'bomb-up', take off, attack the enemy vanguard and return, and this was repeated again and again through the day. Under shaded lights the mechanics worked all night getting the night bombers away. They packed their tents onto trucks and kept everything ready for instant departure and while waiting for the arrival of the enemy tanks, they still kept 'bombing-up' the machines, re- threading the belts of fighter ammunition, filling the tanks and getting the pilots into the air.

In the end they got word that the Germans would be upon them within the hour. Pilots and crews flung their bedding into their machines and took off. They dropped their last bombs and then hastened to other airfields which had been prepared farther back. The ground crews meanwhile jumped into their trucks and drove off a few minutes before their camps were overrun. They slept as they drove back to the rear fields, and then they set to work again. It was a tremendous burst of concentrated effort. These men, half dead with lack of sleep, delayed Rommel for several days.

Those days were vital. They enabled Ritchie to make at least a start on his plans for the defence of Tobruk and to regroup the main bulk of his army on the Egyptian frontier. Tobruk itself was swarming with men. As Pienaar's ten thousand came through he dropped off a battalion from each of his three brigades and this new composite brigade was left behind to strengthen the garrison while the rest of his South Africans hurried on to the border. There was great congestion on the roads.

On June 18th the picture became darker still. The Germans sent out a screen of armoured cars and these rushed Sidi Rezegh and El Duda. Soon they were plunging forward to the cliffs overlooking the sea. A few last British vehicles, through ignorance or courage or desperation, made a bolt down the coast road from Tobruk and some got through and some were caught. Ritchie and all his headquarters were cleared out of Gambut and the Germans quickly had Gambut too. There was no hope of holding a supply route open now. Tobruk was cut off. Those inside the perimeter were forced to stay there and get ready for what was to come. Those outside hurried on to the border throwing up roadblocks behind them, blowing bridges, laying mines. Plan Number One was out of the question. Plan Number Two had to go into action.

Even now it was not certain that Rommel would attack Tobruk at once. All through June 18th his forward elements harried the British toward the frontier. Nazi tanks were seen even as far down the border fence as Sidi Omar. It seemed possible that Rommel might ignore Tobruk for the time being and make straight for Egypt in order to keep the Eighth Army on the run. And bit by bit the Eighth Army was falling back on Bardia, Solium and Halfaya. Ritchie's headquarters were set up anew at Sidi Barrani in Egypt, some sixty miles from the Libyan border. Everyone was ready to move again at a moment's notice.

Then suddenly the Axis thrust toward Egypt turned back. The Nazi tanks and armoured cars wheeled round. They left Gambut and headed due west. If a clear sign was needed that Tobruk was going to be assaulted, it was here. Egypt for the time being was saved. Tobruk was in deadly peril.

Just before this I made my last journey through the town. Driving from Gazala we came first to the tall concrete monument which the Italians built to commemorate the building of the Axen Strasse. The Axen Strasse was the road which the enemy built to bypass Tobruk during the long siege of the year before. It split off the main road at the monument and, running in a great semicircle right round the thirty-five-mile perimeter, it rejoined the main road on the east of the garrison. The road itself was thinly metalled and part of the way it wound up the steep escarpments to the south of the town.

Between the Axen Strasse and the perimeter lay the British minefields, and here and there a little dugout walled with rocks—the watching post of some sentry who had been smuggled out in the darkness.

We did not take the Axen Strasse on this day as we wanted to collect rations in Tobruk and so we drove straight down the coast road until a sentry stopped us on the perimeter. They were dynamiting parts of the road and all vehicles were being carefully checked. The perimeter itself was a series of small slit trenches and sangers—square piles of loose rock that from the distance looked like the crenellated battlements of a medieval castle. Behind this the guns and troops lay pressed to the ground. All these defence works were extremely primitive and flat. There was no built-up wall, no really good system of anti-tank trenches or upright steel spikes, and very few concrete pill boxes.

Indeed, as you went across this flat neutral-coloured ground, you saw very little difference from the ordinary desert. But if you stirred the dust with your toe you would be certain to uncover a spent bullet, a piece of shrapnel or a newly broken bit of rock. For many months the defenders had lived in this waste and their life had been so crude and hard they had left practically no traces behind them.

More minefields lay inside the perimeter and then the flat ground broken here and there by dried-up watercourses swept in a gentle slope to the cliffs above the town.

In the narrow sea plain between the coast and the cliffs, thousands of sand-coloured vehicles were dispersed about. We were in the midst of an immense car park. Crudely painted notices were posted along the road at every sidetrack. These led to ammunition and food dumps, petrol and water points, engineers' and tank stores, hospitals, unit headquarters, ack-ack batteries and rest camps. We stopped to fill up with petrol and take our pick of the first-class rations—tinned tomatoes, peas and potatoes, tinned American bacon and Argentine beef, South African biscuits and the mixture known as 'M and V'—meat and vegetables. We collected sacks of tea and sugar, big tins of cheese, jam and fish. We even got fresh onions and dates. There were enough of all these stores to have maintained twenty or thirty thousand men for three months. There was no shortage of water. The petrol lay around in flimsy square tins—millions of gallons.

That night we camped at Wadi Auda, the one part in this ugly worn-out place where palms and green things flourished by the sea. It was a remote and quiet valley protected by immense yellow cliffs and at its end it opened out onto a white beach perfect for swimming. The beach was heavily mined like all the rest of the Tobruk coast, but there was a spot near a sunken British invasion barge where we peeled off our sand-matted clothes and plunged naked into the transparent water.

All the rest of Tobruk was hideous. We seldom went into the town if we could avoid it, but on this last visit we needed water. Another red-capped sentry stopped us at the entry and then we drove in a slow procession of vehicles onto the rocky promontory where the white houses clustered row on row. Not one house had escaped damage. I saw hundreds that were simply marked 'Out of Bounds' and one look at the sagging roofs and crumbling walls told you why.

Every night the town was raided and although each time another ruin crashed into dust it seemed to make no difference to the general aspect of the place. Tobruk had been bombed into insensibility.

There was little now that anyone could do to increase the wreck and decay in the centre of the tower. Yet still some troops were quartered there. Close to the church the Y.M.C.A. was serving meals, and there was scrawled on the white wall outside—'Hi, Cads, don't park here.' Parked cars attracted bombers.

The mosque was scarred only by blast and a notice warned the troops to keep it inviolate. Most of the Fascist signs and monuments had been defaced or replaced with such ironic descriptions as 'The Red Lion. Free Beer Tomorrow'—the tomorrow that never came. One mauled wreck of a building bore a large notice 'Score—100 not out.' At least a hundred bombs must have touched it. Nearly all the original Italian furnishings in the houses had long since been destroyed or burnt out, and in the empty shells I saw such things as makeshift decontamination centres (lice were getting bad), first-aid posts and a few dumps for spare parts and machinery. I walked down to a cliff above the port and standing there on a ruined tennis court the whole prospect of the wrecked harbour was spread out below. At the wharves immediately beneath, a direct hit had cut a freighter asunder and it spilled its twisted steel entrails.

All around and right across to the other side of the harbour lay the wrecks of good ships with their decks, funnels and masts showing above the water. Even these rusty relics were pitted and twisted by high explosive. After they had been beached and sunk, still they had no rest from bombing, and some of the hulks now were becoming unrecognisable as ships. A red half-sunken Italian monoplane that had been shot down nearly two years ago still perched on a shoal close to that end of the bay the Italians euphemistically called 'The Lido'. There was still a passage through these wrecks and a steamer was unloading onto a pontoon wharf constructed of barrels lashed together. A destroyer was creeping out past the boom at the narrow entrance to the bay.

We left the town and crossed the plain to the high yellow cliffs where the road winds up onto the escarpment. On either side of the dusty, dirty and dispirited land many more lorries and ack-ack guns stood about half embedded in trenches. The soldiers had rigged up nets and were playing soccer close to a cemetery now filled with hundreds of white crosses and surmounted at one end by a concrete monument. A slight sandstorm was blowing and the sand was dirty. A strange sort of atmosphere prevailed over all this ground—a kind of apathy and ugliness one could not describe, but felt very strongly. The very earth looked exhausted.

It was difficult to see any tradition in this squalor, or feel the sense of history and heroic deeds.

The depressing, degrading, levelling influence of war had made this place accursed.

That night the searchlights arched over the town again and bursting colour filled the sky. The ground shook with the weight of bombs. Somehow then Tobruk seemed to be more like its great name in the world, a place of action and excitement. Even the flares could not reveal the full horror of the worn-out earth. This was the war in action—noisy and exhilarating. Only the morning light revealed again the desolation and the hopeless aftermath of war.

Tobruk itself was not the business end of the garrison. These guns and mines and men scattered across the plain above were the town's defences and most of the garrison was stationed up here on the escarpment. Most of the telegraph poles had been cut off as they acted as ranging points for enemy artillery, and so again there was nothing much to see on this eastern half of the perimeter. The crossroads where the vehicles turned off to El Adem airport was still busy when I passed. We were checked by the sentries at the eastern exit on the coast road and drove on smartly toward Gambut. It was always a relief to get out of Tobruk. I think we knew then that the place was doomed.

In command of the garrison was a South African, H. B. Klopper. He had proved himself an able chief of staff to Major-General de Villiers, and a few weeks before the battle of Tobruk he was promoted to major-general and given this all-important post. Throughout the campaign he had under his command two full South African brigades with their artillery. At no time were they employed in the fighting and now on June 19th these fresh troops were disposed mainly on the western and south- western sectors of the perimeter. To them was added the composite brigade which Pienaar dropped off in his passage through the perimeter, various units of the Guards, including the Coldstreams, and about a brigade of Indians who had retired into the south-eastern sector of the perimeter after taking part in the fighting outside. In tanks the garrison was weak. About fifty of all classes were collected out of the workshops and put together as a scratch force. There were in addition the administrative personnel, non-combatants who were employed in the workshops, storage dumps and in the port. In all it was reckoned that Klopper had under his command more than twenty thousand men of whom at least half were fresh. In fire power and actual numbers they were slightly less than the garrison which had held Tobruk through the past year.

There was some doubt in the mind of the high command whether the garrison should be held once again at all costs. For days beforehand I heard doubts expressed among the troops. Everyone wanted to know 'If the Gazala Line falls are we going to try and hold Tobruk?' It was the major question in the desert and as one disaster succeeded another the men felt they were being left in the dark. Few of them would have gladly chosen to go into Tobruk in these circumstances.

In the old days there had been no doubt in the minds of the men defending Tobruk. They had turned the earth with their own hands, had dug the original trenches, embedded the guns, seen their friends killed and wounded in sorties and raids, had faced impending disaster several time, and at the last moment driven it off. They had the habit of defence. They were organised and keyed to it. Tobruk meant a great deal to them. They believed that they were defending London and their own homes across its scarred sulphur-coloured plains and the perimeter was as real to them as the cliffs of Dover.

Now it was altogether different. The new defenders had come as tenants into a strange house and, moreover, a house that had fallen somewhat into disrepair. Thousands of them had bundled pell-mell into the fortress at the last moment and they were tired and hungry and embittered from their setbacks in the past five days. Many came in without their equipment and their guns had been scuttled in the retreat from the line. Communications got into an appalling state and units were badly mixed up. A brigade would find its signallers or its engineers missing. Valuable hours were lost while men waited idly for orders. Ambulances got themselves in the wrong places and the roads were jammed with traffic. Things had gone so badly and so quickly. One defeat had followed another with bewildering rapidity and as is usual in such cases rumours far outstripped the actual facts. The anxiety in men's minds was expressed and passed on from mouth to mouth until it was quoted as a fact. Meanwhile the real urgent business of digging in and getting organised was badly delayed. And it was hours, not days, that counted now.

Moreover, it can scarcely have contributed to the morale of the defenders to see hundreds of lorries filled with troops passing straight through the garrison and on to the east. Inevitably, as these men passed through, they spoke of the enemy on their heels. Just as inevitably it suggested to the defenders that they were being left in the lurch, that they were being used as a rearguard in an action that was already doomed. And one must remember that all around them was the confusion of men seeking orders, of convoys not knowing where to go, of intense congestion round the petrol and water points, of mounting rumours helped on by the actual air raids on the garrison.

One other thing should be mentioned here and this was a broadcast by the B.B.C. When the battle was actually joined, an announcement came over the air from London suggesting that Tobruk was not after all vital and might be lost. How this disastrous and insane broadcast came to go on the air is still unexplained. The encouragement it offered to the Germans and the depression it spread among the isolated British defenders can be imagined. I do not suppose many of the men in Tobruk heard the broadcast at first-hand. But Klopper and his staff heard it and almost the last message that was received from Klopper said, 'I cannot carry on if the B.B.C. is allowed to make these statements.' By then it was too late.

The whole of this campaign had shown that we had in the radio a weapon of war which we underestimated and misunderstood. The B.B.C. was listened to intently every day in the desert because it was usually the only contact the men had with the outside world. The troops formed their opinions from the broadcasts. They listened avidly to everything that was said.

The B.B.C. cannot be entirely blamed for the general confusion into which our propaganda had fallen at this stage; but in their case it was far more serious, for the fighting soldier on both sides heard every word that was broadcast and reacted immediately. Through the delay in the transmission of cables and the absence of an adequate reporting staff in the front line the B.B.C. was as far behind the news as the world's newspapers were. The result was that when tired and dispirited men were coming out of battle they turned on their radios and heard a cheerful and glowing account of a victory that had occurred two or three days earlier. Understandably it infuriated them. They were irritated again when they had successfully gone forward to hear the B.B.C. broadcast a gloomy tale of some earlier setback. The old faith in the B.B.C. began to dissipate around this period and the soldiers began to ridicule the broadcasts. Unquestionably, the same bitter criticism would have fallen on the newspapers had the men seen them, for there were at this time many London commentators who were taking wild guesses at the situation in the absence of any real news. But the B.B.C. came in for all the blame. Two months later it was even alleged that the B.B.C had revealed future British plans, and Auchinleck protested personally to Churchill.

At the moment it was the Tobruk broadcast that counted. Presumably it was thought to be more important 'to prepare the public for a defeat' than try to hold Tobruk itself. Something of the same sort had been done to Czechoslovakia years before, when the London *Times* published a leader suggesting that the Czechs should try to find some compromise with Germany. To the non-combatants in the Middle East it seemed a pity to apply the same treatment to our own men. To the defenders in Tobruk it seemed an outrage.

The British high command was all through this last day making frantic efforts to get the garrison ready. Before the perimeter was sealed General Gott had conferred with Klopper and issued a rousing order of the day. Ritchie could still communicate by radio with Klopper from the outside and he sent across a number of instructions. Auchinleck had visited the front and when he returned to Cairo he sent an urgent order to Ritchie that he was to expect immediate attack on Tobruk, and that it would most likely come from El Duda in the south-east. El Duda was the permanent weak spot in the perimeter. In 1941 the Australians had taken Tobruk from the Italians by attacking through El Duda.

Rommel had planned to assault the garrison from that point in the previous winter. And it was to that point the defenders had sallied out in November. Tobruk, like Bardia, had originally fallen to us in a day. All the recent history of the desert showed that these tight-skinned perimeter fortresses fell very quickly once they were penetrated. Klopper, however, maintained his fresh South Africans on the west and south-west (possibly he had no time to move them), and the defence of the vital south-east fell to tired troops who had fought fairly steadily through the previous week, who were partly disorganised and who had lost quantities of their equipment.

Ritchie also was urged to collect and send out the meagre remnants of our armour from Egypt so that they could create a diversion on Sidi Rezegh and soften the blow on Tobruk when it came. The R.A.F. meanwhile had been forced right out of Libya and for the moment found itself out of range. Given a few more days to organise landing fields, something could have been done to get a fighter screen over Tobruk, but there was no question now of there being a few more days. Tobruk was going to its fate much in the same way as Crete did— without air protection.

Rommel meanwhile was not losing a minute. Now was his time to strike, while the British were still reeling from their series of reverses in the open desert. In thousands, Italian and German troops poured up the coast road. As they swung right along the Axen Strasse they debouched from their lorries and seized every good niche of high ground round the perimeter. The field guns followed.

Soon the Italians were entrenched right round to El Adem and their guns were opening fire on the South Africans. The main part of the Axis striking force—the steel wedge that was going to be driven into the south-eastern perimeter—was rushed farther round to Sidi Rezegh and El Duda. It was a masterpiece of organisation that the enemy could have mounted and adjusted their forces so rapidly.

The Axis assault troops comprised what was left of the Ariete, 21st and 15th Panzer divisions, all armoured, the motorised Trieste division and the 90th Light German Infantry. Naturally they expected that the British tanks outside Tobruk would attempt to take them in the rear so anti-tank guns were set toward the east and south and one of the Panzer divisions detailed to stand by. The Stukas were rushed forward to the former British landing fields at Gazala.

All the German genius for method, order and speed, which had temporarily deserted them in retreat, returned to them now that they were in attack.

It began on the morning of Saturday, June 20th. While yet the sun showed red through the ground mist, German and Italian bombers in numbers unknown before swept onto the fortress. They came over in twenties and thirties, tracing and retracing a pattern of bombs across the wadis, and the sand flats and the entrenchments. And through this tumult of bombs and their great curtains of black smoke the Axis shells began to rake the perimeter from one end to the other. They forced the defenders to the ground, they delayed all movement or stopped it entirely. They painted the clearest of all possible warnings across the Tobruk sky—'This is the zero hour. This is the moment of attack.'

Then something new in the desert happened—whether by design or accident is not known. The Stukas came up. They hung briefly above the barrage and then dived, not on the defenders, but on the minefields in the south-east. Many of the bombs missed entirely and simply made craters in the bare sand. Others went up with a double explosion and whole strings of mines erupted together. Sappers of the German infantry crept forward to drag out with their hands the mines that had not gone up and soon a pathway was opened. Across the skyline of El Duda a line of fast-moving enemy tanks appeared and, wreathed in their own dust, made straight toward the pathway. Guns firing, they ran forward into the gap and halted. Then came the wave of German infantry. Carrying mortars and machine-guns as well as their rifles and hand grenades, they crept up to the tanks and passed them.

Some among them carried smoke machines and these spouted great clouds among the running men so that they were obscured and the British shells and bullets had to be flung haphazardly into the battle arena. And all this time the Axis artillery was laying down a box barrage. It made a wall of explosion and blast and black smoke in front of the advancing men as they hacked through the barbed wire, overwhelmed the British outposts and tore up the remaining mines in the centre of the perimeter.

Then the infantry stopped, their first objective won. They had pierced the perimeter, they had forced and made secure a gap. Now the tanks came on again to exploit it. They ran past the infantry again, bringing their guns with them in this strange and terrible game of leapfrog.

The little scratch force of British tanks was waiting for them in open formation, hull down, the last real barrier between the Germans and the sea. In one cataclysmic rush the full weight of the German armour burst upon them. The British artillery now was giving back shot for shot. The British infantry on either side of the gap was pouring small arms fire and mortar shells into the ranks of the Germans as they rushed through. Reinforcements were coming up from the centre of Tobruk to swing their guns hastily into action. And ceaselessly the Luftwaffe kept dive-bombing, ground-strafing and bombing again.

Outside, near Sidi Rezegh, the remnants of the British armour had attempted their diversionary attack. They had run full tilt into the Panzer division that had been set to lie in wait and soon they were driven off with heavy losses. That was the last attempt to help Tobruk from the outside.

Klopper had his headquarters well inside the perimeter against the cliffs. But at the very earliest moment of the attack he was bombed out and forced to go to another place. Then again the Stukas got onto him. Through these critical hours he was hounded from one place to another, and inevitably his communication broke down. It was not yet midday and his messages to the outside world became fewer and fewer. Back in Egypt Ritchie could do nothing more. As in the Crete action the senior generals had simply to sit and wait for news, and were unable to act upon it when they got it.

At midday the battle touched its crisis. The door was splintered; the enemy was rushing into the fortress. Most of the British tanks lay about burning in their tracks. On either side of the gap the British infantry was brushed aside and large numbers of exhausted prisoners were falling into German hands. And still more and more Germans were pitchforked into the El Duda funnel. Once through they began to fan out, principally to the west. Nothing then could have saved Tobruk. Rommel had a masterly position. All this time the fresh South African troops on the south, south-west and west sectors had not been engaged at all except for shelling and bombing. They had simply heard the distant noises of the battle in the east. Now suddenly fighting began to sound behind them. It was the 90th Light Infantry coming up inside the perimeter, forcing the South Africans to face two fronts at the same time. Through the hundreds of stationary vehicles, machine-gun bullets began to rip back and forth. Soon many lorries were ablaze and little knots of men were running from one place to another seeking cover as the grey-green wave of Germans came on.

In his extremity Klopper radioed Ritchie that the position was hopeless. He said, 'I will try to fight my way out to the west.' Ritchie had no choice but to accept this advice and he agreed. There was a long silence on the radio. Tensely and helplessly, the rest of the Eighth Army waited for the news— news that could only now be bad. Then Klopper's last message came in saying tersely, 'It is too late. Most of my vehicles have been destroyed and it is no longer possible to move. I will continue resistance only long enough to carry out essential demolition.'

This was the last word out of Tobruk that day. As when a ship sinks at sea and the radio splutters and falls silent so now the town plunged into its disaster and was isolated from all the outside world at the end.

Under its rolling battle cloud Tobruk was submerged into an utter chaos of fire and explosion.

Those millions of pounds worth of stores which had been carted to Tobruk at such a painful cost of ships and men were set upon by the demolition squads. Down on the wharves the navy personnel flung themselves into the job with such haste and reckless daring that some of their own men were killed. Water points were blown in. Thousands of gallons of petrol, ignited by electricity or even by hand grenades, leaped burning into the sky and rolled immense black volumes of smoke across the town. Dumps of shells and mines, bullets and hand grenades went up in sheeted flame and with such an unbelievable crack that it sounded above the continuous thunder of the artillery barrage. Now Tobruk had been gashed open, it was being destroyed by its own internal combustion. Yet still all this destruction could not do away with the huge quantities of food and oil and ammunition which lay about the cliffs and beaches.

Four or five small freighters in the harbour were ordered to clear for sea at once. No troops were put aboard—it was simply a matter of saving the ships. It was at this moment that the German tanks and armoured cars reached the El Adem crossroads. Some split off along the track below the cliffs to the west where many hundreds of lorries stood about helplessly. The others made straight for the cliffs overlooking the harbour.

At once the tanks opened fire on the moving ships in the harbour. They flung their shells especially on the little boats and lighters which were trying to reach the larger vessels, already under steam and beginning to slide out through the eastern reaches to the open sea. The wounded and the dead in the upturned boats simply went to the bottom, others struck out and managed to get picked up, some returned to the shore and waited there, wet and helpless, for the moment of their surrender. Four of the larger ships got away.

All this time the bulk of the South African troops in the west and south-west had not been seriously drawn into the battle. They were now astonished and bewildered to receive from Klopper the order 'surrender'. Bitter and confused dispute broke out. The officers who brought the orders were surrounded by angry men saying, 'It's a lie, You've got it wrong. What the hell is happening?' Some declared they would not obey, others urged delay, others again said they had to obey orders. All this time the Germans were creeping closer.

There was little or no difference in the colour of the vehicles of both sides—indeed the Germans by now were using many of our trucks. And so the enemy traffic mingled with the British traffic on the roads and tracks leading into the town, and westwards toward Klopper's headquarters. Men who were riding back to the dumps for supplies heard horns blowing behind them. They waved the approaching vehicles on and as these passed, the British drivers looked up and saw they were full of Germans. By now the enemy was more desirous of infiltrating right through the fortress, of stabbing it in its heart, than taking prisoners. British and German vehicles rode down the roads together and bypassed one another without opening fire. All over the plain and among the wadis, the British were coming out holding up their hands. Klopper himself surrendered, though two soldiers on his staff later escaped in his car. Others held out through the afternoon and night in the remote wadis and were still fighting on the following day.

In defiance of orders, or in their absence, these soldiers simply went on shooting at anything they could see, because they felt there was nothing else to do. When British officers were sent to them by the Germans to demand their surrender a few refused and shot it out to the last. There were many bitter skirmishes.

Some lucky few, including the Coldstreams, took matters into their own hands and under the cover of night fought their way out and escaped to the east. A few more came out in dribbles of fours and fives for days afterwards. But these totalled only a few hundred. All the rest of that garrison of twenty-seven thousand were killed or captured. It was defeat as complete as may be. In equipment alone the enemy had won the richest treasure the desert had ever yielded. Rommel had here enough British vehicles, enough tanks and guns, enough petrol and fuel and enough ammunition to re-equip at once and drive straight on to Egypt. The road lay open before him. He left four Italian battalions behind to handle the prisoners and reopen the port. Then he set out. The smashing of Tobruk had taken just one day.

Thirteen

July in Alamein

ROMMEL'S FORCES were roughly equal to ours when he began the campaign. Now with the fall of Tobruk he was twice as strong. He still had about eight divisions, the best part of a hundred thousand men. As far as one could judge from the disordered state of the Eighth Army, we had about four divisions (Indians, British, South Africans, and composite forces). Rommel still had over a hundred tanks and he was adding to them from captures and his own workshops at the rate of at least a dozen a day. We had practically no tanks at all. Of our losses roughly 45 per cent were South Africans and 55 per cent were British, Indians and others.

It was no longer a question of whether we could hold the Egyptian border but of whether we could hold the old fortress of Mersa Matruh, 130 miles farther back. So Bardia, Solium, Halfaya and the Omars fell without a fight, and in less than a week from the fall of Tobruk, Rommel presented himself before the approaches to Matruh, an astonishing performance.

In a statement issued to his senior officers Rommel had made an estimate of the relative quality of the Allied troops fighting in the Middle East. At the head of the list was the New Zealand division, which had all this time been quartered in Syria. It was this division, hardened in Greece, Crete and the desert, and by common consent the finest infantry formation in the Middle East, that was flung into Matruh at the last moment to peg the Axis tide.

On June 26th, when the British were still far from being ready, a fluid and bloody battle was fought on the cliffs about Matruh mainly between the New Zealanders and the 90th Light German Infantry and the Axis tanks. Freyberg, a man of incredible personal courage, had trained his New Zealanders in the gospel of the bayonet charge. Up to date, both in Crete and in the desert, no troops had been found on the Axis side who were willing to stand up and fight when the Maoris came over the top at the run, yelling their war cries, and lunging out with their bayonets. The Germans were no exceptions. But bayonets could not break tanks. The New Zealanders were forced back in the wake of all the other British forces. The Axis troops rushed into Matruh and within a day or two they had successively entered Bagush, Fuka and Daba, which meant the loss of all our forward landing grounds, of more men, of many more trucks, guns and stores, especially at Daba. Daba always used to be our first halt on the way down to the desert. And still the German drive went on. Only one barrier lay between them and the Delta—the Alamein Line, 150 miles from Cairo, sixty miles from Alexandria. The vanguard of the enemy arrived on the line on the last day of June.

Only now was the full extent of the danger realised. Churchill was in Washington when Tobruk fell, conferring with Roosevelt, and together they heard the shocking news that the whole British position in the Middle East was in danger of immediate collapse. It promised to be the greatest disaster since the fall of France. Into the Middle East for three years the British Empire had poured every man, gun and tank it could spare. Here alone the British had a front against the enemy. The loss of Egypt would precipitate a chain of misfortunes almost too disastrous to contemplate. It would force England back to the dark days of the Battle of Britain.

With Egypt would fall Malta and all British control of the Mediterranean. The Suez Canal would be lost and with it the stores and equipment worth fifty Tobruks. Suez, Port Said, Alexandria, Beyrout and Syrian Tripoli might go. Palestine and Syria could not then hope to stand and once in Jerusalem and Damascus, the Germans would be in sight of the oilwells and Turkey all but surrounded. The Red Sea would become an Axis lake and once in the Indian Ocean the Italian fleet could prey upon all the routes to Africa, India and Australia. India would be approached from both sides by the enemy.

Finally, Russia's left flank would be hopelessly exposed.

All this was possible as the Germans came up to the Alamein Line on July 1st. And on that day, and the day following and the day after that the Alamein Line was in no condition to resist any sort of really determined attack whatever. It was ready to crumple. Such troops as we had left would fight— yes. But if the Germans came on the way they did at Tobruk there was no question but that the line would break. Behind Alamein the road lay fair and straight into Alexandria, a two hours' drive. There was nothing much to stop the enemy on that road.

In the desert itself, beyond Alamein there was nothing much to stop their cutting the Cairo road and driving straight to Cairo.

The British fleet had left Alexandria. The demolition gangs stood ready. The town was emptied of most of its troops and those that remained were put under a curfew. Orders went out every hour for all officers to drop whatever they were doing and rejoin their units immediately.

In Cairo there was another curfew. The streets were jammed with cars that had evacuated from Alexandria and the country districts and military traffic that had come from the front. The British consulate was besieged with people seeking visas to Palestine. The east-bound Palestine trains were jammed. A thin mist of smoke hung over the British Embassy by the Nile and over the sprawling blocks of G.H.Q—huge quantities of secret documents were being burnt. All day a group of privates shovelled piles of maps, lists of figures, reports, estimates, codes and messages into four blazing bonfires in a vacant square of land between the G.H.Q. buildings. Some of the R.A.F. papers being bundled down a chute onto another fire blew over the fence and fluttered down into the crowded street outside. I went into one office and the floor was covered in ashes and the smell of burning rag hung over the whole building.

Long convoys were setting out for Palestine. Every unit that did not have essential business in the fighting was being ordered to get out at once. Part of the United States military headquarters set off in the dead of night for Khartoum and Asmara in Italian Somaliland. The South African women volunteers were hurried onto a south-bound train and elements of the South African army base troops were dispatched after them. The wives and families of British soldiers were warned to get ready for immediate evacuation—some were to be sent to Palestine, the rest put onto ships at Suez.

The British Embassy was going to stay. King Farouk decided he was not going to be a Nazi puppet ruler and was prepared to leave. Auchinleck had in the previous week removed Ritchie from his command and had at last gone down to the desert himself to take charge. Lieutenant-General Corbett was left in command in Cairo, where the new Minister of State, Richard Casey, had just arrived.

There was a great deal of tension and anxiety behind these moves, but no outward panic. The astonishing thing was that the people at large took the crisis so calmly. Beyond the heavy traffic and the queues waiting round the banks there was nothing to show that the enemy might in a day or two be in the town. The Egyptians especially behaved with a fatalism and patience. All that side of the Arab and the near-Arab which bids him say, 'It is the will of Allah' came to the surface at the crucial moment. Many like Nahas Pasha the premier were compromised with the British, and yet they remained in their homes and went about their work. That well-known jelly, the Cairo Stock Exchange, slumped heavily but it did not crash altogether. Prices were pegged but even before this selling had not kept pace with the despairing rumours that flew about. The Exchange previously had fluctuated with every battle in the desert, and one could quite clearly trace Rommel's advance by watching the prices.

On the whole, the Egyptians had much reason to take the situation calmly. Their immediate concern was to avoid being bombed and shelled in their homes and this was not likely to happen. For the rest, there was a definite swing toward the British. Many began to see that they were most unlikely to enjoy such prosperity and opportunities for making money under Axis rule. If the Germans were willing to pay the prices and allow the native a certain amount of leeway, the Italians certainly were not. Then, too, the British in Egypt had become a habit. The Egyptian government had achieved its freedom and there was nothing specific it could hope to get out of the Axis, especially in wartime. By now the German planes were dropping pamphlets. One of these was a facsimile of a Bank of England note on one side. On the other was printed in Arabic something to the effect that once this note had been valuable; now it was not worth a beggar's time to pick one up. Good pamphlets. But they made no great impression.

Domestically then things were not bad; the British did not have to cope with riots as well as the enemy. And all their emergency precautions went forward calmly and briskly because it was judged by the high command that the situation had reached a stage of extreme seriousness. The fall of Alexandria and Cairo had to be envisaged and preparations made to carry on the war from another place.

It was not the intention of the high command to abandon Egypt outright. Even if Alexandria were lost the fight would go on among myriad canals and green fields of the Delta, on the Nile itself, on the desert between the Nile and the Canal, on the banks of the Canal, in Palestine and in the last resort on some sort of a line through Iraq reaching from Basra through Baghdad to Mosul.

Another front could be established in the Sudan in the south. But all these were last-ditch alternatives, and could only delay the overrunning of the Middle East. Egypt was the key to the situation and for the moment the most important place in the world. During this anxious first week of July people simply could not bring themselves to believe that the country could fall. And yet there had been France, the rest of Europe, the Far East.

My wife was now acting as secretary to General Corbett and with some misgiving I left her and the baby to return to the front. After all, I told myself, it's only half a day away now. I will be able to get back in time somehow if the worst happens.

Driving out of Cairo we had scarcely passed Mena House and the Pyramids, when we came on a sight that bore the marks of a full-scale retreat. Guns of all sorts, R.A.F. wagons, recovery vehicles, armoured cars and countless lorries crammed with exhausted and sleeping men, were pouring up the desert road into Cairo. When we reached the halfway resthouse, which was about a hundred kilometres from Alexandria and less than two hundred from the front, the procession thickened instead of slackening. The vehicles were pressed bonnet to tailboard, all coming back from the front, all full of desperately weary men who slept piled on one another oblivious of the discomfort and the jolting. The traffic crawled eastward slowly, an immense lizard over a hundred miles in length, a fantastically easy target for enemy aircraft. Yet no enemy machine appeared. Yard by yard the procession edged its way toward Cairo. There seemed to be no end to it. We asked ourselves, 'Is the whole army in retreat?'

It was nerve-racking to see them go by. There seemed to be no end to the hundreds and thousands who kept pouring back in such haste that they were making no attempt to obey the order that at least a hundred yards should be kept between each vehicle on the road. Some in their anxiety to get through turned off the macadam surface and tried to get by over the loose sand beside the road. But most of them stuck and as the men dug their vehicles out we stopped to ask, 'What is happening? Why are you coming back?' No one could answer us. No one had any news.

The road on our side—the side that carried vehicles up to the front—was clear, and that too, was ominous. We turned off it now and came across a sand track into Auchinleck's headquarters. The general himself was farther forward and we picked up what information we could from the Intelligence officers. A good deal of the traffic going back, it transpired, had been ordered into the Delta to prepare defences there. The battle went on meanwhile at Alamein. The South Africans were in the line in the north and the other sectors were being held by the New Zealanders, the Indians and the British. The Ninth Australian

Division was being flung into the line. This last was good news. It was the Ninth that had held Tobruk. Their reputation was second only to that of the New Zealanders and a very close second at that. There were fresh. They had all their equipment. The only question was whether they would arrive in time.

We felt a little more cheerful about the situation. After all, the line was not turned or pierced yet. There was a tremendous flurry of British bombers and fighters over our heads. At least the R.A.F. was in full action. As we debated, other war correspondents and officers began coming in from the front. One reported that a small group of German tanks had broken through in the south and was headed straight for the Alexandria–Cairo road. A second said that firing had begun on the line and that in the opinion of one of the senior generals there it could be held only another twelve hours. A third said that two Axis thrusts were being made—one in the centre of the line, another in the north. The enemy tanks were coming round the south to isolate all the troops in the line itself.

We decided to drive on to see for ourselves. Back on the road it was the same story again—the endless chain of vehicles on the move eastwards. A sandstorm was blowing up now in the late afternoon to make matters worse. At the junction where one road forks into the desert and the other into Alexandria the going became impossible. Salt marshes lie on either side of the road near this point and now the trucks had packed themselves on the highway, two and sometimes three, abreast. It was impossible to get past, impossible to turn off onto the salt flats where a vehicle would be irretrievably bogged. It was now growing dusk. We decided to give up the attempt to reach Alamein and turned instead into Alexandria. Foot by foot we edged down the road. Sometimes we were forced to stop altogether. Then gradually the traffic thinned out and abruptly died away altogether. I had never seen the approach to Alexandria so empty, so ominous. All those entrenchments, those salt flats that had once swarmed with soldiers were now barren of human life. Even the Bedouin seemed to have fled. Occasionally a military truck or a staff car packed with soldiers would burst round the corner and disappear in the direction of Cairo. But the old camp where the Poles had trained, the compounds filled with newly arrived equipment and vehicles—all these were strangely empty. I caught one glimpse of a company of Indians drawn up to listen to an officer. They looked very like a rearguard or a demolition squad. A little farther on another company of Indians was marching down to a line of trucks. Each man carried his bedding roll.

Then Alexandria itself; overnight the life had gone out of it. The silver barrage balloons still rode above the town but nearly all the ships had gone, many shops were shut and the streets, which normally were bursting with people at this evening hour, were now half empty.

We pulled up at the Cecil Hotel on the waterfront. It had always been our headquarters in Alexandria and was a gay place filled with naval officers and crowds of women. Now it was changed. We got rooms easily. The bar was half empty and those who were there mostly sat around in groups discussing the news—or lack of news. Two military police came in and ordered us to leave at once to rejoin our unit. We told them we knew of no place where we could report except army headquarters, and it was impossible to return there now through the traffic block. It was agreed that like all the other officers staying in the hotel, we were not to go outside again until the morning.

It seemed clear to me now that the battle had touched its crisis. Once the line went Alexandria could not be held. The Germans would not attempt to cross the anti-tank ditches and narrow defiles before the town; they would simply run round the town to the south and cut it off from Cairo. The bulk of the British army would be forced to retreat on Cairo itself. Clearly, too, the next few hours were going to decide the matter one way or the other. There was no point in being cut off in Alexandria.

The state of the roads made rapid communication with the front impossible. The place to be was in Cairo where the news could be gathered and sent off and from there we could set off for the front again—if there was a front to go to. My newspaper now had a staff of half a dozen in the Middle East and these men now had to be disposed to meet any emergency. I was anxious also to make some arrangement for my family. Lucy had been determined not to move so long as G.H.Q. stayed in Cairo, but we were both worried about the baby since, even if Cairo did not fall, the town might be exposed to heavy air attack.

Soon after dawn next morning we set off up the Delta Road toward Cairo, hoping to find it clearer than the desert route. Except for one long convoy of army trucks the route was almost empty.

Apparently in the general confusion this delta road had been forgotten. We had only one vehicle now and Buckley, Hill and myself perched on the roof of the truck like three strange birds on a housetop. It was a fresh and cool morning and the way lay through groves of trees and bright fields, and over many canals where the cotton barges were still floating peacefully by. Even in the remote villages the people had guessed that something dramatic was happening in the war. For one thing the Germans had been broadcasting in Arabic that they would be in Alexandria the following day. They even had the poor taste to suggest that 'the ladies of Alexandria should get out their party dresses.' And now these people came to the roadside and cheered us as we went by. I suppose villagers will automatically cheer or shout at any sort of an unusual procession through their streets, but still these people were definitely friendly. The children gave the thumbs-up sign and we gave it back to them.

We arrived back at the G.H.Q. just as Lucy and Alex Clifford were getting out of the car there. They were much more hopeful than we were but all the same Lucy had been given a box of matches and told to standby to destroy Auchinleck's correspondence with the War Cabinet and Churchill. She was told that she must be prepared to leave. They wanted, at first, to put her into uniform and evacuate her along with the other women in the army, but it turned out that women volunteers cannot take babies with them. We had much argument about what we should do. Finally it was agreed that she and the baby should go to Palestine in a special evacuee train and be prepared to join G.H.Q. there.

This was grossly breaking our word to one another. We had sworn that neither of us should ever suffer the horrors of an evacuee train. In Rome, when we were first married, old Doctor Hubrecht, the Dutch minister, who was not often solemn, said to us, 'Never, never be a refugee. It's always better to stay where you are.' But here we were in the midst of a particularly bad crisis and there seemed to be nothing else to do. We had a nightmarish packing and I drove Lucy and the baby to Cairo station. The special train eclipsed all our forebodings. To begin with it was several hours late. There were also travelling in it members of Casey's staff and a great crowd of Europeans who had thrown in their lot with the British and were therefore likely to face the Gestapo and the firing squad if they were caught. When the train drew in a great wave of Free Italians rushed the carriages and this, as far as I could make out, was followed by successive waves of Free Czechs, Poles, French, Hungarians, Rumanians, Greeks, Germans, Yugoslavs and even Danes.

I got Lucy and the baby a compartment at last and was thankful that Eve Smith, another G.H.Q. secretary, was travelling with her. The enemy plastered the El Kantara canal crossing with a particularly heavy raid that night and Lucy had to trudge into the desert with the baby and wait in a transit camp until morning. A Czech Jew standing next to Lucy at the Customs was told his passport was not in order.

Convinced that he was trapped he tried to commit suicide on the spot by cutting the veins of his wrist, and blood spouted round the baby. It was a triumph of the malicious obstructiveness of some petty official. The man, however, was treated and recovered. A day later Lucy and her fellow refugees were dumped into community wards in Jerusalem.

In Cairo meanwhile it was agreed that Alaric Jacob should go down to Eighth Army headquarters and stick with them whatever they did. James Cooper should follow the fleet wherever it went. Eric Bigio should go to Jerusalem to set up a new bureau there. Henry Buckley would continue on in Turkey. I myself would remain on in Cairo to see which way the cat jumped.

I found that a great fog of anxiety had lifted from my mind with Lucy's departure, and Clifford and I sat down to a reasonably cheerful dinner.

Clifford and I had had a thousand arguments in every sort of situation in the past two years. Without exception he always took the gloomy side. Now, suddenly, he was optimistic and nothing would shake him.

Even while we were arguing the crisis was passing. Like most great dramatic moments of the war, it was not seen for what it was at the time and all the finesse, the luck and dangers of this gamble were only realised when the game was done. Alexandria, perhaps the whole of the Nile Delta, had lain in Rommel's hand for a moment. He stood on the threshold of the greatest victory of the year.

Now, suddenly, and in a few hours, the prize dissipated like a mirage and he was left not among the trees and cities of the Nile but in the arid desert. And all this came about not because Rommel made a mistake or because Auchinleck achieved an eleventh-hour miracle, but because the German army was exhausted. It could do no more. The German soldiers were wearied to the point where they had no more reserves either of body or of willpower, where all the goading and enticement could make no difference, where they were compelled to stop and sleep. It was part of the gamble of the war that they should have reached this extremity when they had endured all the worst hardships and needed only to continue for a couple of days.

The 90th Light German Infantry especially had been tired out. For three weeks they had been in continuous action, fighting, patrolling, travelling. They had fought a dozen separate engagements including the attack on Tobruk. They had come three hundred miles and for a good part of the journey they had had to fight their way through. Always as the shock troops they had been kept in the van, given the toughest jobs.

Recently they had come up against the New Zealand division. For three weeks they had run short of sleep and rest.

Now suddenly it was too much. The drivers of the lorries fell asleep and turned their vehicles over beside the track. The men flung out on the sand lay there too tired to move of their own volition. When they got the order to get up and move on again they did so mechanically and numbly without being very clear about what they were doing or why. They were unkempt and physically dirty. Rommel's officers kept telling them, 'Just a little more. You will be in Alexandria tomorrow. Just one more effort.' And so on tomorrow and the next day until the men slept as they stood and walked dazedly to the guns beyond caring what happened. They had reached the limit of physical despair.

All the mechanical difficulties of supply and maintenance multiplied the farther they advanced. Tank tracks broke. There were no tools at hand to make repairs. Petrol failed to arrive. The British trucks they were using were strange to handle and when they went wrong no one knew how to fix them quickly. The food was late in being prepared and sometimes did not arrive at all. The men were living mostly on hot coffee and cigarettes.

On the British side the reverse influences were gradually taking effect. The Australians were getting into the line and they were fresh and even eager for a fight. All the British forces were right back on their base now and it was the matter of barely half a day to send into Alexandria for a spare part or more rations and petrol. Behind the Germans there was a week's forced march back to Benghazi. Tobruk had not been opened up as a supply port yet.

Because the soldiers in this war were human and no soldier enjoys a defeat, the morale of the Germans and Italians was undoubtedly higher than the British. But now that exhaustion had become a major factor of the battle other matters came into play. The Germans were led on by the hope of reward and the pride of achievement. The British, on the other hand, knew that their last chance had come, that if they failed here then everything would be lost. So they fought with that touch of desperation that had brought wonderful strength to Moscow in the previous summer and to England in the winter before that.

Feeble, half-hearted assaults were made by the enemy at several places along the line. The tanks that had attempted to run through in the south returned to the German lines. An Indian position was overrun in the centre, but the Indians counterattacked. The R.A.F. was working at a rhythm and a speed that eclipsed all their earlier efforts. While the

Luftwaffe was still toiling up the coast to man new airfields, the R.A.F. sat on their home bases and ran riot over Alamein and Daba, over Fuka and Matruh, over the whole of that long weary procession of enemy who were moving slowly and still more slowly up to the Alamein Line.

On July 4th the British position was intact. On the 5th it was still intact and getting a little stronger.

At the end of the week the situation was definitely better. The muddle on the roads behind the lines was being straightened out, communications were getting better. By the opening of the second week in July, the British were set to give battle on the line.

Auchinleck had not done badly since he had taken over. His presence in the desert had spread confidence among the troops and the direction of the battle. After the fall of Tobruk, Auchinleck had simply accepted the situation as he found it. The overriding will of the Axis army was to come forward; of the British army to fall back. Auchinleck, because he had no other choice beyond making a suicidal stand, decided to let these forces have play. He let the Axis army come through. He sought to impede them only at Matruh and when that went wrong he brought his men back again well ahead of the enemy. His whole object was to keep the Eighth Army in being. He believed that for the time being the Eighth Army was more important than all the desert, more important even than Alexandria and the Delta. He was prepared to withdraw even as far as the Suez Canal so long as he kept the army together as a fighting force capable of reinforcement for a counterattack. The proposition was—'If I lose the Delta I have always the hope of winning it back again. If I lose the Eighth Army then I lose everything.' So the general allowed the Germans to come on, hoping that they would wear themselves out. He tried to keep his troops from battle so that they would live to fight another day when they were stronger and the enemy weaker.

There was also excellent tactical reasons for falling back on the Alamein Line. The line was unique in the desert; no other line had a top and a bottom. Every other line, British or Axis, had been turned because its southern end lay in the open desert. The Alamein Line was based at its northern end on salt lakes by the sea and at its southern end on the Qattara quicksands. It was only forty miles in length. The Qattara Depression is a geological freak in the desert. It is a long, lozenge-shaped hollow, some of it below sea-level. The desert here breaks up into steep cliffs and little plateaux and the flats below will not support armoured vehicles. By laying wire netting on the ground, it is possible to get vehicles across, but not a great many in a great hurry. To run round the depression and make the long trek across the open desert to the south was out of the question for Rommel at this stage. He was simply not equipped for it and would have been exposed to the R.A.F. and raiding columns every mile of the way.

So the enemy was forced to come along the coast. The next important thing about the Qattara Depression is that it approaches the coast as one draws near to Alexandria, and Alamein is its narrowest point. It is, in fact, a bottleneck and therefore excellent for defence. Months before, its importance had been realised. Alamein, which is on a ridge, had been formed into a box with a number of concrete underground dugouts and earthworks surrounded by barbed wire and minefields. A number of other positions had been prepared inland.

Let us take a closer look at this line as it was when I arrived on it in the second week of July. The situation, though still very dangerous, had seemed good enough to allow me to alter my plans, by retaining Bigio in Egypt to work with the R.A.F. and by alternating myself with Jacob at the front so that we would have a continuous stream of freshly written messages.

Clifford and I took the train down to Alexandria. It made us both remember the Spanish war when people were able to take trains up to the front at Lerida. At the Cecil Hotel we picked up Kim Mundy and a couple of battered-looking trucks and set off. Coming out of Alexandria we ran first through fig plantations now in full green leaf and a soothing splash of colour in the glaring sand. Then we ran onto the ridge we used to call 'The Ripples'. It always was an appalling bit of road. It ran for thirty miles along a crest of yellow rocks, the gleaming green-blue sea on the right, the railway down below on the left. Since the surface had been built in a slapdash way, even for Egypt, it was an interminable succession of bumps and now these were exaggerated and increased by the heavy traffic. But there was order and method in this traffic now and most of it was going forward. At the end of The Ripples we ran into Alamein Box. It already had a formidable edging of coiled barbed wire and more was being put down. Gangs were nonchalantly digging mines into the ground.

Australians swarmed everywhere and they looked magnificent. None of us had seen such troops before. They had adopted a new uniform during the long months when they were fattening and working in the sun behind the lines. It consisted of a pair of boots, short woollen socks, a pair of khaki drill pants, a piece of string holding two identification disks round the neck, and a wide- brimmed hat turned down all the way round. Their bare backs and shoulders fascinated me. They were burnt brownish-black by the sun. Under the shining skin the muscles bulged like tennis balls.

The long siege of Tobruk had hardened and trained this 9th Division, and given them a pride in fighting. They were the Rats of Tobruk. Their long hibernation had relaxed them, filled them with good food and fresh air. They had grown tired of garrison life. They wanted to fight. They were delighted to be in the desert.

In these two years another subtler change had taken place in these Australians. To Europeans at first they had seemed boastful and quick to take offence, lax in their discipline in the field, and quarrelsome on leave. The usual thing you heard was that the Australians had an inferiority complex, and adopted a truculent noisy manner to hide it. As an Australian living abroad, I had had many arguments about them. I had tried (quite unsuccessfully) to explain to Englishmen that the Australian's manner was the sign of their independence and the freedom of their way of life and that some of their physical vigour might not come amiss in England. To the Australians I tried (even more unsuccessfully) to point out that the Englishman's voice and reserve did not indicate animosity or contempt or weakness, and that some of the Englishman's quiet mental tenacity might not come amiss in Australia. Underneath, I knew the Australians were deeply attached to England. I believed, too, that the English had an affection for Australians that took deep root in the last war. It was usually the officers of both armies who rubbed one another up the wrong way. The men got together as soon as they began to understand one another.

But this 9th Division that came so willingly into the Alamein Line was altogether different from the other Australians I had seen in the Middle East. They spoke much more softly. They were much more sure of themselves and they no longer attempted to impress themselves on a stranger—they knew what they were and who they were. Tobruk had discovered the Australians to themselves. Rest had given them leisure to explore their discovery. Their discipline was far smoother than I had ever seen in Australians before and it was the smooth, definite discipline not of the parade ground but the front line. They worked like blacks and with a new efficiency. They were not two hours in the new positions before Major-General Morshead had them building new fortifications. And with all this they remained among the finest shock troops of the empire.

Those, then, were the men holding the north of the line, and, as we drove on to the centre of the box where the artillery was firing, we came among thousands of South Africans, the men who had held the

Gazala Line and now at last were being given a chance to fight. The Australians held the western primeter of the box, the South Africans the southern sector and a stretch of the line reaching southward outside. We arrived at the moment when the Australians were putting in an attack on the Tel el Eisa ridge to the west of Alamein. The object was to make a 'blister' in the enemy position on the coast so that we should be able to sweep in behind them if they started to drive in on the central sectors of the line.

It was an extraordinary scene in Alamein on that bright morning. The colours ran in vivid parallel lines. First there was the green-blue sparkling sea itself, then the snow-white beach and the sand- dunes, then inside the dunes the grey salt flats that were pitted with shell-holes and bomb craters and looked as the surface of the moon might be. Then came the ultramarine salt lakes edged with floating reeds, then the yellow hogsback of the ridge with the black road on the top, then finally out beyond that the yellow desert. All this area was under fire—fire both going and coming. Choosing a slack moment we crossed a narrow causeway across the lakes to the sea and saw from there the battle clouds roll across the Tel el Eisa ridge. The ridge had fallen to us the night before and now the Germans were coming in with tanks. They had got a new tactic against infantry. Each tank fitted one of its tracks into the Australian slit trenches and tried to crush the men below to death.

'I just held my breath,' one of the wounded told me as he came out of the fight. 'I pressed my face down to the bottom of the trench as hard as I could, but the track touched my back and it was like a series of knives being driven into you. But they didn't get any of us with the first tank or the second. Then when the third one came over we were ready. We pelted the back of it with sticky bombs. One of the boys chased it for a hundred yards to make sure of it. Then it blew up.'

A patrol had gone right into the enemy lines in the dark on foot. They were about to find their way back through the minefields when they saw the outline of an Italian tank against a white limestone cliff. The Italian crew was sleeping on the ground around the tank. The patrol crawled within ten yards of the sleeping men and then gave fire. One of the Italians got his machine gun and answered, but at that moment an Australian engineer crawled up behind the tank and planted his sticky bomb on it. Italians and tank went up together.

I talked to the Germans coming in, wounded and prisoners. Some had bayonet injuries. There had been a series of charges underneath this roof of shells that still kept arching over our heads as we talked. Gun flashes quickly smothered with smoke and dust were flickering right along the ridge ahead of us.

As we turned back across the causeway the battle suddenly veered in our direction. It started in a second and was all over in ten minutes, a bad ten minutes. Thirty Stukas dived in relays and Clifford, Mundy, the driver and myself just flung ourselves headlong where we were. Between the explosions we crawled into ditches and tank ruts. Then the German shelling started. It was sporadic stuff— evidently they were ranging for a new target and our spot was the target. Like heavy hail the shrapnel kept dropping round us. Each time we tried to move another one came over. The Germans were using anti-personnel shells which burst in a black cloud about a hundred feet above the ground and sprayed downward, a damnable weapon. It penetrated to the bottom of slit trenches with red-hot metal. A dud landed a few yards away from me with a dull 'oomph'. I watched it. It did nothing. I ran.

All this time the British gunners alongside us kept firing with their four-point-fives and they stood up to the incoming shells as though they were nothing. I know one feels twice as good under fire when one has a job to do, but this performance was a thing to see to be believed.

The firing quieted presently and we started up the truck again. Through the days ahead Mundy, who stood watching on the top of the truck, was to say many times 'Scram' and we would scram. Driver and all, we would leap straight from the truck onto the ground and then wait for it to heave under the incoming explosions.

Standing on Alamein Ridge and looking south you could clearly see Ruweisat Ridge. This was a second razorback which rose out of the desert parallel with the coast and the scene of the armoured fighting. Soft sand lay between the Alamein Ridge and Ruweisat so you had to double back along the coast road for a bit and then turn inland over a track that was being bound with wire netting.

The Indians held Ruweisat and kept attacking westwards along it. South of Ruweisat there was another flattish plain covered with pink rocks and this was held by the New Zealanders and British motorised units. Beyond that again was the depression. The British armour roved up and down ready to rush in and plug a weak spot in the line. Practically its whole length was covered with minefields.

The rival armies having been equal at the beginning of the campaign, and two to one in favour of Rommel after Tobruk, began to approach equality again. Rommel still had his four armoured formations, but they were much reduced and could hardly muster a hundred tanks in all.

Additionally he still had his 90th Light and elements of all the Italian divisions. They had been rested but were somewhat thinned out partly through losses, partly because they had to man the supply lines and leave garrisons in places like Tobruk, Sollum and Matruh. A second-class German division which had been acting as gaoler in Crete was being flown and shipped across. In all, you might estimate that the enemy had about seven divisions and between fifty and sixty thousand men. On our side the tank strength was gradually getting back to normal with the arrival of reinforcements from America and England. At times we even outnumbered the enemy two to one. In men we had between sixty and seventy thousand in or near the line. In guns both sides seemed about equal since the Germans were using so many of ours they had captured en route.

The quality of the enemy troops was good but very uneven. The Italian Sabrata division seemed to be the one that was always getting into hot water. They were garrison troops anyhow, and it was hardly fair to put them in the front line. It was the Sabrata that had given way before the Australians on Tel el Eisa. They surrendered in hundreds. Down in the centre another group of Italians, who had surrendered, said to an Indian army intelligence officer, 'We are the Brescia division. You think we're poor troops, don't you? Well, you should see the Sabrata.'

Most of the Sabrata were withdrawn after this and the actual front line was given to the Germans to hold while the Italians dug positions behind them. That was the first good sign that the tide was turning. The enemy presumably would not have dug in and spread minefields if they planned to drive into Alexandria.

The Alamein Line, of course, was a reporter's paradise. It was so short and compact that you could visit the whole front in the course of a day and, whereas in Libya we had taken as much as a full day to call on Corps Headquarters, this was now only one of our journeys. If an engagement flared up anywhere we heard about it within a few hours and were able to get to the spot at once.

The correspondents had a wonderful camping spot by the sea about fifteen miles east of the Alamein Line. Each morning the first hot baleful shaft of sunshine used to wake me about six o'clock. Then the first baleful fly. The flies were terrible. This first one would peck at my face, buzz away to call the others, and then sneak up on me again. I would try to escape by shoving my head inside the sleeping-bag and it was too hot. Immediately my head came out again the fly would pounce, and this time he would have a squadron of twenty or more at his back. I would decide to get up.

Every morning in the desert was a beautiful morning full of gold light on the sand-dunes and birds stirring in the clean air. And there were usually shells in the clean air as well, since the morning barrage over Alamein opened about this hour. From this distance, however, it sounded very remote, at any rate not loud enough to wake the others in my party. They slept in a row on camp beds beside the truck and the dew like heavy rain lay on every bed. Reluctantly I peeled off the sleeping-bag and standing at the rear of the truck in my pyjamas I lit the petrol stove and put the kettle on. We shaved every day, and I remember that I was forced to use the rear-vision mirror of the truck as I could never keep a mirror longer than two days in the desert.

For once there was plenty of water for everybody—it was carried in cans looted from the Germans—and by splashing about noisily I knew I could get the driver, Commerford, out of bed. Commerford was a famed cook in the desert. He would go straight to the stove and fix the tea and eggs we had bought from the Bedouin on our way out from Alexandria. Presently I would hear him say, 'My word!' This was his ultimate expression of irritation, the phrase he used in a sort of contempt for the usual swearing and cursing that went on monotonously in the army. It might mean that he was cursing the flies or the enemy barrage or the fact that the stove had gone out or that every other egg was rotten. When he said it for the third time we guessed breakfast was ready, and Clifford and the others climbed out of bed.

As we sat around on boxes eating, the first argument of the day would begin. Clifford would have a hunch that something was doing in the extreme southern sector. Legge, of the *Daily Telegraph*, would have a theory that the enemy was bound to attack along the central ridge. I would want to go up the coast to Alamein because I thought that the barrage might be the beginning of something bigger. We would all produce snippets of information to back up our theories. Mundy, the conducting officer, would stand by saying nothing, but the expression on his face was all too plain, 'For the love of heaven, make up your minds.'

At 7.30 a.m., in the midst of all this, the first dispatch rider came bouncing across the rocks, his greatcoat buttoned up to his chin, and he brought with him the mail tied up in a red cloth bag. The arrival of the mail was a great moment and we grabbed at it eagerly, for it contained cables from our offices in London and New York, letters from home and news from headquarters. I had known correspondents on opening their cables to announce that they had to go to Peru or Moscow, and half an hour later disappear out of the desert forever. Others might glower at some rebuke because they missed a story or again, with heavy modesty, reveal that they had a word of congratulation or a raise.

We handed over our messages to the dispatch rider each morning and he carried them off to an airfield where they were flown to Cairo to be censored, and then cabled and radioed abroad. After that came the business of bundling up the bedding and clothes and stowing the truck. All this time the argument about our day's destination would continue and in the end some sort of compromise would be reached.

It was only a short run down to the Alamein Box, but sometimes the Nazi 105-millimetre guns were shelling the road. One felt a slight constriction in the throat as one rumbled slowly across the target area. The road at this time was full of vehicles and it gave one confidence to see so many others passing back and forth, apparently unconcerned.

At forward headquarters an Intelligence officer would come out of his concrete dugout, map in hand, and explain the previous night's operations…a small enemy attack put in without tank support on Tel el Eisa…the German forward platoons gone aground under our artillery barrage…nothing more expected for the rest of the day. That meant the end of my theory. We would set off for the central ridge to explode theory number two. Several times we would have to jump down from the truck and push it through heavy sand before we got on the ridge. Once there the going was solid but the dust appalling. It made the midday heat seem twice as bad. Often we got lost and wandered for an hour or two among batteries of twenty-five-pounders, petrol dumps, passing jeeps, and ambulances and tank workshops. Every turning would turn out to be the wrong one. It did not take long for everyone to feel hot, thirsty, and irritable, especially if there were enemy planes about. There would be one or two casual dogfights in the distance and always the noise of guns, but still we would have no story and no clear idea of what was happening. The man who favoured going to the southern front would point out that we had lost two valuable hours by going first to Alamein.

Lunch came about 2.30 p.m.—a tin of peaches, biscuits, cheese and a mouthful of warm water taken without getting out of the truck. By this time we were fairly covered in dust and bored with the war. And that would be the moment when something happened.

A new track would take us to an armoured divisional headquarters and there they would be full of the news of a tank and gun skirmish earlier in the day. There would be prisoners to see, freshly come from the fighting. Then, sure enough, a German counterattack would develop in the evening when the setting sun was shining in the eyes of our men. Skirting past the British batteries going at full blast, we would always find a spot from which to see where the shells were falling, and the lines of dust going up about the infantry pressing forward into the enemy barrage. For an hour, while the light lasted, the desert would be full of the noise and movement of battle, and everywhere one turned one gathered a new fact fresh from the fighting.

Coming to the rear as the battle died down, we would check the day's events at brigade, divisional and corps headquarters and gradually a complete picture would form in one's mind.

Reaching our camp by the sea before dusk, there was always that unfailingly pleasant moment which was the reward for all the irritation and strain of the day—when we stripped naked and dived straight off the world's most perfect beach into the world's most perfect sea. In a second the sand was washed out of our eyes and ears and hair, and it was exhilarating just to be cool. A stew of bully-beef, peas, potatoes, tomatoes and onions would be bubbling as we came back from the swim and while it cooked we sat about on the rocks or on the sand typewriting our messages. At this hour the evening barrage over Alamein would start again. Overhead, the first flights of the British night bombers, tightly packed in a V, would go by. Someone would fill half a dozen mugs with whisky and sandy water and at twilight we would eat.

Then, in the rising moonlight, we would knock the dust out of our blankets and rig our beds beside the trucks. We would sit for a while in the warm darkness turning over the day's events, arguing about the war, guessing what was going to happen on the morrow.

At ten o'clock the talk would veer round to books, shop talk, home— anything. Continually it was interrupted by some distant noise of war. Propped on one's elbow in bed, one could sometimes see where the gun-flashes were stabbing in an uneven ring round the high ground to the west. We could hear, too, the convoys of unlighted vehicles making up the coast road to the front. Then, by some chemistry, all of us would get tired together, the talk would snuff out into solid sleep. The next thing would be the same damn fly again.

It was not a bad life, better for us, of course, than for most people in the desert, but still nearly everyone you saw looked healthy and reasonably cheerful.

And so the hot July days went by one after another and every day something was happening. Each side now had adopted the policy of offensive defence—that is, by making limited attacks they meant to break up the immediate opposition and prepare the way for later offensive. Neither army was geared to fighting a static war nor equipped for breaking a line—and neither side would admit it. Six heavy Axis attacks were put in at different points. Six times they were driven off, and at least six times the British tried to roll the Axis back to Matruh.

Every day each side got stronger. The Germans could not shift the Australians from Tel el Eisa. We could not get forward in the centre. Standing on the Alamein Ridge one evening we watched the heaviest of all the German assaults come in along the dusty plain between Ruweisat and the sea. It started with a series of low bombing raids and here and there across the plain trucks burst into flame and the ack-ack shells hummed and spluttered in the evening air.

The artillery followed, and after the artillery, tanks. At one moment the plain was dotted with British vehicles and guns. The next all disappeared under a rolling cloud of smoke and dust and through this dry fog the shells were bursting as lightning will burst through a thunderstorm. Just for a minute the fog would lift and you would marvel to see that the British vehicles on the plain had survived the tumult and were apparently intact. Twenty shells would be in the air together over our heads, you could hear them whining on their course, both toward you and away from you, and sometimes half a dozen of them would come down together. The German infantry reached the edge of the Alamein Box that night and began tearing up the mines. At that moment the combined British artillery got onto them and that was the end of the first big Axis attempt to break the Alamein Line.

Two days later, we made our big effort to break the Germans. It began with the heaviest artillery barrage ever seen in the desert. Clifford and I and the others were standing on the top of our truck on Ruweisat Ridge at zero hour. We knew the general plan of the coming battle. After the barrage the South Africans would attack in the north, the Indians in the centre and the New Zealanders in the south. They were all to go forward about five thousand yards onto a series of low ridges and they were to hold their positions through the night. In the morning the British tanks would attack in the centre.

A sunset made unusually beautiful by the dust delayed the darkness a little that night, and its orange light was still slanting across the sand when the guns opened fire. They came in, gun by gun, and battery by battery, until at dusk there was one continuous uproar, a jagged band of violent explosion. The night bombers passed low above our heads and over the German lines we could see long filaments of smoke reaching up to them and shell-bursts like new stars in the sky. All this time the infantry were going forward under the cover of the barrage and close behind us we heard the rumbling and creaking of many tanks. All day they had been coming up the ridge, a vast procession of vehicles. The armour had to be ready to go in at dawn to meet the inevitable German counterattack.

By now the artillery was firing for twenty miles along the horizon and the gun flashes made a dancing series of lights in the darkness like the lanterns of some garden carnival swaying in the wind. Just before midnight we saw the sign we were waiting for—coloured Very lights and star-shells mounting from the German lines and tracer bullets, mostly red, skidding right and left a few yards above the ground. That meant that the British infantry had engaged. The patter of machine-gun fire came faintly to our ears. At midnight the barrage died away. Somewhere out in the darkness ahead the grim business of 'mopping up' was going on. Hand grenades were being flung into trenches, prisoners were grabbed at the point of the bayonet, men were crawling forward through the rifle fire, others were struggling up the rocks with ammunition. This was the first of our night infantry attacks, and the whole front now was isolated into a number of dark little pockets where the troops fought for their lives, each man for himself, each man entirely alone in the world. There was nothing for us in the rear to do but sleep and wait for news and the morning.

In the morning another batch of infantry went in and we drove forward to the assembly point to see them go. The firing was very heavy out in front now. Clearly the enemy counterattack was developing.

I wonder how many people who are in this war know what it is like waiting to go over the top. As a spectator I can only guess. To me it is always the most highly charged moment of any battle—that infinity of time between the moment when the men are told they will attack and when the actual attack starts. These men were Indian soldiers mixed with some British troops and officers. They sat in their lorries, twenty men to a lorry. They had on their full marching kit and they smoked cigarettes. They sat in rows not talking much, but their eyes were always going from one place to another and they gave the impression that they were listening, listening intently. Each man gripped something with his hands, a rifle, the tailboard of the truck, a cigarette—their hands never lay relaxed and open at their sides.

They did not glance at their watches. They knew the time—each passing second of it. At each new explosion on the ridge before us—the ridge that presently they were going to charge—they did not move or show in any way that they had heard. Only their eyes kept travelling in the direction of the noise.

There was a shouted order. They got down quietly from the trucks and stood waiting. They knew what was coming. Another order. They spread out and began to go over the hill, using that strange crouching walk of men going into fire. It was very undemonstrative, a routine manoeuvre and a small one; yet still I felt this tense constriction in my lungs just watching them go. It was always easier, the men said, when they actually started to use their rifles. As the Cockney put it, 'Yer git yer blood oop.'

With the infantry the British tanks went in…and this was another of those heartbreaking mistakes and misunderstandings that kept occurring in the midst of the British attacks—the little things that you could have sworn would never happen, but yet did happen and made the difference between victory and stalemate.

It was a brand new brigade of tanks from England. The crews had trained and trained thoroughly but they were new to the desert. Only three weeks before they had come ashore at Suez with their Valentines. One wondered if it was a good thing to send troops into action immediately they arrived in the desert. The guns will shoot just the same, of course, but it was not quite like Salisbury Plain. It was not like manoeuvres. If petrol ran out it was not just a matter of running back two miles down the road and taking the first left where there is a filling station. Maybe the petrol-supply vehicles did not arrive in the desert… Maybe you had to take a compass bearing to find the nearest petrol dump, which is just a spot on the map. Maybe you were not too good at reading a compass and you missed the way. Maybe the dump had moved when you got to it.

There was no workshop close at hand if a track broke or a gun stuck. It was hot and the heat played tricks with the eyesight. Then again everything disappeared under dust and smoke once the action was joined, and the best eyesight in the world wasn't much good to you half the time.

Anyway these tanks arrived. The Indian sappers cleared a track for them through the enemy minefields during the night—that was the idea of sending the infantry in first. So in they went at dawn, these fresh-faced boys from England, and they were full of confidence and courage for this, their first real action. Someone gave them the wrong direction. They missed the track entirely and ran instead onto the mines and there the German gunners caught them in a crossfire. Of the eighty-odd tanks that went out, only a score came back. Two years of training, months of building, a voyage halfway round the world—then everything gone in a minute. Because they were given the wrong direction. And one little Cockney among the survivors shoved his head out of his tank and said to me, 'We couldn't understand what had gone wrong. We never had a chance to fire the gun. We couldn't see anything hardly. Shells kept hitting the tank on both sides and throwing us off our course, but we couldn't see who was firing them. We heard the other tanks blowing up all around us. Then one of the officers jumped on board and squeezed into the turret. He said his tank had been hit and just as he said that, a Jerry shell came clean through my turret on the port side and went round and round until it hit the officer on the back of the head and he fell forward on top of the gunner. There was blood all over the place. I was told to go five thousand yards, but when I looked at my speedometer I had done five thousand five hundred. So I turned round and came back again. I seemed to be the only tank that had got through on my sector so I thought I better come back.' And he added quite sincerely and simply, We'd like to have another crack at them, sir.' His name, I remember, was Gordon Redford.[4]

The Germans made mistakes, too, many of them. But still that did not seem to make our own much better, especially as we had plenty of these little Cockneys who wanted, who really wanted, to fight.

In the north, the South Africans had won their objective—indeed, the Germans had withdrawn their front about six thousand yards the previous night. So we turned to see how the New Zealanders were faring. We knew the previous week a battalion of theirs had gone forward to an exposed point and had offered to stay there until the morning, provided that they got support from the British armour.

Something went wrong. The armour never arrived. Most of the battalion was wiped out. And now when we reached the New Zealanders' headquarters in the pink southern desert, we found it had happened all over again. They had attacked the previous night. They had gone in with the bayonet. The Germans rallied and for the first time in desert history tried a bayonet charge of their own. They ran crying, 'Hitler, Hitler'. The New Zealanders cut them up and reported the position was won. They reported that a Nazi counterattack with tanks was likely to come against them at dawn.

Should they stay or retire at once? Stay, they were told. You will have the tanks to support you. Again it went wrong. As the grey light lifted over the desert, the New Zealanders looked back and to their flanks and saw nothing but empty desert. Out in front thirty German tanks came over the hill. In a minute or two the tanks had split the New Zealanders in half. The defenders had a few anti-tank guns with them. The crews decided to stay and fight it out in order to give their comrades a chance of getting away. They accepted the full enemy charge. They did not budge. When the officer died, an

N.C.O. took his place. When the gun-layer died, the man who fired the gun took his job as well as his own. They all died one by one. When the Germans came to occupy the position, they found the gunners laying dead across their guns. I had known some of these men for the past two years and they were really great soldiers, disciplined and firm and wonderfully collected under fire. It was an intense and personal grief to report that they were dead and one railed against the bad luck or stupidity that had let the tanks go astray.

Coming back we ran through a German position the New Zealanders had overrun a few days before. The sand was blackened with shell blast. Burnt-out troop-carriers and wagons stood about surrounded by ashes. Several 88-millimetre guns had been demolished. The nozzles of the barrels were splayed out like tulips. There were a few German graves with swastikas on them. Perhaps the New Zealand gunners did not die meaninglessly, the victims of an error. They had their share in this, too. It might be granted that they have a share in any other victory that is to come on this or any other sector of the war.

When we got back to Corps Headquarters, we found the attack had fizzled out. It was a stalemate. A solitary German prisoner stood beside the Intelligence car, smoking one cigarette after another, and carefully digging the butts into the sand with his toe. He was a deserter. He had had enough. It seemed, too, that for the time being both armies had had enough. They had tried, and tried bravely, to break one another. The fighting had been close and very bitter. There had been casualties of up to ten thousand on the line in these July battles and still neither side was able to get anywhere. As soon as one army made an attack the other drove in behind and the attacker was forced to withdraw. It was a system of stresses and balances. It was something new in the desert. For the first time since the desert war began, there was a front line. Both sides were laying down long entrenchments, hundreds of miles of barbed wire, thousands of mines. Dugouts were coming into fashion. The armour mostly stayed in the rear, while the infantry clashed with the bayonet, the tommy-gun and the grenade. There was even some trench warfare. It was now simply a matter of both sides holding their position until one or the other judged himself strong enough to attack. It had always happened like this in the desert—at Sidi Barrani, at Sollum, at Jedabya, at Gazala, and how here at Alamein. Two or three months' sharp fighting, then four or five months of getting in reinforcements. In the end, the side that got the most and best reinforcements most quickly was the one that was going to win. In the meantime as July drifted into August, the British could at least claim that they had emerged from their blackest hour.

Egypt was safe at last.

Fourteen

August – in Conclusion

WHAT WAS wrong? Why were the British armies constantly forced to retreat? Why had Norway, Dunkirk, Greece, Crete, Singapore, Burma and Egypt followed so closely upon one another? Was it the generals, the equipment, the men, the War Cabinet, the unpreparedness, the structure of the army, or just bad luck?

On the face of it Dunkirk happened because the French and Belgian armies collapsed; Norway, because the expedition was too late and too small; Greece, because we undertook an impossible job for political reasons; Crete, because we had no aircraft; Singapore and Burma, because we held the Far East on a bluff and not much else; and finally Egypt, because the necessary reinforcements were sent elsewhere.

But more and more the public was rejecting these obvious explanations. More and more they blamed the generals. So many had been 'bowler-hatted' or removed to secondary posts since the war began—Gort and Ironside, Dill and Wavell, Ritchie and Cunningham. And now, this August, Auchinleck himself was about to be replaced by General Alexander. In the R.A.F. also there had been many changes in the air marshals. The public drew the obvious inference that the generals were to blame.

I had been in the Middle East since the war started and as an observer had seen something of half a dozen campaigns in western Asia and eastern Africa as well as in the desert. I had met most of the senior generals and had seen their plans in operation. And now when I sat down this August to try and work out an explanation of our failures, I simply could not find the answer in these men. There were so many other factors. Look at just a few of them.

There was equipment. Oliver Lyttleton, the minister of production, put the matter very clearly in his speech to the Commons during the Tobruk debate. He said that England had had to choose between making a great number of inferior guns and tanks or a few of equal or better quality than the Germans. The times were pressing. England chose the great number; she had to get some sort of arms spread round her empire rather than none at all. The factories simply could not change over to new patterns overnight.

Now see how this worked out on the battle-front in the desert. We had as many tanks as the Germans all right, hundreds of them. The only serious difference was that the Germans could shoot a thousand or fifteen hundred yards and we less than a thousand. They had a 75- and a 55-millimetre gun and we had the two-pounder. When the Grants came along with the American 75 they were able to stave off the enemy for a bit, but there were not enough Grants and at the time of Tobruk we were back on our two-pounder again.

We had a new six-pounder anti-tank gun carried on a fast truck and it was a good gun. Again, too few arrived too late. The Germans and Italians had their magnificent all-purpose 88-millimetres, a great many of them, and they had had a long time to train their crews. Our Bofors could not be compared with the 88 as a combined anti-tank and anti-aircraft weapon. Our twenty-five-pounder and our four-point-five were good guns, but they had other good Axis guns against them.

We had at the most half a dozen Spitfires in the desert. Neither the Hurricane nor the Tomahawk nor the Kittyhawk can catch a Messerschmitt 109F. Apart from a few improvised fighters we had no dive-bombers at all. It is useless for military strategists to argue, as they will and fiercely, that the Stuka is a failure and very vulnerable. Ask the troops in the field. Its effect on morale alone made it worthwhile in the Middle East so long as we had insufficient fighters. Anyway, we thought it good enough to attempt to evolve a dive-bomber of our own.

In medium and heavy bombers we undoubtedly had superiority in the desert, but these did not play a leading part until the end of the summer campaign. They could not have saved Tobruk for us.

Our recovery system in the summer showed an immense improvement.

But still the Germans had the better system of front-line workshops. For one thing, their job was easier. Our engineers had to carry the spare parts for half a dozen different types of tank, and necessarily ran short both of tools and replacements. The Germans had standardised their tanks down to two or three types and so were able to carry more spares and distribute them better. This goes for the Luftwaffe too.

There were many other small items…the water and fuel containers, for instance. The Germans experimented and designed what appears to be the best container for the desert. It was a flat, solidly built can holding about five gallons, and so constructed that the last drop could be poured out. It could be used over and over again. By simply painting on each can a special marking—a white cross was employed for water—they were used for diesel oil, ordinary petrol, aviation spirit, kerosene and water. The great bulk of the British army was forced to stick to the old flimsy four-gallon container.

The majority of them were only used once. Thousands were smashed in transit and leaked entirely. Every day in the desert we would have the same trouble. We would put a couple of petrol cans in the back of truck. Two hours of bumping over the desert rocks usually produced a suspicious smell.

Opening the back of the truck there, sure enough, we would find one or both of our cans had leaked and we had to go off hunting for more. It was time as well as petrol we lost.

In general, then, the enemy had a clear advantage in equipment. Whenever the British army took the field, it knew that it would have to face superior weapons, and that makes a certain effect on morale. There is just one other point here. The enemy could get all his replacements and reinforcements three times quicker than we could. Often he used aircraft to carry many of his supplies and reinforcements to the front. They arrived ten times quicker than by land and sea.

Now all this question of equipment had little to do with the general. He specified what he wanted, of course, but he had to take what he could get. No Middle East general would have taken Valentine tanks if he could have got Grants. But he couldn't get the Grants.

Then strategy and tactics. It was no longer the general in the field who decided when or where a campaign should be fought but the War Cabinet in London. In every one of our campaigns political considerations had carried very much importance and the diplomats had had almost as much say in their conception as the generals. We had gone to war on a political and not a military issue. In every case a general had simply been selected and told to get on with the job. Even in the framing of tactics he did not have a free hand. The tactics were those which were recommended by a staff of experts or those which were forced upon the junior commanders at the front by the fortunes of the battle. Before all their Middle Eastern campaigns both Wavell and Auchinleck called upon many technicians to deliver their appreciations of the position. Estimates and reports were sought from the staffs of the engineers and the armourers, from the Royal Army Supply Corps, from both political and military intelligence, from the ministries of shipping and production, from geographers and meteorologists, from the various branches of the R.A.F. and the navy, from the operational staffs and the junior commanders, from the leaders of the Allied forces, from security, from the transport experts, from the Dominions and the American Lease-Lend administrators— to mention only a few. All these reports and estimates were collated and submitted to the central direction of the war in London. The chief duty of the commander-in-chief, Middle East, in this was to see that the best men were giving him these reports and that the facts they submitted were accurately tabulated and assessed. As an experienced man the general's own opinion was of value, but the facts themselves as a rule pointed to the conclusion, and the man in command was forced to accept it. He could not fly flatly in the face of his advisers. He could not say to the meteorologist, 'The moon will not be rising on this date,' nor to the experts in ballistics, 'Your gun will fire three thousand yards, not two,' nor to the Foreign Office, 'It is not politically expedient to attack now.' Once an offensive had been decided upon, the problems of how it should be fought rested not upon one man but fifty or more. The best the general could do would be to see that all went forward smoothly and energetically until the day of the attack and then, like a coach who has sent a football team into play, he could do nothing more but sit back and watch how his men got on.

In actual fact neither the winter nor the summer campaign had produced any vital new tactics. It was the old business of making wide sweeps through the desert, of getting round behind the enemy, of striking him at his weakest point and following up fast. Rommel had revealed no genius in planning or timing. Living at the front he had certainly been in a position to take quick decisions, but if there had been any genius at all on the Axis side it had been the genius of the average German soldier for organisation. In all its branches the German war machine appeared to have a better and tighter control than our army. Many believed that this was because the Germans had been so long in training for this war. One of the senior British generals said to the war correspondents after the fall of Tobruk, 'We are still amateurs. The Germans are professionals.' One saw this talent for organisation in all directions. The Luftwaffe, for example, had a much closer liaison with the ground forces than we, though we made big improvements in this. Time and again, one would note the steady rhythm of a German attack—first the Stukas, then the artillery, then the infantry, then the tanks, then the Stukas following up again. Once the action was joined, the Germans tended to dispense with coded signals which wasted time at both ends. Rommel's own voice could be frequently heard on the air ordering his troops to do this, that, or the other thing. By the time the British could make use of this freely given information the action would be over.

A vast tide of paper clogged the British army. That ancient passion for putting things down in triplicate, that ancient saying, 'Let me just have a chit for that,' sprang largely from one thing—the desire of the subordinate to avoid responsibility, to avoid 'getting a rocket'. If the order was down on paper then the subordinate would not get the blame if anything went wrong. Hours and hours were lost each day by men writing things down on bits of paper because it was the system that they should do so, because they would 'get a rocket' if they failed to do so. It is, no doubt, a wise and necessary part of army discipline that forbids a junior officer to approach his colonel directly—he must go through the officer immediately superior to himself. But to many it has seemed that this system is carried to extremes in the British army, and that the whole question of the relationship between officers and men needs overhauling.

The best discipline I saw was in the front line, where the officers and men lived together and ate the same food and shared the same risks. The worst was far behind the front where men were forbidden to enter officers' restaurants and were reported by military police if they failed to salute an officer in the streets. In the Red army and the German army, every officer must first serve in the ranks. Their discipline is far less a matter of manners than in the British army. Men and officers appear to be far more together among the Germans, to understand one another better and therefore like and trust one another more than in the British army. I remember a pungent little description Mary Welsh wrote for the American magazine *Time*, of the arrival of the first American troops in Ireland. A bevy of British brasshats had come to meet them. When the troops were lined up on the wharf the American commander gave his order for them to move off. It was 'Okay, boys, let's go.' I simply cannot envisage that order being given by a British officer.

It was in the control of tanks that the Germans revealed their greatest gifts. They were tank technicians pure and simple. They were the élite of the Afrika Korps, as compact, as neat and efficient as a team of acrobats. They had been trained to the nth degree and as a group, a group that could be controlled very nearly as easily as one tank. They were self-contained. Stukas, tanks, recovery vehicles, petrol wagons, anti-tank gunners, all went forward together and their senior officers were often in the van. Toward the end Rommel evolved a number of still smaller self-contained armoured groups. There were notably his own bodyguard and the Marx Group. They moved about very rapidly and very successfully. The cooperation between the tanks and the anti-tank gunners was their best achievement. The Germans no longer used tanks to attack equal enemy armoured forces. Let me repeat that— they did not attack with tanks. On the Alamein Line and outside Tobruk they avoided tank action unless they greatly outnumbered us. They preferred always to send out scouts by land and air to plot the positions of our anti-tank guns. Then they used aircraft and infantry to attack those guns. They used artillery too. Then when the British guns were silenced or partially silenced, and the landmines lifted, they used their tanks to mop up the battlefield, and breakthrough to the unprotected British infantry. In defence they used very nearly the same methods—that was how we took our vital losses on June 13th. They had another stunt too—using the tank as a scare weapon. As I remember on that night when we ran into the graveyard at El Adem there was only a handful of German armoured cars and tanks in the German thrust. But they got through to the British infantry and there they made a terrific hullaballoo—shooting off Very lights, firing all their guns, stirring up great columns of dust. They knew that the word would spread through the British lines that the German tanks had cut loose and they exploited the scare for all it was worth. It was effective.

We could not hope to marshal and drive our tanks as the Germans did. We were simply not trained to it and they had years of practice. It was not difficult for us to train the gunners and drivers. Theirs was a mechanical job, and many in the desert were equal or superior to their German opposites. But it takes much longer training and a higher kind of brain to command a tank. The man who can handle large groups of tanks is a much rarer bird still. Among other things he needs experience in actual warfare. About the time of the fall of Tobruk, we found ourselves seriously short of young tank officers, men who knew the desert, and knew their tanks through and through. A number of higher officers in command of the armour were weeded out there and then on the battlefield because of blunders, but no large-scale changes could suddenly be made among the junior ranks.

All these things—the system of the army, the training of the men or the lack of it, the type of discipline—were fundamentals that no general in the field had the time or the means seriously to alter. The system was in being. For better or worse, it had to be used as it was. It would not have helped the commanding general to complain that the army was based on the ideas of 1918, that its methods were redundant and slow, that the men were insufficiently trained and the equipment inferior. He had to accept the situation and make the best of a difficult job.

Morale was important too, but this depended on many factors beyond the general's control. The propaganda system in the Middle East was no better or worse than the rest of the army. It took its defeats in the same way. The Axis army paid the closest attention to morale and the control of morale through propaganda. Where our men in the desert had not seen a newspaper for months, let alone any other reading to divert and encourage their minds, the Axis troops were abundantly supplied. Every one of their camps I saw was strewn with recent magazines and pamphlets. They were filled with good action photographs from all sectors of the war. The airmail came in several times a week. There were thousands of radio sets. About this time there was a girl called Marlene (NOT Marlene Dietrich) who used to sing in a special programme for the Afrika Korps from the Balkans. She was a terrific hit. Not only the German army but the British army too used to tune in to her. She had one lilting song about how she had said goodbye to her soldier underneath the street lamp in Berlin, and how she was still waiting there. You would hear British soldiers whistling the song everywhere in the desert. A slight thing this, but enough to show how badly we needed a more active use of our own radio. The last time I went down to the New Zealanders, Captain Robin Bell, on the general's staff, said something that every soldier in the desert was thinking: 'No, I don't want cigarettes or anything like that, and the food's all right. But for the love of heaven can you send me up any magazines and newspapers?' The men were pathetically eager for even a month-old copy of an Egyptian paper.

Here again we were improving. The radio was putting on special programmes for the troops; four publications—*Parade, Crusader, Gen* and the *World's Press Review*—were being specially printed for them in Cairo. And airgraphs and airmail lettercards were passing to and from the Middle East, sometimes taking less than a fortnight. But still it was not enough. The troops needed more cheering up, more music, more books, more radios. Their food was good.

Beyond this there was the deeper question I have written of before— the need, the really urgent need, to explain to the men the reasons why they were fighting. No German I met ever had any doubt on this point. After all, Germans were not difficult to enthuse, especially as the Nazi party had had eight years in which to work on them. Among the British in the Middle East there was, in August, a general and growing feeling that something was being held back from them, that they were being asked to fight for a cause which the leaders did not find vital enough to state clearly. It's simply no good telling the average soldier that he is fighting for victory, for his country, for the sake of duty. He knows all that. And now he is asking, 'For what sort of victory? For what sort of a post-war country? For my duty to what goal in life?'

It should have been easy to answer. If, for example, the four great allies, China, the U.S.A., Britain and Russia, were to have set out under the names of Chiang Kai Shek, Roosevelt, Churchill and Stalin, a social and political programme for the world and a plan for peace it would have made a remarkable impression on the minds of the men. Morale would have improved. I do not suggest that it was bad. But let us accept that the best morale comes through victory or the hope of victory, and if we could not have victory at once it might have been worthwhile raising a few planned hopes.

In the German army I saw no signs of any breaking in morale. Why should there have been? They were winning. To encourage them they had their loot, the sight of conquered territory, promotion, decorations, all the apparatus of victory. They were solid—woodenly solid if you like. It must be conceded that their morale was higher than ours in the Middle East.

So then in all these things, in equipment, training, organisation and morale, we had to accept a disadvantage through this year of war in the desert.

I cannot see that the weather favoured either side. Both sides had to endure the midsummer heat, both used the moon and the rising and setting sun to their advantage. The sandstorms were impartially damnable. The wind blew indifferently upon Germans and British.

Luck, of course, there was. Luck intervened a thousand times. At moments it took charge of the battle. But if it were possible to assess the good and bad luck that fell to either side, I believe that it would be found that neither Germans nor British had the advantage.

Generals don't control either weather or luck. They and their men can *use* weather and luck, but they can't manufacture it. There was a story in London that the enemy did not suffer so much from the heat as we did because they had some sort of elaborate refrigeration system in their tanks. This was quite untrue. Nor was it true that frequently crews collapsed from the heat inside their tanks. I talked to a number of the troops about this and they were inclined to think that the tank was one of the coolest vehicles in the desert. They pointed out that the tank had its visors down and its turret closed only during that one per cent of time when it was in action. For the rest it travelled with its visors and doors open and most of the crew perched on the roof in the breeze. When they stopped they crawled into the shade underneath and the two-inch armour was the best protection against the sun you could get from any vehicle in the desert.

The further you go into this huge problem, the more factors and influences you discover. Consider the nationalities of the men. The Axis had Germans and Italians—that was all. Just two languages to cope with, two temperaments to consider. And the Italians in all things were entirely subservient to the Germans. There might have been minor irritations but the Italians acknowledged the superiority of the Germans and obeyed their orders. The Germans on their side went out of their way to respect the feelings of the Italians. We captured a fascinating little document from a German soldier. It was a list of instructions for German troops waiting in Naples to embark for Libya. They were to observe the strictest decorum. They were not to remove their caps in the street or their tunics in the restaurants.

They were not to drink too much wine because wine inflamed the passions, and the Italians were very sensitive about their women. At all times the Nazi was to be excessively polite to Italian women— and nothing more. They were not to smoke in the street. They were to understand that the Italians were a very different people to the chosen race. They were warned that they might find things run in a very slipshod manner in Italy, but they were to avoid all criticism or remarks of any sort that might give offence. And so on—the sort of admonition you might give to an adolescent boy on his first trip abroad, but still a measure of the German thoroughness.

On our side there were at least seven different nationalities fighting, at least five different languages used. There were the men from the British Isles, Indians, French, Poles, Greeks, Australians, South Africans, New Zealanders—to mention only the main groups. Every one of these groups had its own way of doing things, its own domestic political problems, its pride—pride that counts for a great deal in war. Of course there were arguments and misunderstandings. I have mentioned only one of these often delicate relationships—that between the Australians and the British. The commander-in-chief had to be a sort of prime minister. He was constantly receiving telegrams from Churchill in England, the viceroy in India, Field-Marshal Smuts in South Africa, Mr Curtin in Australia, Mr Fraser in New Zealand and the Polish General Sikorski in London. There were Americans in the Middle East as well and adjustments had to be made to their way of thinking. And Greeks and Czechs and Yugoslavs and Maltese and Palestinians and Cypriots. There was no question of any one of these people accepting a subservient rôle as the Italians did, unless perhaps it was the Indian soldier, who in any case had such a tremendous reputation as a fighter that he was admired by everyone.

Here, then, was a major problem for the Allied side, a problem that ranks with any other aspect of the war. All these elements had to be composed and organised, the right nationality given the right job at the right moment, and always things had to be adjusted so that no one took offence. The friendly, but non-belligerent, Egyptians and Arabs were another little problem of their own.

Then again a major point of local strategy: always Syria and Palestine had to be guarded. There was no moment when Auchinleck could say (as Rommel could), 'Now we will throw all we have got into the Western Desert.' What about the landing fields the Axis was preparing in the Greek islands? What about the training of parachutists on Crete? What about the massing of caiques and invasion boats in the Dodecanese Islands? Was the enemy going to strike now at Cyprus and Syria? Was he going to make a parachute landing on Palestine and the Canal? These were the questions that went before Auchinleck every day. He had to fight constantly looking over his shoulder. If a successful enemy landing was made in Syria and the Germans spread east then the whole defence of the desert went for nothing, the Middle East was lost, the oilwells were gone. At the height of the crisis, Auchinleck had to take the supreme risk of denuding Palestine of its best troops. There was a time during July and early August when the Axis might well have made successful landings in Syria and Cyprus. But the Axis had sent all it could spare from the Russian front to the desert. They tried to scare the British in July by broadcasting from Berlin: 'Yes, we know the British have removed the Ninth Army from Syria. Syria is defenceless.'

Note the parachutists were not used at any time through these campaigns except in a limited way by the British. One night, a British commando raid behind the enemy lines just missed getting Rommel himself. Throughout our Long Range Desert Group was doing wonderful work, travelling by truck hundreds of miles behind the enemy and striking suddenly in the night at airfields, roads, dumps and camps. The Long Range Desert Group is an epic tale in itself. But it was limited.

Another thing that had a considerable influence on what you might call the 'tone' of the fighting was the German attitude toward British prisoners. Those British who escaped—and there were dozens every other day—all brought back the same story: 'The Germans behaved extraordinarily well. They gave us food and water at once. There was no third degree—nothing like that at all. They behaved far better than the Italians.' One reported that his camera had been taken away from him by a German soldier and an officer had come along and ordered the camera to be given back. Another said that he had been given fifty cigarettes and a glass of beer. A third added that he had had a long and friendly talk with some Nazis who spoke English and said that they thought the British and the Germans should have been on the same side. A British general was captured and he stripped off his badges before the Germans arrived, so that he would pass unnoticed and have a better chance of escaping. When a Nazi officer came along the line of prisoners he stopped at the British general and said, 'You're a bit too old to be in the desert, aren't you?' 'I certainly am,' the general agreed warmly. That night he got away. The wounded also reported that the German hospitals were a miracle of efficiency. They had remarkable stocks of drugs. British wounded were given exactly the same treatment as the Germans. It was not long before one was hearing here and there in the British lines, 'Well, you must admit they treat the prisoners all right. They were damn nice to me.'

Nice and cunning. It was certainly a subtle method of warfare. Presumably, the underlying idea was 'Treat the prisoners well, let a few escape, and the word will soon get round among the enemy that it isn't such a bad thing after all to be taken prisoner. Let them think you are friendly, once they have been caught. Then some of them may desert. Others won't fight so hard.'

The Russians were carrying the idea a step further. They were dropping pamphlets over the German lines saying, 'Try to desert from the Germans. Present this pamphlet to any Russian soldier and you will be guaranteed good treatment.'

It may have been that there was something else in the Germans' 'Be nice to prisoners' scheme. It meant that their own people who were captured could expect reciprocal treatment from the British. (They were getting it anyhow.) It seemed to me that all through this desert fighting the German attitude was, 'This is a clean, clear-cut sort of war... a straight-out fight in the empty desert where there are no civilians and no political considerations. It's a soldier's battle. We're soldiers playing the exciting military game of war for the Führer. It's a game really. Soldiering is what we are born for and this isn't like Europe which is perverted with its Jews, and capitalists and Bolsheviks. Here we can really play the game according to the rules and die gloriously on the clean battlefield for the Führer.'

That, anyway, may have often been in the mind of the young idealistic Nazi officer so long as he was winning. That is what in his better moments he would like to think. And so he welcomed the 'Be nice to the prisoners' campaign. He was playing cricket in a big way.

Back in Cairo I met a young Bulgar who was the correspondent of the *Daily Express* in Sofia. He had escaped through Turkey. The Gestapo had taken off his shoes and socks and sat him on an electric chair. A band was clipped round his calf and it was attached to a rod that extended around below his bare feet. When the machine was set in motion it burnt his calf and beat against the soles of his feet. It wasn't too bad, he said. He had had only two sessions of this before they put him into a concentration camp. He was only limping slightly now after four months' treatment and the doctors said he would be all right again. The Bulgarian socialist leaders had not been so fortunate. The Gestapo had used a new treatment for them. They had soaked squares of flannel with petrol, ignited them and then drawn them slowly back and forth over the private parts. This was especially bad, the young Bulgar said, because the men did not die at once.

Nor was there much cricket being played in Poland, where the worst massacre of modern times was going on. Nor in Russia. Nor in the rest of occupied Europe. Just here in the desert apparently one could have ideals, because they really served quite as well as torture and murder and starvation.

If really bad luck had impeded the British, it was as much among the dead as among the captured.

There seemed to be a curse on the lives of British generals in the Middle East. At a most crucial moment the Generals Gott, Briggs and Lumsden were talking together at the front one day when a Stuka charged them. Briggs and Lumsden were hit and put out of the battle. An aide-de-camp was killed. Only Gott, the man with the charmed life, escaped. Gatehouse took command of the armour. He was putting some of his own fire into it when he, too, was hit and taken back to Cairo. Freyberg was the next casualty—Freyberg who had stood unmoved through impossible risks in this war and survived the last with heaven knew how many wounds. The enemy got him at last at Mersa Matruh.

The old lion continued directing the battle until nightfall and then, so seriously hurt that they had to hold him down, they motored him straight through the enemy lines and got him to hospital.

Added to these were the generals who had been removed because of errors and bad judgment, and the Eighth Army, you will see, was in a bad way over its commanders. It seemed they either died, were wounded, captured, or made mistakes. Only Gott remained of the original men, and he stood out like a giant in this bitter, thankless fighting, the one great name left on the British side, the one man who had survived death, capture, or major error. But Gott could not be everywhere. At a whole series of tense moments the British were without competent leaders. An attempt was made to fly General Morshead into Tobruk at the last moment, but he was too late. He had been the original holder of the garrison during its great days and it is just possible that given a little time he might have got things in better order. Other competent commanders, like de Villiers, the South African, were also absent from the front at crucial moments.

It was unfortunate, too, that Auchinleck should have chosen this moment to institute a scheme behind the lines which might have been an excellent one at another time. He began moving G.H.Q. out of the flesh-pots of Cairo to a spot nearby in the desert. He wanted to get everyone under canvas, the way Allenby had done in the last war, so that the staff men should be less distracted by the baubles of Cairo, and able to devote more time to their jobs. He wanted to remove the criticism that the men at the base were living in ease while others fought their battles for them at the front. Auchinleck was the first to go out. He shut up his town house and moved into a tent. With ironic but good-humoured malice the army immediately dubbed the new G.H.Q. 'The Short Range Desert Group.' It wasn't a bad idea this move to the desert. The trouble was that, coming in the middle of a crisis, it badly disrupted things. At a time when things should have been going with special smoothness at G.H.Q. there was commotion and delay and much grumbling from the staff men who thought the idea crazy anyway.

Then there was this final point which is so obvious that it has been forgotten. This was Rommel's offensive, not ours. Presumably when you make an offensive you hope to get through with it; you hope to gain territory. If you don't, then it is a worse failure, as a rule, than if you never tried at all and merely stood your ground and gave way a bit. Rommel had planned this offensive as far back as nine months before and failed. Tobruk, too, had never before been submitted to an organised, full-scale attack since we held it. It is possible that it might have fallen had Rommel been allowed to attack it as he planned to do when we struck him first in November 1941.

These then were the conclusions I reached when I tried to make a summing up at the beginning of August in Cairo. The list is not exclusive and many of the men who fought in the campaign will disagree with them. But to me they were a full enough explanation. They dispelled in my mind any question of there being a mystery over the fall of Tobruk and our collapse into Egypt. There was no mystery. Everything moved forward step by step, logically and precisely as it was destined to do.

It did not seem to me that our defeat was due to any one cause, such as equipment or tactics, but to a whole variety of causes. A series of events and influences had come into play, and the result could not have been otherwise than it was. Above all, the result was not due to any one man or to any small group of men. One could not blame the British generals any more than one could say, 'Rommel has defeated the British.' These names of generals were merely convenient tags by which the campaigns could be identified and personified. They satisfied the public desire for hero-worship, especially the German desire for hero-worship. The Italians, too, had always been a nation of brilliant individuals and they loved this adulation of generals. Auchinleck had not created the tactics, the equipment and the spirit of the British army any more than Rommel had fashioned the Axis army. Auchinleck had lost and Rommel had won for complicated reasons far beyond the control of the two men.

This is not to say that the German generals were inferior to the British generals. They were superior. They made fewer mistakes and did the right thing more often than the British generals. Rommel was an abler general than any on the British side and for this one reason—because the German army was an abler army than the British army. Rommel was merely the expression of that abler German army.

Just as the German army had produced through long training and a passion for war an abler junior officer and better organisation and weapons to fight with, so at the top it had produced an abler general. It was simply a great pyramid in which every stone had to fit into place and at its apex the rightly shaped stone was set in position. This topmost stone was the one most people looked at because it stood alone at the top and first arrested the eye. But it was no more important than any other stone. Without those stones at the base the whole pyramid could not have existed. Each stone, whether it was at the base or in the middle or at the top, had to perform its function, and no function was more important than another. It was the solid collective mass that counted.

The general, then, was simply the index of his army, the stone that was set at the top to complete the pattern. Just as the German army got the general it deserved, so the British army got the general it deserved. Both Rommel and Auchinleck and all the other commanders were outstanding men. They stood higher in their own pyramids than any others because they were shaped for the high positions.

But even if they had been made of better material than those at the bottom, it would still not have preserved or strengthened the structures greatly; a pyramid weathers at its base as well as at the top. My last conclusion then was this: soldier and general were interdependent. The army and the general were one.

I see no reason for pessimism in this thesis which seeks to prove that not only the generals but the British army, as a whole, was at that time inferior to the German army. In every department, I saw we were making huge improvements. Looking back to 1940, I found it hard to believe the changes that had taken place with us, hard to realise that that little tinpot force of a couple of divisions had grown into the army that now sprawled across an area several times the size of Europe. In every separate department there had been a steady improvement and the rate of improvement was accelerating. There had been no such improvement on the German side. Slowly, and with many pains and disasters, we were overhauling the lead the Axis had held over us from the beginning of the war. This became blindingly apparent in this last summer's campaign. The Axis then produced no new piece of equipment whatever; they simply had overwhelming quantities of the same good material and much training. On our side we had the new Grant tank and there were even better tanks arriving; we had the new six-pounder gun and hundreds of them were beginning to flood into the Middle East. The new Spitfires were starting to come in at last. The Americans, headed by their air force, were taking their positions in the desert.

If we had not had these improvements in the summer, we would have been wiped out of the desert in a quarter of the time. If we had even gone into the campaign with the previous winter's army, the Germans assuredly would have been in the Nile Delta by this.

One other thing—out of the mistakes and the failures there was good metal coming to the top. With every campaign a larger and larger group of experienced men was emerging. Our pyramid had been misshapen and badly built before. Now some of the misfits had been removed. Little by little the pyramid was being groomed and adjusted. Inevitably it was going to be a better pyramid in the end than the German one and at its top it was going to have a better general than Rommel.

When I got back to Cairo the best energy and brains among the Allies was being put into the job of reorganisation. We had had a bad shock. The old business of holding the Middle East on a shoestring was going to cease. There was going to be no more bluffing. So Churchill flew in from London one morning to hold his conference in Cairo. He had with him Averill Harriman, the American Lease- Lend administrator; General Sir Alan Brooke, chief of imperial staff; General Sir Ronald Adam, the adjutant-general; and one or two others. Wavell came across from India. Smuts flew in from South Africa. All the generals, the senior admirals and air marshals of the Middle East were gathered. It was a momentous conference, one that was going to change the course of the war. It meant that at least we acknowledged that we had a second front here in the Middle East, a place where we were immediately in contact with the enemy and able to buttress Russia's left flank.

There was the usual purge of generals—Alexander, a dynamic little man who had done well at Dunkirk and as well as possible at the fall of Burma, took the place of Auchinleck. General Maitland Wilson was given a separate command in Syria and Palestine. More important still, a new and strange leader was given command in the desert—General Montgomery. Several other generals were replaced and reshuffled. This much was announced. But the changes went much further. At this conference a new army of the Middle East was given birth, an army that for the first time was going to include Americans as well as British. A tide of reinforcement such as the Middle East had never known before was going to come in, and from it a better army was going to be built.

An era of the war was over, a bad era, but one from which good was going to come.

I went down to Palestine to fetch Lucy and the baby. They had been staying at a little German Jewish pension by the sea at Naharya in northern Palestine, close to the Syrian border. For the last time I took the Haifa train. I felt very tired. It had gone on so long, this war in the desert. Was there ever going to be an end to it? For more than two years now I had been going down to Sollum and Tobruk, to Sidi Barrani and Benghazi. I felt as though I knew every grain of sand, had seen every possible manoeuvre, experienced all the moods of this monotonous yet not monotonous war. In these two years so many triumphs and bitter disappointments had followed one another, so many friends had come and gone away or been captured or killed. I had seen so many commanders go out there with high hopes and now only Gott was left. He was the only one who had stood the racket from start to finish.

Suddenly, and quite surely, I felt I could not report the desert any more. I had to get away. I could, of course, go on, but it would become a mechanical thing without much meaning for me. I had been too close to it for too long. Clifford, too, who had been there from the beginning, was feeling the same way. We wanted now to see the war from some other point of view than the desert—even a break for just a few months would be enough.

I found Lucy and the baby having a wonderful time by the sea. They were in a place of bright, sunny gardens, fresh fruit and good wines, of sparkling new cottages and trees and flowers. I had a really big fresh egg for breakfast, sitting in the sun on the terrace. Afterwards we bathed the baby in the waves. It made me more determined than ever to get away—a long way from the desert.

Here in the sunshine a little group of Jews flung out by Germany were rebuilding their lives under the lee of the war. They had worked hard. They had turned this barren coast into a lovely place full of good food and good living. There was only the Alamein Line now between them and Hitler, but they did not seem to be afraid. They knew there was no longer any place they could flee to. This, whatever happened, was their journey's end. Their children were growing up here into a new life, a better life than they could ever have had in Germany. At night, looking through their lighted doorways, you could see the families sitting together. Someone would be playing music in the garden.

Perhaps it was for this that in the last analysis we were fighting the war. A cottage, a piece of farmland, the right to work in one's home securely and enjoy it.

As soon as we got back to Cairo I cabled Arthur Christiansen. He saw my point generously. Where did I want to go? I suggested America, and after that anywhere they liked—England, Russia, the Far East, back to the Middle East. It was agreed. Clifford had decided to make use of his leave by going direct to London.

We made one last tour round the familiar places in Cairo—G.H.Q., Shepheard's Hotel, The Turf Club, Gezira, the censorship office. At G.H.Q. we spent half an hour with Wavell. Three years of war had made no difference to him. Nothing, I suppose, will ever shake or change that man.

It was from him that we heard a shocking piece of news, news that somehow more than any other single thing made me feel in a moment that an era in the desert was done and that it was time I went away. Gott was dead. They had killed him in the air. He had talked that morning with Churchill and the others in the desert. Churchill had offered him the greatest opportunity any general in the British army could hope for—command of the Eighth Army—and Gott had accepted. Then after some months of daily danger and unending work he had stepped into a Bombay aircraft to fly back to Cairo for a few days' leave. The enemy had been stopped; he was due for a holiday. Two Messerschmitts returning from a raid saw the slow and cumbersome troop-carrier. The British pilot almost got the Bombay down. As the wheels touched, the Germans fired incendiaries and the machine caught fire.

Gott was dead when they got him out. His body rested on his chosen battlefield, the sand. He was the last of the old desert rats to go. He was a great man for England.

BOOK THREE

The End in Africa: The Year of Eisenhower, Alexander and Montgomery 1942–43

One

Durban

THIS WAS one of the last luxury liners in the world. There would never again be a ship like *Zola*. The company built her in the last year before the war when there was still the hope of peace and the habit of extravagance; and men still believed in a world of luxury and profits because they could not get themselves to face the dreadful prospect of war.

As the last declining months of peace ran out, they streamlined *Zola*'s hull and built a row of luxury shops along the promenade deck. They lined her staterooms with padded silk and placed a flood-lit statue at the end of the great dining saloon, where you might sit over your *huîtres marennes* and *liebfrauenmilch* and watch the sea go past at forty miles an hour through huge plate-glass windows.

And in the hot afternoon you could go through the air-conditioned corridors to play tennis on the upper decks or swim in a marble pool where the artificial waves were kept at just the right temperature.

On *Zola* you could have a mint julep or an electric massage, a love affair or a game of baccarat, a major operation or a Brahms recital. There was hardly an artificial pleasure on earth that you could not have had. She was built to carry only a few hundred passengers, with a huge crew to look after them. Of these passengers just one hundred and fifty were first-class, and to them was given two- thirds of the ship—they would pay for the tennis courts and the burgundy, so let them have everything they wanted. *Zola*, you see, was built to carry millionaires from America to Europe, and she was designed to make that journey across the Atlantic in just a few days. The beef baron could step aboard with his over-jewelled wife and she need never look at the sea or hardly feel its existence until she began arguing with the customs in France. Then Paris; and with Paris the dress shows, the Champs Élysées, the racing at Auteuil, the Bal Tabarin.

Zola, a miracle of white paint and chromium and soundless, vibrationless engines, was ready to put to sea just about the time Hitler was ready. She was one of the last luxury liners in the world.

This was the ship that arrived off Suez at the end of the third year of war. The unbearable heat of the Red Sea in August sweated out of her drab grey plates. Not hundreds of passengers but thousands tumbled down her gangway onto the lighters, and they were young American troops wearing steel helmets and carrying packs. The ship they left behind was as gloomy as a gaol, as comfortless and unlovely as only an army barracks can be. The padded silk, of course, was gone from the walls, but that was only the beginning. In the ballroom crude wooden bunks were piled tier on tier, leaving only two feet six inches between each sleeping man and his fellow passenger above. The swimming pool was full of potatoes, the shops were cabins, six, ten and twelve men to a cabin. The statue was boarded over, and in the first-class dining saloon, where neither oysters nor German wine were ever served, you could see nothing outside, for every window was boarded over with jet-black three-ply wood. The open decks and the tennis court where the men had slept in thousands through the Red Sea were filthy with dust and discarded papers and orange peel. *Zola* was long overdue for fumigation, and she was lousy—lousy with vermin.

Because His Majesty's troopship *Zola* appeared so drab and dirty with her one lofty funnel you would never have guessed as you looked at her from the docks of Suez that she and her fellows were a major factor in the war.

Dirty, lousy, hot and overworked, she had arrived on this sweltering August day to land Americans in Egypt and take on board hundreds of Germans who had been captured in the Western Desert.

These Germans marched through the squalid dockside streets of Suez with great sureness and confidence. They were short and lean little men, and many of them carried under their arms a roll of bedding or an unpainted box containing perhaps an extra shirt and a few personal things they had managed to salvage in the battle. They were still dusty with desert sand, and their thin green-grey gabardine uniforms and cloth caps were soiled and worn. They whistled as they marched. As they crammed into the lighters that took them out to the troopship they sang, 'We March against England Today.' Twenty or thirty officers, including a U-boat lieutenant, were in a little group by themselves. They smoked and contemptuously did what they were told. German privates followed behind carrying the officers' luggage. There was no atmosphere of defeat here, no depression, no apprehension. They were Aryan Germans walking through a rabble of Arabs and Jews and black men, and they wore their medals on their tunics to show that they had fought with Rommel and the Afrika Korps. Lately they had won a great victory in the desert, and even now Marshal Rommel stood at the gates of Alexandria. It appeared almost certain that within a few weeks he would be in Cairo and Alexandria. No, they had nothing to be ashamed of, these Germans, and now they were leaving their comrades to carry on the conquests they had so magnificently begun.

I stood at the rail of *Zola* watching the Germans come aboard from the lighters, and the third mate spat into the oily sea. 'More trouble,' he said. 'I expect we'll be having more trouble with these bastards.'

He had indeed good reason to dislike German prisoners. A remarkable thing had happened aboard this ship on her last trip. In the same way she had arrived at Suez and taken on board a batch of Germans, including General Ravenstein, who had ranked second to Rommel until he was captured outside Tobruk. The German troops had been drafted into quarters between decks at the forward end of the ship and their officers segregated on the boat-deck aft. The officer in charge of the British escort had failed to take proper security measures. There were the Germans under lock and key, he argued, what could they do at sea? That British officer did not know General Ravenstein.

The third day out from Suez a guard who spoke German heard one of the prisoners say quietly, 'It won't be long now.' The guard promptly reported to the orderly room what he had heard. He had the impression the prisoners were plotting something, he said.

The soldier was waved aside with a reprimand by the British officer. He was told not to bring fanciful stories to his superiors and to get on with his job. A Czech doctor who was a member of the ship's crew heard the incident in the orderly room and he was by no means convinced that everything was well. His Czech instincts told him there was likely to be danger wherever you have Germans. He had seen the slovenly arrangements made for the guarding of the prisoners. The doctor went to the captain with the story.

Wars make no difference to the status of captains. The captain is undisputed master of his ship whether he carries a president or a field-marshal or merely an army officer in charge of German prisoners. This captain, being a shrewd and dynamic little Scot, sacked the British army officer on the spot and ordered an immediate search of the ship. Within the hour—the eleventh hour—an extraordinary plot was uncovered.

British Tommies going through the prisoners' quarters found broken chair legs secreted in the stanchions. A score of pepper pots, each one capable of temporarily blinding a man, were dug out of the Germans' bedding. Some had razorblades bedded in potatoes. Others had filed table knives to a point or somehow managed to hide rifle bayonets down their trouser-legs. There were roughly drawn sketch maps showing a plan of the ship's interior. Other charts showed the position of the ship off Africa. The Germans had divided themselves into assault parties, each party under the command of an N.C.O.

All this had been organised by Ravenstein from the upper deck. Under Ravenstein's instructions a German doctor in the officers' quarters had asked permission to attend the German sick and this had been granted. In this way liaison was made between the officers and the troops below decks. To his first patients the doctor said, 'Go back and tell as many of your comrades as you can to report to me with colds and stomach trouble.' To each of these faked patients the doctor passed on orders, 'You will assault this companionway…you will stand here and cause a diversion…you will lead the breakthrough to the upper decks.'

Meanwhile a U-boat officer among the prisoners noted from the speed of the ship and the position of the sun that she was proceeding down the Red Sea and would be off Cape Guardafui on the third night out. He drew up charts accordingly, and the early hours of the fourth morning were selected as the time the mutiny should begin. Ravenstein's plan was very simple. Shortly after midnight a small party of the troops should cause a disturbance along the passages leading to the interior of the ship. The main body of the Germans would then rush and overwhelm the two British soldiers who guarded the two doors leading onto the open decks in the bows. Once outside it would be no difficult matter for the Germans to swarm up over three decks to the bridge and deal with the British officers on duty there. Arms would be found in the bridge.

Then the German N.C.O.'s were ordered to run across the tennis court on the boat-deck and release Ravenstein and his fellow officers. While the remainder of the British escort and the crew were being subdued, the U-boat officer would take control of the vessel and steer her into port in the Vichy- controlled island of Madagascar, which lay a few days' steaming to the south. This was the mutiny which was discovered and put down just two hours before it was to take place on *Zola's* previous voyage. This was what made the third mate spit over the side and say bitterly, 'I expect there will be more trouble.'

But there was no trouble. In the pitiless Red Sea summer glare the prisoners were stowed away. A couple of hundred South African soldiers and women volunteers who were going on leave came aboard. My wife, myself and our baby found a fairly comfortable cabin on the upper decks. We shouldered our canvas life jackets, which we were to have by us day and night for the next six weeks. We gathered in the lounge to hear a lecture on the dangers of smoking on deck at night, of leaving lighted portholes open, of being off our guard with the prisoners, of not having a convenient water bottle in case we were shipwrecked, and of all the other menaces which follow the sailor through the wartime sea.

But it was the heat that governed all our actions, the damp, exhausting Red Sea heat that throws up red spots in front of your eyes in the daytime and leaves you tossing all night in the sweaty damp sheets of your bunk. Sixty Germans between decks collapsed with heatstroke, and as their unconscious bodies were dragged out to the open decks they left behind them on the planks a thin trickle of sweat until they could sweat no more. After that the Czech doctor had to allow the prisoners on deck at night, a highly dangerous move in normal times but at this moment reasonably secure since the men simply lay about gasping and sucking at the dead air like fish that have just been brought ashore from the sea.

In the Indian Ocean the weather freshened. Across the Equator it was almost cold. Each day while the great ship rolled steeply on her beam ends the people of this little moving island grew together, and in their isolation the Germans and the South Africans and the crew came to know one another. Each morning, it seemed, one left behind a little more of the past and the habits of the land fell away. One did not even look forward very far into the future. It was sufficient to fulfil the same daily routine and let one's mind rest in a sort of suspension from the world. The ship would take one back quickly enough. You could feel it all night and all day tugging forward through this immensity of space, and since there was nothing one could do to hasten it or retard it or alter its direction, the natural instinct was to lie back passively and let the sea and the clouds go by.

We saw no other ship, no sign of land. As we crept down into the southern ocean a young albatross swung back and forth over our wake as though it were suspended from a pendulum. Sometimes I would hold my son John up to watch the flying fish spring in shoals from the crest of a wave. There was no other sign of life, and nothing anywhere to suggest that tomorrow would be any different from today or yesterday. We did not think of being torpedoed; we did not imagine we would be bombed.

We seemed to be remote not only from the war but from the peace-time world as well. Neither money nor position nor ambition nor talent could affect one's condition either way in this narrow space; and every day that went by our world grew narrower and more remote.

I imagine that a prisoner in a cell will come to feel like this, and with that idea in mind I began to watch the prisoners on board this ship. Almost imperceptibly they were changing. There was nothing much at first you could point to with certainty, but the general atmosphere of hostility was gone.

Instead of bothering to look contemptuous, the officers used their hours on deck to run and walk about. Once I found them playing hide-and-seek with John, and they seemed to be enjoying it just as much as he was.

The truth was that many on that ship were very tired. A great number had been for a year or even two years in the desert. It had been fighting without decision and without relief. It began to appear that it would go on forever, and that when the armistice came it would still find the Eighth Army and the Afrika Korps swaying back and forth over that dreary worn-out waste. In the minds of the prisoners and their gaolers there was no romance and little excitement left in the desert. Mersa Matruh, Alamein, Solium, Capuzzo, Bardia, Tobruk, Derna, Barce and Benghazi—we knew these places for what they were, broken, wretched, shell-holed villages surrounded by deep clinging dust and a stale atmosphere compounded of heat, flies, petrol fumes and boredom.

Just for a moment in the past month there had been wild hope in the Afrika Korps that they would break through to the green Nile, and there had been a proportionate despair in the British side. The fall of Tobruk had been a disaster for the British and a major triumph for the Germans. But now all that was finished, as all the other great desert moves had finished. We had thrown back the exhausted Germans from Alamein at the last moment. Living in the Alamein Line that August, I had felt again the lift and excitement of the first days of the desert war. The Germans came on again and again and we always held them, and thrust forward on our own account. But gradually that movement levelled down into a tedious war of position. It had been an overwhelming relief to leave it, to come down to the sea and get away in this ship.

More and more one felt 'All that is over and finished with. We can start a new life now— somewhere there are trees and mountains and rivers.' You could see that look forming in the faces of the Germans. They began to relax. They began to throw off the stiff military system that had hemmed in their lives since the day Hitler had marched into Poland. They began to think, and they began the process of becoming normal human beings again.

This change had not yet gone far when we reached Durban. It was winter at Durban and a cold soft rain blew across the bluff, the green headland that blankets the port. As we tied up alongside, a company of troops in battledress began to form up on the docks. These were the

Poles who by some freak of the war had been landed in South Africa on their way from Russia to England. Now they were coming aboard to take over the escort duty from the South Africans who were going ashore on their leave.

Somewhere in the changeover the trouble occurred. There was a hubbub in the middle of the night and much running along the decks and shouting. A porthole on E deck had been prised open and seventeen of the prisoners had slipped over the side into the sea. The hue and cry went on all night and all the next day. Under the ship's floodlights some of the Germans had been picked up with boathooks from the water. Others had drowned near the harbour bar or been taken by sharks. Others had got ashore on to the green headland which at that time was said to be swarming with black mamba snakes. In the end all were accounted for except six, and we sailed without them.

We turned now toward the west around the Cape of Good Hope and into that interminable expanse of the south Atlantic. All the land in the world could be lost in this one ocean, where nothing lies in a straight line between the North and the South Poles. We drove on, day after day, and for many hundreds of miles there was no land in any direction. An island was a tiny unseen speck to the west.

No U-boat had lately been heard of in these latitudes, but still we zigzagged back and forth and sent out a jagged wake behind. And still each morning at ten the ship's siren blew and we went through our lifeboat drill.

Each night the Poles would form up in line on the port deck and with their faces turned toward the sunset they sang their ancient national hymn. It was a lament that might have touched your heart anywhere. But here in this wilderness, sung by these homeless men, mere boys some of them, and without accompaniment except the sound of the waves against the ship, it had a quality of nostalgia and pathos that left you embarrassed and afraid. Each man had lost his family years ago in Poland, and now, dressed in foreign uniforms on a foreign ship, they were divided from their homes not only by the Germans, but by many thousands of miles of sea and land, and their cause looked more hopeless than ever.

The Poles were tough but very correct with the Germans. Put a young lad on sentry duty and he would never budge until he was relieved. The Germans were not allowed to smoke between decks, and one day a Bavarian N.C.O. began taunting a Polish sentry by putting a cigarette in his mouth and pretending to light it. The Pole told him to stop. The German persisted and finally struck a match. In a second the Pole had his gun in the German's back and was marching him up to the orderly room.

There was no more fooling with the Poles after that.

With the handful of British guards on board it was different. The British despite everything were very easygoing, and the Germans seemed to feel more at ease with them. One of the prisoners who had been recaptured at Durban was isolated in a cell as punishment, and he was known as a tough character. There was some surprise therefore one day when he reported to the orderly room that the British sergeant in charge of him had gone off, leaving a rifle and forty rounds of ammunition in the cell.

The Poles never relaxed on duty for an instant. Off duty they never walked about the ship. They simply lay on the deck and slept and ate or played cards quietly, and sometimes they would gather round a man who had a concertina. None of them spoke anything but Polish. They were a strange and secluded group aboard the ship, and although we all had great goodwill for them there was no real point of contact. It was just in the evening when this hymn was sung that one suddenly had a vision of the unconquerable pride that kept these men together. Some of the older men had tears in their eyes as they sang, and if you will concede that these were the tears of men who had nothing to lose except their spirit, you will understand their religious desire to kill Germans. I have seen Poles killing Germans, and they do it with the same passionless coldness with which a surgeon cuts out an ulcer. There is some motive which is beyond hate or revenge. It is a direct physical reaction, something that has made the Germans more brutal in Poland than anywhere else. In the end it is probably the primitive desire for survival.

Soon we were in the Gulf Stream. It was warmer, and clumps of gulf weed, like great bunches of bright yellow grapes, floated constantly by. Points of white phosphorus flashed away from the ship's sides like sparks from an anvil. We went into port to oil. Hills and islands sparkled in vivid sunshine on this morning, a breathtaking pleasure after so many weeks in mid-ocean. From the heights to the pavements in the town below the port glowed with light and fresh colour. We were not allowed ashore. While motor launches plied round and round the ship on the watch for Germans trying to escape overboard, we sat there all day gazing at the lovely scene.

And now at last I began to break off the remaining links that held me to the Mediterranean and the war in the Middle East. This was the New World. For nearly three years I had lived in uniform, and that alone is enough to bind you into army habits so that you do not think very much outside the army, and even the method of your thinking becomes conditioned by the routine. For most people the army is a physically better life than the life of civilian peace, but you lose your mental independence. All of us who had been in the Middle East since the beginning had increasingly felt that our lives were becoming narrower and narrower. We saw the war only from the point of view of Egypt and the desert. We felt we were missing the main thing. For years I had been writing dispatches, articles and books for people I had never seen and whose reactions were almost unknown to me. England was a blur on my memory. I had missed the blitz. America I had never seen. For a long time we had been getting tantalising scraps of information about the great changes that were going on in England and America. It was said there was a great left-wing movement in Britain; that the whole country had swung over to a pro-Russian line. The steel mills and assembly lines of America were simply fables in our minds, things of which we heard with wonder because they were utterly new and we had no points of comparison and assessment. We had seen the American guns fire often enough, but who made them and how many, and when would the new machines they spoke about be delivered?

Above all this, how was the war going to be fought? Were we going to flounder on forever in the desert, getting nowhere? They spoke of a second front from England, but where was it? Where were the Americans going to throw their full weight—in the Pacific or Europe? There were whispers from time to time that Africa and the Mediterranean were going to be made a major front, but you could never believe this entirely any more than you could believe the stories of a new landing in Norway.

It was exasperating never to know for certain. For years it seemed we had blundered on in the darkness, and inevitably a phobia sprang up in our minds that there was no direction anywhere, no plan for the war and no hard prospects for the peace.

And so this was for me a voyage of personal discovery, a voyage round the world to find out what was happening and where the orders were coming from and who was giving them.

I believed in the African war; I knew or thought I knew that if we had enough arms we could clear the Mediterranean and get at Europe through France, Italy and the Balkans at far less cost than by making a frontal assault from England.

433

There were a thousand things I wanted to know and experience, and somehow I felt that I was going to get the answers in America and Britain. For the first time I felt that the story was about to unfold, and I began to look forward to the next few months with the excitement of a child watching the curtain go up on his first pantomime.

That night *Zola* ran out into the Atlantic again and turned north. We had heard many stories of U-boats ranging these seas, but after so many weeks it was impossible to believe that this safe, fast ship would be attacked. They say the crew of a bomber after a number of trips become convinced that their machine is lucky and will never be shot down. Something of the same thought enters the nature of the sailor at sea and he seals up his mind against the prospect of shipwreck.

At all events we saw nothing as we came through this dangerous bit, and in weather that got steadily fresher we passed along the coast of the United States and turned at last toward Halifax in Nova Scotia—our journey's end.

By now the prisoners had become entirely part of the ship's life. We would have missed them had we not seen them exercising on the deck in the morning. We got to know them individually by sight— the short flaxen-haired gunnery officer with the knee-boots, the serious dark-haired group who always played some game with their strange and gay German cards, the Luftwaffe pilot who kept a little apart, the younger ones who could scarcely have been twenty and who used to practise jumps over one of the hawsers. As soon as they filed out from the dim interior of the ship onto the bright deck they smiled and looked at the sea. Then, since they were not allowed to carry matches, they thronged round the British guards to get lights for their cigarettes. The guards and the prisoners had grown through habit to know one another well enough for them to communicate by signs and broken words.

Once the prisoners had complained that their rations were not good enough, but it was not a bitter or mutinous complaint—just the sort of complaint that a group of boarders will make to the landlady at a holiday pension.

God knows we all got tired of the food, but it was still much better than the food in England. I went down to the prisoners' quarters one day, and tasted the meat and vegetable stew and the rice and stewed fruit. There was white bread and occasionally fresh fruit from the refrigerators.

When we had got aboard at Suez only one man, an avowed anti-Nazi, would give his parole that he would not attempt to escape. He was made into a dishwasher and kept apart from his fellow prisoners lest they should molest him. But now the Germans were all willing enough to help with the work.

They were divided into a score or so of 'messes' of about twenty or thirty men each. Each mess appointed its leader, who was responsible for keeping order and getting the men's quarters cleaned out each morning. Two men from each mess collected the food at mealtimes from the galleys, and Germans volunteered to work in the galleys as well.

For the most part they kept their quarters spotlessly clean and most of the men shaved regularly. Their talk now had drifted away from the desert and the war. Mostly they liked to discuss how it would be in camp in Canada, whether they would be able to send and receive mail, what clothes they would be issued with and what the food would be like ashore. They began to look forward to Canada with interest and even pleasure.

One day they sent up word to the orderly room that they had an excellent pianist among their number and they would like to provide a concert for the British officers. All this was a long way from the sort of atmosphere in which we had set out from Suez.

Off Newfoundland we plunged into the heavy fog that hangs off the coast in the late summer. This fog is dangerous, since it lies across one of the busiest sea lanes in the Atlantic and it can descend out of a clear sky within half an hour. Long before we picked up the pilot from Halifax we were creeping very slowly through the grey, wet mist and all around us the sudden eerie blare of foghorns kept sounding. We knew that we had to pass the noise of these foghorns that float at the approaches to the harbour, and for a time we heard them, steadily moaning drawn-out blasts that seemed somehow to accentuate the weight and mystery of the fog. But then other foghorns, coming from many different directions and never remaining in the one place, began to rise and fall over the calm water. These were other ships and they were close. Every available officer on *Zola* stood round the bridge peering vainly through the mist that sometimes lifted for a quarter of a mile and then abruptly closed in again.

Without warning the fog dissipated entirely and the bright sun poured down on the sea like a spotlight coming from the wings of an immense theatre. Within a split second the captain was shouting orders. Ships were all around us. One freighter was right under our bows. Behind them the green cliffs of Halifax glowed strongly in yellow light. We were passing straight through the middle of a convoy setting out for England.

At six or seven knots a great liner answers with painful sluggishness to the helm. There was the freighter a few yards away, a tiny matchbox on the sea; here were *Zola*'s hundred-foot grey bows bearing down on it and there was nothing much anyone could do. I, for one, just stood there holding my breath. Then the freighter vanished from my sight under the bows. We waited. Then the freighter slid out the other side. She trailed a fog-line behind her and this we sliced in half. For a full minute it was possible to look down onto the freighter's decks and see the scared and working face of the commander on his little wooden bridge. He had hoisted a rope-ball to his masthead, which is the signal that a ship is out of control. With that signal aloft the freighter's captain knew that we would be held responsible for any damage that occurred; but who cares for responsibility at the moment of disaster? Can the falling parachutist argue with the manufacturer who supplies him with a parachute that won't open? So, as the tension broke on our bridge, we laughed in a mixture of callousness and relief at the freighter's distress signals.

But still there were other ships all around us. I began to count them and got to six, and suddenly the fog slid down again and where there had been ships now only the angry groan of moving foghorns sounded. In and out of gloom we edged toward the harbour mouth and back into the sunshine. An unemotional pilot took us in. That night while we tied up alongside the railway station there was tremendous commotion on board. The prisoners were to be taken off in the morning. They had to be counted, searched once more and drafted section by section onto a waiting Canadian train. The sick had to be carried ashore.

All the next morning I watched the Germans filing off. They stood in long lines spiralling down the main staircase leading to the gangway, each man with his pack on his back and his prisoner's card in his hand. The prisoners were in high spirits. One flaxen-haired boy winked broadly at my wife, the only woman on board since leaving Durban. You could hardly believe that these were the same men who had fought so bitterly in the desert. They were eager to get ashore, and they kept laughing and making jokes among themselves as they waited.

A ship bringing the wrecked survivors from a convoy which had been attacked outside Halifax a few days before slid into a berth beside us. Haggard-looking women and despondent men with blankets round their shoulders looked across to the prisoners on *Zola* with bitterness and hatred.

There was one last little incident. All the German troops got off first and this left no one to carry the German officers' luggage. (Under the Hague convention captured officers are entitled to have their bags carried.) With a tactlessness that passed all belief the British officer asked the Poles to carry the baggage. He might as well have asked the survivors from the convoy. The Poles refused point-blank.

Now this sort of argument and misunderstanding had been growing aboard *Zola*. There were many differences between the crew, the British escort, and the Poles. While the prisoners had grown more quiescent, the men set to guard them had fallen out with one another. While the Germans in defeat and captivity had been drawn more closely together, we, the victors, were finding points of difference in our victory. It had been like that too at Versailles at the end of the other war. But no one on board was willing to create an incident at this moment, and so the British Tommies were ordered to take the German luggage ashore.

First came the German officers, after them the Tommies lumping their suitcases—and the language of the Tommies was a thing to marvel at. They were angry with the Germans, angry with the Poles, and most of all angry to the point of mutiny with their own officers. It was a slight and silly incident, one of those little things that make men hate the army. A British corporal paused on the gangway and deliberately dropped one of the German suitcases over the side. No one spoke. No officer cared to raise his voice. The corporal, a man with his soul refreshed, continued with dignity up the gangway.

Two

New York

THEY WERE putting the last touches to the North African plan when I arrived in America, and a strange business it was.

While half the newspapers of the country were shouting for a second front the thing was being organised in an atmosphere of secrecy that you would not have thought possible in a democracy. Already, in October, the troops had sailed from the United States, the tanks and guns had been allotted, and the deal with the French generals had been signed, sealed and delivered.

But the country knew nothing of all this. Even in the train journey from Halifax to New York I felt the unrest and discontent at the way the war was going. As the rich pine forests and the lakes of Nova Scotia went past, the man in the next compartment was saying: 'Why don't they DO something? What's wrong with them? Why can't they start a second front?'

There had indeed been no good news for a year.

In the Pacific it had been one calamity after another; Pearl Harbour and Singapore, the sinking of the *Prince of Wales* and the cutting of the Burma Road. Nor had our occasional naval successes been able to stop the Japanese avalanche that swept on over Malaya and Java, Borneo and the Philippines, Burma and New Guinea. Even now things were going badly for the marines on Guadalcanal.

In India the Cripps negotiations had crashed and in the bitter political shambles that followed there was shooting in the streets of Bombay and Calcutta, and sabotage all the way across the peninsula.

Tobruk had surrendered, the worst humiliation in the desert war, and at any moment it seemed likely that Rommel might fling the British out of the Middle East altogether.

The U-boat war had touched its climax. One submarine penetrated far up the St Lawrence. Another destroyed an Allied ship off Long Island, and there was a long list of sinkings right down the eastern American seaboard.

Dieppe, with the swift loss of more than half the British expedition, seemed merely to prove that we could not invade Europe.

The Red armies were reeling back in the face of one massed German offensive after another. The Ukraine was overrun as far as the Caucasus and the Volga; and now the last buildings in Stalingrad were being demolished.

Nowhere on the whole globe was there any real progress or indeed any real sign that the rot would ever stop.

All this was reflected in the harshest possible lines about the time I reached New York, toward the end of September 1942. Morale during bad times is nearly always lowest at the base and highest at the front. I knew that. But for me there had been no chance to make a gradual adjustment in my mind.

I had come straight from the Western Desert, one of the remotest and most changeable of all the fronts. The intervening period at sea had been a vacuum. And now I stepped suddenly into the biggest of all the rear bases, and the shock was much greater than it would otherwise have been.

Everywhere I went people seemed to be gripped by the same sense of irritation and frustration. It made no difference whether you talked to a cab driver on Fifth Avenue or a businessman just in from the Middle West. They were in the war but not of it. They were beginning to suffer the discomforts of war without seeing any definite result. The papers were full of war talk and the streets full of slogans, but where was the action? Where was the money going? Production was coming along fine, but what happened to all the thousands of tanks and guns and jeeps? Why didn't somebody use them? Were the Russians the only people who could fight?

Every stop in the propaganda organ had been pulled out wide in praise of the American soldier.

There was religious fervour in the phrase 'our boys', and while you could criticise everything else on earth even the most hard-boiled columnist or politician would never dare to question the skill and courage of the American soldier. But the ugly, unthinkable thing that nobody dared mention was beginning to creep into the back of people's minds. Did the nation really want to fight? Were not the Germans and the Japs really better soldiers? Look what was happening on Guadalcanal…

And because this suspicion was unthinkable, and I imagine the people in their hearts knew it to be untrue, they vented their discontent with twice the force in other directions. The leadership was wrong, they argued. Washington was a hell's kitchen of double-dealing politicians and war profiteers. The cynicism about Washington was so intense it was bewildering. That was the place where rogues bribed one another to get government contracts, where foreigners intrigued, where men bought themselves out of active service, where fools and incompetents were falling over one another in every government department. American boys were paying with their lives for the mistakes made in the White House. The navy was at loggerheads with the army. There were rows with Russia, rows with Britain, rows with the Chinese. Big business was piling up more big business for after the war.

The draft was crooked. The whole thing was crooked and there was no firm direction anywhere.

What was needed, one was told, was more honest-to-God Americanism in America, and especially in Washington. Once let the Americans get started and they would see this thing through by themselves.

Because they had never seen war, and had been brought up to hate it and fear it more than disease, more even than poverty, many of the people I met imagined it to be far worse than it is. In the absence of facts and in the presence of lurid, exciting propaganda, people's minds were beginning to fill with horrible images—the raped girl in Tokyo, the dying soldier in the mud, the tortured face of the sailor going down for the last time, the blazing homestead and the mother fleeing with her children from the monstrous Jap. These were the subjects of the posters and the daily cartoons, and all the time the long horror of Stalingrad went on, making these images seem all too real.

Nothing it seemed was being done to get on with the war—that was the thing. The boys were being sacrificed without reason, without direction and without care. Unless there was a second front soon, the war might go on forever.

I do not suggest that these feelings were universal or even obvious. I simply say that within a few minutes of talking with the average citizen you began to sense his underlying discontent. It was the same discontent and uncertainty that had assailed every country in Europe on the eve of going into action, the same fear that attacks a patient on his way to the dentist. They say there is no moment for the soldier which is worse than that short period of nervous tension before he goes over the top. Once in action his mind clears and his courage leaps up. To a stranger, America appeared to have reached that difficult moment just before going over the top.

Meanwhile in Washington the plans went steadily forward. Newspaper friends took me to one of Mr Cordell Hull's conferences at the State Department, alongside the White House. The secretary stood patiently behind his chair, and he had the air of a man who feels he is about to say No to a lot of questions which have been asked him many times before.

'Is there any change in our relations with Vichy?' someone asked.

'I have nothing more to add,' said the secretary, and waited for the next question.

There were, of course, the most violent changes with Vichy going on behind the scenes. The matter had been most carefully discussed with Winston Churchill on his visit to Washington in the previous July, at the time of the fall of Tobruk. As the prime minister has since revealed, that conference was the seed of the whole North African adventure— the conference that decided the Americans to put their main effort first into Europe and let the Japanese war wait; the conference that settled the blow should fall in the Mediterranean and that the Vichy generals (and not de Gaulle) should be asked to cooperate in the landing.

One can imagine the prime minister's arguments. Since the days of the Gallipoli landing in the last war he had been an ardent devotee of the Mediterranean policy—of the policy of fighting the war on long lines of communication. Since 1918 he had argued at length and with reason that had the Gallipoli campaign been pressed home it would have considerably shortened the last war by throwing Turkey out of the struggle and opening up a supply line to Russia.

Clearly Churchill had argued these points again in Washington. Just as urgently as in 1915–16 we needed a strong high-road into Russia through the Mediterranean. The Persian and Murmansk routes were slow, difficult and dangerous. Once take the whole North African coast and our shipping tonnage on the Russian supply route would double, since each ship would do two journeys where it had done only one before. Moreover, continuous air cover could be given right down the Mediterranean to the disembarkation points of Haifa, Beyrout and Syrian Tripoli. Not only could we supply Russia rapidly that way, but we could build up a great army in Syria and Palestine for an eventual attack on the Balkans. Turkey was another prize. If she could be induced to come in, Allied vessels could ply through the Dardanelles right up to the Black Sea.

It was a bold and attractive scheme and it required much political preparation. That was where Mr Adolf Berle of the State Department came in. Mr Berle was in charge of French relations. There was already a chain of American representatives and agents through unoccupied France and North Africa. Now, the State Department believed that the way of resurrecting France lay not through General de Gaulle and the Communists and the underground irredentist movements in France, but through France's existing leaders, who were either in prison in Germany or in the service of the Vichy government in France. True, these Frenchmen were not on the whole well disposed towards the British— the battles of Oran and Dakar had never been forgiven—but at least they were friendly to the Americans. The de Gaullist movement had become pretty well a British movement. It had never been regarded with much sympathy in Washington. De Gaulle seemed to have blundered badly in his Dakar expedition, and it was not at all clear what sort of following he had in France.

To the Americans it was all too painfully obvious that de Gaulle had been repulsed in Syria and Jibuti, and indeed almost everywhere he went. Marshal Pétain was still the leader of France, and it was among the marshal's followers, men like Weygand and Giraud and Georges, that the chief hope of advantage lay. Furthermore, de Gaulle was not on the spot and the Vichy leaders were. They had control in North Africa.

There was no frame, no established head of the de Gaullist movement in France and—so one imagines the State Department arguing—there was neither the time nor the means to contact those who regarded the Fighting French movement as their salvation. Far better to win over the Darlans and Girauds, and once in the Allied camp they could be induced to sink their differences with the British. Moreover, once the Vichy government in North Africa came over, you had a working system of government in operation. To put in de Gaulle would mean a political and economic upheaval at the best, and a revolution at the worst. You could do very little work for his cause on the inside until the actual landing took place.

Undeniably the State Department was determined to act in the best way for all concerned.

Undeniably the British and American military leaders on both sides of the Atlantic supported the department's plans for white-anting Vichy rather than raise the standard of rebellion for de Gaulle, since the former move entailed the least military risk. It meant that America was going to raise her own French champion to replace de Gaulle, that America, not Britain, was going to take the dominant political and economic rôle in France not only during the war but afterwards. (Unless, of course, that very elusive imponderable, the Soviet government, had something to say about it.) At any rate, Mr Churchill gave his assent to the deal, a school of American army officers who were to be the future gauleiters of France was set up in the United States, and many a mysterious messenger set off for North Africa and unoccupied France.

So already, in the summer, six months before the North African landing took place, de Gaulle had apparently lost his cause. He was never informed of the preparations. He only heard officially of the landing after it had taken place. To many it seemed that something else was lost at that momentous conference in Washington. It seemed that the fine clear edge of our policy was blunted. We were prepared from now on to parley with the enemy, or at least with those who had been forced to go over to the enemy. We were ready to make concessions. To save the lives of our soldiers we were ready to stretch a point or two in the Atlantic Charter. We still wanted freedom of worship and freedom of race in the world; but if we could gain a short-range military advantage by treating with men who had helped to frame Vichy's anti-Jewish laws, then the end justified the means.

People were saying that de Gaulle before this had damaged his own position by maintaining a pretty stiff and intransigent manner in

London. A black mark was recorded against the de Gaullists for allowing out the secret of the Dakar expedition before the ships had arrived at their destination. But for two years his name had gone out over the radio day and night, and it stood for the ideals of anti- Fascism, of democracy, of the willingness to fight on for principles. We had yet to discover how deep an impression this had made inside Europe and Africa. De Gaulle himself might not be the ideal leader, but his name stood for something. It had become a sort of trademark for liberty. Well, from now on the firm was under new management.

All this time, while all these plans were going forward in secret, the Roosevelt administration was under constant fire. Why no second front? Even Charlie Chaplin came to New York and made a speech calling for a second front. Mr Wendell Willkie, hot from his flight round the world, demanded action. And still people asked, Why do we continue relations with Vichy, which is collaborating with America's enemies? Why don't we recognise de Gaulle?

On the morning of November 8th all the answers came suddenly together. American troops under General Eisenhower had landed in North Africa. Not Dakar, as it was whispered, but Casablanca, Oran and Algiers, which were right on the road to southern Europe. The president had sent a letter to the Bey of Tunis and Tunis was expected to fall at any moment. I was in New York when the news broke, and the effect on the people was electric. They snatched at the newspapers and they hung around their radio sets. They were aglow with the news. America was in it at last. At last we had a second front. At last we were hitting back. Hurrah for the American army, hurrah for Roosevelt and hurrah for the State Department, which in its deep wisdom had kept up relations with Vichy so the boys could make an easy landing.

So it was going to be war in Europe and war from Africa. Knock the Boches out first then all the Allies would turn on Japan together. There was pride and excitement and strong hope on that day.

A fortnight before the landing I had been urgently summoned to London by air. Unknown to me I had been chosen to go down to Africa with the invading troops as a war correspondent for the British press, but bad weather held up my departure from America until it was too late. Now I had to follow as quickly as I could.

I did not want to go. I had discovered the answers to some of my personal questions, but these two months in America had been too rushed, too bewildering and too complicated.

I had seen very little really and probably understood still less. I had developed strong prejudices too quickly. As I packed my baggage I found my mind a confused blur of many chance memories.

The livid golden flood of molten metal pouring from the buckets in the steel foundries; the great sheets of glowing metal roaring through the rollers; the new ships sliding sideways into the Ohio River to make their way two thousand miles down the Mississippi to the sea; the bright clatter of the aircraft plants and the uniformed women on the assembly line snatching at bullets and shells and gadgets while all above them and around them the coloured posters shouted 'Don't Let Them Down,' 'Produce for Victory,' 'Put Ten Per Cent into War Savings.'

There was the monstrous pentagon building across the Potomac at Washington, where I walked a mile and a quarter from the front door to the department I wanted; the squirrels playing in front of the White House as the president drove in; the shocking sight of the burnt-out *Normandie* lying like a beached whale under Manhattan's skyscrapers; the overcrowded trains full of plump men hurrying down to Washington with little leather cases under their arms; the Red Birds returning home from their triumph in the World Series to meet an hysterical crowd at St Louis railway station; Gypsy Rose Lee doing an act called 'I Can't Strip to Brahms.'

Grand Central and the Bronx, that fantastic vision of New York from the Triborough Bridge and the long beautiful drive home in the evening through the autumn colours of the Hudson River; the hellish underground and the hellish overhead; Broadway at six and dinner at eight, sixty-five storeys up; the streets that were German, the cities within New York that were Italian or Jewish, Polish or Czech, Chinese or Negro.

No, it was all much too much. To a stranger there was no cohesion anywhere and the geographical cult of Americanism seemed too new and too superficial to have found its roots. Yet it was there.

I had, too, a strong feeling that there was something wrong about this sudden universal optimism just as there had been something wrong with the earlier pessimism. I had not been in New York nearly long enough to assess the alternative moods that swept the people from one enthusiasm to another with the regularity of the rise and fall of the tide around Manhattan Island; nor had I time to probe deep enough and find something as solid underneath as the seabed.

The most conflicting and improbable news was pouring out of Africa, and, with the exception of one or two military commentators like Hansen Baldwin, the newspaper strategists were discussing the war in a way that bore no relation whatever to the Mediterranean as I knew it. Montgomery's victory at Alamein was now complete. Benghazi was about to fall. The current view of the newspapers was that the British forces from the desert would join hands with the American forces from Algeria within the next few weeks—or days.

The Americans would take Tripoli and, proceeding out into the desert, would scoop up Rommel's retreating Afrika Korps. The meeting between the British and American armies would take place somewhere round the middle of the Gulf of Sirte. Every newspaper published maps showing great arrows pointing across the Mediterranean into Italy, the Balkans and France. Little by little the remarkable story began to come out of how the American fifth column had been organised in France and North Africa, of General Mark Clark's secret and dangerous landing for a rendezvous with the French leaders, of how the United States minister Robert Murphy had sounded out the French generals and brought them to our side, of how we had the great fortune to get Admiral Darlan, and of General Giraud's submarine journey from France. More and more it began to look like the biggest diplomatic coup of the war. France was rising again.

Well, at least I was being given a chance of seeing it. I went down to Grand Central Station for the last time and took the train northward.

At Montreal the first bitter wind of the coming winter was blowing through the streets. It was Armistice Day and a little procession of old soldiers in civilian clothes and young ones in uniform marched down to the war memorial in the central square. The cold was intense. It was agony to stand still for two minutes while the Last Post sounded and the noise of the city fell eerily away. For anyone of my generation it was almost impossible to respond to a ceremony for a war that was finished and fruitless.

The big Liberator bomber smashed through the iced puddles of the airfield as we took off for Scotland. There were sixteen of us, all buttoned up to the eyebrows in helmets, knee-boots, fleece- lined overalls, parachutes, water wings and oxygen masks. We lay full length on the floor so tightly packed that if you decided to turn over, the men on either side of you had to turn as well. Thus, for ten hours over the Atlantic. A miserable, uncomfortable night. We flew only at eight thousand feet because the weather was good, and so needed no oxygen; but it was unbearably hot with all our additional clothing. We were a strange collection—a brigadier, an English peer who had been buying American aircraft, an American armour expert, a Dutch policeman who had escaped from Holland, a fighter pilot and so on. It was the brigadier, if I remember rightly, who was lying on my right side. By accident I pulled the plug in his water wings during the feverish early morning hours and they automatically filled with air. And there he lay quite unable to deflate himself until we slid down on the green, green coast of Scotland.

Three

London

IT WAS eight o'clock on a bright fresh winter's morning when we landed. Within half an hour we had been helped out of our flying kit, passed through the customs and the immigration authorities, given coffee, a bedroom and a bathroom and told breakfast would be ready whenever we wanted it. An

R.A.F. officer said that if we had really urgent business in London he would have us flown down; otherwise sleepers were booked on the overnight train. A girl in W.A.A.F. uniform offered to send cables for us. Another changed dollars for pounds.

One blinked a little dazedly at all this. Since the war began I had travelled many scores of thousands of miles, but nowhere else in the world had there been such efficiency, such courtesy and precision.

True, we were rather rare birds, coming in by air across the Atlantic and travelling on high priority. But still it was remarkable, this atmosphere. The place was alive. The people looked healthy. They were all busy. They were cheerful and there was something else, especially in the faces of the girls, a steadiness, something clear-cut and definite. They were not so pretty as the American women, not nearly so smart, though their complexions were better.

Like nearly everything else in Britain, from the London underground to the British constitution, this airport was the result of a series of compromises and makeshifts. The landing fields were once the fairways of a golf course. The bunkers had been wired off and turned into weapon pits for the anti- aircraft guns. The clubhouse had become the headquarters. There were more aircraft standing about than I had seen in the whole of the Middle East during the first year of war. Every few minutes another military machine swept down from America, from southern England, possibly from France and Germany.

I wandered about in a daze of sentimental memories; Scotland as it was before the war, when I had last seen it. That was gone, of course, but here was the same wet moss on the earthen walls of the country lane, the same grey-white gulls following the ploughman through the field, the same blurred, misty outlines and the incredible greenness of Scotland. For three years, from Gibraltar to New Delhi, I had seen nothing but sharp horizons and strident colours, except very occasionally in the desert at noon when the sand turned into the mirage of an undulating lake. Here every colour was soft and gentle, and one marvelled that one had forgotten this so completely.

Travelling all that night by train to London, I had a bedroom to myself, an air-conditioned bedroom with hot water and a proper bed, and tea in the morning—things you cannot get as a rule in America.

London outwardly was no shock. It had been described to me over and over again by friends who had been in the blitz, so I knew where to look for the holes in the lines of the buildings and the broken churches, and I found them to be just what I expected, bad scars that were healing over. But in the inner workings of London, in its atmosphere and tempo, I found one astonishing thing after another.

The buses careered at speed through the blackout, keeping to a timetable. There were three or four postal deliveries a day. I took a taxi down to Westminster and within an hour had collected all the wartime documents necessary to live in England—ration book, identity card, clothing coupons (plus some additional coupons because I had arrived by air) and registration certificate. There was no queueing up, no waiting, and no hurry. These things were handed out as part of a steady and precise routine.

That night the worst fog in years closed down over the Thames valley. I had accepted two invitations—one for dinner in Battersea, the other for a late party in Kensington—not knowing that most Londoners did not go out at night in winter now because of the sheer difficulty of getting transport. But in my ignorance I set out on this worst of all nights. My taxi got as far as the river before it ran out of petrol and I changed over to a bus that was going vaguely in my direction through the impenetrable gloom. Then I changed over to a tram that ran off the rails on a corner. The passengers with one accord jumped out and lifted the tram back on the rails.

Over dinner—wine, fish and fruit—the conversation was exciting and it was not about the war. Dr Temple, the Archbishop of Canterbury, had made another speech insisting that the Church should concern itself in government, that the banks must be nationalised and that there should be more equal distribution of wealth and land after the war. It sounded more like the Communist Manifesto than the Primate of England, but there it was, and that was not all. The report of Sir William Beveridge was about to be presented in the House. It proposed a scheme by which no man need ever again starve in England, nor fall ill without medical treatment, nor fail to get decent burial when he died. It sounded more like the millennium than the British Conservative Party at work.

Everywhere in the pubs and the factories people were discussing these things. As they worked on munitions, as they trained in the camps or plodded about on A.R.P. jobs at night, they thought about them. The most popular feature on the radio was the Brains Trust. Miraculously the people seemed to know all the placenames of the obscure battlefields in the desert.

By some stroke of good luck a taxi rank sent a taxi for me through the fog and we asked the driver inside for a drink by the fire. He was a wizened little Cockney of sixty, scarf round his neck, cloth cap perched across his head. He had fought through Palestine and Mesopotamia in the last war and in a minute he was down on the floor fighting the battles again with empty beer bottles, comparing those campaigns to these, matching Allenby's strategy with Alexander's.

No fog could baulk this old soldier who had his son in the army abroad and his two daughters working in munitions plants. As we drove on to Kensington I walked ahead with my torch to light him through the worst bits of fog or perched beside him while he furiously discussed the theory of fighting a war on long lines of communications.

And so we wandered through London that night and back to the West End. All through November I travelled about the city and southern England learning and learning, trying to catch up with the tremendous upheavals of thought that had been going on since the blitz. There were only about ten hours of these short winter days when you could meet people, but in that time I contrived to be with as many as possible, politicians and journalists, factory girls and actresses, soldiers and airmen, publishers and stockbrokers. I knew I had to go to North Africa very soon, and there was so much to learn here in such little time.

I went down for a week to see the new British army in training. There was a day when the airborne division put on a full-scale exercise. In a bare and frigid building the pilots sat in a semicircle round a relief map of the terrain on which they were going to drop their troops. It was the same room in which they had been briefed for their drops on Bruneval in occupied France and in Tunisia and Algeria and later in Sicily.

Then we trooped out to the gliders. They were as big as heavy bombers. They carried complete hospitals, lorry-loads of ammunition, workshops, motorcycles, water tanks and men. Each glider was attached by a rope and a telephone line to a bomber. The bombers were warming up, and as we sat waiting the slack on the rope was gradually taken up. The machines went careering forward across the hilltop. Ours was a beautiful take-off. For two or three hundred yards my glider was bumping and wheezing across the rough ground until we were suddenly being towed into mid-air. After travelling so often in aeroplanes, the sensation I had in this glider was that I had moved from a motor boat into a yacht. The wind screamed past, but it was an easy swinging motion. We rode just above the bomber's slipstream and about two thousand feet up through drifting cloud. Over the objective the bomber increased speed. The two pilots—one in the bomber, the other in the glider—checked their position and then we cut the towrope adrift. The glider banked steeply and sailed swiftly down between two copses of beech trees. We hit hard and ran to a standstill in twenty seconds.

All round us men were tumbling out of other gliders. Parachutists were falling and machine-gun shots began sounding round the ring of hills. One glider, landing too steeply, had startled the daylights out of a couple of A.T.S. girls on the ground, and they raced for cover with the glider in pursuit until its wing hit a brick wall. No one was hurt. Other parachutists, lost in the rain, fell on the wrong places or failed to jump at all. Things, in fact, were going wrong just as they always do on the real battlefield, and the test was now whether the men could improvise and make good their mistakes.

There were many brass hats from the War Office watching that day, and they piled into about fifty jeeps to keep up with the exercise. The men who had landed were attacking a low hill through woodland. A good concentrated mortar fire whistled over our heads and from half a dozen directions men came running with machine-guns and hand grenades. They flung themselves prone on the grass every few yards and fired.

At each stage the spectators rushed forward in the jeeps, a wild cavalcade across the fields, and for a time we were hopelessly mixed up with the mock battle. Tracers began skidding past on either side of the jeeps, and in their excitement the jeep drivers kept right up with the forward machine- gunners. The advancing infantry had been told to keep hard up against the shifting line on which the mortar shells were landing, a difficult and dangerous thing to do. The machine-gunners were all the time firing through their own men to protect them up to the edge of the wood. At the wood itself the infantry ran in with tommy-guns. It was very exciting. I closed my eyes when my jeep ran over a grenade that had been flung out a second before and failed to explode. Beyond the wood a bangalore torpedo tore up a slice of wet turf and barbed wire from the ground and a great smoke-ring hung in the air for a moment. Through this the flamethrowers ran to their last objective, and the hill, it was judged, was ours.

These things are not so difficult when there is no fire coming at you, and when men are not dropping out through injury and death. But what a difference from the plodding infantry exercises of three years before. What months and years of training lived in these boys so that they did, in fact, without flinching, keep up with the line of falling mortars. And with only a safety margin of a yard or two, they were willing to run up the line of their own machine-gun fire.

I did not then believe that gliders are an effective instrument except in certain very occasional situations. But these soldiers did believe in them. They did want to fight. They enjoyed it. They believed they were taking part in a great experiment which was to lead to the Wellsian battles of the future.

Another day I joined a battle school. The idea of the battle school was General Alexander's. After their normal training, as many N.C.O.'s and officers as possible went off on three weeks' special training which duplicates war as nearly as possible. On this wet morning the men made a landing before dawn. With smoke bombs and hand grenades falling around them, they rushed the beach. Then they fought their way inland across streams and through hedgerows and farmyards. I can hardly say I enjoyed that day. Once I went down to my thighs in icy mud. Once I was covered with muck from a nearby grenade-burst. When the troops wanted to go through a ten-foot hawthorn hedge they did not hunt for gaps, they walked straight through the thorns. All day until dusk they were at it without food, without rest. They ran and shot and climbed walls with their full equipment until they were tired into speechlessness. At the end of each stage they were called together, told what they had done wrong and then two new students were ordered to lead the next assault. They would simply be given a reference on the map, told roughly what resistance was there and ordered to take the place. Crawling on their bellies, they reconnoitred the farmhouses and the barns. Dropping into ditches and swarming over brick walls, they went in for the mopping-up.

Normally there is something phoney, amateurish and childish about army field exercises, a sort of boy scoutery that sits oddly upon grown men. But not here. This was tough and uncomfortable and extraordinarily real. It was a tremendous advance since the days of the crushing boredom of route marches and parade-ground drill. The enthusiasm was the surprising thing. By some chemistry these youths had been taken from the suburban milk rounds and the city shops and made physically bigger and mentally much more alert. They clutched at any information. I once casually said something about the dispersal of vehicles on convoy. A colonel at once shoved me into an aircraft and, piloting the thing himself, swept me back and forth over his battalion for half an hour to have my opinion on whether they were correctly spaced apart or not. Feeling giddy and far from expert, I shouted that it was first-class, but he continued tree-hopping for another ten minutes before he was satisfied. Clearly these troops were fit for the conquest of Africa and the invasion of Europe.

And so for three weeks I went round England convinced that such a renaissance had overtaken this country as had not happened at least in my lifetime. Just as my first impression of America had been one of confusion and cynicism, so in England it was one of direction and enthusiasm. Both were wrong—at least in part.

Little by little I began to see that. Everything was not all wrong in America, nor was everything all right here. It was during the first days of December, while I was waiting in London for my sailing orders to go down to North Africa, that I began to see the gaps and the wastage in this new England.

The people were tired. No victory in Stalingrad, no breakthrough by the Eighth Army and no landing in North Africa could overnight shake them out of the strain of three years' garrison life in England. Casualties were very few as yet, but many thousands of families had not seen their menfolk for years. Food was sufficient, but it was boring, and beyond everything the abiding interest in everyone's life was food, food, food, how to cook it and how to get it and how to conserve it. Almost every conversation I had was eventually brought round to the subject of food. (It was strange and refreshing to find that the one cabinet minister who was wholeheartedly approved of was Lord Woolton, the minister of food. Woolton had an engaging way of coming on the air from the B.B.C. as soon as some major mess-up occurred like the fish zoning. 'I know the trouble you are having,' he would say. 'It's an awful mess. But we are clearing it up and it won't happen again.')

More people were getting higher wages than they had ever had before, but there was little of any real value you could buy for it. Everyone had work, but it was high-pressure work that went on in endless drudgery, nine, ten or twelve hours a day, six days a week, with fire-watching and other wartime duties on top of it. Women, after a long day in the factory, had to face up to the difficult journey home in the dark, standing in food queues, and the feeding of their children.

There was enough housing for everyone, but most people were cramped for space and decent household facilities were disappearing. If the spouting began to leak, you could get no one to repair it. For almost all the little necessities of life there was a day-long struggle that never let up. Since little or no repairs or painting were being done, every city in England began to look shabby, so that the people were constantly surrounded by ugliness and the atmosphere of neglect and decay. The people themselves were growing shabbier. They were ageing. Young girls leaving school who could normally look forward to the gayest and best time of their lives had never known what it was to put on a party frock and a pair of silk stockings. They felt their youth and attractiveness were fading away in the omnipresent greyness of England and the war.

Nor did things seem quite so bright to me in political England as I had at first thought they were. The Beveridge Report was tabled, but by no means was it adopted. Huge powerful interests like the insurance companies banded against it. Most of the report was supported by the government, but in such a confusing way that half the country had no idea of whether or not they were going to get jobs after the war, which was the real thing they wanted to know. And Beveridge wrote in one of the Sunday papers, 'My principles of security and freedom from want have been abandoned.'

Dr Temple was sharply attacked. The Church was the Church, he was told, and it had no place in politics, let alone revolutionary politics.

Since November I had walked each day through a square in London. When I first arrived I noticed that the iron railings around the gardens had been torn down for salvage and that anyone in London could now walk across those once private lawns and let their children play under the trees. Now, in December, a spiked wooden fence had been placed around the park. And after the war? Would the steel railings come back?

Friends began to explain to me the technique of the rackets and the black markets. Everyone, it seemed, had some sort of small graft; indeed, half of life was spent in working out just how you could pull a string here and exert a little influence there and get an extra bottle of gin over at the other place.

But it was upon North Africa that the public was now concentrating with growing suspicion and uneasiness. Something was being done down there which they did not understand. Why was Darlan in charge?— the professional Britain-hater, the turncoat admiral, the friend of Laval and the German collaborationist. Why were these de Gaullists who had helped us land suddenly clapped into prison? Were we going to advance on one place after another in Europe, raising up Quislings as we went?

The Allied foreigners in England, like the Norwegians, looked on these proceedings with bewilderment. Why stop at Darlan, they said? Why not buy over Quisling himself? Why not the House of Savoy in Italy? And if it came to that, why not Goering, even Hitler himself? Much less vehemently, but very solidly, the British people shared their bitterness.

To some extent the public antagonism to North African politics was hushed by the statement that unless we cooperated with the Vichy French in North Africa thousands of British and American lives would have been lost. To some extent it was diverted by the progress of the war itself, or rather the lack of progress. The First Army, under General Anderson, seemed to be getting nowhere. While Montgomery continued with his great swoops and marches in the desert, the First Army seemed to have stopped dead and was like to remain where it was until Montgomery came to the rescue.

Moreover, the early propaganda on the North African landings had been conducted with the utmost confusion. For some strange reason the authorities in London and Washington had chosen to give the impression that an enormous army had been landed in North Africa. Well, the public began to ask, Why doesn't it do something? Why is it held up by a handful of Germans in the tip of Tunisia?

Still much agitated by these things, I packed my bag at last and went down to Euston Station. My personal quest for information was over and I was going back to the war in Africa not much wiser and a good deal sadder. It seemed to me horribly symbolic that my journey of political discovery, begun so hopefully in the American sunshine, was ending in the black and gloomy emptiness of Euston at midnight. I had got the answers to all the things I wanted to know when I set out from

Egypt; now I had a whole cartload of new questions.

In the train I changed back into uniform. I had not worn it for four months. It suddenly felt very warm and reassuring.

Four

Londonderry

THE LIFELINES of the North African expedition were strung down from a dozen British ports to the Mediterranean. Each week a new convoy put out into the Atlantic and ran between the U-boat packs into Algiers and Oran. Each day some fatal action was fought in the middle of the Atlantic or along the African coast. These battles were never reported. They were, of course, in the essence of our strategy, and unless we won them then everything in Africa was lost; but it was also in the rule of the sea that they should be fought out silently and stealthily with scarcely anyone to know about them except those who had taken part in the fighting.

It seemed to me that if one was going to report the North African war one ought to start here, on the sea, so I asked the admiralty if they could send me down on one of the little ships; not in a big troop-carrying liner where you see very little and hear nothing in addition to being very vulnerable, but in a destroyer or a corvette. And so I went to Londonderry in the north of Ireland two days before Christmas.

The corvette *Exe* (later they called her a frigate) was at her berth in the town and you had to scramble across two sister ships to get at her. *Exe* was brand new and she looked old. There was hardly a day since her launching she had not been at sea and fighting. You could see that from the rust, the peeling paint, the crowded jumble of equipment on her decks and the faces of the men who sailed her.

She was austerely built; instead of planking on her decks she had a chemical mixture that was poured on and set hard and then sometimes buckled under the action of sea water. Even the captain's cabin had been built on monastic and highly economical lines, and the furniture was tubular steel that raced about the deck in a storm like a pack of hounds. All the expense and skill in *Exe*'s building had gone into the equipment, the Oerlikon guns, the asdic, the radio location gear, the depth charges and the instruments that controlled the gunnery, the power and the navigation. She had more power to strike at submarines than anything of her size afloat. She was nothing more than a shell for all these expensive, precious gadgets, and she was the ugliest and most uncomfortable ship I ever expect to travel in. And because I got to know the *Exe* a little I will irrationally defend that corvette against any other, and without reason I will contest any word of criticism I ever hear against her skill, her manners, or her company.

Her company at the moment I got aboard was feeling like mutiny. They had orders to sail on Christmas Day. Not only Christmas Day, but a Friday. Not only Christmas Day, but in lousy weather. Why not Boxing Day? They were bound to be kept hanging about anyway, waiting for the convoy.

They were due for a spell ashore. They needed repairs. They had just come in and they had more sea days in the past year than... The third officer was beyond eloquence. 'It's a bloody racket,' he said.

I had been made welcome as soon as I slid down the companionway into the tiny wardroom. 'Come in. Have a drink,' and—ironically— 'Merry Christmas.'

Like the rest of the crew, most of these officers were in their early twenties. The majority of the men on that ship had hardly seen the sea six months before. They were butchers, bakers, farmhands, milkmen, bank clerks, students and travelling salesmen. Some had grown beards.

The captain had a beard. He was a round, tubby little man, and he was Royal Navy with high seniority in this flotilla of corvettes. Earlier in the war he had been minesweeping. He was born and bred to the little ships and his conversation was racy and gay and often witty.

He came on board with his wife, who had crossed from Scotland, where she was living with her two children. She was snatching just these two or three days' leave with her husband, and then, on Christmas Day, she would go back to Scotland again. Her life had always been like that: a series of brief chance meetings with her husband. They had been shopping in the town, buying flowers for the captain's cabin and holly for the ship. The commanders of the two adjacent corvettes came aboard, and for a while we sat drinking whisky and they talked of their last voyages.

Already when we went ashore for dinner in the town the holly was tied high up on the yardarm and the masts.

We had steaks in Londonderry that night—steaks such as have not been seen in England for years. The pavements were crowded with British and American sailors and in the shops you could still buy fine linen and Donegal tweed. I spent my sweet ration on some hard sticky substance and broke a tooth on it as I wandered in boredom round the town next day. As the naval dentist treated me he discoursed mournfully on teeth in the navy now—'Not like the teeth you used to see.' In the streets the slow, soft, depressing Irish rain fell down. There was slush right along the crowded docksides. There were no cinemas to go to, no books I wanted in the shops. The pubs were closed, and the cold cheerless atmosphere of war seemed to have reached into the grey houses and choked the feeling of Christmas out of the people living there.

The *Exe* was a drab and comfordess place while she was in port, even though I had been given the captain's cabin, since he would naturally sleep in a bunk below the bridge when we were at sea. One could not stay aboard or go on shore—there was nothing but coldness and cheerlessness and boredom everywhere.

But in the end sheer boredom drove me back into Londonderry on this dismal Christmas Eve, and I met a friend in the navy who was living in the town. As we dined at his home the rain stopped falling and Londonderry was suddenly transformed. A huge and boisterous crowd of sailors on leave had flooded into the streets. They poured off the ships in their best uniforms, and nothing could have baulked their determination to be gay.

A clear lamp-like moon rode over the town and it had touched everything with a breathless and unreal loveliness. It was frosty and biting cold on the ramparts, but looking down you could see how the yellow light had touched the wet slate roofs; each homestead chimney breathed up the smoke of a peat fire, and this smoke was turned silver by the moon as it floated over the river and the town. In the streets below there was a wild conglomeration of noise. Since the American sailors had arrived the street boys had discovered a new trade—shoe shining. They waited at the gates to the docks and shouted to the men coming ashore, 'Clean yer shoes for a tanner, mister.' As they shone the shoes the boys would sing to the sailors and their girls in their high, clear Irish voices. They sang the old laments and dirges of county Antrim, and all this sentimental sadness, worth a tanner now, came piping up over the rooftops to the old stone wall on which we were standing. With it came the caterwauling of many drunken men lurching through the dark streets, the high-pitched giggle of the girls, the crash of thrown bottles smashing against the sides of houses, and many other sounds that may have been oaths or tipsy singing or the scraping of trams or the shuffling of many thousands of feet through the slime.

Behind us a narrow sliver of light showed through a chapel door. We went inside, and the place was brightly lit and already filling up with the congregation for the midnight service. The organ was playing, and as we came outside again into the moonlight this music met the drunken noises coming up from the city and for a little triumphed over them.

There was a naval officers' party in the town, and we went in. The guests had been drinking since nightfall, and now they danced or swayed or sat about in all the stages of intoxication from hilarity to complete vacuity and moroseness. People shoved drinks into your hand and forgot you. They began portentous conversations and then lost the drift of their talk until it rambled into nothing. One lad kept saying to me over and over again, 'Dhrink dhrink dhrink.' There were not nearly enough girls, and there were not enough with the sailors in the streets and the pubs.

It is always the same in every British war zone. There are never enough girls, and in the end that is probably doing as much damage as anything else in this war. The men drink out of loneliness and a sense of frustration. They lay about in the gutters of Londonderry that night, having achieved what they set out to do—to reach forgetfulness.

The *Exe* sailed next day. We sailed alone down the river with the tide, and with a weird old Irish pilot at the helm who may have been eighty or a hundred. He came from the Irish Free State, and there could be no secret about our going since there was de Valera's neutral and brightly lit territory on the left bank of the river. There was nothing much to stop German agents from sitting comfortably on the bank and reporting the movement of every British warship up and down the Foyle. It seemed absurd that a few yards away on the right bank, which was the territory of belligerent Northern Ireland, the villages were blacked out.

People passed freely back and forth over the border. Indeed, it was a common practice for the inhabitants of Northern Ireland to cycle across and buy unrationed silk stockings and sweets and liquor, and, provided you did not go to excess, the Eire customs would wink their eyes at the bundles under your coat.

The river was very narrow and sinuous. Sometimes the old pilot called for almost a right-angled turn. Each time we passed another warship moored on the bank the *Exe*'s bosun would sound his whistle and we would stand to the salute on the bridge. Across the water the other vessel's salute would come back, and it seemed to me then a most heartening and dignified farewell.

It was cold, and the manners of the old Free State pilot were cold until we summoned him a double whisky from the wardroom. Then his aged flat face and watery eyes screwed up into a smile. 'Merry Christmas,' he said. The holly was very green and cheerful on the mast. Now that we had actually cast off and accepted the enormity of going to sea on Christmas Day, everyone felt brighter.

The oiler was waiting for us at the mouth of the estuary, and the crew of the oiler was drunk. In some astonishing way the master of the big, ungainly barge had communicated his condition to his ship and she lurched about our thin sides like a sailor on the spree. At length we were safely lashed together and the oil began to flow aboard through the rubber pipes.

We had a turkey for our Christmas dinner in the wardroom that night. It was the last time the captain would leave the precincts of the bridge until the voyage was done, and he sat there benignly at the head of the table, a little man in a little ship, and he was the feudal master of everything around him.

Responsibility seems to lie easily on the men in the little ships. Being so few on board, they have a sense of freedom and independence. Transports carrying thousands of troops and much equipment were at that moment beginning to roll out to a rendezvous somewhere, and we were to protect them; but just tonight, in the warm and lighted cabin, this was of no account. On this night, too, the crew had their last drinks, for they did not take liquor once they were at sea. The sailors were entitled to draw a ration of rum every day at sea, but most refused it and accepted instead a payment of threepence.

In the morning the sea was full of savage, bucketing rollers. We had company now, sloops, another corvette and a destroyer, but of all these the *Exe* appeared to feel the sea the most. She did not even try to cope with the waves. She had a most atrocious roll that pulled up short at its climax and then suddenly swung back the other way. Not for a second was she on an even keel, and there were long hours when it was impossible to stand upright without holding on. When every few minutes an extra large wave bashed her on the side she shivered from one end to the other, and the green sea rushing along the deck made a deep, icy pool in the captain's cabin. This water kept rushing from side to side between the lockers all day and all night.

As a boy I had discovered my own cure for seasickness and I do not recommend it to anyone else. It simply consisted of standing on deck until one was frozen to the bone. Then one bolted down to a warm bunk and fell asleep as quickly as possible. Since a boy I had never been seasick, and I had some pride in my record. The *Exe* upset all that without delay. I felt terrible on the wet and freezing bridge and much more terrible on the damp and heaving bunk. Sleep mercifully came for a few hours at a time, but then the thought and sight of food sent me rushing to the side, where one at least could be miserably alone and wait to die.

A marvellous sight broke on the horizon on the second day out—the convoy, several great ships, apparently untroubled by the storm and apparently without forward motion. For the next week I was going to look out over the starboard side each morning and always see them there, riding majestically and at ease. They became a constant unchangeable backcloth on the western horizon, as though they were painted there, always with the commodore's flagship ahead, the others spaced at just such a distance out astern.

Tiny warships guarded this vital fleet, and except when we were chasing submarines or falling into new positions for the night we never changed our stations—ships out in front, ships lying abreast of the commodore's ship, more on either flank and the last bringing up the rear. The *Exe* was posted to the port side of the convoy immediately ahead of a sloop and astern of the destroyer *Loyal*.

All day the escort ships talked to one another in morse with the lamps. Our orders came from the senior officer aboard the *Egret*, which was riding last in the convoy.

Every so often the whole convoy would alter course and speed according to the weather or the danger or the hour of the day. We were a fast convoy and we had one general order—to get through to Oran and Algiers as safely and as quickly as possible.

For days, while the sea heaved up and blew itself into a climacteric of sleet and wind, aircraft of the coastal command kept passing back and forth searching, as we were, for submarines. Then we steamed into calmer seas beyond the reach of aircraft and beyond the hope of aid if we struck the enemy.

I emerged now from my coma and struggled wanly up to the bridge, where I heard with some pleasure that a third of the crew had been seasick as well as myself. It was Sunday morning, and the captain said briskly, 'We will have prayers on the afterdeck at ten and try out the guns at eleven. "Praise the Lord and pass the ammunition." ' The service went quietly forward among the depth charges, and then the men ran quickly to the Oerlikons, which had not been tested since the previous voyage. 'Fire,' said the captain, and the gunnery officer shouted down the voice-pipe, 'Commence, commence, commence.' For ten minutes they had the low clouds full of tracer bullets and the din on the bridge was unbelievable.

I had come on board dressed in the battledress I used in the winter campaigns in the desert, but now, like the officers, I changed into those heavy padded overalls that keep the wind out while you are afloat and support you on the surface if you are shipwrecked. But still it was cold, and two pairs of gloves could scarcely maintain the circulation in your hands.

Little by little, standing on the bridge all day, I learned something of the art of chasing submarines, which is probably the most desperate battle of wits that modern warfare has provided yet. I learned that submarines will avoid corvettes and destroyers if they can and aim for the convoy. I learned that they prefer to attack on the surface at nightfall and of the means by which they will try to lure the escort away before making their attack from several different directions at once.

In this fantastic game of chess each side knew roughly where the other was moving and in what strength and at what speed and with what destination. Every mile of this vast featureless sea was plotted and checked and though the U-boat packs spoke to one another below water and rarely came to the surface before nightfall, yet they were discovered. Somewhere back in Britain there was a wall chart and day by day a little black speck that was the *Exe* was moved on its course along the wall.

Equally in Lorient or Brest there was very probably a German chart and *Exe* by now was on that too. We never spoke to England lest we should give away the convoy's position, but they spoke to us, and day by day they knew each move we were making on a pre-arranged plan and they kept us informed. Whenever a U-boat pack moved in the Atlantic we were warned. The radio kept buzzing with the news of submarines that moved first toward us then away from us. It was uncanny, this feeling that the enemy was all about us and ready to strike, and yet we could see nothing and hear nothing, and our eyes were in some control room on land a thousand miles away.

By radio location and the asdic we kept peering endlessly into our immediate sea as we went along. The asdic fascinated me.

Crouching in the dark little cabin there beneath the bridge you had the feeling that your nerve centres were projected out and down into the deep water. Mechanically one grew able to measure the sound of the electric impulses going out—ping-ing-ing-...ping-ing-ing...ping-ing-ing…ping-ing-ing. So long as the rhythm kept up it was all right, nothing was there. But once it was interrupted then the echo sounded back and there was an interval in the rhythm. It sounded something like 'Ping…ping- ping. Ping…ping-ping. Ping…ping-ping.' These lacunas showed as gaps in the steady line a mechanical needle was tracing in ink across a chart, so one had a double-check. But it took much sensitivity and training to know when in fact one had a submarine.

Our first alarm rang through the ship on the fourth day. For some time we had been enviously watching the other corvettes go tearing off in pursuit of clues, and we had been feeling rather like the fisherman who never gets a bite while his friends keep hauling them in all the time. But now in the dark, late afternoon I was jerked out of my sleep by that insistent whistle. One never took off all one's clothes at sea, but still one had to fumble for gloves and overalls and then climb through the lurching ship to the bridge. The men were already on the guns and at the depth charges. The tiny bridge was crowded. Our speed had increased enormously and we had changed direction away from the convoy. A black pennant was being pulled to the masthead to warn the other vessels we were going to attack. In the stern I could see the men knocking back the safety catches on the big barrel-shaped depth charges and getting extra detonators ready.

'Pattern,' said the captain, and 'Pattern' one of the officers repeated down the voice-pipe. In the stern they set the charges to spray out over the sea.

The asdic at the captain's feet was switched onto the loudspeaker, and if one leaned down out of the fierce wind one could hear its broken echo. Suddenly one of the men shouted that he had lost contact. I could tell no difference in the rhythm of the echo, but the man kept moving about the direction of his instruments, trying to pick up the contact again.

'Fire,' said the captain, and he nodded as he said it. The big barrels went out almost lazily over the air. They appeared to poise for a minute in mid-career and then they plopped into the waves clumsily and heavily, and the white wake flowed over them. It was no use tensing yourself for the explosions. They were much worse than you expected. At several points the sea humped itself into shivering green hillocks and on the sides of these hillocks the pattern of foam and spume that had formerly rested horizontally on the water was now suspended vertically and distorted into weird shapes. Then each hillock burst asunder into millions of particles and changed from green into sparkling white, so that now it looked like a tall tree after a heavy fall of snow. With the bursting came the noise and a strange rasping shudder that raked the keel from one end of the ship to the other, and for a moment you felt she was about to sink.

'Two hundred and ten revolutions,' said the captain, and he changed course so rapidly a great green wall of water raced waist-high across the men fighting to get a new pattern of charges ready in the stern.

'Pattern ready,' said the officer at the other end of the tube. 'Fire,' said the captain. The barrels floated out lazily again.

Twisting and turning and changing speed we tried again and again to pick up the echo but it was gone.

You do not claim a submarine unless you have something very definite to show for it. A piece of human body preserved in the ship's refrigerator—that is the sort of evidence the admiralty requires. It is not enough to say that oil rose to the surface or that you saw the submarine go into a vertical dive.

So no submarine was claimed here and we steamed back to our station beside the convoy. The black pennant came down from the mast and the men left their action stations.

We were not entirely out to sink U-boats. If we kept them down that would be enough. Kept down and away by the ring of corvettes and destroyers, the submarines would have no chance to fire; and the way to keep them down was to depth charge every suspicious sounding.

That night we had news of a U-boat pack in the Atlantic. It had hovered for the past few days in mid-ocean, apparently awaiting information. Meanwhile two convoys were at sea—ours and another slow convoy of small freighters which was making for America with ordinary civilian cargoes from Britain which would keep up our credit abroad. If one of the convoys was to be attacked then it was preferable that it should be the American one. And now tonight there came word that the American convoy had been spotted by the U-boats.

Hour by hour the news came in. Always the submarines were getting closer to the other convoy. With the slow and paralysing inevitability of a classic tragedy the pack closed in on the freighters.

The admiralty in London knew they were about to attack, the U-boat command in Germany knew it, we knew it—and there was nothing whatever we could do about it. The freighters had to fight out their battle alone and unaided, since no British warship could cross to them in time and no aircraft could reach them. They were remote from the whole world, a private extension of the war.

As we waited the alarm signals rang again through the *Exe*. It was icy dark now and, groping out of the warmth of the cabin to the bridge, the wind seemed to sound more shrilly and the black water was forbidding and malicious. Stray U-boats were about us despite the fact that a pack had gone off in the opposite direction. There was a ragged and misty patchwork of blown clouds that sometimes turned silver but never parted enough to let the full light of the moon come through. One could see only the vague outline of some of the other ships in the convoy and no lights showed. Peering around through this silver and eerie semi-darkness, you could imagine you saw the shapes of a dozen conning towers in the waves, but then the waves fell back and revealed nothing but the empty and interminable sea.

'Well, I'm damned if I know what's going on,' said the captain and he again asked the asdic and the radio location crews if they had picked up anything.

'Nothing, sir.'

The alarm had come from one of the destroyers, and now without warning a lighted shell of incredible brilliance burst out of the sea to our starboard bow and was followed by another and another. These shells mounted to the floor of the low clouds, throwing off a purple light as they swept upward. At their extreme height the parachute flares were released and above each flare was a propeller that regulated the descent. As the propellers turned they interrupted the flow of purple light onto the clouds, so it appeared as though we were looking at some fantastic cinema screen that stretched across the whole sky above. For ten minutes, like the spokes of a moving wheel, the alternate pillars of darkness and light whirled furiously around the clouds and, down below, the *Exe* slid through a purple sea.

'My goodness me,' said the captain lightly. 'Now, who did that?' As he spoke the destroyer *Loyal* emerged suddenly from the darkness and began to move across our bows. She was travelling at fantastic speed, the grey foam flying out astern, and she was a lovely silver streak in the black and purple water. She bounded and heaved herself forward almost in the motion of a greyhound, and we cursed her heartily as we changed course just in time to let her by. Clearly the *Loyal* thought she had found something and was shooting flares in the hope of catching a submarine on the surface.

But again, while we waited in the freezing wind, nothing came out of it.

Twice more that night I bundled out of my bunk as the whistles sounded, and I was still on the bridge when the morning broke and one after another the outlines of the other ships took solid shape. I counted the transports quickly. They were all there. On the radio came the news that the other convoy had taken the full shock of the U-boat attack. A few ships were sunk. The rest of the convoy had scattered.

It was too late for the pack to turn back and catch us, but from now on we were constantly getting alarms. Sometimes depth-charge explosions would fly up from the wakes of the other escort ships. Sometimes, like terriers in a dogfight, all the little ships would scurry across the sea, crisscrossing one another's wakes. Once we raced past one of the great transports and saw the troops in thousands watching us from the high decks. We had a bundle of *Egret*'s mail on board, and she came alongside us and fired a rocket-gun over our stern as we sailed along. But the weather was still rough and only a cylinder of vital documents could be passed across the rope. *Egret* signalled us that she would wait for her mail until we got to port, and disconsolately she steamed back to her station.

It was growing warmer now though still the waves continued. We expected to meet trouble at the approaches to the Straits of Gibraltar, since that was the obvious place for the submarines to concentrate. I was reading in my bunk when a message came down that the captain wanted to see me on the bridge. For a change he was not very light-hearted.

'I have some bad news for you,' he said. 'We have just received orders to leave the convoy and go back to Londonderry immediately.'

Now, this was a sharp disappointment for everyone. It meant that the crew was going to miss the excitement of the Mediterranean and the chance of a spell ashore in the sunshine; it meant much more time at sea for them as they would almost certainly have to set out with another convoy immediately; it meant *Egret* was not going to get her mail; it meant they were going to have a lonely and boring trip home, and much hard work at the worst time of year; and it meant that my own arrival in North Africa was going to be delayed at least another month.

Typically, the captain appeared to be more concerned about me than anything else. 'It's too bad,' he said. 'I am afraid we have let you down badly.' He sent off a signal saying he had myself and thirty ratings bound for Algiers, and could he not at least drop us at Gibraltar? But no, it was no good, *Exe* had to get back.

'I'll tell you what,' said the captain, 'if you like to risk it I will ask *Loyal* to come alongside and we will see if we can't get you across to her in a whaler. The trouble is the weather's too bad; but we can try it.'

You will never get the men in the little ships to abandon anything so long as there is the ghost of a chance. The weather frankly was outrageously bad for this sort of antic. But off went the signal to *Loyal*, out came the bosun piping for the whaler's crew and down I went to the cabin to throw my kit together.

When I got back on deck *Loyal* was coming up on our lee to make what calm water she could between the two vessels. The heavy whaler was slung out over *Exe*'s port side, level with the deck. The mate tied a bulky cork life jacket round my shoulders and I clambered into the stern sheets with my baggage. My kit at this time was a thing of pride and joy to me, selected as a result of three years' campaigning—a flat metal typewriter bought in Macy's in New York that winter, a soft cowhide kitbag made in the native quarter in Cairo and stuffed with such things as shirts and a large silver whisky flask, a featherweight metal stretcher bed and a fleece-lined canvas sleeping-bag just bought in Fortnum and Mason's in London.

It takes years and much travel to design and buy a perfect camping kit, to discover the little things like substituting a light camel-hair dressing-gown for a heavy army blanket; and this was my dream kit, the result of a voyage around the world. Down it all went into the bilge water in the stern of the whaler.

The boat's crew was ready. Each of us gripped a guiding rope with which to ease the whaler down onto the water. But now that *Exe* and *Loyal* had almost stopped, the sea appeared really monstrous— or it did to me at any rate, sitting in the whaler. At one moment we would be poised twenty or thirty feet in mid-air, then, as the *Exe* rolled and the sea came up, we would have the waves rushing about us. The idea was to wait until the sea came up to us and then lower quickly away, and so fall back gently with the declining wave. The men of both *Exe* and *Loyal* crammed the decks to watch this unusually diverting sport in mid-Atlantic. Too far off to see what was happening, the convoy steamed on indifferently.

A young mountain of water came lunging up the side of *Exe*. 'Let go,' snapped the mate. The men on the pulleys relaxed their grip, and it worked like a charm—but only in the stern sheets. My end of the whaler rushed down to meet the wave, the other end stuck fast—the pulley jammed. This left the whaler and us in it suspended almost vertically down the side of the corvette, and the wave fell back without its burden. In the act of falling with the stern sheets some ten foot of corded guiding rope had run through my clenched hand, removing most of the fingerprints.

The next three or four minutes, while the men fought to release the jammed pulley, were unpleasant.

Each wave that rose half capsized the boat and the cold sea water poured in. It was certain that we were going to go overboard when suddenly the pulley gave way and, with a rush and a bang, the whaler hit the water. By some miracle we fell only a few feet and hit the sea right side up. The crew grabbed the oars and pulled away.

We had about a quarter of a mile to get across to the *Loyal*, but this seemed much longer because we were constantly losing sight of both ships in the hollows of the sea. Moreover, the blood from my hand kept staining the water in the boat a vivid red, making me feel things were much worse than they actually were.

In the end we were washed across; and now the full difficulty of our undertaking was apparent. At one moment we would be level with *Loyal*'s bridge and then, after a descent at the speed of an electric lift, we would find ourselves almost surveying the barnacles on her keel. We tried approaching from several different directions, but it was no good; the deck always slid past too fast and there was some danger that we should be smashed against the destroyer's side and capsized.

'It's bloody well impossible,' quoth one of the boat's crew, and I fervently agreed with him.

From the bridge of his ship *Loyal*'s captain shouted down through a megaphone at me a remark which I considered downright frivolous at the time—'I don't see you taking any notes.' The sailors on *Loyal* had now flung a rope net over the side. A lucky wave threw us forward; fright gave me wings; I sprang up and out of the whaler and clutched the net, and the whaler vanished below. A dozen hands dragged me on deck. Then the kit. The bed-roll and the typewriter came up damply and easily on a rope, but the handle of the kitbag gave stitch by stitch as it was hauled over the yawning sea. I was far beyond caring much, nevertheless it was fascinating to see the last stitch give way just as a sailor made a grab at the bag and missed. Someone else below got his hand on the falling bag and there I was, baggage and all, aboard the destroyer.

The whaler's crew put safely back. *Loyal*'s engine-room bells clanged and she leapt on her course. Down in the surgery the doctor put a strong whisky in my left hand and got to work on the right. I felt at home again.

That evening a signal flashed across from the diminishing outline of the *Exe*. She was already miles away. I have kept the signal. It was from *Exe*'s captain and it said simply, 'Sorry you had such a rough passage. We all enjoyed having you on board and wish you all good luck in Africa.'

Poor little *Exe*. I have not seen hide nor hair of you since that day. Wherever you are sailing, if you still sail—and even if you don't—you carry every good wish which I am capable of wishing. I know I will be welcome in your wardroom wherever we meet in this war. And for what it is worth you have my unbounded admiration and respect.

You may remember, captain, standing with me on the bridge one day looking down at your butchers and bakers and bank clerks who were toiling in the waist of the ship. Watching them, you suddenly said with such convinced pride and without any affectation: 'The salt of the earth.'

With complete agreement let us have that here in print—'The salt of the earth.'

Five

Gibraltar

ABOARD THE *Loyal* it was the same routine except that everything was on a larger scale. She was one of the latest of our destroyers. I slept on the bench in the wardroom aft, and all night I could hear the propellers wrenching and tugging at the water, making a perpetual battle with the sea. When we were ordered to increase speed and go into Gibraltar ahead of the convoy to oil, it almost seemed that the great power in the ship would burst her open.

There were no corridors below deck connecting the forward and the after ends of the vessels, and so to get from the wardroom to the bridge one had to navigate a difficult journey along the upper deck, which was often awash. By day you could hold onto the guiding rope and it was easy enough; but at night when the alarms sounded you could see nothing, and you skidded about uncertainly on the slippery decks.

Mostly I stayed aft now, since it was so much trouble to get to the bridge. They gave me an unofficial job of looking after the detonators for the depth charges when we were in action. It was simply a matter of standing there in the wet with the little wooden boxes in my hands while the others did the heavy work of hoisting the depth charges into position for firing.

An aircraft circled round, and as we trained our guns on it the watchers shouted it was British.

Then a gull came out and swept round the ship. We were getting very near to land. When at length we passed into the straits at nightfall everything was much the same as I remembered it during the Spanish war—Tangier and Ceuta on the right, both brightly lit, and then Tarifa to the left, another beaded string of lights. Then into the harbour, Spanish Algeciras on one side, the Rock on the other side, with Gibraltar town clinging on the slopes below. Very little had changed. Gibraltar was not even blacked out. For me Gibraltar had always meant war. When I had first been here, six years before, Franco's troops were fighting their way round to Malaga. There had been shooting in La Linea and Algeciras, the British, sitting on their Gibraltar terraces in the isolation of neutrality, had watched the pleasant spectacle across the bay of the fires and the tracer bullets.

Well, now it was the other way about. The Spanish were sitting placidly on the patios and watching us.

The harbour was much the same except that it was more crowded, and there were more sailors and soldiers about on the docks, more war everywhere.

Later in the year General Mason Macfarlane, the governor of the Rock, took me on a day's tour through the defences. For years miners imported from the Rocky Mountains of Canada had been at work driving a vast network of tunnels through the living rock. It is a staggering thing to see, this underground fortress. Gibraltar now, in an emergency, can close up like a clam and live its life underground. I walked along miles of two-way subterranean roads and saw hospitals and food dumps, workshops and railways buried beyond the reach of any bomb or shell. We walked clean through the Rock and, coming out of a hole on the face of the precipice, looked down into Spain to the north, out into the Mediterranean in the east and the Atlantic in the west.

Caves as big as cinema theatres have been gouged out along the underground roads and sometimes stalactites hang weirdly from the ceiling among the shell-cases and the guns. Great reservoirs of icy rainwater lie in the centre of the Rock. It is all built on a much greater scale than anything in the old Maginot Line.

Gibraltar had become a major crossroad of the war. It was the place where you were quite apt to meet a diplomat from Russia, a general from Washington, or a cabinet minister from London, and every night half a dozen celebrities sat down at the governor's table.

There are many deep secrets about Gibraltar which I am not permitted to write about here. One of the strange things about these secrets was that the Germans knew most of them. Enemy agents sat in La Linea, a few hundred yards away, and presumably telephoned Berlin all the good news about the Rock—how many ships came in and how many went off into the Mediterranean, and so on.

This had once been a pleasant corner of the world, where one could go fishing round at Torremolinos or wander through the sunshine to Malaga for the swimming. In the fondas in the warm hills you could sit for hours over Valdepenas wine and Spanish omelettes, sherry and shrimps. But Spain was hungry now. Suddenly feeling very fed-up with the war, I went back to the wardroom and fell asleep.

When I woke we were already at sea again and trying to catch up with the rest of the convoy that had passed through the straits in the night. We were travelling faster than I had ever travelled at sea before. In clear, sparkling weather *Loyal* was letting herself out with nearly everything she had.

It was an uplifting excitement. At forty miles an hour we ploughed a long white furrow through the sea. The spray turned into millions of flashing diamond points in the sunlight and burst far over the bridge; all the stern sheets were under rushing water, and as the waves came up we cut them clean in half and leaped on the waves beyond. On the bridge that morning one felt a sense of tremendous confidence and light-heartedness, a feeling compounded of speed and sunshine and the sea.

When we turned, half the ship went underwater. It came racing and bumping in a massive plastic wall against the torpedoes and the gun turrets, and it was full of coloured green lights. *Loyal* shook herself and got free of the burden and the water streamed away from her sides in cascades.

There was a man, a young bluejacket, standing amidships working on the torpedoes when we made one of these skating turns. He had his back to the oncoming rush of water. Surely, one thought, he sees, he knows, he has his grip tight on something. At the last split second we realised on the bridge he did not know, he had no grip. Several men cried sharply to him, but their shouts, already too late, were drowned in the roar of the wave. There must have been twenty or thirty tons of water travelling at least forty miles an hour in that wave and its force was unbelievable. It picked up two shell-casings from their lashings and crumpled the solid steel, it gathered up a line of steel fittings and flung them overboard, it tore a spare motor-boat engine out of its steel ropes and smashed it through a lifeboat.

And it grabbed the boy and tossed him into the sea.

He made one cry as he went through the ropes on the starboard side. Then there was a moment when you could see one arm raised in the swirling waves of the wake.

For half an hour we doubled back on our course and cruised around, but already the drowning boy was a mile back by the time we had turned and there was never any hope for him.

So unnecessary and unexpected a death quietened the whole ship. A grim-faced little squad of shipmates patched up the place where the boy had fallen through.

An hour or two later we caught the convoy. It had grown much larger by additions from Gibraltar, and the sea was full of ships wherever you looked—even ships coming in the opposite direction, from Oran and Algiers. The fleet was out. Over against the French coast the *Rodney*'s great bulk showed against the cliffs, and astern of her two aircraft-carriers and still another battleship. They moved through a wide screen of cruisers and destroyers—a majestic sight.

We were at the first degree of readiness all this time, since enemy aircraft were about and we were in bomber range from Italy. Around the guns we pulled on white anti-flash gloves and hoods, so that the ship's company began to look like a gathering of the Ku Klux Klan. Far off to the north-east, near the Italian coast, we could hear the distant sound of gunfire. Over our sector the protective screen of British fighters flew lazily back and forth.

Some of our convoy turned into Oran that night. Ironically, having come all this way, one of the transports fouled another near the entrance to the harbour, and only with great luck and better judgment were the big two ships and their cargoes got to the docks. The rest of us—destroyers, cruisers, aircraft-carriers, battleships, freighters, oilers and transports—sailed on to Algiers.

In line astern this armada rounded the last headland and moved into the channel of the port. Algiers at any time is a beautiful sight from the sea. Today it glistened. Row on row of big white buildings climbed up to the hills above the bay. The white mosques of the kasbah, gleaming in the morning sunshine, made a wavering reflection in the transparent sea.

I had seen this vision only once before—when I crossed to North Africa on the Italian liner *Saturnia*, during the Spanish war. Algiers seemed to have grown since then. For two and a half years it had been shut off from the rest of the world behind the Axis wall. Now it was open and free again with a great fleet at its docks. The tricolour floated very bravely from the roof of the post office.

Two round-eyed English boys who had never been out of England before were detailed to carry my kit ashore. They stepped very cautiously through the hubbub on the docks. Mounting the long ramp to the Hotel Aletti they gazed with increasing wonder at the palm trees, the flamboyant Algerian cavalrymen, the piled-up fruit barrows, the black boys who wanted to clean their shoes, and the Arab women who sidled past with coloured veils over their faces. They screwed their heads round, trying to see everything at once, and drew back in embarrassment when the street vendors offered them necklaces and fly-whisks.

These were two of the boys whom I had seen working waist-deep at the depth charges on the destroyer. In the last few days they had had only four or five hours' sleep. They had done their part in fighting the U-boats all the way from England and they had been quite unmoved and unafraid. I was glad they were getting ashore, if only for an hour or two.

'Look,' I said when we got to the hotel, 'here are some French francs. You are not expected back at the ship for an hour. Have a look around the town.'

The elder of the two, the one who actually fired the depth charge, considered it for a moment. 'No, sorr, thank you,' he said. 'You never know what will happen in these furrin' parts. I think we better be gettin' back to the ship.'

In the lounge of the hotel I came quite unexpectedly on the O.C. troops and his adjutant who had sailed with me in *Zola* to Canada. It seemed that they, too, had just arrived in Algiers and in the same convoy. They had travelled in one of the large transports.

'Dull trip,' said the adjutant. 'Nothing ever seems to happen on these convoys.'

Six

Algiers

IN THE last week of the old year a slim and dark French boy with a sensitive face, named Bonnier de la Chapelle, climbed up the steep road that runs from Algiers town toward the St George Hotel.

Halfway up he paused before the building which Admiral Darlan had made his headquarters, and went inside. He asked by name for a young friend of his who was a junior official in the building. The girl at the reception desk showed him how to make out a form requesting an interview with his friend, and presently he was shown up.

The boy stayed only a few minutes, and, returning to his home in the town where he lived with his parents, he took from his room a service revolver of the type that the Spanish arms makers used to supply to the French government a few years ago. He clipped the breach open and saw that it contained six bullets. Then he put the revolver into his overcoat pocket, ate lunch and returned to the admiral's headquarters. It was by now nearly mid-afternoon.

Again the boy asked to see his friend, and when he had filled up another form he was again invited to mount the stairs. This time he did not go to the friend's room, but continued straight to the admiral's office, which, apparently, he had discovered on his earlier visit that morning.

The admiral's secretary, a French girl, said that her chief was out. 'Never mind,' the boy said. 'I will wait.'

The girl put a cigarette into her mouth and asked de la Chapelle for a light. He drew a box of matches out of his pocket, and having lit her cigarette he said, 'Here, take the box, miss.' This was quite a gesture in a town where matches were rarer than precious metals, but in no other way was the boy's behaviour unusual. He looked composed and at ease as he strolled up and down the corridor waiting for the admiral.

Darlan came in with his aide-de-camp, walking briskly. When he had all but passed, the boy touched him lightly on the sleeve and said, 'L'Amiral...?' Darlan paused and half turned. As he turned, de la Chapelle drew his gun, which was already cocked, and fired three shots diagonally across the admiral's chest. Darlan slumped onto the floor almost without a cry and died soon afterwards. The boy meanwhile ran swiftly back into the office where the girl had risen in alarm from her desk. The A.D.C. followed him.

As de la Chapelle swung his leg over the office window he took careful aim again and fired three bullets at the A.D.C.'s legs. The A.D.C. fell with a crash and de la Chapelle dropped into the courtyard outside.

Many guards and gendarmes had been posted round the building, and a group of these, startled by the firing, now rounded the corner and seized the boy before he could escape to the roadway. Only vaguely realising what had happened from the cries of the girl and the wounded A.D.C., the gendarmes started to beat up their struggling captive, and officials came running in panic from all over the building. The boy's friend shouted to the gendarmes from the windows to stop their baton-play, and the captive was brought into the building without further molestation.

When the doctors had done what they could for the two men who had been shot, all the senior French generals and administrators who happened to be in Algiers were summoned. They at once sat as a court martial—General Giraud, General Noguès and a number of others. No communication was sent to General Eisenhower or the Allies' headquarters at the St George Hotel, and headquarters, in fact, did not hear of the matter until the late afternoon.

Meanwhile the court martial decided to sentence de la Chapelle to life imprisonment. A small minority, led by General Noguès, violently dissented from this decision and forced a reopening of the case. Late that night the sentence was altered to death by the firing squad.

The boy remained in his cell all night in an exalted state of mind and appeared to be full of reckless confidence, not only in his own fate, but in the rightness of what he had done. He asked to see his parents, but this was refused. He then sent a message to the A.D.C. apologising for having shot him and explaining that his quarrel lay only with the admiral. Allied headquarters made no real attempt to intervene, and the French leaders continued to treat the affair as entirely a French military matter in which no foreigner could interfere.

In the morning a priest was sent to talk to the boy and prepare him for his death. But de la Chapelle's confidence was quite unshaken. 'They will not shoot me,' he cried; 'I have liberated France.'

It was in vain that the priest acquainted him with the verdict and sought to make the boy realise that he had only a few hours to live and that the firing squad was even then being assembled.

'They may send the firing squad,' de la Chapelle said. 'They may go through the whole performance of shooting me, but you will see, the bullets will be blank cartridges.'

In the end he accepted final absolution, but he continued to protest: 'They will not shoot me. They will use blank cartridges.' Precisely twenty-four hours after the assassination of Darlan, de la Chapelle was taken out of his cell and shot.

One day there may be monuments erected all over France for Bonnier de la Chapelle, but in Algiers that day only the wildest consternation reigned. The military landing had been made on November 8th at the three keypoints, Casablanca, Oran and Algiers, and there was every sign that it was going to stick. Even the fall of Tunis was envisaged for the following week. But the political plot, the plot to win over the Vichy leaders to our cause, was now bursting wide open at its seams and giving offence to nearly everybody except the Germans.

Mr Robert Murphy, the United States minister, an Irish Catholic of considerable ability and charm, had already lived through a very trying time and now found himself without the machinery or the trained assistants to cope with a situation that was dangerous and rapidly getting worse. The outcry against Darlan had reached full pitch both in America and England. The friendly neutrals were indignant. The Axis propaganda was making great play with the crisis, and now seized upon the assassination as a proof of the perfidy of the Allies and as a means to turn the hesitating French back into the German alliance. Nazi troops were at that moment flooding through unoccupied France.

Valuable units of the French fleet had been unable to get away from Toulon and were now either uselessly scuttled or at the disposal of the enemy. Moreover, disquieting news came in of more German troops being rushed to Tunisia by air. Mr Murphy was faced with a situation which was impossible for one man to handle, and there was at that time no senior British diplomat on the spot to assist him. Nor was he getting much coherent advice from the State Department in Washington where such a grave abortion of the Vichy plan had not been foreseen.

And so in bewilderment, confusion and haste and entirely under the pressure of events was fashioned the Allied design for dealing with the French nation and presumably with the other occupied countries throughout the world.

From the first the Allied authorities stuck to the firm official line which has never since been altered: 'Darlan just happened to be in North Africa attending his dying son. We had not intended to deal with him, but since he was on the spot and manifestly the senior Frenchman we were compelled to use him. Had we not adopted Darlan, thousands of soldiers' lives might have been lost, the landings might have been seriously delayed and we might have been forced to continue for months fighting in Morocco and Algeria.'

There was another point that was developed later: 'We are not invading or occupying French territory. France is our ally, enjoying equal rights. French politics are the concern of the French alone.'

With relief Mr Murphy turned to the only course open to him. He asked General Giraud to step into the admiral's place. Now General Giraud was by no means anxious at that time to become the new French leader in defiance of his old friend Marshal Pétain. His flight from the German cell at Königsberg and France by submarine to Gibraltar and his final emergence in this political madhouse in Algiers had left him shaken and uncertain. He was at first without his uniform, the symbol of authority, and he felt uncomfortable and ill at ease arriving in civilian clothes. No great fuss had been made locally of his coming. He protested, 'I can't do it. I have no following.'

But in the enforced absence of de Gaulle, who was not wanted by the Allied governments, Giraud was our man and no other would do. The minor ex-Vichy figures, Bergeret of the air staff, Yves Chatel, the military governor of Algiers, and others, were rapidly propelled into the breach to persuade Giraud to take over. Reluctantly he agreed, and temporarily at least the situation was saved. The British had nothing against the old general apart from the rapidly being forgotten fact that he was one of the leaders of the French army that collapsed in 1940. Indeed, there was widespread admiration for the old man's indomitable escapes from Germany. At least he was a soldier who had not dirtied his hands in politics as Darlan had.

Without concealment the British cheered the happy assassination of the admiral and applauded the apt appointment of the general. In America, too, there was satisfaction.

Since an iron censorship had closed down in Algiers, very few people at home had any clear notion of the most intricate and dark politics that were going on in North Africa.

Having got their new champion in the chair, Yves Chatel, Bergeret and their companions went one step further. The de Gaullist movement was to them a far greater danger than the Germans. They at once warned Giraud that de Gaullists were dangerously at large in North Africa and that a plot to take the general's life in the same way as the admiral's was on foot. Giraud acted as any general would act in the circumstances. He gave orders that the dangerous characters should be rounded up and imprisoned. Not without logic the general asked himself, 'How can I fight the Germans in Tunisia when I am threatened in my own headquarters?'

And that is how the people who had helped us land, the Frenchmen who were anti-Fascist since the days of the Spanish war, came to be imprisoned. Clearly this was going too far—indeed, the plot at this time was always either stopping short or running ahead of itself. Mr Murphy protested about the arrests.

'What?' said the general shortly. 'Do you not trust me?'

Just about this time I arrived in Algiers and saw the general for the first time. His mere appearance explained a great deal. Of all the graduates of the military academy of Saint Cyr you could scarcely conceive a more polished specimen than this. They were a closed and select group, the Saint Cyr generals—Weygand, Gamelin, Georges, Noguès were all there—men of breeding and strict faith. Of them all Giraud was by far the most distinguished in appearance. Immensely tall for a Frenchman, he had never let himself go to seed, and now in his late sixties he had the slim and graceful figure of a young cavalryman. His greyish uniform with the very long tunic and the broad brown stripe down the trousers was immaculate. In every detail he was precise, formal, stiff and unbending. He appeared to have emerged directly from the barber's shop. His small, bird-like head was beautifully groomed, and he held himself with just a touch of arrogance and independence that only comes from having been a long time in command. He spoke in a light, clipped voice, without gestures, very clearly and distinctly. Perhaps he was unusually icy that morning because he was meeting the press under protest, but on every other occasion I have seen him he had that same unruffled and slightly truculent composure.

Giraud, before anything else, was a general of the old French school, devout, rigidly conservative, the devotee of a set military code of behaviour, a cultivated and severe man who abhorred lawlessness in anything, in appearance, in manner, in behaviour or in thinking. He had been an opponent of the Jews, of the Communists, of all left-wing and untidy movements, but he was never rabid about them, because in his code politics were a slightly shabby form of activity lying outside the soldier's life. He had never been seriously forced to bother about politics; he rather prided himself that he was still no politician and stressed the matter in his speeches. He was, as a result, a little unsubtle, a little narrow and intransigent and very vulnerable indeed to the designs of the skilled political manipulators who at that moment were flooding into Algiers.

The general was a man with an *idée fixe*. He wanted to destroy the German army. All his long life the French army had been pitted in some way against the Germans. The defeat of the Germans was therefore a technical test of the excellence or otherwise of the French army and of the calibre of its generals. He was physically without fear and beyond corruption. And now in the evening of his life, after a most humiliating setback to his strong military pride, he saw a vision—the vision of General Giraud riding his white horse once again as a conqueror through the streets of his old garrison at Metz. Giraud looked forward to that moment with an almost religious passion. He had stripped off his medals and said he would not wear them again until he had made good his pledge. If, after this book is published, you hear of the general making his entry into Metz, you will know that there is at least one man on earth who conceives he has made the perfect poetic conclusion to his life.

It was therefore irritating for him to be bothered with political troubles during these bright winter days when it was so necessary to press on with the war. When Philip Jordan of the *News Chronicle* asked him during a press conference one day if he was going to relax the anti-Jewish laws, he answered tartly: 'That is nothing to do with you, monsieur.'

When Jordan protested that we had been invited to ask questions, and that the Jewish question in North Africa was one of some interest to the world at large at that moment, Giraud snapped: 'It is an affair that has nothing to do with the world. It is a matter for me alone to decide.'

I managed to get the question raised again a little later in the interview, and the general had in the interval apparently reflected that his remarks were going to create a most unfavourable impression in England and America.

'We must proceed slowly and with caution in these things,' he said more amicably. 'We will disturb the Arab section of the community if we act over-hastily. I am not anti-Jewish and I will not continue the anti-Semitic laws of Vichy a day longer than necessary.'

Indeed, steps were taken after that; the Jewish children were permitted to partake of the distribution of free milk and to attend government schools from which they had been excluded. It was still difficult for a Jew to obtain employment, but the more obvious anti-Semitic measures were abolished.

Presently the de Gaullists and the Communist deputies were released, and there followed a general clean-up of the half-dozen concentration camps through Morocco and Algeria where some ten thousand political refugees were imprisoned under conditions that were a disgrace to any civilised nation. A certain relaxation in the censorship was made, and the local French papers even published a photograph of de Gaulle.

A prime mover in these improvements was none other than the remarkable figure of Monsieur Marcel Peyrouton, who had come post-haste from the French Embassy in the Argentine to accept the position of governor-general of Algeria.

Now Monsieur Peyrouton was far from unsubtle. Behind a rather flabby and unpleasing exterior was a witty and most adaptable brain. He had served the French government with distinction, both as an earlier administrator in North Africa, where he had acted with promptitude in the local disturbances, and latterly as Vichy ambassador in Buenos Aires, where he had become a frequent visitor to the German Embassy.

M. Peyrouton had quickly seen which way the wind was blowing on his arrival in Algiers. He was perfectly aware of the animosity his appointment had created in America and England and he set about appeasing it with skill and judgment. He was, in fact, head and shoulders above anybody else in North Africa as an administrator.

Having carried out a number of necessary liberal reforms, he began to establish a government by committee, and Giraud was glad enough to give him a free hand. One after another the committees were nominated and set up—one for the banks, one for the press, another for trade and so on. Each committee contained a government official and was responsible to M. Peyrouton. Above all, good order and efficiency behind the lines was needed at this juncture of our military operations, and this was just what M. Peyrouton was out to provide by means of governing committees all comprised of experts who knew their business.

Obviously this new corporate government had to have its army, and M. Peyrouton and General Giraud were in complete agreement in the matter of getting the army together. As in France in 1939, there was a tremendous call-up throughout North Africa. Allied headquarters suggested that things might be done a little less rapidly since there was as yet no equipment to hand over to the French.

Even uniforms were lacking. But Giraud was determined to get an army of fifty thousand men into the field, and the call-up went on regardless of the fact that many of the men were much more urgently needed to run the railways and keep the ports and telegraph lines open. Peyrouton, on his side, needed an army for his new corporate government against the time when the government moved over to France. Moreover,

none of the recent converts from Vichy were blind to the fact that de
Gaulle already possessed *his* army.

The Duc de Guise arrived in Algiers, but the Royalists never got very
far. Here Mr Murphy, who was now joined by the British minister, Mr
Harold Macmillan, put his foot down. The Duke was removed. At the
same time, the French politicians were losing no point in debate. When
they were told to get rid of the pretender to the French throne they
replied to the British, 'Well, you have a king, haven't you?' And when
some protest was made against Peyrouton's rapidly forming committee
government they asked, 'What, do you wish us to return to the Chamber
of Deputies of 1939?'

The trouble was that no one in Algiers seemed to have any clear notion
of what they wanted. After two years' slow cooking over Nazi fires the
lid had been lifted off the French political stew and it was foul-smelling
and unwholesome to a degree. There was hardly an underground or an
aboveground political movement of the old France that did not flourish
here in the back streets of the big cities. The Cagoulards—the hooded
men of the Ku Klux Klan kidney—were there. And the Croix de Feu.
And the Communists, of several different hues. The traditional trinity
of the Comité des Forges–Banque de France–Four Hundred Families
survived in the very wealthy olive-oil combine which practically
controlled the country financially. There were the Jew baiters and the
Royalists, the anti-Italian and the anti-Arab blocs, the outright Fascists
and the mild Socialists, the Freemasons and the de Gaullists, the regular
army and the Church.

Many political groups of similar views were banded together into
uneasy alliances, but suspicion seemed to be the very air they breathed.
Down in Morocco the Resident General Noguès was openly derisive of
the Americans. 'Political children' was one of his lighter epithets. The
French Foreign Legion was issued with an order of the day instructing
them that they were to stand to their arms, since Marshal Pétain had
by no means been overthrown and the alliances with the Axis still held
good. There was a constant procession of people back and forth to Vichy
by way of Spain where M. Petrie, the Vichy ambassador in Madrid,
acted as a sort of official postbox.

From the hoardings and the placards in every street and in every
public place the unhappy features of Marshal Pétain gazed down on this
unparalleled political mess, and as yet it was a treasonable offence to
utter a word against the leader. The pictures of Giraud which replaced
those of the Marshal came along later, and the Vichy slogan, 'Travail,

Patrie, Famille,' was altered to Giraud's 'Un Seul But—La Victoire.'

The extraordinary thing was that there was no disturbance to speak of anywhere. Apart from a little restrained knife-play in the streets, a little sabotage along the railways and the ports, and a good deal of informing and spying and manoeuvring for position, there was no trouble at all. The French went quietly enough into the army, and bit by bit they grew to accept Giraud as the new leader. The presence of vast numbers of Allied troops who kept pouring off the transports with their modern arms undoubtedly had a strong influence for keeping the peace behind the lines. The people, moreover, were tired with the tiredness of two years of defeat.

Many odd characters, like M. Flandin, who once used to exchange telegrams with Hitler, and Josephine Baker, who had given up the stage, had come here to find what peace and ease they could. There were many thousands of refugees, and the more astute of them had been able to get into the profitable business of supplying North African products to the Germans.

Algiers fairly bulged with the crowds who pressed along the streets. For two years an automobile had been a rarity in the place. Now the traffic was overwhelming, and it often took a good half-hour to get up the steep and sinuous road to General Eisenhower's headquarters. I have known a number of G.H.Q.s, but never one as congested as this. Admirals were working in sculleries, and as like as not you would find a general or two weaving their plans in back bathrooms and pantries.

Half a dozen restaurants ran a merry black-market trade in food for a while, but it soon vanished as more and more troops came in by the thousands. The scent and the champagne disappeared. Prices rocketed. Things like leather goods were unobtainable. Eggs, once sold for a penny a dozen, reached sixpence each. Prostitutes hovering around the bar of the Aletti Hotel—the place where the officers went to relax in the evening—were asking their clients for £10 and £20 and getting it. Apartments became unobtainable, and you had to go twenty miles out of the city into the hills or along the coast to find an unoccupied villa.

Guns sprang up round the lovely town, and they made a brilliant show when the raiders came over at night. Maison Blanche airfield outside the city became an incredible sight—dozens of aircraft of every description stood about in the mud and among the ruined hangars. You could walk into the control room and book a passage for Casablanca, Tunisia, Egypt, India, London or New York.

The galaxy of uniforms in the streets made Algiers look like straight comic opera—Spahis on their white horses and dressed in their flowing red cloaks, the Goums in their brown galabiehs, the green- uniformed Chantiers de la Jeunesse (the Vichy Youth Movement), and the various kepis, caps and berets, pantaloons and cloaks of the Foreign Legion, the regular army and the native battalions. To these were added the whole remarkable parade of British and American uniforms and the blue and gold and white of the British sailors.

No, Algiers was far from boring. Yet, like many others, I found myself hating the place soon after I landed. It was not so much the weather, which was wet and cold, nor our depressing tenth-rate pension, the Regina Hotel, nor the food, which was bulk rations, nor even that milling, noisy throng in the press building where the news was handed out each day. It was the overriding atmosphere of suspicion and bickering argument, the endless ferment in the streets, the indigestion created by bad wine, the rows over censorship and transmission, and, above everything, the feeling that the intrigues of Algiers were a mean and petty betrayal of the men at the front who were fighting for something quite different.

There were many good things, too, of course. I found General Eisenhower's conferences warm, friendly and direct. Both Admiral Cunningham and Air Chief Marshal Tedder went out of their way to emphasise to me that they were delighted to serve under him. Eisenhower, it seemed, had great gifts as a chairman. Mr Harold Macmillan gave me a very shrewd analysis of the whole situation and one felt a slight return to sanity in talking to him.

I must confess, too, that there was a certain perverse professional pleasure in baiting such people as Bergeret, who apparently imagined that press conferences were designed for demonstrating that everything in this rank and unweeded garden was for the best in this best of all possible worlds.

Old friends bobbed up in Algiers from all over the world, and it was pleasant to drive occasionally with them into the bright hills at night and dine off wholly illegal steaks and champagne in a wayside inn we knew about.

This, then, was Algiers—the nerve centre of the North African campaign. But what about the villages? How were they taking it? I got to know one village fairly well—Thibar, just behind the front in Tunisia.

Seven

Thibar

IN THE village of Thibar Brother Mario gathered up his skirts and came running down the main street from the seminary. It was November 9th, and he was in a tremendous state of agitation. Indeed, the news he had to tell the villagers was almost too sensational to be believed.

'They have come!' he announced breathlessly outside the post office. 'They have landed. The Americans.'

Some of the villagers had already heard the news, but with the heavy suspicion of the French peasant they wanted something a little more definite than gossip. There had been so many rumours since France had fallen more than two years before.

'It's not true,' they said, and then, 'How do you know it's true?'

'I have been listening on the radio,' Brother Mario protested. 'Already they have seized the radio station at Oran and I have been listening to the Americans broadcasting. They say they have made landings right along the French coast. They say they have arrived with a huge army, the English as well, and they are calling on the French soldiers to lay down their arms.'

There was a great stir in Thibar that day. The district was administered from the market town of Souk-el-Kemis, about eight miles away across the Medjerda Valley, but Thibar was on one of the more important roads that led from Souk-el-Kemis through the tourist hamlet of Teboursouk to Tunis, and thus in a favourable position to watch events in the neighbourhood. All day the prefect of police and staff officers were careering about at mad speed in their chemical-gas motor cars. There was a company of Zouaves quartered in the district, and these men were now urgently summoned to barracks and confined there.

The most conflicting news came over the two workable radio sets in the village—the one in the seminary and the other in the hotel. From Oran strange announcers kept calling on the people to stay quiet and advising the soldiers to surrender and join the invaders. Radio Mondiale in Paris and Radio Marseilles were saying the most bewildering things. At one moment Radio Algiers was broadcasting that the country was under martial law and that the people must stand firm. The next minute it was playing an endless and meaningless succession of dance records and sugary arias sung by Tino Rossi and Jacques Trênet. Finally it went off the air altogether. Radio Casablanca fell silent too. No newspapers arrived from Tunis, and Tunis radio was simply adding to the confusion by repeating parrot-like all the wild announcements from Paris and Rome. Late in the afternoon three aircraft with strange markings flew very high across the lower end of the valley. Madame Zeni, the postmaster's wife, could get no sense out of the exchange at Souk-el-Kemis, and when she tried to get through to Souk Arras, the main depot, she was told brusquely that the line was commandeered for military traffic and that no civilian calls were to be put through.

That night it was quiet outside, but in the front parlour of the Grand Hôtel de Thibar there was violent discussion over the liqueur they called Thibarene and the rough red village wine that also came from the seminary.

Everyone was disturbed and apprehensive about the news. Monsieur Delafaine, who had come in from his farm to sell Arab stallions to the seminary, was also morbidly bitter. He had been a remote but enthusiastic follower of La Roque and the Croix de Feu before the war, and an avid reader of *Action Française* when he could get a copy from Marseilles. His wife was Italian, and more recently his rich wheat had been shipped across in great quantity to German buyers in France and at an excellent price. 'We will fight them off,' he cried. 'We can have no dealings with the traitors who killed our sailors at Oran.'

The other well-to-do farmers, though less vehement, were inclined to agree with him. Up till now they had not done badly in the war. Olives, vegetables, sheep and especially cattle had sold very well in Souk-el-Kemis, which means in Arabic, Market Wednesdays, and a little farther off in Souk-el- Arba, which means Market Fridays. Price were rising steadily. Moreover, to their minds Marshal Pétain was still the leader, a man of good sound politics who would bring France out of her troubles if given time. The Germans demonstrably were unbeatable. They might have setbacks in Russia, and Rommel might be forced back by superior forces in the empty desert; but Europe was a German garrison now, and North Africa was indissolubly linked to Europe. Look at the length of the coastline from Tunis to Oran, they said—thousands of kilometres. The Allies could not do it. The Luftwaffe would get after their ships and this thing would end as another Dakar. Why should France and North Africa be disturbed? They were out of the war. They wanted peace and a chance to develop their farmlands. This mad war had gone on too long, and the quicker the Americans and the British with their amateur armies were out of it the better. As for the Russians, one knew of old their dealings with the Communist deputies in Paris and what a scandal that had been.

Le Brun, the schoolmaster, was frankly Royalist. The republic was rotten and it was finished, he declared. The only hope now was to bring back the Due de Guise with a firm body of advisers around him, strong men who would settle this Communist nonsense once and for all.

The younger members of the group, the farm hands and the carriers and the young volunteers of Pétain's Chantiers de la Jeunesse, were by no means of this mind though they were divided amongst themselves. True, they wanted no war in North Africa, but it would be pleasant to see the Italians taken down a peg. The macaronis were grabbing everything in Tunisia. Moreover, was it not true that the Arabs were every day getting stronger and more insolent under German patronage? Everything was being taken from the French and given to the Arabs. The Americans would bring in gasoline and movies and there would again be cloth for sale in the bazaars.

This last was by far the larger group, and as the Thibarene went round the more outspoken of them began to shout for de Gaulle. They were fed up with this humiliation of having the Boches in France. Maybe now the time had come to strike back.

From time to time and Arab and French women came in from the kitchen and listened anxiously to the debate. 'Was the village going to be bombed?' they asked. 'Why weren't the men out digging air- raid shelters instead of talking? Should the children be taken away somewhere—to Le Kef perhaps, where it would be safer?'

This really was the big thing at the back of everyone's mind. Was the village going to be bombed? Were the vineyards and the wheat fields going to be ravished by terrible war? Were the women safe? Were food and clothing going to become dearer and harder to get? It was already the good God knew how long since they had had real coffee and enough sugar and jam. And perhaps, worst of all—were the men going to be called to the colours again and made to fight and die in this never-ending war? If only it would end.

The next day still more planes passed over the valley and now the wildest rumours were ranging everywhere. A traveller from the coast came in saying he had talked to a man in Souk Arras who had actually seen the Americans and the British landing at Bougie, and there were bloody battles going on in Algiers and Oran.

Algiers radio had come back on the air, and now the strange

announcer was claiming that the Allies were in possession.

On the other hand the *Dépêche*, arriving from Constantine late that night, printed a long proclamation from General Yves Chatel saying that the French North African forces were resisting heroically, that men were being urgently summoned to the colours and that all traitors to the marshal in this hour of supreme crisis would be shot. The Tunis newspapers also revealed a great commotion.

There was a definite swing toward de Gaulle and the Allies in the village that night. If at last the Allies were going to succeed, and succeed quickly, so that no one need fight, then yes, it might be a great thing for North Africa. France would rise again. There would be more money, more food, more fuel and clothing in the land. One by one the villagers were finding something deep in themselves— some repressed and forgotten hope—coming to the surface again. They grasped at every scrap of news with burning interest, and when an Arab lad brought in a leaflet dropped by a British plane they clustered round to read it with tense excitement. Still the dominant thing was to keep this horrible war out of Thibar—let the British and Americans fight it if they had to—yet it would be a thing of great pride if the French were to have their own land to themselves again.

All over North Africa such vital swaying arguments were going on while the Doughboys and the Tommies splashed ashore at Casablanca, Oran and Algiers. Thibar, a remote and tiny village across the Algerian border in Tunisia, only crudely reflected the tremendous issues that were agitating Frenchmen, Italians and Arabs along the Mediterranean, but the Thibar cleavages were the basic ones. Here, and in a thousand villages, was the Arab in heavy majority and either pro-German or indifferent. And the Italian who sought to score off the French and so supported the Germans. And the prosperous farmer and merchant who was getting good prices on foodstuffs and who felt tired and was willing now to follow the German path since it had for two years been the inevitable path of least resistance. And the petty official who was frightened for his job. That was the opposition. But among the mass of countrymen there was an awakened joy at the idea of freedom from Axis control. The idea of revenge, which had been dampened for so long, began to take fire again. Fear and lassitude were still for the moment the overruling emotions, but the awakened enthusiasm in this sudden change of fate was growing with every hour that went by. However, before they committed themselves irrevocably, the people wanted some sure proof that the Allies were there to stay.

Proof, sure proof, began to come in before the week was out. Allied parachutists had dropped at Bone on the coast, only a day's drive through the mountains. They had come down in hundreds out of the winter clouds and they had seized the airfield. Moreover, strange warships had appeared off La Calle and Tabarka. If this went on they would be in Tunis next. But what was going on in Tunis? The city was only a hundred-odd kilometres away to the north-east, but everyone who came out carried frightening stories. Germans were landing in huge planes on the airfields near Sidi Bou Said, and at the port of La Goulette ships were arriving every day from Sicily carrying Axis troops. There had been shooting in the town. The Bey had gone off to the country and the French army had taken control. One man said de Gaullists had sunk a ship in the mouth of the port. Another from Bizerta said that there had been a naval engagement out to sea. And all the time high over Thibar the planes kept passing back and forth.

The villagers were thrown now into a panic more violent than their first shock. If the Germans were going to fight in Tunisia then who knew?—the whole Medjerda Valley might be turned into a battlefield. Was anyone going to be safe? The villagers looked anxiously across the hills for the first signs of the advancing troops, and as they debated whether it would be the Americans coming from the west or the Germans coming from the east, Madame Schmee, the hotel-keeper's wife, was kept up half the night serving more and more drinks, to oil the talk.

No one, even now in the dead season in the middle of winter, could have gazed down that lovely valley and remained unmoved. The tourist looking up his copy of the *Guide Bleu* would have discovered that the banks of the Medjerda River were rated as one of the six most fertile valleys in the world. But there was a great deal more than cold productivity here.

From Souk-el-Arba right up to Medjez-el-Bab and beyond the land seemed to pour out every rich good thing on earth. It did not matter from which direction you approached—from the dry fir-covered hills near Tebessa in the south or from the wet cork-tree forests around Tabarka in the north—the young wheat rippled across the valley for mile after mile. In the centre of this richness, on a low spur that ran out toward the river from the surrounding mountains, the village of Thibar stood.

Years before, the White Fathers, coming out from France, had chosen this as the finest spot in the whole countryside. On the heights of the spur, just at the point where it flattened out toward the river, they built a seminary, a great pink-and-white storeyed building, the largest seminary in all Africa. To this was added a hospital and presently a pink-and-white village. The fathers worked at the land with inspired energy. They tucked up their robes round their waists and ploughed back and forth along the slopes of the spur until every morsel of rich red soil was under wheat, or vines, or fruit trees, or vegetables. As they collected a little money and more and more students came to them, they invested in modern power-driven tractors and multiple ploughs, in miniature railway lines to feed the piggeries and the horse and cattle stalls, in the latest French machinery to tend the vines.

A gang of workmen came to build a series of huge concrete and steel vats to hold the wine that was now beginning to pour in from the young vineyards. Moved by old monastic tradition they began to brew their own separate sorts of liqueurs—the thick and sticky Thibarene, the yellow Curaçao, a rough brandy. The farm became the wonder of the countryside.

Soon the White Sisters were established in the village, and their handmade carpets began to vie in quality even with those of the famous carpet town of Kairouan to the south. A pink-and-white church was built and two lines of cottages were spaced down either side of the one broad, straight village street. Last came the tiny hotel, just a couple of bare living rooms on the ground floor and a dozen tiny cell-like bedrooms on the first storey. Tourists making the trip from Tunis to the Roman ruins at Dougga would often come on to Thibar to taste the wine and sit for an hour over Madame Schmee's omelettes and *pot-au-feu*. All, or almost all, belonged to the White Fathers and they kept the mixed population of the village—French, Italian, Arabs and half-castes—to a strict and simple way of life.

Everywhere around them was the incredible changing beauty of the valley. Looking down from the stone balcony of the hotel you would see first the white cottages among the firs and then the almond trees that blossomed in such a delicate shade of lilac that the orchard at sunset appeared to be a cloud floating over the land. Beyond this the vineyards, endless mathematical lines of bare, brown twisting stalks that sprouted from earth that was sometimes the colour of chocolate and sometimes vivid crimson. After the vineyards the eye travelled for miles across the swelling green sea of wheat. It flowed across the valley not in a flat pattern but with the gentle undulating contours of a girl's body; every rise and dip in the land was moulded into soft green outlines. Half a dozen farming homesteads were dotted about in this green expanse that poured right across to the foothills on either side of the valley. At the foothills the wheat fell back and wild flowers grew. They grew among the brown and red boulders in startling unbelievable shades of vermilion, canary yellow, sky blue; and in mad African luxuriance. Beyond the boulders lay the last patches of green where the herds of goats browsed with their Arab shepherds right up to the snowline. Snow gleamed in the sunshine right round the mountains, a sharp white edge against the open sky, a painted frame for the green valley.

Throughout the day at every hour the colours were constantly altering. At night when the sunsets were often of monstrous ragged violence the whole valley was for a little lit with a film of red misty light that made the place seem more unreal than ever.

This then was Thibar in the bright cold days of November when the villagers keeping watch down the valley suddenly saw a line of khaki-coloured vehicles appear on the road from the west.

Little Mahmouda, the Arab houseboy at the hotel, was the first to see the strange soldiers turn off the main road and come up the paths toward Thibar. In a sudden instinctive outburst of fear the women in the village ran out and gathered in their children. They bustled them inside and slammed the doors. In an instant the village was cleared. Goats still browsed along the main street. One or two Arab horsemen reined in uncertainly beside the church and a young poilu in uniform bicycled at speed up to the post office and closed the door behind him. There was no sign of the White Fathers anywhere. The nunnery blinds were drawn and you could not be certain whether or not faces were peering through the lace curtains of the other houses. A queer fateful hush settled over the whole village.

Presently the foreign soldiers began to arrive. First a tiny open car with two men in it, both in steel helmets and carrying short stocky guns in their hands. Then more and more vehicles, vehicles with caterpillar wheels that churned up the mud about the crossroads, and filled the air with roaring.

Watching from their windows the villagers could see the officers questioning the Arab goatherds. They waited. There was no shooting. The Arab horsemen trotted with elaborate unconcern toward the soldiers. Gaining courage, the villagers began to come out of their houses. The gendarme appeared.

There was movement up at the seminary and one of the soldier's cars drove up to the main farmyard gate and disappeared inside.

The children somehow escaped and ran onto the roadway. They

shouted 'Vive les Americains.' The soldiers waved back. The street began to fill up rapidly. From the tops of their vehicles the soldiers shouted down at the little crowd and they were smiling and friendly. In a sudden release from fear some of the peasants were shouting 'Vive l'Amerique' now at the tops of their voices and offering up glasses of red wine to the soldiers. The soldiers laughed, drank the wine and handed back cigarettes.

A little group began to gather round an officer in front of the hotel. He spoke French like a tourist, but still one could understand him. He wanted to know if there were any Germans in the village.

'No, no,' they shouted together. 'There have never been any Germans here.' Someone ran off to fetch Brother Antonio from the seminary. He came from England many years ago and spoke English. The Arabs began offering eggs to the soldiers and got in exchange wonderful things— crisp cigarettes with real tobacco in them, handfuls of tea, soap—real soap. The village reached a pitch of excitement.

At the hotel Madame Schmee was frying eggs for the officers and handing round wine. One of the officers had had a long conversation with the gendarme and the postmaster and Brother Antonio. It seemed that the strangers were not Americans after all but Englishmen.

The town was full of soldiers that evening. All night the noise of their vehicles passing along the road went on. There were guns too. The soldiers were very dirty and muddy and tired. They dropped asleep on the ground like cattle. On the orders of the English no lights were shown in the village that night.

Miraculously in the morning most of the soldiers had gone. The stragglers could still be seen passing eastward up the road to Tebousouk and Tunis. There was a distant noise of gunfire from somewhere in the direction of Beja in the north.

Then the war fell on the valley itself. German aircraft swooped on Souk-el-Kemis where the British were trying to fashion an airfield out of the mud. Watching from their safe spur the villagers of Thibar saw the bombs fall and the great pillars of smoke go up from the houses, and from that day onward for the next six months no one in Thibar felt entirely safe.

They grew used to having the war around them. They came to terms with the noise and the sudden scares. They even grew used to the Messerschmitts that swept down the valley scarcely higher than the trees and they accepted that it was dangerous to travel anywhere abroad in a car during the daylight hours.

Some protective divinity seemed to watch over the little colony of the White Fathers. The village was only bombed once toward the end of the war, and even though the Molotov cocktail broke the windows in the seminary and the hotel, no one was seriously hurt. The stables were machine-gunned from the air, but the horses recovered from their injuries.

Wild storms of sleet and snow whirled round the mountains all that winter, but nearly always it was fine weather at Thibar. One after another the surrounding villages were laid waste; Thibar escaped. All through the spring and the early summer the front line lay only an hour's drive away, but this peaceful calm in the centre of the maelstrom remained immune.

The war correspondents took over the top floor of the hotel and as the months went by we grew to know the villagers very well. There was Mahmouda, the sharp little Arab boy, who would beg for chocolate as he swept your room, and Monique, the daughter of the house, who was always surrounded by half a dozen soldiers in the kitchen, a dark and buxom girl, half French and perhaps a quarter Arabic. Monique was a figure of considerable importance in the village, at least to the military quartered there. She had been used to buying her ribbons on occasional visits to the big shops in Tunis and it was her habit to croon such laments as 'Je t'attendrai' as she went about her work. She had lived in an arch and sentimental world compounded of month-old copies of *Marie Claire* and the movies and the cracked mirror nailed on the wall of her tiny bedroom. Already she was engaged to a young Frenchman in the district, but the British troops burst in on this gentle, adolescent love affair with the effect of an avalanche. With amazing poise Monique accepted it all—the gauche and heavy- handed compliments, the awkward gestures of these men who clumped about the kitchen in enormous boots, the gargantuan efforts they made to speak French. Little Monique, with all her rustic chic and her unaffected gaiety, seemed a very modern girl indeed to us in that monastic world and she enjoyed herself hugely.

Monsieur Schmee, a timid and self-effacing little Alsatian, was the head of the house. He divided his time between helping madame with the hotel and working on the books at the seminary. He was more than a little overwhelmed at the change that had overtaken the village and never at any point caught up with the events that rushed by.

Only two other guests besides the war correspondents and our officers stayed at the hotel and these were a bourgeois couple who had taken possession of room Number One, the best in the hotel. They had fled from Bizerta and were awaiting the day when they could go back. The war had turned their lives upside down and they simply took refuge in their old habits and remained remote from the rest of the hotel and as far as possible from the war. Sometimes I would meet the old man in his shirtsleeves taking the air on the balcony before breakfast and we talked stiffly of the weather and the crops and his lawsuit. He lived for the lawsuit, which was an entirely forlorn and hopeless claim for damages he was making against the government because his house had been damaged in the fighting. 'My God,' he used to say wildly, 'it's hard enough to find the government itself these days.' I never discovered his name. His anti-Allied politics were written all over the shiny black bourgeois broadcloth of his suit.

Then there was Honky-Tonk, which was the cruel name the soldiers gave to Monique's Arab grandmother because she had a cleft palate. Honky-Tonk was a lively old party much given to conversing in Arabic at the top of her squawking voice with such matrons as happened to be riding by on their donkeys. The old lady stole the show that terrible night when five over-excited soldiers pursued Monique's sister through the village. Arriving hot and panting at the hotel they rattled furiously on Honky-Tonk's bedroom door. Heaven knew what visions of rapine and death raged through the old woman's mind, for she collapsed with a loud cry and we had to break in to rescue her. Monique's sister, throwing hysterics in the scullery, was quite overlooked in the general astonishment when Honky-Tonk croaked through her withered lips that she was entirely to blame since she had enticed the soldiery in the first place.

The postmaster and his wife became friends of mine from the day I went to the post office to send a *mandat* for four thousand francs to a Russian family I knew in Philippeville.

'What do you want to send the money for?' demanded the postmaster suspiciously.

I explained. The family had been cut off from their bank in New York and needed the money as a loan.

'Send them two thousand,' said the postmaster. 'Four thousand is too much.'

We argued briskly for five minutes. Finally he called his wife and explained the whole business. 'But this is absurd,' she cried indignantly. 'Send them five hundred francs. That will be more than sufficient. Make out the forms, Henri.'

I felt I was losing ground rapidly. 'Please,' I said. 'This is my money and I want to send it and the people need it.'

The postmaster's wife eyed me with sudden coyness. 'There is a girl in this somewhere,' she said firmly. 'Some little thing you met on the way from Algiers. No?'

'No,' I said wearily, 'but if it will help to get the money off then yes, there *is* a girl in it.'

'Aha,' she cried and the postmaster beamed. 'You must have a glass of wine, monsieur.'

The whole family gathered round in the kitchen while we toasted one another. 'Vive l'amour,' cried the postmaster with enormous lechery. He took the money at last. All this was before breakfast. Feeling a little dazed, I went back to my spam and eggs at the hotel.

If I was in love with anyone at that moment it was with Madame Schmee. The hotel revolved round her. It was madame who rose first, at six o'clock, and got the fires going; it was madame who cooked all day in the kitchen, sometimes for a hundred. God knew how the pigeon pies and the hot artichokes and the brandy-soaked cakes were concocted on that ancient cooking range, but they were. She kept the accounts, she fed the children, she issued the wine, she did the marketing, she cooked and served the dinners, she organised the Arab servants, and she continued doing this every day from six until ten or eleven at night.

Madame Schmee adored children. Since she was not having one herself at that moment she adopted a couple. In the evening sometimes fifty soldiers would form a queue into the kitchen. Each soldier carried two eggs he had bought from the Arabs, and these madame would cook with one hand while she handed out wine with the other. Simultaneously she coped with the half-naked babies crawling around her skirts and issued directions to Honky-Tonk and Monique, then flirting in the corner with two dispatch riders. In the next room the radio shrieked at full blast and half a dozen arguments in three languages would be raging over the wine. The uproar and confusion passed description. In the midst of it all was madame, serene, smiling and untroubled. Generosity and kindliness flowed out of her. I never saw her angry or heard her speak sharply. When I was sent as an interpreter to protest at the lateness of the dinner or at the loss of somebody's laundry I found it impossible to maintain the complaint in the face of her distress. Sooner or later dinner would come and the missing shirts would turn up. And then her beautiful face would light up, and as a peace-offering she would timidly produce a cake she had specially baked or a glass of her precious *eau de vie*.

From the first she never made a serious effort to pronounce my name. I remained 'Monsieur Morsel' to the end.

Madame was short and plump and there was Arab and Italian blood in her. Once she had been very pretty. Even now, especially when she smiled, she was as attractive as her daughter.

The seminary had another life of its own. In scores the army trucks would drive into the farmyard and the soldiers would wait to draw wine from Brother Mongo or Brother Antonio. Brother Antonio had been born in Liverpool, and I never discovered by what strange route he had reached this haven in Tunisia. But it must have been a long journey, for he had forgotten most of his English, and what was left of it was a weird mixture of Cockney slang and mongrel verbs.

At first we were the only British in Thibar. But more and more soldiers came every week. First the hospital was taken over. Then another hospital, a vast affair of hundreds of tents, was erected in the valley. Odd units of the Royal Army Service Corps set up their camps and the main street was crowded with men in battledress. Then, toward the end, they gradually fell away. Thibar was practically deserted when I came to leave myself. The vines had come into leaf, the fields had turned yellow and now the crop was already stacked. The vats of wine in the seminary were practically drunk to the dregs and in place of lilac blossom the trees sprouted with full-blown green almonds.

The full blasting heat of summer was beginning to oppress the valley. And the German aircraft had vanished from the sky.

Were the people of Thibar typical of the rest of the villagers of North Africa and France itself? I think they were. Beyond everything else they were bound to a routine of the earth and their narrow daily lives. They were frightened when the landing was made. It meant a break in the routine they had grown to trust. But once they accustomed themselves to the change they welcomed it. They accepted the dangers of being at war in exchange for a new feeling of excited hope. They had been merely existing before. Now they began to live and look forward again. It was only the very old who really resisted the change, and even though they were not prepared to do anything about it they hated and despised the Nazis and the Fascists.

The Arabs of Tunisia were in a special category. For years German agents had been among them, buying off the intellectuals of every village. The German policy was, as the young Frenchman had said, to take everything from the French and give it to the Arabs. I have never believed that the Arabs were a major factor in the Mediterranean war, and the amount of sabotage and spying they did against us was negligible.

As for the bigger political issues, the majority of people in Thibar who sided with us were de Gaullist. For years they had heard his name on the radio, and it was the only symbol they knew for a revived France. Politics and politicians in general they distrusted heartily. But Pétain counted. The 'mystique du Maréchal' had taken hold on their minds, partly because marshals have been pretty imposing and mysterious figures in France since the days of Napoleon, and, anyhow, there was no other 'mystique' at hand.

Nevertheless it was patently absurd to say that these people would have opposed de Gaulle had he been allowed to come instead of Darlan and Giraud in the first place. They knew nothing much of the personalities of these leaders: they simply knew them as the masses will always know their leaders— at second hand and by reputation. De Gaulle was the name they knew as the Frenchman who had sided with the Allies, and they had not yet fully understood what had happened to him.

The French did not hate the British. British and Americans got an equal welcome almost everywhere, though not unnaturally both sides went about imagining each was more popular than the other. There would be occasional swings away from the Americans toward the British and vice versa in certain regions at certain times, but these phases never lasted. I noticed a tendency after the first few months for the French to regard the Americans as an innocent, boyish race in contrast to the more Europeanised and sophisticated British. But it was a fairly obvious distinction, since the Doughboy was a noisy and open-handed visitor and the Tommy rather more reserved in his manner.

At all events Thibar accepted us and grew to like us. They did not fear that we would stay to rule and oppress their country after the war was over. We saw, or thought we saw in those early days, great hope for the peace, not through the political leaders, but through the commonsense of the working people.

Eight

Djedeida

WHEN I arrived in Algiers it was already the first week of 1943, two months after we had made our landing, and only the wildest misconceptions of what was taking place at the front existed in America and England. It is no exaggeration at all to say that the average citizen in New York and London had not the remotest idea of what the fighting was like, of who was doing it, of what weapons were being used, of the numbers engaged on both sides, of what local objectives were being sought or of the prospects for the future.

All this was due no doubt to a mixture of reasons—the inability of the correspondents at the front to get their messages back, the necessity for secrecy which was often expressed in fretful and over- cautious censorship, the strangeness of the theatre, the individual prejudices of the newspapers, the radio and the people, the vast distances involved, the general muddle created by raw staff officers on their first operational jobs, our ignorance of the enemy and—probably most important of all—the fact that the men in charge of the campaign had themselves no really clear-cut picture of a situation that changed from day to day and hour to hour. It was, in fact, a great experiment, and we had to learn as we went along.

If only to be on your guard in the future, just for a minute throw your mind back to some of the simpler misapprehensions the Allied public was labouring under at this time. The authorities had given the impression that we had a huge army in action, thousands of tanks and guns and aircraft. In actual fact only three or four thousand men were fighting at the front and mostly with small arms and practically no air support at all.

In the States it was believed—as it is to this day—that the overwhelming majority of troops doing the fighting was American. In fact, it was very largely a British operation, and from the start of the Tunisian campaign to its finish the Americans never amounted to more than one-quarter of the troops engaged. (This is not to say that the campaign could have been won without American troops and equipment.)

In England the public either could not or would not understand that the battle was being fought in the mountains and the mud, and that northern Tunisia is not flat desert. Almost to the end they continued to make unfavourable comparisons with General Montgomery's rapid advances through Libya.

There was another thing, and this was the fundamental inability of civilians to realise that war is a painfully long, slow business. From the day war broke out people have listened to their radios and read their newspapers, and they have always found news of some description—if the Russian front was quiet, then something was happening in New Guinea or over the Ruhr. Inevitably this gave them the impression that war is a fast-moving thing. It simply is not. All the seemingly quick moves—the Battle of France, the bombing of Pearl Harbour, the collapse of Singapore—were the result of years of planning and manoeuvring for position. This matter seems childishly obvious, but just try to get it across to any gathering in a pub; to explain just how long it takes to get any division from any base to any front line. Try and explain the fact that up to this point only about twenty out of every hundred men sent out from England and America had seen any real fighting, and that the rest were engaged along the vast lines of supply. Try and explain that to keep one heavy bomber with a crew of eight in the air requires about fifty men on the ground. Try and explain that the average ship at sea rarely meets any actual trouble from one month's end to another.

The problems of supply were entirely different from the previous war. It now took double or three times the quantity of machines and explosive to kill a man.

But these things were not understood, and so at every stage of the war the people were impatient for action and irritated by delay.

They were irritated at the New Year because it looked as if the Tunisian campaign was reaching a stalemate. It had indeed. But what a wonderful story these two months had been.

After the first wild rush of landing—and finding everything was all right, the French collapsed— the troops had gone helter-skelter up the coast toward Tunis. It was a difficult journey of six or seven hundred miles, but what did that matter? Get there somehow, and get there quick. No one quite knew what enemy, if any, was ahead or to the flanks, but morale was up to the limits and there was an infectious air of excitement and discovery.

Every available motor vehicle was taken off the ships at Algiers and bundled onto the road. They rushed forward to Setif and Constantine on the inland road through the mountains, and still there was no opposition. Others landed from the sea at Bone and started to spread inland. Others again jumped by parachute into the midst of astonished farming communities. R.A.F. fighters swept down on airfields and, single-handed, the pilots took charge of the surrounding territory, and were quartered there quite happily when the ground troops arrived.

American Rangers and men of their best combat team, British parachutists and battle-school- trained infantry from the British Seventy-Eighth Division and the Sixth Armoured Division—these were the men who raced forward into the unknown mountains. They commandeered civilian cars, got the railways working, reopened the telegraph lines, took over farmhouses as bases, cleared the roads; and always they hurried forward until their lines of supply were stretched to the snapping point and huge unpoliced territories the size of half England were spread out behind them.

So great was the area into which this handful of men was running that units lost touch with one another along the empty roads and every company and platoon seemed to be engaged on a private campaign of its own.

At Bone, the forward port, Axis aircraft came over to bomb, and since no anti-aircraft guns had yet caught up with the front-line troops the place got cruelly mauled. The interior of Bone became a bad shambles for a bit and from the hilltop basilica behind the town down to the docks at the foot of the green cliffs an angry pall of smoke hung over the buildings. The railway station was savaged and wrecked. The town cinema fell in on itself. Ships trying to get into the harbour were caught by bombs and the survivors swam ashore through the icy sea. Along the roads the Luftwaffe kept up a dangerous strafing and the men were leaping to the ditches a dozen times a day.

But still, in mid-November, they were finding no real opposition on the ground. By now they were approaching Medjez-el-Bab, which means the Keys of the Gate. From here two roads led straight into the heart of Tunis. And it was then at last that the Germans began to appear.

General Anderson had rushed his headquarters as far forward as Constantine and even Constantine was now a day's full drive behind the front. Going forward, the general found himself faced with a very serious quandary indeed. His supply lines back to Algiers were in a hopeless state. The railway was not yet working regularly. Bone was being bombed, and very little was coming in there from the sea. His men were wearied and in serious need of everything from bullets to biscuits. There seemed little chance of getting really good supplies up the long mountain roads from Algiers for weeks to come.

But the men were full of determination and eagerness. They were incredibly dirty and short of sleep, but they lived now for the hour when they would enter Tunis.

The American consul-general in the town had escaped to Constantine, and he had a remarkable story. 'Hurry, hurry, hurry,' he said. He had gone to the palace in Tunis as soon as the first landings were made at Algiers and he had read out the president's letter to the Bey. The Bey was noncommittal and disposed to wait and see. He would not say whether or not he would give right of way to the oncoming Allied troops. The officers of the German and Italian armistice commissions were at his elbow.

In the town great things were happening. Some of the French had risen for the Allies. The director of railways had sent as much rolling stock as possible out to Algeria. Other gallant men had attempted to block the harbour by sinking a ship there. Work was at a standstill and there were constant brawls all through the night between Frenchmen and Italians.

As in the rest of North Africa, from Dakar to Algiers, no Axis troops whatever were garrisoning Tunisia. There were just the handful of men on the enemy armistice commission, and these were militarily powerless. The Axis had been caught completely off balance.

But on the third day after the arrival of the Allies in Algiers the Axis had acted, and with incredible thoroughness and speed. A couple of small coasters had put in full of German troops. Others arrived by air troop-carriers on Tunis airport, and as they poured out down the main road to the city more and more aircraft came flying in from Sicily.

The German troops raced through the bewildered cities of Bizerta and Tunis, seizing every keypoint—the post offices, the railway stations, the arsenals, the docks, the airfields, the customs, the police stations. They spread through the back streets, cowing those who had been shouting for de Gaulle. The French soldiers and the soldiers of the Bey had been clapped under German orders before they realised what had happened, and now they were confined to their barracks. The director of railways had been shot, and, one after another, Frenchmen suspected of Allied sympathies were being thrown into gaol. Anyone who resisted was put up against a wall. The people at large were baffled and had fallen back on a sheep-like passivity while the Germans took over.

But still there were only a very few Germans—a few thousand at the most—and they had not yet succeeded in getting in more than a handful of tanks. Scores of Messerschmitts and Focke-Wulf fighters were arriving, but they were still awaiting petrol from Italy. Only twenty-five Germans were spared to run down by sea to the big ports of Sousse and Sfax, and of these ten were split off to occupy Gabes on the Tripolitanian border. Kairouan, the big inland market town, had been taken over by a tiny Italian garrison.

If only we could have landed in Tunis at the beginning, the consul said. The pitifully small enemy vanguard could have done nothing. But now the Germans were pouring in. In desperate haste they were throwing up new airfield runways, digging weapon pits, laying mines, mounting anti-aircraft guns and making anti-tank ditches along the roads.

A German general had arrived and seized the American consul's house, which, unfortunately, had just been redecorated. It was being used as German headquarters now. The consul himself had escaped only by a fluke. When he had gone to read the president's letter to the Bey he had told his wife that she should pack and leave for Constantine if he did not return by nightfall. His wife, seeing the German soldiers in the streets, had packed anyhow. That night, with some French friends, they had driven out of the city. Twice they were stopped by newly posted German sentries on the outskirts. The Germans were under orders to stop all unauthorised outgoing traffic and the soldiers peered suspiciously at the consular party. But the Frenchmen in the car waved nonchalantly and said it was all right, and somehow they had got through to the British lines and Constantine.

That was the consul's story. Clearly it indicated that time was precious. The Germans still might not be ready. Anderson talked to his senior generals—Alfrey the corps commander, Eveleigh of the Seventy-Eighth and Keightley of the Sixth Armoured. They were all keen to advance. And so it was decided to go forward with the gamble.

At once, in these last days of November, there was skirmishing along the roads with the German outposts. This light opposition was overwhelmed, but every mile now the Allies were coming under heavier fire. They met Germans outside Mateur in the north and outside Medjez-el-Bab in the south— these were the two main sectors. The plan was to make the Medjez-el-Bab sector the main one. The two roads that led thence into Tunis were both in excellent condition and apparently unmined. Both were dominated by an isolated series of bare humps which the troops quickly dubbed 'Longstop Hill'—apparently because it bore the same relation to the township of Medjez-el-Bab as a longstop does toward the wicket in cricket.

The Seventy-Eighth Division swept past this obstacle and reached

Tebourba and Djedeida. This was on November 26th, and now, indeed, the battle seemed almost won. The gamble was succeeding. Tunis lay barely twelve miles off up the valley and British patrols going farther forward held the suburbs in view.

At Djedeida the Germans counterattacked, and for a moment stopped the British rush. It was one of those moments of high drama in the war when one stroke can finish the battle. This was match point in this tumultuous game of tennis and the Allies had won all the other sets. I had seen almost the same thing happen the other way about in Egypt the previous summer when Rommel was about to fall on Alexandria and the Nile. Just one more tiny little effort he needed and then he had everything—all Egypt, perhaps the whole of the Middle East. Just one more brigade of men, just another couple of batteries of guns and he might have done it.

It was like that here for our men. The Germans held their ground and attacked again. The seesaw was beginning to balance at last. The Allies had gone on and on and deeper into the German opposition until the few scattered elements that we had at the front were not quite strong enough to deal with the increasing enemy opposition. But no one knew that at the time. Everyone from privates to brigadiers did just what they had to do, and with what means they had, because they were caught up in this game and it had reached the high point of its intensity.

The Germans attacked again, down the Tebourba road. Useless now for the British to cast around for reinforcements—the reinforcements were hundreds of miles away. Tebourba was given up and then Longstop Hill. Feeling baulked and still determined to grasp their prize before it was snatched away, the Allied commanders counterattacked at Longstop. The Guards fought their way up to the top of that vital hill, and, leaving an American unit to hold the place, were retired to strike in another direction. As they were route-marching back to their assembly point dispatch drivers caught up with the Guards' headquarters. They brought the ugly news that the Germans had run through the slender American garrison, and so there was nothing for it but that the Guards should turn round and go back. For a second time that day they swept up to the heights of Longstop, but now the physical strain was too much. They could not hold the position. The Allied line reformed itself at Medjez-el-Bab.

Even now the Allies had an opportunity of returning with a mortal blow. But even as they planned to strike again the matter was taken out of their hands. Rain fell. Not ordinary rain, but the wild torrential rain of Africa. The ground turned to mud, and it was the mud of that same African extravagance, thick, sticky and bottomless. The dead were buried in mud and the living were in it up to their knees. They were wet to the skin all day and all night. They had mud in their hair; mud in their food. When the mud dried it set like iron and had to be beaten off the boots with a hammer or a rifle- butt. Before the astonished eyes of the commanders tanks went down to their turrets in mud. A spell of a few fine days made no difference—the mud was there just the same, and if you sent out a squadron of tanks, you never knew whether or not they would be caught in another downpour and so abandoned to the enemy. The few forward airfields we possessed—at Bone, Souk-el-Kemis and Souk-el-Arba— all lay on the floors of valleys. Rain drained down onto the flat ground, and for days at a time the aircraft were unable to take off. The Germans had no such disadvantage. Their fields were based on porous sand near the coast. And so their fighters kept multiplying in the air while ours were diminishing. Moreover, the Germans were not advancing—they merely sought to hold onto what they had. The rain and mud were for them a godsend. They perched in their foxholes and watched the British tanks come on into the mud-bound belt of fire.

The British foot regiments performed feats of astonishing courage at this time—notably the Hampshires, the Guards and the Argylls. Probably the most ferocious fighters of all were the British parachutists, who were grounded and used—perforce—as ordinary infantry.

It was not easy in this bitter, ruthless fighting for the British commanders to realise that the gamble so gallantly taken was now going against them. They persisted for a time, putting in a series of small counterattacks which got nowhere, largely because battalions were sent to do what only brigades could have accomplished. But by the middle of January it was clear that a stalemate had been reached. Of necessity we would have to put in occasional limited attacks to keep up our morale and worry the Germans, but clearly we had to wait now until much greater forces were brought over from England and America. At last it was seen that we would have to wait until the wet season was over in March or April.

Eisenhower now had to make up his mind on how he should dispose his forces during the lull.

Should he hold onto what he had and make the Germans pay for every yard they advanced? Or should he get clean out of Tunisia and regroup more comfortably and expeditiously in Algeria? He chose to hold what he had.

The stalemate brought all sorts of questions to light. For example, Why had we not landed in Bizerta and Tunis in the first place? The navy's answer to that was it would have meant that the ships were exposed to Sicily-based aircraft and submarines for an extra day of daylight. We were already taking considerable risks in going so far into the Mediterranean as Algiers and Bone.

In the event it turned out that we probably could have got safely through the Sicilian Narrows, and then perhaps the Tunisian war need never have been fought at all. There is no doubt that Tunis would have collapsed almost as easily as Oran and Algiers. But whether the high command was justified or not in taking that risk is only a matter for academic dispute now.

There was another larger question. Had not Montgomery's offensive and Eisenhower's North African landing been staged in exactly the wrong order? Had we gone into Tunisia first, Rommel would have fought his desert campaign knowing that he had no base on which to retreat, and that would have been very bad indeed for German morale and German supply lines from Italy.

The answer to this probably is that the high command expected to conquer Tunisia with the First Army before Montgomery reached Tripoli—even with the First Army's late start. At any rate the Afrika Korps was scooped up eventually. The only man missing from the bag was Rommel himself.

So, then, the first phase of the campaign was over at the end of the first fortnight in January. We had not done too badly considering that practically none of the troops or their officers were battle-trained when they started. Every day they were getting more cunning, eliminating waste effort, taking better cover, striking more shrewdly and with fewer unnecessary casualties.

The front had temporarily stabilised on a line running from Tabarka on the northern Mediterranean coast through the sodden cork-tree forests to Sedjenane and the blasted township of Medjez-el-Bab on the Medjerda River. Thence the line wobbled uncertainly south again over the mountains to El Aroussa and Sbeitla, where the trees became stunted and ground more rocky. After that, with many gaps, the troops were strung through Gafsa until the front petered out into an uncontested no-man's- land in the Sahara Desert.

Roughly speaking, the British held the north and central sectors, down to El Aroussa, the newly formed French force was grouped about the Grande Dorsaale Mountains in the south centre and the Americans held from Sbeitla to Gafsa—an uncertainly balanced three-decker cake.

This was the line I set out to see in the middle of January, the line on which I was going to live for the next four months. To the south of Mareth was Montgomery's Eighth Army, which had now flung Rommel out of Libya. The enemy position, manned with about 200,000 troops of Rommel's and von Arnim's combined armies, was a rough rectangle sixty miles wide, a hundred and fifty miles deep.

Nine

Medjez-el-Bab

IN AFRICA it was always good to be on the road to the front. Once you left the city behind, you had a feeling of escape, even a sense of strong freedom, as though you were a schoolboy setting off for the summer holidays. You knew that in the place you were going money was not going to count any more. There would be no newspapers, no telephones, no buses or trains to catch and life would be lived freely in the open air. Moreover, you had no idea of how long you would be away or of where you were going or of what would happen.

Even in the desert this was so. When we were in Cairo we would say that we hated the desert. But once we got past Mena House on the road to Alamein and Mersa Matruh there would be a feeling of lightness and escape and expectation.

In North Africa it was even better, because in place of the desert the road wound through a country that looked like a garden, and at every twist in the road there was something new.

It was still very early when we got out of the cobblestone clatter along Algiers docks, and then, a map on my knee—one of those Michelin maps I had not seen since my last holiday through France—I charted the course past the airfield at Maison Blanche, past the village with that perfect name, Retour de la Chasse, and down into the long valley, where we would run all morning, keeping the great white range of the Atlas Mountains on our left.

The vineyards were astonishing. They ran on mile after mile, and today the wind coming off the snow blew the white and pink fruit-tree blossoms through the vines. Sometimes through the morning we got involved in long convoys of guns and tanks and trucks that were pushing up to the front. A railway kept winding in and out of the valley, and when a shut railway gate blocked the path and the snorting antique French locomotive went by, you could see that the carriages were full of Doughboys with their outsize helmets and Tommies sleeping on their kits. The black tarpaulins over the open trucks revealed the shapes of more guns, more tanks.

Every few miles Arabs stood beside the road and offered up eggs and tangerines, chickens and oranges, wine and rabbits. The sun streamed down.

Toward midday we came to the head of the valley and a long goods train was stationary on the level crossing, blocking back the traffic for a quarter of a mile on either side. I was new to the road then, and indeed I had to travel that way half a dozen times before I realised what a neat job of sabotage the stationmaster was doing. There was always a train sprawled across the main road at this place, and consequently always a traffic block. The army supply lines lost at least three hours a day there.

We waited on this morning for fifteen minutes. The native engine-driver hung impassively out of his cab and did nothing whatever. I walked up to the head of the line of vehicles on the road and found a military policeman.

'Why can't the train move?'

'I dunno,' the policeman said. 'It's always happening like this and I can't speak their bloody language.'

He tried again. The engine-driver shrugged his shoulders. 'The signal's down.'

'Then who works the signal?' we asked.

With contempt he answered, 'The signalman,' and no amount of persuasion could get out of him the whereabouts of the signal box.

'Divide the train for a few minutes and let the traffic go through,' we said at last. 'We can uncouple this carriage here on the crossing and you pull forward for twenty yards.'

'Can't do that without permission of the stationmaster,' said the engine-driver, and he had a maddening way of talking.

'Where is the stationmaster?'

'He's gone to lunch.'

A sergeant in one of the lorries who was as angry as I was said to the British policeman, 'Just look the other way, will you, chum?' and he unstrapped his tommy-gun. The train was parted and the traffic flowed through.

We passed now into the next valley, an outlandish place of slate-coloured boulders and wild cataracts among the firs. Beyond this the road burst suddenly onto the high plains of Algeria, a great steppe where the wheat rolled like the sea under the freezing wind, and here you could travel at eighty miles an hour along the straight and perfect highway.

Near Setif the air was alive with newly arrived American bombers and fighters, and as we drew petrol in the town we fell in with a platoon of young Americans who had been out on a man-hunt.

German aircraft had been over two nights before dropping Arabs and Germans dressed as Arabs who hid by day in the friendly well-paid farmhouses and by night laid charges under the bridges and railway lines. Two of the saboteurs had been brought in.

In the darkness and with no headlights we crawled into the tourist town of Constantine, which is suspended like a spider's web above and around a spectacular gorge, a town on a massive rock from which in the daytime you could see across Algeria for a hundred miles in every direction.

It was a headquarters town now and full of troops who moved curiously among the tourists and the French refugees who had fled here to get away from the war. As at Aix-en-Provence or any of the towns in the Midi in the old days, the French sat around in the open-air cafés drinking syrupy apéritifs and watching, watching, watching.

At Constantine I began to see just how modern and well equipped this new First Army was. For one thing, there was a transit camp, and that was something new to me. Instead of pulling in beside the road and sleeping in the vehicles or on the ground, you called on the town major and he gave you the address of a place where you could get a bed and a hot meal and food and petrol for the next day's journey. My bed was a wire mattress in a children's nursery school that had been taken over, but there were blankets and the place was warm. Two parachutists who had just come in from behind the German lines lay on the next two beds to mine, luxuriating in the comfort. It was their first night out of the mud for a month.

The place was full of odd characters—motor torpedo boat officers who had been making raids on the Italian convoys in the Sicilian Narrows, awkward and lofty young subalterns just out of England with batmen and bright uniforms, R.A.F. pilots who had been shot down and were on their way back to their squadrons, American intelligence officers looking for their units, and others who had simply got lost. You could pick up a hundred stories in an hour.

It was all so *new*—that was the thing I could not get used to after the dusty and dilapidated-looking Eighth Army. New uniforms, new guns, new vehicles, new men. There were things that never found their way out to the desert—cases of whisky, gin and beer, coffee and coffee-cups, orderlies to cook and orderlies to clean your boots, china plates and eggs and bacon for breakfast, white bread and hot water. Everyone appeared to live in houses or at least in tents. The road was plastered with notices that would have taken the most timid motorist through the wilds of Thibet: 'Dangerous curve ahead...Keep your distance... Bumps ahead...Narrow bridge...Steep hill...Rough surface...Beware of slippery surface...Keep clear of the verges' (which some soldier had naturally altered to 'Keep clear of the virgins').

Everything, it seemed, that could keep the army well fed, comfortable and happy had been laid on. If you broke down on the road it was not an hour or two before your vehicle was picked up by a Light Aid Detachment and mended. Every township had a town major and accommodation, the Naafi stores were full of soap, cigarettes, toothpaste, sweets and even fresh clothing. There was a regular postal service. Every man, especially the Americans, carried around twice or three times as much kit as any soldiers I had seen before. They all looked smart and tidy and well shaven. Generals buzzed about in reconnaissance planes, and jeeps—those jeeps that were beyond price in the desert—were on the road in hundreds.

Now was this a serious army or a luxury parade-ground army? Were these be-monocled young British lieutenants and grapefruit-juice fed Americans quite tough enough? What was going to happen to them when they hit the German 90th Light Division and the Panzer grenadiers?

Well, I was scarcely entitled to say much about it, a non-combatant, sitting on a warm bed with a glass of whisky, three hundred miles behind the front. But in a sudden access of doubt and fear I wanted to get forward quickly and see what was happening.

In the morning when hoar frost was still crunching on the road, I bought the local French paper in Constantine. There was one little item on the front page that more than anything else abruptly made me realise that France was back in the war again. It said, 'A Court Martial, sitting in Constantine yesterday, sentenced to death the two natives, Mahmoud Aly and Hassan Aly, who were found guilty of hiding and assisting enemy saboteurs operating behind our lines. The two prisoners were shot this morning.' Only twenty-four hours had elapsed since our American friends had brought the two natives in and handed them over to the French.

We ran down now out of the cold mountains and the snow into the half-tropical vegetation along the coast at Philippeville. If ever one needed a proof of the insanity of war it was here. A superb vineyard that for twenty years had produced the finest wine of the region had been torn out. Soldiers grubbed at the gnarled old roots and stacked them in neat piles beside the road, where they would dry and be useful for firewood later on. An old peasant farmer hung over the fence watching the soldiers at work and though we tried to talk to him his heart was too full for words. In place of the vines they were laying long runways of steel matting through the mud. When I came by a few months later great bombers were already taking off for Italy.

Beyond the lovely palm-tree port of Philippeville the coast road turns straight into the mountains again and this is the region of the cork-tree forests. Mounds of cork bark were piled along the tracks. The cork had been awaiting export ever since the war began. And to this now was added the high explosive that had been brought ashore for the army.

Never before or since had I seen such quantities of ammunition, so many evil piles of yellow bombs. The trains on the narrow-gauge railway were piled with bombs too, and shells. For thirty miles the ammunition was stacked in heaps on either side of the road under the trees, and more was being dumped as we went along. These were the bombs that, in the end, were not all needed in the Tunisian campaign and later fell on Italy and Europe.

The port of Bone has a huge square Byzantine basilica standing on a high knoll outside the town, but beyond that the place is purely French. Places like Algiers are hybrid growths, luxury resorts where the millionaires have built their villas. But Bone was almost painfully reminiscent of those Provençal French towns we had not seen for years. It was all there—the Saint Raphael advertisements with the hurrying waiters, the signs that read 'Dubo...Dubon...Dubonnet,' the gay umbrellas over the tables on the pavement cafés and the people sitting under the trees in the town square, the piled-up barrows of fish and oranges down by the docks, the men in striped sweaters and the women with bright handkerchiefs over their heads, the graceful façades of the buildings with their sloping Mansard roofs and window boxes, the red and white terracotta cottages by the sea, the cobblestones and the paper-covered books in the shops, the marionette-like gendarmes at the corners and the mad traffic.

A good deal of all this was blown up. The square was roped off because a bombed wall was about to collapse there at any minute. The church was a mass of black and fallen timbers. There was still running water but no electric light as we groped our way to the town major's office through the rain.

He boarded us out for the night with a young Frenchwoman in the suburbs, twenty francs each for the bed.

'I have sent the children into the country while the bombing lasts,' she said. She kept running into our room with odd scraps of conversation. We were her first guests from the British army and she was nervous, excited and gay all at the same time. When the sirens howled and German aircraft raced over the housetops machine-gunning she went into the kitchen and baked us one of those sticky caramel French cakes you have to eat with a spoon, and she stood over us until we had finished it. In the morning we found that the cake had taken the last of her sugar ration.

All day after leaving Bone we threaded in and out of convoys trundling through the rain up to the front. The leading vehicle of these convoys travelled about twenty miles an hour, the regulation pace. Yet by some form of mathematics I don't understand, the last vehicles in the convoys were always travelling between thirty and forty miles an hour in order to keep up. I watched that phenomenon a dozen times as we ran across the border into Tunisia and back into the mountains.

In the afternoon when wild flurries of snow and sleet were breaking across the road we reached the Hôtel Transatlantic, a tiny alpine pension at Les Chênes. We had been travelling three days now, and still we had not reached the front. A handful of officers had come back here from the mud for a few days' rest—men who had exhausted themselves temporarily on night patrols and skirmishing through the woods.

They had been up to their necks in muddy foxholes most of the time with no cover whatever over their heads. There was a Spitfire pilot, the leader of his squadron, who was going home. The other pilots had tried to keep it a secret from the senior officers that the boy's eyesight was failing. In the raids over Tunis he had grown more and more reckless to make up for his deficiency, but it had been impossible to disguise the fact that sometimes, when he got back, he had to make several runs in order to get down. In the end he was ordered to submit to a medical examination and now he was grounded and going home. It had hurt the boy more than he could say, being grounded, for he and his friends had fought together for a long time. He felt he was out of it, disgraced, not good enough any more. The other pilots were giving him a farewell dinner and trying through the conversation to tell him that what he was thinking was not so, that he was still the leader of the squadron. But they made no attempt to disguise the fact that they thought it was bad luck he was not going to have the chance to risk his neck twice a day over Tunisia any more.

In the morning we came down out of the mountains and the storm into the sunshine of the Medjerda Valley. The other correspondents, the veterans who had been on the job since the landing, were drinking gin and lime on the balcony of the Grand Hôtel de Thibar. I was introduced to madame.

'Bonjour, Monsieur Morsel,' said madame cheerfully. 'Bienvenu.'

Each day then we travelled out to the most interesting sections of the front from Thibar. You could get to almost anywhere on the line within an hour or two, gather the story and then drive back to Thibar in the evening to write it.

For a month I could not get used to this front. The geography baffled me. The tactics were an endless riddle. It was, I suppose, a kind of claustrophobia, for I could not accustom myself to the nearness of everything, the fact that while you sat on one hill there was the enemy just across the valley sitting on the next hill. Sometimes you could lift your glasses and actually see the Germans walking about.

For years the enemy had been for me someone remote, a red line on the map, a cloud of dust across the desert horizon. A comfortable no-man's-land dividing the two armies by ten or twenty miles— sometimes by fifty miles—had been the accepted thing in Egypt and Libya. Since the enemy could run across the flat intervening space in an hour or two, you would not willingly bed down for the night anywhere within sight or earshot of him. I had never really seen a battle, only bits of battle; all the rest vanished under clouds of smoke and dust, and spread for a hundred miles across the desert. You never looked down on anyone—or up to them—since there were no hills. Even when the battle joined it was a thing of terribly fast movement that spilled in all directions, so that there would first be firing away to the right, then away to the left, and you might travel for a full day behind the enemy lines and then drive through them back to your own people again.

But here the troops were tumbled on top of one another. They stuck to the roads. They stayed put. They never made great encircling movements. And you could see the fighting. You could climb up on a hill and see your own tanks go out and see the enemy tanks and guns emerge to meet them. The two armies seemed to be forever clutched in a tight embrace. A ferocious skirmish might be going on in one valley, and if you happened to be a couple of miles away in the next valley you heard nothing and knew nothing. If you advanced a thousand yards it was considered a great achievement. Every foot of the front was complicated and dangerous—landmines all over the place, snipers perched in the most unlikely spots, shells and mortars dropping out of nowhere. The pleasure of motoring about the front from one sector to another was gone altogether. You had to keep your frozen head poked through the roof of the car on the lookout, and even then you often got no time to jump out before the Messerschmitt was upon you. And this went on for scores of miles behind the front. At night there was no peace in the forward areas because of the bombing over that confined space.

This compression of the fighting seemed to me to call for much quicker wits and much more vigilance than the desert, except of course when a battle was joined and then perhaps you had to think quicker in the open space. My natural instincts were to seek safety in space—in danger always run for the open desert. Here it was the other way about. Everyone dived for cover under a rock or in a wood.

And there was the mud and the rain. It changed everything. Instead of the freedom of shorts and a shirt you were buttoned up to the ears in a heavy kit. Now I began to understand why men lived in farmhouses and caves when they could, why the roads were so well signposted, and why the army grabbed what comforts it could when it was not actually engaged. This perishing cold, this all- invading mud and this lack of hot food could exhaust and kill a man just as thoroughly as bullets.

I discovered this around Sedjenane where I began a series of tours down the line. Sedjenane was a wayside railway station in the wet cork forest on the way to Mateur. Whoever held Mateur held Bizerta, and whoever held Green and Bald Hills outside Sedjenane held Mateur. The Argylls among others attacked those two hills in the early days. They were bludgeoned and broken up by the most terrible crossfire that entirely governed the one narrow road. There was a long railway tunnel at that point too, and the Germans held one end, we the other. At night, patrols of each side used to go into the tunnel and lay booby traps. By day the constant shelling went on until the very mountain-sides were churned up into craters of red mud. Every time the Argylls emerged from their foxholes and advanced through the mud on foot they were cut up.

Almost to the very end this cruel in-fighting went on, and as in most of the other places along the line, whoever held the high ground held the battlefield. If you won the pass then you won everything. Green and Bald Hills were Number One Pass on the line, and if you care to drive across the mountains there now you will see by the graves how badly we wanted to get through; how determined the Germans were to stop us.

The road near Sedjenane was so often blitzed from the air by German fighters nipping up from their fields ten minutes away, that it was closed to vehicles in the daytime. You had to park your car a mile or two back and walk on foot and under cover to the forward positions.

This was where our parachutists fought when they were turned into ordinary infantry. No prisoners were taken in that terrible skirmishing through the rocks. I called on the parachutists one day, and all around the bush was heavy with the sweet and nauseating smell of bodies that were turning rotten in the sun after the rain. In their whole approach to death these young men had completely altered. They had killed so many themselves and with the bayonet. They had seen so many of their companions die. They had become so well acquainted with death they had no fear of it any longer. The fact that that body lying over there was Bill or Jack or Jim who had eaten breakfast with them this morning was not remarkable or horrible: you either lived or you died or you got wounded, and any one of these conditions was an accepted condition. It was not that pity or grief had gone out of them, but that they were living in a well of danger and their lives were sharpened and lifted up to the point of meeting that danger directly. It was all very largely a technical matter—whether you got your machine-gun burst in first and with the right direction. These men were soaked in war. They were grown old to war in a few weeks, and all the normal uses of peace and the ambitions of peace were entirely drained out of them.

These were the men who were flung into any part of the line that was critical. They led the forward rushes; they stopped the gaps in the retreats. They were feared by the Italians—and by the Germans— as the most terrible animals.

The conditions in which the parachutists lived at the front were barely good enough to keep life going—bully, biscuits, not much else. Once for four days and nights they were in the rain and under fire and unable to heat any food or drink because the smoke of a fire immediately drew snipers' bullets. Some, in the extremity of their hunger and shuddering cold, said, 'The hell with it—I've got to eat,' but they were killed as soon as they got a fire going. At length they were brought a few miles back for a spell. Some huts had been prepared for them and a meal. But when the men got off the trucks they did not want to walk the remaining four hundred yards for the meal and the shelter. They fell onto the mud beside their trucks and slept in the streaming rain.

Once on Jebel Mansour a sergeant of these men led his platoon to the top. He himself was still shooting when he got the order to retire, and his companions were dead around him. From down the hill the others saw him suddenly clip another magazine of bullets to his gun, and he stood upright facing the enemy and in their continuous chain of fire.

'—— this,' the sergeant said, '—— this.' He shouted it straight at the screaming sky, his ultimate expression of human dignity and defiant pride. And he walked straight toward the enemy, firing as he went, one man against a thousand. It was impossible to see how far he got before he died.

The parachutists were a small brigade—perhaps 1500 to 1600 at the front. When the campaign ended they had killed about three thousand Germans and Italians.

Medjez-el-Bab and Longstop Hill were Number Two Pass leading into Tunis, and the Argylls—or what was left of them—were in the line the first time I went there. A providential burst of sunshine had come through and dried out a thick crust on top of the chocolate mud. Coming down either from Testour or from Oued Zarga farther up the Medjerda Valley the township still looked like a township, and the peasants were still tilling their farms round about. Right through this campaign the farmers kept on at their land in the front line. When everything in their world was crumbling about them they clung tenaciously and pathetically to their peace-time habits. If the farmhouse was blitzed the peasants lived in the cowsheds. If an army headquarters moved in on the homestead then the farmer stayed right on and fed his chickens among the anti-aircraft guns. If a field had to be ploughed then he simply skirted round the shell craters. The peasants and the Arabs went to ground somewhat when a barrage or bombing was on, but they would not leave their homes.

There was one young British artillery officer whose position was overrun by the Germans. He put an Arab cloak over his uniform, hitched a plough on to his gun-towing tractor and spent all that day ploughing round and round the field among the Germans. In the night he coupled up one of his guns and drove back to the British lines.

At first then, I noticed nothing abnormal in the approaches to Medjez-el-Bab. But once in the streets one saw a depressing shambles. The old and beautiful bridge had tumbled into the sleepy river and another military bridge had been run up. Every now and then the enemy was lobbing over a shell. For a month they had been trying to hit the new bridge, but even today when one shell made a crater at its western end the structure remained solid, and it stayed intact until the end of the whole campaign. Post office, church, shops, school and mosque—everything was torn about by the tornado of high explosive and reduced to the same dreary colour of the mud. A magnificent grove of eucalyptus, only slightly splintered by the shellfire, led through cratered fields to the railway station where the Argylls had their headquarters. These men, too, had the habit of war. Each night their patrols went out in no-man's-land rounding up hostile Arabs, laying mines, setting ambushes and getting information. The Germans from Longstop Hill were doing precisely the same thing. Standing behind a low garden wall I saw the trenches and the earthworks of the enemy only a mile away. The fighting now had lost its virulence and it was one of those frequent moments in war where both sides, as though by common consent, agree not to attack in force because they know they are too weak.

Equally both sides knew that sooner or later an attack must come and that again men must go out into that field of oats that lay between the two armies.

In the meantime the Argylls drank the petrol tin full of red Thibar wine we had brought and washed their filthy underwear and wrote letters home and brewed that new solution called ration tea which is a powdered mixture of tea, milk and sugar and which tastes, in my opinion, like sweet earth. For the moment we were content to let this pass, too, stay in German hands.

Pass Number Three was at El Aroussa, another battered township in the valley leading up to Pont du Fahs. Something was usually happening here. The Sixth Armoured Division had set up its headquarters in a farmyard and from there General Keightley, knee deep in ducks and pigs, kept up a sort of Red Indian warfare on the enemy. His division was sent out from England with Valentine tanks. It is too late now to ask why his division was given Valentines which had already proved themselves inadequate in the desert. The two-pounder gun was simply not good enough in the hills or on the plains, and no amount of argument either in the House of Commons or the War Office or the factories was going to make them good enough. Later on the division was given the

American Sherman tanks they ought to have had in the first place, and they lost several valuable weeks making the changeover. However, in January, Valentines were all they had, and they made a series of daring but not very decisive forays up the valley toward Pont du Fahs.

Stubbornly—pig-headedly if you like—we were learning here the painful lesson that you cannot attack fixed positions with tanks.

Every day that went by the gun was more and more dominating the fighting in these hills, and the tank was falling into the background. The green floor of the valley looked inviting enough. But send a half squadron of tanks out and then—crash. Out roared the enemy anti-tank guns from twenty different directions.

You would have thought the Germans would have learned this lesson. After all they were the masters of the anti-tank gun technique— the technique of keeping your own tanks out of the battle and luring the enemy tanks on to the guns. But the day I first went down to El Aroussa the German Mark IIIs and IVs came charging down the valley. They had the misfortune to choose the day when we had about seventy twenty-five-pounders in the vicinity all carefully sighted.

Traced on the map afterwards the course of the enemy tanks looked like a heart. They came out of Pont du Fahs as one formation, then split and forked off in two lines on either side of the valley. At the same moment both columns ran into our twenty-five-pounder barrage and turned inwards. Those that were left joined in the centre and ran for home. If ever there was a lesson to every tank commander in the war it was there. And now we proposed to follow up our advantage with an infantry attack on a useful rise called Two Tree Hill (despite the fact that the enemy some days ago had cut down the two trees because they believed we were sighting our guns on them).

The Irish went in under a full moon, and for the next twenty-four hours the valley was full of crossfire and hot skirmishing with the hand grenade and the rifle through the foothills.

As the fighting died down we came back to El Aroussa village, which was much cut about with bombing, and the usual argument broke out about where we were to sleep. One group favoured a great barn-like building in the centre of the village despite the fact that it had had its roof torn off and was now filled with coils of barbed wire. The other group favoured the open countryside away from bomb targets. In the end we compromised with the verandah of a village on the outskirts.

It was an uncomfortable night. The guns kept flashing spasmodically up the valley. Twice I was woken in the early morning—once by a dispatch rider most improbably bringing me a cable from London, and later by a wounded Frenchman who stood dripping blood over our sleeping-bags until we got up and took him to a doctor.

The morning broke unusually clear and I wandered into the village. In the main street half a dozen Tommies were washing in the horse-trough and I fell into conversation with them. They were Londoners, adolescent boys on their first campaign and enjoying a good deal of it. Their backs and chests as they washed were very white but their faces had gone scarlet through exposure. They carried on an effervescent conversation about the only three things that interest a soldier outside his regiment—the mail from home, food and women.

They were friendly and shy and very determined to do well in the war. I declined breakfast with them as my own at that moment was ready.

As I walked back to my camp the Stukas came over. They came very slowly and I suppose about eight hundred feet up, just a dozen of them with one or two fighters up above. There was ample time to run a few yards into the fields and throw oneself into the first available hollow.

It seemed for a moment they were going to sail by the village but at the last moment they altered direction, opened their flaps, and dived. The bombs tumbled out lazily, turning over and over in the morning sunshine. Then with that graceful little jump and a flick each aircraft turned upward and out of its dive and wheeled away. It all happened very slowly. They could scarcely have missed the centre of the village but they were very lucky to have hit a large truck filled with ammunition. The truck caught fire and the bullets kept blowing off in all directions, red for the tracers and white for the others. Half a dozen fires were started and the flames struggled to surge upward through the dust and smoke. One of the explosions performed the remarkable feat of killing a dove which flew through the air and struck down an officer who was in the act of talking to me. One of our men had been carrying a tin of eggs up the road and now he picked himself up ruefully from the sticky mess.

I walked over to the centre of the village keeping care to stay away from the exploding ammunition lorry. A twenty-foot steel water tank had collapsed like a fallen house of cards. The barn-like building in which we had proposed to spend the night had taken another direct hit and the coiled barbed wire had threshed about wildly in a thousand murderous tentacles. The blast had carried these fragments across to the water trough and now my six young friends were curiously huddled up and twisted over one another. It is the stillness of the dead that is so shocking. Even their boots don't seem to lie on the ground as those of a sleeping man would. They don't move at all. They seem to slump into the earth with such unnatural overwhelming tiredness; and I will never grow used to the sight of the dead.

That then was Number Three Pass as I first saw it and now wish to forget it. There remained Number Four, the American sector about Sbeitla and Gafsa. This was unlike the others. The grass was thinner, the trees stunted, the high ground full of brown bare rocks. Gafsa was not, strictly speaking, a pass at all—it was a jaunty little oasis sprawling on the edge of the desert—and at this point our front meandered across the open country. We had good positions on which to fall back at Kasserine and Tebessa but the line itself was exposed and could be flanked.

The Eighth Army had not yet come up from the south to join hands with the First Army and plug Rommel securely into Tunisia. A great empty gap lay between the two Allied armies, and this empty region extended over the salt lakes, called shotts, and ran from Tebessa in the west to Mareth on the coast. Beyond that the Sahara rolled on interminably to the Equator.

So at this stage—the end of January and early February—the stalemate was complete. Our original gamble had failed. Montgomery still had to gear up his army once again at Mareth at the end of its prodigious lines of supply. The four main passes of Tunisia were held strongly by the Germans and they were getting stronger every day.

The fighting along the lines was only a curtain-raiser for the big show that was yet to come.

Everywhere we could we wriggled forward onto a hill so as to be in a better position to launch a full-scale attack when the day came. The Germans on their side counterattacked us off these hills, hoping that we should never establish a satisfactory springboard for the great swoop on Tunis. It was an uneasy shifting line and no one was happy about it. But still there was nothing much we could do until Montgomery arrived. Everyone in the First Army was now asking, 'Where is Montgomery?' 'When does the Eighth Army arrive?'

Ten

Tripoli

WITHIN FOUR months—from October to January—the British Eighth Army had done amazing things in the desert. It had advanced fifteen hundred miles across some of the most inhospitable country in the world. It had smashed the Italian Fascist Empire in Africa. It had fought one major action at Alamein in Egypt and two minor ones at El Agheila and Zem-Zem in Tripolitania.

It had captured 30,000 prisoners including a dozen important generals and killed and wounded something like 40,000 men. In their retreat the Axis lost perhaps 500 tanks, 1000 aircraft, 1500 vehicles and stores worth many millions of pounds. Three vital ports, Tobruk, Benghazi and Tripoli, were in our hands and in operation. We had failed to catch Rommel, but the power of his Afrika Korps was at least halved. Incontestably the Eighth Army was the finest fighting machine in the Anglo-American forces and the name of its general stood higher than that of any other.

Probably it is still too soon to assess this extraordinary crusade across the desert; but at least now we can make a selection of the most vital events and lay them out for analysis.

If you put the story through a critical sieve a whole mass of things that looked important at the time fall through and you are left with half a dozen hard lumps of military discovery. First, there was the personality of the new general. Bernard Montgomery, as we saw him when he first arrived in the desert, was a slightly built man with a thin nervous face, an ascetic who neither drank nor smoked. He was a military scholar who had cut away from himself most of the normal diversions of life, and this left him with a fund of restless energy, part of which he expended in a religious faith in himself and his God and part in a ruthless determination to make battle. Like most missionaries he was flamboyant, and there was in him an almost messianic desire to make converts and to prove his doctrines were the right ones. An unusual man, not an easy companion.

General Montgomery represented central control in the British army as against the democratic ways of most of the other generals—Wavell and Alexander, for example. These last preferred to accept the army and its system as they found it. They tried nothing revolutionary but endeavoured to improve on the existing state of things. They moved on the principle that there is some good in every man and every weapon if they were used in the right way. They consulted their subordinates and left a good deal of the actual control to them. They commanded by a system of compromises and makeshifts which were adjusted to meet each emergency that came up. England and the British Empire had been governed on these lines for several hundreds of years and so the system seemed natural enough.

Now Montgomery was just the reverse. He believed in surgery, not homeopathy. If a thing was not going right or only partially right, then cut it out altogether; don't try makeshifts and slow drugs; sack the man to blame outright. His ideas were a logical extension of the Bedaux efficiency system in America and the Stakhanov system in the Soviet factories. By the Montgomery method the whole art of war was reducible to a pattern and a series of numbers; it was all based on units of manpower and firepower and so forth. He by no means rubbed out the human element; he simply believed that a correct system and good leadership would inspire the troops and draw out hitherto wasted resources of energy.

Montgomery had this system and this faith, and he believed in them passionately. He was itching to put his ideas into practice. Suddenly Churchill gave him the chance.

When the general arrived in the Middle East in August 1942 he had the great good fortune to find a ready-made and experienced army waiting for him. Two years' fighting and training had made many of them wonderful troops and there were plenty of them. The three armoured divisions—the First, Seventh and Tenth—were English, and there were in addition two English foot divisions, the Fiftieth and the Forty-Fourth. The empire had provided five more infantry divisions— two South African, one Indian, one New Zealand and one Australian. There was also the Highland division. A total of eleven divisions, all ready to go into battle. Moreover, the equipment was pouring in at a rate never approached in the Middle East before—British guns, American tanks and aircraft from both countries.

In itself this huge instrument of nearly two hundred thousand men was ready for anything. But the things it lacked badly were a clearly defined purpose and a leader. They got both in Montgomery. 'Follow me,' he cried, 'and we will smash Rommel.' Since the general believed this himself, it was not long before the troops began to believe it too. Before their own eyes great squadrons of tanks and guns were pouring into the desert and naturally the new general was given the credit for it.

From now on the subordinates took a very subordinate position indeed. Everything came straight from the general. Moreover, the new general was a man the troops could understand. He was very much one of the boys. He painted Monty on his tank and he went round wearing a most stimulating array of hats and badges. He harangued the army like a prophet. All this might seem like bad form to the officers of the old school, but the troops loved it. Monty had won them over before the battle started. His shrewdest move of all was to spread the idea that the Eighth Army was an independent striking force, taking its orders from no one. He was their general and he was going to lead them on their own private crusade across Africa.

Behind all this there resided in the general a long and very solid military training. If his battles lacked genius at least they were fought brilliantly and with good sound logic. Enormous experiments, especially in armoured fighting, were being evolved and they were entirely beyond the control of any one man, but Montgomery's battles brought the results to light.

Alamein will be studied in military academies for many years to come. The Eighth Army found itself in front of a short line, barely forty miles long, that could not be turned because the sea lay at one end and a marsh at the other end. Consequently it had to be attacked directly.

The Australians had already made themselves a good big dent in the enemy positions along the coast; so clearly this had to be used. But we needed two lines of attack to prevent the enemy concentrating, and a point halfway down the line seemed to be the best second line of advance.

The Germans on their side had mined their ground in great depth and covered it with artillery and smaller guns firing on fixed lines. Both sides held their armour in reserve, ready to rush critical points once the battle was joined. The British outnumbered the enemy in everything except men by possibly as much as three to two, but still they needed this advantage since they were going to do the attacking.

The British had one other thing in their favour—Marshal Rommel, whose Intelligence staff must have been terrible, was away in Germany, and his substitute, von Stumme, did a thing which Rommel would never have done—spaced his forces more or less equally along the whole line. Whereas the whole basis of his defence should have been to keep his best forces fluid until the battle took shape, he left them lying in static positions, from which they could not be quickly moved.

Montgomery attacked by night. He risked the danger of confusion in the darkness so that he should have the advantage of surprise and so that his striking units could get right up to the enemy without being seen. Before dawn each morning the British dug in furiously in order to meet the inevitable counterattack at daylight. Then at night they attacked again.

We struck not with tanks but with men, aircraft and guns. The tanks for the most part were kept out of it until the guns and aircraft—in this case mostly the twenty-five-pounder and the American medium bomber—had softened up the arena and the infantry had overwhelmed the minefields and anti-tank batteries.

Then once a good solid hole was made in the enemy lines the tanks went roaring through. They fanned out behind the enemy infantry and panicked them, and they forced the enemy armour to do battle in the open ground beyond.

Rommel, who had come racing back from Berlin, took one look at this chaos and apparently decided there was very little he could do about it. Indeed, there was hardly a mistake his subordinates had not made. They had been bluffed by a dummy concentration of vehicles the British had erected behind Alamein. They had confused the position of the real British spearhead, and when they did find it, the situation was too late to be restored. After trying to peg the gaps at one or two places, Rommel wisely abandoned the Italian infantry and got clean out of Egypt and Cyrenaica with the remainder of his tanks and his best mobile units.

I personally was not at the battle of Alamein, but Lieutenant-Colonel J. O. Ewart, one of Montgomery's Intelligence officers, has supplied me with this compact and lucid account:

'The twenty-third of October 1942 was a still and moonlight night in the desert. At 9.40 the roar of 800 guns broke the silence and marked the start of the battle of Alamein. Twenty minutes of flashing, deafening chaos, interrupted by a nervous silence while the barrage lifted from the enemy's forward positions to his gun line. For these twenty minutes the sky was lit by the winking flashes along the horizon, then a quiet, broken by the sound of tank tracks and the rattle of small arms. The Eighth Army was unleashed. Since Rommel had left his hopes of taking Egypt with forty blackened tanks south of Alem Haifa ridge late in August, the army had been waiting and building. There had been endless activity round the back areas and in the workshops of the Delta. More tanks, new tanks—the Shermans— more guns, new guns—the Priests—more and more six-pounders, more men had been pouring up the switchback road. Tracks had been constructed leading up to the assembly area carefully camouflaged, and behind the lines there were as many dummy tanks as real ones, to mislead the enemy as to the point of our attack.

'The Germans, too, had been busy. Rommel had fenced himself in behind barriers of mines and wire, sandwiching Italian battalions between German battalions. It was the deepest defence that either side had constructed in Africa, and there was no possibility of outflanking it. In front of the main position, a strong line with great keeps, there was a forward line. It was not so strong, but was joined to the main line by a series of connecting walls, so that the whole system was like a ladder. The front parts of the line between the 'rungs' were weaker, so that our attacks would be canalized into a series of hollows and would lose direction. Into these "Devil's Gardens" as Rommel named them, a murderous defensive fire was to be laid down. In some areas there were as many as nine successive minefields to overcome.

'General Montgomery had decided to make a break-in in the north, using the 30th Corps which now included the 9th Australian Division (the Rats of Tobruk), the 1st South African Division, the 51st Highland Division (newly arrived in the Middle East) and the New Zealand Division. He chose the north because a break-through in the north threatened the coastal road, the enemy's life, and imperilled the security of all his forces on the southern part of the line. The 30th Corps was to make the gaps, mainly by grinding away at the German defences with infantry supported by some heavy tanks. Then the 10th Corps, consisting of the 1st and 10th Armoured Divisions, which had been reorganized and retained in the Wadi Natrun area half-way from Cairo to Alamein, was to go through the gaps into the open country beyond and there deal with the enemy's armour. On the southern part of the front the 13th Corps with the 7th Armoured Division was to attack to contain the enemy reserves opposite them.

'By first light on the 24th the greater part of the objectives had been gained, and we had bitten deep into the enemy's main defences. Gaps had been made in the minefields and the armour of the 10th Corps had started to move up. We had broken in, but not through. On the enemy side there was confusion. Rommel's deputy, Stumme, had been killed by a stray shot in the first moments of the battle. The Axis command was taken over by von Thoma, who was comparatively new to the desert. His handling of the situation was indecisive. He could not make up his mind whether the main attack was in the north or in the south, or whether it was a seaborne landing west of Daba where light naval forces had been demonstrating. And so he failed to concentrate his reserves. He left the 21st Panzer and the Ariete Divisions in the south, and the 90th Light and Trieste along the coast near Daba, and tried to plug the gap in the line with only the 15th Panzer and the Littorio Divisions.

'The first phase of the battle continued until the 26th. While our infantry ground down the enemy defences slowly and steadily and beat off the counter-attacks of the 15th Panzer Division, the sappers were making corridors for the armour behind. The second phase began on the 27th. A purposefulness appeared in the enemy's movements. We guessed that Rommel was back. Subsequent evidence proved we were right. He took an immediate grip on the situation, and concentrated all his reserves in the north. Meantime Montgomery was building up a hitting reserve behind the "bulge" as it was now called. There were some desperate moments during these days, especially when a battalion of the Rifle Brigade in an advanced position we called Kidney Ridge was counterattacked five times in a day by the 15th Panzer Division, but held out.

'Montgomery was making his plan for the break-through. The threat from the 7th Armoured Division in the south had paid its way, and the division was now brought north into reserve. Everyone moved up one, with the result that there was a spare formation, the 4th Indian Division in the bulge.

The plan had the simplicity of genius. It was to persuade the Germans that we were going one way, and then to go the other. It worked perfectly. On the 29th the 9th Australian Division, after bitter fighting, advanced due north across the coast road almost cutting off an enemy force of about two regiments in a strong point known as Thomson's post. On the map it looked just like a thumb stretched up toward the sea. The Australians were exposed in this precarious salient, but they were told to stay there. Rommel was drawn. All day on the 30th and the 31st the enemy dashed himself against the Thumb. Gradually the whole of the enemy reserve, including the 21st Panzer and the 90th Light, was concentrated astride the road, right in the north. It was tired and battle worn. The Australians had not yielded an inch.

'It was the moment Montgomery was waiting for. After a night attack by the Highlanders and the New Zealanders, gaps were made farther south, and on November 2nd the whole weight of the Eighth Army's armour poured west straight out of the bulge. The Germans were caught off balance. Their attention was toward the north, and the Thumb had become an obsession to Rommel. Before he could re-concentrate to meet the threat from a new direction, the 1st and 10th Armoured Divisions were among him. A fierce battle was fought at El Aqqaqir, and it was here in this flat out, hammer and tongs fighting on murderously open and featureless ground that the final pressure was applied. By nightfall the enemy had cracked, and was starting to disengage.

'But Montgomery had another trump in hand. The 4th Indian Division broke south-west through the Trieste and Trento Divisions, now ripe for surrender, and through the gap poured the 7th Armoured Division. Meantime the armoured cars of the South Africans and the Royals were clean through. Like pirates back in their element after months of waiting they preyed on the enemy soft skinned transport and caused pandemonium in his rear.

'Rommel's main stocks and dumps and workshops were at Daba, some twenty miles up the coast road. To cover their evacuation he tried to stand, but the old, old story had begun. There was no longer a line with two firm flanks. The southern desert flank was open and the 7th Armoured Division was round it before Rommel could call a halt. The Afrika Korps commander, von Thoma, was in the bag, and the retreat for the moment became a rout. Tanks, guns, vehicles, stores were abandoned, burnt out and scattered along the roadside, while Rommel tried to break right away. Past Daba, where the tank workshops were left almost intact, and a train was still steaming in the station, past Fuka, the Axis remnants streamed, pounded ruthlessly by the R.A.F. Tanks were abandoned in panic when they ran out of fuel, aircraft abandoned intact on the Daba landing grounds.

'Nose to tail, two deep, the Eighth Army poured west, back past the old familiar places, tanks, guns without number, without an enemy aircraft disturbing them. In the other direction marched long columns of tattered, tired, dejected Germans and Italians, to join the four divisions Rommel had abandoned in the southern part of the line, and to continue their dreary march into captivity in Egypt, the land they had so nearly conquered. The Axis had suffered its first great defeat of the war, and the tide had turned.'

After Alamein began the usual biannual cross-country race across Cyrenaica. It was an especially brisk affair this year, as the Eighth Army fetched up on the finishing line at El Agheila inside three weeks—a record. But there was just this difference from the other two British advances— Montgomery was given the means to plan his supply ahead so that he would be able to hold what he had already won and eventually push on to Tripoli. Nine-tenths of desert warfare is the battle of supply.

Whoever first gets up most water, food, fuel, guns and men, wins the campaign.

This time the British had engineers waiting to repair the roads, railways, bridges and ports. This time the ships were waiting to put into Benghazi, and the port was open for them to unload three thousand tons a day. This time we had American Douglas aircraft to carry urgent supplies at speed with a rapid shuttle service between Cairo and El Agheila. Despite a violent three-day storm which wrecked the ships in Benghazi, despite the foul and bitter weather all over the desert, Montgomery won the battle of supply.

He was planning to attack again at El Agheila on December 14th. Rommel neatly anticipated the matter by slipping out two days beforehand. Nevertheless, Montgomery very nearly accomplished what he had set his heart on doing—capturing the Afrika Korps—and his plan is interesting because it shows the effect of the lessons learned at Alamein. At El Agheila he developed the tactics which were the distinguishing mark of all Montgomery's actions—a direct blow with the right and an encircling blow with the left. These tactics were more or less forced on the general since he always had the sea on his right and, except at Alamein and his one unsuccessful engagement at Enfidaville, the enemy line could always be outflanked in the empty desert to the south. Like nearly every other innovation in the desert, this tactic was first discovered by Wavell; but Montgomery gave the plan incisiveness and additional speed. Wavell's left-right blitz on the Sidi Barrani Line in 1940, his schemes for the reduction of desert strongholds, and his general plan of striking straight for Benghazi while his mobile forces cut across the desert behind the enemy have become classic desert lore now, and neither Rommel nor Montgomery were able to make any basic improvement on them; but they were supplied with much faster and better machines than Wavell and they controlled very much larger armies.

On this occasion, Montgomery sent the New Zealanders off on a staggering march around and behind the enemy positions at El Agheila. The New Zealanders got into position on time and then found they had been asked to bite off far too big a mouthful. They spaced their infantry brigades around Rommel's rear as best they could and stood by to receive the shock of the full Afrika Korps. Rommel, months before on the Gazala Line, had failed to capture a full British division, the Fiftieth, which was caught in much the same position, so now the Germans, profiting by that lesson, escaped in just the same way. They split into small commandos, each led by tanks, and slipped through the New Zealanders in the dark.

There remained nothing for Montgomery to do but take up the weary chase, and the Eighth Army plunged ahead into regions the British had never entered before. Apart from supply, which dominated everything, the chase developed into a battle of wits between the German and British engineers. A great deal of the German mining technique, which later was a crucial thing in the battle for Tunis, was learned out here in the desert where this one black ribbon of road wound on interminably over the waste of sand. It was a cruel business, mining, a thing that gratified no one's instincts for combat, for it was a stab in the back and the stabber ran no risks himself.

The German S mine projected three prongs above the ground. When a man stepped on it there was a small explosion, a metal ball jumped waist-high into the air and then burst, ejecting small shot in every direction. Its mission was solely to wound and kill soldiers who were off their guard. The German Teller mine was a round metal tin, rather larger than a soup plate, which was buried just below the ground and it contained enough explosive to break a tank track or demolish a lorry. The Italians had a rectangular mine for the same purpose. There were variations of these mines, but all of them were either anti-personnel or anti-vehicle. In addition there were booby traps of half a dozen varieties mostly based on the idea that if a string were pulled unawares the pin was jerked out of a hand grenade which thereupon exploded.

The Germans developed this mining to a science along the road to Tripoli. Everything likely or unlikely was mined or booby-trapped. To give you some idea of the complexity of this mining, here is what would happen when the retreating German sappers got to work on a bridge. First the bridge would be blown up. Then the fallen rubble would be S-mined. Then the approaches to the crater on either side would be mined with Tellers. Then the earthen tracks which wound round on either side of the fallen bridge would be Teller-mined by placing one mine above another so that when the British sappers came along and pulled up the first mine they would be blown up on the second. Then, presuming that the crew of a tank or truck would jump out immediately they struck one of these mines, the Germans spread S mines about at the point where they estimated the Tommies would land. Then, in case they still escaped, tripwires attached to booby traps would be strung between the bushes, or among discarded ammunition cases or in overturned vehicles. Often the road mines would be varied so that they did not go up until several vehicles had passed over and the drivers believed the path to be clear.

The Germans were wonderful toy makers. They made a wooden mine which could not be detected with our usual apparatus which is a flat metal plate on the end of a rod. The mine searcher wears earphones and the electric device in the instrument emits a high-pitched whine if the plate is placed over metal—but not over wood. Still another device of the Germans was to place the detonator for a mine at some distance in advance of the mine itself.

These savage inventions were the things that held up Montgomery on his long march until at last in January he found himself poised over Tripoli and the Germans once again massing in front of him.

The enemy chose a three-pronged wadi called Zem-Zem and mounted their guns on the more westerly of the three ravines. Once more Montgomery struck with a right and a left—the Highland division leading the frontal assault, the New Zealanders making another forced march through the desert to the south. This time the New Zealanders had to go through country so rough that even the desert veterans were left speechless. Tanks had to stand by all day dragging the vehicles up the worst bits.

Meanwhile a third force was converging on Tripoli. General Le Clerc and a brigade of Fighting Frenchmen had made a fantastic forced march from Lake Chad in the centre of Africa, taking one oasis after another, and now they were ready to strike in from the south. A great book and a great movie must some day be written about Le Clerc's march.

Once again Rommel, after a few sharp rearguard actions, withdrew his army and the Allies marched into the open town of Tripoli. The Highland pipers went piping into the main square; and at last, after thirty months of warfare, the ragged and dishevelled desert soldier stood with wonderment and emotion beside the playing fountains. If one excepts the entrance of the Germans into Paris, of the Japanese into Singapore and the return of the Russians to Stalingrad, there can have been no moment in the war equal to this one.

In the swaying battle of the desert, Tripoli had for two and a half years appeared as a mirage that grew strong and now faded away again, and was forever just beyond the Eighth Army's reach. So many had died or been withdrawn through wounds at a time when the struggle looked futile and endless. So many had recovered hope only to lose it again. So many had aged and grown sick and weak. Only those who had suffered the test of the desert, and for a long time, will be able to understand the emotions of the victors at the end—the constricting excitement of the last few hours when the army was about to penetrate the green suburbs, the bursting elation of the actual entrance into the town and the inevitable sense of anti-climax which followed.

This sense of anti-climax came all the more sharply upon the army because it was suddenly made to realise that its job was not yet done. Tripoli had always been for them the conclusion of the African war, the ultimate reward for the men coming out of the desert. But now something more was asked of them. The majority of the army was not even allowed to go into the town—it was obliged to plunge once more into the wastes and pursue Rommel across the border of Tripolitania, into Tunisia.

With alacrity Rommel nipped into the Mareth Line, which the Italians in misplaced optimism had dismantled a year or two before. His Afrika Korps neatly plugged the southern sector of the German front in Tunisia, and a great rectangle of mountain and plain now stood against the combined First and Eighth armies.

The Allied armies, however, had not yet made contact at the end of January. A vast region of desert, dotted with tiny oases, rugged stone ridges and salt marshes, still lay between the two forces. The area along the Tunisian-Tripolitanian border was badly mapped, and except for Bedouin few people had penetrated deep in the Sahara, which rolled away in blistering heat to the south.

Philip Jordan and myself now set out from Thibar into this country hoping that we might find a trail through the shotts and make first contact with the outposts of the Eighth Army. For some reason the military press authorities in Algiers were opposed to the trip and managed to stop us from flying across, though the R.A.F. very kindly offered us a passage. Even when we made the land journey we were punished by having our messages held up for a month or more.

However, there was a strong personal satisfaction in doing what we set out to do since I had spent two years with the desert forces and had a strong nostalgia to see them again.

We drove first to the American headquarters in the dismal town of Tebessa in the south, where somehow the Roman ruins have been made to look more depressing and uninteresting than any I have ever seen. The Americans, who are always open handed, gave us food, clothing, an officer and a driver and two pearls beyond all price—two jeeps. We handed over our Humber station wagon in exchange since it would not tackle the rough country, and set out. The maps were unreliable, to say the least—weird, highly coloured bits of paper drawn by some imaginative Frenchman—but we branched off the main road about twenty miles short of the German positions before Gafsa and struck out across the open country to the south.

It was a fabulous country of stark ravines and crenellated stone ridges that were stained to the colours of pale rose and muddy brown and saffron yellow. A few villages struggled for wretched existence from the bare land and beyond these we sometimes saw a suspicious shepherd clambering among the high rocks. An army might have been held up there forever; however, the jeeps bumped through and the wild camels stared at us with astonishment and malice.

At Metlouie we ran into a company of French Zouaves who were garrisoning the town in a desultory way and two large Doughboys who were roaming unconcernedly about this open section of the front trying to find out if the railway worked. No one had any notion of where the Germans were, and beyond Metlouie the earthen track was entirely deserted except for occasional caravans of Arabs mounted on camels. There were no tracks on the road and it was impossible to know whether the German patrols were operating in this area or not.

There is an excitement in reconnaissance like nothing else. For the most part you are in perfect safety, as we were here, but you are never sure and you keep looking round the horizon and listening, and you have a fine sense of discovery and adventure. And now, after all these months in cities and at sea and in the mountains I saw the desert opening out in front of me again—and it was like coming home. We ran on through two more oases where the date-palm branches had been pegged to the ground to hold the shifting sand back from the miserable crops. The palms yielded almost everything these villages wanted—beams to support their huts, branches for the walls and roofs, shade from the sun and food from the dates.

In the late afternoon, still seeing nothing of any troops, hostile or friendly, we came in sight of the Shott Jerid and ran into the mud-and-tile village of Tozeur.

Tozeur was made for tourists. It is surrounded by a thick belt of date palms, and clear cold water running from the hot sand makes runnels in the shade where peach trees grow and almonds and rich green vegetables. Squatting at their doorways, the Arabs weave baskets and mats from the all- providing palm leaves. Donkeys and camels bray under the snow-white mosque and through the iron grilles of the houses Arab women in brilliant shawls and veils keep peering out.

The Compagnie Transatlantique had built a semi-Moorish hotel with an inner courtyard on the outskirts of the town, and that was where we met my second favourite character of Tunisia.

She was a plump little Frenchwoman with bad teeth and a pretty face, and after a series of involved adventures following the collapse of France she had come down here to run the hotel. We had expected to camp out on this trip, but madame was offering an astonishing array of luxuries— bedrooms, baths, food and even wine. A group of Italian officers had been in the town until a few days before and we were welcome to their rooms.

It was a strange situation. We seemed to be poised between the Germans and the Allies in a sort of vacuum—a vacuum that provided most of the comforts of pre-war Europe. Then into the courtyard strolled a British major in full uniform, followed by a captain. They were alone. They had captured Tozeur for the Allies.

It was from the major that we heard we had stumbled on a great piece of luck, and that our journey was a success. By the merest fluke three men from the Eighth Army—the first to come north in search of the First Army—had arrived in Tozeur on the previous day. We jumped into a jeep and hurried round to their camp, in one of the white huts at the other end of the oasis. I thought I knew every unit in the desert army, but I was altogether unprepared for the shock of this meeting. The three men who got up to meet us were quite unrecognisable as soldiers. They were black bearded up to the eyebrows.

What was left showing of their young faces was burnt almost henna-red by the sun. They wore ragged shorts and shirts bleached white by the sun. On their feet were heavy leather native sandals. In place of helmets—the Eighth Army seldom wore helmets—they had khaki native cloths that kept the sun off the back of their necks. All three were slightly wounded or slightly sick. Two were English boys; the third a New Zealander. They were the survivors of a unit of the Long Range Desert Group which for two years had been making stupendous trips behind the enemy lines.

The Long Range Desert Group were the picked men who set out alone in half a dozen vehicles or more and disappeared for weeks or months at a time. They carried everything with them, including water. They steered for hundreds of miles by compass over a wilderness far south of Tripoli that had never been explored before. They swooped suddenly at night upon isolated German airfields and smashed up the grounded aircraft. They burst into Italian huts and mess rooms hundreds of miles behind the front and, like a gang of desperadoes in a Wild West thriller, shot up everyone and everything they could see. They laid ambushes along the coast road and mined bridges. They blew up ammunition dumps and grabbed vital prisoners. They had a hundred ways of catching the enemy by surprise and deceiving him and filling him with panic. And after each raid they slid silently back into the desert again.

If enemy aircraft picked up their tracks and followed them, they simply dispersed and faced the music as best they could. If they were badly shot up, they had somehow to get their vehicles going again, or they knew that their wounded would die and perhaps the whole party would perish of thirst. It was a recurring miracle the way these desperate little parties always seemed to get back even when they had been overdue for days.

If we were going to make contact with anyone in the Eighth Army it could not be with any troops better than these, who knew the desert better than anyone else. In their speech and their manner and appearance they showed just what the desert will do to white men, how reliant it will make them and how tough. And now this, their last trip, was almost the strangest of all.

They had started, they said, weeks ago, soon after the battle of Alamein, and since then they had barely made contact at all with the main bulk of Montgomery's army, which was working farther to the north, on the coast. Spreading their handkerchief maps on the dust floor of the hut, they showed us how they had struck straight across the desert from a point south of Benghazi, mopping up stray patrols of Italians on their route. Their mission was to go right round Tripoli and cross ahead of Rommel's retreating Afrika Korps into Tunisia. They were to wreck as much as possible of the Mareth Line before the Germans got there, and to make what hell they could with the road and railway line running from Gabes to Tripoli.

At first everything went well. They got right into the Mareth Line and found the place little more than a string of disarmed and sanded-up pill boxes. They roamed right through that region where a great battle had still to be fought and did what damage they could. Then Colonel David Stirling, their leader, and probably the most resourceful adventurer in the desert war, went off Gabes-way to blow up a railway train.

They waited a week at a rendezvous south of Tripoli for Stirling to return, and still they had no news of him. (Stirling, we heard later, had been caught and shipped to Italy, where already he had made one half-successful attempt to escape.) Then they were betrayed by Arabs. Two Messerschmitts dived down on them from Tripoli and shot up all their transport except one jeep. These three sick and wounded lads were piled aboard the jeep and told to get through somehow to the First Army away in the north. The rest of the party, about twenty in all, collected what water and food they could carry and set out to walk, following the tracks of the jeep.

Bedouin guided the wounded men some of the way through the salt shotts. Once they caught and ate a kid goat. At night they stole round Italian encampments, and in the daytime they hid when enemy planes or vehicles appeared. At length they had struggled into Tozeur.

They had been living so long in isolation, living on a cup of water a day and the very barest minimum necessary to keep alive, that they were pathetically grateful and astonished at the meagre things we gave them—a few oranges, a book, a couple of bars of chocolate, a bottle of wine.

They loved their life. All their ambitions were confined to the idea of going on, of discovering new places and breaking open new trails.

'I suppose they won't have any more use for us in Africa now that the desert fighting is over,' the New Zealander said. 'But we got a tip just before we left on this last trip that they may have a job for us in China.' It is quite probable that at this moment these boys are in China or the Balkans or the Caucasus or anywhere where there are no made roads and the winds blow freely.

That evening, as we were sitting in the courtyard of the hotel, a soldier came in and called my name aloud. 'I have letters for you from the Eighth Army,' he said. It was an astonishing meeting. This man was with the walking party which reached Tozeur that night. Weeks before, two friends of mine with Montgomery at Sirte had given him letters for me. He had carried them through the enemy lines and by sheer luck had stumbled across me in Tozeur.

While I was reading the letters the major came over to us and said quietly, 'I have just had a message that I am on no account to go near Gafsa tonight.' This information was official and it had come over the telephone from headquarters. 'You say the road was clear when you came down it today,' he went on. 'Well, it isn't now. It looks as though the Jerries have cut it.'

This was awkward. We knew no other way back, and it looked as though we were cut off unless we cared to head south over the camel tracks the way the Long Range Desert Group had come. Since we had no compass and it was a ten days' trek to Tripoli if you got through the enemy patrols, we did not care for it much, though the American captain with us was keen to go on.

The major then became a mine of bad news. 'I was expecting it, of course,' he said placidly. 'I shouldn't mind betting the Jerries will be in Tozeur—perhaps tomorrow, perhaps the day after.

German patrols have been sniffing round here for the past fortnight. They blew up the bridge on the road down to the shott the night before last. And they have been working along the road you came down on for the past week. Did you see that burnt-out French lorry on the way? They got that. Up till now they have been only mining.'

Now, to me this was downright alarming. I have no nerves for the cat-and-mouse kind of warfare the major liked to play. He had said that he could be up and away within twenty minutes at any time of the night. I was tolerably certain that we could by no means be up and away in anything under an hour or an hour and a half. The jeeps were parked in a remote shed, and I disliked the idea of going to bed knowing that at any hour the enemy patrols, who would be very quick on the trigger, might enter the dark streets. The town was wide open, without any protection whatever, and invading troops would naturally make for the hotel, as we did.

As though to confirm the major's views, a Messerschmitt suddenly sailed out of nowhere, machine- gunning the streets and the railway across the road. We stood under the arches in the courtyard, and he came back for a third run, but this time without firing bullets and obviously taking photographs. The enemy always sent out a reconnaissance plane over a place before they moved in.

The others, however, did not share my qualms, and we stayed on a couple of days and nights in Tozeur with the people from the Eighth Army. And, indeed, it was not for a couple of weeks that the Germans entered the town and Nazi officers took over the bedrooms we had been sleeping in.

Philip and I, with a good story in hand (we did not then know it was going to be stopped by the Algiers authorities), could afford to wait no longer than the second day, and a Frenchman offered to guide us across on a new track to Tebessa through the mountains. I rate this as the coldest drive I have undertaken since the war began. For ten hours we sat in the open jeeps and those beautiful and barbarous mountains flung up at us everything, from frozen rain to iced red mud. I never discovered exactly what route we did take—it gave the

Germans a wide berth, and at times we were running past gazelles in the valleys or looking over cliffs in the mountains. At length we got back, feeling that we had at least seen for ourselves that the junction of the two armies was about to take place and the last stage of the battle for Tunis was about to begin.

Eleven

Casablanca

WHEN WE were at El Aroussa one day in January the war correspondents received a message recalling them by air to Algiers. Just that, nothing more; no explanations, no reason given as to why we should leave the front at a moment when things were going quite briskly.

I personally had not been included in the summons and so, with deep puzzlement, I watched the others go off until I was left almost alone on the front. For a day or two I moped around Thibar feeling a little like Cinderella, and finally, on the third morning, I decided to set off by myself and find out what all the mystery was about.

Flying to Algiers at that time was a rare and wholly unrefreshing experience. The general technique was for the prospective passenger to drive round the front until he saw an aircraft. Then—if he found the pilot and the pilot was willing, and the mud not too deep for the take-off, and the air clear of Messerschmitts—he flew to Algiers.

On this morning I must have pursued a dozen different aircraft down the Medjerda Valley, and then at last someone gave me a clue about Gaston. Gaston was a French pilot who used to fly a decrepit twin-engined Bloch between Algiers and the front.

Sure enough, just when the white ground mists were lifting from the valley, the Frenchman bumped down on a field and I hurried across to the farmhouse in which he had disappeared.

A woman, who, I can only think, was the pilot's mother, came to the door.

'Certainly not,' she said with decision. 'Gaston will not fly again today. He has not even had his lunch yet. Anyway, I will on no account allow him to fly to Algiers in this weather.'

The daughter was more sympathetic. She whispered to me in schoolgirl English that maybe Gaston would fly after all when he had had his lunch. He had several senior French officers as passengers.

After an hour or two Gaston emerged, a rotund and cheerful little Frenchman, and he had lunched amply and well on the rich garlic and the good red wines of the valley. By this time there was quite a crowd of us waiting to get away—a couple of Spitfire pilots, a French naval officer and two full French colonels.

'Why, certainly,' said Gaston briskly. 'Let 'em all come,' and we bundled inside. It was what I can only describe as an austerity take-off. We shot straight across the potato patch with the wind, and by the time our speed was one hundred and forty miles an hour we had climbed roughly to the height of ten feet. If a haystack or a cow or a camel blocked our passage down the valley, Gaston lightly flicked the machine up and over and down again. I will almost assert we could feel the hot breath of the camel on our faces as we went by. Gaston, feeling in need of company, turned round in his seat and conversed animatedly with the two French colonels as we slid in and out of the palm trees. The two Spitfire pilots were full of delighted admiration of this performance, and they sat there loving every minute of it. It appeared that Messerschmitts were prowling about the valley that day and Gaston preferred to keep down low 'out of trouble'—the phrase is his, not mine. Presently we had to climb over the Atlas Mountains, and as we sailed through each pass the tips of the wings had ten, perhaps fifteen, feet to spare on either side. At Constantine something went wrong with one of the engines. When we landed a man came out with a hammer and a piece of wire and fixed it. Finally we arrived at Maison Blanche airfield outside Algiers, which was always an aerial madhouse in those days and looked especially bad that afternoon. But Gaston neatly ran under the wings of an American Douglas transport, slid between two Hudsons that were taking off and finished in a line of Flying Fortresses—a remarkable exhibition.

Poor Gaston. He went on flying his old Bloch like a Paris taxi for many days after that, but the Germans shot him down in the end.

I hitchhiked into Algiers on a jeep and went into the tenth-rate pension the correspondents used as a base in the town. The place had certainly picked up while I had been away. Officers were rushing about in all directions. An American correspondent emerged with two movie stars in tow—Carole Landis and Martha Raye, I think they were. 'To entertain the troops,' the sergeant on the door explained. Major Flood of the Public Relations staff seemed to be the only lucid man in the place. 'We have been trying to get you,' he said. 'You take off at five tomorrow morning.' But where for and why? Nobody was very clear about anything.

Even on the wet and gloomy morning when we took off from Maison Blanche there was some doubt about whether we were headed for Gibraltar, Oran or Casablanca. Some twenty correspondents and officers, mostly American, had climbed into the aircraft. Edward Baudry, of the Canadian Broadcasting Commission, and I found places at the end of one of the hard aluminium benches, and we sat there uncomfortably for a while reading *La Depêche Algierienne* and eating cold bully-beef sandwiches. Above the mountains the wings iced over and the big machine suddenly turned and dived for the coast. It was warmer flying low over the sea. Except for a couple of lone tramp steamers the Mediterranean was very empty and it had a blue and solid calmness on that bright morning. Rapidly we swept by Spanish Ceuta, British Gibraltar and international Tangiers and then we rounded the shoulder of Africa and turned south.

It was a strange flight in every way. Not only were we doubtful about our destination, but we were wholly unable to understand the course the young American pilot was steering. He kept right over the beach where the long swell of the Atlantic was coming in, and the beach was part of neutral Spanish Morocco.

'What's that?' Baudry exclaimed suddenly, and I saw the yellow puff of an ack-ack burst in the air behind us, then another and another. We had just passed by three ships and it was difficult to see whether the fire was coming from them or from the shore. At any rate we were being fired on. We did not know at that time that the pilot had not seen these bursts, and he continued straight down the coast only a few hundred feet in the air. Every now and then a stray volley came up from the ground and passed harmlessly by.

We slid by two villages and reached the Spanish port of Larache, and then things happened very quickly indeed. To our utter astonishment the machine began to descend and circle round the town. This, we thought, could mean only one thing; there was engine trouble and we had to make a forced landing in neutral territory. We went lower and slower, and I was trying to calculate what attitude the Spanish authorities would take—would they treat us as ordinary belligerent soldiers and intern us for the duration, or, since we were civilian war correspondents, would they return us to our own territory? One could read the Spanish words on the shop fronts now, but there was no one in the streets. And then a bright golden burst of tracer bullets broke through the floor of the cabin. Bullets were flying all round us, and now we could clearly hear the rattle of the guns.

I stumbled along to the door of the cockpit and shouted to the pilot, but the noise was too great. As I sat down again another golden ball of fire ripped through the cabin and someone shouted, 'Get down on the floor.' Useless though it was, it seemed to be the only thing to do. Instinctively men under fire will always try and touch something solid with their bodies. Baudry did not get down with the rest of us. With a slight sigh he leaned slowly over backward—and his left temple had been blown away.

Blood and grey brains were pumping out of the wound and spilling down his cheeks.

I struggled again through to the cockpit yelling for a first-aid kit. One of the American crew had blood coming out of a wound across his head and the second pilot was down on the floor bandaging him. After a minute's confused shooting I got an emergency bandage and went back to Baudry. With an effort we lifted him down onto a rough bed of parachutes. It was useless trying to force brandy through his lips for he was unconscious and we feared that the spirit would choke him. Somehow my friend D'Arcy Dawson got the bandage in place while I held up the dying man's head. There was a great deal of blood.

All this time the bullets and tracers had been coming up at us. Even now when we turned away with painful slowness to the open sea the fire kept following, a deadly rat-tat-tat against the fuselage. The Spanish had learned to shoot in their civil war. One felt so utterly helpless in that plane. Those who had nothing to do sprawled in a confused mass of arms, bodies and legs on the floor near the tail, some of them clutching parachute packs to their chests, some wedging themselves under the benches, others clasping their hands over their heads. A British sergeant found a water bottle and began washing Baudry's face. It was better to be doing something.

We got our bearings now and wirelessed ahead to the friendly French port of Lyautey, and an ambulance was waiting there when we put down a few minutes later. From one of the crew I gathered that the pilot had heard nothing of the ack-ack fire all the way along the Spanish coast and had imagined Larache to be Lyautey. The radio operator had sent out recognition signals, but had received only a confused jumble in response, then the bullets.

Feeling shaken and distressed, we saw Baudry taken off. He was buried the next day. The rest of us continued to Casablanca.

Casablanca was in the midst of a witch's brew of rumour and intrigue. We were bustled aboard army trucks to an hotel in the town and told to remove our badges from our uniforms.

A grave-faced American general told us that 'the biggest assemblage of high dignitaries ever gathered together since the war began' was then in Casablanca. We were bound to secrecy and warned not even to talk in our bedrooms since the hotel had once been wired and enemy agents were everywhere.

Thus began one of the most portentous and hollow assignments I ever had. The whole thing was most aptly and pungently expressed a few days later when Osbert Lancaster came out in the London *Daily Express* with a sketch of Churchill disguised in Arab dress but smoking an unmistakable cigar. Everyone in Casablanca who was not entirely indifferent knew that the Allies were having a great conference up there on the hill of Anfa a few miles outside Casablanca. Roosevelt and Churchill had already been there for a week or more and had been seen driving through the town.

For two days we killed time drinking in the pavement cafés, seeing the sights (which included General Noguès at Rabat), talking to the French sailors and looking at the terrible wreckage caused in the port by our naval bombardments. Two fifteen-inch shells had ripped holes in the battleship *Jean Bart* in which you could have built a two-storey cottage.

On the whole Casablanca had had a good war. There was plenty of food. The shops were still stocked with such things as Moroccan leather goods and cheap scent. There was no blackout and the town had only once been raided. Out on Anfa lived the millionaires who had made great wealth out of the traffic to German-occupied Europe. The town was still run by a core of Vichy adherents and military reactionaries. And the sun streamed down.

On the third morning we were taken through the guards and the barbed-wire entanglements at Anfa. We waited for an hour or two in an exquisite villa that was crammed with sculpture and painting, and among other things contained a staggering library of pornographic books bound in the most richly tooled Moroccan leather. Then we walked up the road—about fifty of us—and met the president and the prime minister.

That little tableau still seems utterly unreal whenever I think of it. We squatted in a semicircle on the wet grass, and Roosevelt, Churchill,

Giraud and de Gaulle sat on four chairs facing us. Admirals, generals, diplomats and cabinet ministers perched among the flowerbeds and the orange trees behind. A brilliant sun flowed down and it caught the fixed bayonets of the American sentries who paced along the flower-hung garden walls around the villa. Aircraft kept passing back and forth overhead. Churchill, a little troubled by the sun, kept his dark hat cocked over his forehead; Roosevelt turned his tremendous smile onto the gathering and with a deal of hearty French tried to instil a little cheerfulness into the two stiff, ultra-formal French generals who sat on his left and right hand.

The photographers jumped and frisked through the flowerbeds as they struggled to get their angle shots and plenty of them. With Roosevelt's hands on their arms urging them upward the two lean grim Frenchmen rose at last, touched one another's fingers for a second, and abruptly sat down. It was all rather embarrassing, like the first rehearsal of an amateur play.

The photographers cried that they had missed the shot and Giraud and de Gaulle painfully got to their feet again. This time a wan smile flickered about for a second under the kepis and the generals grasped hands for a little longer. Then they tramped solemnly away across the flowerbeds. 'Bon voyage,' shouted the president. No. It was not a very successful little act. It lacked conviction. It certainly lack showmanship.

Beckoned warmly by the president we clustered closely round the two remaining actors. The scene now was irresistibly like a Sunday-school treat with the children gathered at the feet of their two schoolmistresses. For an hour the president and the prime minister discoursed and told us nothing. It had been a most successful conference—the best they had ever had. Everyone was here—Marshall and Brooke, Eisenhower and Alexander, Tedder and Arnold, Lord Leathers and Harry Hopkins, Mountbatten, Cunningham, King and dozens of others. They had all agreed. We wanted unconditional surrender. Only Stalin and Chiang Kai Shek were missing. And so on. We scribbled and listened and enjoyed the jokes, but no one quite liked to ask the real questions, the only questions:

What sort of any agreement had Giraud and de Gaulle made, if any?

Was the Mediterranean to be made our main theatre of war?

Where was the second front and was there even going to be one?

Had Franco been there and did we have a deal with Spain at one end of the Mediterranean and with Turkey at the other?

Naturally neither Churchill nor Roosevelt raised these points themselves, but since they were the only points that mattered, there was very little else that was worth talking about. The event of the conference itself was news, but after that there was practically nothing that we could write.

Nevertheless we trooped into a large conference room and for the next four hours some twenty or thirty typewriters rattled at the rate of a thousand words per man per hour, a hideous din of noise. The censors sat beside us at a trestle table running through this flood of words until their heads were spinning. That night the messages were flown to London and released a day or two later when the president and the prime minister were safely on their way—one back to America and the other off to another of those still mysterious conferences in Turkey.

Yet vast decisions were taken at Casablanca. It marked a major turning-point in the war. It settled once and for all a matter which I have tried to make a theme in the somewhat addled structure of this book—that America was to fight in Europe first and in the Pacific afterwards, and that in return for this she was to have a fairly free hand in the reconstruction of France (to begin with) and seniority in the military direction of the war.

Again, in his conversation with us, Churchill had repeated, 'I am the president's ardent lieutenant.' The mere presence of the president in Casablanca switched American interest to the Mediterranean.

Given this general understanding—that the Allies were to make their main immediate effort in the Mediterranean—by far the most important event of the conference had been the technical discussions between the naval, army and air staffs.

The plans that were vaguely formed at Washington in the previous July were now given practical and detailed direction. Predominantly, as always, it was a matter of supply—who should get the aircraft and the guns, where should the men go and how many. It was agreed that while an American—General Eisenhower—should retain the high command, the key field positions should go to that seasoned British team which had come to the conference laden with their honours from the desert war— Cunningham for the navy, Tedder and Coningham for the air, Alexander and Montgomery for the army. General Anderson was also retained in his command of the First Army. To these were added a number of Americans of high rank—Smith as chief of staff to Eisenhower, Patton (and later Bradley) with the American Second Corps, which though technically under Anderson was to operate as a separate army, Spaatz with the strategic air force. And there were a number of others.

We were given no opportunity to talk to these commanders at Casablanca, but it was evident that they, being practical men dealing with mechanical problems, had been able to reach a pretty wide field of agreement. Maybe the sunshine and the holiday surroundings had something to do with it.

Maybe it was the fact that we could now plan offensives instead of defensives. At any rate there was a very noticeable amount of goodwill about, and the events since have shown that the Anglo- American leaders did genuinely get to know one another at Casablanca and did achieve a means by which they could fall in with one another's plans. Indeed, the whole story of North Africa indicates that at the top at least the American and British commanders did work well together. A great deal of the credit for this must go to General Eisenhower.

It was only lower down in the scale of command, and usually through ignorance, that the differences occurred.

The Giraud-de Gaulle issue was treated as a minor affair at Casablanca, or at least of secondary importance to the decision that the war should be fought in Europe. Despite the 'we are both determined to win the war' communiqué put out by the two generals under Allied direction, they reached no working agreement. How could they? Giraud, in the eyes of the de Gaullists, was a reactionary general who along with Gamelin, Noguès, Georges and Weygand was responsible for the collapse of the French army in 1940. These generals were of the school that believed that one must call up a vast number of infantrymen and form them into largely immobile lines of defence.

De Gaulle, in the eyes of the Saint Cyr Group, was an upstart who preached much glib nonsense of small, highly mechanised armies, and whose political views were dangerously left-wing to boot. And so that gauche and embarrassing handshake in the garden was as symbolic as any forced gesture of the kind could be. It said as clearly as might be—all right, we will try to combine as long as you, the British and Americans, are in control. But we Frenchmen must settle this in our own way.

All that has happened since between the rival French groups has been an extension of this unhappy beginning.

Still, for the most part Churchill and Roosevelt were justified in coming away from Casablanca well pleased with what they had done. Returning on our plane to the front we knew that every effort was now going to be put into the Tunisian war, and that the Germans were going to suffer such a blitz as they had not yet seen outside Russia.

Twelve

Kasserine

ROMMEL STILL had one desperate chance of holding Tunisia until the autumn. Already he had fought a magnificent delaying action across the desert. Given another seven or eight months in Tunisia the Allied landing in Europe could be delayed until the following year, and in the meantime Germany could launch one more attack upon Russia.

The best that the Axis could spare was now rushed across the narrow eighty-mile sea route from Sicily to Tunis and Bizerta. There were a number of new or almost new weapons, the Mark VI Tiger tank, carrying an 88-millimetre gun, a leviathan of over sixty tons when loaded for battle, with four- inch armour and two-foot-wide tracks. It was also designed to travel underwater, which was necessary since few bridges in Tunisia could stand that weight. There was the improved Focke-Wulf fighter and the Henschel tank-buster, an adaptation of the Russian and British fighters carrying cannon with armour-piercing shells. There was the multiple-barrelled mortar and a great quantity of landmines.

Much of this stuff was brought across in Siebel ferries. These were vessels that looked like two barges lashed together, each with an engine and capable of carrying tanks. They had tremendous ack- ack protection aboard.

Some of the best Axis divisions were then drawn on to bolster up the war-weary garrison in Tunisia. The Hermann Goering division, the German parachutists, the 10th Panzer Division, the Young Fascists—all these were sent, and for the first time the Axis armies in Africa were predominantly German. In addition Rommel had the remnants of his Afrika Korps—the 15th and 21st Panzer divisions, the 90th Light German Infantry (one of the best formations in Africa) and various other units. Large numbers of Germans who had been wounded in Russia and elsewhere and were now recovered were also rushed across and hurriedly formed into battalions at the front. Many of the old Italian divisions, like the Trieste and the Ariete, were still in existence as well as odd groups like the San Marco marines and the Bersagliere regiments. All through the desert war Rommel had never had more than four German divisions, and he had never been able to trust completely the Italians who formed the main part of his array.

541

In fact, he was never nominally commander-in-chief; an Italian held that position. But now he had a very good army indeed, numbering a quarter of a million men, nearly two-thirds of them German, and all in strong defensive positions.

One thing he lacked, and that was serious—artillery. Throughout the fighting in Africa the Germans had pinned their faith to the eighty-eight-millimetre all-purpose gun, the Mark III and IV tank, and the mortar, and aircraft. On his way from Alamein, Rommel had succeeded in bringing back a great quantity of ack-ack guns, but these could never fill the place of a solid phalanx of field guns worked by a well-trained team. Montgomery alone had five hundred guns, and in tanks also greatly outnumbered the Axis. Moreover, Rommel could not hope to compete in the air now that the Desert Air Force was joined to the North African forces and Malta was engaged in its own private blitz in no small way. German bombers could no longer operate from the last remaining patch of Tunisia held by the Axis, and it was becoming increasingly difficult for fighters.

Nevertheless there was a reasonable chance that a defence could be sustained until July or August, and Rommel with all his old resilience prepared to fight. His plan in February was a modern expression of one of the oldest maxims in war—'If you see a superior force approaching, you prevent it from concentrating for a knock-out blow by engaging the enemy in piecemeal attacks along his line.'

Somehow Rommel had to prevent the British, Americans and French from all getting to the starting line together. He had to throw our offensive off balance before it had begun. The story from February onwards is largely the story of the devices by which the Germans sought to hold off the final concentrated blow.

Looking down the line it was obvious that the American sector about Sbeitla was the weakest. Many of the troops there were not battle trained, and moreover they were spread out in a thin straggling line mostly through flat country. It was not a naturally defensive position and it had been maintained because from the first Eisenhower had resolved to fight an offensive action and make the Germans pay for every foot of ground they won back.

Toward the middle of February then Rommel gathered the best of his hard-bitten desert veterans and his new tanks from Germany. On the 14th he fell upon the weak American sector. The results were remarkable—probably even beyond Rommel's highest hopes. At Sbeitla and Sidi Bou Zid, the American guns were overrun before they could be effectively brought to bear, the American tanks were forced back under a concentrated drive toward the Kasserine Pass, and since the American infantry had no proper defensive positions on the open ground they were either taken prisoner or withdrawn. Faid fell in the north and Gafsa and Feriana with its two valuable forward airfields were abandoned in the south. Tebessa, the administrative centre for the whole of this region, was now in real danger despite its protective ring of hills.

For two years Rommel's immediate reaction to any local success had been 'Exploit...exploit...exploit,' and the same exultant order again went out to the Germans who after many weary months of retreat were now experiencing the thrills of victory again. They overran the Kasserine Pass and, splitting into two columns, made for Thala in the north and Tebessa in the west.

For the Allies this was no longer a local menace—it threatened the whole Tunisian line. The Tebessa area was the geographical point of junction for the Eighth and First armies and therefore—as Rommel foresaw—our weak point. If the Germans established themselves in Tebessa, then they might prevent any junction taking place for months. Much worse results would follow the collapse of Thala for, from there, the Germans could advance straight to El Kef. They would then be behind the main Allied line in Tunisia and might easily encircle it entirely by running through to the coast at Bone. Something like a hundred thousand Allied troops could be trapped.

General Alexander had just taken over the field command when this critical situation arose. He knew that General Montgomery would not be able to attack for a month. He knew that once through Thala there were no forces at all to prevent the Axis march on El Kef.

You can judge the seriousness of the situation by the fact that Alexander himself left his headquarters near Constantine and ran along the line looking for someone—anyone—to throw into the gap. He grabbed a battery of guns here, a battalion of infantry there, a fighter squadron in the other place and rushed them to the danger point. The Sixth Armoured Division plus the Guards—our finest fighting formation—were asked to bear the brunt of the shock. They hurried down in the night to join the regrouped American forces in the Kasserine area. Commanders addressed their staffs in the field on the eve of battle telling them frankly: 'The situation is desperate. We are outnumbered and out of position and your chances of surviving are not very good. But you have got to stop the Germans.'

On the very outskirts of Thala the decisive tank battle was fought. It was another of those gambler's moments in the campaign when one side, unknown to itself and its enemy, had reached the peak of its dynamic for the time being—and this time it was the Germans who had reached the end of their tether. Their forward tank units were smashed, and before reinforcements could be brought up, the Guards and the Americans rushed upon the field and turned the German thrust into a local but headlong retreat. The more slender enemy column directed against Tebessa now found its rear communications being cut and this budding shoot withered on its own stalk. The Allies were left in command of the battlefield and the Germans withdrew to Feriana and Gafsa. It had been a near thing.[5]

Alexander worked with frenzy during the ensuing lull which he knew could not last long. He had found the First Army in an appalling mess. Units were mixed up all over the place and all the smooth cohesion that prevailed through long experience in the Eighth Army simply did not exist in this new army. Driblets of French units were under American command and isolated Americans were under British command; a battery of guns would be loaned out here and a squadron of tanks there. A bewildering and overlapping stream of orders was flowing out over the signal wires. The men were willing to fight all right, but they were not being given a chance because of the confusion of the staff work at a high level.

Alexander at once decided that the three very different groups under his command would fight best if they were kept separate and allowed to control themselves in their own way as far as possible.

Accordingly he bunched his four British divisions in the north, his two French in the centre and his two American in the south. The Mareth section remained with Montgomery who had contracted to get four good British divisions up to the line.

Rommel meanwhile was not idle. He struck again—this time in the far north among the rough hills of the Sedjenane sector. Wave after wave of Germans flung themselves on the British infantry and again the enemy achieved a partial breakthrough, not so dangerous as the Kasserine thrust, but still enough to disrupt and delay our concentration in the north. Having achieved this object and having got as far as he could (the key town of Beja almost fell), Rommel suddenly switched to the south for another lightning blow.

He wanted now to throw Montgomery's coming offensive out of gear. On March 8th the German tanks raced forward across the hard flat ground, and to this day there is no satisfactory explanation of why such a master in the handling of tanks as Rommel could have attacked in this way. Perhaps he was misinformed about the number and position of the British guns. Perhaps he was over-elated with his two previous successes and he had forgotten how experienced the Eighth Army was. At any rate, he deliberately broke his own strict rule—which we had learned from him at such cost—never attack fixed positions with tanks.

The British tanks were scarcely used at all that day. A trap was laid for the Germans. When the Axis tanks approached they saw British gunners jumping up from their trenches and running away from their guns. To the German tank commanders this was irresistible and they charged ahead— straight into the real British gun line that was waiting for them. The carnage was horrible. Fifty German tanks were blown up in their tracks and the enfeebled remnants drew off in disorder. We lost no tanks, and in all about two hundred casualties. The gun line had not budged an inch. Rommel's third attempt to break up the Allied concentration had failed with far greater losses than he was able to sustain. This action, which could not be assessed at its true value at the time, was, I believe, the turning-point of the Tunisian campaign. The Germans lost the offensive on that day, and they never again recovered it. It is not too much to say that the battle of Mareth was won in this preliminary tank action, and from Mareth flowed all the rest.

Rommel saw what had happened. He gave up soon afterwards. He surrendered his command and left Africa for good. To von Arnim fell the grisly and thankless job of making a Stalingrad on the Mediterranean.

But still the German high command would not give up. They continued to pour troops and weapons into Tunisia, and with great skill they devised a new method of defence which was ideal for hill country and which the Allies later came against in Europe. This was the minefield-mortar-gun combination. Every valley was strung with minefields. On the heights dominating the valleys machine-guns and anti-tank guns were sighted so that they covered every acre of the ground in which the landmines were laid. The gunners did not have to aim their guns—the guns were already aimed, and all the gunners had to do was to stay below ground and keep loading and pulling the trigger. (This is in theory; of course there were adaptations in practice.) The mortars and anti-tank gunners were also dug into weapon-pits practically invulnerable from the air or shelling, and were free to play their fire where it was most needed. The whole system was most closely interlocked and carried to great depth.

One could not attack such positions with tanks. The sappers had to go forward first and pull up the mines. The infantry had to wipe out the sighted guns. The air forces had to soften up the whole sector. Then, and not until then, could the Allies hope to push their tanks through the gaps into the flat country beyond, where they had room to play about. We had overwhelming superiority in tanks, but they simply could not be brought to bear in the high passes. Not until we broke through at Mareth, at Gabes, at Sbeitla, at Fondouk, at Medjez-el-Bab and in the north could the armour operate.

All through the first weeks of March von Arnim concentrated on strengthening the passes with more and more mines. But the sands were running out quickly now. The rains were stopping and, especially in the south, the ground was drying. As the wheat turned from green to yellow and the first mowers were sent into the fields, the Allies struck.

Thirteen

El Guettar

ALEXANDER'S PLAN was quite obvious to the Germans because it was largely conditioned by the terrain. He conceived German Tunisia as a cylinder with the First Army forming one wall from Tabarka to Gafsa, and the sea as the other wall from Tunis to Gabes. The Eighth Army was to act as a piston pushing up from the bottom. This plan underwent half a dozen modifications with the changing fortunes of the battle, and was eventually abandoned altogether;[6] but that was how the high command looked at the situation in the middle of March, when they were at last ready to move.

I had flown home to England for a few days in a Flying Fortress, and on returning to North Africa I continued straight to Tebessa, where the British and American correspondents had congregated for the opening moves of the coming offensive. The Americans, with three divisions under General Patton, were to strike the first blow. They were to march back into the positions they had lost in the Kasserine action and establish themselves on three key passes leading to the sea—Fondouk, Maknassy and Gafsa. When they had drawn off some of the German units massed in the south the piston would start to shove upward; Montgomery would attack. Then, if the Eighth Army was successful in putting the Germans to flight, the Americans would endeavour to sally out of their three passes and nip off the retreating enemy.

It was still sharply cold and wet at Tebessa as I drove through the hill forests to see the Americans on the eve of the advance. In the drizzling rain little groups of infantrymen were drawn up to receive their last instructions. They were hardly more than boys, most of them, wonderfully tall and proportioned and looking very forbidding under their Nazi-like helmets. Unlike the British battledress and equipment, which tends to hold a man stiffly upright, these boys were in a uniform which gave them plenty of free movement. The short and formless weatherproof jacket was scarcely a garment of beauty, but it allowed the men to walk in the easy stooping way to which they were accustomed.

Most of the American stuff was first-class, and even as good or better than the German. Their mess tins, water bottles, rubber-soled boots, woollen underclothes, shirts and windbreakers were all superior to the British equivalents and their uniforms in general were made of finer stuff. The Garand rifle and the officers' carbine were already regarded by many veterans as the best small arms on the front. As for their heavier equipment, it is doubtful if any army ever went to war so well supplied.

The only general criticism might have been that there was too much of it. Every other truck had a machine-gun mounted on its cabin. The self-propelling guns and the Long Tom rifles were some of the heaviest artillery along the whole front. The diesel Sherman was certainly the best tank of its class.

The jeeps, at the other end of the scale, were unmatched, and the Germans loved to capture them for their own use, just as we had loved to get hold of a Volkswagen. The weapon-carriers and the command vehicles were all brand new, as were the signalling sets, the bulldozers for road-mending, and the electrical workshops. It was the volume of this stuff, the intensity of the firepower that was so impressive. Possibly the troops could have done with a better heavy machine-gun and an improved mortar, but in general there was no question that they were the best equipped allied army at the front. By European army standards the American rations were lavish to the point of extravagance-vast quantities of tinned meats, fruits and vegetables. In any American mess you could be sure of getting an excellent hot meat and vegetable stew, a plate of fruit, white bread and a cup of coffee. Things like cigarettes, chewing-gum and toothpaste were handed out in a way that made the

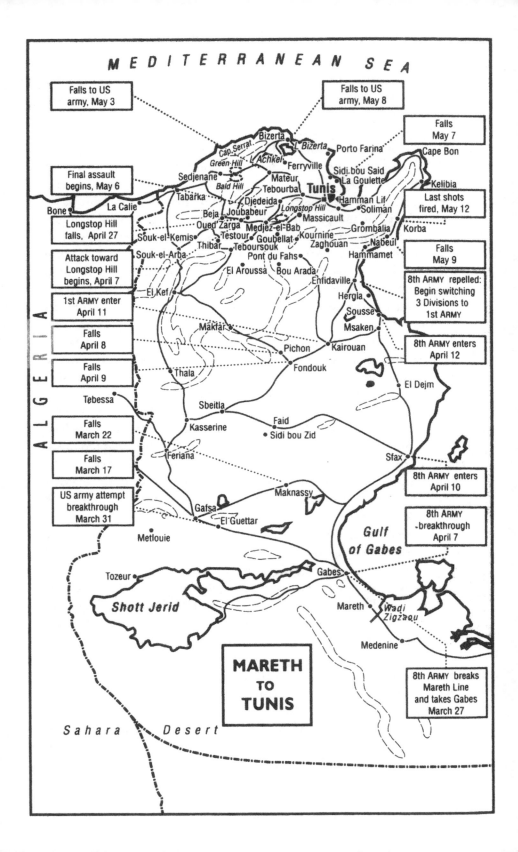

MEDITERRANEAN SEA

Falls to US army, May 3

Falls to US army, May 8

Falls May 7

Cape Bon

Bizerta

L. Bizerta

Porto Farina

Cap Serrat

Green Hill

L. Achkel

Ferryville

Sidi bou Said

Kelibia

Final assault begins, May 6

Sedjenane

Bald Hill

Mateur

La Goulette

Last shots fired, May 12

Tabarka

Tebourba

Tunis

Hamman Lif

Soliman

Bone

La Calie

Beja

Djedeida

Longstop Hill

Massicault

Grombalia

Korba

Falls May 9

Longstop Hill falls, April 27

Oued Zarga

Medjez-el-Bab

Kournine

Nabeul

Souk-el-Kemis

Testour

Goubellat

Zaghouan

Hammamet

Attack toward Longstop Hill begins, April 7

Souk-el-Arba

Thibar

Teboursouk

Pont du Fahs

El Aroussa

Bou Arada

Enfidaville

Hergla

8th ARMY repelled: Begin switching 3 Divisions to 1st ARMY

1st ARMY enter April 11

El Kef

Sousse

Falls April 8

Maktar

Msaken

8th ARMY enters April 12

Falls April 9

Pichon

Kairouan

Thala

Fondouk

El Dejm

Falls March 22

Tebessa

Sbeitla

Faid

Sfax

8th ARMY enters April 10

Falls March 17

Kasserine

Sidi bou Zid

Feriana

8th ARMY breakthrough April 7

US army attempt breakthrough March 31

Gafsa

Maknassy

Metlouie

El Guettar

8th ARMY -breakthrough April 7

Gulf of Gabes

Gabes

8th ARMY breaks Mareth Line and takes Gabes March 27

Tozeur

Mareth

Wadi Zigzaou

Shott Jerid

Medenine

ALGERIA

MARETH TO TUNIS

Sahara Desert

British soldiers gape. The Doughboy was always generous in sharing out his good things. As a British war correspondent I personally was given immediate hospitality wherever I went, and such things as maps and plans were discussed with me without hesitation.

Lieutenant General Patton selected his best trained infantry division—the First—to advance on Gafsa. Early in the morning the division surged forward, an avalanche of vehicles bumping over the flat brown country. They had swept through Feriana without opposition and were already on the outskirts of Gafsa oasis by the time my party caught up with the forward elements, about midday.

General Patton, a large and gregarious man with a fine weather-beaten face, a pearl-handled revolver strapped to his side, stood on a bare rock and surveyed the village of Gafsa a little uneasily. There was no answering gunfire from the enemy. He decided to go forward at once.

'Go down that track until you get blown up,' he said to his A.D.C., 'and then come back and report.' The A.D.C. set off in his jeep, and soon we were all trundling after him. With every minute it became clearer that the enemy had evacuated Gafsa without a fight. We were travelling on a sidetrack and those of us who were landmine conscious kept scrupulously in line. One signalling wagon, eager to get ahead, sheered off into the scrub beside us and by some miracle continued for a couple of hundred yards through a German minefield before it was blown up. We picked our way back off the track to the main road and, skirting the big craters the Germans had left behind, drove into the township in the early afternoon.

Gafsa, after being occupied by three different armies, was still intact, still a pleasant strip of palm trees and flowering gardens beside a watercourse. About fifteen miles farther east, toward the coast, is another smaller oasis, El Guettar. At El Guettar two razorbacked lines of hills come down to the main road and run parallel with it, and that is where the enemy had dug in. They flung their mortar- machine-gun-minefield combination across the valley and prepared to defend. The Gafsa advance came to an abrupt halt.

Meanwhile another American column went up over vile sandy tracks toward Maknassy. There was no real opposition anywhere, but the progress was disappointingly slow. The Americans had not quite got into their stride yet, and there were many delays along the route. Following along in the cavalcade of vehicles, I noticed that whenever an aircraft was sighted in the sky a whistle was blown at the head of each convoy, the vehicles stopped and the troops scattered across the fields.

Since the whistles were frequently blown even for single aircraft and before anyone could determine whether they were friendly or hostile, many hours were wasted every day.

Most of the vehicles were equipped with heavy machine-guns, and the men would have felt very much better firing them than they did taking cover among the wild flowers. But at this stage the order to shoot was not given.

We spent hours on that abominable track digging our station wagon out of bogs and sand-drifts, but in the end we managed to get into Maknassy a few hours after it had fallen. Again the enemy had retreated to the hills behind the town and were shooting down on the valley from their safe positions. The Luftwaffe was very active that day. Six times we jumped for cover among the cactus hedges while the Stukas churned up the road in front or behind us. An American half-tracked vehicle caught fire and began shooting out its ammunition all over the fields. Farther back, at Sened, a series of ragged dogfights was going on in the sky. One of the Germans dived quite unexpectedly out of a strip of low cloud and permitted himself the extravagance of aiming a bomb at my party's one solitary vehicle then travelling on the road. It was, as far as I know, the only bomb which has been aimed at me personally since the war began. We had changed over to a jeep, and by then we were much practised in taking cover. By a system of spontaneous levitation I remember rising directly and without effort into the air, and then travelling sideways until I reached the inevitable cactus hedge. The bomb, only a small one, dropped far behind.

We ran on back to Gafsa, where we had established ourselves in a comfortable Arab house. It even possessed a wood-burning bath-heater, which provided the only hot baths we were going to get for the next two months. Since luxuries were to be had in that pleasant place, I hired, in the absence of a batman, a batwoman. Hyah was without glamour. She was an aged and hideous Arab crone who swept the floors and handled the laundry.

It was a strange, rather pleasant life at Gafsa. Each day we drove up to the hills and looked down on the fighting. Each night while we wrote our messages by candlelight German aircraft swooped back and forth across the oasis dropping parachute flares. Anti-personnel bombs fell through the blinding yellow light. These bombs looked like myriads of big brightly coloured butterflies coming down. They were only the size of a small jam tin, and as each one left its container two metal wings painted yellow began to whirl around. When the wings had made a certain number of revolutions the detonator was released, so that sometimes the bomb would explode when it hit the ground and sometimes it would lie about until a vehicle ran over it or a man kicked it with his foot.

The Doughboys at the front were finding the enemy defence in the high rocks a very tough proposition indeed. Each machine-gun had to be surrounded and rushed before it could be silenced, and although the American barrage became fiercer and fiercer it was not possible to blow the Germans out of the caves and cliffs.

Then, on March 23rd, the Germans forced a crisis. They switched the 10th Panzer Division west and charged straight at El Guettar. Over a hundred tanks ran along the green floor of the valley directly at the American positions and under the cover of a concentrated air and artillery bombardment.

It requires great nerve and training for anti-tank gunners to meet a tank charge. You must hold your fire until, as a rule, you are yourself being shelled. You must select your targets one by one and not be disturbed by the fact that some of the enemy may get through. General Allen's gunners fought the Mark IV tanks down to a distance of several hundred yards—indeed, some of the enemy tanks were already abreast and slightly behind the American positions. Then the Germans broke. More than half of them turned back and groped for the paths through their own minefields. The rest—about forty—were either smashed with direct hits or damaged and left burning on the battlefield. It was as rounded and complete a victory as you could well hope for: and it was all that Montgomery needed. The 10th Panzers had been drawn off. The Eighth Army fell upon the Mareth Line.

Again Montgomery attacked by night. Again he began with an intense artillery barrage. Again he struck first with a direct right-handed blow and then with a left-handed flanking move. And again the air force was very closely interlocked with the advancing troops.

Rommel had already surrendered Médenine and the outlying defences without much argument some weeks before. He had established his real defence on the Wadi Zigzaou, a formidable rift in the land with very steep sides and still treacherous with winter mud.

The battle did not go well. The British Fiftieth Division crossed the wadi, but only with great difficulty—at places the men were clambering over one another's shoulders to reach the opposite side. A slender bridgehead was made, but when morning came the anti-tank guns had still not been got across. When the inevitable German counterattack came in, the British infantry were hopelessly exposed, and Panzer tanks charged right in among their positions. In some confusion the division was withdrawn across the wadi again.

This left the left-hand flanking column in an unhappy position. It was again the New Zealanders who had gone round, with a brigade of tanks, toward their objective—El Hamma—behind the enemy main line. Rommel now wheeled his heavy units on to El Hamma, and General Montgomery was obliged to think very quickly indeed. Those who had grown to believe that the general was incapable of anything more than his standard right-left plan now saw something new put into effect and at speed and in a crisis.

A new sector was opened between the coast and the New Zealanders. At the same time all available armour and aircraft was flung into support of the New Zealanders—possibly the boldest thing Montgomery ever did. Rommel was forced then to withhold some of his strength from the New Zealanders and deal with the new threat in the centre. Immediately he saw the Germans splitting up, Montgomery ordered the New Zealanders and their armour into attack. Again the pressure was applied at the coast, and by March 27th it was all over. The Eighth Army rode into the hamlet of Gabes, taking many thousands of Italian infantry, who had again been left behind, while the Germans retired to their second position on the Wadi Akarit, a few miles farther north. It was a battle that had begun badly and might have bogged down indefinitely but for the quick changeover in the British plans halfway through.

In the meantime the rest of Alexander's plan was not going according to programme. The Americans were repulsed from Fondouk, the most northerly of the passes. At Maknassy they were unable to make headway toward the coast. And at El Guettar the Germans and Italians were holding more strongly than ever. It was decided then to halt the Fondouk and Maknassy thrusts and concentrate on El Guettar. The American armour was wheeled south and the American Ninth Infantry division was also ordered to go to the assistance of the First in the El Guettar hills. In the pattern that was now becoming accepted, the infantry were to mop up the hills on either side of the valley while the tanks broke straight through along the floor of the valley on the Gafsa-Gabes road. It was hoped that the tanks would make the seventy-mile run down to the coast and join hands with the Eighth Army at Gabes.

My party had found an artillery spotting-post right in the centre of the El Guettar valley, and it commanded the most perfect view of a battlefield I have had, before or since. The tanks, we knew, were to attack at noon, and we got onto our grandstand a couple of hours beforehand.

Sprawling there on the ridge in the sunshine we looked right down into the enemy, positions. In front lay the broad green plain dotted with the wrecks of the previous week's tank battle. On either side desultory machine-gunning sounded from the hills. The valley took a turn to the north beyond El Guettar, so that the plain in front of us appeared to finish in another line of hills. These last were being shelled with rising intensity.

I crouched in a dugout with one of the artillery commanders while he gave his orders into the telephone to the American Long Toms a mile or two behind us. It all seemed so easy; just a few figures spoken into the telephone, then the air above us was full of tearing express trains and we grabbed our glasses to watch the hits. They fell among the high brown rocks, first with a quick yellow flash, then with a snow-white column of smoke that streamed steadily upward until it was caught by the crosswind on the mountain crest and billowed out into grey and formless cloud. Sometimes when the smoke cleared you could see the little figures of Germans or Italians running to better cover. They were only a mile or two away, but this was killing by remote control, without the maddening stimulus of hand-to-hand fighting. One could carefully assess the targets and take aim with the same unemotional calmness of a sportsman shooting grouse on the moors. Almost, not quite. In the intervals of our firing the enemy fired back and we ducked into our dugout and hugged the rock.

There was one battery of American medium guns slightly ahead of us on the plain, and they were getting the worst of it. Again and again the German spotters sitting in the hills around us got the range, and those four guns and their crews would disappear in immense shell-bursts. Watching from the ridge we would see first one gun then another emerge unharmed from the smoke, and the gunners, running from their pits, would slap the breeches back and take their revenge.

All morning this artillery duel went on, with the American barrage growing gradually louder and more persistent as more and more guns were brought in, just as an orchestra conductor will draw in more instruments for his crescendo. My head ached with the noise and the dust and the sight of the leaping smoke and flame in the hills.

It was getting very near midday. Four little Stuart reconnaissance tanks—the ones we used to call Honeys in the desert—came casually down the road from our rear positions and moved past my hilltop toward the enemy.

The artillery major picked up his telephone. 'There are four tanks going out now,' he said to the commander of his battery. 'Get Bill to run out after them in a jeep. He might find some more targets for us.'

Presently the jeep came buzzing at speed down the road in the wake of the tanks, three men aboard it.

'Good man, Bill,' said the major; 'he'll find something.'

The Germans now had spotted the tanks, and shell-bursts began groping toward them, making craters among the wild flowers in the plain. Then the enemy saw the jeep scuttling up the road. The first German shell was a hundred yards short, the second fifty yards long. There was a third explosion and the jeep disappeared entirely in erupting dust and fumes. Through the rolling smoke two men came running, and they flopped into a ditch as three more eighty-eight-millimetre shells, whining shrilly, slammed down about them. One dark figure lay prone beside the jeep, and this was Bill. As the firing eased off, the men ran back to him, but Bill was already dead.

A dozen such things were happening around us all the time, but this little tragedy was so personal and so swift that I separated it in my mind from the rest of the battle, and all that day in the dugout we felt guilty for the boy's death.

But there was not much time to reflect. While an ambulance ran out to collect the dead man, all the valleys behind us began to rumble and clatter with heavy machinery on the move. From a hundred wadis and ditches tanks began to debouch into the centre of the valley, first in half-dozens, then in dozens and scores. Some, spaced fifty yards apart, headed up the main road, and they roared and spluttered and grunted as they lurched past our hiding place and out into the fields beyond. Others turned at once into the pastures to our right. As they took up formation, each tank with a column of dust streaming out behind, it was as though one was looking at a battle fleet steaming into action over a green, flat sea—a wonderful sight. Beyond us, all the tanks moved forward together on a mile-wide front and perhaps a mile deep, and they made an exact and changing pattern. I looked at my watch and had to brush the fine dust from the glass. It was just twelve o'clock.

Watching from the heights, the German spotters caught sight of this frightening array that was bearing down on them at a steady fifteen miles an hour. As they went forward, infantrymen, unseen before, rose out of the long grass and for a little kept pace with the tanks. Long lines of dark figures were rising up everywhere from the plain and creeping toward the enemy. Overhead, half a dozen Messerschmitts skidded back and forth over the cavalcade for a moment, little bright shafts of yellow spitting from their wings; but the tanks and the men kept on. A last flight of American bombers swooped upon the end of the valley. One after another the leading tanks topped the horizon and stood briefly outlined against the enemy hills beyond.

'Cease fire,' said the artillery major into the telephone. The tanks were in the target area; they had joined contact with the enemy.

This was the point in every tank battle I had seen where everything vanished into smoke and noise and whirling dust. In Egypt and Libya no onlooker really knew what was going on because the churned-up sand obliterated the desert. But here in the green wheat it was different. The whole scene was played out in fascinating and terrible detail.

For some reason I concentrated my eyes on the tanks that were fighting on the main road. They had dodged round half a dozen wrecked trucks and were following a line of telegraph poles. Just about a mile away from me they came dead in the line of the enemy anti-tank barrage. You could see the enemy gun positions quite clearly from the flashes that leaped out of the rocks and see where the shells hit around the tanks; and see the tanks belch back at them with answering salvoes. As each tank touched the horizon its gun flared out, a bright flame of yellow fringed with black coming out of a black steel hulk. The third leading tank was hit first. I saw the shell hit the turret and a vivid flame flowered out. The tank went on firing. Then again another hit on the tank's port side. It stopped dead, but still its guns kept firing. There were shells now landing every few seconds and the fire had taken hold in the turret. A vast jet-black roll of smoke poured upward and at its base the smoke was red.

The tank stopped firing. Simultaneously a new and wider sort of flame erupted from among the enemy guns and another of our tanks was hit and then another. The two sides were only three or four hundred yards apart, and all along the road between me and the action little puffs of high explosive were making craters and jagged holes in the macadam. Away on the right flank we were not doing so well. The infantry had dropped out of sight again and a squadron of Shermans was shuttling back and forth in front of a continuous curtain of mortar fire. They probed and turned and manoeuvred, but every time they came up to a low brown ridge the mortar shells poured down and there was nothing between the tanks and the enemy but impenetrable bursting shrapnel. In the centre it was better. Our main squadron had almost reached the hills where apparently a dozen Italian tanks had been dug into pits and were being used as artillery. One after another the enemy gun flashes ceased and where there was flame before now only acrid smoke rose up. Shifting my glasses back to the road, I saw that the first tank was now completely alight and two others were smoking nearby. But other Shermans had passed through and were now fighting out of sight. A steady procession of vehicles raced up the road carrying ammunition. Ambulances began to stream back from the other direction. Over everything sounded the same quick staccato coughing of the guns. And now in the full light of the afternoon the sun was misted over by the battle cloud and the battle itself seemed to be illuminated with its own gun flashes and the flames of the burning vehicles that were running with molten white-hot steel.

For two hours it went on and then, imperceptibly at first, one gun after another fell silent. The fields in front of me began flooding with hundreds of vehicles that were spreading out to take over the newly won ground. A lorry-load of Italian prisoners came back, followed by six ambulances. The dust lifted a little and a shaft of sunlight came through again, turning the hollow in the hills into purple and the dark rocks into yellow. A heavy and unnatural silence began. There was still the noise of machine-gunning, still an occasional explosion. But compared with the uproar that had filled the valley for the past two hours this was silence.

I got into a jeep and went forward down the road. There was a pungent smell, a mixture of burnt oil and steel and clothing and cordite, welling out of the burning vehicles. Odd little things—a toothbrush, a table knife, a charred packet of cigarettes—were scattered over the ground in a jumble of telegraph wires and things too blackened and burnt to be recognised. The burning tanks were still too hot to approach and occasionally a shell came tearing out of the flaming débris. American soldiers were turning over broken bits of Italian weapons with their boots. A major-general tore by in a jeep. Two signallers carefully paid out their wire round a crater where a dead man was lying and walked on, chewing gum. A dud shell was upended grotesquely in a pool of sand.

Two or three aircraft went by, but scarcely anyone bothered to look up. A German newspaper, the *Oasis*, lay on the road beside a pile of empty shell-cases. This was the most forward gun position and now the enemy had gone back five thousand, perhaps six thousand, yards. He had broken off the battle and we were not yet able to follow up. There was a tugging weariness over the valley, a subsiding nervous tension. It was oppressive. As the light failed and the shooting died entirely away, the fires on the battlefield stood out more clearly. Everywhere the front-line troops were digging fresh trenches and rolling the guns into pits and hollows in the blackened wheat. As we drove back in the evening the rain started again. It extinguished the fires. It left the battlefield cold, and very quiet.

The tanks did not get through to Gabes that day. In the night fresh opposition mounted up before them, and for the time being the U.S. armoured thrust was abandoned.

Still, it had done its main job by reducing the pressure on Montgomery.

Fourteen

Kairouan

IT WAS now the first week in April and Alexander judged that he could safely go ahead with the second leg of his plan—to make the western wall of the cylinder contract a little more and get the piston to shove again from the bottom.

Our attempt to nip off the bottom section of the cylinder by driving down the Gabes road from Gafsa had apparently been halted indefinitely, but that did not spoil the general plan. The line was getting stronger every day, and indeed we had held off a renewed assault on the Sedjenane position and even captured new ground there. The fighting now was to spread along the whole front. This second stage required that we should clean up a line of hills along the northern side of the Medjerda Valley running from Oued Zarga to Longstop. Simultaneously Montgomery should attack on the Wadi Akarit just north of Gabes. Then we would strike again at Fondouk and attempt to cut off the enemy routed by Montgomery in the Akarit battle.

The First Army's best and most experienced infantry division—the Seventy-Eighth—was chosen to do the job in the Medjerda Valley, with the support of about a hundred and twenty-five Churchill tanks and some five hundred guns. This time instead of attacking down the valley we were going to fight across it. Since we held the southern line of hills and the Germans the northern line it would be necessary for our infantry and tanks to surge across the open floor of the valley and fight their way up the slopes on the opposite side. Four a.m., April 7th, was given as zero hour.

It was a very still night before the battle, no wind, no sound of firing. We drove almost to Medjez- el-Bab looking for a vantage point and then ran across a major in charge of the ack-ack and anti-tank guns.

'Come on,' he said, 'the brigadier's picked the best lookout on the whole line. I'll lead you up there.'

It was a rugged hollow in the hills, too rough for farming, and it overlooked the whole length of the valley. We got down into our sleeping-bags early and it was not yet 2 a.m. when I was wakened by a noise. Not fifty yards away British infantry were filing down to their assault positions just over the brow of the hill. They moved with expert quietness, a long broken line of upright silhouettes winding in and out of the gorse, and there was just the soft rhythmical sound of their boots on the earthen goat track. No one smoked. No one talked. Every so often as they filed by my bed an officer would say, 'Companee…halt,' and the moving shadows stopped dead and melted in the surrounding darkness. Then 'Companee…forward,' and the silhouettes broke away from the shadow again and vanished over the hill. For an hour they filed past.

Feeling too restless and expectant to sleep, we got up into the bitter, stinging cold and clambered to the crest of the hill. The valley below was in purple darkness. Far over to the right the R.A.F. was bombing Tunis and the searchlights or the bomb explosions—we could not tell which—made flickering lights against the clouds. There was no moon.

At ten minutes to four a battery of twenty-five-pounders, some twenty miles away to the west, opened fire; then someone nearer at hand opened up. A clump of bushes, a few hundred feet directly below us, suddenly lit with flashes and in the brief purplish light we could see the guns jumping with the recoil under the camouflage nets.

'They are a little earlier than I thought,' said the major. 'They are supposed to have ten minutes' slow, then ten minutes' intense firing. The mediums will come in, in a minute.'

They came in with a roar, and now the firing made a deep, measured beat right along the valley, a strange play of noise on light, a spectacle that you could not analyse because you could not see where the shells were landing and you had no notion of what was being hit in the darkness. Once or twice there was a steady flare in the distance that indicated something had been hit, a petrol dump perhaps; perhaps a German lorry. There was no sign of answering fire.

A few minutes after four the barrage abruptly broadened and redoubled. More guns came in, hundreds of them. Up to this moment the guns had made a series of flashes that danced along the foothills, but now it was almost a continuous band of light that kept renewing itself and seemed to be constantly growing brighter. The noise of single explosions blended into one continuous roar.

Hundreds of shells were tearing through the air together and I remember thinking then: 'No one can suffer this barrage and still fight.'

The first grey shafts of the morning came from over Tunis. As this light steadily increased, the noise of the guns fell away, battery by battery, and in its place the dark valley below was filled with the noise of tanks. The attack had started. The infantry were due on their first objectives at dawn.

When at last the morning came, it was an astonishing thing to look down and see that the valley was exactly the same. The farmhouses still stood. The rows of trees were unaltered. The wheat fields still spread out in a neat pattern and there were even Arabs at work about the homesteads. It was in the foothills beyond that the action lay. Already the infantry had rushed the first enemy outposts and we heard the steady rattle of the machine-guns. One or two fires had started. In the centre three lines of soldiers were creeping up to a farmhouse and we saw the men leap to their feet and rush forward over the last hundred yards. They emerged out the other side a moment later, running hard among the outbuildings, in pursuit of escaping Germans. The Churchills on the right were performing staggering feats of hill climbing. One group appeared to be almost upended in a steep wadi. Every time the leading tank shoved its nose over the top, a storm of mortar shells came down, and now the tanks were settling into hull-down positions and firing back. Away to the left a line of British trucks was moving slowly across a wheat field when the German gunners got onto them. A squadron of tanks, moving like prehistoric lizards, came crawling back to silence this fire, and presently it stopped and the trucks moved on.

The Luftwaffe, whose efforts had been gradually growing weaker and weaker over the past few weeks (the dive-bomber had almost disappeared), made a spasmodic effort to delay the attack. I remember this clearly because of a very ordinary but graphic little incident that happened to my party as we were driving from one part of the front to another. We had run back toward Testour in our station wagon, and I think it was Philip Jordan who was keeping watch through the roof—a job we took in turns for about half an hour at a time. The car had run down into a partly wooded valley beside a Bofors anti-aircraft gun when Philip shouted something, and as he shouted pale yellow tracer-bullets began to skid down the road on either side of us. The driver automatically jammed his foot down and grabbed the handbrake. The car skidded to a standstill and we tumbled out. The German aircraft, a Messerschmitt with silver wings, was only fifteen or twenty feet above our heads and as it roared on down the road the Bofors gun fired into its belly. For half a minute the machine continued straight onwards. It rose slightly, executed a graceful half-circle in the sky and then slithered down to a belly-landing among the wild flowers. We jumped back into the car and drove a couple of miles to the river where we judged the plane had fallen. From many directions troops who had seen the incident were running through the shoulder- high wheat which was dotted with red poppies and sweet mustard and tall white lilies. In a few minutes we found the Messerschmitt. It had landed practically unharmed on the soft wheat, but the pilot had vanished. I clambered into the cockpit and felt the joystick and the trigger; it was still warm from the pilot's hand, still warm from the grip with which he had fired his guns at us along the road, a minute or two before.

On the bank of the river an Arab peasant was gesticulating and shouting and everyone ran across to the direction in which he was pointing. They found the pilot hiding in a dung heap under a lip in the bank and he made no effort to resist. He lay there until the pursuers found him and then he got up slowly with his hands above his head and walked back toward his machine with a pistol pressed in his back.

He was a strikingly good-looking boy, not more than twenty-three or four, with fair hair and clear blue eyes, and he wore flying boots and overalls but no cap. The soldiers searched him and took from his pockets his revolver and his belt of bullets and a leather wallet. As they searched the German fumbled for a cigarette and made motions for someone to light it for him. He did this mechanically and without attempting to speak, and the hand which held the cigarette was shaking badly. Someone lit the cigarette and for some reason I could not understand the man with the pistol motioned the pilot to a place in the wheat about twenty yards from the fallen plane. Then quite accidentally everyone stepped back from the pilot at the same time and he was left alone standing in the wild flowers.

You could see very clearly what he was thinking. He was thinking, 'They are going to shoot me now. This is the end. The one with the pistol will fire at my body.' He stiffened and the hand holding the cigarette was tensed and shivering. Little globes of sweat came out in a line on his forehead and he looked straight ahead.

All this took only a moment and then, in the same involuntary way, the British troops moved toward him again and motioned him to march with them back toward the road.

The pilot did not comprehend for a moment. Then he relaxed and drew deeply on his cigarette, and it was again quite clear that he was saying to himself in a spasm of half-understood relief, 'It's all right. They are not going to shoot me.' Then we all walked back to the road. We felt pleased that the matter had ended so well and that punishment had come so quickly to the enemy who had fired at us on the road; but this actual physical contact with the pilot, his shock and his fear, suddenly made one conscious that we were fighting human beings and not just machines and hilltops and guns. Nearly always the battle to us was a mechanical thing and the enemy a sort of abstract evil in the distance.

But now, having captured a human being from that dark continent which was the enemy's line, one wanted to talk to the pilot and argue with him and tell him he was wrong.

As it was, we simply drove on again through the hills and the continuing gunfire again brought the war into focus as a thing of maps and calibres and tactics.

In this way then the First Army's attack went in along the Medjerda Valley on the morning of April 7th. It was a successful attack inasmuch as all the objectives set for that day were won. But this was only the beginning. For days afterwards that bitter hill skirmishing went on. Yard by yard the infantry fought their way steadily upwards, through minefields, taking machine-guns at the bayonet point, rushing tiny upland villages with hand grenades, always going up and up until at last they stood on the crest. A whole division of men—fifteen thousand—was swallowed up in those hills, and they struggled on desperately among the crags and boulders, often without food or water or even ammunition. There was nothing wildly spectacular about it—no towns to take, no massed formations in pitched battle, no great hosts of prisoners. It was just a painful slogging fight that had to be fought before we could get at the last great obstacle on the way to Tunis—Longstop Hill. It was the slow contracting of the cylinder.

Montgomery meanwhile went crashing in for his last great battle, in the south at Wadi Akarit. This time he charged head-on with his Highland division, the Indians and the Fiftieth. The Eighth Army was a wonderful machine when it was geared up to fight. It went forward with a terrible momentum and in a wonderfully adjusted rhythm—first the bombers, then the guns, then the infantry, then the tanks. Six gaps were blasted in the enemy line along the Wadi Akarit, and then the First Armoured Division and the New Zealanders poured through for the kill. Once again the German line broke under the stroke of the piston. For one hundred and fifty miles along the coast north of Akarit von Arnim had no defensive position. It was every man for himself now in the enemy camp. If you were lucky enough to possess a truck, you jumped aboard with your pals and lit out for the north with all the speed you could make. The R.A.F. fell on that retreat, but it was too great to smash entirely. A vast crocodile of German vehicles filed northwards day and night. It ran into Sfax and out again. It streamed into Sousse and still flowed northwards.

On April 8th Alexander made a bid to cut off that fugitive German crocodile. He switched his Sixth Armoured Division (which had just re-equipped with Sherman tanks) and some of his finest infantry, the Guards and the Hampshires, into the Fondouk sector for a combined operation with the French and the Americans. The proposition was the standard Tunisian thing—the French and the British were to take the village of Pichon and the high ground on the left, the Americans were to take the high ground on the right and the British armour was to drive up the middle straight at Fondouk. Once through Fondouk, the army would enter a broad, cultivated plain where the tanks could manoeuvre. Once in the plain, the key town of Kairouan would fall and the First Army could rush across to the coast.

It was strange country, this valley—half dead and brown, a patchwork of gaunt red rocks and cactus and broad wheat lands. There was some quality in the dust, its fineness possibly, that made it abominable. Running down to the starting line with the armour was a hot and sweaty business. The lads in the tanks were full of excitement over their new toys. They had also managed to get a higher percentage of high-explosive shells in place of armour-piercing shells. For some time the tanks had been finding that it was not enemy tanks they had to deal with but enemy guns. High-explosive and wide-spreading shrapnel was the thing to drive the gun crews away. These boys went to this bloody business with the excitement of a troop of boy scouts out for a day's hike through the woods.

The Hampshires started the thrust with a flanking attack on Pichon. It was as neat and balanced an engagement as any in the Tunisian war. Following them into the scrawny and unlovely village one could clearly read the story of the assault written in the debris left behind—a gun here that had been rushed, another in the cactus fields that had been knocked out, a Churchill and a Bren carrier that had been caught on the minefield and then the shell-holes in the village itself. Already, though it was hardly midday and the attack had only begun at dawn, the regiment was beyond the village and blazing away with mortars at the hills.

The prisoners were Austrian. It was interesting to notice, the deeper we cut into the German defences, the order in which they were prepared to sacrifice their troops. At the start of this offensive most of the prisoners were Italians, not young Fascists but the unwarlike types from the south who made good base troops and not much else. Then we began to pick up Germans who had recently been released from concentration camps in Germany on the condition that they would fight in Africa. These were all (in Nazi eyes) politically unreliable and therefore expendable. There were Poles and Czechs among them. Now we were gathering in Austrians, many of whom had no hesitation at all in saying how delighted they were to be out of it. The hard core of the Germans—troops like the Panzer grenadiers—still remained at large. They were always withdrawn from tight corners so that they could fight another day.

General Crocker, a lean, tall and quietly spoken Englishman, in charge of this operation, had one general order from Alexander: 'You must hurry. You must get through to Kairouan by the ninth or earlier, or the Germans retreating from Akarit will escape you.'

He therefore very smartly rushed his Guards up to the heights on the left where the German gunners were in hiding. The job for the Guards was exactly the same as for the Americans on the other side— to silence the German gunners in the hills so that our sappers could pull up the minefield in the Fondouk Pass and let our new tanks burst through.

It was the Welsh Guards I especially remember that day, though there were others in the fighting as well. In a steady, unflinching line the Welshmen went up the last bare slopes on foot, and they faced a withering machine-gun fire all the way up. When a man fell, someone was always there to step in, and the line went on until it reached the top.

'You can see them up there now,' Crocker said proudly. He had come into the front to get a first- hand view, and more especially to find out what had gone wrong. It seemed that the American troops had not arrived on the starting line, and their sector, a vicious line of hills to the right, was still in enemy hands. This meant that the German gunners were still operating across the minefield and the pass. Anything coming in a frontal attack straight down the valley was going to run into murderous fire. But Crocker was under orders to press on. He waited twenty-four hours, but when the southern hills still remained untaken he decided to sacrifice his tanks. Some would be lost for certain, but there was a strong chance that in being lost the leading tanks would blast a way through. A young squadron leader was chosen to lead the assault. Spaced wide apart, the tanks ran forward for a mile over heavy sand. Then, as they began to come under fire, the squadron leader reported over the radio: 'There's a hell of a minefield in front. It looks about three hundred yards deep. Shall I go on?'

'Go on,' he was told. 'Go on at all costs.' The cost in the end was not too bad—less than one hundred tanks, many of them quickly repairable, since only their tracks had been blown off. The bad thing was that as soon as a tank fouled a mine and its crew jumped outside they were caught in mortar fire from close range. Beyond brigade headquarters I came on several little groups of the lads who had set out so bravely that morning. They were badly beaten up, even those who could walk. Their faces were black with burnt tank grease and oil, they were half deaf and their uniforms were cut about in an extraordinary way by blast and near misses.

Then the young squadron leader was carried by. He had lived just long enough to break a passage through the mines and see the reinforcements flow through, and this man is remembered now in his regiment with great affection and pride.

Fondouk fell that night.

It was reported later that the Americans had failed to arrive on time partly because there was some confusion about the zero hour and partly—so American friends later told me—because of the slowness of their vehicular traffic on the road and of getting the men into position. This was the low- water mark of American arms on the Tunisian front, and only if one understands and knows about these early mishaps is one able to appreciate the extraordinary change that took place later on. These very units that failed at Fondouk were the ones that swept through to a brilliant victory in the north only a few weeks later. If ever there was proof of the need of field training and the ability of the Americans to profit by it, it was here.

There comes a moment in nearly every campaign when the atmosphere along the front, suddenly alters. For days, or even weeks or months, one has gone into the line and seen the same old things, the same guns firing at the same targets, the same patrols going out, and inevitably you give way to the despondent feeling that it will all go on indefinitely. Then, one morning you notice everything has changed. First, probably you notice the rear workshops and casualty clearing stations have moved from their old positions under the trees. Farther down the road more and more trucks are pouring in from the sidetracks and there is a general and accelerating movement toward the front. No enemy aircraft appear. Staff cars, ambulances, water carts, lorries, signalling vans are all racing to get ahead. You call at divisional headquarters and find it has moved forward to the spot where brigade used to be; and brigade has moved. Everything is moving, and as you run past the procession the troops on the lorries are grinning and shouting. At the danger spots, where you never drove in daylight if you could avoid it, more and more vehicles are pressing down the road and there is no shelling, no machine-gunning.

It was like this now. The break had come. I found myself in the midst of the most exultant and exciting spectacle a war can offer—a victorious army rushing forward over its battlefields in pursuit of the broken enemy. Every deserted German gun pit, every tangle of broken barbed wire, is a milestone on the way and a visible proof that you have won and the enemy is beaten.

A strange, buoyant excitement seizes the army then. Men in their eagerness to rush on do reckless things like running blindly through minefields. They feel they can't be stopped now, that every gun has twice the power it had before, that every man is equal to a dozen of the enemy. 'Get on…get on…' You hear the order everywhere, and in the dust and the shouting and the confusion the men are laughing and talking at the top of their voices.

General Alexander pushed by in a big American command vehicle and shouted across at us, 'How are you getting on?' He was gone before we could answer. An English officer in a jeep joined us at a traffic block, saying, 'There's a complete madhouse in the hills over there. The American Rangers, the British Commandos and the French Goums are all stalking one another round and round the mountain-tops and no one knows who is supposed to be fighting who. They have just ambushed the general.'

Farther on, the sand was very deep and we could only get by in single file by sticking to the steel netting that had been hastily pegged down through the night. We were in the midst of the burnt-out tanks now—the tanks that sacrificed themselves for this breakthrough—and lines of white tape laid down by the sappers showed where the German minefields were.

Another friend joins us in the procession and says, 'There are a lot of our dead out there and we can't get to them because of the mines. Two of the sappers were blown up half an hour ago.'

The scene at Fondouk is quite inexplicable. The Americans have arrived and are marching south while we march north. The two columns cross one another on the crossroads and there is a most extraordinary mixture of vehicles being straightened out by the military police. Still, it is a great pleasure to be on a good macadam road again—and the road leads straight into the Mohammedan city of Kairouan, the fourth most holy Moorish city in the world, the centre of the great mosque and the Moorish carpet industry and, what is more to the point, the crossroads town on which the German army is converging.

Realising it was late, the army made a great effort to reach Kairouan that night. As my party ran forward to join the vanguard others kept coming back with the usual conflicting news: 'Kairouan has fallen... No, it has not...We attack tomorrow...We attack tonight,' and so on. In those circumstances there is only one thing to do—go and find out for yourself.

This is always the most difficult moment for the war correspondent. Shall he isolate himself with the troops at the head of the hue and cry?— in which case he will get a better story but be unable to get it back until days afterwards—or shall he stop and get a story off and then resume the chase on the following day? I personally was all for pushing on, since this was the First Army's first big breakthrough after many bitter months of being stuck in the mud. In the end it was agreed that we should use two more hours of the precious daylight in going forward and then return to get our messages away. For once it was a sensible decision.

Outside the ruined hamlet of Fondouk we careered across a flat, soft countryside that was at last beginning to bloom with the spring wild flowers, a cascade of sweet yellow mustard that stretched mile on mile into the distance. The vehicles on the road grew fewer and fewer and already many units had turned aside into the breast-high wheat to camp for the night. Dark puffs of smoke began to show on the horizon on either side of the road, and occasionally we caught the distant sound of gunfire. Enemy aircraft were about, travelling very low and fast.

We ran forward to the head of the column, still a dozen miles from Kairouan, and found the tyred vehicles stopped by a sand drift in the bottom of a wadi. Everyone piled off the trucks and got to work with shovels. A huge German troop-carrier, towing an 88-millimetre gun, had been knocked out only an hour or two before and the wreckage still smouldered beside the road. Twice we ran in panic along the wadi when fighters swooped by, twenty feet above the ground. Then we got through and raced north to find the tanks. The road was empty now, but there was still no sign of the enemy. A lone British dispatch rider held us up. 'I shouldn't go any farther if I were you,' he said. 'Not at any rate in that' (a slightly contemptuous reference to our rickety station wagon), 'as there are Jerry tanks ahead.'

Content then that Kairouan was not going to fall that night, we ran back to Fondouk, where we had noticed a particularly good-looking white villa outside the village.

A group of American anti-tank gunners had got there first, but they did not seem to want the place. Cautiously kicking open the doors we searched inside with a torch, but apparently the Germans had left too much in a hurry to mine or booby trap the place. From the papers lying about we discovered that until the previous day this villa had been the Nazi headquarters for the region. A German general's breakfast things were still lying about. A lamb had just been skinned and cleaned for him and was hanging up in the kitchen. In the bedrooms there were packets of 'louse powder,' and they were marked for use in Russia. The villa shook a little that night as the Germans bombed our end of the valley and we bombed their end, but it was a pleasant night, and we were on the road early next morning. On a slight rise that commanded a view of the white walls of Kairouan shimmering in the distance we found General Keightley, the commander of the British armour.

General Keightley could give a more lucid and entertaining account of a battle than any field commander I have met. In ten minutes he told us the position. Sfax, the big port to the south-east, had fallen without a fight and the Eighth Army was now pushing up the coast road to Sousse. The First and the Eighth armies were therefore running parallel with one another, but unfortunately the Germans had put on an additional turn of speed. We were too late to catch them at Kairouan. We had nipped off one of their rear columns an hour or two before, but the bulk of the enemy had got away. Kairouan was declared an open city, and our patrols would enter it within the hour.

At that we hurried down the road again. Ahead of us a Stuka with the most improbable good luck dived on a Sherman tank and put a bomb through the turret. After that we drove peaceably and cautiously into Kairouan. At first there was no sign of life among the glistening white tombstones that surrounded the town. Then, penetrating past dozens of German noticeboards into the central square, we were surrounded by a crowd of mingled Jews, French and friendly Arabs who gave themselves entirely to hysteria. They did all the things the crowd usually does when a town is taken. They gave the V sign, they shouted and waved flags, the girls kissed the soldiers and the men ran out with bottles of wine and fruit. But here the demonstration was so spontaneous and so genuine it was somehow most moving and most gay. It was the first glimpse we were going to have of the delighted relief that swept the whole countryside at the departure of the Germans.

Not everyone welcomed us, of course. Indeed, that evening I had this shattering experience. A Frenchwoman ran up and said that her two baby girls wanted to kiss me. I had hoisted the first one up on my knee when out of the corner of my eye I caught sight of a little Arab girl watching the proceedings. And with elaborate malice she slowly pulled the back of her hand across her throat and disappeared.

It took me a day or two and much enquiry to find out what had been going on in Kairouan since the Germans occupied the place four months before. Then I sent the following message to my paper:

'KAIROUAN, *Wednesday*.—This is the story of what happens when the Germans take a village. I write it just as it fell out here—and at half a dozen places I have been in in the past two days.

'First, Messerschmitts come over very low and very fast and two Arab A.R.P. wardens run to the roof of the town's tallest building beside the mosque. They turn over the petrol motor that works the town's one siren, but by then the people in the earthen streets below are already slamming their doors, picking up their children and running blindly to the rough trenches they have dug in the main square. Twice more the Messerschmitts go by, but it is quiet toward evening.

'Rumours are passing everywhere around the souk and the bazaar, where the men sit cross-legged at their doorways. Eventually the French civil controller gets his counsellors together. They order the people to be calm. They warn them to hide their flags and anything that might anger the Germans. None is to carry weapons lest the Germans should grow suspicious and start shooting…and what are half a dozen long-barrelled rifles from the Berber wars against German tanks?

'Presently there is dust on the empty road leading into the town, and from the north a German armoured car slowly edges its way through the outer streets. A German officer stands in the open turret with a pair of binoculars round his neck and a revolver in his hand. All his men are at their machine-guns.

'Arabs in the doorway smoke, look up and do nothing. A few excitable children run into the street, shouting and cheering at the big strange motor car. In their doorways and from behind their lace curtains the French watch and wait. In the main square the car stops, and as the crowd gathers round the German officer asks in broken French for the mayor.

'The mayor is there in his best suit, and he tries hard to understand the German orders: "No lights at night…Hostages and immediate death if there is trouble…Are there any British here?"

'More and more armoured cars come into the square, and as the crowds gather round to stare the officers flock into the little tenth-rate hotel. They want wine. They want dinners. Madam does what she can. The wine is sour, the eggs hardly fresh—but…they will pay.

'The Germans have a great deal of money. They pay thirty francs for four eggs apiece, which works out at ninepence an egg, a fantastically high rate in this land of chickens.

'The tension breaks quickly in this hotel as the Germans eat and drink. They start making jokes with madame and her daughter.

'All this time more and more Germans are coming in, infantrymen in dusty green gabardine uniforms who start pitching tents on the outskirts of the village and digging holes for their guns. They park their vehicles carefully under the trees and hedges, and throw branches over the guns. A few gather round a pump with flat five-gallon tins, and they try to talk to the Arabs as they draw water.

'By the morning quite a lot more Germans have arrived. Some go to the town hall and tell the mayor that he must be out by noon, for his offices are requisitioned. Half a dozen other buildings are taken over through the morning, and the Germans are asking questions everywhere around the town. And they are very busy talking to informers. Always they have plenty of francs for information. In the afternoon the arrests begin.

'First, the mayor. It turns out that he is a de Gaullist. Then half his counsellors, just to be on the safe side. Then the corn merchant. Apparently he has been saying things about the Nazis recently. A Jew, of course. There seem to be quite a lot of Jews. An informer obliges with a list.

'The Germans are very correct and very methodical. In all the surrounding farms they ask: "How many sheep, how many pigs, how much grain?"

'It is all paid for at high prices. The villagers find that prices have doubled overnight. Next day they have tripled. It is no longer possible to buy wheat.

'But why worry? There is plenty of work. The Germans are offering Arabs up to five shillings daily to work on their new airfield, three miles outside the town. The Jews get work, too. Not in return for money, of course, but still they are not killed so long as they are willing to work a ten-hour day digging drains. They can keep going by buying vegetables with their savings. Frenchmen, too, find it difficult—all favours seem to be going to the Arabs.

'It seems to get tougher every week. The wine vanishes. Meat is unobtainable. The bread goes brown and then black.

'But the young German officers are tremendously good-looking, and tremendously full of confidence. They have a series of good jokes about how the English ran away, first in France, then in the Far East, and then in the desert; and if anyone suggests they are not about to run away again in Tunisia—well, then, that is another good joke.

'And here are newspapers to prove it—newspapers in French, German and Arabic appear by magic, filled with the latest news of the U-boat war and raids on London. The bazaar gets a free gift of two strong radio sets so that the villagers can hear special broadcasts from Berlin.

'As the days go by the village slips into the gradually tightening routine. Each Jew has his badge of David pinned to his coat. Each day he struggles a little harder to get food.

'Even the first R.A.F. raid fails to shake the boyish high spirits of the Germans. But they grow irritable when eggs and wine fail to appear at the hotel. Nor are the local people so pliant. They have plenty of francs. But now there is nothing to buy. An Arab will work for a full day for just one handful of tea.

'There is no great Axis advance, but instead, rumours begin to fill the bazaar—rumours that the British are approaching. There is a second air raid, and then a third. More than one hundred civilians are in hospital, and the women in their grief grow recklessly critical of the Germans. The Germans themselves stop making jokes, and there is much movement of Wehrmacht traffic in the village. All trucks seem to be headed north, and that is not the direction of the front. Ambulances keep passing through. The atmosphere grows sullen and morose and apprehensive.

'There is no more talk of what Marshal Rommel is going to do.

'A Jew dies of weakness. A Frenchman is knocked down in the street. A German is shot for trying to desert. Bazaar rumours go on and on.

'Then one night there is the distant sound of artillery, and as it grows louder, and more and more dusty vehicles rush through the village, no one can pretend that this is a great German advance to throw the British out of Africa.

'Suddenly German gunners who have idled for three months around the village walls pack their guns and vanish. Flares keep showing on the southern horizon, and there is heavier gunfire. 'Only a few Germans are left now, and it is hard to believe that these tense, drooping men are the boyish officers who arrived laughing and shouting only a month or two ago. The colonel drives away with his staff. Work ceases on the airfield. Odd parties of Germans, looking exhausted and dishevelled, walk into the village and snatch bicycles, carts, horses—anything that moves—and depart. They do not pay now.

'Suddenly the villagers find they are alone. A single Spitfire rushes across the white, flat roofs, and presently is back with ten more fighters, weaving back and forth just above the mosque.

'The mayor gets his counsellors together. "There must be no excitement…Wait until we are certain it is all right…Get the flags ready."

'As he talks, two armoured cars burst through the dust in the south and make toward the town. An

A.R.P. warden on the roof shouts, "It's the British"—and the people rush into the streets.

'This is not an imaginative short story. It has happened. It is being made to happen, more and more, as every day goes by.'

Fifteen

Sousse

BEYOND KAIROUAN the good hard road ran straight to Sousse on the sea. All my instincts now made me want to meet the Eighth Army again. I had left them eight months before at Alamein, and at a moment of indecision and defence. Now they rode on a great victory, and I was curious to see if my friends had changed. Sousse lay only eighty kilometres away from Kairouan, but the road was empty and no one yet had passed along it. The First Army's tank battle had veered away to the north and west and General Keightley had told us that he was not going to the coast at all, but continuing inland. On the seaboard Montgomery was presumably about to take Sousse, if he had not already done so, and the patrols of the First Army were too busy on their own sector to take a joy-ride and find out.

Meanwhile it was known that odd groups of Germans were still straggling northwards across the Kairouan-Sousse road between the two British armies.

My party was as keen as I was to reconnoitre across to the sea by ourselves, but on the first night we turned back after going only a few miles. A patrol leader of a group of Valentines told us firmly that German tanks were reported down the road, in addition to minefields, and it seemed stupid to go on.

Next morning we set out again, and it was all plain sailing for a while. Humps that appeared from the distance to be tanks turned out to be haystacks or Arab huts. The road ran over gentle hills and dales and it was deserted except for odd civilian cyclists who gabbled incomprehensibly in Arabic and could give no accurate information.

After an hour a jeep and an ambulance overtook us. They were searching for one of our armoured patrol cars which had fouled a minefield, and we followed on. The broken car lay in the fields near a place where the enemy had blown a series of craters in the road. It was the old story. The car had turned off along a sidetrack to get around, and now it was completely capsized over an exploded mine and the dead driver was stretched on the turf.

We picked our way past cautiously. The country here had burst into a wild fantasy of colour, and that overworked cliche 'a carpet of flowers' became a proven fact. It was just that, a rich deep Persian carpet woven of bluebells and poppies, of sweet peas and tulips, of daisies and lilies; and these grew so thickly that for miles you could not see the ground or the grass, only flowers. They made patterns that swept over hilltops, hilarious, shouting bands of colour. Partly to rationalise our astonishment and partly because we were unable to express our delight we fell back on our old game of out-clicheing one another.

'A veritable carpet of flowers.'

'A regular Brocks benefit.' And finally:

'Good enough for *Punch*.'

It helped to relieve the tension of travelling in an open vehicle into enemy country. As we talked we always kept watching for strange vehicles on the road ahead or out in the fields on either side. Then, quite unexpectedly, we had a great stroke of luck. A British artillery officer whom we had known in the Middle East casually drove up in a truck from the east.

'Yes,' he said, 'Sousse fell an hour or two ago. I have just come across country from the coast and as far as I know the main road is clear.'

After that we came on scattered villages where the people ran out and waved flags as we went by. Twice we ducked into a wood and hid from aircraft. The country began to break up a little into hills, and then at last we turned into the town of Msaken and saw the Eighth Army. We had come in off a side road and just for a moment it seemed that we had made a bad mistake. The vehicles running up the main road were all German or Italian. Then drawing closer I saw the British troops in the lorries. The British desert soldier looks like no other soldier in the world. He looks at first sight like a rather rakish and dishevelled boy scout, the effect, I suppose, of his bleached khaki shorts and shirt and the paraphernalia of blackened pots and pans and oddments he carries round in his vehicle which is his home. He practically never wears a helmet, and he has a careless loose-limbed way of walking which comes from living on the open plains and which is altogether different from the hill troops weighed down by heavy battledress. The desert is a healthy place especially if you can camp by the sea. These youths were burnt incredibly by the sun and they had that quality of brimming health that made them shout and sing as they went along.

Very content to be among them again, I struck up conversations with the troops as we bumped along in the cavalcade. It seemed that they had taken over the enemy vehicles when their own had broken down. Montgomery's forces had split into two halves, one going directly into Sousse on the coast, the other splitting off northward here at Msaken because the main bridge was blown by the enemy.

For an hour or more we coasted along over a rough and filthy track, and after many months I felt almost pleasurably my lungs filling up with dust again. It was much warmer here on the coast and the palm trees still gave the flavour of the desert. The progress was very slow and sometimes we ran into traffic blocks, for ten minutes or more. The Eighth Army was swarming through the countryside and every side road was choked.

At last we cut through a field of cactus and joined the main road north of Sousse. With the main road we hit the New Zealand division coming head-on toward us—in the way the enemy would see it coming. They rolled by with their tanks and their guns and armoured cars, the finest troops of their kind in the world, the outflanking experts, the men who had fought the Germans in the desert for two years, the victors of half a dozen pitched battles. They were too gaunt and lean to be handsome, too hard and sinewy to be graceful, too youthful and physical to be complete. But if ever you wished to see the most resilient and practised fighter of the Anglo-Saxon armies this was he. This wonderful division took a good deal of its fighting morale from its English general, Freyberg, the V.C. who through two wars had probably been more critically wounded more often than any other living man.

After Freyberg had defended Crete and carried his gospel of the bayonet through half a dozen campaigns in the Middle East, the Germans very nearly killed him at Mersa Matruh. By continuing to conduct the battle with a wound through the back of his neck, the general practically threw away his chance of survival, but somehow he had been patched up. And now the old gentleman himself rode up the road standing in the open turret of a tank, and he looked a good deal younger and tougher than I had ever seen him before.

Against this tremendous flood of vehicles, all painted a brilliant light desert yellow, we rode into the blasted town of Sousse. For months this place had been attacked by the R.A.F. and the United States Air Force; and now driving in through the target area along the docks it was a frightening sight, a vision of what we were one day going to see in the Ruhr, in Germany. It was not so much the general devastation, it was the violence with which everything had been done. A grand piano had been picked up from a basement and flung onto a housetop. The roof of one apartment building had been flung bodily onto the next building. The palm trees on the waterfront looked like those photographs one used to see after a hurricane had passed through Florida. The ships in the bay were set in a frame of blackened warehouses and they were in all stages of decomposition—the ships that had been merely hit and sunk, those that had been beached by a near miss and subsequently broken up by the waves, those that had been entirely disintegrated. Bits of cork, broken scraps of lifeboats and rope and spars were mingled with the tangled mess of the railway lines that ran down to the docks. The walled Arab section—the Kasbah—had been split open and the midday sun poured in over all its tawdry and shabby secrets; the labyrinthine brothels, the sweet- vendors' shops, the miserable foetid courtyards where the Moorish women wasted their obscure and furtive lives.

Beyond this, away from the port, the modern city had been untouched, and now the civilians were in the excited high tide of their relief that at last the hell of bombing was over. And so they made the soldiers welcome. A day or two later when Montgomery drove through the town in a jeep a great crowd saluted him, 'Vive Mong-goum-ree, vive Mong-goum-ree,' and an unusually attractive little French girl offered a bouquet and flung her arms round the general's neck.

But today they were still a little stunned.

I hunted about through the ruined streets looking for my friend, Alexander Clifford. I was quite certain he would turn up. Long before all this, before even Italy had entered the war, we had met in Athens and flown across to Cairo and the desert. For two years we had covered all the campaigns together as correspondents, until finally we had both got fed up with the war and managed to get leave, he to go to England, myself to America. Then he had rejoined the Eighth Army and I had gone to the First. I had failed to get a rendezvous in Tripoli and now I felt sure he would turn up in Sousse.

He had, of course, entered the town within an hour of its fall and we met in the main street. With him came the other two men with whom we always played bridge in the desert—Geoffrey Keating and Russell Hill. I had had many journeys with these three. We had camped alone for long periods in many difficult places, and there had grown up between us quite unawares a network of tacit understandings and little habits. Within the hour we had broken open and entered a comfortable villa by the sea; one man had gone off to ferret for wine, another to clean the house, a third to cook. Each one fell naturally into the job he had always done. I would no more have dreamed of interfering with Clifford's cooking than he would have thought of instructing me on the lighting of the stoves or the unpacking of the trucks. Keating always procured the petrol and the rations, and so it went on. I do not know if we were efficient or not, but our personal lives were made easier and pleasanter by these naturally formed habits, and when we worked as a team we seldom missed any vital incident on the front.

It was only after many months of mistakes and errors that we had learned how to live on a campaign, to know how to interpret a line of rising dust on the horizon, to know when to go forward and when to stay back, to know the key men in each division and to have a certain feeling that told you whether the battle was going well or badly.

And now on this night, sitting back after dinner with my friends, I began to understand the differences between the First and the Eighth armies. Already there was a good deal of superficial jealousy and fundamental misunderstandings.

In Kairouan a friend of mine from the First Army had gone up to a sergeant from the Eighth Army and said, 'Hullo! Pleased to see you. I am from the First Army.' To which the desert sergeant replied lightly, 'Well, you can go home now. The Eighth Armys arrived.' Again, a young officer from Montgomerys staff who joined us on this night was full of derision for the First Army. He asserted that the Eighth Army would have to take Tunis since the First Army was incompetent.

Such obvious boasting usually came from men who had only recently arrived in the desert, but it antagonised the soldiers who had been struggling all winter in the mountains and the mud of northern Tunisia. They regarded the desert soldiers as noisy and over-confident, an army that was sunning itself in publicity, and they looked forward with grim and unfriendly relish to the moment when the desert fighters struck the mountains.

In the same way the First Army men themselves were not understood. They appeared to the veteran soldiers in Montgomery's forces as a parade-ground army, beautifully equipped but not much good at fighting.

I do not say that these feelings went very deep, but the antagonism was there, and it continued until the troops went into action side by side. Then they began to know one another.

The fact was that the Eighth Army was not a European army any more. To a great extent it had become an overseas army, an army based not on London but on Cairo. For months and years it had been cut off from Europe, and in their isolation the troops had developed a complicated set of private habits, and even a slang language of their own.[7] Anyone who did not fit into these habits, who had not shared their adventures, was an outsider. The Eighth Army had been encouraged for the past few months by Montgomery to regard itself as invincible, as an independent and private expeditionary force knowing no law except its own. It was irksome, therefore, for this vigorous and victorious force, to learn, following the Casablanca conference, that it had been placed under the command of Algiers. They felt a little aggressive about it and showed it. In other words, they had a superiority complex just as the First Army at that time had an inferiority complex.

But the thing went deeper. The Eighth Army was very largely an empire army comprised of Australians, South Africans, New Zealanders and Indians. The settlers who had gone out to Australia in the nineteenth century learned and earned their independence. When they returned on visits to England the Australians appeared to the English as aggressive, boastful and a little uncouth in manner. To the Australians the English appeared as more than a little effete and soft. Yet the Australian was very often aggressive solely in order to hide his sense of insularity. And the Englishman very often admired the virility of the Australian. Then when the Tommy demonstrated his toughness in Flanders, the English and

Australian troops got on very well indeed.

Something of the same sort happened in Tunisia. When the Eighth Army saw the fine equipment, the new guns and tanks and uniforms of the First Army, a slight sense of insularity was forced upon Montgomery's men and to stifle it they boasted a little. In other words, an inferiority complex existed inside their superiority complex.

This was the argument I developed over dinner that night and the others would not agree. They asserted that the bulk of the Eighth Army—the part that had existed before Montgomery's arrival— were simply veterans who were sure of themselves. They had come through much fighting to a seasoned maturity and they sought no one's good opinion but their own.

Either way we agreed that the Eighth Army, despite the fact that its fighting had mostly been done in the desert, was the better force because of sheer experience. This dispute which was at that moment a favourite topic throughout Tunisia was happily going to be settled in the best possible way before the end of the month.

For the next ten days or so I hunted with the Eighth Army. It was to me a never-ending pleasure to see again the units I had known so well. Fundamentally nothing had changed, but on the surface there were many differences. Montgomery had given the men a tremendous eagerness and there was always a stir along the road when the general drove past, a black beret on his head, his lean ascetic face looking always intent and preoccupied. Driving up to the three caravans he used as a travelling home one day, I heard that he had got his Flying Fortress, as strange a story as any that came out of the campaign.

It seemed that after his conquest of Tripoli the general was dining with some American officers and for some reason the conversation turned on the subject of the town of Sfax.

'What will you give me if I take Sfax by April 15th?' Montgomery said suddenly to the Americans. He had still to fight the battles of Mareth and Wadi Akarit and the distance alone made it unlikely that the Eighth Army would get there so soon.

'We'll give you anything you like,' the Americans said lightly.

'Will you give me,' Montgomery said (I am paraphrasing his words), 'a Flying Fortress for the duration, its crew to be on the American payroll?'

'Sure,' they said, and forgot about the matter. Montgomery did not allow himself to forget. He gave Sfax the code name of 'Fortress' in his messages, and when he duly arrived there two or three days ahead of his bet he sent a signal to Eisenhower in Algiers, 'Fortress, please.'

Now this was distinctly embarrassing. It was not quite in the province of American generals to go betting in American government Fortresses. So it was suggested that Montgomery should wait for the machine until the campaign was over. The general, however, was adamant. He insisted on the Fortress at once, and after a somewhat brusque correspondence it arrived. The crew was delighted and at once set about flying Montgomery between Algiers, Tunisia, Cairo and subsequently London.

Meanwhile the fascinating spectacle of the desert army entering the mountains was going on. The enemy had halted about thirty miles north of Sousse around the village of Enfidaville. It was an obvious place in which to make a stand, for at that point the mountains came down almost to the sea.

The attack began long before dawn on April 19th. Feeling our way forward in the darkness of the New Zealand headquarters we heard enough to know that it was not going too well. Enfidaville itself fell quickly enough, but beyond that the enemy were dug into fearsome hills, hills that had to be assaulted directly. For an hour I watched them sending down concentrated mortar fire and the Eighth Army's guns bayed back in force until the hills were full of teeming smoke from the shell-bursts. The Indians, the New Zealanders and the Guards went in and soon found themselves obliged to swarm up sheer cliffs. The enemy above had merely to fire their guns straight down on the climbing men. The Gurkhas were in their own country here, and when they did get to grips with the Italians they did terrible things. They used the knife. There were even hand-to-hand struggles where men sought to throw one another from the heights. For the rest of the men their first contact with the hills was not easy. Some confessed they even had that same feeling of claustrophobia I remembered on arriving in Tunisia, the feeling, too, that one was being constantly overlooked—as indeed one was. Clifford and I were involved in one little antic by the sea. We were travelling into Enfidaville when the troops in the lorries on the road suddenly began to dismount and disperse across the fields. They split up into platoons, the Bren-gun crews out on the flanks, the stretcher-bearers drawing up behind. It was a tense little scene. The men crept forward yard by yard, taking what cover they could. They held themselves ready for the command to rush forward with the bayonet and the hand grenade. Suddenly a major jumped up and hurried to the main road. 'God damn it,' he shouted, 'we have debussed two miles too soon. Get back into the vehicles.' Rather tamely everyone filed back to the road and the cavalcade rolled on through the peaceful landscape.

It is doubtful if any army could have broken through that Enfidaville position without support from the left flank. Unit after unit was sent in. Some reached the caves where the enemy were in hiding, but there were always more caves higher up, more mortars, more open slopes to cross against machine- gun fire. By the end of two bitter days of many casualties it was evident that the first attack was not going to break through.

Tanks could not operate in this congested space, and it was at this point—about April 21st—that Alexander diverted the First British Armoured Division away from Montgomery's army and attached it to Anderson's forces in the Goubellat Plain.

Again and again the desert fighters thrust forward, always making a little ground, but never forcing a decisive action.

Most of the trouble concerned a hill feature known as Garcia. The fighting turned on this spot and whoever held it was in possession of the battlefield. A fresh division of British troops was called up to assault Garcia, and it was agreed that once they had taken the hill the New Zealanders and Indians would go forward for the kill. There was bloody fighting. Each time we got onto the hill the enemy counterattacked us off it. The commanders of the New Zealand and Indian divisions both agreed that it was entirely impracticable to go ahead until the feature was definitely won and they told Montgomery so. Montgomery was inclined to agree, and the matter went to Alexander.

There followed a number of rapid conferences among the generals. Clearly now we were in sight of victory. The enemy was compressed into the last tip of Tunisia. We dominated the air—it had been a wonderful sight seeing our machines flying out all day over Enfidaville. We outgunned the enemy and we out-tanked him. But still he stood on the vital passes—Green and Bald Hills in the Sedjenane sector, Longstop Hill in the Medjerda sector, Pont du Fahs farther south and then finally at Enfidaville.

It was no longer a matter of friendly rivalry—who should get into Tunis first, the Eighth or the First Army. It was a question of whether we were going to get in at all and of how to do it with the least loss of life and machines.

There were three known centres of interior enemy resistance which were capable of standing even when the outer passes had gone—Bizerta, Tunis and Cape Bon Peninsula. No one at that time exactly knew von Arnim's intentions, though it was fairly clear that Cape Bon was going to be used as an evacuation area. Our reconnaissance machines had brought back many photographs of the jetties that had recently been built round the cape.

Standing on the coast one day in the purple and white village of Hergla I looked across and saw the heights of the Cape Bon mountains, but that did not mean we could get there. Already by April 21st it was becoming pretty evident that we were never going to break through on the coast. The Medjerda Valley still appeared to be the best way in. But the Medjerda Valley was blocked so long as the Germans held Longstop Hill. On April 23rd Alexander attacked the hill.

Sixteen

Longstop

WHAT A legend Longstop had become. We checked it on a dozen different maps. We explored the roads and tracks around the hill. We talked about it: 'Once we are on Longstop…' The veterans who had mounted the hill before we were thrown off in the early days declared that on a clear afternoon you could almost see Tunis from the heights.

In the German ranks too, Longstop was a great thing. When an officer of the Panzer grenadiers was taken prisoner he declared, 'You will never take Longstop. It is impregnable now.'

For five months it had lain right in the front line, the fortress of the Medjerda Valley, the locked gate on the road to Tunis. We climbed the surrounding hills and looked down upon the hill and it always appeared darker than the surrounding country and more sinister, a great two-humped bulk that heaved itself out of the wheat fields like some fabulous whale beached on the edge of a green sea.

All through April the Seventy-Eighth Division had been edging its way along the heights toward Longs top. One after another the mountain peaks had been cleaned out. Toukabeur village and Chaouach had fallen, and while the donkeys and the mule teams dragged up ammunition and food the men crept forward on to Jebel Ang. At last, on April 22nd, the men in the forward platoons could look right into the German defences of Longstop itself.

To launch his final assault General Eveleigh, commanding the

Seventy-Eighth Division established his headquarters high up in the mountains and very close to his operational brigades. To get to this place you had to turn off the main road just short of Medjez-el-Bab and take a winding earthen track through Toukabeur. The track began in a field of poppies that spread in a blood-red pool across the floor of the valley; it finished in miraculous alpine fields where a flower of the most delicate lavender bloomed among the rocks.

We called on the Intelligence major we knew best. 'It's started,' he said. 'You can have a look at it if you go round that corner. Don't go on to the top of this hill because there's a lot of red flannel up there.'

'A lot of red flannel' presumably meant General Alexander and his staff, who usually wore their red bands at the front, had come to watch the battle; so we took a lower track and moved through the stunted mountain trees looking for a good commanding point. The British twenty-five-pounders were making vicious cracking echoes through the rocks. Heaven knew how the guns had been dragged to those heights. Beyond the last battery we crept around the crest of a steep hill until we were in view of the enemy in Heidous village across the valley and Longstop lay below us on the right.

From that height everything appeared to happen in miniature. The Churchill tanks climbing on Jebel Ang looked like toys. The infantry that crept across the uplands toward Heidous were tiny dark dots, and when the mortar shells fell among them it was like drops of rain on a muddy puddle. Toy donkeys toiled up the tracks toward the mountain crests, and the Germans, too, were like toys, little animated figures that occasionally got up and ran or bobbed up out of holes in the ground between the shell explosions.

Most of our shells were falling on the near slopes of Longstop. The barrage kept rushing over our heads and falling among the black gorse on the hill, and at times it was so heavy everything disappeared in grey-black smoke and the hill became a cloud of fumes and dust.

On Longstop the Germans had dug trenches which had a horizontal shelf deep below the surface. During a barrage such as this the Germans lay under this shelf and waited in safety. Their guns were fired from below the surface so that it was only in the very last stages of an assault that they had to put their heads out. They had ample stores of food and water and ammunition. The Germans knew that the British infantry would have to cross the minefields first and that they would have to expose themselves as they climbed upward. It was no use our ignoring Longstop by going round it. The Germans would still be able to shell the two roads running into Tunis. They would break up our convoys. They would launch counterattacks from the hill. And so it was necessary now, even at great cost, for the Seventy-Eighth Division to make a direct assault.

On the second morning of the battle, when the British guns had done all they could, I went with my party down onto the plain before Longstop to see the infantry go in. The brigade in charge of this operation had taken over a farmhouse in a little grove of trees. The command vehicles were drawn up against a wall close to a ruined tennis court.

The enemy seemed to be aware that this was a headquarters because they kept firing at the place, occasionally with 88-millimetre shells, occasionally with mortars that sent up puffs of black or white dust according to whether they landed on rock or soil. It was never quite clear until the last second whether shells would fall over the farmhouse or short of it. As we came up the road a padre said to us, 'It is very difficult at the moment. I have been trying to get to some of our dead, but every time I go out they can see me and they start mortaring. I shall have to wait until it is dark.' The padres were very brave on this front, and some had been decorated for it. They were armed only with their helmets and their faith, and often they went forward with the attacking infantry to be at hand to help with the wounded. At these times they did not pray or preach on the battlefield: they dealt out brandy to the dying and administered morphia and helped bind the wounded and get them back in trucks and Bren- gun carriers to the dressing stations. They carried food and water and medical supplies. In return for this the men looked on the padres with an affection and respect which they had never felt at home.

We could see the lower slopes of Longstop quite clearly from brigade headquarters, and even here, only half a mile off, the hill looked dark and uncouth. Zero hour for the attack was 1.30 p.m., but the Germans above could see our infantry massing, and they were already firing very heavily upon them with mortars. The West Kents, the Surreys and the Argylls were making this attack, each taking a separate part of the hill, and they had a few Churchill tanks in support as well as the artillery that kept banging away at the places where the German mortars seemed to be hidden.

At one o'clock the artillery increased, and for the fiftieth time the hill disappeared in dust. At 1.20 the guns fell silent. There was a long pause. The shell-dust lifted slowly off the hill. At 1.30 a flare rose out of the foothills and at that signal the attack was on. In little quick ripples of noise the machine-guns sounded first from one side of the hill then the other. Sometimes the bursts went on as long as a full minute, and always the machine-gunning would be drowned eventually in the crump of the enemy mortars. The mortars fell in sprays of half a dozen or more, and, watching from behind a cactus hedge at the farmhouse, you would see roughly from the mortar-fire how far our men had advanced. At 2 p.m. little dark figures appeared spasmodically on the skyline at the crest of the first slope. They stood silhouetted for a second and then dropped away. Near the top there was a patch of yellow open rock. Men were running across this, always going upward. Then they disappeared for a moment until they were on the skyline and dropping down over the other side.

In a calm, reasonable voice the brigade major was calling over the telephone for a bombing raid to help the advance. His phone was ringing all the time now. Little scraps of coded information were coming back from the battalion headquarters. They were map references, jumbles of figures. You could not tell from the faces of the officers whether the attack was going well or not, but it was obvious that we were advancing.

It was hot, and presently through the dust Bren-gun carriers came rattling down the track that led from the hill. The wounded were piled on the carriers just as they had been lifted there in the midst of the firing. They lay quite still on their backs, staring upwards, and the blood dropped down among the instruments inside the carriers.

The drivers sat fixedly in their seats and said nothing. They brought the vehicles to a standstill beside a line of ambulances sheltering under the cactus hedge, and the stretcher-bearers lifted the wounded onto stretchers and slid them into the ambulances. Then the Bren-gun carriers turned and went back through the dust into the battle again.

One of the officers who came back took his helmet off and let it drop on the ground. 'The men are very tired,' he said. 'It's not the opposition so much, it's sleep. They have been going for a long time now.'

'How long?'

'I don't know—a long time.' The officer himself was very tired. He had been in the line for a week, and during the previous night some of his men had just fallen on the ground and cried. They cried because they had no strength any more, not even the strength to stand up. They had continued without sleep for two days under the compulsion of their brains and beyond the point where the body will normally function. But now, when their minds would not work any more, they discovered that the strength had already gone out of their bodies and that, in fact, they had no control of anything any more, not even of tears. The tears came quite involuntarily and without any sense of relief because the body was incapable of feeling anything any more, and what became of the body now was of no consequence. And so they had lain about the hill for an hour or two in a stupor. The cold and the dew bit into them through the night and brought them back to consciousness. Then they had stumbled about in the darkness until they found their platoons. They ate a little cold bully without tasting it and took swigs from their water bottles. By morning their brains were operating again, not their bodies, but their brains, and they were able to contemplate themselves and consider what still had to be done.

Some of them slept in the sun through the morning and this brought back a little strength into their bodies—enough to cooperate with their minds and give obedience. At noon then, they had regrouped, and they mechanically registered the order that they had to attack again, and they assessed their strength against what was required by the order. These were the men we had seen running across the top of the slope and the men who came back in the Bren-gun carriers.

The wounded were not just yet in great pain because the shock of the bullets in their flesh was still taking effect. They were very dirty, and the dirt ran in lines in the sagging hollows of their faces.

Their hands dropped over the edges of the stretchers, lumpish hands, coloured a greyish yellow colour that was inhuman. No one could look at them without protesting.

The German prisoners came next. Black jackboots, green gabardine uniforms, wings on their chests, cloth caps with the red, white and black badge, the Afrika Korps. They marched stolidly in columns of three, the officers in front. They were not so tired as our men, since they had been lying in provisioned dugouts, and they marched mechanically, but well. One of the officers started to argue.

He wanted to see a British officer. A Scots sergeant waved him on bleakly with the tip of his bayonet. The Germans stood stolidly beside the ambulances, waiting their turn to go into the cowshed. In the cowshed British military police were running their hands over each prisoner, taking away from him his combined knife, fork, spoon and tin-opener, a neat gadget, also his pocketknife and any weapons he carried. The Germans submitted to this, automatically raising their hands above their heads. The pile of knives and forks got larger and larger on the floor. Some of the Germans started smoking after the search; and they sat quietly on a fallen log. There was something in their faces that registered not fright or fear, but deep tiredness, a sense of relief. Only the German officer was still arguing. A British captain who had been tending the wounded came over to him.

'You bastard,' he said. 'Get back in your place.' The German, not understanding, offered the British officer a cigarette.

The British officer said again, 'Get back.' It was quite clear that, having come so recently from the fighting and the wounded, he wanted to shoot the German.

There were many scenes like this that day. The Germans were firing their machine-guns until the British got within thirty yards or so—near enough to kill. And then the Germans surrendered. This meant that we were taking many casualties but not killing many Germans, and the physical presence of the prisoners did not entirely satisfy the desire of the British troops for revenge.

That night they took three-quarters of Longstop Hill. As soon as it was light in the morning I drove to brigade headquarters. A young signals officer was going up to the hill in his truck and he offered to take my party with him. We got only half a mile in the truck and then, leaving it under the cover of the high wheat, we began climbing on foot, keeping to the right-hand side of the hill. We followed the line of the signal wires so that we could check for breakages. Every few yards the wheat had been torn up and blackened as though some sort of plague had blighted it; this was the effect of the mortars, which were fused so that they exploded immediately on contact and were therefore more likely to kill men.

It was very hot. The dust rose up out of the wheat, and when it had coated one's face and body little runnels of sweat ran over one's cheeks and under the armpits.

Now we were on the hill, I saw that it was much more thickly covered with scrub than had appeared from the distance; and it did not consist of two big humps, but a whole series, seven in all, with many subsidiary ridges. As soon as we pulled ourselves to the top of one slope another appeared above us. Over all this ground the troops had fought the day before, and now the carriers were bringing up water cans that had to be lugged the last half of the journey by hand.

On the lip of the third rise we came suddenly upon a scene so dramatic, so complete in itself that I recall it now, detail by detail almost as I would remember a painting or a play in the theatre. It was a front-line trench. The Germans had dug it, but our men had occupied it the day before. It was a shallow trench and it made a zigzag suture through the blackened grass on the slope of the hill. On the piles of freshly turned yellow soil the men had thrown their battledress jackets, the tin mugs and plates from which they had been eating, the empty salmon and bully-beef tins.

A profusion of things lay about all the way up the trench—empty packets of cigarettes, both British and German, water bottles and hand grenaders, half-used boxes of cartridges, German steel helmets, bits of notepaper, discarded packs and torn pieces of clothing. Through this mess the rifles and machine-guns were pointing out toward the next slope, but the men were not firing. The sun was shining strongly and they sat or leaned half in and half out of the trench. Some smoked. One man was mending a boot. Another was sewing on a button. But mostly they leaned loosely on the earth and rested. Every time an enemy gun sounded they cocked their heads mechanically and waited for the whine that would give the direction of the shot. It was only a slight movement and you did not notice them doing it at first. Sometimes the shells landed short, three or four hundred yards away, sometimes very near, perhaps only fifty yards down the slope, but anyway not on the trench. No one commented on the nearness of the shells. They had had much heavier shelling than this all night, and these spasmodic shots were only a nuisance that still had the power to hurt unless one watched.

There were several old London papers lying about. One, the *Daily Mirror*, had its last page turned upward and its thick headline read: ' "No more wars after this," says Eden.'

Seeing me looking at it, the soldier on the end of the trench said bitterly, 'They said the last war was going to end all wars. I reckon this war is supposed to start them all again.' The others in the trench laughed shortly and one or two of them made some retort. The men had greeted us with interest, but without enthusiasm. When they read the war correspondent badges on our shoulders they were full of questions and derisive comments. 'Why weren't you up here yesterday? You'd have seen something!' Then another, 'You can tell Winston Churchill we have been in the bloody line ten bloody weeks already.' Then a third, 'Are you the bastard that wrote in the paper that we're getting poached eggs for breakfast every morning?' And a fourth, 'Where's the Eighth Army? Aren't they doing anything?' And several of them, 'How's the war going, mister? Is there anyone doing anything besides us?'

They were hostile, bitter and contemptuous. Every second word was an adjective I have not quoted here, and they repeated it *ad nauseam*. They felt they were a minority that was being ordered to die (a third of them had been killed or wounded in the night) so that a civilian majority could sit back at home and enjoy life.

It was useless to picture these men who were winning the war for you as immaculate and shining young heroes agog with enthusiasm for the Cause. They had seen too much dirt and filth for that. They hated the war. They knew it. And they were very realistic indeed about it. Instead of sitting on an exposed hilltop in the imminent danger of death they would have much preferred to have been on a drunk, or in bed with a girl, or eating a steak, or going to the movies. They fought because they were part of a system, part of a team. It was something they were obliged to do, and now that they were in it they had a technical interest and a pride in it. They wanted to win and get out of it—the sooner the better. They had no high notions of glory. A great number of people at home who referred emotionally to 'Our Boys' would have been shocked and horrified if they had known just how the boys were thinking and behaving. They would have regarded them as young hooligans. And this was because the real degrading nature of war was not understood by the public at home, and it never can be understood by anyone who has not spent months in the trenches or in the air or at sea. More than half the army did not know what it was because they had not been in the trenches. Only a tiny proportion, one-fifth of the race perhaps, know what it is, and it is an experience that sets them apart from other people. If you find the men do not want to talk about the fighting or what they have done, it will be for this reason only—they want to forget it.

We went higher onto Longstop to join the Argylls, and as we moved off, the men shouted at us to keep down so that we would not draw the fire onto their position.

The Argylls, too, were resting after the bad night, and their eyes were red-rimmed with fatigue. The commanding officer had been killed. His deputy, a tall major who was a Highland farmer, had been drinking wine with us at Thibar only a few days before, but now a great gulf of experience separated us. He was still as hospitable and level-headed and kind, but there was something he could not communicate. We were very near the top of Longstop here. From the surrounding caves Germans were still being routed out. We overlooked a German gun-pit, empty now of men, but the black snouts of the guns still pointed toward us. In every direction the rocks were chipped with shell-blast and the camel thorn was rooted from the ground. A light heat haze hung over the far end of the hill, where the Germans were still hiding and shooting.

Below us the Medjerda Valley spread out majestically, and we looked for miles across the enemy lines and deep into our own. At that moment, surprisingly, half a dozen enemy shells whistled over our heads and landed on the brigade headquarters we had just left at the bottom of the hill. The cowshed, where the prisoners were, was enveloped in great billows of smoke, and all that part where the ambulances lay appeared to be in the range of fire. There had been so much killing all around here that the only emotion I felt was: 'I'm glad I'm not still in the cowshed.'

It was a shock, then, to look across the valley and see that an entirely separate battle was going on. Longstop had for the past forty-eight hours so absorbed our interest that we had begun to think that it was the whole battle. But now I remembered Alexander had sent two armoured divisions into the Goubellat Plain, and other formations were working up from Medjez-el-Bab to the villages of Crich- el-oued and Sidi Abdallah in the centre and southern side of the valley. Tanks were moving about very briskly and firing, but from that distance we could not see exactly what they were doing.

Bombers kept coming in low and adding to the turmoil on the plain. Crich-el-oued (inevitably the troops called it Cricklewood) was having an especially rough time, and it was surprising to see the minaret of its little mosque survive the constant salvoes.

As we watched, another officer of the Argylls came up, a major named John Anderson. Just before he introduced us our friend whispered, 'Here's the man who did the whole thing. Don't say anything about it, but we have put him in for the V.C.'

It was not much good asking Anderson how Longstop had fallen. 'Oh, I don't know,' he said vaguely. 'I shouted "Come on!" and the boys jumped up and ran forward shouting at the tops of their voices. We found the Germans cowering in their trenches—it was probably the noise that made the Jerries give in.'

Anderson, to look at, was not very different from the other officers in this battalion except he was still alive and most of the others were dead or wounded. He himself had been slightly wounded. His uniform was in a bad mess and his beard was matted with sweat and dirt. What he had done was this. He had led the frontal attack at night up the first slope. With so much fire coming from every direction and so many confusing explosions and flares, the only thing that was clear was that the enemy was somewhere above. Anderson, armed with a revolver, did the thing that sounds so mundane in words. He stood up in the fire and shouted to his men. They swarmed up after him as men will when they find a leader. He ran straight through the minefield and up through the darkness to the points where the yellow streams of bullets were coming out. He and his men yelled and screamed as they flung themselves upward. They got caught in barbed wire and clawed it aside. Some were shot down. The others jumped down into the dugouts on top of the Germans, firing as they jumped. That was one hill. There were still men left, and Anderson jumped up again. Sheer rage carried them up the next slope, and again they broke through the wire and killed with the bayonet. Even then there were a few of the Argylls left who had not died or been wounded, and a third time Anderson ran on and upward until he had achieved this height.

Many such things happened on Longstop during this terrible three-day battle, but this was one of the great charges. When the third day came it was evident that the enemy defences were pierced, and as we stood near the summit that afternoon new units were going in to mop up the rest. Longstop was taken in the only possible way, by men going in yelling with the bayonet and meeting the enemy face to face.

Anderson got his V.C. and died fighting in Italy six months later.

Seventeen

Mateur

I CAN imagine something snapping in Alexander's mind when he heard of the fall of Longstop. At all events he went to work in a tornado of energy, as one who has suddenly seen the light. Just as a player of bridge or chess will parry and thrust for position here and there, and then suddenly see the way clear before him, so now Alexander moved forward with a touch and sureness that had not been apparent in the battle before.

He had already ordered a wholesale regrouping of the armies and at urgent speed. All the Americans, three divisions, were swung into the northern sector around Sedjenane. The French, with their new Valentine tanks and American vehicles, were wedged into the Pont du Fahs gap. On the coast Montgomery's forces were ordered merely to maintain a series of holding attacks. This left only the Medjerda Valley, and upon the Medjerda the general concentrated all his great hopes for a knockout blow. He wanted only the best of his British forces here. Already the Seventy-Eighth Division, the Fourth and the First Infantry divisions were in position. To these were added the Sixth Armoured Division from the First Army and the Seventh Armoured Division and the Indian division from the Eighth Army.

These last two desert divisions were obliged to make a spectacular forced march from the coast in order to reach the Medjerda Valley in time. They were unable to pause even long enough to camouflage their vehicles from the desert yellow to the mountain blacks and browns.

The scene on the roads during these days was bewildering. Tens of thousands of vehicles crammed the passes day and night, and, when after darkness fell, we were sometimes caught in the mountains away from our base at Thibar, it was an unnerving thing to drive past the immense convoys of blacked-out trucks and tanks. Not infrequently vehicles tumbled headlong into the valleys and ditches below, and the strain upon the drivers was intense.

The battle plan was quite simple. Now that the line was barely a hundred and thirty miles long, we were going to apply severe and continuous pressure along its whole length—the Americans striking toward Mateur, the British along the Medjerda Valley, the French at Pont du Fahs and the British again at Enfidaville. As soon as the pressure was applied in force then the blitz would go in up the Medjerda Valley, a needle-thrust aimed straight at Tunis. Two infantry divisions, the Indians and the Fourth, were to break the crust of the German line. Then the two crack armoured divisions, the Seventh and the Sixth, would pour through and continue until they reached the sea.

A sector only three thousand yards wide was chosen for this thrust, and it was to go directly up the road from Medjez-el-Bab through Massicault and St Cyprien to Tunis.

That was the broad plan. Although surprising and unpredictable things occurred and the plan had to be altered and extended, its essential structure remained the same to the end.

No one man could hope to watch the whole of this spectacle. During the first week in May my party found itself buzzing about agitatedly all over the front, never quite certain that we were in the right place, never quite sure that if we went to the Mateur sector something more important might not be happening in the Goubellat Plain, never able to resolve whether or not Bizerta would fall before Tunis. In the end I suppose we did not do badly. At least we got a superficial view of most of the preliminary moves and we were in the right place when the final blow fell.

One day we drove onto the hills south of Medjez-el-Bab, and all the Goubellat plain spread out below us. It looked like a bright flypaper with thousands of black flies stuck on it. Two whole divisions were dotted across the valley and sheltering on the edges of the mountains, perhaps ten or fifteen thousand vehicles. They had run through Goubellat village and spread in a flood of armour and guns across the plain. At the spot where we sat there was a burnt-out German Tiger tank. The Tigers were a failure in Tunisia. We even stopped them with two-pounder guns. They were too cumbersome, too slow, too big a target, too lightly armed to meet modern anti-tank weapons. And yet as I clambered over this vast wreck I found it frightening in its sheer enormity. It was the biggest and the ugliest vehicle I had ever seen on land. Like a London bus or a sixty-thousand-ton liner, it had that quality of largeness that never diminishes, no matter how familiar it becomes.

A little group of British Tommies seeing battle for the first time had put up an exemplary defence here, on the edge of Goubellat.

They had been surrounded in the night by a great weight of German tanks and infantry—it was one of these final desperate efforts the enemy made to disorganise our coming attack. The hilltop where the Tommies were defending disappeared in shell-bursts. In the morning, when our reinforcements drove off the Germans, a column was sent up to the hilltop to see if any of the defenders had escaped death or imprisonment. As the rescuers appeared, the defenders bobbed up cheerfully and unharmed from their foxholes. They had fired off all their ammunition. They had flung back successive waves of German infantry all night long. They were greenhorns no longer. It was a perfect demonstration of what you can do with really tough training in the battle schools at home.

Across the other side of Goubellat, where our tanks had touched the lakes, things were not going so well. A jagged and precipitous ridge of rock called Kournine rose out of the plain beside the lakes, and it bristled with German guns. Every time our tanks approached they were caught, and from our eyrie we could see them burning. Every time the infantry tried to infiltrate they were swept back with small-arms fire. Across the plain itself the Germans were using their new Henschel tank-buster—the fighter with the cannon—with devastating effect. Just as at Enfidaville, it was obvious that we were going to do no more at Kournine than keep the enemy busy.

The sappers at this time were completing a job which had the importance of a battle. They had to prepare a series of springboards from which the final offensive could be made. With bulldozers, with dynamite and the pick and shovel they ran roads right out into no-man's-land. They worked in pitch darkness and under mortar-fire, throwing up new steel bridges, making fords across the streams, driving cuttings through the rocks. The sappers were in the forefront of everything; they were out ahead of the infantry making passages through the mines; they went out on patrols to plot the country; they made tunnels and set new minefields right under the German guns. From the days of the Abyssinian war I had seen the sappers getting more and more expert, taking on bigger and bigger jobs and often working under fire without the time or the means to protect themselves or hit back. In this last week they reached a climax of effort.

One day we got ourselves entirely out of position. We knew the final assault was some days ahead and the front seemed quiet. We decided to take a few hours off, and we ran up to Cap Serrat, on the northern coast. It was a beautiful day—no sign of war. Nightingales were piping in the bushes. We plunged into the sea among the washed-up wrecks of invasion barges and rusting guns. We loitered over lunch—the lunch which I had designed as the best and easiest for these long daytrips when we were often twelve hours on the road: a bottle of Thibar wine diluted with water, a chunk of American cheese from Vermont, a loaf of madame's white bread, a tin of margarine and a slab of chocolate. Easily and pleasantly we drove back toward Thibar in the evening. On the road we all got an attack of conscience through staying away from the war for so many hours, and we turned into an American headquarters near Sedjenane. And that was when we first heard the astounding news about the Americans. In defiance of everyone's predictions they had made a full-scale breakthrough toward Bizerta. You might wonder how on a narrow front like this we could not have known about so big an event beforehand. The truth was that no one expected the Americans to break through. They were faced with some of the roughest country in Tunisia. Moreover, we did not know then that two major events had happened. First, the Germans were already beginning to draw back from the Bizerta area toward Tunis and Cape Bon; and secondly, the Americans, profiting by what they had learned in the south, had suddenly become some of the most adept and determined fighters in the whole battle.

There was nothing much that we, as correspondents, could do about the breakthrough that night. We could only gather the astonishing story at headquarters—Green and Bald Hills had fallen, Mateur had been entered. The Americans were on the borders of the Bizerta lakes and had the city itself in view.

We drove hard next day to catch up. The Beja-Mateur road was one long hue and cry of army vehicles pushing forward. We ran over the old front line—a graveyard now of dynamited German tanks—and then into the great hills we had never been able to reach before. Others, turning back, said it was hopeless—the traffic was jammed all the way to Mateur—but we edged on, often being bawled out by the military police for getting out of the single line of traffic, but more usually sneaking past when nobody was looking. The enemy gunners were still firing out of the line of hills to our right, but somehow they could not get onto this perfect target, these thousands of vehicles jammed on the road.

Near Mateur the traffic thinned out at last and the town itself appeared dramatically through the hills. It lay at the mouth of the valley on the edge of Lake Achkel. Between the town and the lake Jebel Achkel rose up, a fabulous mass, dark, precipitous and isolated, a rock skyscraper that made an island in the sky. Beyond this, in the narrow causeway of land between Lake Achkel and Lake Bizerta, the clean bright town of Ferryville was clearly in view, and beyond that again the haze that was Bizerta.

As we looked, most of this area was under fire of some kind. A Messerschmitt dived on Mateur, blew up a jeep and then, caught by anti-aircraft fire, it dived in streaming yellow flames to the ground. Shells were bursting steadily round Ferryville, and the German fire, both from guns and dive- bombers, fell heavily on the outskirts of Mateur. They were aiming at the one bridge we had to cross to get into the town.

An American Doughboy was sitting on that bridge as we made our dash across between salvoes. God knows what he was doing there. He just sat grinning on the rails, with smoking bomb-holes all around him and more shells due any minute. Decidedly the American soldier had got his teeth into the war this time.

Mateur was devastated and deserted. A few stray dogs and cats ran among the tottering walls, a handful of gendarmes and a plucky French girl had taken refuge in a cave decked with the tricolour. In the streets jeeps and Sherman tanks were milling about. Shells were landing haphazardly round the town, and we drove out quickly to the north, following the shores of the lake. It was hard to make out what was happening and nobody had any accurate information. Some said there were Germans on the Jebel, but we rode under the mountain without interference. It was much softer country here in the north, well cultivated, with large prosperous homesteads, more European. We were now entirely alone, and I did not like it much. But of my two companions, one, A. B. Austin,[8] seemed to derive a strange satisfaction from being fired at, and the other, Christopher Buckley, had for years been quite unable to resist a craving to explore anything and everything whether it lay inside enemy territory or not.

And so we rode on round that lovely lake until we came on an American reconnaissance unit. They had taken cover in a farmhouse which had been vacated by six hundred Germans the day before.

There was a touching domestic scene going on in the French family circle in the house. Madame Verdier, a charming woman, half-English, drew us into the parlour to act as judges in the matter. It seemed that her husband had escaped to England two years before and joined the Free French. In the meantime his son Robert had grown up, and now, at seventeen, was determined to set off and find his father and then join the R.A.F., for which he had conceived an intense admiration. He had wanted to pass through the German lines at night, and with difficulty his mother had dissuaded him. She had been forced to promise that as soon as the Allies reached the farmhouse he could set off. Now her son was holding her to her promise. The boy, a thin, sensitive lad, stood tensely in the corner while it was all explained.

We said the obvious things. The front was in a turmoil at the moment. He would be lost for days, even weeks, if he tried to find his way without passes through the army to Algiers and then to England. If he would just wait until Tunis had fallen, then everything would be easier. The French authorities would be able to help him then.

I don't think we made much impression. The boy was keyed up to a state of excitement that could not have been brooked. I was sorry for his mother. All the time we were talking the guns were going outside, but she had no thought for these, only for the boy. She was gripped with her anxiety to do the best she could for him. Already she had faced up to the fact that she was going to lose him anyhow. I never heard what happened. We were swept back at once into the prodigious moving spectacle outside that little farmhouse parlour. But still the incident sticks in my mind for, just as in the case of the German pilot who had been shot down, it forced one for a moment to see that all the machinery of war, all the organisation and the outward show, was in the end based on such little family matters as these—and the spirit of them.

Beyond the farmhouse we took the empty road again, and at last caught up with the front on the banks of the Sedjenane River. I call it a front, but in reality it was a quaint little pocket of the war. A column of Frenchmen had come through the thickets along the coast and had been stopped by mortar- fire outside Bizerta. We were unable to join them because the bridge across the river was down, and the enemy was shelling the river. Shells fell now among a group of frightened horses, now around an American Doughboy who was trying to build a ford across the river with a bulldozer, and now close to a French poilu who was squatting on his haunches and throwing hand grenades into the river. Each time a grenade exploded, a few muddy-looking fish floated to the surface and the Frenchman dragged them in with a stick. A line of American shock troops sat under the lee of the bank watching with interest. Nobody seemed to be paying the least attention to the shelling or the war. Clearly we were not going to get into Bizerta that night, and we turned back.

We had had such a day of reconnoitring on our own that we decided to push our luck a little further. Since Green and Bald Hills had fallen, it was reasonable to presume that the road linking that pass to the lakes was open, so we turned up it. As we climbed into the mountains I saw through the back of the car that there was a battery of German guns firing out of the hospital in Ferryville. The shots kept falling in the lake and sending up columns of water that were pink and shining in the sunset light.

We were now approaching Green and Bald Hills from the enemy direction, and we ran full tilt into a vast crater across the road. Beyond that, a stray American colonel told us, the road MIGHT be clear of mines. But then again, he said, it might not. We pushed on cautiously, and then at the crest of the pass saw something that made the driver jam on his brakes. A party of American sappers with mine detectors was approaching us from the opposite direction. Walking in front of the car and studying every foot of the ground, we got through to the Americans and continued home. When we passed that spot on the hills the following morning, two of the American sappers lay dead beside the road. They had been killed by a mine which our car had harmlessly gone by the night before.

It had been a curious thing passing through Green and Bald Hills, and seeing the dugouts of both sides where so many had died in the winter in the mud and the cold. At the end the Germans made no attempt to hold the two bastions. A handful of Americans had struggled up both hills and reported back the astounding news that the enemy had decamped in the night. It seemed an anticlimax that the great battle of the Sedjenane sector, which had cost thousands of lives, should finish so quietly and without display. The little wayside graves, some with swastikas on them and some with British or American helmets, are practically all that is left to mark that terrible battlefield now.

For three days we hunted in the Bizerta district, hoping every hour that the town would fall. Enemy troops and civilians, we knew, were pouring southward out of the town along the one road that lay open to them into Tunis. But a rearguard fought bitterly. To everyone's astonishment it turned out that there was a garrison of Germans perched on the black heights of Jebel Achkel. A lavish French homestead stood on the slopes opposite the mountain, and we drove up there to watch the battle.

It was quite a set-piece, this affair—the infantry spread in lines across the wheat fields, the guns and the tanks closing in, the shells bursting on the heights of the jebel, and the enemy hitting back, sometimes by casting shots off the heights, sometimes by dive-bombing and strafing along the roads. In perfect safety we looked down on the arena from this homestead, and then the bizarre figure of Monsieur Louis Roederer appeared. He came out onto the verandah, an elderly Frenchman, a cosmopolitan who contrived to look like an English country squire by wearing riding breeches and a voluminous tweed jacket. Monsieur Roederer was one of the Champagne family. He had come to Tunisia years ago, and, apart from his town house in Paris and his estates in France, he had devoted most of his life and his great wealth to this farm. He had built himself this lovely home. He had drained and cleared the land with the cheap native labour, and now his neat and orderly fields spread away to the jebel.

'That is my land you are fighting your battle on now,' he said. 'I hope they don't do too much damage.'

He spoke in English, almost as well as he spoke French and German. 'Come inside,' he said, 'and I will show you General Manteufel's room.'

It was a charming countryman's study. The walls were lined with books in three languages. There were many sporting prints, a collection of stuffed game-birds, and a shelf crowded with the stocks of old Moorish hunting guns. Here, among the fishing nets and the sporting prints, the German General Manteufel had conducted the defence of the whole Bizerta area until he had been forced to leave hurriedly two nights before. 'He did not appear worried,' Monsieur Roederer said; 'he remained very correct and charming to the end. I used to have breakfast with him every morning, but of course we never discussed the war or politics—we just talked about fishing and shooting and sports. He was very correct. I was sorry in some ways to see him go. The Germans paid for everything during the four months they were here, and did far less damage than your troops have done in a single morning.

Just look at this,' and he led the way out onto the verandah again. Pointing down to a grove of trees, he said:

'Ruined—all ruined—by your tanks when they broke in here and sheltered this morning. When I protested, the American officer in charge said that I was a pro-Nazi. I replied that it was only because I was friendly to your cause that I could be so frank and open with my complaint.'

A good deal of Monsieur Roederer's conversation ran like this. We were to meet more of his kind among the wealthy people of Tunis later on. It was not so much that they were pro-Nazi, it was that the sole consuming interest of their lives was to safeguard their property. They gave hospitality to the Allies and the Germans with an equal mind. They were prepared to talk in German, French, Italian or English. Before the war they had divided their lives between London, Paris, southern Europe and New York, always with one eye on their investments. They were simply not interested in the war.

They were waiting with impatience for the day when they could enter into the full use of their frozen wealth again.

To Monsieur Roederer the spectacle of wounded American soldiers being brought into his house from the fighting on the jebel was more of an inconvenience than an appeal for his assistance. He did everything to help, of course, in a perfunctory way, but he was glad, profoundly glad, when the battle of the jebel was finished. What a difference between this cultivated and cynical old man and the burning enthusiasm of the young French boy who wanted to join the R.A.F.

By May 4th it was clear that Bizerta was not going to fall at once, and since Tunis was fifty times more important, we returned to the Medjerda sector to await the zero hour. Alexander had wheeled the main bulk of the American forces eastward, directly toward the coast and away from Bizerta. His object was to bottle up the German army in the Medjerda Valley, which was now being invested from all sides, including the sea. It was ferocious country the Americans entered now, but still they forged on, and finally got astride the road between Bizerta and Tunis. Simultaneously the last obstacle in the Medjerda Valley was mopped up. This was an ugly jebel called Bou Aoukaz, just outside Tebourba.

In a series of hectic rushes the British infantry swept onto the crest. On the night of May 5th the enemy's last battleline around Tunis lay exposed to immediate assault. At dawn on the following day the British blitz went in.

Eighteen

Tunis

AS I say, we had taken a sector of only three thousand yards for his last assault. This cauldron seemed to us at that time the whole battle and the whole world, but in reality it was a tiny piece of the line, not two per cent of its entire length. Like the arc of a bubble now, the German line stretched round Tunis, and Alexander proposed to prick it in this one place.

Von Arnim was issuing printed orders of the day to his men: 'Behind you lies the sea; before you lies the enemy. You must go forward. You must fight to the last round and the last man'—the sort of pamphlet they issued at Stalingrad. But the German position was not desperate. The minefield-mortar- machine-gun combination still stretched like a web around Tunis and Cape Bon. There was still a quarter of a million Axis troops on the field of battle. They had petrol, food, guns, tanks and ammunition. Only the Luftwaffe seemed to have packed up. Most of it had already gone off to Sicily, and there were rumours that a dispute was going on between the Luftwaffe and the German army command. For the rest, the German morale was not bad. I glanced through some letters we had taken from prisoners. One sergeant wrote from Tebourba: 'We are all right here. We can hold them off for months if need be. It's only those bastards back at base and on the lines of supply. The cowards are already making jokes about "Tunisgrad". Our lieutenant sent for a gun replacement and the fellow at base workshops sent back word, "What do you want replacements for? All the guns are going to be spiked in a fortnight." We will know who to deal with in our own ranks when we have won the victory here.' There was another letter addressed to a soldier from his father in Berlin. It described street by street the damage done by the R.A.F. in Berlin, and it ended, 'Be pitiless, for the English know no pity.'

Up to a point this was true. The Allied army had no pity now. It was a machine, a great mill pressing down, and now a blade was going to come out of the press.

Alexander made his last reshuffles behind the lines. The corps that was going to deliver the first blow leapfrogged over Number 5, the one that had done all the serious fighting up the Medjerda Valley until now. The new corps, Number 9, had two fine infantry divisions and two armoured divisions. One half of the force was from the Eighth Army and one half from the First. That was right. Both armies should share in this honour. Lieutenant-General Horrocks was made the corps commander. He had been borrowed from the Eighth Army because he was a veteran, an aggressive man, a successful commander with three or four recent victories to his credit.[9]

In the same way Air Marshal Coningham bound his two air forces together, the one from the desert and the one from the mountains, and it was an instrument of air war such as Africa had never seen before—thousands of aircraft. They had three jobs: to smash the enemy in Tunisia, to prevent what was left taking to the boats, to knock out the enemy ports and airfields in Sicily and southern Italy. The navy likewise was ready with hundreds of motor boats, destroyers, corvettes, cruisers and even aircraft-carriers and battleships to deal with the Italian fleet if it came out (it never did).

It was the air force that started the battle and the air force which brought back the first indication of the way the battle was going to go—though we did not at the time fully understand the indication. On the morning of May 6th 1000 sorties were made on the enemy lines before breakfast. That is to say, some of die squadrons were used twice or several times, but in all 1000 trips were made before 9 a.m. They rose in swarms out of the clearings in the vineyards and the cork-tree forests, out of the beaches and the sandy plains to the south.

Before 9 a.m. the pilots were coming back with extraordinary reports—'We have nothing to bomb. The enemy have dragged all their remaining aircraft off the airfields and hidden them under the trees. There are no enemy aircraft in the sky. There is no movement of vehicles along the road. There is no sign of German activity at the front. There is practically nothing we can see to hit, nothing to strafe.'

The Wehrmacht had gone to ground. It was dug into its trenches and weapon pits, and heavily camouflaged. From the air the ground appeared dead and deserted. It was one more demonstration that you cannot accurately bomb a stationary army in the field because you cannot see it. I do not say that some of the pilots did not find targets, but for the most part the bombs had to be dropped at places where the enemy was believed to be, but where no enemy was visible.

Coningham did not change his plans. He went right on bombing. From the opening of the battle to the end I saw something I had never seen in a campaign before—shoals of Allied fighters patrolling back and forth, protecting the ground troops every hour of the day. You must certainly give a good deal of the credit for this Tunisian blitz to the fact that the army was not bombed as it went forward.

General Horrocks had spaced one gun about every five yards along his tiny front. The actual spot for the breakthrough was just to the southeast of Medjez-el-Bab on the southern side of the Medjerda Valley. The land was gently undulating at that place, and between the scattered villages the wheat was now breast-high and beginning to turn yellow.

The guns had begun bellowing soon after midnight on May 6th, one shell landing every five yards every few seconds. It is simply not possible to explain the effect of that. Even if one is there, the full enormity of the noise and the brilliance of the light does not persist in the memory;

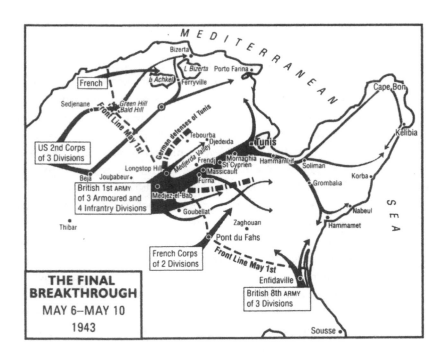

THE FINAL BREAKTHROUGH
MAY 6–MAY 10
1943

and the Germans receiving the barrage do not speak clearly of it because each shell that fell near them was every shell; they could see nothing beyond their immediate trench and hear nothing except the monstrous noise of the explosions near at hand.

Under this roof of shells the sappers went forward at 4 a.m. In the flickering light of the explosions they cut the barbed wire and felt on the ground for the mines. Then the Indians and the British infantry charged through. In the midst of the web of mines and mortars and bullets, the battle was on.

All this time the Germans had never been sure of the precise point at which the main shock of the British assault was coming. They expected it somewhere in the Medjerda Valley—but just where, they could not foretell, because the whole front was in an uproar. And the men in the direct path of our onslaught never had time to realise what had struck them.

In that triangle of villages around Sidi Salem, Sidi Abdallah and Peter's Corner the Germans were manning their positions in the usual way when the British fell on them. While it was still dark the Indians and the Tommies came creeping through the wheat. Over the last few hundred yards they rose to their feet and rushed the enemy positions. They swarmed into the enemy dugouts. They yelled their war-cries, each man taking courage from the excitement of his neighbour, and they poured a hail of bullets across that three-thousand-yard front that was more terrible than the earlier barrage.

By sheer weight of numbers and the exhilaration of the charge, the British infantry swept through the German outposts and got up to the main chain of machine-gun posts. As dawn broke they were leaping from one German weapon-pit to another, shooting as long as the Germans shot, and killing so long as they had to kill. When a group of Germans round a machine-gun gave up, the British ran onto the next knot of opposition without waiting to collect prisoners or wounded—someone coming on behind would do that.

The German line was perhaps a mile or two miles thick—that is to say, there was a loosely connected series of trenches and defended positions of that depth. At daylight the British were right in the midst of this line and our penetration was being measured in thousands of yards. And still it went on, the hacking and thrusting, the hand-to-hand fighting, the overwhelming of the enemy positions one by one. It was scarcely noon when the leaders of the forward companies were reporting over their portable radios that they were meeting reduced opposition.

They had burst clean through the German line and come out into the vacant space behind.

It was only a narrow breach, but that was all that Horrocks wanted: he had pricked the bubble; he was behind the German line; he was through the minefields. For seven or eight hours the tank crews of the Sixth and Seventh Armoured divisions had been waiting. A few tanks had gone in with the infantry, but the bulk of them were waiting in the rear under the cover of the trees. He now turned to these vital reserves and said 'Go.'

The tanks charged ahead. They went straight at the gap the infantry had made for them, and they passed through practically unscathed. It was like releasing the floodgates of a dam. In scores, in hundreds, this vast procession of steel lizards went grumbling and lurching and swaying up the Tunis road. Tunis itself lay barely thirty miles away, the line was pierced. Visors down, dust streaming out behind them, they shot ahead straight for Tunis. They took no account of the Germans on either side of them, no account of the fact that the road behind them might be closed. The line was pierced, and that was enough. They roared on. With them flowed the artillery and the anti-tank guns, the fuel and the ammunition wagons, the workshops and the recovery vehicles, the jeeps and the command cars. Out in front and on either flank rode the armoured cars on reconnaissance. When night came they were all on the road to Tunis.

On the morning of the 7th the Medjerda Valley had become a hateful place: it had turned from green to dirty yellows and greys; the fields of wild flowers had withered entirely; the ripening wheat was flattened; the dust was appalling. Nearing Medjez-el-Bab visibility was barely two hundred yards, and on the dozens of newly made sidetracks it was much worse than that. Huge trucks lurched suddenly out of the gloom and we turned aside fifty times at the last moment to avoid a collision.

General Alexander, driving a jeep, shot past us over a culvert. He was travelling at almost reckless speed, both his hands tight on the wheel and his face was whitened like a baker-boy's with white dust. We felt our way onto corps headquarters, but it had vanished. A solitary red-cap simply said, 'They moved on two hours ago. They've got to Furna.' To Furna? Furna was behind the enemy's old line. It scarcely seemed possible. If corps headquarters had gone as far as this, where, then, were the front-line troops? For the first time we thought, 'Can Tunis fall today?' No one said this. No one liked to say it. But we all thought it as we raced down the sidetracks toward the main road.

Inside half an hour we were on yesterday's battlefield and no enemy anywhere, just empty trenches and gun-pits. Past the villages which the Germans had held for months, past Sidi Salem and Sidi Abdallah, where there had been nothing but death and killing the week before. Over a ruined bridge and round by Peter's Corner that was once an enemy stronghold. Nothing there now. Nothing but the rusting broken tanks around which the wheat and flowers had grown tall, as if the earth itself wanted to hide those hideous machines.

And then, on the main road, there it was again, for the third time in one month—the army careering forward in pursuit of the enemy. But this made the other cavalcades look puny and of no account. Miles before Furna the vehicles were touching almost bonnet to tailboard. They stacked themselves two and three deep along the road. The infantry lay sprawling on their kits on top of the lorries and their rifles lay stacked together as though the war was over. At Furna still the procession went on; it was not so thick now, but still it stretched away in the distance. Only twenty miles to go. It was there on the white stone: 'Tunis 33 kilometres.'

We wanted no part of corps headquarters now. We wanted only to get to the head of this incredible race. Brief scraps of information came to us on the road—the troops were through Massicault. The tanks were moving into St Cyprien. Where, then, were the enemy? Who was on either side of this narrow thrust? We asked and asked and got no reasonable answer. Only 'God knows.' 'Who cares? It's Tunis we want.'

In Massicault the traffic had definitely thinned out, but the village was entirely ours. Two Tunisian girls hung over a wicket fence talking to a group of Tommies as though the army had been there for weeks. There were only a few shell scars on the white buildings along the single street. The tanks had blitzed clean through. Sixteen miles to Tunis.

Presently a mosque and another group of white farmhouses showed up across the plain—St Cyprien. We ran into the village and stopped at the first farmhouse. That was a pleasant moment. We had found the front—if you could call it a front. Standing there were the men and the guns of the Royal Horse Artillery—the Desert Rats, the original Desert Rats. The men I had seen in Syria and Abyssinia and the desert. The guns that had fired from the very beginning of the African war for Wavell and Straffer Gott, for Jock Campbell and Alec Gatehouse. The twenty-five-pounders that used to accept and turn back the German tank rushes in the desert though they were never meant to fire at tanks. They had come all the way from Alamein and they had been through everything: young Cockneys and Lancaster boys in shorts and shirts and burnt by the sun, men of the Seventh Armoured Division who had fired the first shots in the African war, some of the finest gunners in the world.

They were excited. 'We're going to get into Tunis somehow.'

But as we turned back to their brigade headquarters for information my spirits sank. German shelling began. There was resistance still. It was already midday. We could hardly round up those enemy guns before dark. Even as we stopped in a wheat field to gobble a quick cold lunch the shells began coming in our direction. A line of German prisoners was marching into the camp, and each time a shell cracked into the field they broke ranks and went to ground, not in panic, but mechanically and automatically, as men do when they have been shelled too much, too often, too recently. After each burst they formed ranks again without bidding from the guards.

There was more firing away to the right where it was said a tank battle was going on. All this time, while we ate cheese and bread on the steps of the car, more and more desert vehicles kept flowing into the fields behind St Cyprien and dispersing. We decided to go forward again to the hills outside the town to get a better view of the fighting before we turned back to Thibar to send our messages away.

It was there on the hilltops in the early afternoon that we saw for the first time what a wonderfully professional thing this advance was. All around us the army was flowing forward—first the tanks in squadrons of fifteen or twenty nosing up to the hills, then splitting and going around into the next valley, then lying stationary and hull down for a bit and firing. Behind them the guns came up and settled into positions on the newly won hill. In fifteen minutes they were firing. Up the road came the ack-ack guns and the supply wagons and they too dispersed, waited and then went forward again. It was all most impressive, this weaving in and out of the hills. Every commander seemed to know exactly what to do. There was no rushing, no overstraining. Everything worked. Each hill was checked on the map, invested, surrounded and passed by.

A thin rain came down and it made no difference except that it settled the dust a little. We ached to see Tunis, but we were too far off. A mountainous column of black smoke was going up from the sea, that was all. As we watched we saw other vehicles going ahead of us down the road. Was it possible then we were going to get a little nearer? The trail was very warm as we followed on. Outside St Cyprien there was a German cemetery, row upon row of neat graves divided by flowerbeds and gravel paths, and you could read the history of the Tunisian campaign there.

Near the ornamental gate were the old graves of the past year. Oberleutnant Hans this and Corporal Fritz that from the Hermann Goering division, killed in the early skirmishes at Green Hill and Tebourba. These graves had elaborately painted swastikas. Then others, Stuka pilots, with their black emblem of the diving plane, the laurel wreath and the German eagle. Further inside the cemetery the graves were increasingly newer, the paths ungravelled. The last graves had crosses, but these had not been erected or painted, just little tabs lay on the ground giving the dead man's name. Beyond that a series of gaping holes in the ground waiting for more bodies. At the end of the cemetery a Mark IV tank had taken shelter behind the cactus hedge, and it had been destroyed an hour or two before. It still smouldered. I looked inside the smoking wreck and saw the nauseating sight of the dead crew.

The war had caught up with and passed this cemetery too quickly for the recent dead to find a grave. Across the road two French children were playing with an ack-ack gun and a British reconnaissance plane that had just put down.

As we drove on and still there was no impediment on the road our hopes began to rise again.

Perhaps it would be Tunis tonight. I felt a twinge of conscience about Clifford and Keating. For the past three years we had entered most captured towns together. We had always been together at the last. Clifford was definitely out of the running. He had gone off with the French down at Pont du Fahs miles away across the mountains. Keating I had not seen for days. It was hard on them, I thought, to miss Tunis after coming two thousand miles from Alamein.

We were getting very close. Kilometre 14. The village of La Mornaghia. A notice in German, 'Danger—Typhus in Village.' The villagers were standing on the steps of the Café aux Délices de Mornaghia in the Place des Carnieres and cheering. Out ahead there was a series of new explosions—tanks fighting possibly; perhaps the enemy blowing up dumps. Smudges of smoke crept up through the rain on the northern horizon.

The first man I recognised in the village was Clifford. He was standing on a bit of raised ground watching a fight between Shermans and Mark IVs on the next hillside. 'I hitchhiked up from Pont du Fahs,' he said airily. 'I got a tip Tunis was going to fall.' It must have been a monumental bit of hitchhiking in that traffic jam, experts though we all were in getting lifts from the army and the air force.

I saw Horrocks arrive in the main street and made a beeline for him. Except for the crown and crossed swords on his cap you would never have recognised this slight thin-faced man as the controller of the huge machine that was fighting around us. Like every really able general in the British army, he had time to talk and patience to explain. I believe that he had genius that day. You can never attribute success in battle to any one man or any group of men. It is the system and training of an army that takes it forward, not the general, since not one per cent of the army ever sees or hears from its general once the action is joined. But this general at this moment was the ultimate and essential cog in the machine, the governor from which the machine took its rhythm and its pace. And what was important to us, he had more information than anyone else.

I believe he had genius because he not only planned the thrust and sent it in, but he now made it clear that he understood the significance of what he had done.

'We have captured the headquarters of the Hermann Goering division and eighty staff officers, though the general got away,' he said. 'We have penetrated right through the enemy line. It is simply the blitz method confined to a narrow space that has paid us here. The Germans along our line of advance were paralysed by yesterday's shelling and bombing, and they have been overrun by the tanks before they could recover. Speed was the thing. There was one moment last night when they could have held us by counterattacking at Frendj, but we broke through again before they could muster. They might have erected gun positions in these hills if they had had a little more time. We have captured a great number of 88s and vehicles. The prisoners are demoralised. It is the blitz. After the shelling and bombing the first thing they saw was hordes of Churchill and Sherman tanks coming over the horizon and they gave in.'

He added unemotionally, 'The Eleventh Hussars signalled me at 2.25 p.m. that they were on the outskirts of Tunis. I have given them as their objective for the day Tunis Central Railway Station. They may be there now. The Derbyshire Yeomanry are also in the suburbs.'

This was electric news. Could we go in?

'I don't see why you shouldn't try,' Horrocks said. 'But don't blame me if anything happens.'

We hurried into the vehicles. Ten miles to go. We were standing in the cars now, poking our heads through the open roofs and terribly anxious not to miss anything. This moment had been a long time coming.

Presently on the wet and winding road we fell in with a group of armoured cars reconnoitring the road. That was good; our own cars could not even stop a rifle bullet. They were travelling fast and we went with them, each vehicle spaced about fifty yards away from its neighbours. I counted the kilometre stones. Only eight miles now. It was gentle country, almost market-gardening country. The Arabs stared out of their huts without comprehending. The smoke ahead got heavier and heavier.

At Kilometre 9 all Tunis broke into view—the wide bay, flanked by mountains, the spreading town, one of the largest in Africa, not much harmed by bombs, but smoking now with a score of large fires. We stood poised on the summit for a moment before we dipped down into the suburbs. I remember thinking over and over again as I stood in the rain, 'Tunis has fallen.' That simple thought seemed to be quite enough in itself, as complete as a curtain falling on a play, and if one had any sense of triumph, I do not remember it. I can recall only a sense of relief and gratitude.

Someone, the retreating Germans probably, had piled brushwood round a bungalow and it was burning brightly. In all directions there were fires and occasional explosions. Clearly the enemy was destroying his dumps before he got away. More and more houses appeared. The crew of a tank had pulled into a piece of waste land and the crew were boiling a pot for tea with a ring of curious Arabs squatting around them.

In the Avenue de Bardo there were more vehicles, armoured cars mostly, that had arrived before us, and as we ran to the head of the line I saw, without any surprise, Geoffrey Keating driving a jeep. I wondered then how I ever doubted that he would arrive.

Looking around, I saw I was again among the Desert Rats. The Red Jerboa in the red circle was painted on the battered mudguards, the most famous symbol in the whole desert war. And the men in the vehicles were the Eleventh Hussars, the reconnaissance unit that had led the Eighth Army across the desert since Wavell's time. With them were the Derbyshire Yeomanry, the men who had led the First Army through all the hard fighting in Tunisia, and they carried the symbol of the mailed fist.

It is useless and stupid to argue which of these units was the best or debate who got into Tunis first.

They arrived together. They were the representatives of the two most famous British divisions, the Sixth and the Seventh Armoured. They were both magnificent reconnoitring units. It was almost poetic that the Hussars and the Yeomanry should have come up to Tunis together.

For those who had been in Africa from the beginning, there was something else, an incommunicable thing. It was beyond excitement or the immediate sense of triumph. Some of the men there were only by chance alive. They had fought so often, taken so many risks, seen so many of their friends die in the desert. They knew almost too well what it was to have hope and lose it, to hang on blindly and then to recover hope again. And so this was a moment of extraordinary emotional fullness and it was a thing of deep pride to see the men from the hills and the men from the desert come into Tunis together.

The vehicles had pulled up and at the head of the line a British officer stopped us. 'No farther,' he said. 'There are German snipers down the street. Wait until they are cleared up.' We waited in the rain, but no firing sounded and one or two of the armoured cars moved on again. In his excitement my driver tried to get ahead of the armoured cars, but I held him back, as we were already third in line and the only unarmoured vehicle on the spot except for Keating's jeep. We waited until two tanks and a Bren-gun carrier had gone ahead and then we followed.

Quite suddenly the Avenue de Bardo sprang to life. Crowds of French people rushed into the street and they were beside themselves in hysterical delight. Some rushed directly at us, flinging themselves on the running boards. A girl threw her arms round my driver's neck. An old man took a packet of cigarettes from his pocket and flung them up at us. Someone else brandished a bottle of wine. All the women had flowers that they had hastily plucked up from their gardens. A clump of roses hit me full on the mouth and there were flowers all over the bonnet of the car. Everyone was screaming and shouting and getting in the way of the vehicles, not caring whether they were run over or not. A young Frenchman, his face working with excitement, hoisted himself onto the roof of our car with a Sten gun in his hand. He screamed that he was an escaped prisoner and something else in French I did not catch, but I pushed him off, not sure whether he was friend or enemy. There were Germans walking about all over the place. They stood gaping on the pavements, standing in groups, just staring, their rifles slung over their shoulders. A Bren-gun carrier shot past us and it was full of Germans whom the Tommies had picked up, and in their excitement the crowd imagined that these Germans in the British vehicle were British and so they threw flowers at them. The Germans caught the flowers, and they sat there stiffly in the Bren-gun carrier, each man with a little posy clutched in his hand.

The double doors of a big red building on the right-hand side of the street burst open and at first I could not understand—the men who ran out, scores, hundreds of them, were British, in flat steel helmets and British battledress. Then it came to me—they were prisoners whom we had rescued.

They stood in an undecided group for a moment on the sidewalk in the rain, filling their eyes with the sight of us. Then they cheered. Some of them had no heart to speak and simply looked. One man, bearded up to his eyes, cried quietly. The others yelled hoarsely. Suddenly the whole mass of men were swept with a torrent of emotional relief and wild joy. They yelled and yelled.

Handing out cigarettes, we caught their story in broken phrases. 'Four hundred of them, all officers and N.C.O.'s…due to sail for Italy today. Another big batch of them had sailed yesterday.'

There was an Italian lying in blood at the doorway and I asked about him. A major answered. 'He and another Italian were on guard over us. An hour ago a German armoured car went down this street and they put a burst of machine-gun bullets through the door, hoping to hit us. They didn't care about the Italian sentries and they hit this one in the head. He's dying. His friend went crazy. He rushed off down the street shooting any German he could see, and I think they killed him.'

We drove on again. On our left there was a tall and ancient stone viaduct and piles of ammunition were burning at the base of the pillars. A railway line ran beside the road. On our right there was a four-storeyed red building, a brewery. We were just level with this when the shooting started.

It started with a stream of tracer bullets, about shoulder high, skidding across the road between my vehicle and the armoured car in front. We stopped and jumped for the gutters. The crowd melted from the street, the cheering died away with a sort of strangled sigh. After the first burst there came another and another, and soon there must have been half a dozen machine-guns firing at very close range. The trouble was that one had at first no notion of where it was coming from. This was my first experience of street fighting, but I felt instinctively I wanted to get up against the wall. There were five of us in our car, Austin, Buckley, the driver and Sidney Bernstein, none of us with arms, and we groped our way along one of the side walls of the brewery.

The shooting now was continuous. Three lads suddenly jumped out of the nearest armoured car with a Bren gun. They dashed across the road, flung themselves down on the railway line, set up the gun and began firing. The Germans from the Bren-gun carrier had also jumped into the ditch beside the railway and they lay there on their backs, each man still holding his posy.

Looking up, I saw a line of bullets slapping against the brewery wall above us. As each bullet hit it sent out a little yellow flame and a spray of plaster came down on top of us. At the same moment my driver pointed up. Directly above us two German snipers were shooting out of the brewery, and we could see the barrels of their guns sticking out of a second-storey window. As yet the Germans had not seen us. Since at any moment they might look down, we crawled back to the main street. Keeping pressed against the wall, we edged our way from doorway to doorway until we reached the building where the British prisoners were kept. It was raining very heavily. There was now a second wounded man on the wooden floor. All this time the engine of our stationary car was running and the windscreen wipers were swishing to and fro. The bullets kept screaming past and above and below the car. It was in a very isolated position and directly in the path of the shooting.

After ten minutes or so the firing eased off. The tank had let fly with a couple of heavy shells and that had sobered up the snipers. We began to edge back to the brewery, hoping to get our car out before it caught fire from the tracers.

A German with blood pouring down his leg popped out of a doorway in front of me and surrendered. We waved him back toward the British prisoners. Two more Germans came out of a house with their hands up, but we were intent on getting to the car and took no notice. At the corner of the brewery two sergeants, one American and the other British, who were staff photographers, ran across the open road to their vehicle, grabbed their tommy-guns and began firing. They were enjoying the whole thing with a gusto that seemed madness at first. Yet I could understand it a little. This street fighting had a kind of Red Indian quality about it. You felt you were right up against the enemy and able to deal with him directly, your nimbleness and marksmanship against his. The American was coolly picking his targets and taking careful aim. The young Frenchman with the Sten gun turned up, and I realised now that he had been warning us about these snipers in the first place. He led the two sergeants into the brewery, kicking the door open with his foot and shooting from the hip. They sent a preliminary volley through the aperture. Presently the three of them came out with the two snipers who had been shooting above our heads. They had wounded one.

The sergeants then offered to cover us while we ran for our car. My driver was quick. He whizzed it backwards up the street, and we ran to the point a quarter of a mile back where the rest of the British column was waiting.

Clifford had been having a busy time at the crossroads. He had stopped one car with two German officers in it. They had pointed to the red crosses on their arms, but Clifford found the vehicle full of arms and he lugged them out. At the same time two snipers had run across to the house on the corner. A Tommy with a neat burst killed them as they ran. Mad things were going on. Two Italian officers marched up and demanded, in the midst of this confusion, that they should be provided with transport to return to their barracks, where they had left their waterproof coats.

Meanwhile another patrol of armoured cars had taken the right fork, the Rue de Londres, down to the centre of the town. They took the city entirely unawares. Hundreds of Germans were walking in the streets, some with their girlfriends. Hundreds more were sitting drinking apéritifs in a big pavement café. No one had warned them the British were near. The attack had gone so quickly that here in the town there had been no indication that the Axis line was broken. Now, suddenly, like a vision from the sky, appeared these three British armoured cars. The Germans rose from their seats and stared. The Tommies stared back. There was not much they could do. There armoured cars could not handle all these prisoners. In the hairdressing saloon next door more Germans struggled out of the chairs and, with white sheets round their necks and lather on their faces, stood gaping.

The three armoured cars turned back for reinforcements.

In this mad way Tunis fell that night. Here and there a German with desperate courage emptied his gun down on the streets and hurled a grenade or two. But for the most part these base troops in Tunis were taken entirely off their guard and there were thousands of them. All night there was hopeless confusion in the dark, Germans and British wandering about together, Italians scrambling into civilian clothes and taking refuge in the cellars, saboteurs starting new fires and igniting more dumps, men putting out to sea in rowing boats, others grabbing bicycles and carts and making up the roads to Cape Bon, and others again, bewildered and afraid, simply marching along until they could find someone to whom they could surrender. All night the fires burned, and they were still going in the morning when the British infantry began to flood into the town in force.

An extraordinary scene of havoc and confusion was revealed by the morning light. The town itself was pretty well unscathed, but the waterfront had been savaged by bomb-fire out of all recognition. Six-storey buildings had collapsed like pancakes. For days hardly a man had dared to approach the docks. The port of La Goulette outside the town, near the site of ancient Carthage, was even worse. Ships or parts of ships were blown out of the sea and flung upon the hulks of their sister ships. The stone wharves were split up and pocked with immense craters.

At the two airfields scores of smashed German planes were lying about in the soaking rain— Messerschmitts, Dorniers, Macchis, Focke-Wulfs, Junkers, Stukas and communication machines of every possible sort.

My party had not stayed to explore these things. We had entered the city at fifteen minutes to three on May 7th. The street fighting had held us up until nearly dark, and then, through the evening, we made that endless tedious drive back to Thibar to send our messages. We were so tired we scarcely glanced up when a Spitfire crashed close by us at Medjez-el-Bab. On the way we heard that the Americans had reached Bizerta. It was just six months since the landing in North Africa, just on three years since the African war had begun.

Nineteen

Bizerta

BY MAY 8th the front was falling to bits in every direction. Even at Alexander's headquarters they did not yet know the overwhelming nature of the breakthrough. The Allied army had simply picked itself up like a colossal tidal wave, and now the wave had burst uncontrollably over that last corner of Axis Africa. No force on earth could have checked its onward course at that moment. The Axis defence was pricked to its heart, and now from every direction an ungovernable flood of men and weapons was spilling up the valleys and the mountain roads.

Like everyone else we were swept into it that morning. We fondly imagined we could drive back into Tunis and then turn northward up the coast road and enter Bizerta. An hour after leaving Thibar we disillusioned ourselves. There was a sixty-mile traffic jam. This was a traffic jam to end all traffic jams, a solid mass of vehicles blocking every sidetrack. At Medjez-el-Bab there were only two makeshift bridges, and the procession was practically stationary for twenty miles on either side of the bottleneck. Neither persuasion nor cunning could get us through, and we turned up the northerly road hoping we could open up a new way across country. If Tebourba had fallen, then we knew we might get through. Tebourba had fallen all right, but the enemy were still around it. We exchanged a few words with the men who had taken the town and then doubled back on our tracks to Beja.

Somehow we felt we had to see the fall of Bizerta. Tunis had been a great triumph and we were greedy for more. By some miracle the back roads were clear. Three hours' headlong driving brought us to Mateur. No firing ahead. We ran straight into Ferryville. The people there were cheering and waving madly, but still we could not be sure whether Bizerta had fallen or not. It looked quiet enough across the lake. We doubled round behind the airport and ran through groves of olive trees where thousands of casks of German oil were lying. We were almost into the town before we heard shellfire—shellfire coming toward us. We were rather childishly pleased that we had arrived in time to see the end.

It was an odd situation. An American patrol had entered the town the previous day about the same time as Tunis fell, but they had cqme out again in the night. Now, ten hours later, Germans were still fighting in the streets and it was a moot point as to whether the place had fallen or not. The thing was additionally complicated by the fact that more German tanks and gunners were barely a quarter of a mile away across the narrow channel that runs into Bizerta lake. They had a clear view up all the north and south streets running through the town, and anyone who crossed those lines of fire was in for trouble. Early in the morning of May 8th eighteen guns of the Thirty-Ninth British Light Anti- Aircraft Regiment had made a dash through the enemy shells and reached the town where the guns were turned upon the snipers. At the same time about two hundred French colonial troops crept through the suburbs and got to work with the bayonet.

A company of Doughboys, moving in single file, was now going to have another shot at cleaning up the situation. We parked the car and went along with them.

For the first few hundred yards inside the city wall it was all plain sailing, and there was leisure to look around as we went forward, keeping close to the walls. What a difference there was here. Tunis was alive; this was dead. No town that I had seen in the war had ever been knocked flat, but Bizerta was the nearest thing to it. The very earth had been churned up and broken into dust by high explosive. Tunis was marred at the edges; this was ravaged throughout. I looked at house after house as we walked by, and nothing had escaped. Some buildings were turned upside down. The roofs had fallen to the floors and the floors had been blasted up against the walls. Fire had done the rest. The palace, the bank, the administration centre—they were all holed with direct hits, and it looked as though some giant claw had scraped away the façades of the buildings. The church steeple still stood. And in the steeple a little group of Germans were sitting around a machine-gun. Down below that they had another gun, a full-sized anti-tank gun poking through the grating of a cellar. There were other snipers about.

A Sherman tank lunged down the street of the church and came back with its nose chipped. Every time a Doughboy shoved his head round the corner a bullet flicked by. A Frenchman blithely wished to guide us in a jeep to the upper reaches of the town. We followed until there was another burst of machine-gunning, and it was borne in upon us that the snipers were letting the Frenchman go by on his bicycle and holding their fire until we got conveniently close. Our day in Tunis had given me a lively distaste for street fighting, and we crawled back to the Doughboys. They were working very neatly and smoothly, creeping up on the houses and flinging their hand grenades from the cover of the doorways. Already they had silenced two snipers and the church steeple was cleaned out. Across the river we could see the enemy tanks pulling into a wood and taking the track southward in the wake of the rest of the Axis army. Well, they would not get far. At that we reckoned Bizerta had fallen and was in American hands. The lovely port and its docks had paid the heaviest price that is possible in war. Had the Romans come again with their firebrands and ploughed salt into the ground, they could scarcely have done more damage. Bizerta was destroyed. Its inhabitants had fled, and not until long after this war will they be able to repair the damage that was done in a few hours of hellishly precise bombing from the sky.

Again we drove back to Thibar in almost a coma of weariness, for we had been on the road almost continuously for forty-eight hours. We were forced to a long detour in the darkness, because an ammunition lorry had caught fire on the main road and it was again long after midnight before we had our messages done.

Tunis, when we got back to it on May 9th, had given itself up to song and dance. The town's population had been doubled by refugees, and to these was added now a horde of exultant soldiery. The men who had been in the desert or in the mountains for months on end stared with amazement at the riot of hilarity raging along every street, and then joined in themselves. The French soldiers who came in were nearly smothered with kisses. Staid old French dowagers leaned over the balconies and screamed 'Vive de Gaulle'—they had not yet heard about General Giraud, and our propaganda units were busy plastering the town with coloured posters showing Girauds features. The V sign, enclosing the Fighting French Cross of Lorraine, was being chalked up everywhere, and it was with some difficulty that one explained that General de Gaulle was not, after all, the man who had liberated them, but another general—Giraud by name. He was just as good, one explained, and they would grow to like him. Heavens, how the politics of Algiers stank in this exuberant atmosphere. It was especially embarrassing when some of General Le Clerc's hard-bitten warriors came in after their three years' fight for de Gaulle in the desert.

But no one was going very deeply into politics at this moment. The Germans were gone; that was the main thing. How the French of Tunis loathed the Germans. It was just one black wall of choking hatred. Not that the Germans had been brutal, just arrogant and very strict. I went into the local newspaper office and the French compositor showed me a copy of that week's *Oasis* he had been obliged to print for the Afrika Korps. One of the headlines was 'Fair play—Nein.' The compositor showed me a pile of anti-British and anti-American printing blocks. With one superb gesture he swept them off the table and spat.

There was a curfew at night and a car with a loudspeaker kept driving through the streets to enforce it. But up till eight the people were free to let themselves go—and they did. Tens of thousands swarmed across the main streets cheering every truckload of soldiers that came in.

Tunis still had food and liquor of a sort and the troops made pretty free with it.

One night I drove out to the headland where the village of Sidi Bou Said is built, and after six years of travelling round the Mediterranean I would say that it is the most beautiful village on all the shores of that sea. The snow-white Arab houses are stepped up the cliffs in a haphazard pyramid, and in this vision of bougainvillea and orange groves and terraced gardens the very wealthy people of France and Italy have built their holiday houses. The villas hang above that perfect bay and, standing on the balconies, one feels suspended between the sea and the sky and the mountains. The showplace is the palace built by the international banker d'Erlanger. A niche for this delicate and lovely house was carved out of the cliffs above the Bey's seaside residence. All the old arts of Arab carving in wood and marble and plaster were revived to decorate the interior. A cooling stream plays along a channel through the reception rooms. The books are bound in the rarest leather. A waterfall of flowers and cypresses and orange trees falls down to the sea.

In the midst of this cultured splendour dwelt La Baronne. She was living in a remote wing of the house when I met her—just a bedroom and a sitting room. Like herself, the sitting room was fragile and charming and in excellent taste. It was entirely feminine, and everything had been chosen with care, even the English books which had just been laid out. The servant, in voluminous white trousers, a turban, a red sash and slippers that turned up to a point, brought us whisky and soda.

'Thank heavens I have some left,' the baroness said. Her English was faultless. 'The Germans and the Italians drank all the champagne. I had the pilots living here, you know. They were very correct, but there were just a few things…The peacocks, for instance. I had ten lovely white peacocks, and one day I noticed there were only seven of them on the terrace. It turned out the Italians were killing and roasting them to eat. I had to ask them to stop.'

Below us a Moorish fountain, richly tiled, stood among the orange trees of her private garden, a grotto in the palace. No bombs had fallen here but, away below, the port of La Goulette was an ugly mess. The baroness used to watch the Allied aircraft sail in and plant their bombs on that festering mass of twisted steel.

'But it was all so quick,' she said. 'Only the day before yesterday the Germans were here and we had no sign at all that anything was wrong. My maid brought my breakfast to me in bed as she always does, and she said to me, "The Germans are going." I said to her, "Nonsense. What do you mean?

Why should they go?" The next thing she came running in to say that the colonel himself had set off. I looked out of the window, and sure enough they were throwing their belongings into the trucks and driving off. In an hour or two none of them was left. I had no notion of what was happening. And then, a few hours later, I looked out again—and there they were, the British troops. It was almost too sudden to be believed. I have had such a lot of your generals coming in to see me. They all seem to want to stay here.'

I rested luxuriously in another villa a little higher up the hill that night. The bed, as I noted from the books and papers lying about, had been used as late as the Wednesday night by the officer in charge of the peacock-eating pilots. An Italian military telephone stood beside the bed.

Back in Tunis, one event came crowding on another. The ship that had set off for Italy with the cargo of British prisoners had taken one look at the British destroyers lying in wait outside the harbour and put back into Tunis, its crew preferring imprisonment to death, its precious passengers safe. Everywhere refugees from the Axis were coming out of the cellars and back rooms where they had been living for months—an English clergyman, leaders of the French Socialist party, de Gaullists, Tommies who had escaped and found shelter with friendly French people.

General Giraud arrived, and when he drove through the streets to the city monument in a fine cavalcade of Spahi horsemen the crowds gave him a good welcome. Already he was becoming well known, and it was clear the people would accept him since he stood for revenge on the Germans.

Many hostile Italians were hidden in the city. A proclamation went up stating that all enemy soldiers in hiding were to give themselves up by the following night. Otherwise they would be shot.

Outside the town the prisoners' cages were filling up. Not since Wavell's days had I seen such swarms of men. The compound on the Massicault road overflowed beyond its barbed wire and cactus hedges, and the Germans and Italians simply hung around the outskirts waiting to be taken in. A German band, complete with its instruments, had arrived. The bandsmen stood in a square and played soothing Viennese lieder. There must have been five thousand prisoners in that camp and more were coming in at the rate of five hundred an hour. The prisoners were being issued with tins of bully beef, packets of biscuits and tins of fruit. There seemed to be plenty. Since neither I myself nor anyone in the army had been able to get his hands on more than a spoonful of tinned fruit for the past few weeks, I found myself unreasonably annoyed with one German who was pouring away the juice in order to get at the pears in his tin more easily.

At that moment I had not yet begun to know the full story of the prisoners or I would not have been so excited.

While all this peaceful sorting-out was going on in Tunis tremendous events were happening outside the town. The Americans had broken clean through the mountains to the west and north of Medjerda Valley, and were mopping up prisoners in uncounted thousands. The Seventh Armoured Division wheeled northward from Tunis and pursued its old enemy, the 15th Panzer Division, up the coast road as far as Porto Farina, outside Bizerta. The Germans made one abortive attempt to escape by sea—bodies were being washed ashore for days afterwards—and then surrendered. Those two divisions had been fighting one another across the desert for years.

The Fighting French had come through Pont du Fahs in one epic rush and were counting their prisoners by the truckload. On the coast the skeleton Eighth Army was again locked in a most bloody battle around Enfidaville.

But all this did not account for the main bulk of von Arnim's forces. They were in a state of disorder, but they were still intact. In a vast disorganised mob the majority of them had made for the Cape Bon Peninsula, where arrangements for evacuation ought to have been made. Cape Bon was defensible. A stiff double line of hills ran across its base, and von Arnim's last coherent plan was to get as many of his men and weapons as possible behind those hills before the British arrived. There were only two feasible passes through the hills—one at Hamman Lif, where the Bey had his palace, on the northern coast outside Tunis, the other at the lovely tourist town of Hammamet on the south coast at the base of Cape Bon. Von Arnim himself had retreated to the Zaghouan area and was fighting a hot rearguard action back toward Hammamet. His northern armies meanwhile were slipping through the Hamman Lif gap in the north.

This was the moment when Alexander turned his decisive thrust on Tunis into a *coup de grâce*. It is fascinating to me now to look back and see a guiding hand in all these vast movements. At the time, everything to me was pretty confused; indeed, travelling as I was with the onward sweep of the troops and being without general information from hour to hour, it was impossible to know what plan, if any, was being carried out. All I knew was that a major breakthrough had occurred and, willy-nilly, one followed the general advance wherever it went.

It was not until a few days later, when General Anderson explained to us personally what had happened, that I realised what a masterpiece of design the breakthrough had been, and what enormous risks had been taken. In our headlong thrust to Tunis we had left huge numbers of the enemy in pockets on either side of us. It was an extremely narrow thrust, and the major risk was that the enemy might close in behind us and entirely surround the head of the British army. Fifty things might have gone wrong. As it turned out, the sheer depth and swiftness of the thrust entirely disorganised von Arnim's command. Von Arnim himself was put to flight. So were his corps and divisional headquarters.

The result was that the big pockets of fresh fighting troops on either side of the British breakthrough were without orders. They saw a great column of enemy vehicles and tanks rushing past them, and they simply deduced that the game was up. They headed at full steam for Cape Bon.

Now, having taken this first major risk and got away with it, Alexander and Anderson decided to go one further.

They decided to split the German army in two halves by occupying the Hamman Lif–Hammamet line across the base of Cape Bon Peninsula before von Arnim could. In that way one-half of the Germans would be bottled up in the peninsula, the other half would be isolated outside, and neither would even get a chance of getting to the boats. There was, of course, not an instant to lose, and already, before Tunis fell, the orders went out to the Sixth Armoured Division: 'You will break through the enemy position at Hamman Lif and then, wheeling south between the hills, proceed to Hammamet.' Even on paper it seemed to be a fantastic thing to ask of any division. For one thing, it meant their tackling an enemy at least ten times numerically stronger. But Alexander had the Germans on the run and he meant to keep them running even if it cost him an entire division or more. Some of our finest infantry—the Guards—without waiting for daylight, set off into the unknown. The subsequent march of the Sixth Division must place it and its general in the very highest place in the military history of the war.

They arrived outside Hamman Lif at nightfall, the evening after Tunis fell. The village straggles along the main road and the seashore, and it is dominated by the Bey's white palace on the road and a tall apartment house standing near the sea. There are half a dozen blocks of smaller buildings and the streets run at right angles. The Germans had set up about twenty 88-millimetre guns in a field beyond the town. They had also established snipers in every one of the six storeys of the apartment house, and there were fighting troops in the village as well. It was an extremely strong defensive position since it had to be attacked frontally, after the surrounding heights were taken.

The general waited until the moon had risen. Then he placed tanks at the mouths of each of the village streets. The Guards infantry clambered up on the outside of the tanks. Then the tanks charged. At each intersection infantry dropped off and went down the side streets mopping up with the grenade, the bayonet and the tommy-gun. Others continued to the apartment house and dealt with it in the same way. The tanks engaged the 88s at short range and knocked them out. In that one epic moonlight charge the town was taken. Someone went into the Bey's palace and apologised to the hysterical officials for the damage that was done, and the rest of the division swept on.

They broke clean through to Hammamet inside the next ten hours. They roared past German airfields, workshops, petrol and ammunition dumps and gun positions. They did not stop to take prisoners—things had gone far beyond that. If a comet had rushed down that road, it could hardly have made a greater impression. The Germans now were entirely dazed. Wherever they looked, British tanks seemed to be hurtling past. Von Arnim's guns would be firing south only to find that the enemy had also appeared behind them—and over on the left—and on the right. The German generals gave up giving orders since they were completely out of touch and the people to whom they could give orders were diminishing every hour. In what direction, anyway, were they to fight. Back toward Zaghouan? Toward Tunis? Under the German military training you had to have a plan. But there was no plan. Only the boats remained—the evacuation boats which had been promised them. The boats that were to take them back to Italy. In a contagion of doubt and fear the German army turned tail and made up the Cape Bon roads looking for the boats. When on the beaches it became apparent to them at last that there were no boats—nor any aircraft either—the army became a rabble. The Italian navy had not dared to put to sea to save its men. The Luftwaffe had been blown out of the sky. In other words, the Axis had cut its losses and the Afirika Korps was abandoned to its fate. On May 10th I set off up the peninsula through Hamman Lif to see one of the most grotesque and awesome spectacles that can have occurred in this war—an entire German army laying down its arms.[10]

Twenty

Cape Bon

TEN KILOMETRES outside Tunis we began to meet Germans and Italians coming toward us on the road; at Hamman Lif their vehicles had thickened to one every hundred yards; outside Soliman it was one solid mass and there was hardly a British soldier to be seen anywhere.

All the Axis soldiers were driving. They drove in ten-ton diesel lorries, and by standing upright and close together, they had managed to jam about forty or fifty men into each vehicle. Many of the lorries towed a trailer of the same size and an equal number of men were crowded into the trailer.

For eighty miles this procession was crawling slowly along the roads of Cape Bon Peninsula toward the British lines. Most of the German officers were travelling in blunt-nosed little staff cars adapted from the Volkswagen. Others had ordinary touring cars and saloons and there was a good sprinkling of command vehicles. The Italian officers were in Toppolino Fiats and Lancias. Some of the trucks were very old and much battered by desert wear. They staggered along under their unusual burdens, emitting great jets of acrid brown smoke. In the smaller cars the officers had piled up their bedding and any chance thing they had laid their hands on at the last moment—extra gallons of petrol, packets of cigarettes, a favourite folding-chair, a violin, a basket of oranges, a suitcase full of civilian clothing. There were many motorcycles and sidecars.

When a vehicle broke down, its passengers went along the line begging lifts, and when they were all absorbed in the overcrowded lorries the procession went on again. The soldiers still wore their insignia, showing that they were sailors or soldiers or airmen, but they had thrown away their weapons and their steel helmets.

No one was in charge of this horde, not even the Axis officers. No one had accepted its surrender. It was a spontaneous and natural sequence of the Allied victory, a result no one could have foreseen, but still a natural result. The Axis mob had retreated to the tip of the peninsula and found itself unable to get away. They were trapped. They had no orders. The finely balanced Wehrmacht system, the careful stepping down of responsibility from corps to division and from colonel to regiment, from N.C.O. to soldier, had disintegrated into a thousand pieces.

By a natural instinct the men sought the preservation of the last thing left to them—their own lives.

In the absence of orders they obeyed their instincts. They clambered into their vehicles and drove back toward their conquerors to surrender. The tide in which they had flooded, like some driven herd of cattle, up to the beaches of Cape Bon now began to ebb back toward Tunis.

A gap—a military vacuum—had been left on the roads by the Sixth Division in its dramatic breakthrough to Hammamet. The returning Germans and Italians now filled that gap, and there were no British troops to take them in charge. Throughout this day my party was outnumbered on the roads by about one thousand to one by Axis troops. None made the slightest attempt to molest us. They shouted instead, 'Who do we surrender to? To you?' We were willing to accept anyone's surrender, but there was nothing that we—four people—could do about it. Like the rest of the British troops scattered here and there along the roads, we simply waved the prisoners on and they kept going. I am making no attempt here to write of the astonishment and incredulity with which we saw this mass of beaten men flow by all through May 10th, the 11th and the 12th, and even for days after that. I want only to explain how it looked and why they surrendered. The prisoners I saw—and I suppose I passed thirty thousand on this first day, mostly Germans—were not exhausted; they were not hungry or shell-shocked or wounded; they were not frightened. I saw their dumps under the trees from Soliman to Grombalia and away up the peninsula, and the weapons they had thrown away—they had ammunition and food and water; they had enough weapons and supplies to make a series of isolated stands in the mountains for weeks had they chosen to do so.

But they did not choose because they had lost the power of making military decisions. From the moment of our breakthrough on May 6th orders had stopped flowing through the German machine. It was like a motor-car engine running out of petrol. The machine was still there all right, but there was no one to put it into motion again. The orders were not given because von Arnim and all his senior generals were forced to strike camp and flee at the most critical stages of the battle. There is nothing new about this. Precisely the same thing happened at Tobruk. Rommel made a swift, narrow and deep penetration of the Tobruk perimeter, and the South African general in command of the British garrison, General Klopper, was obliged to keep moving his headquarters during the vital stages of the battle.

During that time he received no information and was unable to give orders. In the absence of any battle plan, in their complete ignorance of what was happening and because they did not know when to fire or in what direction, the Tobruk garrison was mopped up piecemeal by the Germans and surrendered in one day.

That is precisely what happened to von Arnim. In each case the general and the troops were oppressed by the fact that they had their backs to the sea and that they were trapped without the chance of escape or reinforcement. In each case the bulk of the defending troops had come recently and hurriedly into their new positions, and at a time when the enemy was victorious everywhere else. Each position was designed to act as a bulwark in a rout, a peg to halt the retreat. Both at Tobruk and in Cape Bon the defenders were never given time to man their defences, to settle into the trenches, to acclimatise themselves and get the habit of resistance.

With very few exceptions this war seemed to have demonstrated that armies are brittle things.

Crack them smartly at the outset and they fly to bits. The knockout finishes the fight before the opponent has time to settle into his defences; thus France; thus Norway; thus the Low Countries; thus Singapore— but not thus in Russia and not thus in Rommel's retreat across the desert, and the difference here was this—the retreating armies had somewhere to retreat to. Behind Singapore and behind Cape Bon was only the sea. At neither place could the defenders play the old game of stretching out the enemy's lines of communication to the point where the enemy was starved and exhausted, a prey to the tactic of throwing in strategic reserves. The Germans had played that game once in Tunisia in the very beginning and got away with it. But now they could retreat no more.

There were a dozen other factors in the Tunisian victory, like our dominance of the air and sea, but this question of the breakdown of the German system seems to be the governing one.

It appeared to me as I travelled among the prisoners, especially the Germans, that they lacked the power of individual thought and action. They had been trained as a team, for years the best fighting team in the world. They had never been trained to fight in small groups or by themselves. They were seldom forced to make adaptations and makeshifts on the spur of the moment, because they were usually on the winning side and their almost perfect supply machine had placed the finest weapons in their hands. The German army organisation had been a miracle of precision in every phase of the African war. The fighting men always got their ammunition and their food. It used to come by air while we were still using carts. They even got their mail twice a week from home. And so they leaned heavily on the machine and trusted it. They never tried out the odd exciting things that we did—things like the Long Range Desert Group. They were never much good at guerrilla fighting or patrolling at night. They liked to do things en masse.

I do not want to support that old and easy saying that once the Germans crack they go to pieces.

Rommel has shown for all time that the Germans will go on fighting against impossible odds and take impossible risks so long as they are well controlled and officered. Most of the story of the African war shows that the Germans don't crack. They were split up at Alamein and they managed to regroup.

I simply state that the Germans were not trained to band themselves into small autonomous groups, whereas often our own troops and the Americans will do so. The British battle schools forced men to take independent action in a crisis. The Germans apparently had either not had that training or did not like it. At any rate, in Tunisia, when the orders stopped coming, great doubts took hold of the German mind and their discipline collapsed. Especially in war it is the unknown that men fear more than anything. As a lonely sentry will imagine a thousand terrors in the night, so an army will flounder uncertainly and weakly so long as it is in doubt about the position and strength of the enemy. That is why every battle is preceded with a long period which is called 'trying out the enemy'. Big operations are laid on with the sole object of getting the enemy to demonstrate his strength and the nature of his weapons. All through this battle we had aircraft and tanks ranging back and forth to tempt the enemy to shoot so that we would know how many guns he had in a certain spot and where they were placed. From May 6th onwards the Germans were forever in doubt, and doubt created despair.

I stress the Germans in all this. The Italians at the end showed much more initiative. Indeed, the young Fascists were indignant at several places when their German companions gave up. A few of the Italians at least wanted to fight it out, guerrilla fashion, to the death.

However, the Germans prevailed because of their greater numbers, and so for the next two or three days we came on an endless succession of these amazing scenes along the road. At Grombalia the Axis troops were pouring in from the side roads and grouping themselves in a cactus field outside the village. There were, I suppose, thirty British guards for about five thousand prisoners. No one had been able to get word through to a battery of Italian gunners on the heights above that the game was up. They kept firing first in this direction, then in that, and you could almost feel the gunners saying to themselves, 'Well, what *are* we firing at anyway?'

In the orchards beside the road the enemy encampments were lying just as they left them—vehicles and tanks dispersed round in a circle, motorcycles lying on the ditches, signals vans standing under camouflage nets and the telephones still working. In their blitz through the Sixth had knocked out an odd truck here and a tank there, and these still smouldered beside the track. An ammunition dump had blown up and the sparks had set a haystack alight. At Rebka, near to the southern coast, we found the vanguard of the Sixth at last. They were entirely surrounded by prisoners, and more coming in every minute. A handful of harassed tank men were forming them into a crocodile that wound slowly away to the north for a mile or two. 'God knows where they are supposed to go,' a British sergeant said to me. 'I just put 'em on the road and tell 'em to keep going.'

There was shooting still along the coast to the south-west of Hammamet, and we joined a squadron of Shermans that was streaming off in that direction. In the distance a long dark column of enemy vehicles was approaching. The British artillery spotter had just decided on the range and was about to open fire. With his glasses to his eyes he was opening his mouth to give the order when he suddenly snapped, 'God damn it. They've seen us and they're hanging out white flags. Cease fire. Try and get someone to round them up.'

We turned back and ran into Hammamet, which is more like a landscape painting in watercolours than something in real life. Flowering shrubs and laden fruit trees hung over the winding lanes. By the tiny beach and the old fort the white villas cluster together in their walled gardens, and the sea was shining, transparent blue. Just a few hours before we drove in, a violent argument had raged among the German soldiers in the garrison. Some were for surrendering, others for fighting, other for getting away in a fishing smack.

'It was terrible, that dispute,' the hotel-keeper said. 'In the end they all crowded aboard the boat. They just got round that corner an hour ago.' The boat was lucky if it got more than ten miles. By this time the British navy had put a complete blockade across the Sicilian Narrows. Allied aircraft were passing back and forth every half-hour. Both the navy and the air force were feeling a little baulked that the Germans had not at least made one decent attempt to put to sea, and that fishing smack would be a welcome sight for a pilot.

Nabeul, the next port, was to have been the major embarkation port, but the town was empty when we drove through. Always we kept passing Germans and Italians. At Korba a group of German and Italian specialists and vital experts had been promised air transportation. They were still waiting on the airfield when the British arrived—along with fix or six thousand other prisoners.

Clifford and I were keen to do a little looting, a sport at which we had become adept in the desert. We knew we would have to give the things up to the British military police, but still it was great sport to wander about picking up radio sets, cameras, binoculars and typewriters.

Everything you saw was yours. If there is such a thing as feeling you are a millionaire for a day, then this is it. On this day we wanted cars. 'Take your pick,' said a British officer who was battling with a disordered mob of prisoners. 'Turn out any passengers you like.' We did indeed need one car, so we selected a Fiat. The Italian officer at once scrambled out with his belongings and we drove off. The Fiat was not much of a success. It blew up after a bit, and then we went hunting for Volkswagens. There were dozens lying about, wonderful little cars with the engine in the back, and they were pleasant to drive. The ignition keys were missing from most of the Volkswagens, but in the end we got one going and that was the Volkswagen in which we eventually drove six hundred miles through the mountains from Cape Bon back to Algiers.

Beyond Korba was Kelibia, the most distant of the abortive enemy evacuation ports. A great crowd of Germans were stranded there with their vehicles. Some were forming up to make a convoy on the road, others were rifling a food dump under the olive trees. Enemy colonels and generals seemed to be bustling about in all directions, and utterly failing to get any order out of the confusion. Some of the Germans showed us where the cases of choicest food were lying, and helped us to extract tins of pork and fruit, and packets of wholewheat biscuits. I lived on German and Italian rations once—they were always first-class. The soldiers got real Danish butter, not margarine. The Italian tinned fruit and cheese were especially excellent.

The extraordinary thing was that once the enemy troops had decided to surrender they had no thought whatever of taking up arms again. Two days before they were concentrating all their minds and bodies on killing Englishmen and Americans. At this moment they were entirely free to pick up their rifles and shoot us. But they did not seem to be even morose or resentful. They were eager to be pleasant. In dozens they came up to explain the workings of the Volkswagen to us. They were delighted to find Clifford spoke German, and they talked with him as though the war had never occurred. Their attitude was: 'Well, it's finished for me now. I don't have to fight any more. I can relax a bit.'

They had lived such a practical and physical life in the field that they had had no time to develop any grandiose theories about the war and the honour of Germany. They did not worry about the future. Since whole armies were surrendering, it did not seem to any one man that he was doing anything extraordinary by giving up. Indeed, the whole astonishing spectacle was more and more like another army manoeuvre. They were simply going off to another place—America, they hoped.

They had heard well of the food and conditions there, and they had always wanted to see America.

Indeed, the prospect before these prisoners was not a bad one. They had had three years' fighting and they were fortunate to be unwounded and alive. Those who had been in Russia never wanted to go back. They were all sick and tired of army life. They looked forward to having a rest. For the moment the escape from the terrible bombing and shelling was all they asked. They knew their wives and families would be looked after in Germany and Italy as well as might be—they seldom saw them anyway when they were fighting in the Axis armies, so being a prisoner of war would not make much difference.

These men were not soft. They simply felt: 'I have done my bit. Let someone else carry on now.' They honestly did not have any fixed ideas about whether Germany was going to win or not. If you questioned them, they said they thought the war would go on for years. They certainly did not feel that Germany was already beaten. They were glad to be out of it—that was all there was to it. There was, in fact, a malaise among these men, a malaise of the spirit brought on by too many hard trials that had gone on too long.

We rode back at last to Tunis, past the prisoners, who now stretched in a procession reaching from the tip of Cape Bon far into Tunisia. Weeks were going to elapse before a final count revealed the total at over a quarter of a million prisoners, the biggest single haul made by the Allies since the war had begun. In all, the Axis had lost close on a million men in Africa. Now they had nothing, absolutely nothing, to show for it.

I personally had expected the African war to finish in havoc, a cataclysm of destruction and death and frightfulness. These friendly, peaceful scenes at the end were almost an anticlimax. In the British army alone the doctors had budgeted for six thousand casualties in the final breakthrough. Actually they got the astonishingly low number of two thousand.

There remained still, on May 11th, a large knot of resistance in the mountains between Zaghouan and Enfidaville, where the Eighth Army was still fighting. But in the afternoon General Anderson called us to his headquarters outside Medjez-el-Bab and gave us the momentous news that von Arnim had been captured near the aerodrome of St Marie du Zit and had asked for terms.

'I told him we want unconditional surrender,' General Anderson said. 'In my message I said that all destruction of war materials must cease, and that we must have a plan of their minefields immediately. Von Arnim has refused these terms. He has asked to see me. He will be here in a minute. I don't think it will make much difference what he says.'

The fact that von Arnim himself had not been able to get away was proof of the speed and completeness of our victory. No Axis aircraft had been able to take off into a sky filled with British and American aircraft, no Axis ship of any size had been able to put to sea. All the Axis generals, with only one notable exception, had now been taken. One after another the famous units, like the 10th Panzer Division, gave up en masse. It is doubtful if more than one thousand enemy troops got away to Italy at the last. In the end a quarter of a million prisoners were taken.

In the southern sector the New Zealanders and the German 90th Light Division broke off their fighting at last. These two divisions were the élite of the British and German armies. For two years they had mauled one another across the desert. We had killed two of the 90th Light's commanders. The 90th Light had almost killed Freyberg. They had charged up to the gates of Egypt in the previous summer, and it was the New Zealanders who broke the German division's heart outside Mersa Matruh. There is hardly a major battlefield in the desert where you will not find the intermingled graves of the New Zealanders and the men of the 90th Light. And now at last it was all over.

Eight minutes to eight o'clock on May 12th is the official time given for the cessation of all organised enemy resistance in Africa.

No special incident marked that moment. This tragedy of three years and three acts simply ended with all the actors crowding onto the stage too exhausted to be exultant or defiant or humiliated or resentful. At the end the battlefield fell to pieces and lost all pattern and design, and those who had fought hardest on both sides found they had nothing to say, nothing to feel beyond an enveloping sense of gratitude and rest. The anger had subsided at the surrender, and for the first time the German and Allied soldiers stood together looking at one another with listless and passionless curiosity.

The struggle had gone on so long. It had been so bitter. There were so many dead. There was nothing more to say.

The last of the German generals came down to the landing field and was flown off to captivity. The last of many thousand enemy soldiers trudged into the internment camps.

And in our ranks the soldiers stripped off their uniforms, washed, and fell asleep in the sunshine.

All Africa was ours.

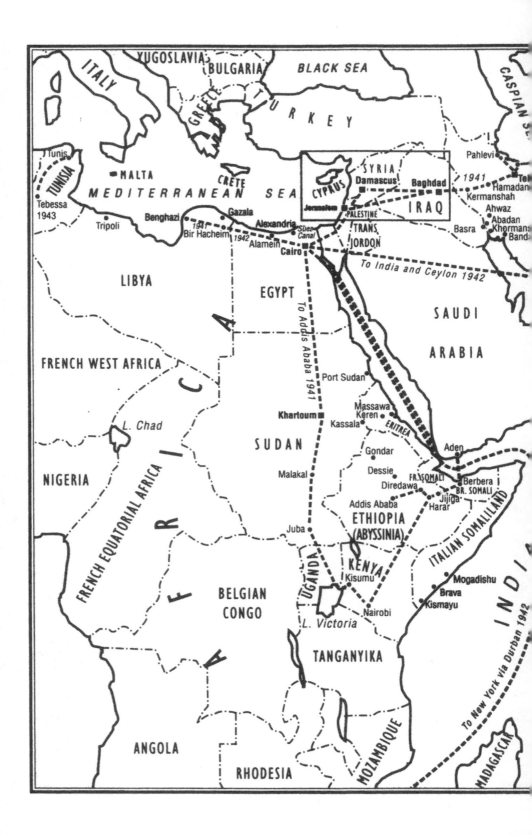

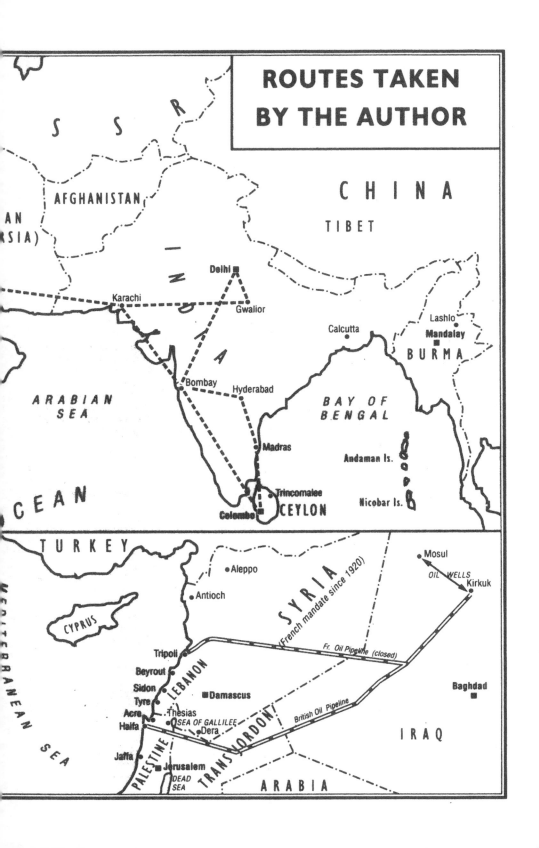

ROUTES TAKEN BY THE AUTHOR

ENDNOTES

1. Major-General E. P. Nares, in charge of supplies, contests this paragraph in an interesting letter to me. He says the forward troops always got 90 per cent of their supplies, and that when we re- conquered this territory the following year we found our old ammunition dumps intact and they were most useful to Montgomery. He adds: 'Petrol—or rather the "flimsies" it was carried in—was the real cause of our downfall. 80,000 gallons was my daily requirement in the forward area. I rarely got more than 60,000 gallons of which 50,000 reached the units.'

2. Again, General Nares writes that all that was humanly possible was done at Benghazi. Of our retreat he says: 'My last act before leaving Msus was to put a match to seven million cigarettes and a large consignment of mail and stores which had arrived the previous day. Three six-ton lorry-loads of rum went back in the same lorries it arrived in. Had we held Rommel for ten days, or had he put back his attack for that period, I still believe we could have come through.'

3. Chandra Bose, who was broadcasting to India from the German radio stations, was reported killed in an aircrash near Tokyo about this time. Later the report was denied. Significantly Gandhi sent a warm message of congratulation to Bose's mother and had the telegram published.

4. We lost between ninety and a hundred tanks on this day. It was subsequently found that their batteries had not been charged and there was a wireless failure.

5. As a result of the Kasserine action one or two subsequent mishaps, an ignorant and malicious controversy sprang up in Europe about the fighting qualities of the American troops. They were said to be 'green,' which was true enough; but doubt was also thrown on American courage and skill and willingness to fight, which was grossly unfair. It was said that the Americans had boasted before they had seen real action. The truth of the matter was, of course,

that the Americans were at the same stage as the British were a year after they had entered the war—slow, awkward and apt to be thrown off balance on experiencing hostile fire for the first time. There was just this difference—the Americans were much better armed than we were in1940 and they learned much more quickly. The two temperaments will probably never be the same. The best statement on the matter I have seen appeared in a German military magazine we picked up in an enemy barracks in Tunis. It said: 'The British soldier is still the best soldier in Africa. The Americans entered this war without any conception of its grimness and hardship. Once they learn this they will become very good soldiers indeed.' General Terry Allen's First American Infantry Division provided a brilliant proof of this in Tunisia.

6. I am challenged on this point by staff officers who state that Alexander foresaw the actual course of events and never intended the Eighth Army to act merely as a piston. They say that the general wanted the Germans to fight on a right-angled line and that the Americans were never expected to break through to the sea. It is a difficult and academic point.

7. For a long time the desert soldiers had been using Egyptian Arabic terms such as 'moy-ah' for water, 'shufti' for look and so on. They used the Western Desert Bedouin expression 'say-eeda' (which means 'Go with God') as a form of greeting. These Arabic words were perverted or lost entirely in the passage of the original Moorish invasions around the Mediterranean from Arabia to Spain. The word 'wadi,' for example, had become 'oued'. In Thibar I found some of the older Arabs knew a word of greeting, 'seeda,' but it was obviously not in use. The Eight Army troops now imported the bastard Nile Delta Arabic into Tunisia. The Tunisian Arabs naturally thought these expressions were English words, and began to use them as such. When a soldier saw an Arab he at once shouted 'say-eeda' and the Arab after a little began to say 'say-eeda' in response, thingking it was the English for hullo. Within a few weeks of Montgomery's arrival, 'say-eeda' was in pretty general use in southern Tunisia.

Mr Evelyn Montague, the correspondent of the *Manchester Guardian* and the *Times*, made a study of this battle on the spot, and he sends me this valuable amplification:

'Actually it took the Sixth Armoured Division all of thirty-six hours to break through Hamman Lif and another thirty-six-odd to get to Hammamet. This was the time-table. On the afternoon of May 7th the Derbyshire Yeomanry were yanked out of Tunis (where they had to abandon five hundred prisoners) and the whole of the Sixth Armoured moved toward Hamman Lif and were held up on the outskirts by tanks hull-down behind the breakwaters as well as by a minefield, anti-tank guns and heavier guns on the hills above the town. The armour therefore waited while the Welsh Guards, the divisional artillery and some tanks attacked the overlooking hills and, after a struggle lasting all day, took them against mortar and machine-gun opposition. Meanwhile the Yeomanry gave the First Armoured Division a hand to get through the Creteville Pass, the next pass further south.

'At first light on May 9th the armour of the Sixth Armoured had another sniff at Hamman Lif, but found the enemy had reinforced during the night. Meanwhile the Guards held their hills securely enough, but could not advance eastward along with them without coming under heavy fire from higher ground. So Keightley switched the entire divisional artillery on to Hamman Lif, after which he sent in three squadrons of the Lothians. One squadron could not penetrate the town at all; the other two fought their way through it yard by yard, knocking out each gun as they came to it.

'The remaining squadron of Lothians with infantry riding on the tanks was then put in to clear a way for the armour, the infantry jumping off at each corner to clear garrisons from houses. This was too much for the Boches, who began to retire about mid-afternoon, and the rest of our armour went through apparently unmolested, while the Guards cleared the high ground.

'By dusk on this day (May 9th) the armour was three miles short of Soliman, but on May 10th they took three hours to fight their way into its outskirts against tanks and eighty-eights well dug in.

'They had less trouble with Grombalia, and late this afternoon (May 10th) a light group of tanks and armoured cars went through Grombalia with orders to push on day and night to occupy the road junction three miles west of Hammamet which would completely cut off Cape Bon from the mainland. They got within five miles of the road junction that night, and next day reached it and pressed on toward Bou Ficha, which they reached after overcoming heavy opposition three miles north of it.

During this day the Sixth Armoured's fire was observed and corrected by the Eighth Army.

'On May 12th the division advanced south from Bou Ficha, meeting heavy fire at first, which died down soon after midday, and mass surrenders began, culminating in the junction of the First and Eighth Armies at 5.15 p.m. and the surrender of von Sponeck, the commander of the German 90th Light Division, at 5.20 p.m.'

8. A shell fired at point-blank range killed him near Salerno the following winter.

9. Horrocks was later badly wounded by bomb splinters in Bizerta when he was about to lead a party of the Allied forces on the invasion of Italy.

INDEX